EAL

13140005425375

KT-413-766

ENEMIES WITHIN

Also by Richard Davenport-Hines

Dudley Docker
Sex, Death and Punishment
The Macmillans
Glaxo
Vice
Auden
Gothic
The Pursuit of Oblivion
A Night at the Majestic
Ettie: The Intimate Life of Lady Desborough
Titanic Lives
An English Affair
Universal Man: The Seven Lives of John Maynard Keynes
Edward VII: The Cosmopolitan King

Speculators and Patriots (edited)
British Business in Asia since 1860 (co-edited)
Hugh Trevor-Roper's Letters from Oxford (edited)
Hugh Trevor-Roper's Wartime Journals (edited)
One Hundred Letters from Hugh Trevor-Roper (co-edited)
Hugh Trevor-Roper's China Journals (forthcoming)

RICHARD DAVENPORT-HINES

Enemies Within

Communists, the Cambridge Spies and the Making of Modern Britain

EAST AYRSHIRE LEISURE TRUST	
542537	
Bertrams	15/02/2018
327.12	£25.00
	D1

WILLIAM COLLINS

William Collins
An imprint of HarperCollins*Publishers*
1 London Bridge Street
London SE1 9GF

WilliamCollinsBooks.com

First published in Great Britain in 2018 by William Collins

1

Copyright © 2018 Richard Davenport-Hines

Richard Davenport-Hines asserts the moral right to be identified as the author of this work.

A catalogue record for this book is available from the British Library

ISBN 978-0-00-751667-4 (hardback)
ISBN 978-0-00-824556-6 (trade paperback)

All rights reserved. No part of this publication may be reproduced, stored in a retrieval system, or transmitted, in any form or by any means, electronic, mechanical, photocopying, recording or otherwise, without the prior permission of the publishers.

This book is sold subject to the condition that it shall not, by way of trade or otherwise, be lent, re-sold, hired out or otherwise circulated without the publisher's prior consent in any form of binding or cover other than that in which it is published and without a similar condition including this condition being imposed on the subsequent purchaser.

Set in Minion by Palimpsest Book Production Limited,
Falkirk, Stirlingshire

Printed in Great Britain by CPI Group (UK) Ltd, Croydon CR0 4YY

MIX
Paper from
responsible sources
FSC™ C007454

This book is produced from independently certified FSC™ paper
to ensure responsible forest management.

For more information visit: www.harpercollins.co.uk/green

With love for † Rory Benet Allan
With gratitude to the Warden and Fellows of All Souls

CONTENTS

PART TWO
Asking for Trouble

PART THREE
Settling the Score

Author's Note

In MI5 files the symbol @ is used to indicate an alias, and repetitions of @ indicate a variety of aliases or codenames. I have followed this practice in the text.

Glossary

Abwehr	German military intelligence, 1920–45
active measures	Black propaganda, dirty tricks
agent	Individual who performs intelligence assignments for an intelligence agency without being an officer or staff member of that agency
agent of influence	An agent who is able to influence policy decisions
ARCOS	All Russian Co-operative Society, London, 1920–7
asset	A source of human intelligence
BSA	Birmingham Small Arms Company
C	Chief of the Secret Intelligence Service
case officer	An officer of an intelligence agency responsible for operating a particular agent or asset
Cheka	Extraordinary Commission for Combating Counter-Revolution and Sabotage, USSR, 1917–22

CIA	Central Intelligence Agency, USA, 1947–
CID	Committee of Imperial Defence, London, 1902–39
CIGS	Chief of the Imperial General Staff, London, 1909–64
Comintern	Third Communist International, USSR, 1919–43
CPGB	Communist Party of Great Britain, 1920–91
CPUSA	Communist Party of the United States of America, 1921–
cut-out	The intermediary communicating secret information between the provider and recipient of illicit information; knowing the source and destination of the transmitted information, but ignorant of the identities of other persons involved in the spying network
dead drop	Prearranged location where an agent, asset or case officer may leave material for collection
double agent	Agent cooperating with the intelligence service of one nation state while also working for and controlled by the intelligence or security service of another nation state
DPP	Directorate of Public Prosecutions, UK
DSO	Defence Security Officer, MI5
FBI	Federal Bureau of Investigation, US law enforcement agency, 1908–
FCO	Foreign & Commonwealth Office, 1968–
FO	Foreign Office
Fourth Department	Soviet military intelligence, known as the Fourth Department of the Red Army's General Staff, 1926–42

Friend	Source
GC&CS	Government Code & Cypher School, 1919–46
GCHQ	Government Communications Headquarters, 1946–
GPU	State Political Directorate, USSR, 1922–3
GRU	Soviet military intelligence, 1942–92
HUAC	House Un-American Activities Committee, USA, 1938–69
HUMINT	human intelligence
illegal	Officer of an intelligence service without any official connection to the nation for whom he is working; usually with false documentation
INO	foreign section of Cheka and its successor bodies, USSR, 1920–41
intelligence agent	An outside individual who is used by an intelligence service to supply information or to gain access to a target
intelligence officer	A trained individual who is formally employed in the hierarchy of an intelligence agency, whether serving at home or abroad
legal	Intelligence officer serving abroad as an official or semi-official representative of his home country
MGB	Ministry for State Security, USSR, 1946–53
MVD	Ministry of Internal Affairs, USSR, 1953–4 (as secret police)
negative vetting	background checks on an individual before offering her or him a government job
NKGB	People's Commissariat of State Security, February–July 1941 and 1943–6

NKVD   People's Commissariat for Internal Affairs
                          (responsible for state security of Soviet Union
                          1934–February 1941 and July 1941 to 1943)

NUPPO   National Union of Police and Prison Officers,
                          1913–20

OGPU   Combined State Political Directorate, USSR,
                          1923–34

OSINT   open source intelligence

OSS   Office of Strategic Services, Washington, 1942–5

PCO   Passport Control Officer: cover for SIS officers
                          in British embassies and legations

positive vetting (PV)   The exhaustive checking of an individual's back-
                          ground, political affiliations, personal life and
                          character in order to measure their suitability
                          for access to confidential material

principal   Intelligence officer directly responsible for
                          running an agent or asset

protective security   Security to protect personnel, buildings, docu-
                          ments, communications etc. involved in classified
                          material

PUS   Permanent Under Secretary

PWE   Political Warfare Executive, UK

rezident   Chief of a Soviet Russian intelligence station,
                          with supervisory control over subordinate intel-
                          ligence personnel

rezidentura   Soviet Russian intelligence station

ROP   Russian Oil Products Limited

SIGINT   Intelligence from intercepted foreign signals and
                          communications. Human intervention is needed
                          to turn the raw product into useful intelligence

SIME	Security Intelligence Middle East
SIS	Secret Intelligence Service (MI6), 1909–
SS	Security Service (MI5, under which name it was founded in 1909), 1931–
tradecraft	Acquired techniques of espionage and counter-intelligence
vorón	Literally 'raven': a male Russian operative used for sexual seduction

Illustration Credits

- Sir Robert Vansittart, head of the Foreign Office. (Popperfoto/Getty Images)
- Cecil L'Estrange Malone, Leninist MP for Leyton East. (Associated Newspapers/REX/Shutterstock)
- Jack Hayes, the MP whose detective agency manned by aggrieved ex-policemen spied for Moscow. (© National Portrait Gallery, London)
- MI5's agent M/1, Graham Pollard. (Esther Potter)
- MI5's agent M/12, Olga Gray. (Valerie Lippay)
- Percy Glading, leader of the Woolwich Arsenal and Holland Road spy ring. (Keystone Pictures USA/Alamy Stock Photo)
- Wilfrid Vernon, the MP who filched aviation secrets for Stalinist Russia and spoke up for Maoist China. (Daily Mail/REX/Shutterstock)
- Maurice Dobb, Cambridge economist. (Peter Lofts)
- Anthony Blunt boating party on the River Ouse in 1930. (Lytton Strachey/Frances Partridge/Getty Images)
- Moscow's talent scout Edith Tudor-Hart. (Attributed to Edith Tudor-Hart; print by Joanna Kane. Edith Tudor-Hart. National Galleries of Scotland / Archive presented by Wolfgang Suschitzky 2004. © Copyright held jointly by Peter Suschitzky, Julie Donat and Misha Donat)
- Pall Mall during the Blitz. (Central Press/Getty Images)
- Andrew Cohen, as Governor of Uganda, shares a dais with the Kabaka of Buganda. (Terence Spencer/The LIFE Images Collection/Getty Images)
- Philby's early associate Peter Smolka. (Centropa)
- Alexander Foote, who spied for Soviet Russia before defecting to the British in Berlin and cooperating with MI5. (Popperfoto/Getty Images)

- Igor Gouzenko, the Russian cipher clerk who defected in 1945. (Bettmann/Getty Images)
- Donald Maclean perched on Jock Balfour's desk at the Washington embassy, with Nicholas Henderson and Denis Greenhill. (Popperfoto/ Getty Images)
- Special Branch's Jim Skardon, prime interrogator of Soviet spies. (Associated Newspapers/REX/Shutterstock)
- Lord Inverchapel appreciating young American manhood. (Photo by JHU Sheridan Libraries/Gado/Getty Images)
- A carefree family without a secret in the world: Melinda and Donald Maclean. (Photo by Keystone-France/Gamma-Keystone via Getty Images)
- Dora Philby and her son in her Kensington flat. (Photo by Harold Clements/Express/Getty Images)
- Philby's wife Aileen facing prying journalists at her front door. (Associated Newspapers/REX/Shutterstock)
- Alan Nunn May, after his release from prison, enjoys the consumer durables of the Affluent Society. (Keystone Pictures USA/Alamy Stock Photo)
- The exiled Guy Burgess. (Popperfoto/Getty Images)
- John Vassall. (Trinity Mirror/Mirrorpix/Alamy Stock Photo)
- George Blake. (Photo by Central Press/Hulton Archive/Getty Images)
- George Brown, Foreign Secretary. (Clive Limpkin/Associated Newspapers /REX/Shutterstock)
- Richard Crossman. (Photo by Len Trievnor/Daily Express/Getty Images)
- *Daily Express* journalist Sefton Delmer. (Photo by Ronald Dumont/ Express/Getty Images)
- Maurice Oldfield of SIS – with his mother and sister outside Buckingham Palace. (©UPP/TopFoto)

The lie is a European power.

FERDINAND LASSALLE

Great is the power of steady misrepresentation.

CHARLES DARWIN

No great spy has been a short-term man.

SIR JOHN MASTERMAN

Men are classed less by achievement than by failure to achieve the impossible.

SIR ROBERT VANSITTART

Men go in herds: but every woman counts.

BLANCHE WARRE-CORNISH

Aims

In planning this book and arranging its evidence I have been guided by the social anthropologist Sir Edward Evans-Pritchard. 'Events lose much, even all, of their meaning if they are not seen as having some degree of regularity and constancy, as belonging to a certain type of event, all instances of which have many features in common,' he wrote. 'King John's struggle with the barons is meaningful only when the relations of the barons to Henry I, Stephen, Henry II, and Richard are also known; and also when the relations between the kings and barons in other countries with feudal institutions are known.' Similarly, the intelligence services' dealings with the Cambridge ring of five are best understood when the services' relations with other spy networks working for Moscow are put alongside them. The significance of Kim Philby, Donald Maclean, Guy Burgess, Anthony Blunt and John Cairncross, and the actions of counter-espionage officers pitted against them, make sense only when they are seen in a continuum with Jack Hayes, Norman Ewer, George Slocombe, Ernest Oldham, Wilfrid Vernon, Percy Glading, Alan Nunn May, William Marshall and John Vassall.

Enemies Within is a set of studies in character: incidentally of individual character, but primarily a study of institutional character. The operative traits of boarding schools, the universities of Oxford and Cambridge, the Intelligence Division, the Foreign Office, MI5, MI6 and Moscow Centre are the book's subjects. Historians fumble their catches when they study individuals' motives and individuals' ideas rather than the institutions in which people work, respond, find motivation and develop their ideas. This book is not a succession of character portraits: it seeks the bonds between individuals; it depicts mutually supportive networks; it explores the cooperative interests that mould thinking; it joins ideas to actions, and connects reactions with counter-reactions; it makes individuals intelligible by placing them in sequence, among the correct types and tendencies, of the milieux in which they thought and acted.

In addition to Evans-Pritchard I have carried in my mind a quotation from F. S. Oliver's great chronicle of Walpole's England in which he refers to Titus Oates, the perjurer who caused a cruel and stupid panic in 1678–9 by inventing a Jesuitical conspiracy known as the Popish Plot. 'Historians', wrote Oliver in *The Endless Adventure*,

> are too often of a baser sort. Such men write dark melodramas, wherein ancient wrongs cry out for vengeance, and wholesale destruction of institutions or states appears the only way to safety. Productions of this kind require comparatively little labour and thought; they provide the author with high excitement; they may bring him immediate fame, official recognition and substantial profits. Nearly every nation has been cursed at times with what may be called the *Titus Oates* school of historians. Their dark melodramas are not truth, but as nearly as possible the opposite of truth. *Titus Oates* the historian, stirring his brew of arrogance, envy and hatred in the witches' cauldron, is an ugly sight. A great part of the miseries which have afflicted Europe since the beginning of the nineteenth century have been due to frenzies produced in millions of weak or childish minds by deliberate perversions of history. And one of the worst things about *Titus Oates* is the malevolence he shows in tainting generous ideas.

One aim of this book is to rebut the Titus Oates commentators who have commandeered the history of communist espionage in twentieth-century Britain. I want to show the malevolence that has been used to taint generous ideas.

This is a thematic book. My ruling theme is that it hinders clear thinking if the significance of the Cambridge spies is presented, as they wished to be, in Marxist terms. Their ideological pursuit of class warfare, and their desire for the socialist proletariat to triumph over the capitalist bourgeoisie, is no reason for historians to follow the constricting jargon of their faith. I argue that the Cambridge spies did their greatest harm to Britain not during their clandestine espionage in 1934–51, but in their insidious propaganda victories over British government departments after 1951. The undermining of authority, the rejection of expertise, the suspicion of educational advantages, and the use of the words 'elite' and 'Establishment' as derogatory epithets transformed the social and political temper of Britain. The long-term results of the Burgess and Maclean defection reached their apotheosis when joined with other forces in the referendum vote for Brexit on 23 June 2016.

The social class of Moscow's agents inside British government departments was mixed. The contours of the espionage and counter-espionage described in *Enemies Within* – the recurrent types of event in the half-century after 1920 – do not fit Marxist class analysis. To follow the communist interpretation of these events is to become the dupe of Muscovite manipulation. The myths about the singularity of the Cambridge spies and the class-bound London Establishment's protection of them is belied by comparison with the New Deal officials who became Soviet spies in Roosevelt's Washington. Other comparisons are made with the internal dynasties of the KGB and with MI5's penetration agents within the Communist Party of Great Britain.

The belief in Establishment cover-ups is based on wilful misunderstanding. The primary aim of counter-intelligence is not to arrest spies and put them on public trial, profitable though this may be to newspapers in times of falling sales or national insecurity. The evidence to the Senate Intelligence Committee tendered in 2017 by James Comey, recently dismissed as Director of the Federal Bureau of Investigation by President Donald Trump, contains a paragraph that, with the adjustment of a few nouns, summarizes the policy of MI5 during the period of this book:

> It is important to understand that FBI counter-intelligence investigations are different than the more commonly known criminal investigative work. The Bureau's goal in a counter-intelligence investigation is to understand the technical and human methods that hostile foreign powers are using to influence the United States or to steal our secrets. The FBI uses that understanding to disrupt those efforts. Sometimes disruption takes the form of alerting a person who is targeted for recruitment or influence by the foreign power. Sometimes it involves hardening a computer system that is being

attacked. Sometimes it involves 'turning' the recruited person into a double agent, or publicly calling out the behavior with sanctions or expulsions of embassy-based intelligence officers. On occasion, criminal prosecution is used to disrupt intelligence activities.

For MI5, as for Comey's FBI, the first priority of counter-espionage was to understand the organization and techniques of their adversaries. The lowest priorities were arrests and trials.

The Marxist indictment of Whitehall's leadership takes a narrow, obsolete view of power relations. Inclusiveness entails not only the mesh of different classes but the duality of both sexes. In the period covered by this book, and long after, women lacked the status of men at all social levels. They were repulsed from the great departments of state. The interactions in such departments were wholly masculine: the supposed class exclusivity of the Foreign Office (which is a partial caricature, as I show) mattered little, so far as the subject of this book is concerned, compared to gender exclusivity. The key to understanding the successes of Moscow's penetration agents in government ministries, the failures to detect them swiftly and the counter-espionage mistakes in handling them lies in sex discrimination rather than class discrimination. Masculine loyalties rather than class affinities are the key that unlocks the closed secrets of communist espionage in Britain. The jokes between men – the unifying management of male personnel of all classes by the device of humour – was indispensable to engendering such loyalty. Laughing at the same jokes is one of the tightest forms of conformity.

Enemies Within is a study in trust, abused trust, forfeited trust and mistrust. Stalinist Russia is depicted as a totalitarian state in which there were ruthless efforts to arouse distrust between neighbours and colleagues, to eradicate mutual trust within families and institutions, and to run a power system based on paranoia. 'Saboteurs' and 'wreckers' were key-words of Stalinism, and Moscow projected its preoccupation with sabotage and wrecking on to the departments of state of its first great adversary, the British Empire. The London government is portrayed as a sophisticated, necessarily flawed but far from contemptible apparatus in which trust among colleagues was cultivated and valued. The assumptions of workplace trust existed at every level: the lowest and highest echelons of the Foreign Office worked from the same openly argued and unrestricted 'circulating file'; in the Special Branch of the Metropolitan Police, until the 1930s, matters of utmost political delicacy were confided to all men from the rank of superintendent downwards.

At the time of the defection of Burgess and Maclean in 1951, the departments of state were congeries of social relations and hierarchical networks. They were deliberate in their reliance on and development of the bonding of staff and in building bridges between diverse groups. Government ministries were thus edifices of 'social capital': a broad phrase denoting the systems of workplace reciprocity and goodwill, the exchanges of information and influence, the *informal solidarity*, that was a valued part of office life in western democracies until the 1980s. The era of the missing diplomats and the ensuing tall tales of Establishment cover-ups chipped away at this edifice, and weakened it for the wrecking-ball that demolished the social capital of twentieth-century Britain. The downfall of 'social capital' was accompanied by the upraising of 'rational choice theory'.

This theory suggests that untrammelled individuals make prudent, rational decisions bringing the best available satisfaction, and that accordingly they should act in their highest self-interest. The limits of rational choice theory ought to be evident: experience shows that people with low self-esteem make poor decisions; nationalism is a form of pooled self-regard to boost such people; and in the words of Sir George Rendel, sometime ambassador in Sofia and Brussels, 'Nationalism seldom sees its own economic interest.' Rational choice is the antithesis of the animating beliefs of the British administrative cadre in the period covered by this book. The theory has legitimated competitive disloyalty among colleagues, degraded personal self-respect, validated ruthless ill-will and diminished probity. The primacy of rational choice has subdued the sense of personal protective responsibility in government, and has gone a long way in eradicating traditional values of institutional neutrality, personal objectivity and self-respect. Not only the Cambridge spies, but the mandarins in departments of state whom they worked to outwit and damage would be astounded by the methods and ethics of Whitehall in the twenty-first century. They would consider contemporary procedures to be as corrupt, self-seeking and inefficient as those under any central African despotism or South American junta.

The influence of Moscow on London is the subject of *Enemies Within*. As any reader of *The Oxford Handbook of the History of Communism* will understand, Soviet communism was only one version of a Marxist state. 'As the twenty-first century advances,' writes Stephen A. Smith, editor of the *Oxford Handbook*, 'it may come to seem that the Chinese revolution was *the* great revolution of the twentieth century, deeper in its mobilization of society, more ambitious in its projects, more far-reaching in its achievements, and in some ways more enduring than its Soviet counterpart.' All this must be acknowledged: so, too, that Chinese revolutionaries took their own branded initiatives to change the character of western states. These great themes – as well as reactions to the wars in Korea and Vietnam – however lie outside my remit.

If I had attempted to be comprehensive, *Enemies Within* would have swollen into an unreadable leviathan. Endnotes at the close of paragraphs supply in order the sources of quotations, but I have not burdened the book with heavy citation of the sources for every idea or judgement. I have concentrated its focus by giving more attention to HUMINT than to SIGINT. There are more details on Leninism and Stalinism than on Marxism. The inter-war conflicts between British and Soviet interests in India, Afghanistan and China get scant notice. There are only slight references to German agents, or to the activities of the Communist Party of Great Britain. There is nothing about Italian pursuit of British secrets. Japan does not impinge on this story, for it did not operate a secret intelligence service in Europe: a Scottish aviator, Lord Sempill, and a former communist MP, Cecil L'Estrange Malone, were two of its few agents of influence. The interference in the 1960s and 1970s of Soviet satellite states in British politics and industrial relations is elided. Although I suspect that Soviet plans in the 1930s for industrial sabotage in the event of an Anglo-Russian war were extensive, the available archives are devoid of material. The Portland spy ring is omitted because, important though it was, its activities in 1952–61 are peripheral to themes of this book. The material necessary for a reliable appraisal of George Blake is not yet available: once the documentation is released, it will need a book of its own. I have drawn parallels between the activities of penetration agents in government departments in London and Washington, and have contrasted the counter-espionage of the two nations. There is a crying need for a historical study – written from an institutional standpoint rather than as biographical case-studies – of Soviet penetration of government departments in the Baltic capitals, of official cadres in the Balkans and most especially of ministries in Berlin, Brussels, Budapest, Madrid, Paris, Prague, Rome and Vienna.

Enemies Within is not a pantechnicon containing all that can be carried from a household clearance: it is a van carrying a few hand-picked artefacts.

PART ONE

Rules of the Game

CHAPTER 1

The Moscow Apparatus

When Sir John ('Jock') Balfour went as British Minister to Moscow in 1943, he was given sound advice by the American diplomat George Kennan. 'Although it will be very far from explaining everything,' Kennan said, 'it is always worthwhile, whenever the behaviour of the Soviet authorities becomes particularly difficult, to look back into Russian history for a precedent.' Current ideas and acts, he understood, encase past history. Similarly, in 1946, Frank Roberts surveyed post-war Soviet intentions from his vantage point in Britain's Moscow embassy. 'Basically, the Kremlin is now pursuing a Russian national policy, which does not differ except in degree from that pursued in the past by Ivan the Terrible, Peter the Great or Catherine the Great.' The chief difference between imperial and Stalinist Russia, according to Roberts, was that Soviet leaders covered their aims in the garb of Marxist-Leninist ideology, in which they believed with a faith as steadfast as that of the Jesuits during the Counter-Reformation.[1]

Although Tsar Alexander II had abolished serfdom in 1861, most of the subjects of his grandson Nicholas II lived in conditions of semi-vassalage in 1917. It was the promise of emancipation from Romanov controls, exploitation, injustice and ruinous warfare that made the Russian people give their support to the Bolsheviks. Lenin's one-party state faced the same crisis of economic and institutional backwardness that had overwhelmed the last Tsar: industries, agriculture, bureaucracy, the armed forces and armaments all needed to be modernized, empowered and expanded at juddering speed. As Kennan and Roberts indicated, a sense of the historic continuities in Leninist and Stalinist Russia helps in evaluating Moscow's ruling cadres and in appraising the function and extent of communist espionage. It matters as much to stress that the pitiless energy and ambition of the Bolshevik state apparatus surpassed any previous force in Russian history.[2]

Tsarist Russia

Russia's earliest political police was the Oprichnina. It was mustered in 1565 by Ivan the Terrible, Grand Duke of Muscovy and first Tsar of Russia. Ivan's enforcers dressed in black, rode black horses and had saddles embellished with a dog's head and broom to symbolize their task of sniffing out and sweeping away treason. During the European-wide reaction after the Napoleonic wars, a new apparatus called the Third Section was formed in 1826. It was charged with monitoring political dissent and social unrest, operated in tandem with several thousand gendarmes and employed innumerable paid informers. Annual summaries of the Third Section's surveillance reports were made to the tsarist government. 'Public opinion', declared the Third Section's Count Alexander von Benckendoff, 'is for the government what a topographical map is for an army command in time of war.'[3]

From the 1820s political dissidents, criminals, insubordinate soldiers, drunkards and vagabonds were deported in marching convoys to Siberia. They were consigned to this harsh exile (often after Third Section investigations) partly as condign punishment, but also to provide labour to colonize and develop the frozen wastes beyond the Ural Mountains. The rape of women, male and female prostitution, trafficked children, flogging, typhus, tuberculosis, the stench from human excrement, the hunger and destitution that occurred inside the penal colony became notorious as the number of exiles mounted (in the century before the Russian revolution of 1917, over a million indi-viduals had been sent to Siberia).

After the fatal stabbing of the Third Section's chief in 1878, a new state security apparatus named the Okhrana was instituted to eradicate political crime. Its draconian prerogatives were exercised with restraint in some respects: only seventeen people were executed for political crimes during the 1880s; all were assassins or implicated in murderous plots (a youth hanged for conspiring to kill Tsar Alexander III in 1887 was elder brother of Vladimir Ilyich Ulyanov, who took the alias of Lenin). But Okhrana's policemen were empowered to imprison and exile suspects in Siberia on their own authority. Thousands of deportees died there of disease, hunger and exhaustion. The overseers of one gang of convict roadbuilders starved their men into cannibalism. Exiles were regularly flogged with the cat-o'-nine-tails.

Not everyone suffered intolerably. Conditions were generally ameliorated at the time of Lenin's exile in Siberia in 1897–1900. While living in a peasant hut surrounded by steppe, swamp and the village dungheaps, he was able to borrow statistical, political and economics books from libraries, and published *The Development of Capitalism in Russia*, which established him as a Marxist ideologue. He secured a lucrative contract to translate into Russian *The History of Trade Unionism* by Beatrice and Sidney Webb. The authorities allowed him to keep a two-bore shotgun, cartridges and an Irish setter to hunt duck and snipe. Throughout his exile, Lenin played chess by correspondence across Russia and abroad. His letters were intercepted but seldom stopped: he maintained contacts with conspirators and subversives far away in Moscow, Kiev, Geneva and London. 'Lenin's letters from Siberia make strange reading,' writes Victor Sebestyen. 'They might be the letters of an indolent country squire of outdoor tastes but gentle epicurean philosophy which forbade him to take such tastes too seriously.'[4]

At 1 January 1901 there were as few as 1,800 political exiles confined in Siberia, with a few thousand more kept under police supervision, in remote provincial districts, as punishment for political crimes. About 10 per cent of those confined in Siberia in 1901 had been condemned to hard labour. Trotsky, who was exiled to a forlorn village in 1904, used his time to study Marx's *Das Kapital*, to father two children and to play croquet. In the aftermath of the revolutionary uprisings of 1905 there was renewed and intensified repression. The total of those sentenced to exile rose from 6,500 in 1905 to 30,000 in 1910. The living conditions of exiles deteriorated hideously. Some sixty of the leaders of the October revolution in 1917 were, like Lenin and Trotsky, former Siberian exiles. They learnt there to be merciless and vengeful, to cherish personal enmities, to bide their time, to foster fratricidal resentments. Bolshevism was Siberian-made.[5]

During the 1890s anti-tsarist conspirators developed new underground networks, which no longer plotted to seize power by sudden violent blows against the authorities but sought instead to topple tsarist absolutism by organizing the oppressed workers in a mass movement that would be too populous for Okhrana repression. They adapted the methods of German social democracy for the Russian environment. Okhrana agents continued to penetrate the revolutionary movement, report on discussions and remit secret material (the young Stalin, it has been suggested, acted as an Okhrana informer and agent provocateur). The Okhrana's foreign agency – based in the Russian embassy in Paris – kept émigrés and fugitive revolutionaries under trans-European surveillance. To counter the Okhrana's countless paid informers, revolutionaries became expert in running clandestine groups, holding undetected meetings and evading surveillance. Bolsheviks learnt, as one example, to write secret letters, which were to be sewn into the lining of clothes, not on paper, but on linen, which did not rustle incriminatingly if a courier was searched.

The Bolsheviks' organizational culture was conspiratorial from top and bottom. Their leaders acted under protective party disguises: Iosif Vissarionovich Dzhugashvili took the revolutionary pseudonym of Stalin because it resembled the sound of Lenin; Leon Trotsky had begun life as Lev Davidovich Bronstein; Grigory Yevseevich Zinoviev was the fighting name of Hirsch Apfelbaum alias Ovsei-Gershon Aronovich Radomyslsky; Maxim Litvinov was born Meir Henoch Mojszewicz Wallach-Finkelstein, and had the intermediate alias of Max Wallach; Vyacheslav Scriabin took the hard man's name of Molotov, meaning 'hammer'. Bolsheviks were indoctrinated with the need for secrecy: they grew adept in subterfuge and misdirection, and remained hyper-vigilant about enemies long after seizing power in 1917. As revolutionaries they pursued both overt and covert operations to weaken the institutions and governments of their enemies. The necessary crafts for survival in tsarist Russia, including secret cells and the transmission of secret material, were adaptable for foreign espionage.

Leninist Russia

Marx belittled the *Lumpenproletariat* who made mid-nineteenth-century revolutions: the urban forces that brought Louis Bonaparte to power in 1848 were, he wrote, a rabble of decayed roués, bourgeois chancers, ferret-like vagabonds, discharged soldiers, ex-prisoners, spongers, drifters, pickpockets, confidence-tricksters, pimps, literati, organ-grinders, rag-pickers and tinkers. Marx regarded universal suffrage as a fetish, Bonaparte as a reckless gambler, his election by popular vote as head of the French state as a pathological symptom, and Bonapartism as little different from tsarism. He regarded the working of economic laws as the paramount and predestined cause of revolution, and considered assertions of collective social will as subordinate factors. 'The strength of Marxism', wrote R. C. ('Robin') Zaehner, a Secret Intelligence Service (SIS) officer in Iran during the 1940s, 'is that it is a revolutionary creed which offers an earthly paradise here and now, which claims to be scientific, and which would have us believe that the classless society is the *inevitable* result of the evolutionary process'. Communism, continued Zaehner, repudiates individualism, self-regard, personal enterprise and the rights of private property: indeed considers them as condemned at the bar of historic destiny.[6]

The Bolshevik revolution in 1917 did not fit the principles of *Das Kapital*. Mechanized slaughter rather than, as Marx predicted, the breakdown of capitalism brought communist revolution to Russia. It was not the Bolshevik insurgents who made the revolutionary situation, but the European 'total war', which overwhelmed tsarist autocracy, brought military collapse, civilian exasperation, hunger and fatigue, and forced the abdication of Nicholas II in March 1917. The decision of the provisional government, which replaced the Romanov monarchy, to continue participation in that war led to the swift rise of several distinct mass movements: the urban proletariat (organized in 'soviets', viz. councils elected by manual workers), the peasantry, soldiers and sailors, non-Russian nationalities and a numerically small number of bourgeois all coalesced into different groups. The war-induced crisis discredited monarchism, liberalism and moderate socialism in turn. The collapse of state authority in 1917 had little resemblance to the military coups of politically minded soldiers, such as overthrew the Obrenović royal dynasty in Serbia in 1903 or mustered for the Young Turk revolt of 1908. Nor did it resemble the crowd pressure represented by the March on Rome led by Mussolini in 1922. It arose from the mass mobilization of peasants, soldiers and workers who were provoked by the injustice, exploitation, inequity and incompetence of their rulers, and yearned to be freed from a failed autocracy.[7]

On taking power the Bolsheviks sought to placate the mass movements. They signed the Brest-Litovsk peace treaty with Germany, devolved power to the soviets, redistributed confiscated lands to the peasantry and tried to vest control of factories in their workers. A giddying spiral of economic collapse, unemployment and mass privation renewed urban proletarian and peasant discontent. 'In the course of a bitter civil war, the Bolsheviks forged a Red Army that defeated a succession of enemies, including the Socialist Revolutionaries, the Whites, Allied interventionists, and peasant partisans,' as the historian of communism Stephen A. Smith has put it. 'In so doing, they instituted key elements of what would become the generic communist system: a highly centralized state under a single party, the crushing of dissent, and the curtailment of popular organizations.' Some scholars argue that this outcome was the result of Lenin's determination to concentrate power in a single party and to eliminate political opposition. Others contend that the totalitarian state was necessitated by 'the desperate problems the Bolshevists faced in defeating the counter-revolution, in feeding the Red Army and the urban population, in maintaining production for the war effort and in combating tendencies to crime and social anomie'. Once the Bolsheviks had trounced their adversaries, they did not revert to the decentralized socialist structures that had achieved the revolutions of 1917.[8]

Other preliminary points must be stressed in contextualizing the history of communist espionage in England. Nicholas II, whose Romanov dynasty had ruled since 1613, believed that he was a divine instrument, and that it was by God's command that his subjects owed unconditional submission to his autocracy. He preferred sacred duties, mysticism and superstition to secular expertise: specialist cadres of ministers and bureaucrats were anathema to him. The Russian Orthodox Church had been a temporal instrument of the Romanov empire since the reign of Peter the Great: icons and local saints – but also devils and sprites – were vivid, active forces in the lives of the peasantry; apostasy was a criminal offence. Bolshevik Russia was the antithesis of the Tsar's ramshackle theocracy: it was the first state in world history to be atheistic in its foundation and to deny the merit in any religion. 'The working class has elaborated its own revolutionary morality, which began by dethroning God and all absolute standards,' Trotsky declared in 1922. Although the Orthodox Church was one of the few Romanov institutions to survive 1917, its influence was truncated. Atheists across Europe welcomed the ruthless hostility of the pioneer socialist state to religious hocus-pocus. Kim Philby particularly but also Anthony Blunt, Guy Burgess and Donald Maclean were drawn to Marxism by its repudiation of Christianity.[9]

Secondly, the civil war of 1917–22 was the crucible in which the Soviet Union was forged. By one reliable computation, deaths in combat, endemic disease, disappearances and emigration led to a fall in population of 12.7 million between 1917 and 1922. During those years of savage combat the Bolshevik leadership made the communist party into a disciplined fighting force: they shed the vitiating residue of revolutionary romanticism and utopianism; they abjured clemency, lenience and individualism; and they asserted the historical inevitability of victory. Bolshevism was set on breaking the sovereignty and capitalism of nation states, installing an international workers' dictatorship and thus accomplishing global revolution. These great aims were used to justify the exaction of huge sacrifices by the present generation for the benefit of their successors; to justify, too, forced labour and show-trials.

During the 1920s Litvinov developed a diplomatic negotiating style suitable for the dictatorship of the proletariat: exhausting, outrageous insistence on predetermined objects, regardless of truth, reason or facts. Soviet officials had neither the training nor the capacity to argue with foreign negotiators. They declared their position with immovable aggression, and never deviated from it. Molotov was true to his *nom de guerre* and during the 1930s and 1940s continued this hammering, defiantly mendacious manner of diplomatic exchanges. Andrei Gromyko, who in 1957 began his twenty-eight years as Minister of Foreign Affairs, was a past-master in the old Bolshevik brand of brutal diplomacy and ersatz furious indignation.

During the civil war, the Bolsheviks lost control of large parts of the Romanov empire to the anti-Bolshevist, monarchist and nationalist forces known as the White armies. At first the Ukraine, the Caucasus, the Baltic provinces and central Asia were wrested back; but by the treaty of Riga in 1921 Ukraine was partitioned between the Soviet Union and an expanded Poland. Ground was lost in Finland, the Baltic littoral, western Belorussia and Bessarabia. Soviet Russia was seen by the Bolshevik leadership as a dismembered version of imperial Russia. Russian military advances into Poland and Finland in 1939–40 show the Stalinist priority in regaining the lost territories of 1918–20. In the spring of 1945 Russia was able to reoccupy Poland, Estonia, Latvia and

Lithuania, and to begin renewing its territorial and ideological control elsewhere. Britain, with its history of intervention in the civil war and as the only western European power with a major Asiatic empire, was a primary adversary, which needed to be met with espionage, subversion and ultimately sabotage.[10]

'How can you make a revolution without firing squads?' Lenin asked in 1917. 'Do you really believe that we can be victorious without the very cruellest revolutionary terror?' he demanded a year later. Soon he instituted so-called People's Courts, which have been described by Victor Sebestyen as 'essentially *ad hoc* mob trials in which twelve "elected" judges, most of them barely literate, would rule less on the facts of the case than with the use, in Lenin's words, of "revolutionary justice"'. After issuing a decree in 1918 permitting the summary shooting by Red Guards of enemy agents, profiteers, marauders, hooligans and counter-revolutionary agitators, Lenin regretted that it would be impolitic to rename the Commissariat of Justice the Commissariat for Social Extermination.[11]

Walter Krivitsky, the first major Soviet intelligence defector, said in his MI5 debriefing of 1940 that the moment when Bolshevism swung from socialism with benevolent hopes to an entrenched tyranny occurred in 1921, with the crushing of the revolt at Kronstadt naval base. A mass meeting of sailors of the Baltic fleet demanded free parliamentary elections, the establishment of non-communist trade unions and the abolition of internal political police. Their defiance was suppressed by 20,000 Red Army soldiers whom Trotsky had promised would shoot the sailors like partridges. The quashing of the Kronstadt protest was nasty, brutish and short: reading Trotsky's book *Whither England?* in 1925, the political theorist Harold Laski reflected that 'the whole Bolshevik psychology is merely Hobbes redressed in Marxian costume'. The Hobbesian absolutist system was intended to optimize the subject's peace and security; but, as Locke said, the tranquillity of Hobbes's ideal commonwealth was the peace and security of a dungeon.[12]

Dissidents across *ancien régime* Europe had to contend with 'perlustration' (government interception and reading of mail to discover what the population is thinking and writing). The Okhrana had *cabinets noirs*, or 'black chambers', where private and diplomatic correspondence was intercepted and read, in the ten main post offices of tsarist Russia, although this involved a total staff nationwide of only forty-nine people in 1913. After the Bolsheviks had attained power in 1917, they found that a state monopoly of propaganda was the best way to monitor thoughts, control the masses and inculcate them with socialism. By 1920 they had 10,000 officials trained to read the post in Russia. They destroyed letters that criticized the regime, and quoted from representative samples when compiling summaries of mass opinion. Surveillance reports were indispensable to policing public opinion in inter-war totalitarian states, whether Bolshevik Russia, Nazi Germany or fascist Italy, and to maximizing the effects of state propaganda. Most militant Marxist revolutionaries before 1917 were 'staunch fighters for political freedom', as Lars Lih, the historian of Leninism, has written. 'One of the most important political facts about the rest of the twentieth century was that the most orthodox and militant advocates of revolutionary Marxism were devoted to regimes that crushed political freedom to an unprecedented degree.'[13]

'Russia is a country which it is very easy to invade, but very difficult to conquer,' Lloyd George told parliament in 1919. 'Starvation, bloodshed, confusion, ruin, and horror' had been the outcome of the revolution two years earlier: he loathed 'Bolshevik teachings', but 'would rather leave Russia Bolshevik until she sees her way out of it than see Britain [go] bankrupt' as the result of military intervention against the revolutionaries. Soviet Russia nevertheless felt itself to be the target of relentless encirclement by capitalist forces and secret agents. This federation of socialist republics covered a huge area without natural defensible frontiers. Amid multitudinous evidence of London's malign intentions, there was the agreement in 1920 between the English armaments company Vickers and its French counterpart Schneider-Creusot to develop the Polish metallurgy firm Starachowice into a munition works. Similarly, in 1921–3, Vickers invested in the privately owned naval yards at Tallinn in Estonia, becoming sole technical advisers and purchasing agents as recompense for its investment: they were, said their manager in Estonia, seeking orders for their British factories, but 'also guided by the necessity of safeguarding as far as lay in our power the higher interests of British influence'. Both ventures proved unprofitable; but it is not surprising that the Soviets felt defensive security measures were needed.[14]

The Bolshevists' first Soviet intelligence agency, named the Cheka, was formed in December 1917 with the intention of defending and extending the dictatorship of the proletariat. Much of the Cheka's trade-craft was derived from the Okhrana, including the use of agents provocateurs to identify, incriminate and eliminate opponents. 'Every Bolshevist should make himself a Chekist,' Lenin once said. This was tantamount to saying that every communist must spy, steal, cheat, falsify documents, double-cross and be willing to kill. The Cheka's emblems of a shield to defend the revolution and a sword to smite its foes were used as the insignia of its ultimate successor organization, the KGB. Until the disbandment of the KGB in the 1990s, many of its officers, including Vladimir Putin, described themselves as Chekists.[15]

The Cheka's priority was arresting, shooting, imprisoning or exiling in forced labour camps Russian counter-revolutionaries, class enemies and putative conspirators whom they accused of being financed by foreign capitalism. As one of its internal documents asserted in 1918: 'He who fights for a better future will be merciless towards his enemies. He who seeks to protect poor people will harden his heart against pity and will become cruel.' The Chekists of the 1920s believed themselves superior to bourgeois scruples about guilt and innocence, or truth and lies. 'Give us a man, and we'll make a case,' their interrogators said with pride. As Nadezhda Mandelstam testified, the pioneer generation of Chekist leaders had modish cultural pretensions. 'The Chekists were the avant-garde of the new people and they revised, in the manner of the Superman, all human values,' she wrote. After their liquidation in 1937, they were succeeded by a very different type of political-police enforcer.[16]

The tsarist Okhrana had been anti-semitic, stoked pogroms and thus drove many Jewish people into revolutionary sympathies. Under the Romanovs, Jews were barred from Russian citizenship and forbidden to print in Hebrew. Violent persecution, injustice and exclusion caused retaliatory resentment, which took political form. Many of the Chekist avant-garde were Jewish. If the fact that Lenin's maternal grandfather was Jewish was then unknown, the identification of Kamenev, Litvinov, Radek, Trotsky and Zinoviev as Jews led to widespread European perceptions of Bolshevism as a Judaic influence. Lord D'Abernon, British Ambassador in Berlin, reflected in 1922 that Jewish small-traders in Germany felt 'sneaking affection for the Bolsheviks. Many of them are inclined to regard their co-religionaries at Moscow as rather fine fellows, who have done something to avenge the misfortunes of the Jewish race;

they consider Trotsky and the Cheka the apostolic successors to Judith and Deborah.'[17]

During the civil war of 1917–22, the Cheka was responsible for as many as 250,000 executions (possibly exceeding the number of deaths in combat). Lenin took a close interest in its operations, and discounted its brutality. He was less concerned by five million Russians and Ukrainians starving to death in 1921 than by his paranoia that the American Relief Administration was a front for subversion and espionage. In Odessa captured White officers were tied to planks and used to feed furnaces. In Kiev cages of rats were attached to prisoners' bodies, and the rats then maddened by the heat until they gnawed their way into the prisoners' intestines. In Tiflis the Cheka hauled persons of superior education from their beds, tied them head to foot, piled them into the back of a lorry, laid planks cross-wise over their captives so that the firing-party could clamber on board the lorry too and motored to a nearby agricultural college. There the victims were thrown into trenches and shot through the cervical vertebrae. 'The Russian government is composed of utter brutes,' wrote Sir Eyre Crowe, Permanent Under Secretary (PUS) at the Foreign Office, in 1924. It is important to add that atrocities were not all on the Red side. Between 50,000 and 200,000 Jews were massacred during the civil war period, and another 200,000 injured. Anti-Bolshevik forces seized the Jews from some soviets and boiled them alive in what they called 'communist soup'. Peasants disembowelled members of Food Requisition Detachments sent by Lenin from the cities to harvest or collect grain. Violence, as Stephen Smith shows, had variable purposes: it killed enemies, intimidated opponents, punished 'speculators' who intruded into peasant communities, protected criminals, enabled the seizure of booty, settled neighbourly disputes, enforced ideological convictions, gave depraved pleasure and bonded group loyalties.[18]

The history of Soviet espionage is disfigured by permutations of acronyms. In December 1920 the Cheka formed a new foreign department, known as INO, to run operations outside Soviet frontiers. In 1923 the Cheka was reconstituted as OGPU. George Slocombe, who spied for the Soviet Union during the 1920s, paid his only visit to Russia in 1926. Kept awake by Moscow's summer heat, he gazed through his open window: 'the red star burning in the tower of the OGPU headquarters, a sign of the never-relaxed vigilance of the defenders of the revolution, shone steadily, like a great red eye above the roofs and chimneys of Moscow'. Reader Bullard, who arrived in Moscow as British Consul General in 1930, was oppressed by a huge placard outside the opera house urging Muscovites to 'strengthen the sword of the dictatorship of the proletariat – the OGPU'. In 1934 OGPU was reincorporated into the NKVD. The later permutations were the NKGB (February 1941), NKVD again (July 1941), NKGB again (1943), MGB (1946), MVD (1953) and, from March 1954 until December 1991, the KGB. These bodies had a counterpart in the military intelligence section, which was known as the Fourth Department until it was renamed the GRU in 1942. The breaking or foiling of Fourth Department activities in Austria in 1931, in China in 1931–2 and in Latvia, Germany and Finland in 1933 was a chain-reaction caused by weak security between different cells. It proved ruinous for the department's standing with Stalin, who transferred it in 1934 from the superintendence of the Red Army to INO and limited its remit to Finland, Poland, Germany, Romania, Britain, Japan, Manchuria and China. As Jonathan Haslam reminds us, the KGB 'may have been the largest intelligence service in the world, but it was heavily weighted in favour of its domestic role, a role never played by its military counterpart, the GRU, the second largest intelligence service in the world'. KGB sources give a valuable if incomplete sense of events: the Fourth Department archive is unavailable to historians.[19]

The career of one Fourth Department man must represent hundreds of his colleagues. Ivan Zolov Vinarov @ Josef Winzer @ MART was born in 1896 to a family of prosperous Bulgarian landowners. He fled to Soviet Russia in 1922 to escape arrest for his part in the Bulgarian communist party's arms-smuggling. He was trained in military intelligence, sent on clandestine missions and involved with the communists who detonated an 'infernal machine' beneath the dome of a cathedral in Sofia during the state funeral of an assassinated general in 1925. A total of 123 people (including thirteen generals and seven children) were killed in the atrocity, which failed in its objective to liquidate Bulgaria's Prime Minister, Prince Alexander Tsankov, and his political cadre. Nor did it spark the intended communist revolution. The outcome was thousands of arrests, hundreds of executions and bitter destabilizing misery.

Two Labour MPs visiting Bulgaria, Josiah Wedgwood and William

Mackinder, failed to dissuade Tsankov's government from reprisals. Returning to Bradford, Mackinder told journalists that he would not revisit Bulgaria under Tsankov's government for a million pounds, but was not quoted as condemning the communist bomb outrage. Wedgwood contributed a report on 'Bulgarian vengeance-politics' to the *Manchester Guardian*. 'A Communist is outside the law, and the hunt is therefore up for Communists,' he told liberal-minded readers. Torture was being used to obtain confessions and denunciations: 'prisoners come back from Bulgarian prisons maimed for life, the bones of the feet all broken with the bastinado [caning the soles of feet]'. Wedgwood judged that Bulgaria's leaders were less frightened of Bolshevism from Russia than of western European radicalism. He found patriotic solace, amid the reprisals following the explosion, in noting that the English community in Bulgaria 'are doing their best to stem the spate of horrors. It is on occasions such as this that even the Labour member may thank God for an English gentleman.'[20]

The Communist International, abbreviated to Comintern, was established in Moscow in 1919–20 to act as the 'global party of the proletariat' organizing communist revolutionary activism across Europe and America. From the outset it stipulated that its affiliates must expel moderates, conform to Leninist domination and obey Moscow's orders. Disbursements to foreign communist parties in the Comintern's first financial year exceeded five million rubles: far more than was allotted for famine relief in 1921–2 when some five million Russians starved to death or died in epidemics. In accordance with Leninist paranoia, it developed its own spy network during the 1920s. The Comintern's enforcement of the 'Bolshevization' of foreign Marxist parties, its inordinate demands of fealty and its rejection of collaboration with European social democrats all proved major obstacles to the spread of socialism, enabling left-wing parties to be depicted by their opponents as the dupes or fifth columnists of Moscow. The insistence on mental submission certainly alienated intellectual members of the Communist Party of Great Britain (CPGB) in the late 1920s, and caused defections from the party. The Comintern made headway in colonial territories with predominantly peasant economies. Factory workers in European capitalist economies proved averse to risking their limited prosperity and security by rising in support of revolutionary socialism, which had proved so impoverishing in Bolshevist Russia. Until 1934 the Comintern

forbade cooperation with anti-fascists in Mussolini's Italy or with anti-
Nazis in Hitler's Germany; thereafter it accepted a Popular Front policy,
of which the first great achievement was the formation in 1936 of a
French government supported by communists. The Comintern became
Stalinized in the 1930s, it received directives from the Politburo and
its officials and agents increasingly cooperated with Soviet diplomats
in Europe and the USA.[21]

'In our era,' the Comintern propounded, 'imperialist wars and world
revolution, revolutionary civil wars of the proletarian dictatorship
against the bourgeoisie, wars of the proletariat against the bourgeois
states and world-capitalism, as well as national revolutionary wars of
oppressed peoples against imperialism, are unavoidable.' Many of the
officers and agents in the Comintern's international department were
able linguists and seasoned travellers of central or eastern European
birth. Cities like Prague produced alert, responsive men who noticed
changing tendencies and were effective in getting what they wanted
because their ambitions and insular pride were never as exorbitant as
those of Londoners, Berliners and Muscovites brought up in imperial
capitals. They were resourceful in selecting targets, laying plans and
reading motives. By contrast, many of their counterparts in INO, OGPU
and the NKVD were ill-educated, with the guile and brutality that fitted
them for suppressing dissidents in provincial Russia and harassing
counter-revolutionaries overseas, but less apt for collecting foreign
intelligence material.[22]

Stalinist Russia

Shrewd appraisals of Marxism-Leninism were provided by Sir Robert
Hodgson, Britain's resilient diplomatic representative in Moscow during
1921–7. He chronicled the Bolshevik government's continuous conflicts
with its founding principles, and the pressures which forced it to forsake
the revolutionary ideals of 1917. It was a huge challenge to misdirect
attention so that 'a trusting proletariat' could continue to cherish the
illusion that they, rather than a hefty, humdrum bureaucracy, governed
Russia, Hodgson reported after the May Day celebrations of 1926, when
Lenin had been dead for two years. 'Moscow, however much nonsense
is exhibited on red banners, stuffed into youthful brains, or poured out
through loud-speakers to the populace, has to deal with precisely the

same problems as any of its neighbours – and is dealing with them in very much the same way.'[23]

This focus became less helpful in assessing events after Stalin achieved undisputed supremacy in the Soviet Union in 1928–9. Wars, civil wars, threats of foreign wars and domestic class warfare were constant factors in the political careers and personal experiences of all Bolshevik leaders. Marxist-Leninist theory propounded the inevitability of wars between empires, of socialist revolution as a result of these imperialist wars, and of warlike interventions by capitalist powers against socialist states. Fears of internal adversaries and external encirclement were never assuaged. Stalin, though, intensified and invigorated this aspect of the Bolshevik mentality. He convinced the party cadres and general membership that he was a relentlessly industrious pragmatist who could manage the domestic and foreign crises that threatened the Soviet Union. He gained a well-deserved reputation for achievement. 'He was assiduous in consolidating his power base throughout the party, state, secret police and military hierarchies,' writes the historian of deStalin-ization Kevin McDermott. 'His increasingly radical policies in the years after 1928 proved attractive to the new brand of militant unschooled proletarians who formed the base of the party at that time.'[24]

Stalin's supremacy was characterized by crisis-paroxysms of socialist modernization. He sought to transform a ravaged agrarian economy into a global industrial power. The upheaval of forced agricultural collectivization and accelerated manufacturing capacity were akin to social and economic mobilization on a war footing. The first of Stalin's Five Year Plans for headlong economic expansion was ill-considered, and caused huge instabilities. Bolshevik fears of counter-revolutionary plots, of foreign saboteurs and internal wreckers, of encirclement by hostile foreign powers all grew in ferocity. Opposition was equated with terrorism. Frank discussion and rational argument were precluded within the Moscow apparatus. Britain's paramount instrument of civi-lized administration, the 'circulating file', which will be discussed later (p. 78–9), was unthinkable in communist bureaucracy.

A new ruling echelon was consolidated by Stalinism. Economic and social hierarchies were restored. The early Bolsheviks had been anti-patriarchal, had promoted the emancipation of women by improved educational and work opportunities, and had attempted to punish drunken wife-beaters. These advances halted after 1928. Stalin, whose wife shot herself in 1932 after being humiliated by him at a banquet, reconfigured masculine authority with his notions of motherhood and the criminalization of abortion in 1936. The early Bolshevik rejection of bourgeois morality ceased. Creative experimentation was stifled: stereotyped party hackwork dominated the arts; nonconformity was penalized. 'Crucially', as Stephen Smith summarizes the development, 'although the institutions of rule did not change, personal dictatorship, the unrestrained use of force, the cult of power, paranoia about encirclement and internal wreckers, and the spiralling of terror across an entire society, all served to underline the difference between Stalinism and Leninism.' Smith sees Stalinism as a reversion to an earlier type: 'the resurgence of . . . a patrimonial regime in which the tsar's absolute and unconstrained authority derived from his ownership of the country's resources, including the lives of his subjects'.[25]

Bolshevik foreign policy tactics were innovative. 'The Soviet Government', reported Sir Esmond Ovey soon after his appointment as the first British Ambassador to the Soviet Union in 1929, 'have inverted the normal methods of diplomacy, and are past-masters in the fanning of hostility to a point which is useful for their internal political plans, without actually provoking an armed attack from outside.' The desirable norm of Soviet diplomacy was a 'vociferously cantankerous state of peace', Ovey judged after some months in Moscow. Relatively minor incidents, such as the defection of Gregori Bessedovsky, the Soviet Chargé d'Affaires in Paris, could excite 'a fever of alarm' at 'the sinister intentions of the ring of capitalist countries who are waiting, watching, scheming and plotting to destroy them'.[26]

Intelligence-gathering and subversion managed by SIS representatives, under cover of passport control officers, in Scandinavia and the Baltic states, made Moscow feel beset by fears of foreign capitalist intervention. This feeling was shared by members of the CPGB, which was founded in 1920. Norman Ewer, a loyal upholder of Bolshevist ideology who ran a spy network for Moscow in London during the 1920s, felt sure that capitalist governments *must* be plotting to overthrow the world's first and only worker-peasant state by either invasion or secret subversion. As he wrote in 1927 in *Labour Monthly*, a magazine edited by a CPGB founder, Rajani ('Raymond') Palme Dutt: 'I would lay heavy money that to-day the War Office, the Admiralty and the Air Ministry are very busy with their plans for a Russian war. For a variety of Russian wars, I expect. There would be one plan for a war in defence of "gallant little Esthonia": another for a war to safeguard India from the Afghans . . . another for Manchurian possibilities; all these plans quite possibly interlocking and correlating, as did the pre-1914 plans for the aiding of France and for the conquest of Mesopotamia.' Ewer saw the Tory government as pushing 'a continuous movement in one direction and to one end. That end is war. War will come as certainly as harvest follows sowing.'[27]

After his defection from the Soviet embassy in Paris in 1929, Gregori Bessedovsky published his revelatory 'Souvenirs' in *Le Matin*. Summary translations, which were supplied to the British counter-espionage agency MI5 by the SIS station in Paris, show the ferocity of communist extremism. Ivanov, one of the Cheka chiefs, had confided to Bessedovsky 'that passing sentences of death was not so difficult as one might think. It was all a matter of getting used to it. At first, of course, it made one feel a bit queer, but afterwards one no longer thought of the man – the living person – in front of one, and the only thing one saw was a "dossier" of documents and papers.' Ivanov admitted that he never attended executions, although he was nominally in charge of them, because 'he feared the madhouse'. Ivanov's executioner-in-chief Gourov, who had killed 3,000 people and intended to reach the figure of 5,000, 'could no longer "work" unless he made himself drunk'. Ivanov continued: 'every Saturday night it is Hell', with the condemned in the cellars shrieking like beasts in a slaughter-house. Ivanov's assistant, who attended most executions, proposed gagging the prisoners' mouths to stop their cries; but, so Ivanov told Bessedovsky, 'I forbade him doing so. It would look too much like ordinary murders.'[28]

Maurice Dobb, an economist and pioneer Cambridge communist who was a key influence in assembling his university's spy network, minimized these enormities in a lecture at Pembroke College. He admitted the famine, executions and reprisals against hostages – undoubtedly 'the Red Terror has been at times exceedingly brutal' – but most stories, including those of 'torture' or 'the massacre of everyone with a white collar', were fables spread by tsarist exiles. His optimism was not ignoble, although time would discredit it. The Bolshevik programme was committed to the abolition of standing armies and to establishing the workers and peasantry as the new ruling class. Dynastic absolutism and bigoted theocracy had already been replaced by a federation of soviet socialist republics. Ownership of the means of production had been transferred from exploitative capitalism to the socialist state. Reactionary hereditary landowners had been usurped by peasant uprisings. In consequence of these revolutionary changes, Dobb averred, 'the extremes of riches & poverty exist no longer'. Although there were food shortages, rations were equitably shared. In Moscow 'there are no slums; their former inhabitants having been accommodated in the flats & palaces of the former bourgeoisie . . . children are especially well cared for'. Dobb idealized Lenin as 'a stern realist. Siberia & exile no doubt have tended to embitter him to a considerable degree. His political writings, which display acumen, erudition & logical reasoning, are invariably marred by virulent vilification of his opponents.' Lenin resembled a Jesuit priest, continued Dobb, 'with all the Jesuit's sincerity & idealism, and at the same time the Jesuit's callousness, casuistry, & bigotry'. He was 'a man with a mission, subordinating all else to a single goal . . . a great leader, a great thinker and a great administrator'; but withal 'a modest man, who regards himself as the mere instrument of the inexorable forces of social progress'.[29]

By contrast the diplomat Owen O'Malley, who journeyed through Russia in 1925 and 1941, described it as 'a spiritual gas-chamber, a sinister, unnatural and unholy place'. People trudged through the streets of Leningrad with averted eyes: they had to efface themselves to stay safe; greeting a neighbour might prove fatal; children spied on parents. A red-bearded Cheka agent dressed in an engine driver's peaked cap, black drill blouse and blue serge riding-breeches was charged with watching and eavesdropping on him in 1925. O'Malley believed that after he threw this tail, the 'poor fellow' was put to death. Even as a temporary visitor to the 'Worker's Paradise' he grew nerve-racked by 'the horrible feeling of being alone and in the power of these revolting barbarians'. After a few months as Consul General in Moscow in 1930, Reader Bullard felt repelled by what he saw: 'the unscrupulous deception, the unrelenting despotism, and above all the cruelty'.[30]

The Great Illegals

Between March and June 1927 the Chekists suffered major reverses in their clandestine work in Poland, China, France and London. Stalin attributed these setbacks to hidden traitors: 'London's agents have nestled in amongst us deeper than it seems.' The detection of espionage and subversion by accredited members of Soviet embassies, consulates and trade missions resulted in bad publicity and diplomatic tension. Accordingly, in August, the Politburo ordained that secret agents from OGPU, INO, the Fourth, the Comintern and cognate international bodies could no longer be members of embassies, legations or trade delegations. Top-secret communications must henceforth be transmitted as encrypted letters carried in the diplomatic bag: never by telegraph or wireless traffic. Although these orders were only partially implemented in 1927, they inaugurated the era of the Great Illegals.[31]

The illegal system had been pioneered in Berlin from 1925, and had subsequently been developed in Paris. The designation 'illegal' referred not to the illegality of agents' intentions or conduct, but to the nature of their foreign posting. These were men and women who worked and travelled under false documentation and had no official ties to Moscow. If their activities were detected or they were arrested, they had no incriminating direct link to Moscow and could be disavowed. The presence of illegals did not obviate the use of agents and officers who were designated as 'legal', because they operated under the cover of a diplomatic post in a legation, consulate or trade delegation. (The exception to this was the USA, where successive administrations refused diplomatic recognition to Soviet Russia until 1933: perforce Soviet agents working in Washington or other locations had no official ties to Moscow, and usually worked and travelled under false documentation.) 'Legal' officers and agents had the advantages of easy communications with Moscow through official codes and by diplomatic bags. If their espionage activities were detected, they could claim diplomatic immunity. The chiefs of both legal and illegal operations based in European capitals were denominated the *rezident*. It was usual for each country to have both a legal *rezident* and an illegal *rezident*. These *rezidents* supervised a spying apparatus called the *rezidentura*.

The illegal *rezidenturas* were seldom involved in actual recruitment, but ran paid and unpaid agents, and cultivated sources who might unwittingly provide them with information. Many illegals had canny psychological insight, which they used to assess the ability, temperament and vulnerability of potential sources. These informants might receive an explicit approach or else be tapped for information without realizing the nature of their contacts. Officials were targeted, but also sources in journalism, politics, commerce and manufacturing. Informants were recruited by appeals to ideological sympathies or by exploiting the vanity of people who felt superior if their lives involved the exciting secret cleverness of espionage. The illegals identified people who needed money and would supply material in return for cash. They used sexual enticement, too. The illegals and their sub-agents often had to forfeit their human decency by cheating, lying, betrayal and abandonment of the weak. They rationalized their loss by arguing that only exploitative capitalists who were secure in power could afford scruples. Leninists or Stalinists who baulked at orders or confessed to scruples were betraying their cause and doubting its supreme value.

Following the Sofia cathedral massacre, the Bulgarian Vinarov served in 1926–9 as an illegal in China, where his wife worked as a cipher clerk in the Soviet legations in Peking and Harbin. During 1930–3 he was the senior illegal in Austria, where he riddled the French alliance system in eastern Europe and the Balkans with a network of agents and sources. He formed a trading company as cover for illicit movements across national frontiers, and penetrated the radio-telegraphic departments in Balkan capitals handling ciphered wireless traffic from foreign legations and embassies. This yielded good product until 1933, when the activities of Vinarov's penetration agents were discovered, although misunderstood, in Bucharest. In 1936, after further training, he went to Spain under the cover of a commercial attaché, but was purged in 1938. Recalled to guerrilla warfare in the 1940s, he was appointed the Bulgarian communist government's Minister of Transport and Construction in 1949.[32]

The illegals never travelled to and from Moscow under their own names. Nor did they use the passport attached to their primary alias. If Walter Krivitsky, who was the illegal in The Hague using the alias of Martin Lessner, had to return to Moscow, he travelled via Stockholm using the cover and documentation of an Austrian engineer named Eduard Miller. Elizabeth Poretsky, in her moving group memoir of Krivitsky and her husband Ignace Reiss, who served as an illegal in Austria, Poland, Czechoslovakia, France and the Netherlands (with oversight of England), shows that local conditions and the aptitude of the *rezident* counted for much. 'Soviet agents', Poretsky recalled, 'were convinced that their historic role gave them an innate advantage in dealing with world politics.'[33]

The illegals' commitment is incomprehensible unless one understands their certitude in their historical destiny. They all experienced the reality of the Soviet Union under Lenin and Stalin while they underwent indoctrination and training in Moscow. They knew the cruelty, hardship and scarcities while never doubting the future abundance. In their temporary Red Army accommodation in Moscow, Reiss and Poretsky gave parties at which they could serve only bad herring, horsemeat sausages, salted fish which made their gums bleed, and beetroot. On one occasion a visitor from Kiev described conditions in Ukraine to them: 'the famine in the cities, the bloated corpses in the streets, the hordes of abandoned children hanging around the railway stations, the ghostly villages where people were dying of starvation and typhus'. Their other guest was a Red Army colonel who, hearing this recital, started sobbing. 'He, he, is doing this,' the colonel raged between sobs and obscenities, 'he is ruining the country, he is destroying the party.' Then he opened a window and vomited his meal outdoors.[34]

The development of this ramified illegal apparatus was required because Soviet military attachés dispersed in European capitals were otiose for intelligence work. Active combat in the war of 1914–17 or in the civil war of 1917–22 was poor training for gathering and evaluating political intelligence reports. The military attachés despised capitalism, but seldom understood it. They were easily duped by spurious material, especially forgeries emanating from White Russian émigré organizations or local counter-intelligence. Poretsky recalled one document, purportedly composed by the French General Staff, outlining a secret agreement between Poland and France on military collaboration against the Soviet Union, which was couched in excruciating French, with blunders of syntax and spelling which no Frenchman could have committed. This palpable fraud was bought, photographed and sent to Moscow because no one working for military intelligence at the Soviet embassy in Vienna knew a word of French. Poretsky considered that 'a surprising number [of Soviet military attachés] showed signs of mental instability'.[35]

A costly apparatus watched its citizens, monitored public opinion, identified recalcitrant individuals and determined whom to kill. A Cheka circular of 1920–1 declared: 'Our work should concentrate on the information apparatus, for only when the Cheka is sufficiently informed and has precise data elucidating organisations and their individual members will it be able . . . to take timely and necessary measures for liquidating groups as well as the individual who is harmful and dangerous.' Moscow killed their own. The illegal Fedia Umansky @ Fedin @ Alfred Krauss predicted in 1929, 'there are only two things in store for the likes of us. Either the enemy will hang us or our own people will shoot us.' None of the illegals was executed by western imperialism: most were killed by the cannibal paranoia of the dictatorship of the proletariat. This phenomenon led to several damaging Soviet defections.[36]

In January 1930 Georges Agabekov (born Grigory Sergeyvich Arutyunov @ Nerses Ovsepyan @ Azadoff), who was chief of OGPU's eastern section in 1928-9, tried to defect to the British in Istanbul. He was motivated by both ideological estrangement and infatuation with an Englishwoman whom he had met in Turkey. Defectors at that time were treated as despicable funks rather than valuable assets. They ranked as the civilian equivalent of selfish deserters who had been put before the firing-squad in wartime. Accordingly Agabekov was rebuffed by his girlfriend's compatriots, although six months later he successfully defected in Paris. The French government, rather than cultivating him as a source, expelled him as a trouble-maker after the girlfriend's parents denounced him as a heartless seducer. Before his deportation, it was recognized in London by Guy Liddell of Special Branch and by MI5's Kathleen ('Jane') Sissmore and Oswald ('Jasper') Harker that, as the most senior OGPU officer to have defected, he was worth monitoring and interviewing. The Home Office warrant of 27 July 1930 requesting the interception of his mail was phrased in the patronizing, mistrustful terms with which foreign sources were often approached: 'The individual named, who states himself to have been a member of the Russian OGPU, has made a rather theatrical "escape" from Constantinople to Paris. He has given a lurid account of orders from his former chiefs including the liquidation of recalcitrant Soviet employees. It is strongly suspected . . . that he may be acting as agent provocateur.' London's *Morning Post* newspaper sent its Paris correspondent to interview Agabekov, 'chief of the OGPU for the five Mahomedan countries', and duly reported: 'He calls himself an American, and is a typical Levantine with yellow eyes and a coffee-coloured complexion.' These were yet further expressions of that British condescension – a complacent amalgam of pride and insularity – that had led Robert Bruce Lockhart, the British acting Consul General in Moscow, to liken Lenin to a provincial grocer in 1917.[37]

The deaths or flight from Russia of the tsarists' world-leading cryptographers lowered the quality of Soviet code-making and code-breaking. Partly as compensation for this deterioration in SIGINT (signals intelligence), but also as an outcome of their inclinations, the Bolsheviks collected excellent HUMINT (human intelligence) from other countries' missions, legations and embassies both in Moscow and in other European capitals. There is a myth, as Christopher Andrew and Oleg Gordievsky write, that brilliant mathematicians achieved the major code-breaking successes. The reality is that HUMINT had a part in most major breaks of high-grade code and cipher systems. During the 1930s Moscow's informants in the Communications Department of the Foreign Office supplied plain-text British diplomatic telegrams which Soviet code-breakers could, in some instances, compare with the ciphered versions as an aid to breaking the ciphers. Soviet SIGINT experts were, however, decimated during Stalin's Great Terror. The cryptographer Gleb Boky, who led the SIGINT operations of the NKVD and the Fourth Department, was shot in 1937 together with his deputy. Boky's successor survived in post only a month.[38]

Soviet espionage in foreign missions

Britain's Secret Intelligence Service (SIS) did not have a Moscow station in the 1920s or 1930s. Muscovites were too cowed to be approachable by foreign diplomats. Sir Robert Hodgson reported in 1924 on Soviet espionage on diplomatic missions in Moscow: 'It is unfortunate that, in order to establish the new régime – the so-called dictatorship of the proletariat – the Soviet Government should find itself compelled to . . . extend on an unheard-of scale the most revolting expedients of dilation, espionage and administrative tyranny which disfigured the old régime.' Foreign missions in the capital were beleaguered 'panic-centres', he said. Russians were afraid to attend Hodgson's lawn-tennis tournaments; musicians were scared to perform at evening concerts. He regarded the Soviet regime as akin to a fundamentalist religious cult at the height of its zeal: a year later he told Lord D'Abernon that he hoped Russia's government 'will be laicised, and that normal human interests will resume their sway'. When Anglo-Russian diplomatic relations were temporarily severed in 1927, all but two of the Russian staff of Hodgson's mission were given diplomatic protection with jobs at the Norwegian legation. Dire punishment for collaborating with capitalism befell the unfortunate pair who were not hired by Norway: the doorkeeper Vera Rublatt was exiled for three years in Siberia; the messenger Surkov was sent to the dreaded penal camp in the Solovetsky Islands.[39]

Security measures were primitive for most of the inter-war period not only in British embassies and legations but in those of the other powers. The need for specialist advice or strict procedures occurred to almost no one in the 1920s. In 1927 it was found that Soviet diplomats in Peking had recruited Chinese staff in the British, Italian and Japanese legations to supply copies of secret diplomatic documents.

The most grievous lapse began on the watch of Sir Ronald Graham, who was the Ambassador in Rome for twelve years from 1921. Graham made the embassy at the end of the Via XX Settembre, with its beautiful garden shaded by the city wall, into a salon for literary and artistic connoisseurs as well as a political and diplomatic congregation point. Amid these amenities Francesco Constantini, an embassy messenger, was recruited by INO in 1924 and given the codename DUNCAN. When two copies of the diplomatic cipher went missing shortly afterwards, diplomats did not think to suspect him. In addition to cipher material, he stole dispatches on Anglo-Italian relations and often supplied the 'confidential print' which was circulated from London to heads of its overseas diplomatic missions giving up-to-date material from important Foreign Office documents and selected dispatches and summaries. Constantini was a mercenary who wanted to enrich himself. Some 150 pages of classified material left the embassy on average each week by 1925. In Moscow, Constantini was reckoned to be INO's most valuable agent, whose material would betray British plots to destroy the Soviet Union and provide early warnings of the expected British invasion. 'England is now the organizing force behind a probable attack on the USSR in the near future,' Constantini was instructed by Moscow in 1925. 'A continuous hostile cordon [of states] is being formed against us in the West. In the East, in Persia, Afghanistan and China we observe a similar picture . . . your task (and consider it a priority) is to provide documentary and agent materials which reveal the details of the English plan.'[40]

Security did not improve after Sir Eric Drummond had succeeded Graham as Ambassador in 1933. Slocombe's pen-portrait of the new chief in Via XX Settembre evokes an unassuming, dejected, exact and unimaginative Scot who was heir-presumptive to the earldom of Perth: 'the least elegant Foreign Office official who ever carried a neatly rolled umbrella in Whitehall . . . he had a small head, a long neck with a prominent Adam's apple, a long nose'. Drummond and his staff could not think how to react to the brazenness of Mussolini in 1936 in publishing a secret British report on Abyssinia which had been filched from the embassy. They were confounded when Il Duce bragged that he had a copy of a memorandum 'The German Danger' circulated to the Cabinet by the Foreign Secretary Anthony Eden. They did not know that the Italians forthwith gave the text of Eden's paper to Hitler.[41]

No action was taken to improve security until in 1937 a necklace belonging to Lady Drummond vanished from a locked red box in the Ambassador's office. Valentine Vivian of SIS, who was sent by the Foreign Office to report on the Rome embassy, warned that there was no 'such thing as an expert in security measures, and I make no pretensions to being one'. He nevertheless made sound recommendations – of which one is especially notable. Although diplomats assumed that telephone conversations were tapped, they were unaware that telephones might be doctored so as to act as microphones recording conversations in embassy offices. Vivian suspected a new telephone on the cipher officers' table, and after Foreign Office discussions, the PUS Sir Robert ('Van') Vansittart instructed that henceforth telephones should be excluded from the cipher-room. A month after Vivian's visit to Rome, the Foreign Office discovered that the summary of a confidential talk with the Regent of Yugoslavia about his policy towards Italy had been leaked to Mussolini's government.[42]

When Vivian inspected British embassy offices in Berlin a few months later, he found them vulnerable to breaches. Security in embassies, legations, consulates and the Foreign Office was seen as a matter of lowly office administration. Officials of mature judgement were dismissive and even scornful of crude espionage scares. Basil Liddell Hart was military correspondent of *The Times*, adviser to the Secretary of State for War and one of England's most up-to-date tactical planners. 'This ugly rash is again breaking out on the face of Europe,' he warned of 'spy-mania' in 1937. 'Its justification is probably slender, as usual.

For the knowledge that matters is rarely gained by the methods that thrill the lover of sensational spy-stories: safer, in every sense, is the knowledge that comes by the application of ordinary deductive methods to a mass of data that is common property.' It took the discovery in September 1939, after the outbreak of war, that for ten years Moscow had been buying secrets from the Foreign Office's Communications Department (see Chapter 5), and the further belated revelation by SIS in January 1940 that Berlin had (during the previous July and August) received secrets from the Office's Central Department, for an embryonic Security Department to be formed. 'I can trust *no one*,' exclaimed the Office's exasperated Permanent Under Secretary, Sir Alexander Cadogan, who had been equally astounded on first hearing the long history of betrayals in Rome.[43]

It is easy to disparage these attitudes with hindsight. These were men, though, who never purged an enemy, and were never deluded that history was on their side. Their arrangements were no more defective or naive than those of the United States. William Bullitt was appointed as the earliest American Ambassador to Soviet Russia in 1933: he had earlier been psychoanalysed by Freud, and had co-authored with Freud a psychoanalytical biography of Woodrow Wilson. 'We should never send a spy to the Soviet Union,' Bullitt advised the State Department after three years in Moscow. 'There is no weapon so disarming and so effective in relations with the Communists as sheer honesty.' The corporate lawyer Joseph Davies, who replaced Bullitt in 1936, was a dupe who attended the Moscow show-trials and believed the evidence. The embassy at first had no codes, no safes and no couriers, but sent messages through the Moscow telegraph service where they could be read by anyone. The US Marines who guarded the embassy, and some of the cipher clerks, were provided with NKVD girlfriends. When an FBI agent, posing as a courier, visited the embassy in 1940, he found that the duty code clerk had left the code-room unattended, with the door open, for forty-five minutes. At night the code-room safe was left open with codebooks and messages on the table. It did not occur to the FBI agent to search for listening devices. When this was belatedly done in 1944, a total of 120 hidden microphones were found in the first sweep of the building. Further sweeps found more microphones secreted in furniture legs, plastered walls and elsewhere.[44]

The political culture of everlasting distrust

The most effective British Ambassador to Stalinist Russia was Sir Archie Clark Kerr, who was created Lord Inverchapel as a reward for his success. 'Nearly all of those who now govern Russia and mould opinion have led hunted lives since their early manhood when they were chased from pillar to post by the Tsarist police,' he wrote in a dispatch of December 1945 assessing diplomacy in the new nuclear age. 'Then came the immense and dangerous gamble of the Revolution, followed by the perils and ups and downs of intervention and civil war.' Later still came the deadly purges, when 'no one of them knew today whether he would be alive tomorrow'. Through all these years Soviet apparatchiks 'trembled for the safety of their country and of their system as they trembled for their own'. Their personal experiences and their national system liquidated trust and personal security.[45]

Stalin achieved supremacy by implementing a maxim in his book *Concerning Questions of Leninism*: 'Power has not merely to be seized: it has to be held, to be consolidated, to be made invincible.' To Lev Kamenev, whom he was to have killed, he said: 'The greatest delight is to mark one's enemy, prepare everything, avenge oneself thoroughly, and go to sleep.' Dissidents who had fled abroad were assassinated. In 1938, for example, Evgeni Konovalets, the Ukrainian nationalist leader, was killed in Rotterdam by an exploding chocolate cake. Stalin compared his purges and liquidations to Ivan the Terrible's massacres: 'Who's going to remember all this riffraff in twenty years' time? Who remembers the names of the *boyars* Ivan the Terrible got rid of? No one . . . He should have killed them all, to create a strong state.'[46]

Stalin rewarded his associates with privileges so long as they served his will. 'Every Leninist knows, if he is a real Leninist,' he told the party congress of 1934, 'that equality in the sphere of requirements and personal life is a piece of reactionary petit-bourgeois stupidity, worthy of a primitive sect of ascetics, but not of a socialist society organized on Marxist lines.' But Stalin was pitiless in ordering the deaths of his adjutants when they no longer served his turn. The first member of his entourage to be killed on his orders was Nestor Apollonovich Lakoba, who was poisoned during a dinner at which his attendance was coerced by Stalin's deadly subordinate Lavrentiy Beria in 1936. Beria then maddened Lakoba's beautiful widow by confining her in a

cell with a snake and by forcing her to watch the beating of her four-
teen-year-old son. She finally died after a night of torture, and the child
was subsequently put to death.[47]

The enemies of the people were not limited to saboteurs and spies,
Stalin said at the time that he launched his purges. There were also
doubters – the naysayers to the dictatorship of the proletariat – and
they too had to be liquidated. The first of the notorious Moscow show-
trials opened in August 1936. Chief among the sixteen defendants were
Zinoviev and Kamenev, who had agreed with Stalin to plead guilty and
make docile, bogus confessions in return for a guarantee that there
would be no executions and that their families would be spared. They
were faced by the Procurator General, Andrei Vyshinsky, the scion of
a wealthy Polish family in Odessa, who had years before shared
food-hampers from his parents with his prison cell-mate Stalin.
Vyshinsky was 'ravenously bloodthirsty', in Simon Sebag Montefiore's
phrase, producing outrushes of synthetic fury at need, and using his
vicious wit to revile the defendants as 'mad dogs of capitalism'. The
promises of clemency were ignored, and when all sixteen defendants
were sentenced to death, there was a shout in court of 'Long live the
cause of Marx, Engels, Lenin and Stalin!' Stalin never attended executions, which he treated as 'noble party service' and which were officially
designated the Highest Measure of Punishment. Vyshinsky seldom saw
the kill, for he too was squeamish. At the Lubianka prison, Zinoviev
cried: 'Please, comrade, for God's sake, call Joseph Vissarionovich
[Stalin]! Joseph Vissarionovich promised to save our lives!' He, Kamenev
and the others were shot through the back of the head. The bullets,
with their noses crushed, were dug from the skulls, cleaned of blood
and brains, and handed (probably still warm) to Genrikh Grigorievich
Yagoda, the ex-pharmacist who had created the slave-labour camps of
the Gulag and was rewarded with appointment as Commissar General
of State Security.[48]

Yagoda, who was a collector of orchids and erotic curiosities, labelled
the bullets 'Zinoviev' and 'Kamenev', and treasured them alongside
his collection of women's stockings. At a subsequent dinner in the
NKVD's honour, Stalin's court jester Karl Pauker made a comic re-
enactment of Zinoviev's desperate final pleading, with added anti-
semitic touches of exaggerated cringing, weeping and raising of hands
heavenwards with the prayer, 'Hear oh Israel the Lord is our God.'

Stalin's entourage guffawed at this mockery of the dead: the despot laughed so heartily that he was nearly sick. A year later Pauker himself was shot: 'guilty of knowing too much and living too well: Stalin no longer trusted the old-fashioned Chekists with foreign connections'. When Yagoda in turn was exterminated in 1938, the 'Zinoviev' and 'Kamenev' bullets passed 'like holy relics in a depraved distortion of the apostolic succession' to his successor Nikolai Ivanovich Yezhov. Two years later Yezhov was convicted of spying for Polish landowners, English noblemen and Japanese samurai. When taken to a special execution yard, with sloping floor and hosing facilities, Yezhov's legs buckled and he was dragged weeping to meet the bullet. Similarly the executioner who shot Beria after Stalin's death stuffed rags in his mouth to stifle the bawling.[49]

Denis Pritt attended the first Moscow show-trials of 1936. A former Tory voter and a King's Counsel with a prosperous practice in capitalist Chancery cases, he had turned Red, and became the barrister chosen by the CPGB to defend party members accused of espionage. For fifteen years he was MP for North Hammersmith: after his expulsion from the Labour party in 1940 he continued for a decade to represent the constituency as a communist fellow-traveller; he was rewarded with the Stalin Peace Prize. 'The Soviet Union is a civilised country, with . . . very fine lawyers and jurists,' Pritt reported of a criminal state which deprived its subjects of every vestige of truth. The Moscow trials were a 'great step' towards placing Soviet justice at the forefront of 'the legal systems of the modern world'. Vyshinsky, he said, resembled 'a very intelligent and rather mild-mannered English businessman', who 'seldom raised his voice . . . never ranted . . . or thumped the table', and was merely being forthright when he called the defendants 'bandits and mad-dogs and suggested that they ought to be exterminated'. Any doubts about the guilt of Zinoviev and Kamenev were dispelled for Pritt by 'their confessions [made] with an almost abject and exuberant completeness'. None of the defendants had 'the haggard face, the twitching hand, the dazed expression, the bandaged head' familiar from prisoners' docks in capitalist jurisdictions. Bourgeois critics who vilified socialist justice exceeded the bounds of plausibility: 'if they thus dismiss the whole case for the prosecution as a "frame-up", it follows inescapably that Stalin and a substantial number of other high officials, including presumably the judges and the prosecutors, were themselves guilty of a foul conspiracy to procure the judicial murder of Zinoviev, Kamenev, and a fair number of other persons'.[50]

Stalin's obsession with 'wreckers' and 'saboteurs' working within the Soviet Union is certainly a projection of Moscow's activities abroad: plans and personnel for sabotage of British factories, transport and fuel depots in the event of the long-expected Anglo-Russian war were probably extensive. More than ever, after the purges, Stalin used gallows humour to intimidate his entourage. At a Kremlin banquet to welcome Charles de Gaulle in 1942, he proposed a toast: 'I drink to my Commissar of Railways. He knows that if his railways failed to function, he would answer with his neck. This is wartime, gentlemen, so I use harsh words.' Or again: 'I raise my glass to my Commissar of Tanks. He knows that failure of his tanks to issue from the factories would cause him to hang.' The commissars in question had to rise from their seats and proceed along the banqueting table clinking glasses. 'People call me a monster, but as you see, I make a joke of it,' he chuckled to de Gaulle. Later he nudged the Free French leader and pointed at Molotov confabulating with Georges Bidault: 'Machine-gun the diplomats, machine-gun them. Leave it to us soldiers to settle things.'[51]

Soviet Russia killed its own in their millions, tortured the children of disgraced leaders, urged other children to denounce their parents for political delinquency, used threats of the noose or the bullet as a work-incentive for its officials, and built slaughter-houses for the extermination of loyal servants. 'There are no . . . private individuals in this country,' Stalin told a newly appointed Ambassador in Moscow, Sir Maurice Peterson, in 1946. The best-organized and most productive Stalinist industry was the falsification of history. Blatant lies were symbols of status: the bigger the lies that went unchallenged, the higher one's standing. Communist Russia liquidated trust throughout its territories. Every family constantly scrutinized their acquaintances, trying to spot the informers and provocateurs, or those who by association might bring down on them the lethal interest of the secret police. By the culmination of the purges in 1937, people were too scared to meet each other socially. Independent personal judgements on matters of doctrinal orthodoxy became impermissible. As Hugh Trevor-Roper noted in 1959, 'the Russian historians who come to international conferences are like men from the moon: they speak a different language, talk of the "correct" and "incorrect" interpretations, make statements and refuse discussions'. When after thirty years of internal exile, Nadezhda Mandelstam returned to Moscow in 1965, she found that fear remained ubiquitous. 'Nobody trusted anyone else, and every acquaintance was a suspected police informer. It somehow seemed as if the whole country was suffering from persecution mania.'[52]

In Stalin's toxic suspicions we reach the kernel of this book: the destruction of trust. Purges, so Nikolai Bukharin told Stalin in 1937, guaranteed the primacy of the leadership by arousing in the upper echelons of the party 'an everlasting distrust' of each other. Stalin went further, and said in Nikita Khrushchev's presence in 1951, 'I'm finished, I trust no one, not even myself.' Soviet Russia's ultimate triumph was to destroy reciprocal trust within the political society of its chief adversary.[53]

CHAPTER 2

The Intelligence Division

Every power system must defend itself against spies, traitors, rebels, saboteurs and mutineers. Cunning ambitions – both internal and external – threaten every sovereignty. Individual vanities endanger national security. Accordingly, hidden away inside the great machinery of states, there have always been the smaller apparatuses of espionage, counter-espionage and counter-subversion. Yet spies, double agents, couriers and informers are little use abroad or in the homeland, nor can the collection by licit means of foreign and domestic information be made intelligible, without offices to process material and turn it into intelligence. In England, as in Russia, the organized collection of reports and intercepts on exiles, foreign enemies and domestic rebels reached maturity in the sixteenth century.

Pre-Victorian espionage

One of the ablest men in Elizabethan England, Sir Francis Walsingham, was the country's earliest spymaster. When in 1571 the Florentine banker Roberto di Ridolfi led an international conspiracy to kill England's Protestant Queen Elizabeth and to crown the Catholic Queen of Scotland, Mary, in her stead, Walsingham's organization foiled the plot, with the help of informants, torture, intercepted messages and deciphered codes. He had fifty-three agents at foreign courts, and was adept at persuading Catholics to betray one another. His apparatus detected further plots to depose Elizabeth. After the foiling of the most notable of these conspiracies, led by Anthony Babington in 1586, the Queen told her parliament, 'Good Neighbours I have had, and I have met with bad; and in Trust I have found Treason.'[1]

Sectarian animosity between Catholics and Protestants, and dynastic rivalries between adherents of the Tudors, the Stuarts and the Hanoverians, involved foreign conspirators, aggrieved exiles, domestic malcontents and headstrong adventurers. European power-centres were monitored from London. The Lord Protector, Oliver Cromwell, used countless paid spies during the 1650s and was said to have 'carried the secrets of all the Princes of Europe at his girdle'. The Venetian Ambassador in London, reporting on the Protectorate, declared that 'no Government on earth discloses its own acts less and knows those of others more precisely than that of England'.[2]

During the 1720s the South Sea Company financial scandal set other precedents in the spiriting away from prosecutors of malefactors with disturbing secret knowledge. The company's cashier, Robert Knight, after attempting to blackmail government ministers into protecting him, and reluctant to undergo close interrogation, took ship for Calais with his son and namesake. The two Robert Knights then hastened to the Austrian Netherlands, where a junior English diplomat acted on his own initiative, pursued the elder Knight with a troop of hussars and had him incarcerated, under heavy security, in the citadel of Antwerp. Although the House of Commons sought Knight's extradition, their purpose was not punishment but political gamesmanship: the opposition wished him to divulge material incriminating office-holders. The monarch and the government were correspondingly anxious to prevent his repatriation and to silence the disruptive stories that he might tell. There followed an intricate 'screen': the Georgian word for a cover-up. After negotiations between London and Vienna, Knight was transferred to Luxembourg, and then taken at night to the Ardennes and set free. The authorities meanwhile arranged for a hole to be dug in the wall of the Knights' cell, and for a rope-ladder to be lowered from it, in order to bolster the pretence that they had escaped. The determination of London office-holders that the secrets of Knight's financial chicanery should not be publicly aired was akin to the aversion of twentieth-century authorities to sharing security failures.[3]

Eighteenth-century uprisings by Scottish Jacobites against the government in London were defeated by secret intelligence, disinformation and betrayals as well as by force of arms. Both sides employed messenger-spies, such as the Jacobite innkeeper who in 1745 tried to cut his throat after being captured with papers from Charles Edward, the Young Pretender, hidden in his glove. The London government gained an important advantage when the Jacobite cipher code was seized by a mob in Cumberland from the Duke of Perth's travelling servant. After two years of imprisonment in the Tower of London, the clan chief Alastair Ruadh MacDonell of Glengarry was turned, and under the alias of Pickle acted as a secret informant on Jacobite activities after 1747. 'Tall, athletic, with a frank and pleasing face, Pickle could never be taken for a traitor,' wrote his biographer. 'The man was brave, for he moved freely in France, England, and Scotland, well knowing that the *sgian* [small dagger] was sharpened for his throat if he were detected.' He was not a paid informer, but a conceited man who enjoyed the secret importance of double-dealing. His second alias was Random, which suggests his liking for risk. Collectors of antiquities and works of art, who roamed Europe in pursuit of their avocation, as well as the dealers from whom they bought their rarities, had good cover for underhand activities as political agents. There were ample opportunities for gossip, covert surveillance, gambits and counter-espionage by connoisseurs who encountered Jacobites in exile. Much useless tittle-tattle from Rome or Florence about the Old and Young Pretenders was sold to London at high prices, which were paid tardily or not at all.[4]

The Home Office employed informers and agents provocateurs during the French revolutionary wars and their turbulent sequel. Lord Sidmouth, Home Secretary during 1812–22, became convinced by his sources, so he told the House of Lords in 1817, that 'scarcely a cottage had escaped the perseverance of the agents of mischief'. Radicals, warned Sidmouth, 'had parliamentary reform in their mouths, but rebellion and revolution in their hearts'. The Cato Street conspirator Arthur Thistlewood was incriminated by a bevy of police spies, including John Castle, a maker of paper dolls for children, who was also a bigamist and pimp, and George Edwards, a maker of plaster figurines, whose bestselling line was a bust of the headmaster of Eton which pupils bought to use in the manner of a coconut shy. The defence of the realm from internal foes has always needed its Pickles, Randoms and Castles.[5]

Mid-nineteenth-century London became a haven for political exiles (predominantly German, but some Italian). Most were quiescent refugees who sat smoking, talking, eating and drinking in Soho dives, but one account of 1859 presents a minority group of active conspirators gathering in a small Whitechapel *Gasthaus* known as the Tyrants' Entrails: 'the incandescent ones, the roaring, raging, rampaging, red-hot refugees; the amateurs in vitriol, soda-bottles full of gunpowder, and broken bottles for horses' hoofs'. The surveillance of these irreconcilables was the preserve of foreign police spies. A Prussian spy reported in 1853 on one exile who had been born in the Rhineland, had been radicalized in Berlin and was living in two rooms in Dean Street, Soho: 'everything is broken down, tattered and torn, with a half inch of dust over everything . . . manuscripts, books and newspapers, as well as children's toys, and rags and tatters of his wife's sewing basket, several cups with broken rims, knives, forks, lamps, an inkpot, tumblers, Dutch clay pipes, tobacco ash – in a word, everything top-turvy'. As to the paterfamilias, 'Washing, grooming and changing his linen are things he rarely does, and he likes to get drunk. Though he is often idle for days on end, he will work day and night with tireless endurance when he has great work to do. He has no fixed times for going to sleep and waking up. He often stays up all night, and then lies down fully clothed on the sofa at midday and sleeps till evening, untroubled by the comings and goings of the world.' It was in this squalid chaos that Karl Marx did the preliminary thinking that led to *Das Kapital*.[6]

Victorian espionage

Every successful military leader valued intelligence reports. 'I am always preceded by a hundred spies,' the all-conquering Frederick the Great of Prussia said in the 1750s. His decision to go to war in 1756 was based partly on the intelligence received from his spy in the Austrian embassy in Berlin, and from the interception and decoding of messages sent by the Dutch envoy in St Petersburg to The Hague. Half a century later Napoleon declared, 'one spy in the right place is worth 20,000 men in the field'. International diplomacy also suborned well-placed informants among the desk-bound officials of other great powers. As one example, Lord Cowley, Ambassador in Vienna during the 1820s, had the private secretary of the Austrian Foreign Minister Metternich in his pay.[7]

An intelligence department to measure, limit and manage the risks entailed by the territorial rivalry in Asia between England and Russia was developed in London from the 1850s. This department worked with successive prime ministers and the Foreign Office to inform and strengthen imperial policy-making. William Beaver, in his pioneering study of Victorian military intelligence, argues that the *Pax Britannica* was intelligence-based and intelligence-led. The London government's success during Victoria's reign in protecting its ideals of progress, prosperity and peace was achievable only by investigating, watching and listening to hostile powers, and by collating, interpreting and acting on intelligence about potential foes. The efforts of this War Office sub-division meant that for over half a century the British Empire waged colonial wars in Asia and made localized interventions in Africa, but avoided major warfare in either Europe or Asia. 'Britain', says Beaver, 'played her cards well because she sat facing the mirror.'[8]

This systematic intelligence-gathering was instigated by Thomas Jervis, a retired Indian Army officer of whom it was said that cartography was second only to Christianity as the ruling passion of his life. Shortly before the outbreak of the Crimean war, he bought copies of the Russian army's secret map of the Crimea and of the Austrian staff map of Turkey-in-Europe from a source in Brussels. At his own expense he then provided the War Office with tactical maps of the seat of war. These proved invaluable at a time when British military inadequacy in the Crimea was being exposed by *The Times* war correspondent and by war artists whose drawings dismayed readers of illustrated magazines. The politicians sought to deflect public anger at the maladministration and tactical failures in the Crimea by incriminating the military. Sidney Herbert, the reform-minded Secretary of State for War, told the House of Commons that responsibility for the bungles 'lies with that collection of regiments which calls itself the British Army and not with the Government!'[9]

Jervis campaigned for peacetime map-making, fact-gathering and tactical analysis. In 1855 he was appointed director of a new Topographical & Statistical Department (T&S) charged with supporting reconnaissance in war and intelligence-gathering in peacetime. This was reconstituted in 1873 as the Intelligence Department (ID). Although the Horse Guards generals were relentless in disliking the ID as an incipient General Staff which would reduce their prerogatives, the ID soon proved its value to the great offices of state by discounting the bellicose opinions of the military hierarchy. It provided prime ministers and foreign secretaries with evidence-based intelligence shorn of the generals' bluster. 'If you believe the doctors, nothing is wholesome,' the Foreign Secretary and future Prime Minister Lord Salisbury said in 1877: 'if you believe the theologians, nothing is innocent: if you believe the soldiers, nothing is safe.' By the 1880s the ID was a major supplier of intelligence to the Foreign Office as well as a prototype general staff for the War Office.[10]

ID officers scoured the foreign daily press, and weekly and monthly periodicals, for material on foreign armies, territories and thinking. This was later known as open source intelligence (OSINT). Interesting items were indexed under four or five headings, and pasted into cuttings-books. The cellars of the nondescript ID offices at 16–18 Queen Anne's Gate, Westminster, two minutes' walk from the Foreign Office and Downing Street, bulged with the largest secret military library in the world. Within months of the advent of the Dewey Decimal system of cataloguing in 1876, the ID had begun cataloguing the information in its holdings to as much as seven decimal points. Its officers took pride in map-making, and established cartography as a valued precision craft. Their voracity in amassing facts, and their canny analysis of material, provided the Foreign Office, the Cabinet and ministries with product that was both hallmarked as reliable and based on innovative thinking. The ID was a paper-bound bureaucracy, in which lucid, clarifying desk-work brought promotion: Sir John Ardagh, Jervis's ultimate successor as the ID's mastermind, was renowned for producing 'beautifully expressed far-seeing memoranda on the most abstruse questions'.[11]

The Indian Army remitted recurrent scares about Afghan uprisings and the mustering of Russian battalions. Lord Dufferin was rare among viceroys in discounting the likelihood of a Russian invasion of India: he protested in 1885 against 'putting a frightful hole in our pocket' by mobilizing the Indian Army 'every time that a wretched Cossack chooses to shake his spear on the top of a sand-hill against Penjdeh'. Prime ministers learnt to trust ID reassurances about Russian intentions. Responding to an Indian Army alarm that Russia was preparing a major invasion of Afghanistan and India, the ID obtained and analysed the annual contract for procuring flour for the Russian army. It ascertained that there were no plans to build or expand flour points for bakeries on the trajectory of the planned invasion. As bakeries on lines of march to the Hindu Kush were indispensable to invasion plans, the ID advised the Foreign and India offices that without bread supplies there would be no military advance. This was a radical new way of assessing risk and laying plans.[12]

Politicians like to rely on instinct, which is inherently a primitive force, or on flair, 'which means you guess what you ought to know', as Robert Vansittart noted. The ID countered the makeshifts of instinct and flair with factually grounded intelligence assessments that gave reassurance about imperial security when rabble-rousers, apoplectic generals and press stunts seemed to presage impending Russian invasions of India. In the words of an ID paper of 1880 dispelling rumours of Russian expeditions into Afghanistan, 'Ignorance is weakness, and this weakness we constantly show by the undignified fear displayed at every report of the threat of Russian movements.' Just as military reverses were often attributable to poor field intelligence, so British diplomacy was sometimes outwitted by other European powers through deficient information.[13]

The ID attracted a new breed of 'scientific officers', mainly engineers and artillerymen. Unusually for the nineteenth-century army, at least a dozen had attended Oxford, Cambridge or Dublin universities; almost all were good linguists. Humour was prized: each section kept a screen on which were displayed 'screamingly funny' cuttings from foreign newspapers, such as an Austrian officer's account of a Gibraltar cricket match and a Spanish scheme to train swans to tow reconnaissance balloons. The ID during the last quarter of the nineteenth century eventually produced three chiefs of the Imperial General Staff, two field marshals, six generals, eleven lieutenant generals and fifteen major generals. Over half were gazetted with knighthoods or peerages. Fewer than half ever married. Beaver identifies the ID as 'the first real meritocratic cadre in modern British government'. As Stalin told the graduates of the Red Army Academy in a Kremlin speech of 1935, 'cadres decide everything'.[14]

The ID trained men who later attained non-military but intelligence-informed positions of power: Vincent Caillard, an ID officer who served on the Montenegrin frontier commission, was rewarded with the presidency of the administrative council of the Ottoman Public Debt (1883–98), which brought him rare influence and privileged information in Constantinople. He corresponded with Salisbury on Turkish affairs, and was knighted at the age of thirty-nine. After 1906 he became central to military and naval preparedness as financial comptroller of the armaments company Vickers. In 1915–18 he was involved with the arms dealer Sir Basil Zaharoff in a fruitless scheme to bribe the Young Turks out of the war.[15]

After the European powers began to scramble for African territories in the 1880s, the Intelligence Division (as the Intelligence Department was renamed in 1888) became active in that continent. Its officers knew how to hold their tongues, said Ardagh, and could commit crimes while remaining gentlemanly. Theirs, he continued, were 'the qualities disowned by the bishop who "thanked God that Providence had not endowed him with the low cunning necessary for the solution of a quadratic equation"'. All this was accomplished despite the Treasury keeping, in the words of an ID section head in the 1890s, 'a frightfully tight hold on every sixpence'.[16]

'Spies have a dangerous task, and not an honourable one; consequently, except in very rare and extreme cases, officers will not accept the invidious duty,' wrote Captain Henry Hozier in 1867 after espionage had helped Prussia to its battle victories over Austria. Nevertheless, 'adventurers and unscrupulous men will, if well paid, do the work, and, for the sake of a sufficient sum, run the risk of certain death'. Despite this disavowal, in the last quarter of the nineteenth century ID officers traversed the globe, ran networks in Egypt, the Sudan, the Upper Nile and the new French spheres of influence along the west coast of Africa. Always and everywhere they drew maps: cartography was an English weapon to box the French, the Germans and the Italians in Africa, the Austrians and Turks in the Balkans, and the Russians in Asia. Medals were bestowed in order to distinguish officers who were willing to reconnoitre enemy positions from those whom Hozier stigmatized as 'mercenary wretches who will sell friend and foe alike'. Claude Dansey, the Vice Chief of SIS during the 1940s, had a soldier uncle who was awarded the Victoria Cross for his courage as a scout in the Ashanti war of 1874, and a military cousin who won the VC in 1914 for reconnaissance of enemy positions in the German West Africa protectorate.[17]

Clive Bigham, Lord Mersey's young son and heir, who had distinguished himself in China during the Boxer rebellion of 1900, was recommended by the Foreign Office to Ardagh, and served in the ID until 1904. Almost his first task was to go to Paris, where he bribed newspaper editors to halt their abuse of Queen Victoria (his expenses for this task were put under the heading 'Remounts'). Next he was posted to ID's Section E, which covered Austria, Hungary, the Balkans and the Ottoman Empire, and commissioned to compile handbooks on Abyssinia, Morocco and Arabia. 'These were long and interesting jobs,' Bigham recalled, 'for I had to sift, check, compile and arrange a mass of material; but the work attracted me and taught me a lot.' Section E was headed first by George Forestier-Walker, who rose to the rank of major general, and then by George ('Uncle George') Milne, afterwards CIGS, field marshal and Lord Milne. Among Bigham's colleagues William ('Wully') Robertson also became field marshal and CIGS, while Herbert ('Lorenzo') Lawrence became both a general and chairman of Vickers from 1926.[18]

In contrast to the Soviet Union's confidence after 1917 in communism's inevitable triumph over capitalism, the rapidly expanding British Empire showed imperialism at its most pessimistic. Bravado about national destiny and chauvinism about the British genius for world leadership were super-abundant; but they always raised countervailing voices which decried the interminable wars against the weak: Zulus, Ashanti, Benin, Afghans, Burmese and others. The colonial expansion and 'scramble for Africa' of the 1880s and 1890s were both vaunted and beset by misgivings. 'Military adventure . . . is extremely distasteful to me,' commented Dufferin when in 1885 he was instructed by London politicians to annex Burma. 'The Burmese are a nice people, easily managed, and I cannot bear the thought of making war upon them.' After the conquest of Burma, Dufferin anticipated 'nothing but trouble and annoyance'. Sir Cecil ('Springy') Spring Rice, future Ambassador in Washington, wrote in 1899 after the outbreak of the South African war: 'We are surrounded in the world by a depth and intensity of hatred which is really astonishing. If we fall we shall have a hundred fangs in our throat.' He disliked the new bellicosity: 'Imperialism is not so bad a thing if you pay for it in your own blood, but spending 3 per-cent out of your stock exchange gains to buy people to fight for you in picturesque places, in order to provide you with interesting illustrated papers (or new investments) is a different thing.' On the eve of the twentieth century Spring Rice saw 'great danger threatening' and wished British imperialists 'hadn't boasted and shouted so much and spoilt our own game and turned the whole thing into a burglar's prowl'.[19]

In the post-mortem after the South African war of 1899–1902, the

ID was the only branch of the army to avoid censure. Scorching public anger at the humiliating defeats of British imperial forces by Boer irregulars required the Edwardian generals to submit to organizational reform: a general staff was belatedly instituted in 1904. This coincided with the reorientation of British foreign policy, which embraced its traditional enemies France and Russia as allies against its new chief adversary, Germany. The Directorate of Military Intelligence, which replaced the ID, continued the old successful methods of combining reports of British officers travelling overseas, the gleaning of OSINT from newspapers and gazettes, diplomatic and consular reports, and espionage. The Admiralty's Naval Intelligence Division (NID) relied on similar sources, supplemented by commercial and business informants. The Foreign Office however disliked the use of military and naval attachés for espionage, fearing that they might be entrapped by counter-espionage officers and thus embarrass their embassy. Accordingly, in Berlin and other power centres, service attachés collected open material by legal methods, but shunned covert or illicit acquisition of official secrets. It was partly to keep attachés clear of spy work that new security agencies were established in 1909. It is indicative of the relative standing of military and naval intelligence that the 'MI' in the designations 'MI5' and 'MI6' represents Military Intelligence, not Naval Intelligence.[20]

The ID had further long-term influence for the good in the quality and activities of military attachés appointed to foreign embassies. They were skilled in using the well-tried ID techniques: they cultivated cordial contacts with the military officers of the countries to which they were posted; they attended manoeuvres, and watched new tactics and armoured formations; they were politically aware and kept alert to changing social and economic trends in their territories; they read newspapers and monitored specialist periodicals. Linguistic skills were a prerequisite. Noel Mason-MacFarlane, who was Military Attaché at Vienna and Budapest in 1931–5 and at Berlin in 1937–9, spoke excellent French and German and was conversant in Spanish, Hungarian and Russian. His Assistant Military Attaché in Berlin, Kenneth Strong, began intelligence work as a subaltern in Ireland in the early 1920s. During the struggle against Sinn Fein he ran informants such as railway porters, shopkeepers and barmen who would warn him of suspicious strangers in his district. He was fluent in four foreign languages and had smatterings of others. During the 1930s he was instrumental in starting the War Office's Intelligence Corps. 'The task of the Intelligence Officer', Strong wrote, 'is to exercise a spirit of positive inquiry and faculty of judgement, above all in discarding that large part of the incoming material which does not appreciably alter the known or anticipated situation, and from the residue to form a coherent and balanced picture, whether for a Supreme Commander, a Prime Minister . . . or for someone less elevated.'[21]

Edwardian espionage

The power, the pride and the reach of the British Empire seemed in constant jeopardy after the defeats in South Africa. Lord Eustace Percy, who began his diplomatic career in Washington in 1911, recalled Edwardian England as always 'overshadowed by premonitions of catastrophe'. He had been reared in a ducal castle, but 'whatever privileges my generation enjoyed in its youth, a sense of security was not one of them'. There was no time 'when a European war did not seem to me the most probable of prospects, or when I forgot my first ugly taste of public disaster in the Black Week of Colenso and Magersfontein, which had darkened the Christmas school holidays of 1899'.[22]

The temper of Edwardian England remained apprehensive. Newspapers profited by intensifying public anxieties. In 1906 the *Daily Mail* paid columns of morose men to march along Oxford Street in London wearing spiked helmets, Prussian-blue uniforms and blood-stained gloves. They carried sandwich-boards promoting a new novel of which the newspaper had bought the serialization rights, William Le Queux's *The Invasion of 1910* – a novel catering, as the *Daily Mail*'s shameless proprietor said, to his readers' need for 'a good hate'. *Daily Mail* readers were urged to refuse to be served by German waiters: 'if your waiter says he is Swiss, ask to see his passport'. Le Queux was a bombastic sensationalist who pretended to intimate knowledge of European secret services. The fearful insecurity aroused by his next booming scare-stunt, *Spies of the Kaiser* (1909), overcame the Liberal government's sentiment that domestic counter-espionage was a mark of despotic regimes. In October 1909 a Secret Service Bureau was established in rooms in Victoria Street.[23]

After months of dispute over purposes and responsibilities, the

Bureau was sub-divided. The home section, which was known as MI5 from 1915 and also after 1931 as the Security Service, was given the purview of counter-espionage, counter-subversion and counter-sabotage in Britain and its overseas territories. The foreign section, known as the Secret Intelligence Service (SIS or MI1c, also later as MI6) was charged with collecting human intelligence (HUMINT) from non-British territories. In addition, Indian Political Intelligence (IPI) was formed to monitor the activities of Indian nationalists, revolution-aries and anarchists and their allies not only in Britain but across Europe. There were also three divisions of Scotland Yard's Special Branch, which had been formed in 1883 in response to Irish dynamite attacks in London. A draconian Official Secrets Act of 1911 was a further signal that national security was being treated more systemat-ically, and also being kept determinedly from informed public comment.

Vernon Kell, the first Director of MI5, was a graduate of the Royal Military Academy at Sandhurst, whose father had been an English army officer and whose maternal grandfather was a Polish army surgeon. After his parents' divorce, he travelled widely in Europe with his mother, visiting exiled members of her family and mastering French, German and other European languages. The War Office in the late 1890s posted him to Moscow and Shanghai to learn Russian and Chinese. There was no insularity about this multilingual man of action. He had the type of keen, alert efficiency that allows no time for showiness. The great hindrance to his work was that he had funds for only a small staff. Sir Edward Grey, Foreign Secretary when European war erupted in 1914, said with revealing naivety: 'if we spend anything on Secret Service, it must be very trifling, because it never comes to my knowledge'. As Lord Eustace Percy noted, the 'Secret Service' account at the Office was devoted to the financial relief of impoverished British subjects over-seas.[24]

There was a clear understanding by the new intelligence services of the benefits of watch-and-learn. In 1911 Heinrich Grosse was convicted of spying on the Royal Navy at Portsmouth, but the network of which he was part was left all but undisturbed. Identities were established, addresses, correspondence and activities were monitored. One or two individuals were arrested, when it was considered unavoidable, but the majority were allowed to continue transmitting inaccurate material. 'In other words, we just played them,' recalled Superintendent Percy Savage of Scotland Yard. Karl Ernst, a hairdresser at King's Cross, who acted as the postbox for this spy network, was arrested in the first round-up of German agents in August 1914. Once the two nations were at war, it was no longer safe enough to keep him under surveillance: he had to be detained.[25]

England's *cabinet noir* for intercepting and reading private and diplomatic correspondence, the Decyphering Branch, had been abolished in 1844 after parliamentary protests at the opening of the correspondence of the exiled Italian nationalist Giuseppe Mazzini and the sharing of their contents with the Austrian and Neapolitan governments. Perlustration was not resumed for seventy years. At the outbreak of hostilities in 1914, the Post Office (which was a government department, headed by a minister, the Postmaster General) employed a single censor intercepting, opening, reading and resealing suspect letters. By the Armistice in 1918 the Censor's Office employed over 2,000 staff, who were expected to open at least 150 letters a day each.

At the outset of war MI5 comprised Kell, six officers, its chief detective William Melville (formerly the Metropolitan Police superintendent in charge of Special Branch), two assistant detectives, six clerks and a caretaker. Its initial priority was to catch spies and saboteurs; but from 1916–17 its political masters were equally anxious about civil unrest and subversion. By 1918 MI5 had a staff of over 800, including 133 officers. Jervis would have rhapsodized at the amplitude of their records: over 250,000 index-cards cross-referencing 27,000 personal files in its central registry by the time of the Armistice that halted the European war in November 1918. Similarly Kell's counterpart at SIS, Sir Mansfield Cumming, numbered his staff (exclusive of agents) as 47 in June 1915 and 1,024 by October 1916.

The months after the Armistice were a time of political instability, strange alliances and imponderable risk. Exterior perceptions might mislead. In the east London slum district of Limehouse, during the last months of the war, Irish nationalists combined with socialists to organize a militant constituency cohort led by a pharmacist called Oscar Tobin. One day in January 1919 a newly demobilized soldier, carrying a nondescript suitcase like the terrorist in Conrad's *Secret Agent*, visited Tobin's shop, went up the backstairs with him and laid plans for socialists to take control of Stepney Borough Council. Tobin was a Jewish Romanian who was to be refused naturalization as a British subject in

1924. To a watcher the confabulation above his shop might have seemed the inception of a revolutionary cell; but the demobbed soldier was Clement Attlee, and this was the first step in a political career that always upheld constitutionalism and culminated in his leadership of his country during the Cold War. History is full of misleading appearances. The balance between trust and treason, as Queen Elizabeth said, is seldom easy to get right.[26]

CHAPTER 3

The Whitehall Frame of Mind

The age of intelligence

At the acme of dynastical insecurity in November 1918, when the monarchies in Austria, Bavaria, Hungary, Prussia, Saxony and Württemberg followed the Romanov empire into extinction, Sir Basil Thomson, the bristling, pushy head of Special Branch at Scotland Yard, wrote a memorandum intended for the eyes of King George V. 'Every institution of any importance has depended during the war for its existence on an intelligence organization,' he began with his usual bounding confidence. The Foreign Office, the Admiralty, the War Office and the Ministry of Blockade all had departments collecting data, evaluating rumours, making predictions and trying to stabilize the future. Additional officials in Downing Street were amassing political intelligence for the Prime Minister, Lloyd George. His predecessor, Asquith, had fallen from power in 1916, Thomson continued, 'not so much because he failed in policy, as because he had no intelligence organization to keep him warned of the intrigues and movements around him'. Similarly, among factors in the recent Russian revolution and overthrow of the Romanov dynasty, defective intelligence had a leading part: 'Petrograd was in the hands of the revolutionaries before any hint of trouble was heard at Tsarsky' (Tsarskoye Syelo, the imperial compound outside the capital). Thomson's lesson for the Royal Household was terse:

(1) The only safe organizations are those that possess an efficient intelligence system.
(2) Those persons or organizations that have failed to develop such systems have been destroyed.

Statecraft had mutated. Europe's age of intelligence had begun.[1]

Opposing power blocs had different explanations for these new necessities. Soviet Russia attributed the world's great changes to the communist revolution of 1917, and to the irresistible impetus towards the dictatorship of the proletariat. The European powers attributed them to the convulsion of continental warfare in 1914–18. Certainly the clashes of the Russian, British, German and Austro-Hungarian empires, and of the French and American republics, had changed their governments' attitudes to their populations. For centuries monarchs had levied troops to fight wars, governments had repressed civil disorder and reformers had tried to harness popular sentiments. But the military, industrial and transport mobilization of 1914–18 turned the civil population into a new concept called manpower. People of working age – women as well as men – were deployed as a war resource in factories and transport systems as well as on battlefields. The Defence of the Realm Act was enacted in London in 1914, and extended at intervals so as to manage the mass of adults to an unprecedented extent.

When the Russian revolution erupted in 1917, MI5 was focused on German espionage, subversion and sabotage. With the start of the Comintern's international activities and the foundation of the CPGB in 1920 it changed target to Bolshevism. It relied on the police officers of the Metropolitan Police's Special Branch, which chewed communists, anarchists, Indian nationalists, pacifists, atheists, self-important but insignificant cranks, Soho rakes, unemployed marchers and mutinous merchant seamen in its greedy, indiscriminate maw. Special Branch reports were often unimaginative if not obtuse. 'I should wait a long, long time before acting on the advice of the present authorities at Scotland Yard,' wrote a Tory MP, Sir Cuthbert Headlam, at the time of a botched police raid on the offices of the Soviet trading agency ARCOS in 1927. Special Branch lost control of monitoring domestic subversion after the discovery in 1929 that it had been betrayed by two Bolshevik informants, Hubert van Ginhoven and Charles Jane. Complicated cross-jurisdictional clashes between MI5 and SIS were considered at ministerial level by the Secret Service Committee in 1919, and again by senior officials in 1921, 1922, 1925 and 1927. Committee members found it hard to adjudicate between the two agencies. A resolution was not reached until Kell's organization was named as the lead national security service in 1931.[2]

MI5 was primarily an advisory agency, which existed to inform government decisions and to assess and manage risks. Its staff collected, filtered, indexed and filed information gleaned from confidential informants, passport and customs officers, intercepted mail, the garbled chatter heard by covert bugging of offices and telephones, watching of addresses, shadowing of individuals and surveillance of bank accounts, public meetings and publications. Counter-intelligence officers used this data to assess the risks posed by individuals who might be subversives or spies. They resembled historians scouring documentary fragments, unravelling confused memories, checking false trails, re-evaluating doubts and discounting persecution complexes. Their re-examination of past bungles was often more informative than success stories. In the search for long-term patterns, material from multitudinous sources was assembled, allowed to fester, pondered, evaluated, deconstructed, rejected and revised. Every intelligence service was a paper-driven bureaucracy. Officers in MI5, the Cheka, OGPU and the NKVD commissioned reports, compiled profiles, read and reread their dossiers. Every small detail was committed to paper. Successful counter-intelligence usually means following a paper-trail.

The arrest of spies was not the invariable first object of counter-espionage. It was often more profitable to watch and learn. If a spy was allowed to go free, watchers could study his methods and identify his contacts. That was why SIS betrayed its inexperience of domestic counter-espionage when, in 1927, its men arrested Georg Hansen, the Soviet handler of the spy Wilfred Macartney, three days after his arrival in England, before he had found his bearings or met his contacts. Arrests might lead to exciting public denouements, but counter-espionage officers prefer to accumulate and refine intelligence rather than arrest suspects, put them on trial and thus risk disclosure of their methods.

One early example of their watch-and-learn procedure can be given. Theodore Rothstein was 'a short, stumpy, bearded, bespectacled revolutionary who looked like Karl Marx'. Before 1914 he had collaborated with Wilfrid Scawen Blunt's campaigns against British imperialism in Egypt and India: during the war he was a triple agent working for Lenin's Bolsheviks, British military intelligence and the Turkish secret service. In 1919 he wished Leonard Woolf, a former colonial official turned radical activist, to publish Lenin's recent speeches and insisted on delivering the texts in person. Woolf was instructed to walk on the inside of the pavement along the Strand eastwards towards Fleet Street on a Wednesday afternoon, timing it so that he passed under the clock of the Law Courts at 2.30. At that exact moment he met Rothstein walking westwards from Fleet Street on the outside of the pavement. Rothstein carried in his right hand an envelope containing Lenin's speeches, which, without either man speaking or looking at each other, he transferred into Woolf's right hand. These precautions were in vain, for Rothstein was shadowed everywhere by Special Branch and the handover was seen. A few days later the police raided Woolf's printers and seized the documents. Although Rothstein was kept under surveillance, he had been neither arrested nor dismissed from his wartime job at the War Office: officials judged that it was better to keep him in sight rather than expel him to Russia, where out of reach he might prove a dangerous opponent. This was a pattern of behaviour that was to be repeated in cases over the next century.[3]

In 1919 there was a sensation when the miners' leader Robert Smillie, as a member of the Royal Commission on the Coal Industry, browbeat three coal-mining magnates, the Duke of Northumberland, the Marquess of Londonderry and the Earl of Durham, and quoted egalitarian extracts from the Christian gospels at them. 'The public is amused by the spectacle, but few realize its sinister significance,' commented Hensley Henson, Bishop of Durham. 'The very foundations of the whole social fabric are challenged. The tables are plainly turned; and it requires very little to transform the Commission into a revolutionary tribunal, and Smillie into an English Lenin . . . preparing an immense catastrophe.'[4]

Lord D'Abernon, who was an eyewitness to the Russian advance into Poland in 1920, felt sure that 'Western civilisation was menaced by an external danger which, coming into being during the war, threatened a cataclysm equalled only by the fall of the Roman Empire.' He had little hope that the European powers would forget their rivalries and combine to prevent 'world-victory of the Soviet creed'. The communist threat to 'England's stupendous and vital interests in Asia' was graver than those posed by the old tsarist regime, judged D'Abernon, for 'the Bolsheviks disposed of two weapons which Imperial Russia lacked – class-revolt propaganda, appealing to the proletariat of the world, and the quasi-religious fanaticism of Lenin, which infused a vigour and zeal unknown to the officials and emissaries of the Czar'.[5]

There was no English Lenin. The nearest home-grown version of him was the foolhardy Cecil L'Estrange Malone. Born in 1890, the son of a Yorkshire clergyman and nephew of the Earl of Liverpool, he entered the Royal Navy in 1905, and trained as a pioneer naval aviator in 1911. He flew off the fo'c'sle of a battleship steaming at 12 knots in 1912, planned the historic bombing raid by seaplanes on Cuxhaven harbour on Christmas Day of 1914 and commanded the Royal Navy's converted packet-steamer from which the first seaplanes flew to drop torpedoes from the air and to sink enemy vessels in 1916. He became a lieutenant colonel aged twenty-seven, and the first air attaché at a British embassy – Paris – in 1918. With this reputation for derring-do Malone was elected as a Liberal MP in the general election after the Armistice. Crossing frontiers illicitly, making night marches through forests and swamps and armed with a Browning automatic, he reached Petrograd in 1919. There he met Litvinov, Chicherin and Trotsky, visited factories and power stations under workers' control and was converted to communism. He forsook the Liberals and joined the CPGB at its formation in 1920. He was thus the first communist MP to sit in the House of Commons (two years before the election of Walton Newbold). In October 1920 Special Branch raided his flat in Chalk Farm, and arrested Erkki Veltheim, a twenty-two-year-old Comintern courier from Finland who was in possession of seditious literature. Although Veltheim was evidently staying as a guest, Malone pretended that he was a burglar who had broken in while he was away. The young Finn was sentenced to six months' imprisonment, and then deported. During the police search of the flat in Wellington House, they found two railway-cloakroom tickets wrapped in plain unmarked paper inside an envelope addressed to Malone. The tickets led them to parcels containing a booklet, probably written by Malone, which was a training manual for officers of a British 'Red Army'. It contained instructions on improvised guerrilla tactics, street-fighting, execution of provocateurs and traitors, machine-gun drill, building barricades by overturning buses and trams, blockading coal-mines, seizing banks and post offices, cutting telephone and telegraph lines, and instigating naval mutinies.[6]

At a meeting organized by the CPGB and the Hands Off Russia Committee, held at the Royal Albert Hall on 7 November 1920, Malone made an inflammatory speech extolling the Bolshevik revolution and denouncing 'the humbug' of traditional parliamentary candidates. Capitalist manipulation of the proletariat was foundering, he averred:

'the day will soon come when we shall pass blessings on the British revolution, when you meet here as delegates of the first all-British congress of workers, sailors and soldiers. When that day comes, woe to all those people who get in our way. We are out to change the present constitution, and if it is necessary to save bloodshed and atrocities we shall have to use the lamp-posts.' From the Albert Hall stage he promised vengeance to an audience of over 8,000 Bolshevik sympathizers: 'What, my friends, are a few Churchills or a few Curzons on lamp-posts compared with the massacres of thousands of human beings? . . . What is the punishment of these world-criminals compared to the misery which they are causing to thousands of women and little children in Soviet Russia?' At this juncture there were cries of 'Hang them', 'Burn them' and 'Shoot them'.[7]

Malone was arrested and tried for sedition. The prosecutor at Malone's trial, Travers Humphreys, suggested that 'young alien East End Jews of a disorderly type' in the Albert Hall audience might have been roused by Malone's violent exhortations. As to the revolutionary pamphlet, Humphreys warned that in many large British towns there were 'persons of weak intellect, of vicious and criminal instincts, largely aliens, who will . . . act in response to any incitement for looting, murdering and brawling'. Malone was sentenced to six months' imprisonment: his mother died of dismay a few weeks later. On his release he went abroad to recover, refused to respond to CPGB overtures and failed to organize a campaign to defend his parliamentary seat at the 1922 general election. Subsequently he travelled in the Balkans, visited Siberia, China and Japan, and rethought his ideas. As a Labour candidate avowing constitutionalism and disavowing extra-parliamentarianism, he was re-elected as an MP in a by-election of 1928 but lost his seat three years later. He then became an international wheeler-dealer, working for the Armenian oil millionaire Calouste Gulbenkian to extend Soviet influence in the Persian oilfields, and from 1934 served as the paid propagandist of Tokyo, running the venal East Asia News Service, defending Japan's invasion and atrocities in Manchuria, acting as London agent of the South Manchuria Railway and operating the Japan Travel Bureau.[8]

Malone was a Lenin who took two years to fizzle out. The civil war in Ireland in 1920–2 caused little disruptive aftermath elsewhere in the British Isles. The workers' challenge to capitalism represented by the

General Strike in 1926 was only moderately divisive. The extension of the parliamentary franchise to younger women in 1927 was a voluntary act by the government rather than a sop to appease civil unrest. Demonstrations against high regional unemployment did not erupt into riots. Men parading in Trafalgar Square holding aloft banners bearing empty slogans – 'Workers of the World, Unite', 'Long Live the World Solidarity of the Proletariat', 'Walthamstow Old Comrades', 'Balham Branch of the Juvenile Workers League' – never endangered national security.[9]

Westminster and Whitehall worried, though, about Walthamstow and Balham. The police strike of August 1918, the return of demobilized troops after the Armistice in November 1918 and firebrand propagandists led to the inauguration of the Cabinet's Secret Service Committee in February 1919 and to the formation of the Home Office's Directorate of Intelligence, which was charged with combating domestic sedition. The Directorate's chief Sir Basil Thomson (hitherto head of Special Branch) reported direct to the Cabinet. His summaries of opinion and sentiment from across the country – intelligence from human sources (later called HUMINT) – were a piecemeal version of the Cheka's surveillance of opinion. In time his reports were recognized by their recipients as opinionated, subjective and contradictory. His animosity towards workers, foreigners, theoreticians, voters and those elected leaders who had the temerity to disagree with him led to increasing mistrust of his product. Suspicions that he had made disruptive, unauthorized leaks of foreign signals and communications (since known as SIGINT) prompted his dismissal in 1921. As a reaction to Thomson's biased HUMINT, Cabinet ministers and senior officials preferred SIGINT because it seemed neutral and enabled them, if they chose, to assess it themselves without tendentious interpretations urged on them by forceful outside advisers.

Good intelligence officers remind their customers that they cannot give iron-clad guarantees about the future, although they can make informed predictions. This wariness does not make them beloved by politicians in search of certainties or by officials who want to limit the risk of mistakes. In the 1920s particularly, when Westminster politicians and Whitehall officials were still inexperienced in the techniques and benefits of intelligence-collection, SIS and MI5 were not cherished. There was more concern about subversion than about espionage. It seemed preferable to pay for police to control social disorder than to fund counter-intelligence work by MI5 or SIS. The Armistice brought slashing cuts to intelligence agencies and soaring expenditure on policing. The Secret Service Vote (money voted by parliament for the purchase of secret information in the British Isles and abroad to thwart the machinations of enemies of the nation) fell from £1,150,000 in 1918 to £400,000 in 1919 and £300,000 in 1921. It sank to £180,000 a year from 1925 to 1929. SIS expenditure fell from £766,247 in 1918 to £205,200 in 1919. It lost fifty-eight staff in the first quarter of 1919, although its Chief Sir Mansfield Cumming claimed that its commitments had increased by 300 per cent. Cumming volunteered in 1921 to reduce SIS expenditure in the coming year from £125,000 to £87,500. SIS operated from a relatively cheap house at 1 Melbury Road, on the edge of Holland Park in Kensington, during 1919–25, but thereafter found the means to occupy larger and more costly offices in Broadway, near St James's Park and a few minutes' walk from Whitehall and Westminster.

MI5's budget was cut from £100,000 in the last year of the war to £35,000 in the first year of peace: it was £22,183 in 1921. These budgetary cuts were made despite the unrelenting efforts of the Bolshevik regime throughout the 1920s to spread world communist revolution, with propaganda, subversion and espionage deployed to weaken the British Empire and sundry groups and individuals enlisted to give overt or covert help in damaging British imperial capitalism. As an economy measure MI5 moved in 1919 from its offices near Haymarket, close to Whitehall and Westminster, to smaller, cheaper premises at 73–75 Queen's Gate, Kensington, where it remained until shifting in 1929 to Oliver House at 35 Cromwell Road, Kensington. In contrast to the reduced spending on domestic counter-espionage and security, police outlay in England and Wales rose from £106,521 in 1917 to £1,159,168 in 1918, to £5,511,943 in 1919 and to £6,679,209 in 1921. Thereafter, it edged upwards to £7,239,694 in 1929.

The need to impress politicians in order to protect or expand budgets contributes to a perennial failing of intelligence services. 'What we want', Desmond Morton of SIS instructed the head of station in Warsaw in 1920, 'is absolutely *inside* information or none at all . . . if you start with the idea that nothing that ever appears in a newspaper is of the least value, I am sure everything will be all right.' This was not invariably sound procedure. 'S.I.S. values information in proportion to its secrecy, not its accuracy,' Stuart Hampshire was recorded as telling his wartime intelligence chief Hugh Trevor-Roper in 1943. 'They would attach more value, he said, to a scrap of third-rate and tendentious misinformation smuggled out of Sofia in the fly-buttons of a vagabond Rumanian pimp than to any intelligence deduced from a prudent reading of the foreign press.' The eighth of the ten commandments of intelligence propounded by the SIS veteran Brian Stewart made the same point more prosaically: 'secret and official sources have no monopoly of the truth. Open, readily accessible sources are also important.' This was a lesson that the Intelligence Division had first taught in the 1870s.[10]

With depleted budgets, the activities of both MI5 and SIS were kept peripheral to central government, although anxieties about Bolshevism were rampant throughout the 1920s. 'We naturally ascribe all of our ills to this horrible phantom,' wrote the industrialist-aristocrat and former Cabinet minister Lord Crawford in 1927, 'always lurking in the background, and all the more alarming because it is tireless and unseen.' Diplomatic relations between London and Moscow were likened by Vansittart in 1934 to that of card-players whose opponents kept a fifth ace up their sleeves and a Thompson sub-machine gun under the table. Yet there was no anti-communist section operated by SIS in 1939.[11]

Special Branch officers were often prejudiced, but unlike J. Edgar Hoover's Federal Bureau of Investigation they had no programme to harass, entrap and incriminate. State underfunding of the intelligence agencies during the 1920s nudged them into closer reliance on right-wing individuals and organizations than was desirable. Instead of picking and paying trustworthy agents, they had to use (although they dared not rely on) dubious informants. There were unsavoury, self-dramatizing confidence-tricksters making quick improvisations on their way to the main chance. One example is a young public schoolboy named James McGuirk Hughes. In 1923 he posed as 'a Red', and claimed membership of the CPGB so as to penetrate Liverpool trade unionism and remit secret reports to the super-patriotic British Empire Union. He was part of a gang associated with the future MI5 agent-runner Maxwell Knight which repeatedly burgled and wrecked the Glasgow offices of the CPGB. Hughes supplied 'oddments of information' to MI5, which mistrusted him as a boastful and indiscreet 'windbag'. When in 1926 he failed to get on to the payroll of MI5 or the *Daily Mail*, he convinced Sir Vincent Caillard, financial comptroller of the armaments company Vickers and former officer in the old Intelligence Division, that he could supply dirt on workers' militancy. Caillard gave him a retainer of £750 a year, with an additional £750 to pay informants (which Hughes probably pocketed).[12]

Another unreliable informant was George McMahon @ Jerome Bannigan, who supplied Special Branch and MI5 with bogus information about gun-running to Ireland and about a communist plot to disrupt the Trooping of the Colour. He was arrested in 1936 after hurling a loaded revolver at King Edward VIII in St James's Park as part, so he claimed, of a Nazi conspiracy. At McMahon's trial Sir Donald Somervell, the Attorney General, was determined to suppress mention in court of either Moscow or Berlin and to stop indiscretions about McMahon's earlier use as an informant: 'We did not particularly want the names of our emissaries whom he had seen to come out, or the previous history,' Somervell noted.[13]

The security services understood – as Special Branch seldom did – the necessity of evaluating the trustworthiness of informants. Material from a paid informant named Kenneth Stott @ MARMION began to be supplied, through a trusted intermediary, to Desmond Morton of SIS in 1922. Stott informed on militant Scottish trade unionism, secret German industrial activities, the Brotherhood of Russian Truth, German secret agents and the French intelligence service. 'He is badly educated, his personal conceit is enormous and his methods are unscrupulous and peculiar,' Morton was warned in 1923. 'While Stott's knowledge of the Labour movement in this country is undoubtedly very extensive . . . his knowledge of foreign espionage methods seems to be sketchy.' When he named suspects he allowed colourful 'imagination and animus to have full play'. He was accordingly dropped by SIS in 1923; but, like Hughes, he continued to be paid by a credulous rich man, Sir George Makgill, for titbits on trade union conspiracies until 1926.[14]

Most British military attachés were intelligent in their collection and sifting of material. Charles Bridge, the cavalry officer who was Military Attaché at Warsaw and Prague until 1928, when he went to run the foreign intelligence operations of the Vickers armaments company, spoke French, German and Italian, with a smattering of central European languages. When he left Vickers in 1934, it was to become inaugural secretary general of the British Council, in which post he was able to place informants and cultivate 'Friends' across Europe. Bridge, it was said, had 'the energy and exactitude of a first-rate staff officer, the courtesy and knowledge of the world expected of a military attaché, and . . . an indefinable mixture of devilry and charm.'[15]

Equally impressive was James ('Jimmy') Marshall-Cornwall, the Military Attaché at Berlin in 1928–32, who spoke French, German, Italian, Dutch, Norwegian, Swedish, Turkish, modern Greek, Chinese and colloquial Arabic. Although he knew how to open sealed envelopes without detection and how to tap telephone and telegraph lines, as Military Attaché he had no need of ancillary skills such as burgling safes, forging passports and concocting invisible ink. His reports never failed to interest. 'The National-Socialist Movement is a real danger, and far more of a menace to the present constitution than is Communism,' he reported from Berlin to the Foreign Office as early as 1930. 'The trouble about the "Brown Shirts" is that their principles and theories are entirely *destructive*. They wish to destroy the present fabric of the State, but have no constructive programme with which to replace it, except a sort of mad-dog dictatorship.' The Nazis were, Marshall-Cornwall advised, 'far more akin to Bolshevism than to Fascism'. As to Hitler, 'He is a marvellous orator, and possesses an extraordinary gift for hypnotizing his audience . . . Even though his policy is a negative one, his personal magnetism is such as to win over quite reasonable people to his standard, and it is this which constitutes the chief danger of the movement.' Subsequently Marshall-Cornwall wrote a thoughtful treatise on geography and disarmament. In 1943 he was transferred from a post in the Special Operations Executive to be Assistant Chief of SIS.[16]

The Admiralty's grasp of naval intelligence was weaker than the War Office's hold on military intelligence, perhaps for lack of the sound traditions derived from the old Intelligence Division and possibly for lack of brainpower. 'All simple-minded, religious, semi-literate, and amazingly unadaptable', concluded Harold Laski of the London School of Economics after lunching at the Admiralty in 1929. 'No doubt they are technically superb,' he conceded, 'but they never see beyond their noses.'[17]

Sir Robert Bruce Lockhart, who had been acting Consul General in Moscow when it became the Soviet Union's capital in 1918 and survived a month's imprisonment in the Lubianka, exchanged confidences during the 1930s with 'Commander Fletcher . . . of the Secret Service'. Reginald ('Rex') Fletcher had become a Royal Navy cadet in 1899 aged fourteen. After wartime service on destroyers in the Dardanelles, he became post-war head of the Near East section of the Naval Intelligence Division. He sat as Liberal MP for Basingstoke in 1923–4, became an SIS officer supervising overseas operations, joined the Labour party in 1929 and was elected as Labour MP for a Midlands mining constituency in 1935. During the 1930s he worked at SIS headquarters in Broadway during the morning before crossing Westminster to the House of Commons in the afternoon. Fletcher and Bruce Lockhart agreed in their response when, in 1936, Admiralty intelligence became excited by obtaining 'absolute proof' of a secret treaty between Italy, Germany and Franco whereby Italy was to receive the Balearics and Ceuta and Germany the Canary Islands in return for helping the Nationalists in the Spanish civil war. 'No intelligence reports can be taken at more than twenty per cent of truth,' commented Bruce Lockhart, when the story reached him. 'Secret treaties, etc., are the kind of thing intelligence officers keep supplying all the year round.' Fletcher of SIS told him, 'Admiralty Intelligence is particularly bad, no grey matter in it.' Rear Admiral Sir James Troup, Director of Naval Intelligence, 'however good he may be as a sailor, is an absolute child about intelligence'. In 1938, using SIS sources while explicitly denying that he had access to any intelligence sources, Fletcher contributed an essay on European air power (containing strictures on the Air Ministry) to a rearmament survey entitled *The Air Defence of Britain*. The savagery of his Commons speech in January 1939 attacking Chamberlain's policy of appeasement was remarkable as coming from an SIS man. The Foreign Office's liaison with SIS Patrick Reilly perhaps had Fletcher (afterwards Lord Winster) in mind when he later wrote of 'that dangerous type often found in Naval Intelligence, the Commander passed over for promotion, bitter because he thinks, probably rightly, that he is cleverer than his contemporaries who have been promoted'.[18]

Starting in 1919 SIS officers were installed in British embassies and legations under the guise of passport control officers (PCOs). Many heads of diplomatic missions mistrusted the PCOs' activities being run under cover from their buildings. A few PCOs were gung-ho buffoons, several were spivs, but others were discreet and conscientious. Ambassadors and heads of legations however preferred formal sources of official information, received unofficial confidences which they could evaluate for themselves and disliked material of obscure and untested origins which might mislead when transmitted to London. They further feared that *sub rosa* activities by PCOs might cause diplomatic incidents or compromise the mission. This attitude was so pronounced that in 1921 the Foreign Office (codenamed ZP inside SIS) sent a circular to all its embassies and legations in Europe which outlined its attitude to espionage during the 1920s. 'Today the old type of Secret Service has disappeared, and melodrama has given place to a more sober style of enquiry from which the diplomat need no longer, as he was very properly required to do before, withdraw the hem of his garment,' wrote the PUS, Sir Eyre Crowe. 'It is largely concerned with subterranean revolutionary movements and individuals, and instead of spying on the military defences of individual countries, devotes itself principally to detecting tendencies subversive of the established order of things, irrespective of whether these are directed against the United Kingdom or are International in character.' This circular did little to reduce the hostility of traditional diplomats to spies operating in their territories. As one example, Sir Tudor Vaughan, the British Minister to Latvia, was outraged by the breach of propriety and possible complications when the files of the SIS station in Riga were moved for safety to the legation after the ARCOS raid in 1927.[19]

In addition to the PCOs, Admiral Sir Hugh ('Quex') Sinclair, Chief of SIS in 1923–39, financed the parallel Z Organization – a network of businessmen based overseas, acting as informants and collecting Friends who could amplify their reports. Claude Dansey, the PCO at Rome, left his post in 1936 with the cover story that he had been caught embezzling SIS funds. He subsequently opened an import-export business based at Bush House in the Strand, from which he ran the Z Organization. Dansey was a self-mystifying and sinister man: 'I'm sure he's very clever & very subtle, but I have no proof of it because I can't hear 10% of what he says', wrote Sir Alexander Cadogan, PUS of the Foreign Office, at the time of Dansey's appointment as wartime Vice Chief of SIS.[20]

The successes of the Admiralty's wartime code-breakers, known as 'Room 40', are celebrated. Their greatest SIGINT coup came in 1917 with the interception of the Zimmerman telegram, in which the German Foreign Minister promised to award three southern USA states to

Mexico if it joined the Germans and declared war on the USA. The War Office's MI1B did equally important work. The two sections, which veered between cooperation and rivalry between the wars, were merged into one agency, the Government Code and Cypher School (GC&CS), in 1919. It was swiftly recognized as the most secretive and effective British intelligence agency. The Russian section of GC&CS was led in the 1920s by a refugee from the 1917 revolution, Ernst Fetterlein, who had decrypted British diplomatic material in the tsarist *cabinet noir* before decrypting Bolshevik diplomatic messages for the British. For most of the inter-war period the Chief of SIS, Admiral Sinclair, was also Director of GC&CS. GC&CS had no more immunity from histrionic fantasists craving attention than other security services. One Cambridge mathematician and GC&CS officer, who committed several indiscretions in 1938–40, had 'a kind of secret service kink', Guy Liddell noted. 'He likes to imagine himself as a cloak-and-dagger man, and is given to relating hair-raising stories about himself which have absolutely no foundation in fact.' He also drank Chartreuse by the bottle.[21]

Lord Curzon of Kedleston, Foreign Secretary in 1919–24, was as peremptory and touchy as minor royalty, but unfortunately without their laziness. During 1920 he became wrathful about the deciphered wireless messages exchanged between Moscow and the Soviet trade delegation in London. 'That swine Lloyd George has no scruples or shame in the way he deceives,' Lenin declared in one intercepted message. 'Don't believe a word he says, but gull him three times as much.' Lloyd George was nonchalant about the insults; but eight messages from Lev Kamenev, the head of the Moscow communist party (who was in London for the trade negotiations), referring to the CPGB and to Moscow's secret subsidy of the *Daily Herald*, inflamed Curzon and other extreme anti-Bolsheviks in the Cabinet. They insisted on publication of these incriminating messages: a rash, flamboyant gesture which betrayed to Moscow that its codes had been broken. Alastair Denniston, head of GC&CS, blamed the short-term Kamenev publicity coup for the plummeting output of deciphered Soviet radio traffic after 1920. Thereafter, although GC&CS intercepted much secondary material on Asia and Bolshevik subversion in the British Empire, it was weak on central Europe. In addition to Curzon's blunder, it seems likely that White Russians, who had been captured by Bolshevik forces in Crimea and had been indiscreetly told by their English contacts of

GC&CS's cryptographic abilities, disclosed that the English could understand most secret Bolshevist signals.[22]

Further political indiscretions jeopardized GC&CS's good work in decoding intercepted signals traffic: in 1922 more Soviet decrypts were published by the London government; on 2 May 1923 Curzon sent a formal protest about Bolshevik subversion in Britain to the Soviets. This so-called Curzon Note was the first protest by one government to another that acknowledged that it was based on the intercepted radio traffic of the recipient nation. There were further calamitous revelations about signals interception at the time of the police raid in 1927 on the London offices of the All Russian Co-operative Society (ARCOS) searching for purloined secret official documents. Cabinet ministers quoted from Soviet diplomatic dispatches that had been sent from London to Moscow in code. The Soviet Union dropped its encryption procedure and introduced the more secure one-time pad method.

The Foreign Office replaced the Admiralty in 1922 in its supervision of GC&CS. There was no one of sufficient seniority there to halt the misjudged disclosures of 1922–3 and 1927. The three old-guard diplomatists who served as PUS at the apex of the Office hierarchy during the 1920s, Sir Eyre Crowe, Sir William Tyrrell and Sir Ronald Lindsay, regarded intelligence as a subordinate aspect of diplomacy. They doubtless agreed with the Berlin Ambassador, Lord D'Abernon, that 'the Secret Service' product was 'in a large majority of instances of no political value, based mainly upon scandal and tittle-tattle, and prepared apparently with no discrimination as to what is really important'. By contrast, the rising younger men of the 1920s understood the value and necessity of secret intelligence. Vansittart, who replaced Lindsay in 1930, and Cadogan, who succeeded him, were the first PUS to value this new ingredient in statecraft. This was held against them by officials and politicians who preferred to work by their own settled assumptions and hunches. 'No one questions Van's patriotism,' wrote the Cabinet Secretary, Sir Maurice Hankey, in explanation of his enforced retirement in 1938, 'but he is apt to get rather jumpy. He pays too much attention to the press of all countries and to S.I.S. information – useful pointers in both cases, but bad guides.'[23]

The Flapper Vote

One momentous fact is always overlooked: for MI5's first two decades Britain was not yet a full parliamentary democracy. Property-owning qualifications restricted the franchise, and all women were excluded from parliamentary elections. In 1910, at the first general election after the formation of the security services, the electorate numbered 5.8 million for England, 357,566 for Wales, 785,208 for Scotland, 698,787 for Ireland, making a total of 7.6 million. The combined population of England, Scotland and Wales was about 40 million (this includes children). During the war of 1914–18, Britain was depicted as the world's leading parliamentary democracy, although only about 40 per cent of its troops had the vote, whereas universal male suffrage had prevailed in Germany since 1871. In Britain in 1918 the franchise was extended to all men over the age of twenty-one and to women aged over thirty. The English electorate accordingly rose to just over 16 million, the Welsh to 1.2 million, the Scottish to 2.2 million and the Irish to 1.9 million – a total of 21.3 million. There was subsequent discussion of equalizing the franchise for both sexes at twenty-five, but in 1927 'the Cabinet went mad', as one of its members, Lord Birkenhead, explained, and authorized the extension of the vote to women above the age of twenty-one – 'a change so dangerous and so revolutionary' that Churchill fought it. This was called the Flapper Vote.[24]

The general election of 1929 was the first in which the British parliamentary franchise was extended to all men and women aged over twenty-one, except for prisoners, peers and lunatics. For the first time women comprised the majority of the electorate: 52.7 per cent were female and 47.3 per cent were male (15.2 million women and 13.7 million men). There had been an almost threefold increase in the electorate in under twenty years. Conservative activists believed that the Baldwin government's defeat by Labour was made inevitable by the extended franchise. Other conservative thinkers saw this as part of a wider *dégringolade*. 'The two most important happenings in my lifetime', said Hensley Henson, Bishop of Durham, 'are the revolt of women against their natural and traditional subordination, and the repudiation of Christianity lock, stock and barrel in Soviet Russia. The one destroys the family, and the other banishes God.'[25]

'The Flapper Vote . . . had to come, but came too soon,' Vansittart judged. After the election of 1929, 'electoral power passed from the thoughtful – pessimists said the educated – in a crucial decade, which first popularized the impracticable'. His deputy Sir Victor Wellesley was likewise convinced that the instability of British foreign policy during the 1930s was 'largely due' to the recent expansion of the electorate to include women. 'The pressure of an uninstructed public opinion' after the Italian invasion of Abyssinia resulted in policy swerves and a fatal diplomatic crash which forced the resignation of the Foreign Secretary. 'We like to think of democracy', wrote Wellesley, 'as the best guarantee against war. The events of 1935 prove that it can be as dangerous as a war-minded autocracy.' Wellesley, writing from the perspective of 1944, made a further point: universal adult suffrage was obtained just at the moment when 'the authority and prestige of parliaments' were declining in democratic countries; legislatures were 'steadily losing their sovereign power'. The volume and intricacy of public business required such specialization that parliaments were slackening control of the administrative machinery: real power had shifted to highly capitalized international companies, argued Wellesley, who founded the Foreign Office's Economic Relations section in 1933. Britain's epoch of full democracy began just as the deification of the nation state was occurring elsewhere in Europe: Italy had its Duce, Germany its Führer, Spain its Caudillo and Hungary its Serene Regent; but the most enduring absolutism was in Soviet Russia, where the dictatorship of the proletariat became the dictatorship of Generalissimo Stalin.[26]

One fact about the departments of state was so enormous, omnipotent and matchless that it is seldom mentioned. Whitehall was overwhelmingly masculine. The departmental culture was a body of assumptions, judgements, tastes and habits that, even when they underwent adaptation and reformulation, remained irrefragably male. No woman exerted any influence within any ministry. The security services were exceptional in employing women – Jane Sissmore, Ann Glass and others – in positions that mattered. Women were required to resign from the civil service if they married: their first thoughts must henceforth be for their husbands and their homes, so the Home Civil Service judged, and they should not be taking a salary into a household which already had a male breadwinner. The first marriage waiver was given to a principal at the Ministry of Labour in 1938. A year or so later Jane Sissmore, afterwards Jane Archer, became an outstanding exception to this rule. The former Oxford communist Jenifer Hart at the Home Office obtained a marriage waiver in 1941 with the support of her boss, Sir Alexander Maxwell, who advised her to announce in *The Times* that she wished to be regarded as married although she was barred by the civil service from being so. (She also endured sexual advances in the office from Sir Frank Newsam, who succeeded Maxwell as PUS in 1948.) Under wartime conditions most other women were required to resign on marriage, and were then re-employed as temporary civil servants for the duration of the war.

The married-women ban was formally lifted from the Home Civil Service in 1946, although it endured unofficially for many years longer. In the 1960s officials of the Civil Service Commission justified the bar in the Diplomatic Service on married women as necessary to clear the way for men to get promotion. The interdiction on married women continued in the Service until 1973. There were three women Cabinet ministers between 1919 and 1964 with a combined length of service of seven years. The first female PUS was installed at the suitably domestic Ministry of Housing in 1955. Although the bicameral Westminster legislature was idealized as 'The Mother of Parliaments', women were excluded from membership of its upper chamber, the House of Lords, until 1958. Such were the sacrifices expected of mothers that all the early life peeresses were childless. Hereditary women peers, unlike their male counterparts, were debarred from the Lords until 1963. The first woman judge was appointed in 1962, the first woman ambassador in 1976 and the first married woman ambassador in 1987; the first female chief of a security agency was Stella Rimington of MI5 in 1992; the Whitehall mandarins' preferred club, the Athenaeum, admitted its first women members in 2002. Women were excluded from full membership of Cambridge University until 1948: the first all-male colleges there began admitting female undergraduates in the 1970s.

These facts were more important to departmental temper, to office procedures and to relations between colleagues than the fluid or ductile gradations of class. It is compelling to note that critiques of the Whitehall ministries – starting in earnest after 1951, when Burgess and Maclean absconded from the Foreign Office – as class-bound in their recruitment, sectional and exclusive in their operations, inimical to modern technological progress, averse to private enterprise were all written by men. The position of women in government employment was seldom raised before a woman prime minister took office in 1979. Even then, it was treated as an issue for women writers, whose criticisms were discounted, sometimes with contempt, as a minority issue – despite Disraeli's axiom that the history of success is the history of minorities. The hegemony of class explanations belonged to a phase of thinking that should be long gone. As this book will show, gender exclusivity – not class exclusivity – helped men in their espionage for Soviet Russia. Whitehall's response to the discovery of such espionage was fashioned by male affinities, not class connivance.

The ideal of fraternity among men was fundamental to the way that everything worked. Collin Brooks, editor of the *Sunday Dispatch*, was among thirty journalists invited to the Treasury for a briefing on gold-conversion policy in 1932. 'We had tea and plum-cake in the Chancellor's room, talking very informally over pipes,' Brooks recorded. 'It was an interesting confidential pow-wow, and a beautiful example of the informality of British government.' This relaxed manliness in action required gender exclusivity: women subordinates may have prepared the tea and plum-cake, but they were not present to inhibit the men pulling on their pipes.[27]

Manliness can be defined in many ways: virility, fortitude, enterprise, aggression, logical powers, compassion, gullibility, boorishness, sentimentality, lumbering thoughts. 'They can laugh at anything – including themselves,' Vansittart said of his male compatriots. 'They boast of their smallest possession, common sense, and win victories for which no foresight qualified them.' Among colleagues, in offices and committees, nicknames proliferated as a way of bringing cheerful cohesion: 'Waterbeast', 'Snatch', 'Moly' and the rest. (Unaffectionate nicknames, such as 'Sir Icicle' for Alexander Cadogan, were not used openly.) Manly good humour was prized. 'I doubt if he has a very powerful head,' the Solicitor General, Sir Donald Somervell, said of the Home Secretary, Sir John Gilmour, in 1934; but 'he has a very robust & humorous outlook . . . & knows how to deal with men'. This seemed preferable to the volatility of brilliance.[28]

Masculine hardness was especially valued by Conservative leaders: their admiration for fascists and Nazis was expressed in gendered terms. Speaking of 'national glories' to the Anti-Socialist Union in 1933, Churchill thundered: 'I think of Germany, with its splendid, clear-eyed youths marching forward on all the roads of the Reich, singing their ancient songs, demanding to be conscripted into an army; eagerly seeking the most terrible weapons of war; burning to suffer and die for their Fatherland.' He praised, too, the Italian hard man Mussolini for inspiring his fascists with their 'stern sense of national duty'. This was men's stuff.[29]

Security Service staffing

What of the officers and men who worked for MI5? Edwin Woodhall joined the Metropolitan Police at the age of twenty in 1906. Before the war he worked for the Special Branch squad protecting Cabinet ministers from suffragette aggression and for MI5. Later he was personal protection officer to the Prince of Wales in France. He described the auxiliary officers with whom he served in wartime counter-espionage as drawn from 'the best class of educated British manhood' procurable in wartime: 'stockbrokers, partners of big business houses, civil, mechanical, and electrical engineers, artists, journalists, surveyors, accountants, men of travel – men of good family, men of the world. In fact, the finest types.'[30]

Typical of wartime MI5 officers was William Hinchley Cooke, who had been born in Germany to an English father and German mother. He attended school in Dresden and university in Leipzig, spoke German with a Hamburg accent and was fluent in French and Dutch. Like Woodhall he spent much of the war in counter-espionage on the Western Front. After his release from full-time government service, he had an attachment with the Birmingham city police; studied law at Gray's Inn, but was never called to the bar; and then joined the staff of the armaments company Vickers, which gave him cover for travelling in Austria, Belgium, Czechoslovakia, France, Germany, Italy, the Netherlands, Switzerland and Yugoslavia.

Vernon Kell sought the finest types for MI5: he liked men to be linguists, to enjoy outdoor life, to be shrewd readers of character, to be monuments of solid sense. In 1912 he recruited Reginald ('Duck') Drake, an army officer who spoke excellent French and passable German and Dutch, and whose listed recreations included hunting, shooting, beagling, skiing, golf, cricket, hockey, polo, otter-hunting, swimming, tennis and squash. Another recruit of 1912, Eric ('Holy Willy') Holt-Wilson, was an Old Harrovian, an instructor in military engineering at Woolwich Military Academy, a champion revolver shot and a keen skier. Holt-Wilson was seconded to the Inter-Allied Intelligence Bureau in Paris in 1915, and headed the Rhineland police commission after the Armistice. MI5's first graduate recruit, in 1914, Maldwyn ('Muldoon') Haldane, studied at Jesus College, Cambridge and the University of Göttingen, spoke German, French and Hindustani, and gave his recreations as trout-fishing, rowing, rugby, walking, poultry-farming, gardening, history, ethnology, palaeontology and biology.[31]

Haldane's recruitment belies the story that Dick White, who had read history at Christ Church, Oxford, was the earliest graduate to join the Security Service in 1936. Criticisms that Kell recruited from a narrow social group are similarly unfair. His budget for salaries was tight, and became more constricted by the funding cuts of the 1920s. Few men could live on the sums offered unless they had other income: White, then a young bachelor schoolmaster, rejected the first approach to him because he was offered the puny sum of £350 a year (albeit in cash, and tax-free). It was pragmatic of Kell, after the European war, to recruit men who were in receipt of army, navy or Indian police pensions. They had not only shown their trustworthiness in public service, but could afford to accept low salaries, which did not divert too much of the budget into personnel. MI5 got the only officers that it could afford. The retired Indian police officers have been disparaged as 'burnt out by the sun and the gin', and their colleagues as 'washed-up colonial administrators' and officials in 'the twilight of their careers'. Such denigration is partisan. No doubt they were conventional-minded and responsive to discipline, or persevering to a fault, but they took pride in trying to do a good job. There is little evidence for the reiterative assumption that they were obtuse or inflexibly prejudiced (which is perhaps to mistake them for Special Branch). On the contrary, MI5 looked for multiple meanings, burrowed beneath superficial statements, used intuition in their relentless paperwork and knew the place in counter-intelligence work of paradox. They were never lazy or corrupt. Kell assembled an efficient body of men who worked well together on meagre budgets. White, who became head of MI5 a dozen years after Kell's retirement, was well placed to appraise him. 'Kell', he judged, 'was a shrewd old bugger.'[32]

The pre-eminent example of an MI5 officer bolstered by income from an Indian police pension, Oswald ('Jasper') Harker, was recruited by Kell in 1920. Born in 1886, Harker was the son of a professor at the Royal Agricultural College at Cirencester, and had been invalided home from the deputy police commissionership in Bombay in 1919. He was a hard, astute, dutiful, prudent man, who headed B Branch (or Division), which ran investigations and inquiries with a staff of six officers and a three-man Observation section charged with shadowing suspects and pursuing inquiries. When the ailing Kell was dismissed in 1940, Harker, who was by then his deputy, had the sense to recognize that he was not the best man to succeed as Director, but took charge until a stronger leader was found. Harker's appointment in 1920, like White's in 1936, occurred years before security vetting of new staff was considered necessary. Vetting was not introduced until the 1940s: initially, there was negative vetting (background checks on potential new employees) and then, with reluctance, positive vetting. Checking the backgrounds, affiliations, personal habits and character of all civil servants with access to confidential material (which is what is meant by positive vetting) is a laborious, time-consuming, costly procedure, which diverted over-stretched personnel from their traditional priorities. There were neither security men vigilant at the entrances to MI5 offices nor security passes for its staff.

Intelligence officers in both Moscow and London understood the melodramatic stupidity of the officers of the Austrian General Staff after they proved in 1913 that Colonel Alfred Redl, the head of their Intelligence Bureau in Vienna, had been spying for tsarist Russia. They left him alone in a room with a pistol and waited for him to shoot himself. He took with him to his death any chance of identifying his accomplices, contacts, informants and tradecraft. Worst of all, the Austrians never learnt how many mobilization plans, armaments blue-prints and transport schedules had been betrayed by him. Unlike these pre-war Vienna blunderers, MI5 practised patient watchfulness, psycho-logical shrewdness and discreet understatement in preparing people to give them intelligence without exerting sanctions or threatening pain.

From 1925 onward MI5 preferred to identify traitors, establish under-standings with them, draw information from them and amass knowledge of their procedures and contacts. It disliked the confronta-tion and finality, to say nothing of the uncontrollable public disclosures and reckless speculative half-truths in newspapers, which arose from criminal trials. This was not a matter of class loyalties and corrupt cover-ups, as has been suggested with the Cambridge spies, but a tech-nique of accumulating, developing and sifting intelligence rather than introducing unnecessary crudity and spoiling sources. None of the Englishmen who spied in Britain for communist Russia was executed. In several trials – Glading in 1938, Nunn May in 1946, Marshall in 1952, Vassall in 1962 and doubtless others – prosecuting and defence counsel settled in advance what evidence was to be aired in court and how it was to be interpreted. The public disclosures in such trials often bore scant resemblance to the reality of what had happened.

In many cases public trials were avoided. The two Special Branch officers, Ginhoven and Jane, who were discovered in 1929 to be supplying secret material to Moscow were dismissed from the force after a disciplinary hearing in camera, but kept out of court. In conse-quence of this debacle, Special Branch responsibilities for monitoring and countering domestic communist subversion were transferred in 1931 to MI5, which was thereafter known as the Security Service. SIS reaffirmed in 1931 that it would not operate within 3 miles of British territory, and that all such territory across the globe came under the ambit of the Security Service. The new service was invested with enhanced status within Whitehall as an inter-departmental intelligence service providing advisory material to the Home, Foreign and Colonial offices, the Admiralty, the War Office, the Air Ministry, the Committee of Imperial Defence, the Attorney General, the Director of Public Prosecutions, chief constables in the United Kingdom and imperial police authorities.

In 1929 MI5 had only thirteen officers, including Kell, Holt-Wilson and Harker. Its operations were divided between A Branch (adminis-tration, personnel, records and protective security) and B Branch (investigations and inquiries). The transfer of the SS1 section from Special Branch into MI5 in 1931 brought two notable officers into MI5, Hugh Miller and Guy Liddell. Miller had been a pre-war lecturer at the universities of Grenoble, Dijon, the Sorbonne and Cairo, and had joined SS1 in 1920. When he died after a fall in 1934, his cryptic obit-uary in *The Times* called him 'a man of high intellectual interests' who had since the war 'devoted himself to sociological research applied to the domain of politics' – a striking euphemism for defeating subversion. 'The services he rendered to his country, though anonymous, were of great value.' Miller was admired by his colleagues as a connoisseur of

Japanese prints rather as Liddell was respected by them as an accomplished cellist.[33]

'When I joined MI5 in 1936 it was Guy Liddell who persuaded me to do so,' Dick White recalled over forty years later. 'He was the only civilising influence in the place at that time & I think this was felt by all the able men & women who joined MI5 [after 1939] for their war service.' Liddell had 'infinite diplomatic skill', his Security Service colleague John Masterman judged. 'At first meeting one's heart warmed to him, for he was a cultured man, primed with humour.' His years in Special Branch had made Liddell contemptuous of policemen: the Metropolitan force, as he saw first hand, was saturated by corruption as well as bungling. Somerset Maugham lunched with him in 1940: 'a plump man with grey hair and a grey moon face, in rather shabby grey clothes. He had an ingratiating way with him, a pleasant laugh and a soft voice.' If one had found Liddell standing in a doorway, apparently sheltering from the weather, one would mistake him, said Maugham, for 'a motor salesman perhaps, or a retired tea planter'.[34]

All the European powers recognized that their safety required intelligence systems; but the traditions, assumptions and values of the ruling cadres in different capitals diverged. The variations between Bolshevik Russia, Weimar Germany, Nazi Germany and the Third Republic in France – to take obvious examples – affected every particle of the espionage and counter-espionage operations of those countries. William Phillips, the head of MI5's A Branch, took over the files of Special Branch's SS1 section in 1931. It seemed wrong to him that Scotland Yard had compiled files on atheists, Scottish nationalists, conscientious objectors and what he called 'Hot Air Merchants'. The spying by the Bolshevik and Nazi regimes on their citizens, and the terrifying system of vengeful denunciations and violence, enormities that were emulated in parts of Vichy France, had more systematized ferocity than the crass incarceration and maltreatment of 'enemy aliens' in 1939–40 or the racist killings and colonial torture that were perpetrated by soldiers and officials in the British Empire.[35]

Office cultures and manly trust

What was the political and bureaucratic environment in which Kell's service operated? What were the institutional mentalities that prevailed in inter-war Whitehall and Westminster? How was national security evaluated and managed before the Cold War?

Political assessments were often crude during the 1920s. 'Everyone who is not a Tory is either a German, a Sinn Féiner or a Bolshevist,' declared Admiral Sir Reginald ('Blinker') Hall, wartime Director of Naval Intelligence at the Admiralty, and post-war Conservative MP for Eastbourne. Winston Churchill, as Chancellor of the Exchequer in 1924–9, denied any 'fundamental difference between the "moderate" Labour men and the Communists: the managers and leaders of the Trades Union movement are now nearly all of them Socialists and the "moderate" Socialists are aiming, in effect, at the same thing as the Communists: the only difference is their method of procedure'. Churchill's supreme fear was of outward moderation, which 'by so-called constitutional methods soothes public opinion while stealthily and by smooth words it proceeds step by step to revolution'. This assessment was not wholly unfair, for Lenin in a pamphlet of 1920 had recommended that communists should urge the British proletariat to vote Labour: in doing so communists would support Labour leaders 'in the same way that a rope supports a hanged man'. Churchill's absolute incapacity for irony or scepticism – his avidity for intense and dramatic beliefs – made his judgement too belligerent. His compulsion to treat weekly incidents as if they were historic events made him equally unsound in his use of intelligence reports. As one of Churchill's Cabinet colleagues confided to the Viceroy of India in 1927: 'I don't believe Winston takes any interest in public affairs unless they involve the possibility of bloodshed. Preferably he likes to kill foreigners, but if that cannot be done he would be satisfied with a few native Communists.'[36]

After 1929, although the British Empire had been made by conquest and was ruled by force, its leaders were committed to rule by democratic consent. Conservative politicians of the period, in the words of a Cabinet minister in 1929, wanted to trust an 'electorate trained by the War and by education' to work together without class antagonism. After 1929, British leaders began an experiment in the art of parliamentary rule. They attempted to solve, as the art historian and administrative panjandrum Kenneth Clark said in a different context, 'one of the chief problems of democracy: how to combine a maximum of freedom with an ultimate direction'. Their purposes were at odds with communists such as J. D. Bernal, who wrote in *Cambridge Left* in 1933: 'the betrayal and collapse of the General Strike combined with the pathetic impotence of the two Labour governments had already shown the hopelessness of political democracy'. Communists wanted to reduce liberty, limit parliamentary sovereignty and tighten party directives. The dictatorship of the proletariat was the aim. An MI5 summary of a bugged conversation at CPGB headquarters in 1951 reports James Klugmann, the party stalwart who animated Cambridge undergraduate communism, 'holding forth about "The British Road" saying that . . . "we" could *make* Parliament – transforming or reforming it as "we" went – into an instrument to give legal sanction to the people, as they took the power into their own hands'.[37]

Humour or lack of it was a leading point in appraising public servants. Thus Vansittart on 'the Bull', Lord Bertie of Thame, Ambassador in Paris: 'Snobbish, sternly practical, resolutely prosaic, he knew no arabesques of humour or irony, but only hard straight lines'; Sir David Kelly, Ambassador in Moscow during the Cold War, on Vansittart: 'his witty comments always imparted a cheerful and soothing note into our frenzied conveyor-belt of files boxes'; and the insider who wrote the enigmatic obituary in *The Times* of Hugh Miller of MI5: 'Captain Miller's marvellous knowledge of human nature . . . [and] his never-failing humour . . . established his undisputed authority in a select circle'. It was recognized that geniality might help in handling Stalinist officials. Alan Roger of MI5, recommending cooperation with the Russians in running a deception campaign from Tehran to Berlin in 1944, insisted that a measure of mutual trust could be won from Soviet officials 'by persistent good humour, obvious frankness, personal contact and a readiness to be helpful in small things'. Jokes all but extenuated communist activism. Charles Moody was a dustman in Richmond, Surrey who was industrial organizer of the Thames Valley branch of the CPGB in the 1920s and took subversive literature to army barracks, went underground in the 1930s, and in the 1940s was used as an intermediary when the atomic scientist-spy Klaus Fuchs wished to make emergency contact with his Russian cut-out – a go-between who serves as an intermediary between the leader of a spy network and a source of material – or to defer a meeting. After 1950 he underwent several interviews with MI5's prime interrogator without any incriminating admissions. 'Mr MOODY continues to impress as being a very likeable man,' declared an MI5 report of 1953, before praising his 'quiet sense

of humour'. It is hard to imagine US or Soviet counter-espionage investigators appreciating a suspect's jokes.[38]

Trust was an important civilizing notion in the 1920s and 1930s.
Men subdued expression of their feelings if they could. 'We possess
one thing in common,' Masterman had been told in adolescence, 'the
gorgeous . . . power of reticence, and it binds, if I may say so, tighter
than speech.' The initiators of personal conversations were distrusted
by the English: the poet, painter and dandy Villiers David advised his
godchildren in 1943, 'Never speak first to anyone you really want to
know.' If men refrained from intimacies, they often talked without guard
of impersonal matters. The inter-war years were a period of careless
Cabinet talk. Speaking at a dinner of parliamentary correspondents in
1934, George Lansbury, then leader of the Labour party, 'derided the
superstition of Cabinet secrets – had, he felt sure, told many because
he hadn't realised that they were secrets'. Collin Brooks of the *Sunday
Dispatch* described the Cabinet of 1935 as 'a chatterbox Gvt'.[39]

Senior ministers discussed at dinner parties confidential material
which had been circulated to them, including Foreign Office telegrams
and dispatches, without any glimmering that they were being culpably
indiscreet. The position of Sir Eric Phipps as Ambassador in Hitler's
Berlin was weakened because Cabinet ministers were circulated with
his dispatches about the Nazi leadership and recounted them for laughs
at social gatherings. Above all there was Phipps's famous 'bison despatch',
in which he described a visit to Göring's country estate:

> The chief impression was that of the most pathetic naïveté of General
> Göring, who showed us his toys like a big, fat, spoilt child: his primeval
> woods, his bison and birds, his shooting-box and lake and bathing
> beach, his blond 'private secretary', his wife's mausoleum and swans
> and sarsen stones, all mere toys to satisfy his varying moods . . . and
> then I remembered there were other toys, less innocent though
> winged, and these might some day be launched on their murderous
> mission in the same childlike spirit and with the same childlike glee.

After Phipps's transfer to the Paris embassy, he was cautioned by
Vansittart against candour about French politicians in telegrams that
had a wide circulation among members of the government.[40]

Embassies and legations, like the Office in London, were cooperative, hierarchical organizations in which mutual trust was indispensable. This was not a matter of class loyalty or old-school-tie fidelity, but an obvious point about raising the efficiency of its staff. Sir Owen O'Malley estimated that about one-third of his ambassadorial energy went into making his embassy work well. 'It begins to lose power whenever one man gets discouraged or another too cocky or a third jealous . . . when wives quarrel it is hell.' It was indispensable for an ambassador to be trusted by the government to which he was accredited. 'One of the many illusions about diplomacy is that it consists in diddling the other fellow. Nothing could be further from the truth. It consists more than anything else in precision, honesty, and persuasion, which three things should hang together.'[41]

'Democracy is not only a theory of government, but also a scale of moral values,' the economic historian Sir Michael Postan insisted in a 1934 essay on Marx. As someone born in Bessarabia under tsarist despotism, who had escaped from the dictatorship of the proletariat in 1919, Postan valued parliamentary democracy as a flower of the European tradition of humanitarian individualism. 'It accepts human personality and individual man as an end in themselves, the sole purpose and the only justification of a social system. It judges political actions by the good or evil they do to individuals, rather than by their effects on the collective super-individual entities of race, state, church and society.' Postan countered the modish communists in his university who excused collective authoritarianism: 'majority rule, representative institutions, government by consent and respect for opinions are merely broad applications of humanitarian ethics to problems of state government'. Social networks were central in Postan's model society, where transactions were characterized by trust, reciprocity and the absence of avarice – but never led by the popular will. Maynard Keynes, Cambridge economist and Treasury official, thought on similar lines to Postan. 'Civilisation', he said during the looming European catastrophe of 1938, 'was a thin and precarious crust erected by the personality and will of a very few, and only maintained by rules and conventions skilfully put across and guilefully preserved.'[42]

After the transformative crisis of 1914–18, and despite the widespread earlier qualms about Victorian imperialism, most of the administrative leaders who helped to govern inter-war Britain believed that they represented a civilizing force in the world: 'all my life and all my strength', as Eric Holt-Wilson declared with staunch sincerity of his work for MI5, 'were given to the finest cause on this earth – the ennoblement of all mankind by the example of the British race'. There were self-seekers and time-servers, of course, but also efficient, modest men, who took pride in doing the best possible job that they could. Sir Alan Brooke, the most effective Chief of the Imperial General Staff in history and afterwards Lord Alanbrooke, wrote on New Year's Day of 1944: 'Heard on the 8 am wireless that I had been promoted to Field Marshal! It gave me a curious peaceful feeling that I had at last, and unexpectedly, succeeded in reaching the top rung of the ladder!! I certainly never set out to reach this position, nor did I ever hope to do so, even in my wildest moments. When I look back over my life no one could be more surprised than I am to find where I have got to!!'[43]

Such men as Holt-Wilson and Brooke were convinced upholders of values which required the practice in their working lives of such personal virtues as pride in service, individual self-respect and group responsibility. Cynicism was thought a sign of mediocrity. It is easy to scoff that these beliefs covered hypocrisy, selfishness, bullying, prejudice and inefficiency; but many public servants upheld these beliefs, which were at the core of their self-identification and a vital motive in their work. They were rich in the social capital of group loyalty, and therefore rich in trust. Although the British Empire rested on force, and its diplomats exerted coercion, it was the pride of Whitehall that it worked by influence rather than power.

'Power', to quote Lord Beveridge, 'means ability to give to other men orders enforced by sanctions, by punishment or by control of rewards; a man has power when he can mould events by an exercise of will; if power is to be used for the good, it must be guided by reason and accompanied by respect for other men.' Beside the power of money, exerted by giving or withholding rewards, stood governmental power: 'making of laws and enforcing them by sanctions, using the instrument of fear'. In contrast, Beveridge continued, 'influence . . . means changing the actions of others by persuasion, means appeal to reason or to emotions other than fear or greed; the instruments of influence are words, spoken or written; if the influence is to be for good, it must rest on knowledge'. It was believed that the official integrity and impartiality of men of good influence would not be warped by personal preferences. When Burgess and Maclean disappeared from the Foreign Office in

1951, the former Foreign Secretary Anthony Eden told the Commons that all ministers trusted the neutrality of their officials, and felt sure 'that the civil service has no part in political views'. His apparent implication was that it was irrelevant if the two missing diplomats – or any of their colleagues – were secret communists, because their partisanship outside the Office could not have tinged decision-making within the Office.[44]

In 1940 the Home Defence (Security) Executive, newly constituted by Churchill's War Cabinet to oversee the defence of the nation from fifth columnists and best known as the Security Executive (SE), recommended that a regulation be implemented making it an offence to subvert government authority. This was opposed by Sir Alexander Maxwell, the PUS at the Home Office, as 'inconsistent with the historic notions of English liberty. Our tradition is that while orders issued by the duly constituted authority must be obeyed, every civilian is at liberty to show, if he can, that such orders are silly or mischievous and that the duly constituted authorities are composed of fools or rogues'. Maxwell had a first-class degree in politics and ancient philosophy from Oxford, and was married to a Quaker physician: together they gave an annual party for the Home Office charwomen with their sons acting as waiters. He was humorous, gentle, unruffled and a model of upright neutrality who always remembered that Home Office decisions affected, not an undifferentiated mass of citizens, but individual lives, each of which had peculiar problems and potentialities. Maxwell respected, as few officials in his department have done since 1997, 'historic notions of English liberty'. Activities which showed the authorities as contemptible were not necessarily subversive in Maxwell's judgement. 'They are only subversive if they are calculated to incite persons to disobey the law, or to change the government by unconstitutional means. This doctrine gives, of course, great and indeed dangerous liberty to persons who desire revolution . . . but the readiness to take this risk is the cardinal distinction between democracy and totalitarianism.'[45]

A description of Algernon Hay, chief of the Foreign Office's Communications Department during 1919–34, shows the Whitehall ideal personified. Hay mastered 'the supreme art of making others obey him without knowing they were obedient', recalled one of his subordinates. 'He knew how to talk, not merely to those in his own station of life but to everyone, from a royal duke to a scullery maid. He never let

anyone down or gave anyone away . . . true loyalty, such as his, needs
qualities of the head as well as of the heart.' Hay and his kind inculcated
an *esprit de corps* that had admirable elements. What distinguished the
Office in 1936, so Gladwyn Jebb recalled, 'was an intellectual liveliness
and complete liberty, inside the machine, to say what you thought and
press your own point of view, provided that outside you were reasonably discreet about the official line'. No one questioned the motives – as
opposed to the judgement – of colleagues in public service, or impugned
their loyalty. Colleagues 'regarded themselves as a band of brothers
who trusted each other . . . the great thing was that all, however junior,
would express an individual view which, if it was intelligently voiced
and to the point, might come up to the Secretary of State himself'.[46]

The fact that senior members of the Diplomatic Service were clas-
sically educated has been condemned by later generations, but it had
advantages. 'Latin is a thrifty language and demands a keen eye and
ear for the single word which contains so much,' as John Drury has
written. Latinists were invaluable in finding and making sense of the
key words embedded in the evasive rigmarole of diplomatic exchanges:
trained too in detecting fallacies, making distinctions between major
and minor propositions, and giving clarifications in eloquent, impartial
prose. A tone of festive irony was not inimical to these exacting standards. Junior officials who were verbose, or offered fallacious reasoning,
found that their seniors could be crushing. Ivone Kirkpatrick, who
joined the Western Department of the Office in 1919, had his draft
papers returned with cutting comments: 'rejected with contumely'; 'this
seems to me the bloody limit of blatant imbecility'. On one occasion
Kirkpatrick was telephoned by the PUS, Sir Eyre Crowe, about a draft
memorandum. 'Either you do not mean what you say, in which case
you are wasting my time,' Crowe snapped at him, 'or you do mean it,
in which case you are writing rot.' With that, Crowe put down the
receiver. He was anxious that his young staff would not be disillusioned
by exposure to politicians. When Lloyd George asked that a junior
official should attend meetings of a Cabinet committee, Crowe
demurred: 'if young men from the Foreign Office go to Cabinet committees, they will learn what Cabinet ministers are like', Crowe warned.[47]

These vivacious exchanges were enabled in the Office and other
departments of state by an admirable tool of orderly, discriminating
administration: the circulating file. All but ultra-secret dispatches, tele-

grams and incoming letters went first to the most junior official in the responsible department, who read the document, wrote a minute (that is, a comment or preliminary recommendation) and perhaps made annotations. Then the document would rise through the hierarchy, with each official adding comments, exploring alternatives, adding emphasis or making retractions, in order to improve the recommendation. Having started at the bottom, the file would finally reach the Secretary of State. Evidence and arguments were sieved, weighed, evaluated and refined like rare metals. In some ways the ministries resembled the court of a Renaissance humanist monarch in which learned experts proposed, replied, explained, objected, discoursed and resolved. This system of calm, self-contained reciprocity relied on trust. 'In most foreign ministries,' wrote Sir Owen O'Malley, 'the presiding politician, less confident in the loyalty of officials or more apprehensive that his doings should be known outside his own personal entourage, often employed in confidential or shady transactions a small group of adherents who could be as dangerous to themselves as to him.' Such shenanigans impaired the trust between ministers and officials, caused delays, confusion and duplicated labour, and devalued the objective advice of those excluded from the inner ring. (The circulating file is a grievous loss in the age of emails and 'Reply all' circulation lists.)[48]

Condescension and chauvinism were ubiquitous. When the British Minister in Prague was asked if he had many friends among the Czechs, he was incredulous. 'Friends!' he exclaimed. 'They eat in their kitchens!' Sir Alexander Cadogan, lunching at the Ritz Hotel in 1940, was irritated by the proximity of 'Dagos and Coons'. Assumptions of racial superiority were treated as a national virtue. 'It looks as if the peak of white supremacy has been reached and that recession is now inevitable,' lamented Sir Victor Wellesley, Deputy Under Secretary at the FO until 1936. 'Of all the calamities which that gigantic struggle [in 1914–18] inflicted upon Europe, none in the end may prove to have been greater than the loss of prestige which the white race has suffered in the eyes of the coloured world.' Even communist informants thought that the exceptionalism of the Anglo-Saxon kingdom was part of the natural order. 'Nature has put Great Britain at the cross-roads of civilization,' declared a Labour MP Wilfrid Vernon in 1948 (eleven years after he had been caught leaking aviation secrets to the Soviets). Duff Cooper, Ambassador in Paris during 1944–7, 'has a tremendous feeling about

the superiority of the British race and about our system of government,
Guy Liddell noted. 'He thinks the old school tie is one of the finest
institutions we have got, and that widespread education is a mistake.'[49]

Racism was a majority pleasure. In 1940 the Duke of St Albans, after
a day on guard at Admiralty Arch, went in battledress to dine at Brooks's
club. 'I hate all Europeans, except Scandinavians,' he growled to a fellow
diner; 'of course I loathe all dagoes.' Dining at the Blue Train Grill, one
Fleet Street editor endured 'a cabaret which consisted of two niggers
at a piano – one a full-blooded fellow and the other a chocolate-coloured
coon. It was odd how my old Tory blood revolted at these self-satisfied
niggers ogling our women, and at our women mooning over them.'
Foreigners were called Fuzzy-Wuzzies, Levantines, kaffirs, chinks and
worse. They were identified with failure, contraceptives, trickery, idle-
ness, perversion, cowardice, absenteeism and disease: Balkanization,
Dutch caps, French letters, Greek gifts, Greek ease, Hunnish practices,
Dutch courage, French leave, Spanish influenza, German measles, the
French disease. 'Egyptian PT' (physical training) was afternoon sleep,
and a 'Portuguese parliament' was where everyone talked but no one
listened. Orientals were wily, Hindus were lazy, Hungarians were reckless, and Slavs were dreamy and lethargic. Treachery was sincerely
thought to be unEnglish: it was the trait of subject breeds. 'Don't trust
the natives: they're treacherous,' the war correspondent Philip Jordan
was told when he visited Ceylon in the 1930s. 'It's only when you've
been out here as long as I have', said expatriates who thought themselves
kind and good, 'that you will realise how little you know about "our
coloured brethren" as we must call them now.'[50]

London was the capital of 'the greatest democracy in the world', the
Cabinet minister Sir Samuel Hoare averred in 1936. 'If British liberty
and democracy collapse in a catastrophe, liberty and democracy will
be exterminated in the world.' Few people in England thought such
Anglocentrism was absurdly overblown, or that Hoare was insular and
foolish. After all, Germany and Italy were already autocracies, Austria
and Spain were being overwhelmed by anti-democratic forces, and the
Second Republic in Portugal and the Regency in Hungary were author-
itarian regimes. King Alexander I had imposed personal dictatorship
on Yugoslavia in 1929. There had been a military seizure of power in
Bulgaria in 1934, although by 1936 King Boris III had engineered a
semi-democratic counter-coup which prevailed until 1939. A fortnight

after Hoare's speech a military junta in Greece proclaimed the dawn of the Third Hellenic Civilization, which meant the abolition of the constitution, the dissolution of parliament and the suppression of political parties. King Carol II was preparing to suppress all democratic pretences in Romania. Britain, with its new constitutional settlement of 1927–9, was indeed one of the leading survivors among the diminishing number of free European democracies. It was to prevent resurgence of the dictatorial nationalism of the 1930s that the European nations coalesced economically, judicially and politically in the late twentieth century.[51]

There was justified pride in the intelligence, neutrality and inviolability from corruption of Whitehall. 'The Greeks, like many other races, lack a competent civil service with established traditions of hard work and integrity,' wrote Sir Daniel Lascelles from the Athens embassy in 1945. After years of Turkish domination, their political tradition was 'to evade and thwart governmental authority'. It was said in their favour, continued Lascelles, that Greeks had 'plenty of guts. So, I believe, have the Irish'. There were a few exceptions to this patriotic unity: Goronwy Rees, who spied for Moscow in 1938–9, disparaged the land mass of England, Scotland and Wales as 'Bird's Custard Island' because it was thick, tasteless and sickly. Millions of his compatriots however believed that British was best. Sometimes for sound reasons, but often with the benefit of self-assured inexperience, they presumed that the English language was the richest in the world, and that the nation's policemen, beer, pageantry, countryside, sense of fair play, engineering, handshakes, comedians and parliament were unmatched. Nationalist pride permeated every social group: 'the lags were as uncritically patriotic as book-makers or actors', said Wilfred Macartney of his fellow inmates in Parkhurst prison, where he was detained in 1927–35 after trying to obtain RAF secrets for Moscow. 'Everything English was best, from a Rolls-Royce to a cigarette.'[52]

Such unreal assumptions vitiated national influence throughout the Cold War period. 'The British have a great liability: so many of us still believe in the "effortless superiority" . . . of all British men and some women,' wrote the sociologist Michael Young in 1960. 'This terrifying attitude is not confined to Bournemouth. Many solid working-class people have it too, Labour voters as well as Tory.' When, during the Suez crisis of 1956, Young conducted an opinion survey in the inner London suburb of Hornsey, he was 'dismayed by the number of manual workers who backed Eden wholeheartedly, talked of Wogs, Dagoes and Gyppies as vituperatively as they did when they were "seeing the world" in the Army'.[53]

Pretensions of English singularity, coupled with the delusion that public institutions could be made inviolate from continental influences, beset the cruder politicians, virulent editorial journalists and the more ignorant voters. Officers in Special Branch may have been hoodwinked by such ideas, but they made less headway in MI5, where most officials were well-travelled linguists rather than the blockheads imagined by the agency's detractors. Diplomatists from Crowe, Vansittart and Cadogan downwards, though they were patriotic, saw the best hopes of peace lay in supra-nationalism, not nationalism. 'The only sure guarantee against a renewal of fratricidal strife lies in the realisation, not only of the economic, but of the social solidarity of Europe,' Don Gregory (the former Foreign Office expert on Soviet Russia) wrote in 1929. He warned against the special danger of Britain being lulled into complacency because 'we are almost the only Europeans who have no traditional hatreds, who have no land frontiers to bother about, who need never be dragged into a war unless we wish to be'. European ideas and power had mastery over British destiny.[54]

CHAPTER 4

The Vigilance Detectives

The first English network of communist espionage reporting to Moscow came into existence because of a commotion in a Pimlico side-street in 1909 some eight years before the Bolshevik revolution in Russia. Wolverhampton, Chatham, Hornsey and Bristol – not Cambridge colleges – spawned the earliest Soviet spy ring. Renegade policemen worked for Moscow first. The covert activities of these policemen and their journalist associates, and the way that MI5 handled them, is fundamental to understanding secret service priorities and techniques in the seventy years before the dismantling of the Soviet Union in 1991.

The uprising of the Metropolitan Police

One night in the year of the foundation of the British secret services two patrolling constables detained two rowdy men who were ringing doorbells in Pimlico. The miscreants were taken to the local police station, where they were identified as neighbours who had been locked out by their irate wives after carousing too late at the pub. The Metropolitan Police inspector on duty that night at Pimlico, John Syme, sent the men home without charge. The rumpus ought to have ended there. Instead, it led to rebellion inside the Metropolitan Police, demonstrations, strikes and the first organized network of Englishmen spying for the Bolsheviks.

After Syme had rebuked the constables for being officious, they made counter-complaints against him. A tortuous disciplinary procedure ended with his demotion to the rank of sergeant. When he protested, he was suspended from duty for insubordination. In 1910 he was dismissed for declaring that he would take his grievances outside the force to his MP. Sir Edward Henry, the fingerprint pioneer who was

Chief Commissioner of Metropolitan Police, threatened resignation in 1911 when Winston Churchill, as Home Secretary, seemed inclined to reinstate Syme. In June that year Syme was arrested after sending a letter to Churchill which threatened murder. He was put under police watch lest he offer violence to King George V. He and his wife Nellie were evicted from their police flat. He protested at the Palace of Westminster. There were terms of imprisonment. Twice he went on hunger-strike. He was sent to Broadmoor criminal lunatic asylum. Scotland Yard's determination to crush a man who had, under stress, threatened violence is comprehensible: a barman shot and wounded Sir Edward Henry in 1912 after his application for a licence to drive a motor-bus had been rejected at Scotland Yard.

Jack Hayes, a Liverpool MP and former London policeman, using the language of racism and sportsmanship that connoted manliness to his generation, told the House of Commons in 1923: 'Inspector Syme, one of the whitest men who ever wore a police uniform, a man who has undergone untold suffering, was really playing the game as an inspector of the Metropolitan Police.' Three years after Syme's death in 1945, his misfortunes were again debated in parliament. 'I remember him away back in the years before the first world war – tall, fine, handsome he was, and . . . very clean in his character,' said the communist MP Willie Gallacher. 'Injustice wore down that strong body and practically destroyed the mind and soul of that fine man.'[1]

Syme's treatment was seen as a travesty by many London policemen, who projected a workplace association to resist victimization and favouritism. The authorities responded in 1913 by forbidding policemen from union membership, under penalty of dismissal. Money became a pressing issue, too. Although policemen considered themselves to be a class above the urban labouring poor, they were paid at similar levels. From the declaration of war in 1914 to the outbreak of the Russian revolution in 1917, the cost of living in London rose by 76 per cent but police pay by only 20 per cent. Policemen resented losing prestige to munitions workers earning three times as much. They fainted on duty from hunger.

These pressures led to the formation of the National Union of Police and Prison Officers (NUPPO), which declared a strike in August 1918. Almost all of the 12,000 Metropolitan Police withdrew from duty. So, too, did the 1,200 men of the City of London force guarding the capital's financial institutions. These police 'revolters' were, thought Hensley Henson, the politically minded bishop, 'a very ominous sign of social disintegration'. The wartime coalition government, which feared that police disaffection would spread to the army, sent a detachment of Guards to protect Scotland Yard from the mutineers. Lloyd George, as Prime Minister, conceded most of the strikers' demands on pay, pensions and war bonuses, and was understood by negotiators to have given an oral promise of union recognition. Sir Edward Henry, who had underestimated NUPPO's support, was replaced as Chief Commissioner by General Sir Nevil Macready. Hayes and other policemen were soon riled by Macready's declared intention to raise the force's discipline to the standard of a Guards regiment.[2]

Hayes left the Metropolitan Police on his election as general secretary of NUPPO in March 1919. Born in 1889, he was one of the seven children of a police inspector at Wolverhampton, and had been educated in the town. At the age of thirteen he became a clerk with the Wolverhampton Corrugated Iron Company. By attending evening classes he learnt shorthand, book-keeping, accountancy and French. In 1909 he joined the Metropolitan Police, in which he reached the rank of sergeant within four years. He was an imposing man whose elaborate waxed moustache suggested vanity. The success of the 1918 strike imbued him with over-confidence. On the Sunday nearest to May Day in 1919 NUPPO assembled the largest crowd seen in Trafalgar Square for years. In addition to thousands of Metropolitan policemen, who marched along Whitehall bearing banners with defiant slogans, they were supported by crowds of colonial soldiers and by some sailors. The most insistent protesters were policemen who had recently been demobilized from regiments on the Western Front and found reversion to military drilling to be an intolerable prospect. Hayes denounced Macready to the demonstrators: 'being an army officer, the Chief Commissioner was introducing a system not of discipline, but of tyranny, brutality and Prussianism'.[3]

The Police Act of 1919, which came into force in August, granted higher wages, but made it illegal (with a penalty of up to two years' imprisonment) for policemen to join a trade union concerned with pay, pensions and conditions of service. The government-subsidized Police Federation was formed. NUPPO responded by calling a national strike which flopped everywhere except Merseyside. There the strike

endured for three weeks, during which troops made bayonet charges
to quell looting in rough districts. When the Merseyside strike collapsed,
every striking policeman there was dismissed with total loss of pension
rights. Lloyd George said that 'all England' should feel indebted to
Liverpool's resilient municipal leadership. He saw Merseyside's police
strike 'as perhaps the turning point in the Labour movement, deflecting
it from Bolshevist and Direct Actionist courses to legitimate Trade
Unionism. Had Liverpool been wrongly handled, and had the strikers
scored a success, the whole country might very soon have been on
fire.'[4]

All NUPPO activists in London were dismissed. Several of them,
including its former general secretary James Marston, took jobs with
the All Russian Co-operative Society (ARCOS), the Soviet government's commercial agency which opened in London in 1920 and acted
as a front for espionage and subversion. Historians of British
communism imply that these men were Special Branch plants, and
mock 'the wave of Bolshevism coursing through Scotland Yard and
the Metropolitan Police at this time', as if the recent victimization,
strikes, demonstrations and dismissals were not sufficient causes of
radicalization. Special Branch did have two informants planted inside
ARCOS, Karl Korbs and Peter Miller, while MI5 had its own double
agent embedded there, Anatoli Timokhin. None of them had been
Metropolitan policemen.[5]

After the collapse of NUPPO, Hayes started the Vigilance Detective
Agency, which was based at Clapton Common, where he lived. A
festering shared grievance is a powerful unifier of men. Vigilance was
manned by a rump of NUPPO loyalists, notably Walter Dale and Arthur
Lakey. Dale became Vigilance's chief investigator. Lakey's wife joined
Marston in the ARCOS offices, where she worked under her maiden
name of Kitty Reynolds. In Paris before 1914 the Okhrana's surveillance
of dissident émigrés had been delegated to a private detective agency,
Bint et Sambain, in order to distance the Russian embassy in Paris from
the watch. After 1920 the Cheka determined to use Vigilance in post-war
London rather as the Okhrana had used Bint et Sambain in pre-war
Paris. The agency's detectives were soon recommended by Hayes to a
young journalist named William Norman Ewer.

Norman Ewer of the *Daily Herald*

Norman Ewer had been born in 1885 in the middling London suburb of Hornsey. His father dealt in silk, and later moved to Muswell Hill. The family kept one live-in housemaid. Ewer rose up the rungs of the middle class by passing examinations. He attended Merchant Taylor's School in Charterhouse Square in the City of London, and Trinity College, Cambridge, where he won first-class degrees in mathematics and history. From an early age, he was nicknamed 'Trilby' because, like the heroine of George du Maurier's novel, he liked to be barefoot. After Cambridge he became private secretary to an exotic plutocrat known as Baron de Forest.

Born in 1879, de Forest was ostensibly the son of American circus performers who died of typhoid when their troupe visited Turkey. After a spell in an orphanage, he was adopted in 1887 by the fabulously rich Baroness Hirsch, who believed that he was the illegitimate child of her dead son. He inherited a castle and many millions in 1899, was created Baron de Forest by the Austrian Emperor and converted from Judaism to Catholicism. Subsequently he settled in England, where he held the land-speed record and was the victorious radical candidate at a parliamentary by-election in 1911. He forthwith spoiled his political prospects by suing his mother-in-law for slander. In 1912 de Forest contributed to the fund launched by the Labour MP George Lansbury to save the fiercely partisan *Daily Herald* from insolvency. Ewer was installed as de Forest's nominee in the *Daily Herald* management: he soon became, together with the young Oxford graduates G. D. H. Cole, Gerald Gould and Harold Laski, one of 'Lansbury's lambs' working as a journalist there. His idealism became the overworked centre of his existence.

After the outbreak of war in 1914 Ewer opposed conscription, registered as a conscientious objector, became an indentured agricultural worker in Waldorf Astor's pigsties at Cliveden and published anti-war verses. He was aghast at the mayhem of the Western Front, was revolted by the militarism of the Austrian, British, German and Russian monarchies, and loathed the inequities of free-market capitalism. He saw the undoubtable humbug of the British claim to be fighting for liberal democracy when its main ally was tsarist Russia, which had sponsored the pogroms of 1903–6 and sent dissidents into captivity and internal exile. As Ewer wrote in 1924, Lenin emerged as the greatest historical leader of the epoch because he saw world revolution, not national victory in the European war, as the primary aim. German socialists collaborated with German capitalism, British socialists exerted themselves for national interests, and pacifists strove for peace. 'Only the great voice of Lenin cried from Switzerland that all were wrong; that the job of Socialists was Socialism; neither to prosecute the Imperialist war nor to stop the Imperialist war, but to snatch a Socialist victory from the conflicts of Imperialism; to turn war into revolution.' For Ewer, like Lenin, imperialism was the apotheosis of capitalism.[6]

When Ewer applied for a post-war passport to visit the Netherlands and Switzerland, Gerald Gould assured the Foreign Office that the 'extreme' socialism preached in the *Daily Herald* was a bulwark against Bolshevism. Counter-espionage officers assessed him differently. 'EWER is pro-German principally on the grounds that other Governments are not less wicked than the German,' reported Special Branch's Hugh Miller. 'He preaches peace with Germany, followed by "*revolution through bloodshed*".' In Miller's estimate, Ewer was a risk to national security: not only 'a clever writer and fluent speaker' but 'a dangerous and inflammatory agitator'.[7]

In 1919 Ewer was appointed foreign editor of the *Daily Herald*. He collaborated during that year with the pro-Bolshevik MP Cecil L'Estrange Malone and a director of the *Daily Herald* named Francis Meynell in formulating a programme for a Sailors', Soldiers' & Airmen's Union which would certainly have been revolutionary in intent. Ewer became a founding member of the CPGB in 1920, and liaised between the newspaper, CPGB headquarters in King Street and Nikolai Klyshko, who was both secretary of the Soviet delegation that arrived in London in May 1920 to negotiate a trade agreement and the Cheka chief in London. Klyshko controlled Soviet espionage in Britain, and funded subversion, until his recall from London in 1923.

George Lansbury visited Moscow and met Lenin in 1920. 'I shall always esteem it the greatest event in my life that I was privileged to see this fine, simple, wise man', he wrote in besotted terms in his memoirs. Lenin was 'a great man in every sense of the word', who held supreme national power and yet remained 'unaffected and without personal pride'. Lansbury, who became chairman of the Labour party in 1927 and its leader in 1932, told the party conference at Birmingham in 1928 that the Bolshevik revolution had been 'the greatest and best thing that has ever happened in the history of the world'. Socialists should rejoice that the 'fearful autocracy', which ruled from the Baltic to the Black Sea and from the Volga to the Pacific, had been replaced by that magnificent venture in state socialism, the Soviet Union. 'The peasants and workers of that great nation, encircled by implacable foes who ceaselessly intrigue, conspire and work to restore Czardom, need our sympathy and help, and we need theirs.' It was the role of the *Daily Herald*, thought Lansbury and his lambs, to provide and receive sympathetic help.[8]

In August 1920 GC&CS intercepted and deciphered a signal from Lev Kamenev, the Bolshevik revolutionary leader and acting head of the Soviet trade delegation, reporting that he had given to the *Daily Herald* a subsidy of £40,000 raised by selling precious stones. In return, it was understood that the newspaper would be the mouthpiece of Moscow on Anglo-Russian relations and would support Bolshevik agitation and propaganda against the Lloyd George government. Meynell, the courier used to smuggle many of these jewels, made several visits to Copenhagen to meet Moscow's star diplomat Maxim Litvinov. The surveillance of these meetings was comically blatant: a window-cleaner appeared on a ladder, and a banister-polisher on the landing, whenever Meynell entered Litvinov's hotel suite. Once Meynell returned from Copenhagen with two strings of pearls secreted in a jar of butter. On another occasion he posted a box of chocolate creams, each containing a pearl or diamond, to his friend the philosopher Cyril Joad. All these shenanigans were known to Ewer, although it may have been kept from him that £10,000 of the jewels money was invested in the Anglo-Russian Three Ply and Veneer Company run by George Lansbury's sons Edgar and William. Edgar Lansbury was a member of the CPGB, who in 1924 was elected communist mayor of Poplar. His mother-in-law, Hannah ('Annie') Glassman, was used to convert the jewels into cash.[9]

MI5 resorted to family connections and social contacts in order to handle Kamenev and the *Daily Herald*. Jasper Harker had recently married Margaret Russell Cooke at a Mayfair church. She was the sister of Sidney ('Cookie') Russell Cooke, an intellectual stockbroker and Liberal parliamentary candidate, who had inherited a fine house on the Isle of Wight called Bellecroft. Russell Cooke had been a lover of Maynard Keynes, whose lifelong friend and business associate he remained, and was the son-in-law of the captain of the *Titanic*. Virginia

Woolf called him 'a shoving young man, who wants to be smart, cultivated, go-ahead & all the rest of it'. Harker used his brother-in-law to compromise Kamenev. Russell Cooke invited Kamenev and the latter's London girlfriend Clare Sheridan, who was a sculptor, Winston Churchill's cousin and a 'parlour bolshevik', first to lunch at Claridge's and then to stay at Bellecroft for an August weekend. Lounging on rugs by the tennis court, Kamenev spoke vividly for over an hour, 'stumbling along in his bad French', about the inner history of the revolution in 1917, recounting the 'secret organizations' of Lenin, Trotsky, Krasin and himself, and depicting the Cheka's chief Felix Dzerzhinsky: 'a man turned to stone through years of *travaux forcés*, an ascetic and fanatic, whom the Soviet selected as head of *La Terreur*'. Kamenev inscribed a poem in which he likened Sheridan to Venus on a £5 banknote. He signed Bellecroft's visitors' book with the slogan, 'Workers of the World Unit [sic]'.[10]

Next month, on the eve of Kamenev's scheduled return to Moscow with Sheridan, Lloyd George upbraided him for his part in the contraband-jewels subsidy. In order to gain political advantage, Lloyd George's entourage spread the notion that he had given Kamenev peremptory orders to leave the country. The Prime Minister also yielded to pressure to publish the intercepts in order to justify his confrontation with Kamenev, although this compromised future SIGINT by betraying the fact that GC&CS could read Moscow's ciphered wireless traffic. Journalists duly raised uproar about the *Daily Herald* diamonds under such headlines as 'Lenin's "Jewel Box" a War Chest'.[11]

When Kamenev and Sheridan left together for Moscow, Russell Cooke found an excuse to meet them at King's Cross station, to accompany them on their train and to see them on to their ship. Sheridan's handbag went missing on the journey, and was doubtless searched. At Newcastle it reappeared in the clutches of Russell Cooke, who claimed to have traced it to the lost luggage office. In Moscow Sheridan sculpted heads of Lenin, Dzerzhinsky, Trotsky, Zinoviev and other Bolshevik leaders. Soon afterwards, the Cheka informed Kamenev that Sheridan had lured him into staying with the brother-in-law and informant of an MI5 officer, and she found herself shunned when she returned to Moscow in 1923.[12]

Meanwhile, on 28 February 1921 the *Daily Herald* published a photograph of an imitation of the Bolshevik newspaper *Pravda* which was circulating in England. The identifying marks of printers in Luton proved this issue to be a forgery which, as the Home Secretary admitted in the Commons, had been prepared with the help of the Home Office's Director of Intelligence, Sir Basil Thomson. This trickery was adduced by Ewer, when MI5 interviewed him in 1950, as his reason for starting his counter-intelligence operation. In fact the groundwork had been laid before the forged *Pravda* incident; but it is true that his network coalesced in 1921.[13]

Hayes was the talent-spotter who put Ewer in touch with dismissed NUPPO activists and disaffected Special Branch officers willing to undertake political inquiries. Ewer in turn exerted his jaunty charm to inspire his operatives with team spirit. They wanted to prove that they could do a good job for him, both individually and as a group. Their skills were a source of pride to them. Shadowing and watching in the streets of London was akin to a sport that needed brains as well as agility. Smarting from their dismissals by the Metropolitan Police, they were glad to join an organization that appreciated team-work. The Vigilance brigade of detectives believed in manly self-respect and masculine prowess.

Ewer's security officer Arthur Lakey had been born at Chatham in 1885. His father came from Tresco in the Scilly Isles: his mother was an office cleaner and munitions worker from Deptford. He worked as a railway booking clerk and in a brewery office before enlisting in the Royal Navy in 1900 and serving on the torpedo training vessel HMS *Vernon*. He left the navy to join the Metropolitan Police in 1911, but was recalled for war service, and spent eight hours in the sea when his ship was torpedoed in 1916. After this ordeal, he kept to land and was employed as a sergeant in Special Branch. During the NUPPO struggles of 1918–19, Lakey entered General Macready's office at Scotland Yard, rifled his desk, read confidential papers and reported their contents to NUPPO.

In 1921, while Lakey was in the Doncaster mining district raising relief funds for dismissed NUPPO activists, he was summoned by Hayes to meet Ewer in the *Daily Herald* offices. Ewer asked him to investigate the circumstances of the *Pravda* forgery, implying that the inquiry was on behalf of the Labour party. When Lakey tendered his report, Ewer told him that the work had been commissioned on behalf of the Russian government and established that he had no misgivings about undertaking further work for the same employer. He was put in contact with Nikolai Klyshko, who paid the rent of a flat at 55 Ridgmount Gardens, Bloomsbury, where Lakey lived and worked to Klyshko's orders. Walter Dale and a policeman's daughter named Rose Edwardes worked with Lakey in Ridgmount Gardens.

Hayes also introduced Ewer to Hubert van Ginhoven and Charles Jane, who held the ranks of inspector and sergeant in Special Branch, and were discreet NUPPO sympathizers. Ewer began paying them £20 a week to report on Special Branch registry cards on suspects, on names and addresses subject to Home Office mail intercept warrants, and on names on watch lists at major ports. They also furnished addresses of intelligence officers and personnel, and gave forewarnings of Special Branch operations. In addition Ginhoven and Jane supplied material enabling Ewer to deduce that communist organizations in foreign capitals were under SIS surveillance, which made it easier to identify SIS officers or agents abroad who were targeting these foreign organizations. Leaks were facilitated by the Special Branch practice of trusting officers with delicate political information. This guileless, unreflecting camaraderie had nothing to do with the old-school-tie outlook or class allegiances (Guy Liddell and Hugh Miller were rare within Special Branch in being privately educated). It was how men at work were expected to behave with one another.

Ginhoven, who worked under the alias of Fletcher within the Ewer–Hayes network, was a familiar visitor to the Special Branch registry, where he flirted with women clerks and snooped when they had gone home. Every week or ten days Ewer dictated an updated list supplied by Ginhoven of addresses for which Home Office warrants had been issued. These were typed in triplicate, with one copy going to Chesham House (the Soviet legation in Belgravia), another to Moscow via Chesham House and the third to the CPGB. It was found in 1929 that traces of Home Office warrants issued for Ewer's associates, together with any intercepted letters, had vanished from the files at Scotland Yard. So, too, had compromising documents which had been seized during the police raid on CPGB headquarters in 1925.

The Vigilance detectives resembled tugs in the London docks, sturdy and work-worn, speeding hither and thither, but taken for granted and therefore unseen. The material collected by them served as tuition lessons for Soviet Russia in British tradecraft. By watching targeted individuals, Vigilance operatives identified SIS and MI5 headquarters. They shadowed employees from these offices to establish their home addresses. They tracked messengers, secretarial staff and official cars. In 1924 they realized that Kell was MI5's chief by tracking him from his house at 67 Evelyn Gardens: surveillance was easy, because his address was in *Who's Who* and the *Post Office London Directory*, and his chauffeur-driven car flew a distinctive blue pennant displaying the image of a tortoise with the motto 'safe but sure'. They watched MI5 and Special Branch methods of monitoring Soviet and CPGB operations, and thus helped the Russians to study and improve the rules of the game. They checked that Ewer and his associates were not being shadowed by the British secret services. They observed embassies and legations in London, and tracked foreign diplomats. Possibly this surveillance led to the recruitment of informants, although no evidence survives of this. Vigilance men monitored employees of ARCOS, CPGB members and Russians living in England who were suspect in Moscow eyes. 'If a Russian was caught out, invariably he was sent home and shot,' boasted Ewer's chief watcher in 1928.[14]

Ewer, under the codename HERMAN, was Moscow's main source in London. He accompanied Nikolai Klyshko to Cheka headquarters in Moscow in 1922, and visited Józef Krasny, Russian *rezident* in Vienna. He returned to Moscow in 1923 in the company of Andrew Rothstein @ C. M. Roebuck, a fellow founder of the CPGB and London correspondent of the Soviet news agency ROSTA. He also became the lover of Rose Cohen. Born in Poland in 1894, the child of garment-makers, Cohen had been reared in extreme poverty in east London slums. After studying politics and economics, she joined the Labour Research Department, and was a founder member of the CPGB. Harry Pollitt, who became general secretary of the CPGB in 1929, was among the men who became infatuated with this ardent, clever and alluring beauty, whom Ivy Litvinov described as 'a sort of *jüdische* rose'. Cohen crisscrossed Europe after 1922 as a London-based Comintern courier and money mule. Eventually she committed herself to a monstrously ugly charmer, Max Petrovsky @ David Lipetz @ Max Goldfarb, a Ukrainian who translated Lenin's works into Yiddish and went to England, using the alias of Bennett, as Comintern's liaison with the CPGB. Together Cohen and Petrovsky moved in 1927 to Moscow, where her manners were thought grandiose by other communist expatriates.[15]

Ewer returned from Moscow in 1923 with boosted self-esteem and instructions, or the implanted idea, to run his espionage activities under the cover of a news agency. Until then, it had been based in Lakey's Bloomsbury flat, or later in premises at Leigh-on-Sea: Ewer had met Lakey and other operatives either in cafés or at the *Daily Herald* offices. Accordingly, in 1923, Ewer leased room 50 in an office building called Outer Temple at 222 The Strand, opposite the Royal Courts of Justice at the west end of Fleet Street. There he opened the London branch of the Federated Press Agency of America, a news service which had been founded in 1919 to report strikes, trade unionism, workers' militancy and radical activism. The FPA issued twice-weekly bulletins of news, comment and data to its left-wing subscribers. It was based first in Chicago, shifted its offices to Detroit and then Washington, before settling in New York. The FPA had developed reciprocal relations with socialist, communist and trade union newspapers internationally and acted as an information clearing-house in the United States and Europe. It may have served broad Comintern interests, but was not a front organization for Moscow. According to Ewer, the only American in the FPA who knew that its London office operated as a cover for Russian spying was its managing editor, Carl Haessler, a pre-war Rhodes scholar at Oxford.

Moscow sometimes sent money to Haessler in New York, who remitted funds either to the communist bookshop-owner Eva Reckitt in London or to the Paris correspondent of the *Daily Herald*, George Slocombe. Usually dollars arrived in the diplomatic bag at Chesham House and were distributed to the FPA and the CPGB by Khristian Rakovsky, Soviet plenipotentiary in London from 1923 and Ambassador from 1925. An associate of Ewer's named Walter Holmes (sometime Moscow correspondent of the *Daily Herald*) converted the dollars into sterling by exchanging small amounts at travel agencies and currency bureaux. These arrangements ended after the ARCOS raid in 1927.

For a time Ewer had a source in Indian Political Intelligence (IPI), who was dropped because the product was suspected of being phoney. Ewer had a sub-source in the Foreign Office, who reported confidential remarks made by two officials, Sir Arthur Willert of the Press Department and J. D. Gregory of the Northern Department; but his network never obtained original FO documents which could be sent to Moscow for verification. Probably the remitted material from the

Foreign Office and India Office was limited to low-grade gossip. Don Gregory, the Office's in-house Russian expert until 1928, enjoyed his half-hour briefings with Ewer, whose facetious anti-semitism amused him: 'he is an admirable and loyal friend, though I have heard him described as a dangerous bolshevik'. The only diplomatic documents obtained by Ewer's network came from his second prong in Paris, where his sub-agent was the *Daily Herald* correspondent George Slocombe.[16]

George Slocombe in Paris

Slocombe had been born in 1894, and grew up in the semi-industrial northern districts of Bristol called Horfield and Bishopston. He was baptized in a Wesleyan Methodist chapel. His father was a commercial traveller (who left an estate worth only £268 in 1929). He attended the Merchant Adventurers' Technical College at Bristol, where his best friend was a lively peasant boy from Touraine on a government scholarship. In July 1909, aged fifteen, Slocombe was appointed as a boy clerk in the Post Office Savings Bank, behind London's Olympia, which had recently been converted from a hippodrome into an exhibition centre for motor-cars and furnishings. According to the 1911 census, he lived nearby at 63 West Kensington Mansions, as a friend rather than a lodger, with Emma Karlinsky, who had come to England from the Crimea in 1909 with her two daughters, Fanny and Marie. Her husband Joseph was an attorney at Yalta and business adviser to a grand duke.

Young Slocombe arranged nearby accommodation for his French friend, who had meanwhile adopted the name of Henri Gaudier-Brzeska. He was proud of being the sculptor's most intimate English friend: when he started a Post Office Savings Bank internal magazine, a Gaudier-Brzeska drawing decorated its cover. Slocombe's sonnet raging against tyrants and celebrating the assassination of the Russian Prime Minister Pyotr Stolypin in 1911 was published in the Marxist magazine *Justice*. 'Nobody then foresaw', Slocombe recalled a quarter of a century later, 'the day when the theories contained in the badly printed, red-covered volumes of Marx's *Das Kapital* would become the official religion of a hundred and sixty million people seated astride Europe and Asia.'[17]

As an impressionable youth, Slocombe was drawn by the anarchism of Kropotkin. He found a mentor in a stern, gloomy Scottish-Italian recluse, who lived, worked and slept in a book-lined cellar under a Hammersmith tailor's shop. This underground cell, which daylight never reached, was the haunt of nihilistic young workmen, French, Russian and Spanish exiles, and the anarchist Errico Malatesta, who had escaped from an Italian prison-fortress and worked as an electrician in Soho. Slocombe's youthful eagerness won him the trust of 'men who lived in dread of informers, who distrusted strangers, who walked warily from bitter knowledge of the world's prisons'. He learnt the mentality and methods of the plotters who created European despotism. 'When, long afterwards, I met Mussolini for the first time, we met on common ground,' he claimed. 'We spoke the same secret language, the language of the men working blindly in cellars, in prisons, writing burning words to be printed on small and hidden presses, talking burning words at street corners, ardent, disdainful, self-righteous.'[18]

In 1912, aged eighteen, Slocombe married seventeen-year-old Marie Karlinsky, who was pregnant with their son Ralph. He joined the staff of the *Daily Herald* at about the same time, and the Royal Flying Corps as a second-class mechanic in 1916. He had a winter digging roads in Lincolnshire before deployment in France, where he spent eighteen months in intelligence translating German military wireless messages. When the first attempts were made to bug prison cells with microphones, Slocombe was told to eavesdrop, and felt relief that the stone paving of the prison cells caused such echoes that the indiscretions of captured German aviators were incomprehensible. He found headquarters life to be monotonous, and compared the staff officers to golfing stockbrokers.[19]

Slocombe wrote an empurpled 'Letter to Lenin', published in the *Daily Herald* of 24 August 1918. 'Your first proclamation, after the Second Russian Revolution, was a deep blast upon the Bugle of the Army of the World's Freedom,' he apostrophized Lenin. 'You are aiming, as I believe sincerely, at the liberation and the redemption of man. The hate you have been shown by the rich, the monopolists, the concession-hunters, the feudalists, the diplomatists and the Press of all countries – German and allied alike – is a sure sign of your earnestness in the cause.' These ebullitions seemed suspicious to the security services in London, but Slocombe's commanding officer Lieutenant Colonel Harry Goldsmith defended him to Stewart Menzies of SIS: 'he was a

M.T. [motor-transport] driver, but having crashed a senior officer into a ditch, was taken off cars & put to clerking. He is an educated man & . . . writes verses, patriotic & not bad at that for the *Tatler*.' Goldsmith, who was a future military ADC to King George V, continued with the tolerance that often characterized authority's attitude to oddballs: 'I don't think he is a bad chap on the whole, & I am rather inclined, if you agree, to talk to him myself & tell him I know he wrote this article addressed to Lenin & ask him if he think it's playing the game to butter up a fellow whose actions caused very heavy losses to the French & ourselves by setting free troops hitherto employed on the Russian front, who is now assisting the Germans to enslave the Poles & Ukrainians etc.'[20]

After demobilization in 1919, Slocombe returned to the *Daily Herald* as news editor. 'He was a timid and anxious man,' recalled Francis Meynell, 'until he grew a beard to hide his receding chin. The change was immediate and remarkable: he became master of his scene.' In the spring of 1920 Slocombe went as the *Daily Herald*'s special correspondent in Paris, which he loved as the capital of rumour. His work took him roaming in Europe: everywhere he resisted standardization and vapidity. The suicide of millionaires and dethroning of monarchs enlivened him. He liked to meet currency smugglers, concession-hunters, bankers-condottieri, political grafters, stock-exchange tipsters, swagger beaux, faithless men with awkward principles, and idealists who uttered only flippancies. He savoured the furtive exiles found in every European capital, 'nursing midnight dreams of liberty, power and martyrdom' and conjuring vengeful conspiracies.[21]

A Home Office warrant was issued in 1921 to intercept letters to Slocombe's house at Sutton in Surrey on the grounds that he was bringing Bolshevik literature into Britain and communicating with 'leaders of the Red Trade Union International movement'. In 1922 a major international conference was held at Genoa to promote the economic stabilization and revival of central and eastern Europe, and to reconcile European capitalism with the Bolshevik economy. Shortly before the conference convened, Ewer sent Slocombe 'hints about Genoa for your private ear' which he intended to be passed to Soviet contacts. These hints comprised information from Edward Wise, a civil servant who was Lloyd George's economic adviser during the Genoa deliberations and sympathetic to Bolshevism, that London hoped to use the

Genoa meeting to parlay an agreement between the Soviet Union and the other European powers. The French embassy in London reported in 1923 that Slocombe had visited Lausanne under the alias of Nathan Grunberg. The French tied him to Clare Sheridan, who was reputed to have been his lover. His expulsion from France was contemplated in 1926 after he was seen in regular meetings with a Bolshevik agent.[22]

Slocombe's sister-in-law Fanny Karlinsky was the object of further suspicions. She won a scholarship to St Paul's Girls' School in Hammersmith, and read modern languages at Somerville College, Oxford in 1913, but fell ill and spent much of 1914 in the French Pyrenees recuperating. During 1916–19 she worked as an Anglo–Russian translator and interpreter. In 1919 she became a telegraph coder and decipherer for ARCOS, and worked in its offices for twelve years. She was anonymously denounced to Special Branch in 1924 for her alleged association with Edith Lunn, wife of Andrew Rothstein. There were two separate code-rooms in ARCOS offices, one for purely commercial traffic and the other for political messages: Fanny Karlinsky claimed to have worked only in the first room. She was present during the police raid of 1927, was listed for possible expulsion to Russia by the authorities and had her application for British citizenship denied. She continued working for ARCOS until 1931, when she refused orders to return to Russia and was stripped of her Soviet passport. Guy Liddell, then still in Special Branch, noted in 1928: 'although she is not a full member of the Party, she is in close touch with party circles and ready to assist in any way she can'. MI5 suspected her of being a sub-agent of Lenin's State Political Directorate, the GPU. Later she ran a board-ing-house, but in the 1950s needed an allowance from Slocombe in Paris to keep her from privation.[23]

The Zinoviev letter and the ARCOS raid

The Ewer–Hayes network first attracted MI5's interest in 1924 in the aftermath of the Zinoviev letter scare. The background was this. A Scottish communist named John Ross Campbell, acting editor of the *Workers' Weekly*, was arrested on 5 August on the instructions of Sir Archibald Bodkin, the Director of Public Prosecutions. He was charged under the Incitement to Mutiny Act of 1797 with seducing members of the armed forces from their allegiance. He had done this, Bodkin alleged, by publishing 'An Open Letter to the Fighting Forces', expressed in terms similar to Cecil L'Estrange Malone's speech of 1920 at the Hands Off Russia meeting. Campbell urged 'soldiers, sailors and airmen, not merely to refuse to go to war, or to refuse to shoot strikers during industrial conflicts', but also to join with urban proletariat and rural labourers 'in a common attack upon the capitalists, and to smash capitalism forever, and institute the reign of the whole working class'. Bodkin's motives were mixed, according to A. J. P. Taylor: 'perhaps stupidity (and the director of public prosecutions is usually a stupid man); perhaps also to embarrass the government'. Certainly Campbell was arrested on the same day that Ramsay MacDonald's Labour government reached terms for an Anglo-Russian trade treaty, which communism's adversaries were determined to thwart. When the government withdrew the prosecution on 13 August (on the pretext that Campbell was a decorated soldier, who had been crippled by war wounds), its opponents protested at political interference with the law. A general election was called when on 8 October MacDonald's government opposed and lost a parliamentary motion calling for an independent tribunal to inquire into the handling of Campbell's prosecution.[24]

Amid the furore over the proposed Anglo-Russian treaty and the Campbell case, a message was supposedly sent from Moscow, dated 15 September 1924, from Grigory Zinoviev, the head of the Comintern, to the CPGB's general committee. The message conveyed Comintern orders to prepare for revolution by subverting the armed forces and by duping Labour party leaders. It was obtained by the SIS station in Riga, which sent it to SIS headquarters in London on 2 October. SIS circularized copies to the Foreign Office, Admiralty, War Office, Air Ministry, MI5 and Scotland Yard (which failed to pass it to Special Branch). The letter was spurious, probably concocted by White Russian forgers in Riga, and possibly planted by die-hard intelligence anti-Bolshevists, but it differed little from genuine Moscow messages to the CPGB. Lakey told MI5 that the CPGB gave Ewer a categorical denial that it had received any such letter. As both the army and MI5, even without the Campbell case, feared subversion of troops, MI5 on 21 October sent copies of the Riga letter to General Officers Commanding in Britain. A copy certainly went to Conservative Central Office (most probably by the hand of Sir Joseph Ball, head of MI5's investigative branch); Desmond Morton of SIS may have meddled alongside Ball; and another copy of the letter was, according to Morton, given by Stewart Menzies of SIS to the *Daily Mail*. The *Daily Mail*, which doubtless received a confirmatory copy from Conservative Central Office, published the forgery four days before the general election on 29 October. Publication did not swing voters against socialism: the financial terms of the doomed Anglo-Russian treaty aroused more suspicion. Labour got 5.3 million votes, compared with 4.3 million in 1923; but the collapse of Liberal support since 1923 gave a majority of seats to the Conservatives, and created a bitter Labour feeling that they had been cheated out of power by the *Daily Mail*'s Zinoviev stunt.

In the final meeting of the Labour Cabinet after their defeat, Lord Parmoor, Sir Charles Trevelyan and Josiah Wedgwood voiced their suspicion that 'Crowe and Gregory had stooped to a mean political trick in order to damage the Labour Party,' reported the official taking the minutes, and 'were quite prepared to blow up the F.O. if they could get rid of the spy system'. (During the 1930s Trevelyan was one of the most gullible of fellow-travellers to Bolshevist Russia, who described Stalinist penal colonies as a 'grand method of human regeneration', while Parmoor was an apologist for Stalinist slave labour and religious persecution.) In fact Gregory had opposed publication, and Crowe was so mortified by his mismanagement of the letter's distribution that he broke down in tears as he apologized to MacDonald for contributing to the election defeat. 'The Zinoviev letter killed Crowe,' MacDonald said in 1928. 'He never lifted up his head after that.'[25]

Generations of Labour activists nurtured festering resentment of MI5 for plotting to install the Conservatives in power: the party's antagonism towards the intelligence services continues to this day. But it was suspicions of the financial terms of the Anglo-Russian treaty, and MacDonald's refusal to institute a tribunal of inquiry into the Campbell case, coupled with Liberal voters transferring to the Conservatives, that lost Labour power: not the Zinoviev stunt. On the other side, from 1925 onwards, SIS collected ample and reliable evidence that in response to the Riga forgery Moscow sought to discredit, mislead and confuse the British intelligence services by providing forgers with blank Soviet and Comintern writing-paper with which to concoct bogus material for the misdirection, humiliation and weakening of SIS and MI5.

A trades union delegation left for Moscow in mid-November 1924 to investigate the authenticity of the Zinoviev letter. On 21 November the *Daily Herald* carried a small advert placed by Ewer: 'Labour Group carrying out investigation would be glad to receive information and details from anyone who has ever had any association with, or been brought into touch with, any Secret Service Department or operation.' A box number at the *Daily Herald* was given for replies. Probably this small-ad was a clumsy attempt to investigate the machinations behind the forgery either in parallel or in association with the trades union inquiry in Moscow. MI5 set its agent D to reply. He received a message signed 'Q.X.' fixing a rendezvous outside St George's Hospital at Hyde Park Corner on 1 January 1925. D waited there for an hour in vain. He was kept under surveillance by an MI5 colleague, who spotted another man (later identified as Walter Dale) also keeping covert watch. Following a second approach, D met Q.X. in a wine bar. Q.X. was soon identified as Ewer. They had several meetings, during which Q.X. questioned D about intelligence, until Dale, who was tracking D after meetings, discovered his MI5 connection. Ewer dropped him and, if challenged, could have pretended that he was investigating a possible story for the *Daily Herald*.

Ewer and his network were put under surveillance. Ewer himself kept short hours at the *Daily Herald* office, punctuating his working day with visits to Fleet Street pubs, notably the Cheshire Cheese, lunches in the Falstaff restaurant in Fleet Street and tea-breaks in cafés. MI5 collected genealogical and financial data on the families of FPA operatives, checked addresses, obtained Home Office warrants on their correspondence, shadowed them, compiled physical descriptions and took photographic head-shots. The shadowing of Dale led to Rose Edwardes, who in turn led them to room 50 of Outer Temple, for which a Home Office warrant was issued in February 1925. Telephone intercepts revealed the FPA's regular dealings with ARCOS, Chesham House and the Vigilance Detective Agency. On 11 February the FPA office received a package addressed to 'Kenneth Milton, Esq.' containing typed reports in French on Morocco, Bulgaria, Romania and Serbia.

It became evident that 'Kenneth Milton' frequently received packets from Paris. These enclosed copies of French ambassadorial dispatches from various capitals, confidential news on French politics and finance, unsigned typed letters accompanying English plain-language codes, and occasional letters from Indian revolutionaries to comrades living in England. The material justified Vansittart's quip: 'in France official secrets are everybody's secret'. Codewords in the letters were often food-related. 'Spaghetti' indicated an agent inside the Quai d'Orsay, paid 5,000 francs a month, who supplied product on Italy. 'Goulash' was an agent supplying material on the Balkans. 'Native grown cereals' meant an informant from within French political circles. 'Hospitality' or 'footmen' indicated occasional informants. 'Bristol' was the codeword for Warsaw. 'Glasgow' indicated Moscow or Russia. 'Leicester' meant Paris. Halifax, Cheltenham, Nottingham, Exeter, Hereford and Gloucester were other towns with coded meanings.[26]

Then, on 8 May 1925, Ewer's inadvertence exposed his Paris sub-agent. He published an article on French Morocco in the *Daily Herald*, under George Slocombe's byline, which was barely distinguishable from a note to 'Milton' intercepted two days earlier. The Home Office issued postal warrants for Slocombe's private and business addresses. They found that Ewer sent him about £210 a month, of which one-third was spent on bribes to obtain copies of secret documents from the Quai d'Orsay or embassies in Paris. The trusting fealty between Ewer and Slocombe was helped by juvenile matiness. They disdained upper-case typing in their unsigned missives, in which the keynotes were bluff irreverence and Jew-baiting.

In November 1925 Slocombe became infuriated by the Bolshevik – whom he codenamed 'flivverman' – who had arrived in Paris to run him. 'He's a thin-lipped hebrew who despises politics of which d'ailleurs [anyway] he's supremely ignorant and is interested only in originals of whatever value,' Slocombe told Ewer. Flivverman had conveyed Moscow's dissatisfaction that Ewer's network seldom obtained original diplomatic documents. 'He despises the London food service as too costly thinks you are all a lot of reckless spendthrifts is sceptical of your efficiency, and is generally jewish, but without the hebrew wit.' Ewer replied on 20 November that he had seen 'the chauffeur' (his controller at Chesham House): 'He's damned angry with the yiddisher brat whom I think he does not love.' Slocombe added a covering note with the batch sent on 26 November: 'Yid improves slightly on acquaintance but . . . entirely preoccupied with first editions regardless of value. hope however to train him. our personal relations cordial enough. inferiority complex characteristic of his race responsible i think for his preliminary rudeness.'[27]

Moscow sent almost £1.25 million to fund the miners' strike of 1926, which developed into the General Strike. The consequent industrial disruption and civil strife, ample proof of Soviet-inspired subversion within the British Empire and Moscow's support of Chinese communist revolutionaries against British control in Shanghai determined the Conservative government to break off diplomatic relations with Moscow. In January 1927 an ARCOS employee named Edward Langston informed Herbert ('Bertie') Maw of SIS that he had been instructed to photocopy a secret Signals Training manual obtained from Aldershot barracks. This information was passed to MI5, where Kell and Harker spent weeks checking its authenticity, interviewing the informant and consulting an ARCOS accountant who was a reliable SIS source in ARCOS. The Home Secretary, Sir William Joynson-Hicks, was an impulsive populist well described by his parliamentary colleague Cuthbert Headlam as 'a miserable creature – a shop-walker attempting to pose as a strong man'. When the situation was explained to him (as the result of an intervention of the Secretary of State for War, Sir Laming Worthington-Evans), Joynson-Hicks initiated a raid on the ARCOS offices, with the intention of finding evidence for a prosecution under the Official Secrets Act.[28]

Compton Mackenzie, who had worked for SIS in Greece during the war and wrote an insultingly farcical novel *Water on the Brain* (1933) about Sir Mansfield Cumming's regime, commented on the ARCOS raid: 'anti-Russian propaganda was being worked up solely with the object of persuading the country not to vote for the Labour Party at the next election; but the Russian government, less aware than ourselves of the unscrupulousness concealed by the pleasant masks of party politics in Great Britain, might be forgiven for supposing that the mind of the country was being prepared for a declaration of war against the U.S.S.R.'. Mackenzie exaggerated by using the word 'solely', but his phrases expressed a widespread and justified suspicion of the motives of Joynson-Hicks, Worthington-Evans and other ministers in Baldwin's Cabinet.[29]

Ginhoven and Jane were unable to warn the FPA of the impending raid, because Special Branch received misdirection, when they were deployed, that the target of the swoop was contraband in the London docks. The raid, on 12 May 1927, was hastily prepared and ill-executed. Desmond Morton was one of the SIS officers who participated in the descent on 49 Moorgate: his biographer Gill Bennett depicts uniformed City of London constables, Special Branch men and SIS officers hurtling around in strenuous, uncoordinated activity. One squirted ink on to a portrait of Lenin's face hanging on the office wall. No one took charge; almost no one knew the extent of their legal powers to seize materials or detain individuals; few searchers knew what documents to seek. The seized items proved 'inconclusive and confusing', once they had been translated, Bennett reports. The stolen Signals Training manual, which it was the primary object of the raid to retrieve, was not found.[30]

'An immense quantity of police descended on the place, searched the inmates, impounded documents, and for 48 hours have been occupied in smashing up concrete walls in order to break open concealed safes,' noted Lord Crawford. 'Secret hiding-places existed all over the building – behind panelling, under floors, in thicknesses of walls; and the place has been throbbing with pneumatic road-breakers, and with expert safe-breakers working acetylene gases.' The rupture of diplomatic relations with Russia, which was the sequel to the raid, made the 'Clear out the Reds' section of the Conservative party rejoice. 'At last we have got rid of the Bolsheviks,' a Cabinet minister Lord Birkenhead rejoiced. 'We have got rid of the hypocrisy of pretending to have friendly relations with this Jewish gang of murderers, revolutionaries and thieves. I breathe quite differently now that we have purged our capital of these unclean and treacherous elements.' Birkenhead's cooler-headed colleague Neville Chamberlain considered the raid 'farcical'.[31]

The raid was a blunder, which breached with disastrous results the intelligence principle of watch and learn. Having failed to find any clinching proof of espionage, subversion or schemes of sabotage, the government, which was set on severing diplomatic relations with the Soviet Union, had to justify its decision by producing, instead of the incriminating documents expected from the ARCOS raid, communications between the Soviet Mission at Chesham House and Moscow, which had been secretly intercepted by GC&CS. This proved to be a grievous error. As Gill Bennett has summarized the position, 'The production in Parliament and publication of these documents for all to see in a Command Paper, revealed their source beyond question, leading to the immediate abandonment by the Soviet Foreign Ministry of its methods of encipherment in favour of unbreakable one-time pad systems for its communications; thereafter no high-grade Soviet diplomatic messages could be read by the British authorities.'

Admiral Sinclair, the head of both SIS and GC&CS, deplored this heedless political irresponsibility. 'The publication of these telegrams automatically stops their source of supply,' he wrote. 'It was authorized only as a measure of desperation to bolster up a cause vital to Government, which had the facts been fully known at the time, needed no such costly support.' Both SIS and MI5 had been watching and learning from ARCOS, which had been a promising source of intelligence for the British secret services. Sinclair characterized the ARCOS raid as an 'irretrievable loss of an unprecedented opportunity'.[32]

After the raid, Ewer sent James Marston, Hayes's predecessor as general secretary of NUPPO, to visit the former ARCOS employee Edward Langston, who was rightly suspected of being the source of the leak and had just started a new life as a publican at the Dolphin in Uxbridge. When Marston began hanging around the Dolphin, disguised as a tramp, Langston sent a panicky telegram to Harker, addressed to the chambers in the Temple of Harker's brother-in-law Sidney Russell Cooke, asking to be sent a revolver for self-defence. Rose Edwardes had meanwhile ceased deliveries of material from the FPA to Chesham House. Instead, secrets were written in invisible ink in a book which she or Walter Dale took as couriers to Paris. From thence it went underground to Warsaw and thence to Moscow. The expulsion of the Soviet delegation after the raid left Ewer's network short of funds. The CPGB secretary Albert Inkpin began travelling to Berlin to collect dollars, which he then took to Paris. There Slocombe arranged for Rose Cohen, or other women couriers, to smuggle the dollars to London, where Holmes laundered their conversion into sterling. But this procedure was too complex, and despite obtaining £100 from Slocombe in Paris, the network had shrivelled by October 1927 for lack of funds.

MI5 investigates the Ewer–Hayes network

Lakey, who with his taste for disguise was by now established in the new identity of Albert Allen, was left in financial straits after the FPA's diminuendo. Ewer provided £20 to finance his move to Bournemouth, where he managed Dean's Restaurant at 261a Wimborne Road, Winton. Jane Sissmore suggested a Home Office warrant to monitor Allen's decline into debt, and a carefully timed approach to debrief him when he needed financial extrication but would not be too expensive to rescue. After an approach by Kell to Sir William Tyrrell, PUS of the Foreign Office, MI5 was granted £250 for this purpose.

The first approach to Allen was made by John Ottaway, the chief of MI5's observation section B6. Ottaway had been born in 1870 in a Midland Railway cottage at Hitchin in Hertfordshire, the son of a pointsman and signalman. In 1891 he became a constable in the City of London Police, lodging in a police boarding-house in Bishopsgate hugger-mugger with other young constables. He rose fast in the force, for ten years later he was already a police inspector, living in Leyton with a Scottish wife by whom he had at least five daughters. While City of London constables managed the formidable traffic congestion of the financial district, officers like Ottaway tracked forgers, swindlers and embezzlers. City of London detectives tended to be well-groomed men, suggesting the managing clerk of a solicitor's office, rather than burly, heavy-footed plodders. In 1909 Ottaway was appointed detective super-intendent – effective head – of the City of London Police, and his family were allotted apartments in Cloak Lane police station. In 1911 he participated in the search for the murderous anarchist Peter the Painter. During 1916 he joined a Freemasons lodge and received the freedom of the City of London. He was recruited to Kell's department in 1920, and died in retirement at Bournemouth in 1954 leaving the notable sum of £12,000.[33]

In 1942 Ottaway's successor Harry Hunter described Section B6's surveillance techniques to Anthony Blunt, who was then working for MI5. 'His methods are very unscientific and depend above all on the experience and patience of his men,' Blunt informed Moscow. 'Recruiting is usually through a personal recommendation from some contact of Hunter's, or by recommendation of Special Branch.' The training for watchers was 'primitive'. Hunter inducted new recruits with a few lectures, but relied on practice making perfect: 'new men are sent out almost immediately on minor jobs accompanied by more experienced watchers, from whom they learn the methods in the actual process [of] following'.[34]

Ottaway approached Allen in June 1928 offering to pay £75 for each interview that they had. In July Ottaway took Harker to meet Allen. As Harker reported to Kell, he and Ottaway motored to the Bournemouth suburb where Allen lived. He sat in his car in a small side-road, surrounded by half-built houses and wasteland, while Ottaway, who was masquerading as Mr Stewart of the Anti-Socialist Union, fetched Allen to the car. Harker then explained that he represented Kell, whose position in MI5 Allen knew. He decided that it might inhibit Allen, who talked for over an hour and a half, if he tried to take notes. He knew how often confession is a kind of pride. Interrogators can seem therapeutic: they encourage their subjects to talk about themselves and how they relate to other people; they discourage introspection; they do not lead the conversation by questioning or responses; they try to maintain an appreciative impassivity, never looking too keen, as their targets reminisce, boast, grumble, explain, retell rumours and produce telling anecdotes about other people. 'I very quickly found', Harker reported, 'that we were on quite good terms, and, by treating him rather as my opposite number, found that he was quite ready to talk up to a point. He is, I think, a man who is extraordinarily pleased with himself, and considers that the work which he did for some eight years for the Underground Organisation known as the F.P.A. was admirably carried out, and has not received quite the recognition from its paymasters that Allen considers it deserves.' Harker recognized Allen's relief at talking 'openly about his past life to someone who is not only a sympa-thetic listener, but also appreciates the technical side, and can thus see what an admirable Intelligence Officer Allen has been'. Harker was careful not to prompt or steer Allen, because 'entirely spontaneous remarks' were more useful than answers to questions. 'Before we got down to talking generally, I explained to Allen that I understood from Mr Stewart that there were names that he did not wish to give away, and that this naturally would considerably impair the value of his information, if it was to be made with reservations.' Allen reflected for a moment before replying, 'I do not want to give away my late boss, because personally, I was very fond of him.' Harker responded, 'Perhaps I could tell you the name of your late boss, in which case you would not be placed in such an awkward position,' then wrote the initials 'W.N.E.' on a piece of paper, and showed them to Allen asking, 'That was your late boss, wasn't he?' Allen said: 'Yes, Trilby. Trilby is a good fellow and damned smart!'[35]

After further corroborative investigation Dale, Jane and Ginhoven were arrested on 11 April 1929; but Scotland Yard was determined to obscure as far as possible the infiltration of its Special Branch. After the three men's detention Harker went straight to Bournemouth, where he asked Allen to tell all that he knew about the leakages from Scotland Yard, and the names of those responsible. 'I explained to him that this information was of interest to me if given at once, but that if not given at once I was not prepared to pursue the matter further. I also stated that if ALLEN told the story in a manner which appeared to me to be correct, I would hand over to him the sum of £50, and that if the story which he told me was found to be of use to the authorities, I would consider giving him a further £50, but that, in any case, until I had heard his story, I was prepared to give him nothing.' Allen accepted Harker's terms. Before Allen began to tell his story, Harker asked him to note the time (5.10 p.m.) and that he was writing on a blank piece of paper. Harker then wrote, out of Allen's sight, the names of Ginhoven and Jane together with the time. As Harker reported, 'I then asked ALLEN to tell me his story straight away without any questions on my part and to preface it by giving me the names of the individuals in Scotland Yard who were known to have been passing on information to the F.P.A. organisation in the past. ALLEN at once gave me the names of GINHOVEN and JANE, whereupon I handed him the paper on which I had written these same names. ALLEN expressed considerable surprise and then continued with his story.'

The watch on Rose Edwardes had meanwhile revealed that she was running a new front for Ewer's group, the Featherstone Typewriting Bureau in Holborn, which had been started soon after Ewer's closure of the FPA. Ewer, Holmes, Dale and Edwardes often conferred in Holborn; Dale, under cover of a Shoreditch Borough Council investigator, acted as Ewer's intermediary with the Special Branch informants. When Allen had ended his account, Harker revealed that the other FPA personnel had continued working together at the typewriting bureau. 'In all my previous dealings with him, he has always been calm and collected and rather humorous . . . but on receipt of the information that the show had practically been going on minus himself, his self-control broke down,' Harker reported. 'He stamped round the room, swore and expressed the opinion that he, ALLEN, had been double-crossed, even going so far as to say he would give evidence against the — — — who had let him down in this scandalous manner.' Harker doubted if there was much risk of this. 'ALLEN is not a fool and he realises that, were he to come into the open with his full story, it would be quite impossible for him to lead subsequently a quiet life in this country, and in order to induce him to come into the open, it would be necessary . . . to arrange for him to retire to some other country where he could start life again under a new name.' When Harker paid the £50, Allen 'went out of his way to express his gratitude to [sic] my generosity in coming down and giving him the chance of telling a story which I had found out already for myself'.[36]

After his arrest Ginhoven contacted Hayes, who defended him in an article in the *Police Review* and used him as an intermediary to contact Ewer. Harker became convinced that Moscow had 'some hold' over Hayes – perhaps evidence that Hayes had always understood the nature of his men's work for Ewer although, in Harker's words, 'as he began to get on more in the world, HAYES ceased to interest himself in the [undercover] organisation, and latterly apparently had little if anything to do with it'.[37]

Hayes had made a success of politics in the previous six years. It will be recalled that NUPPO's strike of 1919 had taken hold only in Merseyside. Hayes, who had worked in youth at a corrugated-iron business at Ellesmere Port, stood unsuccessfully in the Liverpool munic-ipal elections of 1919 as a NUPPO-sponsored Labour candidate and again unsuccessfully for the Liverpool parliamentary constituency of Edge Hill at the next general election. In 1923, when a by-election was called in Edge Hill, he was elected as Liverpool's first Labour MP. Arriving in London by train to take his seat in the House of Commons, he was hoisted shoulder high and carried across the station concourse by 200 cheering NUPPO members blowing bugles.[38]

In parliament Hayes was counted as a moderate socialist. Appointed as an opposition whip in the Commons in 1925 and elected to the party's national executive in 1926, he became a reliable, sapless party hack. As the government's third most senior whip after Labour's victory at the general election of 1929, his duties included the compilation of a daily summary for King George V of Commons debates. The Tory MP Sir Henry Betterton, afterwards Lord Rushcliffe, had a story of seeing two Labour whips on a visit to Palestine. 'Jack Hayes (the Liverpool policeman), now Treasurer of the Household, was very drunk and staggering about on the platform. As a train drew in, his pal urged him to pull himself together and said, "the Treasurer of Palestine is on

this train." Hayes clicked his heels and stood at attention with his hand
at the salute and said "Treasurer be b—d. I am His Majesty's Treasurer",
and added fervently, "Gawd bless 'im".[39]

The general election of May 1929 was approached with heavy apprehension by many Conservatives because it was the first contest with
the enlarged franchise of the so-called Flapper Vote. 'Votes for women
at 21 is alarming people up here and there is no doubt that we are
taking a big leap in the dark,' judged Cuthbert Headlam, a Tory whose
constituency lay in a northern mining county. He expected 'a big
increase in the Socialist vote. In our pit villages the women are far
wilder than the men – they are hopeless to argue with – they listen to
the sob stuff with open ears.'[40]

The involvement of a popular Labour whip in a spying scandal during
election year would have aroused suspicions that the arrests were a
pre-election stunt by intelligence mavericks similar to those behind the
Pravda and Zinoviev forgeries. The government was to prove chary in
1934 when the CPGB member Edgar Lansbury, late of the Anglo-
Russian Three Ply and Veneer Company, was prosecuted under the
Official Secrets Act: as the Solicitor General, Somervell, noted, 'The
Cabinet are very apt to be afraid that a quasi-political prosecution will
lead to a row.' Similar squeamishness was one reason for the decision
not to prosecute Ginhoven and Jane who, after hearings by a disciplinary
board, were dismissed from the police on 2 May (the general election
was to be held on 30 May). Another good reason for disciplinary
proceedings rather than a criminal trial was to avoid discomfiting
public revelations in court. It would have harmed future MI5 investigations if the extent to which Allen had been turned by MI5 and had
informed on his former employers, both English and Russian, had
been publicized. MI5's improving tradecraft was saved from public
exposure. The agency was enabled to continue watching and learning
from its adversaries.[41]

Ginhoven and Jane expected demotion to the ranks of sergeant and
constable, and were indignant at their dismissal from Special Branch.
Harker was disquieted to find that 'both inside the Special Branch and
outside, there is a good deal of sympathy with the two men, who – by
the majority ignorant of all . . . the *true* facts – are considered to have
been punished with unjustifiable severity'. This reaction resulted from
'the Scotland Yard policy of concealing all the true facts as far as possible.

One begins to wonder how far the very clumsy investigation may not have been inspired by a desire to produce such a state of mind with the Disciplinary Board itself!' Another puzzle is the fate of Sidney Russell Cooke. In July 1930 he was found in the dining-room of his chambers in the Temple dead of an oddly angled gunshot wound to the abdomen. It was unlikely that the wound was accidental; hard to believe that 'Cookie' had killed himself; but the possibility that he died as the result of his association with Harker has never been aired.[42]

Labour's electoral victory encouraged Ewer, who in the weeks afterwards seemed to the incoming junior FO minister Hugh Dalton to be 'a tiresome busybody', lobbying for the restoration of diplomatic relations with Moscow, which had been severed after the ARCOS raid. Disillusion with Marxist orthodoxy came soon. In August Ewer took a reflective holiday in Warsaw and the Carpathian resort of Zakopane. After returning in September, he wrote an article for the communist *Labour Monthly* in which he argued that Anglo-Russian tensions were not simply an ideological clash of capitalism and communism, but also derived from their nineteenth-century rivalry as Asiatic powers. The piece was denounced as counter-revolutionary and Ewer was expelled from party membership. In a letter to Rajani Palme Dutt, the Stalinist doctrinaire in the CPGB, possibly written in the knowledge that his words would be intercepted and read by MI5, Ewer declared his apostasy. Communists 'have come to talk only in an idiom, which, once a powerful instrument of thought, has become so worn and so debased that – like the analogous idiom of the Christian Churches – it no longer serves for thinking, but only as a substitute for thinking'. In all disputes 'they rely upon the repetition of phrases which have come to be as mechanical – and yet, to them, as magically authoritative – as the formulae of the Athanasian creed'. He rejected the authoritarianism which enforces doctrinal conformity, 'condemns all "deviation" as a moral offence' and imposes obedience by the 'apparatus . . . of confession, of absolution, of excommunication'.[43]

Slocombe's success in conducting 'secret work unmolested for such a long period is proof of the high standard of his efficiency as an espionage agent', MI5 concluded in 1930. 'His high standard and reputation as a journalist give to him, as to EWER, most excellent cover for his treasonable activities and unrivalled opportunities for the collection of valuable confidential information.' In August that year Harker cautioned

Sir Arthur Willert (the Foreign Office's press officer) about Ewer: 'I considered him by far the most dangerous individual from a S.S. point of view that the Russians had in this country, and that Sir Arthur Willert might rest assured that anything he told Ewer, would go straight to the Soviet Embassy.' Willert responded by asking unprompted if Harker knew Slocombe. Harker replied that Slocombe was Ewer's deputy, and 'very nearly as dangerous'. Willert thought the pair were 'the ablest and most entertaining journalists he had ever met', and offered to introduce Harker to them. 'Though nothing would please me more personally, I did not think it wise at this juncture,' Harker said.[44]

Around this time Lord Southwood's profit-driven printing combine Odhams Press bought control of the *Daily Herald*. Ewer continued as the paper's foreign editor, in an editorial office in which communist affiliations were less acceptable and commercial considerations had higher ranking. Slocombe, however, left the *Daily Herald*: he was later foreign editor at the *Sunday Express* and a *Daily Mail* special correspondent. Ewer was summoned to a disciplinary meeting with Pollitt and Willie Gallacher in the Lyons tea-shop next to Leicester Square tube station in September 1931. 'They parted on very bad terms,' MI5 understood. 'Ewer stated that from now on he was going to be bitterly anti-Communist.' Pollitt subsequently described Ewer as 'a posturing renegade who never loses a single opportunity of getting his poison over', while the *Daily Worker* was to denounce him as 'pro-Nazi'.[45]

During the purges of 1937 Rose Cohen, the former lover of both Ewer and Pollitt, was arrested – apparently to stop her from meeting Pollitt in Moscow and reporting that her husband Max Petrovsky had been arrested as a Trotskyite 'wrecker' and was awaiting execution. The *Daily Herald* made a weasel defence of Soviet maltreatment of her. British officials were disinclined to help this '"Bloomsbury Bolshevik" or "parlour pink"', as they called her: one of them asked, as a marginal joke in her file, 'I wonder whether Miss Cohen is now solid or liquid?' Ewer convinced himself that she had been sent to a Siberian camp (in reality she was shot after months of abysmal terror), and felt haunting distress about her fate. He did not know that Pollitt had made strenuous private appeals on her behalf, and therefore found it unforgivable that CPGB leaders knew how hard she had worked for 'the Cause' but, as he told MI5, never intervened on her behalf.[46]

In the late 1940s Ewer worked with the Foreign Office's Information

Research Department in countering communist propaganda and apologetics. He broadcast for the BBC and wrote commentaries expressing the bitterness of a betrayed and disillusioned idealist. Younger diplomatic correspondents, who consulted their amiable doyen 'Trilby' for interpretations of official opacities, never guessed that this urbane man had once been an inflammatory communist zealot. It was suggested in September 1949 by Ann Glass and Jane Archer that given the leakages attributed by Soviet defectors to highly placed government circles, Ewer and Slocombe should be questioned in the hope of establishing whether some of their sources in 1919–29 had since reached senior positions. The task was allotted to Maxwell Knight, a former naval midshipman, preparatory school teacher and journalist, who during the 1930s had become MI5's pre-eminent agent-runner. Knight invited Ewer to lunch at the Connaught Hotel in Mayfair in January 1950.

For the first hour they exchanged 'trivialities about the war and the comparative efficiency of the German and Russian Intelligence Services'. When lunch was over, Ewer said jokily, 'Well now, disclose the great mystery.' Finally, some quarter of a century after MI5 had first rumbled his network, one of its officers confronted him. 'He had no inkling of the real purpose of the interview,' Knight reported.

As he is a very highly strung person, in spite of his experience and undoubted intelligence, I thought it might be a good idea to deal him a rapid blow at the outset. I therefore said to him that what I really wanted to talk to him about was the Federated Press of America. This certainly took him by surprise, and it was on the tip of his tongue to pretend some difficulty in remembering what this was; but as he hesitated, I took out from my dispatch case a rather formidable bundle of typescript, whereupon, with a slightly self-conscious smile he changed his tone and said, 'Oh yes, of course, I can remember the Federated Press of America very well.'

Knight made clear to Ewer that 'there were "no strings" at all attached to this interview . . . and that if he felt he did not wish to discuss the matter with me, he had only to put on his hat and go home, and there would be no hard feelings on my side. I explained that, on the other hand, if he would be kind enough to discuss the case with me, I felt it might be extremely helpful.'

Knight explained that MI5 'made a habit of going over what might be termed "classic cases" in the light of new information or the general trend of international politics, as by doing so we not only frequently re-educated ourselves, but also obtained new information and clearer interpretations of matters which were originally obscure'. Ewer listened attentively, and nodded his agreement. Knight said that two or three recent cases indicated that there might be persons in high government positions who were giving information to the Russians. Ewer agreed to help, with the reservation that he felt hesitant about naming individuals. 'I passed lightly over this, saying that I quite understood,' Knight recorded. Ewer talked slowly and quietly, as if weighing every word. He seemed to Knight evasive, forgetful, 'obstinately vague' and sometimes 'unconvincing'. He claimed that, with the exception of Slocombe's activities in Paris, his group did not touch espionage, but only undertook counter-espionage. The limit of their interest was the actions and plans of the British intelligence services against Soviet and CPGB activities in Britain. This was hard to disprove (certainly in a criminal trial), but sophistical.[47]

There was no official discrediting of Ewer. His fifty years of diplomatic journalism was marked in 1959 by his investiture as a Commander of the Order of the British Empire. Colleagues hailed him as a fearless anti-communist who had once quenched Andrei Vyshinsky's verbal outpourings at a Moscow press conference. Thirty years after the arrest of Dale, Ginhoven and Jane, their spymaster was honoured with a special pass to the Foreign Office which was valid for the rest of his life.

Years later Brian Stewart, the SIS officer who nearly succeeded Maurice Oldfield as Chief in 1978, declared that objectivity was the first necessity for successful intelligence work. 'Report nothing but the unvarnished truth and, as far as possible, the whole truth. Understand, but do not pander to, the prejudices and preconceptions of the customer.' Stewart was equally emphatic about the assessment of intelligence material: 'beware of intellectual laziness, mirror imaging, prejudice, racial or professional arrogance, bias, groupthink, and the sin of assuming that the future will develop, broadly speaking, along the same lines as the past'. These commandments were the result of a century's experience by the intelligence services, including MI5's treatment of the Ewer–Hayes network. MI5 officers showed themselves as shrewd, efficient and decent in their questioning and turning of informants. Contrary to the caricature, they did not behave like clumsy oafish schoolboys playing rough sport. Effective counter-espionage needs tact and patience. Mistakes occur when time is short, or opponents are demonized. Although MI5 has often been depicted as blimpish, rigid, reactionary and thick, in reality its ductile liberalism ought to impress. There was a culture of respecting individuals. Secret policing was not oppressive. The security services were usually more considerate than Fleet Street reporters in minding people's feelings.[48]

CHAPTER 5

The Cipher Spies

The Soviet Union's earliest spies inside the Foreign Office are the subject of this chapter, which is avowedly revisionist. The security failings of the Office and of the intelligence services have been treated in the terminology of class for over sixty years. Public schoolboys supposedly protected one another in obtuse, complacent and snobbish collusion. The secrets of Whitehall were lost on the playing-fields of Eton, so the caricature runs. This, however, is an unreal presentation. The first Foreign Office men to spy for Moscow – in the years immediately after the disintegration of the Ewer–Hayes network – were members of its Communications Department. That department was an amalgam of Etonians, cousins of earls, half-pay officers, the sons of clergymen and of administrators in government agencies, youths from Lower Edmonton and Finchley, lower-middle-class men with a knack for foreign languages. Their common ingredient was masculinity. The predominant influence on the institutional character of the department, its management and group loyalty, its fortitude and vulnerability, all derived from its maleness. As in the Foreign Office generally, it was not class bias but gender exclusivity that created the enabling conditions for espionage. The Communications Department spies Ernest Oldham and John King, and the later spy-diplomatists Burgess, Cairncross and Maclean, had colleagues and chiefs who trusted and protected them, because that was how – under the parliamentary democracy that was settled in 1929 – public servants in a department of state prided themselves on behaving to their fellow men.

The Communications Department

Reader Bullard reflected while Consul General in Leningrad in 1934: 'Schools are not meant to give boys a good time, but to teach them to be happy together even when they are not having a good time.' The office culture of the Communications Department was an extension of school: the staff there tried to be cheery in a hard place, valued cama- raderie and professed individual self-respect as their creed; its vulnerabilities were easy for Oldham and King to exploit. Their male colleagues swapped banter and chaff, forgave and covered each other's mistakes. They aspired to be tolerant, unflappable and conscientious. The departmental spirit precluded grudges and doubts among colleagues. They were not social equals, but they found their common ground as men. As a nationality, the English had too high and yet too juvenile a reckoning of themselves. 'The strength of the British lies in never quite growing up,' Vansittart, PUS of the Foreign Office, said with satisfaction: 'the cause of our mercifully arrested development is that we have not been liable to introspection.'[1]

Boyish ideas about good sports were ubiquitous. The deputy governor of Parkhurst prison during the detention there of the spy Wilfred Macartney was nicknamed 'Jumbo' and was popular with most inmates. In 1930, on Jumbo's last Sunday at Parkhurst, after his promotion to be governor elsewhere, the prisoners held a farewell concert to honour him. 'I've found you fellows a jolly fine set of sports in playing the game,' he told them after the concert in his pronounced Oxford accent. 'Cheer up, and don't forget that the game is not over till the stumps are drawn or the final whistle blown.' Although these virile sentiments may seem laughable in the twenty-first century, in the early 1930s they meant the world for many men: Jumbo was cheered for a full five minutes by the Parkhurst prisoners.[2]

The office culture of the Communications Department is richly evoked in the memoirs of George Antrobus. 'Bozo' Antrobus was born in 1892, the only child of an official in the Crown Agents for the Colonies. He was educated at Westminster School before reading history at Oxford. He lived as a bachelor with his parents a short walk from Leamington Spa station, and commuted daily by train. He appeared punctually at the Foreign Office in suits shiny with age, with a tattered umbrella and greasy bowler hat. He liked musty smells: wet straw, tar, coal-dust, oil, dead rats, fried fish, sweat and spilt beer are all praised in his memoirs. He was an obsessive compiler of railway statistics whose tabular reports on the punctuality of trains are still used by train-spot- ters today.

Antrobus joined the Foreign Office in 1915 as a temporary clerk in the Parliamentary Department. This designation was a classic of misdirection, because the department had sole charge of the urgent, heavy wartime traffic in ciphered messages. He soon learnt the skills necessary for decoding or encrypting messages at top speed. By 1917 he had some forty temporary wartime colleagues, including 'gentlemen of leisure', the filmstar Athole Stewart and the portrait-painter John Collier. Antrobus was one of the minority who stayed in government service when, in 1919, a new Communications Department to handle coded messages was organized. He was at the same time appointed a King's Messenger.

King's Messengers were the men – often ex-officers – who carried confidential material to and fro between the Foreign Office and its embassies and legations in Europe. They travelled by train and steamer, bearing a red passport marked *courier du Roi*, transporting versions of Post Office bags, which were known as 'crossed bags' because their labels bore a conspicuous black cross. Under the 1919 arrangement of the Communications Department, these couriers spent the intervals between their European journeys working on encoding and deciphering in the Office. This was craft work, for which they were adequately but not lavishly paid. Members of the department were ranked with diplomatic staff, but unlike other officials they were not pensionable, and received on retirement lump sums computed on the length of their service. Their status in the building was ambiguous, their financial position felt precarious and these anomalies intensified their *esprit de corps*.

Outgoing Office telegrams were enciphered and incoming messages were deciphered in Room 22. It was a gaunt and lofty space lit by two vast, rattling windows looking northwards. The furniture was hard and plain: half a dozen tables, a dozen chairs, two ranges of cupboards 9 feet high. All was fuggy and frenetic. The clerks were 'a hard-bitten lot', recalled Patrick Reilly. They chain-smoked pipes and cigarettes, working in pairs, one calling aloud from the codebook and the other transcribing the message, at a speed of thirty codewords per minute when encoding and fifty words per minute when decoding – all this hour after hour. The pressure left them, said Antrobus, 'sweating like pigs, with hair awry and shirt-sleeves rolled up, cheeks aflame and collars pulp'. Their finished work was taken to a cacophonous adjoining room, where it was typed on noisy machines using wax stencils rather than paper to enable mass duplication. A careworn official checked every document for its sense: 'Take this back to Room 22, and ask them what the hell they mean by this tripe,' he would shout when he found errors, shouting because behind him dispatch boxes were being slammed shut, before being taken by special messenger to the King, to every Cabinet minister, to departmental heads.[3]

Because of the incoming and outgoing coded messages, Room 22 had as clear a sense of international events as any other section in the Foreign Office. The latest news of treaty negotiations, conference adjournments, troop movements, armaments contracts, political chicanery, financial hanky-panky, sudden deaths, reprisal raids, incendiary speeches and ultimatums were decoded in that austere, noisy department.

Before the European war the Office had resembled 'a small family party', recalled Don Gregory, who joined the Diplomatic Service in 1902 and resigned in 1928. But the European war and subsequent worldwide dislocation required huge expansion of Office responsibilities, activities and personnel. 'Nowadays,' Gregory lamented in 1929, 'with its multifarious new activities, its ramifications, divisions and sub-divisions, its clerks and short-hand typists running here, there and everywhere, its constant meetings and interdepartmental conferences, its innumerable visitors, it is tending to resemble a large insurance office or, in times of stress, a central railway station on a bank holiday.' With the exception of Lord Curzon, foreign secretaries and junior ministers in the Office were notably honeyed in their dealings with officials before 1929. Increasingly thereafter, complained Vansittart, diplomats encountered political chiefs 'seemingly fresh from elevenses of vinegar'.[4]

In reaction to this hectic and unmanageable environment, some officials tried to rehabilitate the pace and temper of Edwardian England in the Office. 'Its keynote was Harmony rather than Hustle,' said Antrobus. Efforts to revive pre-war poise were personified by the Foreign Secretary, Sir Austen Chamberlain, whom Lord Crawford described in 1927 as 'urbane, a little more mysterious and stand-offish than most Foreign Secretaries, and moreover getting into the bad habit of making French gestures with very English-shaped hands'. George Slocombe, who met Chamberlain in Geneva and Locarno, likened him to Talleyrand striving to restore 'the old *douceur de vivre*' to a continent rent by war and revolution: 'from his early readings in European history, Austen Chamberlain had formed, entirely in the tradition of Talleyrand, his own highly personal conception of diplomacy as the guardian of the necessary amenities of life, the custodian of the gracious conventions, the urbanities'.[5]

The chief of the Communications Department from 1925 until 1940 was Harold Eastwood, a product of Eton and Trinity, Cambridge, and brother of a Conservative MP. Eastwood believed that his staff would work best if he trusted them to do their jobs without his fretful interference: 'Everyone was treated as a man of honour; he had his work to do, and if he did it well and quickly, it mattered not the least how he did it or, within limits, when he did it.' There was less change of staff in Communications than in any other Foreign Office department: they knew every speck of one another's capacity and temperament.[6]

Eastwood's deputy Ralph Cotesworth was the son of an Anglican chaplain in Switzerland. His health had collapsed in 1915 while he was a commander in the Royal Navy, and when, after twenty years of encroaching illness, he died in 1937 aged forty-nine, his lungs were found to be rotted away. Cotesworth became a King's Messenger in 1920, grew expert in the use of ciphers, and was in 1925 chosen as Eastwood's deputy. Antrobus noted his 'naval ideas of discipline and duty, large heart and quick sympathy'. Another colleague said with an affectionate tease that Cotesworth's conscientiousness was 'appalling': 'his quasi-boyish gaiety and his shrewdly humorous outlook' contributed to the mood of Room 22.[7]

Algernon Hay, head of the cipher-room from 1919 until 1934, believed in 'the tonic effect of crusted jokes'. He tried to unify his socially variegated staff by managing them in a 'gentlemanly' way. His successor as cipher-room chief was Antrobus, who averred: 'Clever men, strong men, brave men, even good men, are all more readily come by than your man of the world with a conscience.' This was all of a piece with a phrase of T. E. Lawrence's to describe the British Empire: 'the Power which had thrown a girdle of humour and strong dealing around the world'.[8]

Men found different ways to slacken the tension of a strenuous day in the Office. Curzon, as Foreign Secretary, prepared for his working day by going to Christie's auction house and appraising the exhibited artworks that were going under the hammer. Vansittart spent the hour after work every evening playing fierce bridge at the St James's Club. In the Underground railway carriage taking him home, Sir Owen O'Malley sat knitting woollen socks with purled ribs and basket-stitched heels. Sir Archie Clark Kerr liked talking and thinking about sex. Sir Maurice Peterson never stopped puffing his pipe, and enjoyed living in a converted pub in Belgravia called the Triumphal Chariot. (Sir Alan Brooke, Chief of the Imperial General Staff in 1941–5, liked to start his long days with an action-packed *Daily Mirror* strip cartoon about a private investigator, Buck Ryan.) The encryption and decryption clerks, who worked long hours without break, unwound by chain-smoking and hard drinking. They resorted to the Mine, a drinking-hole in the basement of the Foreign Office run by the head office-keeper and his wife. The bar resembled a shabby French *estaminet* with just a pair of broad planks resting on upturned barrels. The tolerance of alcoholism in the Office went to the top: it was said in 1929 that Tyrrell, recently retired as PUS, 'has not done a stroke of work for years, and has sometimes been so drunk that J. D. Gregory had to smuggle him out of the office'.[9]

Ernest Oldham

One of the leading figures in Room 22 and the Mine was Ernest Oldham. Born in 1894 in Lower Edmonton, he was the son of schoolteachers. Most of his education was at Tottenham County School, although he spent some months at an obscure sixth-form boarding school near Staines in Middlesex. In 1914, aged nineteen, he joined the Chief Clerk's Department at the Foreign Office. As a junior officer on the Western Front in 1917–18 he endured bombardment and poison-gas attacks amid the trenches, dug-outs, shell-holes and mine-craters. He was never one of those Englishmen who were reconciled to the carnage of the Western Front by leaving wreaths of Haig poppies at the base of war memorials.

In his determination to rise from the ranks, Oldham made himself into a proficient French-speaker. His bilingualism resulted in his appointment in 1919 as a clerk at the Paris Peace Conference. During his six months in the French capital he mastered its streets and by-ways, which was to prove helpful when years later he needed to escape surveillance. After returning from Paris, Oldham applied for admission into the Consular Service. There seemed a chance of his appointment as Third Consul at Rio de Janeiro, for in addition to good French he had reasonable knowledge of Spanish, Italian and German. After some hesitation, he was rejected by the promotion board in 1920, but offered a post in the Communications Department. This was insufficient salve, for Oldham aspired to the social cachet of the Consular Service.

Like other men in the department, Oldham doubled as a King's Messenger. He visited Constantinople and other Balkan capitals as well as closer destinations. In May 1922 he was sent by air – travelling in a fragile single-engine biplane – to deliver a document intended for King George V, who was visiting war cemeteries in Belgium. These travels made him adept at buying and selling foreign currencies at good rates. The offices of every embassy or legation in a foreign capital were alike, with similar stationery, filing cabinets, pencils, punches and calendars and the same red copies of the *Foreign Office List* and *Who's Who*, as Owen O'Malley recounted. 'In the residential part of the house too, though the servants may be white or black or yellow, there will be the same kindly discipline, the same Lux [soap], Ronuk [floor-polish], chintz, pot-plants, water-colours, large bath towels and Bromo [a patent cure for hangovers and upset stomachs], which the Englishman carries round the world like a snail its shell: which form indeed the temple and fortress of his soul.' To these familiar surroundings King's Messengers brought office talk from Whitehall and from other European capitals, and exchanged it for local gossip. All the staff, from the Ambassador downwards, pumped Oldham about diplomatic trends, promotions, political currents and whatever was afoot in London.[10]

Oldham was given charge of managing the routes for King's Messengers across Europe. The location of the League of Nations in Geneva required his frequent visits to Switzerland, either as a courier of documents or as an encrypter and decrypter. For ten years meetings of the League there were held in the Hôtel Victoria. 'By day the hotel was a babel of strange sounds,' as Slocombe remembered: 'conversations in many languages, the machine-gun rattle of typewriters, the shrilling of telephone bells, and the whine of the mimeograph machines multiplying copies of speeches just made in the drab hall beyond the faded plush of those Victorian sitting-rooms'. At night there was heavy drinking and poker. It was into this mêlée that the boy from Tottenham County School was pitched.[11]

A change in Oldham's circumstances came in 1927 when, falsely describing his father as a gentleman and giving the Foreign Office as his home address, he married a prosperous Australian widow twelve years his senior. With his wife's money, they bought 31 Pembroke Gardens (near Kensington High Street) and employed two housemaids and a chauffeur for their Sunbeam coupé. Oldham filled his wardrobe with monogrammed clothes, and could afford to drink spirits more deeply than ever. 'He arrayed himself, if not in purple, at least in fine linen, and fared sumptuously,' said Antrobus. 'So sumptuously . . . that he contracted delirium tremens.' As an auspicious sequel to this marriage, Oldham was promoted to be Staff Officer of the Communications Department in 1928.[12]

In October 1929 Gregori Bessedovsky, the Soviet Chargé d'Affaires in Paris, who had been ordered back to Moscow for punishment after being denounced for criticizing Stalin's maltreatment of the peasantry, fled over the embassy wall and was granted asylum by the French government. Maurice Oldfield, a future head of SIS, used to say that 'defectors are like grapes; the first pressings are always the best'. Wilfred ('Biffy') Dunderdale, SIS's station head in Paris, who had spent his boyhood in Odessa and spoke Russian fluently, interviewed Bessedovsky three days after his defection, but did not press him well. Dunderdale discounted Bessedovsky's material because he found him sharp, 'but neither frank nor principled'. Although Dunderdale had a reputation for shrewdness, he was prone to SIS's cultural contempt for foreigners. 'British intelligence', recalled Elizabeth Poretsky, 'appeared to consider the Soviets mere rabble.'[13]

Early reports of Bessedovsky's revelations were garbled, but indicated that some months earlier an Englishman had called at the Russian embassy offering secret cipher books of the British government. The 'walk-in', as such unheralded visitors were called, was seen by the OGPU Director Vladimir Ianovich (born Wilenski), a coarse man who had previously been a dock-worker. Ianovich's wife managed OGPU finances in Paris (she received large dollar bills in the diplomatic mail, and exchanged them for francs). Her impersonations of a Hungarian countess in Berlin, of a Persian diplomat's wife in Vienna and of a diamond merchant's widow in Prague were admired by the illegals, although her husband was not. Ianovich took away the codebooks, saying that he had to show them to the Ambassador, but gave them instead to his wife, who had a brightly lit room for taking photographs and a well-equipped darkroom for developing them. After she had copied the codebooks, Ianovich – either suspecting an agent provocateur's trap or wishing to save OGPU money – threw them back at the walk-in Englishman and ejected him from the embassy in an insulting fashion.

SIS continued to assess Bessedovsky as shifty, talkative and imprudent. This was not far wrong: years later he tried to make money by forging the journals of Maxim Litvinov, the former Foreign Affairs Commissar of the Soviet Union. Accordingly, in 1929, Special Branch did not investigate his tale of purloined codebooks. Norman Ewer's *Daily Herald* on 29 October pooh-poohed Bessedovsky's information in a manner that suited Russian interests: it depicted the fugitive diplomat as an opportunist whose stories were derided in Whitehall. If leakages had occurred, the Communications Department was a likely source, and its Staff Officer, Oldham, should have led an investigation. He was however both the walk-in with the codebooks and absent undergoing treatment for alcoholism from mid-October until March 1930. It can be surmised that his collapse began with a panicky binge after Bessedovsky's story appeared in London newspapers.

Bessedovsky's warning was duplicated in 1930 by Georges Agabekov, then the most senior OGPU officer to have defected. The English parents of his young girlfriend complained to the French authorities that he was a seducer who had alienated her loyalty to them: he was deported to Belgium (more on grounds of public morality than national security) in July 1930. After his deportation, Jasper Harker, head of MI5's B Division (investigations and inquiries), Guy Liddell of Special Branch and Jane Sissmore, who was MI5's specialist in Russian community activity, agreed that Agabekov and his correspondence should be put under surveillance. Liddell was sent to interview him in Brussels, and maintained telephonic contact with Sissmore while in the Belgian capital. Agabekov was pressed about the Soviet agent who was obtaining Foreign Office secrets (now known to be the Rome embassy servant, Francesco Constantini). He described OGPU's network of agents and their operations to Liddell. He also reported that Moscow received copies of the secret exchanges between the Foreign Office and the High Commissioner in Egypt, Lord Lloyd. This renewed confirmation of a breach in coded traffic was reported to the Foreign Office. It is known that the Communications Department led an internal investigation, but the identity and report of the investigators are unknown. Agabekov made similar revelations in newspaper articles and in two essays which were published together in a garbled, facetious English edition in 1931.

The truth behind the tales of Bessedovsky and Agabekov was that in July 1929 Oldham had gone to the Russian embassy in Paris with two books bound in red buckram containing Foreign Office, Colonial Office and Dominions Office ciphers (in some accounts the codebooks were those of the FO and of the India Office). He presented himself as a typesetter called 'Charlie Scott', disguising his status by speaking bad French, and demanding first £50,000 and then £10,000 for his material. 'Charlie Scott' was paid $11,000 in two instalments, and thereafter $1,000 a month. Oldham averted insolvency, and maintained his pretensions in Kensington, by making renewed visits to Paris in order to deliver secret material, which the Russians found patchy and low-grade. They did not trust him enough to risk giving him a handler in London who might be trapped. Oldham protected his true identity from his Paris handler, Dimitri Bystrolyotov.

After the ARCOS raid in 1927 London had severed official relations with Moscow, and ordered all diplomats and trade representatives to leave the country within ten days. OGPU thereupon ordained that only illegals could be used in Britain, but that there was to be no illegal residency there. All activities had to be run from the European mainland, usually from Amsterdam or Paris, but under the control of the Berlin *rezidentura*. Although Anglo-Soviet diplomatic relations were restored by the incoming Labour government in 1929, Moscow remained doubtful about sending permanent illegals to London, and continued running operations there from other European capitals.

Bystrolyotov was born in Crimea in 1901, the son of a village schoolmistress: he knew nothing of his paternity. In 1919 he smuggled himself into Turkey in the coal-hole of a ship, worked as a stoker, and got some education at the American College for Christian Youth. He had a nervous breakdown after witnessing massacres of Armenians, worked for the Red Cross in Prague and then as a cemetery worker. Around 1925 he was recruited to OGPU with the cover of a post in the Soviet trade mission in Prague and the task of collecting secret material on armaments production at the Franco-Czech Škoda factory in Pilsen.

He was a clever linguist and perceptive student of character: his black eyes and dashing masculinity brought him success as a *vorón* (a 'raven', or male seducer of women with access to confidential material). In 1930 he was transferred to the illegal *rezidentura* in Berlin headed by Basil Bazarov (born Shpak), whose OGPU codename was KIN. The Greek Consul in Danzig, an Odessa-born swindler and drugs-smuggler, provided Bystrolyotov with a Greek passport and the false identity of a Salonika businessman, Alexander Gallas.

Bystrolyotov was instructed to elicit the identity of 'Charlie Scott', who was being run under the codename of ARNO. To this end, he adopted the alias of a Hungarian count, Lajos József Perelly, and went to Budapest to learn his part. He introduced himself to 'Scott' in a Paris restaurant as a nobleman who had been ruined by the war and who performed services for OGPU in return for an income that enabled him to keep caste. He felt that he was more acceptable to 'Scott' posing as a Hungarian hireling than he would have been as a Russian or Ukrainian communist. After months of patience, 'Perelly' discovered that 'Scott' was staying in a particular Paris hotel, where his luggage was stamped with the monogram 'EHO'.

The scene shifted from Paris to Geneva. When Slocombe depicted Geneva as Europe's 'most secretive city', he was indulging in an old spy's misdirection. It was hard to keep secrets there. The lifeless official verbiage and stiff protocol surrounding League of Nations sessions there encouraged men to unbend with confidential admissions and gossipy indiscretions when they went off duty in bars and brasseries. 'A vast concourse of politicians . . . is bound to bring all the ragtag and bobtail of the earth sniffing at their heels,' as Antrobus recorded. 'All the paraphernalia of leakage on a grand scale there assembled . . . the place swarmed with spies and secret agents who, I imagine, got what they wanted handed to them on a plate.'[14]

Bystrolyotov @ Gallas @ Perelly arrived in Geneva for a League meeting in, it seems, July 1931. He deduced that 'EHO' would attend the League sessions, found that a man with those initials was staying at the Hôtel Beau-Rivage, spotted 'Scott' in the hotel bar and sat next to him there in silence. 'Scott' looked aghast on catching sight of 'Perelly' and realized that OGPU had broken his anonymity. Bystrolyotov intended to consolidate his advantage by visiting Oldham at home and asserting OGPU control over him, but when he called at Pembroke

Gardens in September with false credentials identifying him as a Dresden banker, Lucy Oldham, looking tense, explained that her husband was away from home. The courteous foreigner invited her for lunch at the Ritz. Amid the restaurant's gilt and mirrors she revealed that Oldham was undergoing an expensive cure for alcoholism in a sanatorium in Suffolk called Rendlesham Hall.

She besought 'Count Perelly' to visit Oldham at Rendlesham, and insisted that he take the spare bedroom in Pembroke Gardens. On the night before Oldham's return home in October, Lucy Oldham rolled up the hem of her dress, spread her legs and begged the Count not to waste time. He obliged, and reported his performance to Moscow, where the codename of MADAM was bestowed on her. Bystrolyotov came to suspect that she had instigated her husband's approach to the Russian embassy in Paris in 1929, and that she had encouraged the subsequent espionage as a way of perpetuating their Kensington prosperity.

OGPU in Moscow and the *rezidentura* in Berlin continued to assess Oldham as too dicey to risk agents receiving material direct from him in London. Instead, he was required to travel to Bonn, Ostend, Paris, Calais, Trouville, Madrid, Amsterdam and Switzerland for handovers of purloined documents. Throughout he insisted that he was only an intermediary, acting on behalf of the material's true source. Oldham became such a valued source that Bystrolyotov was joined in London in 1932 by two well-tried agents. Joseph Leppin @ PEEP @ PEPIKA, a young Prague journalist who was then working under Boris Bazarov in the Berlin *rezidentura*, was fluent in French, English and German, had intellectual and artistic interests and was used by Bystrolyotov as the courier carrying Oldham's product out of England on its journey to Moscow. Leppin was married for 'operational purposes' to a fellow Czech agent, Erica Weinstein (ERIKA), who collaborated with him on operations for Bystrolyotov. Bazarov (presenting himself as an Italian communist called da Vinci) and Theodore Maly also came to London to help in running Oldham.[15]

Theodore Stephanovich Maly @ Theodore Mally @ Tivadar Mály @ Willy Broschart @ Paul Hardt @ Peters @ der Lange @ Mann is the most famous of the illegals. Born in 1894, the son of a provincial offi-cial in the Hungarian Ministry of Finance, he trained for priesthood in a seminary before his military mobilization at the age of twenty-one. He was an ensign-cadet by the time of his capture by tsarist forces in

1916. After gruelling train journeys, he was held in a prisoner-of-war camp at Astrakhan by the Caspian Sea, and later was transferred to the frontier town of Orenburg at the southern end of the Ural Mountains. 'I lost my faith in God,' he later said of his incarceration, 'and when the revolution broke out I joined the Bolsheviks. I broke with my past completely. I was no longer a Hungarian, a priest, a Christian, even anyone's son . . . I became a communist.' Maly was a Chekist for ten years before joining INO in about 1931. He could pass as Austrian, Hungarian, German or Swiss. As described by his biographer William Duff, a special agent of the FBI who specialized in Soviet bloc espionage, Maly had 'a tanned and strangely aesthetic face highlighted by deep-set but sad, almost childlike eyes'. For Elizabeth Poretsky, '"Teddy" . . . combined extreme sweetness with a great deal of determination, so that one felt at ease and protected in his company.' OGPU admired Maly's abilities, but felt perturbed by his outbursts of drunken and indiscreet remorse. They forced him to marry a woman whom he disliked because she kept him under watchful guard and kept him from binge-drinking.[16]

During the Lausanne Conference of June–July 1932, at which the British, French and German governments discussed the suspension of German reparation payments, Oldham provided Bystrolyotov with coded messages, dispatches and even a British passport bearing the invented name of 'Sir Robert Grenville'. The strain of duplicity drove Oldham into dipsomania. His department began investigating the disappearance of a codebook from a basement safe, in a part of the building where Oldham had been seen when he was on sick-leave. He was reported for using the Office's ambassadorial side-entrance so as to avoid the doorkeepers who maintained security at the main doors. Other reports had him in a drunken stupor. On 30 September 1932 he was summoned to a disciplinary meeting, confronted with a list of transgressions, including unexplained visits to the cipher-room and losing confidential material which he claimed to have taken home. He was asked to resign without any gratuity. Like other members of his department, he had no pension rights.

Oldham did not admit to the illegals that he had been sacked. On 18 October, avid for more OGPU money, he flew with his wife from Croydon aerodrome to Berlin for a rendezvous with 'Perelly'. During their meeting he was so helplessly drunk that he could hardly move or speak, and vomited. MADAM subsequently revealed to her partner in adultery, 'Perelly', that Oldham had been fired from his job. She added that she was leaving him, would sell the house and go to work in a French resort either as a lady companion or, if that failed, as a prostitute. Just before Christmas 1932 Oldham tried to strangle her when she refused to give him brandy. He was sent for another cure at Rendlesham.

After drying out, Oldham revisited his old department to jaw with friends there, notably Thomas Kemp, who was in charge of the King's Messengers' itineraries, and a clerk named Raymond Oake. He had a further excuse for visits, because he had been allowed, incomprehensibly to modern thinking, to keep a safety-deposit box in the building after his dismissal. He used the pretext of examining personal papers in the box as the justification for two or three further visits. One evening in May 1933, he arrived at 6 p.m., loitered around Room 22, his speech slurred with drink, waiting for other clerks to go home. He asked for the combination number of the safe where keys were kept at night and briefly got custody of the keys to the cupboards known as 'presses' containing confidential material. Those ex-colleagues who saw him felt a mixture of pity, embarrassment, annoyance and suspicion at his conduct, but the blokey 'good form' of the department meant that his manoeuvres were watched but not challenged. During one of these forays he obtained documents which he sold in Paris to the Soviets in May 1933. He and his wife commuted by air between London and Paris during May and June to see Bystrolyotov. OGPU became so alarmed by the likelihood of Oldham's exposure that all illegal operatives, including Bazarov and Maly, were withdrawn from England.

On 13 July 1933, desperate for OGPU money and under incitement from Bystrolyotov, Oldham returned to the Office in an attempt to lay hands on the cipher codes for the following year. He arrived just before 6 p.m., ostensibly to see Kemp who had already gone home, got hold of a set of keys left momentarily in the door, rushed to the lavatory and there took wax impressions of them. When he reappeared with the keys, he was sweating and his hands shook. Wax was found on the wards of the keys. Eastwood reported the incident next day to Sir Vernon Kell of MI5, who set Harker on the case. Oldham's correspondence was intercepted, his telephone was tapped and he was put under John Ottaway's surveillance. Bystrolyotov met Oldham on a bench in

Hyde Park, and urged him to try again to get into the safes to obtain up-to-date codes. At lunchtime on Sunday 16 July Oldham was refused admittance when he called again at the Office.

Some days later he was heard in a bugged telephone call to say that he was going to Vienna. He evaded his watchers by instead flying from Croydon to Geneva. From there he hastened to Interlaken, where he met Bystrolyotov calling himself 'Perelly' and Bazarov calling himself 'da Vinci'. After returning from Basel to Croydon on 4 August, Oldham was traced by Ottaway to the Jules Hotel at 85–86 Jermyn Street, St James's, and tracked to a nearby pub, the Chequers, off a narrow alley joining Duke Street, St James's to Mason's Yard. At the poky bar in the Chequers, two MI5 operatives, Herbert ('Con') Boddington, a bookie's son who had been Chief of Dublin Special Branch targeting the IRA in the early 1920s, and Thomas ('Tar') Robertson, set to work on Oldham. Robertson (born in Sumatra in 1909) had only recently joined MI5 after working in the City, and was known to his new colleagues as 'Passion Pants' because he wore Seaforth tartan trews at headquarters. 'Con' and 'Passion Pants' got Oldham hopelessly drunk in the Chequers, put him to bed in the Jules Hotel and searched his belongings while he was comatose.[17]

Oldham was not questioned or detained, although it was obvious to his watchers that he was falling apart. MI5 wished to learn from watching his activities and contacts. Probably the Foreign Office shrank from discovering the extent to which diplomatic secrets had been broached. Still striving to earn OGPU money, dosing himself with paraldehyde (a foul-smelling, addictive sedative taken by alcoholics and insomniacs), Oldham finally broke. He went to his former marital home at 31 Pembroke Gardens, now vacant and unfurnished, and gassed himself in the kitchen. The suspicions of some of his Room 22 colleagues and Russian handlers that he had been killed by MI5 seem unwarranted. In retrospect Antrobus despised his department's first traitor. 'A clever little upstart,' he called him, 'with a face like a rat and a conscience utterly devoid of scruples.'[18]

Until Oldham's attempted break-in, members of the Foreign Office were often visited at work by friends. After 1933, however, visitors were filtered by policemen and doorkeepers: once admitted, they were escorted everywhere by hardy factotums. The locks and keys of the 'presses' were changed. Algernon Hay was retired from overseeing Room

22 in 1934. His replacement Antrobus thought of his staff as a 'little brotherhood' of 'learned friends'. He explained: 'everybody gave of his best, although (very properly) he got no credit for it beyond his own satisfaction'. He believed that 'in all classes of life and among all sorts and conditions of men', especially 'in teams, regiments, and ships', the best-performing organizations had consciously developed 'the Spirit of the Old School Tie'. This Spirit motivated and unified men without appealing to class bias: public schools did not hold 'a monopoly of true fellowship and devotion to an ideal', insisted Antrobus. A minority of his staff had attended public schools.[19]

The Foreign Office conducted an internal, amateurish and self-protective investigation of the Oldham case without MI5 or Special Branch assistance. There was little investigation of Oldham's overseas air journeys, or of his ultimate destinations and contacts, which might have given leads to Bystrolyotov and Bazarov. In gathering clues from outsiders, such as Oldham's solicitor, it was represented that he was suspected of drugs-smuggling. No hint was permissible that he had been betraying official secrets to a hostile power. There were few leads, as 'Count Perelly' and 'da Vinci' had vanished and reverted to their true identities as Bystrolyotov and Bazarov. 'I could have ended up in the Tower, but only if Vansittart had been willing to wash his dirty linen in public,' Bystrolyotov judged; but the Foreign Office saw no benefit in publicizing the lax security. As to Moscow, OGPU had been exasperated by Oldham's alcoholic volatility. At times the risks for his handlers seemed nightmarish. His low status in the Office hierarchy had moreover limited his access to secret material. OGPU's frustrations with him perhaps contributed to the strategy of placing more reliable penetration agents in the Diplomatic Service through the device of recruiting young Cambridge high-fliers.[20]

Hans Pieck and John King

Oldham had supplied personal assessments of his colleagues. One of these was Raymond Oake, born in 1894 in Finchley and the son of a railway clerk. After wartime naval service, Oake joined the Communications Department as a clerk in 1920. He was used as an occasional King's Messenger without being promoted above the level of clerk, amassed debts and borrowed money from colleagues. His bank manager told MI5, when it was investigating Oake's finances in 1939, that his customer was 'a weak, foolish man, whose vanity leads him to live above his income, which is about £600 per annum. On one occasion when he was warned as to his account, he created a wild scene and ended by bursting into tears.'[21]

Bystrolyotov delegated the task of cultivating Oake to Hans Pieck, a Dutchman codenamed COOPER. Pieck, who was the son of a naval officer, had joined his country's communist party in 1920 under the alias of Donat. He had visited Moscow on party business in 1929. He spoke German, English, French, Danish and perhaps Italian. He was a man of culture and charm, well reputed as a decorative artist, architectural designer and cartoonist, who lived with his wife in The Hague in style (subsidized by OGPU money). 'He is a good actor who plays his role naturally, sometimes masterfully, finds his bearings quickly in conversation, manoeuvres well and is already ready for initiative,' Bystrolyotov declared. Pieck was not a staid communist: rather he was 'Bohemian, disorderly, untidy, inaccurate, incoherent and undisciplined'. Although effective as a talent-spotter and recruiter, he was too fastidious to coerce targets, to kidnap them, to apply blackmail or to threaten lives. Bystrolyotov attributed to Pieck 'Love for intelligence work bordering on a passion, a romantic attitude to his role close to that of an actor's enjoyment'.[22]

Pieck installed himself at the Hôtel Beau-Rivage in Geneva, befriended Communications Department men and consular officials in bars and brasseries, spent a fortune on hospitality and gave handsome presents. In the summary of Valentine Vivian of SIS, Pieck 'allayed suspicion by posing as the prince of good fellows, habitué of the International Club, always "good" for a drink, a motor expedition, or a free meal – a histrionic effort worthy of a better cause'. Pieck moved deftly towards his target of Oake, who was given the codename SHELLEY. On Christmas Day of 1933 Pieck visited him in Room 22. They had festive drinks together in a nearby pub, where Pieck learnt that Oake had already spent his December wages and loaned him money to cover some cheques. Six years later, under interrogation by MI5, Oake described Pieck as 'absolutely a white man', whose lavish generosity had sometimes embarrassed him. Pieck posed as the representative of a Dutch bank interested in collecting economic and political intelligence, but although Oake agreed to supply him with material, it was always meagre pickings.

Security had been tightened after Oldham's disgrace. Sitting at a table in Room 22 with four other men, Oake found no opportunities for clandestine work. He was so chary of being caught that he was dropped by OGPU in December 1934.[23]

Three months earlier, in Geneva, Oake had however introduced Pieck to another clerk in the Communications Department, John King. King had joined the Rhineland High Commission, a supra-national body based in Coblenz and supervising the Anglo-French occupation of the Rhineland, as a cipher officer in 1923. He was promoted to be personal clerk to the High Commissioner, the Earl of Erroll, in 1925. After Erroll's death in 1928, he had a posting in China. 'He is about fifty years of age, an Irishman who lived in Germany for about ten years and speaks German perfectly,' reported Bystrolyotov. 'A lively and inquisitive person . . . he draws a sharp distinction between himself with his cultured ways and the "pompous fools" of Englishmen.' He was keen on the theatre and liked magic tricks. His salary was too small for his needs, he cadged drinks and tried to touch people for loans.[24]

After dropping Oake, Pieck approached King to provide political information and weekly summaries for use by a Dutch bank. King agreed, and a secret bank account was opened for his remuneration. He received the codename MAG. King's first delivery of secret material included an account of Hitler's conversations with the Foreign Secretary, Sir John Simon, in March 1935. 'His conviction that he is destined to bring about the moral rehabilitation of the German people after being crushed and humiliated by the treaty of Versailles', Simon noted,

> is very dangerous to peace in Europe, and it is all the more dangerous for being very sincere. And he is adored by those who follow him as no German Emperor has ever been adored. Hitler made it perfectly plain that he would never agree to enter into a pact of 'mutual assistance' with Russia. Communism, he declared, is the plague: unlike National Socialism, which he claims seeks only to embrace Germans, it is a contagious infection which might spread over all Europe and all Asia. He has stamped it out of Germany, and Germany is the barrier to prevent the pestilence coming westward.[25]

King, like Oake, found it hard to obtain the Foreign Office daily bulletins which Oldham had been able to supply. Files, registers, the flimsy

papers on which decrypts were scrawled – all were now guarded by
the men who had responsibility for them. Any official found in a part
of the department where he had no business was challenged. In order
to justify his frequent visits to London, Pieck started a flimsy cover
business called the Universal Barter Company. He then devised a better
front after Oake had introduced him to Conrad Parlanti, with whom
Oake often commuted by train from Herne Bay to Victoria station.
Pieck suggested that he and Parlanti should go into business together
as shopfitters. Among other commissions, Pieck and Parlanti revamped
the shop-window displays at Marshall & Snelgrove's department store
in Oxford Street. At Pieck's insistence Parlanti rented offices at 34a
Buckingham Gate, close to Victoria station but also a few minutes'
stroll across St James's Park from the Foreign Office. Parlanti was puzzled
by Pieck's insistence on leasing these offices, which were a secret amenity
for spying rather than for the shop-window design business. Pieck kept
a floor there for his own use, with one room which was always locked.
King could walk over from Room 22, let himself in with a key and
draw the curtains to indicate that he had left papers to be photographed
in the locked room. Buckingham Gate was only a small deviation from
King's homeward route to Flat 9, St Leonard's Mansions, Smith Street,
Chelsea. Copies or originals of the documents were collected from
Buckingham Gate by Brian Goold-Verschoyle, a communist electrical
engineer and Comintern courier. The more important material was
telegraphed to Moscow from the Soviet embassy.

   Parlanti eventually picked the door lock when Pieck was away. Inside
the mystery room he found a Leica camera fixed to photograph articles
on a table. When he confronted Pieck, he was told that the Leica was
for photographing 'dirty pictures'. On another occasion Parlanti saw
Pieck receive documents typed in red from a man in the lounge of the
Victoria Hotel in Northumberland Avenue, off Whitehall. Pieck invited
him to visit The Hague, but then made a show of being suddenly called
to Germany. As Parlanti told MI5 in September 1939, 'Mrs Pieck began
very soon to make love to him, in order, as he is now convinced, to
get him to entangle himself. He resisted her wiles, and finally lost
patience with her.' Mrs Pieck then wept, and told him that she and her
husband were engaged in financial manipulations, 'with big people and
for big money', and received official secrets from a man in the Foreign
Office's code section.[26]

At a party in London in January 1936 Pieck was approached by William John ('Jack') Hooper, a British-Dutch dual national whom he believed to be the British Commercial Attaché at The Hague but who in fact worked for SIS there. In a quiet corner at the party Hooper referred to Pieck's Comintern activities in the 1920s: 'We know about your past and keep a constant watch on you. I want to know if you are still in the same business.' Pieck insisted that he had abandoned his youthful political enthusiasms, but was sufficiently rattled to stop using the Buckingham Gate office as King's drop-off because Hooper knew of its existence. Possibly Hooper was exploring Pieck's availability to inform on his old communist friends without knowing that Pieck was an important communist agent.[27]

In September 1936 Hooper was dismissed by SIS after the head of station in The Hague, Major Ernest Dalton, shot himself. As Passport Control Officer, Dalton had been selling visas to Jewish fugitives from Hitler who wanted to reach Palestine. When Hooper had spotted the racket, he was given a cut by Dalton, whose corruption was discovered during a routine audit. After being discarded by SIS, Hooper enlisted as an NKVD agent and went to work in Pieck's Dutch office, where he watched his employer, asked questions and amassed material which he gave piecemeal to SIS as a way of vindicating himself after the Dalton scandal and regaining official British employment. SIS ignored his information and did not rehire him, because of his complicity with Dalton. The NKVD decided that Hooper was untrustworthy or compromised, and dropped him later in 1937. Rejected by both London and Moscow, Hooper turned to Berlin. In 1938-9 he worked for the Abwehr, to which he divulged that the Soviets had a source in the Communications Department.

For two years, as the head of SIS's counter-espionage section Valentine Vivian noted in a retrospective of the King case, SIS had known Hooper's information about Pieck's clandestine activities in London, which 'could have been acted upon then had it been credited. It was, however, treated with coldness and even derision, largely as a result of the prejudice against X [Hooper] himself.' Vivian was impressed that Pieck had 'included in his confidences one conscious and artistic lie – for the purpose undoubtedly of discrediting "X's" story in the unlikely event of his passing it to the British authorities – i.e. he gave the name of his "inside agent" in the Foreign Office as Sir Robert

Vansittart'. Pieck embroidered this critical misdirection with other absurdities, including an imaginary mistress of Vansittart's who acted as a cut-out in transmitting betrayed secrets.[28]

Hooper's activities resulted in Pieck being withdrawn from handling King. The Dutchman was next sent by Moscow to Athens, where he tried to induce the Minister of War to order forty fighter planes, ostensibly for the Greek government, which were to be shipped to Republican forces in Spain with the Minister's connivance. This intrigue failed, and Pieck had to leave Athens in a hurry, according to an SIS source; but he proceeded to Paris, where he found a South American legation ready to help.

The eminent illegal Walter Krivitsky, codenamed GROLL, was briefly charged with delivering the photographic film for use on King's material in London. Theodore Maly, who succeeded Krivitsky in London, reported to Moscow Centre that King wished to 'rid the world of poverty, hunger, war and prison', but was not left-wing. Socialism meant 'the terrors of Bolshevism, it is chaos, the power of the mob, Jews and endless bloodshed', he told Maly. 'I am against Fascism but if here, in this country, I had to choose between Sir Oswald Mosley and British Labourites, I would choose the former, for the latter logically lead to Bolshevism.' He assessed Hitler as 'a maniac but an honest person' who had saved Germany from the Reds. The English aristocracy was 'good for nothing, in the first place because it was English, and in the second because it is mixed with Jews and other lower classes'. The Irish and Scottish nobility was however 'clear of foreign taint, and it has preserved its race'. King, like Oldham, was a mercenary who needed money, and had no interest in communism. He was conceited like Oldham too, but had stronger nerves: he enjoyed the sense of superior but secret privileges that accompanied his hidden life; he did not get rattled by the dangers of discovery and launch himself into panicky binges.[29]

King's influence may have been world-changing. Donald Cameron Watt believed that the material supplied by King in July and August 1939 to his Soviet controller, reporting on the Anglo-French tripartite negotiations with Russia for a pact against Germany, was leaked by Moscow in a selective fashion to Berlin. The intelligence gobbets given to Germany were among the enticements that led Berlin into the Nazi–Soviet non-aggression pact of August 1939.[30]

Walter Krivitsky

Krivitsky was the link joining Oldham and King to Maclean and Philby. His original name was Samuel Ginsburg. He was Jewish and Russian-born, with a Polish father, a Slav mother and a Latvian wife who was a dedicated Bolshevik. In youth he was an active Vienna socialist while training as an engineer. After the launch of the illegal system in 1925, he became illegal *rezident* in The Hague, under the alias of Martin Lessner, an Austrian dealer in art and rare books. His house was furnished with stark minimalist modernity as visible support for his cover. He had enough culture to sustain the mask of connoisseurship. From the Netherlands Krivitsky directed much of the espionage in Britain. He became convinced of the insanity of Nikolai Yezhov, whom Stalin appointed chief of the NKVD in 1936 with the remit to purge the party. In 1937 Ignace Reiss @ Poretsky, the Paris-based illegal who was Krivitsky's boon comrade, protested against the Great Terror and denounced Stalin. As a test of Krivitsky's fealty, Moscow ordered him to liquidate Reiss. He refused, was summoned to Moscow for retribution and fled for his life to the USA.

It was at this time that a Cambridge luminary, the novelist E. M. Forster, wrote a credo that has been lampooned, truncated in quotation and traduced by subsequent writers. His remarks in their entirety carry a message of individualism, conscientious judgement and anti-totalitarianism that might have been a text for Whitehall values in the 1930s. 'One must be fond of people,' said Forster, 'and trust them if one is not to make a mess of one's life, and it is therefore essential that they should not let one down. They often do.' Writing in 1939, when totalitarian nationalism was rampant, Forster continued: 'Personal relations are despised today. They are regarded as bourgeois luxuries, as products of a time of fair weather which is now past, and we are urged to get rid of them, and to dedicate ourselves to some movement or cause instead. I hate the idea of causes, and if I had to choose between betraying my country and betraying my friend, I hope I should have the guts to betray my country.' Krivitsky had the guts.[31]

The Americans were more obtuse about Krivitsky's defection even than Dunderdale had been with Bessedovsky's. He reached New York with his wife and children on the liner *Normandie* on 10 November 1938 (travelling under his real name of Ginsburg). Immigration officials rejected the family's entry on grounds of insufficient funds. He was eventually released on bail provided by his future writing collaborator Isaac Don Levine, who had been born in Belarus, finished high school in Missouri and worked as a radical journalist but had become hostile to communist chicanery. Krivitsky funded his American life by producing articles and an autobiography which were ghosted by Levine and sold by Paul Wohl, a German-Jewish refugee who had worked for the League of Nations and was trying to scratch a living as a New York literary agent and book reviewer. In an article of February 1939 Krivitsky predicted the Nazi–Soviet pact seven months before it was agreed.

Roosevelt's Secretary of State Cordell Hull had relinquished his department's responsibility for monitoring communists and fascists to the Federal Bureau of Investigation in 1936: 'go ahead and investigate the hell out of those cocksuckers', he had told its chief J. Edgar Hoover. This decision left the FBI with the incompatible tasks of policing crimes that had already been committed and of amassing secret intelligence about future intentions and possible risks to come. In practice, the Bureau concentrated on law enforcement and criminal investigation rather than intelligence-gathering and analysis. This bias and Hoover's insularity meant that there was more interest in pursuing Krivitsky for passport fraud than in extracting intelligence from him.[32]

After a nine-month delay, on 27 July 1939 a special agent of the FBI questioned Krivitsky for the first time in Levine's office in downtown New York. Their exchanges were too crude to be called a debriefing. The debriefing of defectors is slow-moving at the start: character must be assessed, trust must be gained, affinities must be recognized and motivations must be plumbed. Only then, when the participants are speaking rationally and with the semblance of mutual respect, can reliability be gauged and evasions be addressed. Perception, patience and tact are needed to overcome psychological resistance and to elicit information that can be acted on. But the FBI agent did not engage in preliminary civilities to reach some affinity with his subject. Instead he fired narrowly focused questions about Moishe Stern @ Emile Kléber @ Mark Zilbert, who was believed to have run a spy ring in the USA. Krivitsky was diverted from volunteering information on other matters. When his replies contradicted the conclusions drawn in previous FBI investigations, or expressed his certainty that Stern had been purged, the special agent concluded that he was ill-informed, wrong-headed and obstinate. The FBI agent did not listen with an open mind; he would not revise his own presuppositions. Hoover dismissed Krivitsky as a liar.

Krivitsky's memoirs *In Stalin's Secret Service* had an ungrateful reception from reviewers: 'his words are those of a renegade and his mentality that of a master-spy', *Foreign Affairs* warned in response to his indictment of Stalinism. Communist sympathizers were especially hostile: Malcolm Cowley in *New Republic* decried the fugitive from Stalin's hit-squad as 'a coward . . . a gangster and a traitor' to his friends, and elsewhere labelled him 'a rat'. Edmund Wilson called Cowley's review 'Stalinist character assassination'; and certainly such tendentious pieces harmed Krivitsky's credibility. The book was nevertheless read by Whittaker Chambers, a former courier for a communist spy ring in Washington who had turned against the Stalinist system of deceit, paranoia and executions, and had gone into hiding after being summoned to Moscow for purging. Later he was to write his own memoir, *Witness*, in which he presented the object of a secret agent's life as humdrum duplicity. 'Thrills mean that something has gone wrong,' he wrote. 'I have never known a good conspirator who enjoyed conspiracy.' Chambers contacted Levine, who introduced him to Krivitsky. After the shock of the non-aggression pact signed by Nazi Germany and Soviet Russia on 23 August, Levine asked Assistant Secretary of State Adolf Berle to meet Chambers and hear his information.[33]

War in Europe began on 1 September: next day Chambers visited Berle and named eighteen New Deal officials as communists, including a Far Eastern expert at the State Department, Alger Hiss @ LAWYER @ALES, and Laurence Duggan @ 19 @ FRANK @ PRINCE, chief of the American Republics Division of the State Department. It is likely, but not certain, that the senior Treasury official Harry Dexter White was another of the communists denounced by Chambers. Berle reported the denunciation to President Roosevelt, who took no action, and waited seven months before alerting the FBI, which also took little action. In consequence of Berle's inattention and the FBI's laxity, Russian communist spies riddled the Roosevelt administration until the Cold War, damaged US interests and contributed to the post-war paranoia about communist penetration agents. Washington officials had an antithetical group mentality from their counterparts in Whitehall: most were

political appointees; many were career lawyers; they lacked the procedures, continuities and group loyalties that were the pride of English
civil servants; they had no administrative tradition of minuting inter-
departmental meetings, and often avoided recording decisions on paper.
Although more diverse in their backgrounds and less hidebound in
their management, in handling Russian communist penetration of
central government Washington's oversights were as grievous as
London's.

The day after Chambers met Berle, on 3 September, Victor Mallet,
Counsellor at the Washington embassy, wrote to Gladwyn Jebb, who
was then private secretary to Sir Alexander Cadogan (Vansittart's
successor as PUS at the Foreign Office). Mallet noted that Krivitsky
had foretold the Russo-German pact: 'he is clearly not bogus as many
people tried to make out'. Mallet reported Levine's information that
Krivitsky knew of two Soviet agents working in Whitehall: one was
King in the Office cipher-room, who 'has for several years been passing
on everything to Moscow for mercenary motives'; the other man was
said to be in the 'Political Committee Cabinet Office'. (Levine was to
recall in 1956 that when he told the British Ambassador in Washington,
Lord Lothian, about two Foreign Office spies, Lothian smiled in superior disbelief.) Mallet warned Jebb, 'Levine is of course a Jew and his
previous history does not predispose one in his favour, as he was
[newspaper owner William Randolph] Hearst's bear-leader to a ridiculous mission of Senators to Palestine in 1936 and a violent critic of
our policy. But . . . he seems quite genuine in his desire to see us lick
Hitler.'[34]

Cadogan asked Harker of MI5 and Vivian of SIS to investigate the
Communications Department. Vivian, with SIS's patriotic mistrust of
foreigners, thought Krivitsky sounded 'at the best a person of very
doubtful genuineness'. King stymied his questioners during his first
interrogation on 25 September, without convincing Vivian, who ended
by telling him, in the rational bromide style of such interviews, 'We
had hoped that you might be able to clear up what looks like a very
unfortunate affair, and if you can at this eleventh hour tell us anything,
it will, I think, be to everybody's advantage. I don't think you will find
us unreasonable, but it is depressing to find that you have been unable
to tell us anything, except the specific things we have asked you about.'
They detained King overnight in 'jug', to use the slang word of Cadogan,

who noted on 26 September: 'I have no doubt he is guilty – curse him – but there is absolutely no proof.'[35]

Spurred by the emphasis on national security that had followed the declaration of war on 3 September, and independently of the information received in Whitehall from Krivitsky, Parlanti approached the authorities of his own volition and volunteered his strange story of the Herne Bay train and the Buckingham Gate lease. Hooper's denunciation of Pieck was resuscitated from a moribund SIS file. Decisively 'Tar' Robertson got King drunk in the Bunch of Grapes pub at 80 Jermyn Street, rather as he had done six years earlier with Oldham at the Chequers pub a few yards away. Robertson got temporary possession of King's key-ring, which enabled MI5 colleagues to visit King's flat in Chelsea and find incriminating material. King was arrested next day. On 28 September, under what Cadogan called 'Third Degree' questioning in Wandsworth prison, he gave a full confession. MI5 witnesses at his secret trial in October were driven to the Old Bailey in cars with curtained windows to hide their identity. There were no press reports of the trial, which was kept secret for twenty years. King was sentenced to ten years' imprisonment.[36]

Harker and Vivian suspected several of King's colleagues, but had no evidence for prosecutions. The 'awful revelations of leakage' appalled Cadogan and his Foreign Secretary Lord Halifax: in December 1939 they swept all the existing staff out of the Communications Department, although most remained as King's Messengers, and installed a clean new team. Dorothy Denny and other women were appointed to the department to dilute its masculinity, and thus to moderate its office culture, although the top departmental jobs remained in male hands.

Then on 26 January 1940 SIS informed Cadogan that there had been leakages from the FO's Central Department to Germany during the preceding July and August. On 8 February Cadogan persuaded William Codrington (chairman of Nyasaland Railways and of the London-registered company that held the Buenos Aires gas supply monopoly) to accept appointment as Chief Security Officer at the Foreign Office, with the rank of Acting Assistant Under Secretary of State and direct access to the PUS. One of Will Codrington's brothers travelled across Europe for Claude Dansey's Z Organization under cover of being a film company executive.[37]

Codrington was unpaid. He had no staff until in 1944 he enlisted

Sir John Dashwood, Assistant Marshal of the Diplomatic Corps, 'the most good-natured, jolly man imaginable' in James Lees-Milne's description. Dashwood handled the security crisis at the embassy in Ankara, where the Ambassador's Albanian valet Elyesa Bazna, code-named CICERO, filched secrets and passed them to the German High Command. Codrington retired in August 1945, resumed his City direc-torships and accepted the congenial responsibilities of Lord Lieutenant of the tiny county of Rutland. It is hard to imagine that he and Dashwood scared anyone who mattered.[38]

Meanwhile Krivitsky had been summoned by the House Un-American Activities Committee (HUAC), then better known as the Dies Committee (named after its chairman, the Texan congressman Martin Dies). When he testified on 11 October 1939, naive and rude questions were pelted at him. One senator decried him as 'a phony', who ought to be deported. Krivitsky afterwards called HUAC 'ignorant cowboys' and Dies a 'shit-head'.[39]

There was a different assessment of Krivitsky in London. The star among Harker's officers was MI5's first woman officer Jane Sissmore: she had taken the surname of Archer after her recent marriage and was so precious to the Service that she had been kept in her job at a time when women civil servants were required to resign if they married so that they neither neglected their husbands nor continued to take a man's place and salary. In November 1939 Archer convinced Harker that Krivitsky should be invited to London for debriefing. Krivitsky reached Southampton in January 1940, and was installed at the Langham Hotel in Portland Place under the alias 'Mr Thomas'. Krivitsky's four weeks of debriefing was MI5's first experience of interrogating a former Soviet illegal about tradecraft, networks and names. As Brian Quinlan explains in Secret War, 'The seamless nature of the debriefing's planning and execution, the expertise and diligence of the officers who conducted it, and the quality and quantity of the information it produced have led some MI5 insiders to regard this case as the moment when MI5 came of age.'[40]

Krivitsky's trans-Atlantic journey and accommodation in the Langham Hotel were tightly managed by his English hosts, who knew that a controlled but not oppressive environment improves the prospects of counter-intelligence interrogations. The FBI had waited nine months before interviewing Krivitsky and gave little forethought to the meeting.

MI5 and SIS made meticulous preparations for his arrival at the Langham Hotel. They compiled preliminary character assessments of a kind that has since evolved and become standard operating procedure for defectors, foreign agents and foreign leaders. They exerted themselves to help Krivitsky's wife and children, who were living in Canada while US immigration issues were resolved. Archer and her colleagues sought to impress Krivitsky with their understanding, competence and judgement. As Quinlan recounts, 'their motivation was not simply pride; they understood that Krivitsky was a professional, and they hoped to gain his respect and cooperation by showing their own professionalism'.[41]

The debriefing was conducted by Archer, who was well informed about Stalin's Russia and about Soviet espionage and approached Krivitsky from an international perspective. Her first task, which took several interviews, was to reassure him that he would not be arrested if he made admissions about spying on the British Empire. She then won his respect by her expertise in his field, and encouraged his explanatory candour by listening appreciatively to his account of all that he knew or had done. During debriefing, Krivitsky described the organization, tradecraft, tactics and personalities of the Fourth Department, the NKVD and the system of legal and illegal residents in the European capitals. He spoke of forged passports, secret inks, agent-training, penetration, counter-espionage and subversion in the British Empire. He predicted that in the event of an Anglo-Russian war the CPGB would mobilize a fifth column of saboteurs. Krivitsky made clear that the Stalinist aim was to support and fund colonial liberation movements, which would bring revolutionary change in territories under imperial rule and thus accelerate revolution in the west. He expressed 'passionate hatred of Stalin', Archer reported. It was his 'burning conviction that if any freedom is to continue to exist in Europe, and the Russian people freed from endless tyranny, Stalin must be overthrown'.[42]

Krivitsky supplied new material on Oldham, Bystrolyotov, King, Pieck, Goold-Verschoyle and others. There were clues to the activities of both Maclean and Philby in his account. Krivitsky felt sure that the source of Foreign Office leaks was 'a young man, probably under thirty, an agent of Theodore MALY @ Paul HARDT, that he was recruited as a Soviet agent purely on ideological grounds, and that he took no money for the information he obtained. He was almost certainly educated at

Eton and Oxford. KRIVITSKY cannot get it out of his head that the source is a "young aristocrat", but agrees that he may have arrived at this conclusion because he thought it was only young men of the nobility who were educated at Eton.' Krivitsky imagined that since the announcement of the Nazi–Soviet pact in August 1939, 'the young man will have tried "to stop work" for he was an idealist and recruited on the basis that the only man who would fight Hitler was Stalin: that his feelings had been worked on to such an extent that he believed that in helping Russia he would be helping this country and the cause of democracy generally. Whether if he has wanted to "stop work" he is a type with sufficient moral courage to withstand the inevitable OGPU blackmail and threats of exposure KRIVITSKY cannot say.' No one connected the supposed Eton and Oxford aristocrat to Maclean, the non-Etonian, non-Oxford politician's son.[43]

Krivitsky repeatedly alluded to a young 'University man' of 'titled family', with 'plenty of money', whose surname began with P. He was 'pretty certain' that this individual was in the same milieu as the Foreign Office source. In Archer's summary of Krivitsky's remarks, Yezhov had ordered Maly to ask this young Englishman – 'a journalist of good family, an idealist and a fanatical anti-Nazi' – to murder Franco in Spain. No one had the time to connect this information to Philby, who met many of the criteria but had no titles or fortunes in his background. It is usually forgotten that at the time of the Krivitsky interrogations Philby was working as a war correspondent in France and six months away from his recruitment to SIS.[44]

Doubtless at Vivian's request, Archer omitted from her summary of Krivitsky's debriefing all reference to Hooper, who had been rewarded for informing on Pieck by being re-engaged in October 1939 by SIS. Both Vivian and his SIS colleague Felix Cowgill trusted Hooper, and did not want him incriminated. Vivian insisted that Hooper was 'a loyal Britisher'. Cowgill concurred that he was 'above everything . . . absolutely loyal'. In fact Hooper was the only man in history to work for SIS, MI5, the Abwehr and the NKVD. He was sacked from SIS in September 1945, after post-war interrogations of Abwehr officers revealed that he had worked for them until the autumn of 1939.[45]

The earliest MI5 material supplied by Blunt to Moscow in January 1941 included a full copy of Archer's account of debriefing Krivitsky. A month later Krivitsky was found dead, with his right temple shot away and a revolver beside him, in a hotel bedroom in Washington, where he was due to testify to a congressional committee. Moscow's desire for revenge must have intensified after reading all that he had said in his debriefing, but suicide is equally probable. MI5 felt a moral responsibility to give financial help to his widow. Ignace Reiss had already been ambushed near Lausanne and raked with machine-gun fire in 1937. Joseph Leppin, Bystrolyotov's courier for Oldham's material, disappeared in Switzerland in the same year. The courier Brian Goold-Verschoyle was summoned to Moscow from the Spanish civil war and never seen again. Liddell's informant Georges Agabekov vanished in 1938 – perhaps stabbed in Paris and his corpse put in a trunk that was dumped at sea, perhaps executed after interrogation in Barcelona, perhaps butchered in the Pyrenees with his remains thrown in a ravine. Theodore Maly, with his hands tied behind his back, dressed in white underclothes, kneeling on a tarpaulin, was shot in the back of the neck in a cellar at the Lubianka in 1938. Bazarov, who had been transferred from Berlin to serve as OGPU's illegal *rezident* in the USA, was recalled in the purge of 1937 and shot in 1939. Bystrolyotov was luckier than these colleagues: recalled in 1937, he was tortured and survived twenty years' hard labour in the camps (although his destitute wife and mother killed themselves). After Krivitsky's death his refugee literary agent Paul Wohl told Malcolm Cowley: 'We are broken men; the best of our generation are dead. *Nous sommes des survivants.*'[46]

George Antrobus was at home with his parents in Leamington Spa, celebrating his father's eightieth birthday on 14 November 1940, when a bomb fell on their house – dropped by a German aircraft during the night of the great aerial blitz on Coventry. Antrobus and his father were killed. In the same week Jane Archer was sacked from MI5 for insubordination. Earlier that year, at MI5's instigation, Vernon Bartlett, a diplomatic correspondent who had been elected as a Popular Front MP, tried without avail to inveigle Pieck into visiting London, where he would have been interrogated. Instead, in May 1940, Germany invaded the Netherlands, Pieck was taken into Nazi captivity and incarcerated in Buchenwald. Somehow he survived the barbarities of camp life, and resumed his design business in peacetime. In April 1950 he was induced to visit London for interview by MI5 about King. His clarifications may have contributed to a final death.

Armed with Pieck's information, MI5 reinterviewed Oldham's

ex-colleague Thomas Kemp. Kemp, whose account of his contacts with
Pieck was disingenuous, had been Lucy Oldham's confidant and may
have kept in touch with her. She had sunk towards destitution in the
1930s and spent the war years in the grime of Belfast, but in 1950 (aged
sixty-seven) was living in a drab Ealing lodging-house. Perhaps because
she was in desperate straits for money, perhaps after a tip-off from
Kemp that MI5 were reinvestigating her complicity in the old treason,
probably because both converging crises were intolerable, she drowned
herself in the River Thames at Richmond in June 1950 before MI5
resumed contact.

Despite the determination of Antrobus, Cotesworth, Eastwood and
Hay to coast through life with jokes, there was no laughter at the end.

CHAPTER 6

The Blueprint Spies

Industrial mobilization and espionage

The design of new weapons, the quantities produced, their export to foreign powers and the capacity of munitions works to expand production were subjects for the War Office's nineteenth-century Intelligence Division and for its counterparts across Europe. As early as 1865 two young men were dismissed from Armstrong's naval shipyard and armaments factory in Newcastle for copying secret plans: 'for some time past much annoyance has been felt from similar malpractices', complained a director of Armstrong's. Forty years later, when the naval shipyards at Kiel were ice-bound, Sir Trevor Dawson, the Edwardian naval ordnance director of the armaments company Vickers, skated round the docks, like a pleasure-seeker on a spree, making mental notes of what was visible. Arthur Conan Doyle's story 'The Adventure of the Bruce-Partington Plans' (1908), about secret submarine designs missing from Woolwich Arsenal, showed the increasing awareness of industrial espionage in a mechanized age. The earliest known intelligence report from SIS, issued in January 1910, concerned Vickers's German counterpart, Krupp.[1]

The crisis over the shortage of artillery shells in 1915, and general battle experiences during 1914–18, demonstrated that armaments manufacturing capacity was as important to victory as fighting manpower. 'National armies cannot even be collected without the assistance of the whole modern machinery of national industry, still less equipped,' wrote the first communist MP, Cecil L'Estrange Malone, after returning from his visit in 1919 to the Soviet Union. Russian revolutionaries knew they had to match the industrial potential of the British Empire, the USA, France and Germany, for 'without equipment on the modern scale great armies are sheep for the slaughter', Malone explained. 'The next war will be won in the workshop,' General Sir Noel ('Curly') Birch, Master General of Ordnance at the War Office turned director in charge of land armaments at Vickers, told Lord Milne, Chief of the Imperial General Staff, in 1929. 'If we are honest as a nation we must pay just as much attention to the industrial mobilisation for war as we do to our armed forces.' If the productive capacity of British armaments companies continued to be depleted, as it had been for the ten years of attempted world disarmament, Birch asked, 'where will be the force behind diplomacy?'[2]

Intelligence services exist to monitor risks. They amass, collate and analyse information covering the fluctuations of public opinion and national sentiments, they collect diplomatic and strategic secrets, they foster subversion and they practise counter-espionage; and more than ever after 1918, they have supplied industrial intelligence. The remit of British military attachés in Prague included the monitoring of the Škoda munitions works at Pilsen. In 1928 and 1929 James Marshall-Cornwall, then Military Attaché in Berlin, visited Sweden to inspect and report on the Bofors works, which had a working arrangement with Krupp as regards munitions and ordnance. Edwin ('Eddy') Boxshall, who was both SIS and Vickers representative in Bucharest, was a director with inside information on the privately owned Copşa-Mică & Cugir arsenal and the Reşiţa company, in both of which Vickers had invested. Noel Mason-MacFarlane, Military Attaché at Vienna, Budapest and Berne in 1930–4, recalled his office being besieged by inventors of warlike devices. A few were technically well versed with sound ideas: 'the vast majority of my visitors were either ignorant optimists, charlatans, or even rogues, while some gave every indication of being borderline mental cases'. He became accustomed to mysterious rendezvous with strangers wearing odd adornments – in one case being instructed to meet an intermediary at Zurich station who signalled his identity by sporting a carnation the size of a cabbage.[3]

Section VI of SIS, the economic section, was formed in 1925–6 to collect material on the manufacturing strength and adaptability of European powers. Section VI was the brainchild of a senior SIS officer, Desmond Morton, who was struck by the number of reports emanating from France about 'this new thing' called industrial mobilization, for which the Germans had already coined a word, *Wehrwirtschaft*. In 1928

the Committee of Imperial Defence formed its sub-committee on industrial intelligence in foreign countries (FCI) charged with establishing
the armaments manufacturing reserves and wartime expansion plans
of antagonistic European powers. Developments within the FCI led to
Section VI of SIS evolving in 1931 into the Industrial Intelligence Centre
(IIC) headed by Morton. The IIC made a resounding debut with its
first major report, compiled from secret sources and official publications, on Russia's preparations for wartime industrial mobilization. This
memorandum was beyond the capacity of naval or military intelligence.
'The level of detail, imparted with a peremptory authority and with a
lavish sprinkling of acronyms and Russian designations' (to quote
Morton's biographer Gill Bennett), brought an unimpeachable new
standard to British industrial intelligence-gathering and analysis.[4]

'War has now become a matter for the whole nation,' Charles de
Gaulle of the Conseil Supérieur de la Défense Nationale wrote in a
detailed survey of European plans to mobilize armaments production
in wartime. 'Politicians, soldiers, businessmen and economists increasingly proclaim the comprehensiveness of National Defence nowadays
and the necessity accordingly for preparations to utilise all the resources
of the country.' Moscow knew these truths too, and never relented in
its espionage directed against the machinery, blueprints, personnel and
order books of the munitions factories of the European powers. Its
best-known industrial spy in France was Jean Cremet, known as
L'Hermine rouge or Le petit rouquin (the Red Ermine, or the Little
Ginger). Cremet was a munitions worker whose war experiences had
converted him to trade union militancy. By 1924 he was secretary
general of the French communist party and running a spy network
specializing in munitions design and manufacturing capacity. Against
Kremlin rules, he was both a member of the local Politburo and head
of the Fourth Department's illegal rezidentura in France. When the
Sûreté shut his group down in 1927, he fled to Moscow with his two
lovers, the sisters Louise and Madeleine Clarac. After serving as the
French representative on the Comintern, he was sent to Shanghai in
1929 to organize activities in China, Japan, Korea and Indo-China; but
two years later, fearing for his survival under Stalin, he disappeared.
He was thought to be dead, but returned to Europe by circuitous routes,
took a new identity and survived in Brussels for forty years.[5]

In England Jack Hayes asked his brother Charles, a Midlands

policeman, to collect information on the Birmingham Small Arms Company's sales of weaponry to Balkan or Baltic states bordering Russia. BSA had been licensed by the Labour government in 1924 to supply 200 new Lewis guns to Russia (an order worth £20,000), but the incoming Conservative government embargoed arms exports to the Soviets and revoked the export licence in 1925. BSA had all but ceased armaments manufacture after 1918, because of the huge post-war European glut of weaponry; but it operated as the War Office's agent to sell surplus rifles and machine guns. Charles Hayes was instructed to monitor these exports. In the mid-1920s another investigator tied to the Vigilance network, David Ramsay, used the cover of a travelling salesman of office accessories to visit armaments factories, including those of Vickers and Hadfield at Sheffield, to obtain confidential information and blueprints on war-material construction. He was equipped with a miniature photostat machine. Usually he took his material direct to the Soviet mission, Chesham House, from whence it went in the diplomatic bag to Moscow.[6]

The ARCOS raid of 1927 intensified the Bolshevik's pre-existent siege mentality. At the May Day rally in Hyde Park a few months later, one CPGB activist, Charles Moody, a council dustman, made an inflammatory speech advocating propaganda among transport workers and merchant seamen to prevent troops and munitions from being sent abroad in the event of war. Moscow's fear that British shipments of munitions to Estonia and other Baltic states presaged a London-concerted attack on the Soviet Union resulted in a recently converted young communist, Wilfred Macartney, approaching a shifty marine insurance underwriter named George Monkland for information on the value of such shipments. Macartney was the son of an electrical engineer who had made a fortune installing tramways in Malta. His boyhood was spent in the Levant, Panama and other exotic locations. In Odessa in 1905, aged six, he was traumatized when, as a result of officious blundering, his mother was seized before his eyes by tsarist policemen and carried off for interrogation as a suspected spy. He inherited about £70,000 in adolescence, but lost his fortune to swindlers, partly because he was always 'one over the eight' and in a state of reckless, drunken elation. He paid income tax of £8,000 in 1923 but was penniless by 1925, when two fervid CPGB recruiters got hold of him. 'Communism became Macartney's religion,' wrote Compton

Mackenzie, who had once employed him in secret service work in Greece; but he continued to consort with share-pushers, confidence tricksters and cat burglars, and in 1926 was jailed after an inept smash-and-grab raid on a Mayfair jeweller's shop.[7]

After his release from Wormwood Scrubs prison, Macartney made his approach to Monkland, who took fright when inquiries about insurance cover for armaments shipments were succeeded by a detailed technical questionnaire about Royal Air Force aircraft. Monkland scurried to the former Director of Naval Intelligence 'Blinker' Hall, who passed him to SIS – not to MI5. 'Throughout the summer of 1927 Macartney was buzzing about between London, Paris and Berlin, writing idiotic letters to Mr. Monkland, all of which the Intelligence Department had photographed by the Post Office in transit,' as Mackenzie noted. SIS watched but remained inactive until November, when a young German named Georg Hansen came to London. Two or three days later, without any attempt to discover Hansen's contacts or intentions, SIS had him and Macartney arrested at their first rendez-vous at Hampstead tube station. As Mackenzie commented, 'either Hansen was an unimportant supernumerary in a trivial affair or the British Intelligence authorities displayed an inexplicable neglect in their manner of dealing with him'. Their clumsy impatience was in contrast to MI5's handling of the Vigilance detectives.[8]

Western capital-intensive manufacturing became more than ever a communist target after the inauguration in 1928 of the Five Year Plan, which made industrialization central to the self-induced modernization crisis of the Soviet Union. 'The whole country is machine mad,' reported Sir Esmond Ovey soon after reaching Moscow as British Ambassador following the restoration of Anglo-Soviet diplomatic relations by the incoming Labour government in 1929. A Birmingham audience would not, he thought, be as enthused as 'primitive and simple-minded' Muscovites were by a documentary film showing hundreds of whirring wheels: 'in the machine the Communist enthusiast sees the future salvation of humanity'. Ovey was not hostile to the Soviets, whom he admired for pursuing 'the greatest industrial experiment ever tried by mankind'. Defeatists were 'reprimanded out of political existence', he reported; for 'Marxism is a religion to the Russian Communists,' and no leniency could be afforded to doubters.[9]

Propaganda against armaments manufacturers

As early as 1926, speaking in a parliamentary debate on the Royal Navy, a Labour MP, Hugh Dalton, had declared: 'directors of armament firms are the highest and completest embodiment of capitalist morality'. In the era of Five Year Plans, similar sentiments were used by communists and their allies to campaign against the munitions makers whose research and development expertise and reserve productive capacity were essential for rearmament. *The Secret International* (1932) and *Patriotism Ltd* (1933) by Dorothy Woodman of the Union of Democratic Control, *The Bloody Traffic* (1933) by Fenner Brockway of the War Resisters' International and polemics by the communists J. T. Walton Newbold and Harry Pollitt were part of a heavy propaganda assault. The Labour Research Department's *Who's Who in Arms* (1935), published in a blood-red cover adorned with a black skull, argued that 'dominant capitalist groups' were the arch-manipulators behind the warmongering armaments firms. As the finance director of Vickers remarked in 1935, 'the motive of the attack on the armaments firms is an attempt to get at the banks and financial houses'.[10]

The campaign against armourers entered popular culture. The villain of Graham Greene's *A Gun for Sale* (1936) is a venomous munitions manufacturer called Sir Marcus, 'a very old and very sick man with a little wisp of white beard on his chin like chicken fluff', who is trying to engineer a European war. 'He gave the impression that very many cities had rubbed him smooth. If there was a touch of Jerusalem, there was also a touch of St James's, if of Vienna or some Central European ghetto, there were also marks of the most exclusive clubs in Cannes.' Similarly, in Leslie Charteris's thriller *Prelude for War* (1938), the machinations of Kane Luker, the aptly named financial kingpin of the Merchants of Death, are defeated by the all-action hero Simon Templar ('the Saint'). Christina Stead, in perhaps the best-informed novel about hot money ever written, *The House of All Nations* (1938), depicts armaments manufacturers as 'apaches of commercial life, profiteers of war, rapine, and fratricidal slaughter'.[11]

In Washington Senator Gerald Nye led a Special Senate Committee of Investigation into the Munitions Industry during 1934–6. 'Mr. Nye is undoubtedly on the make,' the British embassy in Washington reported in 1935. His committee's wild innuendoes about warmongering by bankers, profiteering by manufacturers and European ruling-class duplicity had made front-page headlines. The senators, reported the British Ambassador, 'overshot themselves in pursuit of the macabre, and a discreditable amount of loose talk was allowed, the names of prominent persons . . . being bandied about with incredible levity'. A few years later Isaiah Berlin, then posted to the British embassy in Washington, described Nye as 'a notorious fire-eating Anglophobe isolationist'. The Nye Committee's legal assistant, Alger Hiss, was a member of an underground communist cell in Washington. In 1934 the US Ambassador in Berlin, William Dodd (whose daughter Martha @ LIZA and son William @ BOY @ PRESIDENT were Soviet agents between 1934 and 1949) urged London to emulate Washington by setting up a Nye committee to expose the corrupt warmongering of arms manufacturers. Peter Rhodes, an American communist studying at the University of Oxford, urged fellow undergraduates to form study groups on the revelations of the Nye inquiry, 'with the avowed aim of studying the root causes of war, so that the attack [on rearmament] may be directed sanely and efficiently'.[12]

The Baldwin government capitulated to this clamour by appointing the Royal Commission on the Private Manufacture of Armaments in 1935. The commissioners investigated allegations that capitalists fomented war, suborned civil servants, negated national sovereignty and defiled international politics. The preparation of testimony to the Commission and its prolonged deliberations during 1935–6 were a damaging distraction for both Whitehall and the private companies when the need for rearmament was becoming urgent. In May 1935 the pre-war alliance between France and tsarist Russia was revived by a Franco-Soviet treaty of mutual assistance if either nation was attacked by any European power. Although the pact contained no military protocols, Germany felt more ominously encircled than at any time since 1917. In March 1936 Hitler used the Franco-Soviet pact as a pretext for repudiating German obligations under the Locarno treaties and for reoccupying the Rhineland with troops. This was the moment when France might have arrested the Nazi advance by confronting the militarization of the Rhineland. Instead its Popular Front government shrank from military action, but nationalized its private armaments sector. All this at a time when Hitler was (in his own words) arousing in Germany 'the spirit of proud self-assertion, manly defiance and

passionate hate', and igniting a 'blazing sea of flame from which would
. . . rise one cry: "WE WANT ARMS AGAIN!"'[13]

MI5 watch Wilfrid Vernon

In 1932 MI5's deep informant within the CPGB, Graham Pollard,
reported that a party of staff from the Royal Aircraft Establishment
(RAE) at Farnborough – the Air Ministry's research and experimental
works – was to pay a summer visit to Russia. The RAE tourists included
a draughtsman and technical officer, Wilfrid Vernon. The Security
Service took little further interest in him until 1934, when he organized
hospitality for the communist-led National Unemployed Workers
Movement's protesting Hunger Marchers as they proceeded towards
Aldershot. An MI5 informant codenamed HOPS, who had infiltrated
local left-wing study-groups, was set on him. Vernon liked talking, and
soon became frank in his confidences to HOPS. Vernon was distributing
Russia To-day, *Moscow News* and the *Daily Worker* within the RAE and
among RAF personnel when he could. 'I take four copies of the "Daily
Worker" to the office every day,' he told HOPS. 'We spread the "Daily
Worker" on the Mess Table, and discuss the King, munitions manufacturers and "Robber Barons" etc., and raise argument. A few
disapprove, but we are gradually getting a number over to our way of
thinking.'[14]

Vernon supported communist-front bodies such as the League
against Imperialism and the Relief Committee for Victims of German
Fascism. Background checks showed him to have been born in 1882
in the lower-middle-class London district of Stroud Green, Hornsey.
His father's work as an editorial clerk in a publishing office qualified
him for a reasonable education at the Stationers Company School in
Hornsey Vale. His early employers included the Siemens electrical
combine and the Bristol Aeroplane Company. During the first war he
joined the Royal Naval Air Force as an engineer officer, learnt to fly,
worked on the development of flying-boats and served in RAF headquarters during 1919. He was demobilized with the rank of major, RAF,
and continued to use his military title in civilian life until his death.
He joined the Aircraft Inspection Department of the Air Ministry in
1924, and was transferred a year later to the RAE.

Major Vernon lived in a glade in the middle of a wood in Farnham, sleeping during warmer months in a tent by a pretty pond and retreating in winter to a bungalow-hut constructed of asbestos sheeting on a wooden frame. In socialist study circles and at self-help clubs for the unemployed he advocated workers' power and revolutionary overthrow of the bourgeoisie. One of his RAE colleagues, who was in the group that visited Russia in 1932, was an Ulsterman called Edward Calvert. Their political views diverged and their friendship ruptured in the mid-1930s. 'VERNON was a hale, red-faced, tweedy individual and looked rather like a country gentleman,' an MI5 officer summarized Calvert as saying during an interview in 1952. 'He used this impression to good effect when he was engaged in propaganda work.' Vernon did not forgive Calvert for telling him, 'the trouble with you is that you have not got the surface markings of a snake in the grass'.[15]

After the fascist violence against the Vienna socialists in February 1934, a refugee named Gessner came to live with Vernon. Immediately after the Nazi murder of the Austrian Chancellor Engelbert Dollfuss in July 1934, Gessner determined to make a hurried, clandestine return to Vienna with the Major's help (apparently travelling in the side-car of the Major's motorbike). As the latter recounted in a lantern-slide lecture to the Friends of the Soviet Union at Aldershot later that year, 'We thought it would be easier if the Party contained two Englishmen to back our Austrian friend and bustle the frontier officials, so "George" and I fixed our Austrian friend up with a Trinity College tie, English cut grey suit, cap, and glare glasses, and called him "Toby". "Toby" speaks excellent English and it was all very easy.' 'Tar' Robertson of MI5 attended a similar lecture given by Vernon at Woking: he thought his target was hard-faced, untrustworthy, a poor public speaker, but mild rather than vindictive.[16]

In 1935 the Chief Superintendent at Farnborough addressed all the RAE departments with a remonstrance against political conversations in office hours. 'He blamed the youngsters recently down from colleges with degrees, etc., imagining that they knew so much more than the older hands and trying to run the show,' Vernon told HOPS. 'Of course, it is not the youngsters; they are too full of science and technical cramming to have any room for politics yet.' Gaining confidence, the Major persuaded a young soldier named Thomas Ford to distribute seditious literature and collect names of communist sympathizers in the Royal Army Medical Corps. Ford was given the codename RIVER. When after several months Ford became conscience-stricken, Vernon (fearing that the youth might denounce him to the authorities) persuaded him to desert and gave him the money to take refuge in the Irish Free State. Ford seems then to have volunteered as a gunman for the Irish Republican Army.[17]

In 1936 the Major began supplying aircraft blueprints and other official secrets to Ernst Weiss @ David Lock and to an agent known to MI5 only as HARRY II. Vernon seems to have been secondary in the value of his purloined material to another RAE official, Frederick Meredith, who was introduced to Weiss by that scourge of munitions companies Dorothy Woodman. Ford meanwhile fell in with a group of Blackshirts – that is, adherents of Sir Oswald Mosley's British Union of Fascists – whom he enraged with tales of Vernon's sedition. In August 1937 Ford and three Blackshirts broke into the asbestos bungalow, ransacked it and stole books, political pamphlets, correspondence and documents in the hope of incriminating him as a subversive. They also took money, cutlery, a watch and a telescope. Their burglary was spotted by a neighbouring farmer, and their getaway car, with its fascist flag on the windscreen, was stopped by police at Staines. It was found to contain a wood-chopper, a knuckle-duster, a dummy revolver and a stash of Vernon's belongings.

In these higgledy-piggledy papers the police found a blueprint of the Hawker Horsley single-engine torpedo bomber (an obsolete wooden machine that was no longer used by the RAF), pencil notes on the thoroughly up-to-date Avro Anson aircraft, information on aircraft performance and assessments of anti-aircraft equipment apparently prepared for anti-war propaganda. There were also receipts from Harry Pollitt of the CPGB, and lists of contacts. Vernon told HOPS that the Blackshirts, who were prosecuted for their burglary in September, were a blind to misdirect attention from the 'Whitehall authorities' who had instigated the burglary. This seems unlikely. The trial of Ford and his fascist associates had undoubted peculiarities: prosecuting and defence barristers seem to have worked in tandem; the defending counsel was rough in cross-examining Vernon about his communist sympathies; the prosecutor announced just before the jury retired that 'certain documents' had been discovered in the stolen stash – 'I need not say anything more than that, but I think it is right to say that there was a discovery made of some importance that has not been referred to here.'

This mysterious and prejudicial remark may have helped the four burglars to avoid imprisonment: they received the lenient sentence of being bound over to keep the peace for twelve months.[18]

This was a lighter penalty than that imposed on Vernon when, in October, he was tried under the Official Secrets Act on a specimen charge of having retained official information (by keeping pencilled notes on bomb-dropping exercises), and another of not taking due care of documents. These charges were light, because the authorities had no wish to make a drama of the case. Denis Pritt was briefed to defend Vernon, who was fined a total of £50. This conviction enabled the RAE to dismiss him from the civil service, which was the chief purpose of prosecuting him. *The Strange Case of Major Vernon*, a pamphlet published by the National Council for Civil Liberties, argued that he had been the victim of injustice engineered by Whitehall mystery-men. In fact Vernon continued helping Weiss and Meredith in their aviation spy network until the Nazi–Soviet pact of 1939.

The foe of armaments manufacturers and industrial preparedness Fenner Brockway, who spent his early manhood imprisoned in the dungeons of the Tower of London, Chester Castle and Lincoln Castle's isolation wing, ended in the House of Lords; Vernon was elected as Labour MP for Dulwich in 1945; Hiss became Director of the State Department's Office of Special Political Affairs; but Percy Glading, England's equivalent of Cremet, party activist and industrial spy, was condemned to penal servitude and spent his old age in the inglorious recesses of the London suburbs.

MI5 watch Percy Glading

Glading was born in Wanstead, Essex in 1893. His father was then a railway labourer. After a boyhood in Henniker Road, Stratford, he worked as a grinder in the Royal Ordnance Factories at Woolwich until 1918. In 1921 he was employed as an engineer by the Belfast shipyard of Harland & Wolff, but thereafter had spells of unemployment. He was known to MI5 by 1925, when he was best man at Harry Pollitt's wedding and travelled as the earliest CPGB courier to India using the alias of Cochrane. There he met the activists who later figured in the Meerut conspiracy trial of 1929, which centred on plans to start Comintern operations in India. After his return, Glading rejoined Woolwich as an examiner in the naval ordnance department. Research, design and testing remained significant functions there, although Woolwich's limited productive capacity made it obsolete as a national arsenal according to the new doctrines of total wartime mobilization. His dismissal from Woolwich in 1928, on account of his revolutionary beliefs, was the occasion for the CPGB to issue an indignant manifesto denouncing capitalist exploitation and praising class war.[19]

Sabotage was one of Moscow's interests. The Soviets' paranoia about foreign saboteurs was partly a projection of their own plans for their western enemies. In 1924 a company called Russian Oil Products Ltd was registered in London. All of its shareholders were Russian subjects. Ostensibly it was to act as a trading organization, but it collected technical, scientific and commercial intelligence for Moscow: in one case in 1932 an employee of ROP's Bristol branch – Iosif Wolfovich Volodarsky using the alias of Olsen – posed as a Romanian journalist and was fined for offering bribes to staff at Shell Mex House in the Strand in return for confidential data on the petroleum business. (Volodarsky subsequently moved to Canada, where he was known as Armand Feldman, and helped Soviet illegals to obtain false Canadian passports.) The activities of ROP were monitored by MI5 and Special Branch. By 1930 ROP had a network of thirty-three offices, installations and depots which were being operated at an estimated loss of up to £390,000 a year. MI5 feared that if Britain went to war with the Soviet Union, ROP lorry tankers filled with petrol would be detonated at fuel storage depots and munitions works. It was also apprehensive that ROP ship tankers might be exploded at British ports.

ROP laundered money as well as preparing for large-scale sabotage. After the ARCOS raid in 1927, Moscow's cash subsidies for communist organizations in Britain had to be funnelled through the London branch of the Moscow Narodny Bank. They were then distributed by Thomas Quelch, whose father had provided work-space in his Clerkenwell print-shop for Lenin during the latter's exile in London, and by Frank Priestley; both men were employed by the Soviets' London-based trading company known as Centrosoyus (the Central Union of Consumers' Co-operative Societies). Quelch and Priestley were dismissed from Centrosoyus in 1928 as scapegoats when the money-laundering was under investigation by Special Branch, but soon had new jobs at ROP. MI5 believed that from 1929 cash from Moscow was collected from Soviet oil tankers, after they had docked at ROP port storage depots, by Richard ('Dick') Beech. Beech's cash haul was then distributed by Priestley, Quelch and a Scotsman, Alec Squair. (Before joining ROP, Beech had been twice torpedoed in the Atlantic, fought with the Red Army in the Russian civil war, served as a Soviet spy-saboteur in Finland and as a Comintern courier, and worked at ARCOS. His father-in-law was James Connolly, the Irish republican executed in 1916.)[20]

Glading, after his dismissal from Woolwich, became an employee of ROP. He was one of about 1,000 staff, of whom approximately one-third were (like him) members of CPGB. He combined the three leading traits that Moscow thought promising in a potential undercover source: idealism, vanity and greed. In 1929 he was elected to the London party's Politburo and went to Moscow to study at the Lenin School under the alias of James Brownlie. After returning to London in 1930, he was given a cover job in the CPGB's colonial department. There was nothing stealthy about his allegiance. He became an officer in the League against Imperialism, alongside Brockway, and an activist in the Anti-War Movement. Installed in offices on the top floor of 23 Great Ormond Street, he served as a conduit between ROP and the CPGB, and worked for the illegals as a cut-out obtaining military intelligence which was funnelled to Moscow.

In 1933 Eric Holt-Wilson, by now Kell's Deputy Director at MI5, prepared a memorandum on 'Seditious and Revolutionary Incitements to Public Violence' about such insidious threats as ROP. 'Not all of our enemies work in the light of day. Those . . . most dangerous to our public security and peace today are doing evil work in the dark.' It exasperated him that these hidden adversaries, while working to break the English legal system, exploited English laws for their personal protection. 'In this free land of ours in recent years we have been permitting the growth of the most sinister organisation for evil the world has ever seen. An organisation with . . . one object and one only: the forcible destruction, at first by secret methods and then by open methods, of our liberty, our constitution, our laws, our religion and our heritage.' The conspirators' intent was, Holt-Wilson warned, 'that we shall be subjected to the tyranny of a powerful alien body which has never enjoyed our freedom or any freedom, and is determined that we shall enjoy it no longer'.[21]

One such plotter was Glading, who was kept under observation. On

a Sunday evening in July 1936 he was seen loitering at Cambridge
Circus on the edge of Soho until he was joined by Charles Moody. Part
of MI5's file on Moody was burnt when a German bomb set fire to the
Service's archives stored in Wormwood Scrubs prison, so his significance
can only be surmised. He had been dismissed in 1920 from a job with
Richmond Council as a communist. After his reinstatement, he drove
a lorry emptying rubbish bins, was communist nominee to the Trades
Union Congress in 1927 and sat on the executive committee of the
CPGB in 1930, but thereafter went undercover. SIS reported to MI5 in
1933 that Moody was a CPGB member charged with weakening the
armed forces in south-east England. He had five or six party members
answerable to him, SIS believed, and had been provided with a car and
money for petrol to make night-time visits to Chatham, Aldershot,
Portsmouth and Southampton, where he threw subversive literature
over barracks walls.

The purpose of Glading's meeting with Moody is unknown. They
went to a Charing Cross Road newsreel cinema, where they probably
heard reports about the deadlock between Britain, France, Italy, Russia
and Turkey at the Montreux naval conference on access to the Black
Sea, and about a speech at Southampton by the First Lord of the
Admiralty, Sir Samuel Hoare, on the urgent need for rearmament. 'The
Bolsheviks in Russia have embarked upon an armament programme
in comparison with which ours is a mere bagatelle,' declared Hoare. 'As
our life depends upon free passage through the seven seas, the Fleet
must be strong enough to go anywhere.' Hoare deplored socialist leaders
voting against rearmament: 'this miserable, this inconsequent, this
improvident attitude shows how far the Labour Party has drifted from
reality'. From the cinema Glading and Moody repaired to a public house
in Glasshouse Street, no doubt to discuss the implicit threats to Soviet
security being revealed at Montreux and Southampton.[22]

Glading prospered during the 1930s, as many people living in south-
east England did. He bought a salubrious, newly built house in Warwick
Avenue, South Harrow. There were Crittall windows, front and back
gardens, instalment-plan furniture, a neat porch. It was part of a development of semi-detached houses for quiet, respectable bourgeois, which
had been built when the Piccadilly railway extension to South Harrow
brought the area within commuting distance of central London in 1932.
Although Glading is usually seen as an ideologue, the comforts of his

existence suggest that he prospered from his Moscow connections. The comment by Sir Anthony Hawke, the judge at his trial, that he had been money-motivated may not be completely awry.

At this point the duo of Maxwell Knight and Olga Gray must be introduced. Knight was a former sports master at a preparatory school, a former jazz clarinettist, an ex-member of the British Fascists and failed manager of a hotel on Exmoor. The discovery by Special Branch that Knight, whom it employed, was also being used by SIS to run a small network of domestic informants had resulted in an inter-departmental storm and the repromulgation in 1931 of the rule that all domestic intelligence work was reserved for MI5 and must not be encroached upon by SIS. Knight was a Pied Piper figure who exerted almost mesmeric charm over wild creatures (he lived in a small flat with a fascist bride named Gwladys, a mongoose named Rikkitikki, a sherry-drinking bush baby named Pookie and a wheezing bulldog named Fattie). He studied the kinks of human nature with the keenness that he afforded to the responses of wild animals. After 1931 he became MI5's best agent-runner. Unlike many of his colleagues, he had faith in women agents.

Olga Gray was a young secretary in the Automobile Association office in Birmingham. There was little remarkable about her, except that she had been treated with savagery by her long-dead father, who had been night-editor of the northern edition of the *Daily Mail*, and she had in consequence been an unruly schoolgirl. 'I say, old thing, have you ever thought of working for the secret service?' she was asked by a woman called Dolly Pyle while playing clock golf in Birmingham in 1931. 'Gosh, Doll, that sounds jolly exciting, I'd love to,' she replied without realizing that Pyle's question was in earnest. She was contacted by Knight, whose preferred strategy for infiltrating a penetration agent into a subversive body was to put the agent in a place where the target body would make the first recruitment approach.[23]

Knight induced Gray to move to London, where she worked as a secretary, joined Ealing Ladies' Hockey Club, attended meetings of Comintern front organizations, volunteered as a typist for the Friends of the Soviet Union, and waited. In time Knight's strategy succeeded. Gray was approached to do paid secretarial work at the League against Imperialism, where she achieved the enviable position for a penetration agent, said Knight, of being as unremarkable as a piece of furniture. In 1934 she was sent on a mission to India carrying funds and instructions for Indian communists. Next year she became Pollitt's personal secretary at CPGB headquarters, but found the strain of her double life too much and withdrew from secret work. She had the less nerve-racking job of advertising agency typist when in 1937 she telephoned Knight to report that Glading had asked her to arrange a safe-house for communist meetings. She took a flat in her own name at 82 Holland Road in April 1937. The rent of £100 a year was paid by the CPGB. Holland Road was a busy, dingy traffic artery running north from Kensington High Street. In a fit of depression Lord Loughborough had defenestrated himself from a bedroom there a few years earlier. Lord Lee of Fareham, a poor man until as Military Attaché in Washington he had married a New York banker's daughter, had lived in the next street, which he called an 'unromantic neighbourhood'.[24]

After Gray had been installed at 82 Holland Road, Glading brought a foreigner called 'Mr Peters' to vet her. 'Mr Peters' then arranged for a Viennese-born photographer and London talent scout for Moscow, Edith Tudor-Hart, to provide the flat with a Leica camera to photograph secret material. Gray reported that 'Peters' had a bumptious colleague, whom Glading disliked. Krivitsky, during his debriefing by Jane Archer at the Langham Hotel three years later, identified these two men as Theodore Maly and Arnold Deutsch.

Deutsch, who had been born in 1904, had a PhD in chemistry from the University of Vienna, but psychology was his primary interest. He was a votary of the Vienna sexologist and communist Wilhelm Reich, who sought to integrate Freudianism with Marxism and outraged Austrian Catholics by opening advisory clinics offering contraception, sexual enlightenment and erotic pleasure to Vienna's proletariat. Deutsch believed that sexual and political repression were intertwined. He described himself at university as a practising Jew to mask the fact that communism was his true faith. He envisioned humanity as freed from capitalist exploitation and bourgeois sexual ethics, both of which were (he felt sure) historically doomed. In 1932 he left Vienna for Moscow, where he was assigned to the Comintern's international department and trained as a secret agent.

Two years later, in 1934, Deutsch reached London as an illegal under the cover of an academic researching psychology at the University of London. He moved among radical theorists, and took Flat 7 in the newly opened Isokon Building in Hampstead's Lawn Road with his

Sir Robert Vansittart was the first head of the Foreign Office to give his full trust to intelligence material.

Cecil L'Estrange Malone, Leninist MP for Leyton East, was later an agent of influence for imperial Japan.

Jack Hayes, the MP whose Vigilance Detective Agency was manned by aggrieved ex-policemen who spied for Moscow.

MI5's agent M/1, Graham Pollard, may have been first cultivated at a Putney school sports event.

Agent M/12, Olga Gray, was first approached while playing clock golf at a Birmingham garden party.

Percy Glading, leader of the Woolwich Arsenal and Holland Road spy ring, which M/12 penetrated for Knight.

Wilfrid Vernon, the MP who filched aviation secrets for Stalinist Russia and admired Maoist China.

The Cambridge economist Maurice Dobb was a dedicated communist proselytizer among undergraduates of the 1930s.

'A. Blunt was the life and soul of the party,' said Lytton Strachey, who took this snap of a boating party on the River Ouse in 1930.

Moscow's talent-scout Edith Tudor-Hart first spotted
Philby's potential, and later worked with Glading.

Cambridge spies and MI5 officers alike endured the Blitz in London. This scene in Pall Mall is yards from the Athenaeum, Reform and Travellers clubs, of which the Cambridge quintet were members.

Andrew Cohen was a pre-war Oxford communist who later came under Peter Wright's indiscriminate suspicion. Here, as Governor of Uganda, he shares a dais with the Kabaka of Buganda.

Philby's early associate Peter Smolka, who (as Peter Smollett) worked for Moscow in the wartime Ministry of Information.

wife Josefine, a Comintern-trained wireless operator. The architect of the Isokon Building, Wells Coates, was defiantly anti-bourgeois: 'that idea of property – so much of this little garden is for you, m'dear, and this tweeny little wishy bit is for me, so there! – is dead, dead, dead. It's that idea which makes peoples, nations, set up borders, and put troops on them, and forts too, and makes wars between nations.' The building was designed as a prototype for high-quality proletarian dwellings, as pioneered in Vienna. Early tenants included the Bauhaus refugees Walter Gropius, László Moholy-Nagy and Marcel Breuer; Agatha Christie; Nicholas Monsarrat; and Henry Moore. Other residents were communists involved in espionage: Jürgen Kuczynski, who recruited the atomic spy Klaus Fuchs; Andrew Rothstein; and Eva Reckitt, Moscow's money-launderer in London. For four years Deutsch worked as a London illegal under the aliases of STEPHAN, LANG, ARNOLD and above all OTTO. He looked people straight in the eye, made them feel important and was shrewdly humorous.[25]

Glading subsequently introduced Gray to 'Mr and Mrs Stevens'. 'Stevens' was the alias of a member of the NKVD's scientific and technical section, Mikhail Borovoy @ Abraham Hoffman @ Willy Brandes, who had recently arrived in London using a false Canadian passport. His cover was that he was London agent of the Phantome Red Cosmetics Company of New York. He was accompanied by his wife Mary, who was supposedly a photographer for the Charak Furniture Company and was handy with the Leica camera which Edith Tudor-Hart had supplied. In London Maly and his wife (whom Moscow had coerced him to marry in order to restrain his drunken bouts), posing as Paul and Lydia Hardt, lived at 8 Wallace Court, 300 Marylebone Road. A few minutes' walk away 'Mr and Mrs Stevens' occupied 31 Forset Court, 140 Edgware Road.[26]

Harry Hunter, Ottaway's successor as head of MI5's surveillance section B6, allotted his two best watchers, named Hutchie and Long, to follow and report on visitors to 82 Holland Road. Glading brought secret documents and blueprints, which had been filched overnight from Woolwich Arsenal, to be photographed in Holland Road before the originals were smuggled back into the arsenal next morning. He sometimes stored illicit material in a safe-house at Finchley belonging to Melita ('Letty') Norwood, the secretary to the director of research at the Euston headquarters of an armaments sector supplier called the British Non-Ferrous Metals Research Association.

Norwood had been born in Bournemouth in 1912, the daughter of an exiled Russian revolutionary called Sernis. She studied Latin and logic at the University of Southampton, and was politicized after visiting Heidelberg in the early 1930s. Living with her mother and sister at 173 Hendon Way (a house similar in style to Glading's in Harrow), she went on Friday evenings and Saturday mornings with Hilary Nussbaum, a chemistry student at North London Polytechnic, to tout the *Labour Leader* and the communist *Daily Worker* outside Golders Green station. Nussbaum introduced her to Andrew Rothstein, who was then forming a scientific and technical intelligence network which had the Non-Ferrous Metals Research Association as one of its targets. In 1934, at a discussion of collective farms held by the Friends of the Soviet Union in Finchley, Melita Sernis approached Rothstein with an offer to supply secret material from BNFMRA. She and Nussbaum joined the CPGB in 1935, and married two months later after Nussbaum had changed his surname to Norwood.

Stalin wanted battleships with heavy guns to establish Soviet Russia as a naval super-power with an intimidating ocean fleet. In an epoch before atomic bombs, battleships symbolized world power for him; but although Soviet shipyards had the capacity to build shipyard hulls, they were forced to import armour plate and heavy guns. The Washington and London disarmament treaties of 1922 and 1930 had set a maximum of 13 inches on naval guns, but Germany, Japan and Italy began to break this settlement after Hitler's ascent to power in 1933. In order to evade the tonnage restrictions which limited the size of warships, German naval constructors substituted welding for riveting when building new vessels. This gave them battle-cruisers, with the capacities of battleships and the tonnage of cruisers, which could fire 14-inch shells without breaching the terms of the London treaty. The Russians had been dogged by fears of naval disaster ever since Japan's pre-emptive strike at Port Arthur in 1904. They were determined that other naval powers, especially Germany and the British Empire, should not steal an advantage. Accordingly they laid meticulous plans for Deutsch, Maly and Borovoy to obtain blueprints of the latest technology on 14-inch guns for the Royal Navy.

On 21 October 1937 'Mrs Stevens' arrived at 82 Holland Road with the 14-inch naval gun mounting plans. Only five copies of the plan existed: Woolwich had received its copy only a few days earlier; Glading was both well informed about its arrival and prompt in obtaining it. 'Mrs Stevens' photographed the blueprint in sections requiring forty-two exposures. Gray brewed a pot of tea while the films were hung in the bathroom to dry. At 10.35 p.m. 'Mrs Stevens' left Holland Road with the plan secreted in a bundle of rolled-up newspapers. MI5 watchers tracked her to Hyde Park Corner, where she met her husband and George Whomack, a gun examiner at Woolwich Arsenal, to whom she returned the plan. Whomack had smuggled it past the guards at the end of his evening shift some hours earlier, and was to return it the following morning. Next evening, on 22 October, Glading collected the naval gun mounting negatives from Holland Road.

MI5 decided to delay the arrest of Glading and his network until they had finished tracing all its tentacles. Hunter's watchers were present at Victoria station on 6 November when 'Mr and Mrs Stevens' boarded the boat train. They did not stop them, or search their luggage which probably contained the copied plans for the 14-inch gun. (Some espionage historians have pounced on the failure to detain or search the illegals involved with Glading: their criticisms rest on factual errors or retrospective wisdom; the allegation that Borovoy was warned or protected by MI5's Guy Liddell is absurd.)[27]

Five months earlier Gray had reported a drunken visit by Glading to Holland Road. He was probably upset because Edith Tudor-Hart had lost a diary which Deutsch had given her for safe-keeping together with a folder containing his itemized expenses, including payment to agents. Subsequently Tudor-Hart found the folder secreted beneath the cushions of her sofa. But after this alarm Moscow considered the network compromised: Deutsch was accordingly recalled as a security measure. Stalin's purges were under way, and Borovoy was summoned in the same month for liquidation. Finally Maly was ordered to return to Moscow, where he was shot for Trotskyism. Such horrors seemed remote to Glading. 'These blokes', he told Gray by way of explanation for the disappearances from Holland Road, 'live on a volcano the whole time they are over here, and when they do go home you do not know if they will ever come back.'[28]

Much of what civilians describe as leadership qualities is simply masculine vanity. 'Most persons set themselves a part and overplay it,' as Vansittart said. Glading found it hard to relinquish his leading role in the Woolwich shadow-play. He did not accept that in obtaining the naval gun mounting plans he had accomplished all that Moscow wanted of him. In November, when Deutsch and Borovoy left for Moscow, he received instructions from the CPGB to sever his connections with the 'secret' party (that is, to cease underground activities) and to resume open party activism. Instead, he began a solo spying spree. He decided, without authority, to use his contacts to obtain more material from Woolwich Arsenal. Some years later the French resistance organizer Pierre ('Guillain') de Bénouville wrote a memorandum listing the fatal temptations for a secret agent. 'He is keyed up and treats himself too well . . . He believes that he is important, and hates to be utterly obscure.' These were the failings of Glading, who objected to receding into obscurity and wanted to show his sponsors what he could achieve by himself.[29]

Glading did not last long. Acting on information from Gray, he was arrested at Charing Cross station on 21 January 1938, while a Woolwich employee, Albert Williams, was handing him a brown-paper package. This parcel contained blueprints of a pressure bar apparatus for testing the detonators of anti-submarine bombs. Williams was arrested with Glading, and Whomack shortly afterwards. All of Moscow's illegals who were relevant to the case had left London months before: none could be detained, questioned or involved in court proceedings. This met the desires of the Chamberlain government, which wanted nothing to exacerbate Anglo-Soviet relations at a time of mounting Nazi pugnacity. That government did not want the Woolwich spy case to turn into a rerun of the ARCOS raid of 1927, when Russians had been expelled and diplomatic relations had been severed between London and Moscow. At a time when Hitler was courting a general European war, an outright breach in March 1938 would have been destructive.

The trial of Glading

At their committal proceedings on 29 January, Glading, Williams and Whomack pleaded not guilty. Olga Gray testified under the soubriquet of 'Miss X'. There was not as much melodrama as at the trial in 1927 of Wilfred Macartney and Georg Hansen, when the Attorney General, Sir Douglas Hogg, had asked Major General Charles Bonham Carter of the War Office if reading aloud exhibits of evidence in open court would be 'prejudicial to the safety of the court'. The General replied

with categorical absurdity, 'Yes, certainly,' whereupon Lord Chief Justice
Hewart ruled that the case should be heard in camera. The intention
in 1927, thought Compton Mackenzie, was 'to make the flesh of the
public creep by letting down the black curtain of *in camera*', and to
impress the public with the notion that 'nothing except the vigilance
and acumen of a Secret Service, [and] the devotion and patriotism of
a Conservative Cabinet' had saved the nation from being overrun by
Reds. Politicians 'would not hesitate to work up popular feeling by
staging political trials *in camera*', continued Mackenzie, 'and the
spoon-fed public would presumably accept such an attack on liberty'.[30]

Glading, Williams and Whomack probably thought themselves lucky
when the CPGB arranged for two eminent barristers, Denis Pritt and
Dudley Collard, to be briefed for their defence. In fact both lawyers
were happy to subordinate justice to party needs. Pritt was a staunch
admirer of the Soviet legal and penal systems, in which (as he had
reported in 1932) cells were decorated with flowers and labour camps
provided 'the quiet encouragement to reform that comes from decent
surroundings'.[31]

Collard had been born in 1907, in Chestnut Grove, New Malden, a
middle-class commuter suburb: his father was a managing clerk in a
wool warehouse and scraped the money to send him for a board-
ing-school education at Cheltenham College. Collard provided legal
advice to ROP, the front company for Soviet saboteurs, in 1932; he
represented the Union of Democratic Control in anti-capitalist testimony to the Royal Commission on the Private Manufacture of
Armaments in 1935; and was an appreciative tourist in the Soviet Union
in 1933, 1936 and 1937. After this last visit he had written (for the Left
Book Club) a volume entitled *Soviet Justice and the Trial of Radek*. 'To
assert that Stalin finds it necessary to bump anyone off, besides betraying
complete ignorance of conditions in the Soviet Union, is in my view a
malicious slander,' he averred. Some defendants in the Moscow trials
were 'mere gangsters': others 'through their lack of confidence in the
creative power of the working class, [were] genuinely apprehensive of
the policy that was being adopted, and started engaging in sabotage
and terrorism'. After an 'eloquent appeal' by that model prosecutor
Vyshinsky for death sentences for those guilty of these 'appalling crimes',
'there was enthusiastic applause for about two minutes', which for
Collard clinched the impeccable justice of the trials. Collard had a

'one-track mind on political subjects', according to Maxwell Knight's undercover informant M/7. M/7 was the MI5 designation of Vivian Hancock-Nunn, legal adviser and libel reader of the *Daily Worker*, who was thoroughly trusted by Collard and the CPGB despite being a scion of Tory squires. 'An utterly ambitious man who sees himself as a legal leader under some socialist regime', reported Hancock-Nunn in 1938, 'COLLARD is very obviously extremely jealous of D. N. PRITT.'[32]

The Attorney General, Sir Donald Somervell, who led for the Crown in the Woolwich case, was a Conservative MP and member of the Chamberlain government. He had reflected in his journal a year earlier: 'In our curious & admirable system the prosecution very often helps the defence.' He was describing his pre-trial arrangements in the case of the Security Service informant George McMahon @ Jerome Bannigan, who had pulled a loaded revolver on King Edward VIII as he rode down Constitution Hill and claimed to have been instigated by German Nazis. Somervell, who thought that the defendant was more a communist, suggested to defence counsel in private conference 'that we might leave the foreign power unnamed', and undertook in return that he would not probe McMahon's story in cross-examination.[33]

Similarly, Somervell discussed the Woolwich case before trial with Collard and Pritt, who gave Glading, Whomack and Williams instructions from the CPGB to rescind their pleas of not guilty, and to plead guilty when they reached the Old Bailey. This was at Moscow's behest to avoid publicity about their espionage. Disclosures in court were minimized so as to reduce this risk. The trial on 14 March took only a few hours. There were addresses from counsel, and questions from the judge, Sir Anthony Hawke, but none of the defendants uttered a word in their own defence. Because of the guilty pleas, it was unnecessary to hear any evidence in court. After the men had been sentenced, Collard told Hancock-Nunn that he and Pritt had bargained with Somervell over the guilty pleas and were relieved that Somervell 'had refrained from bringing in the Communist Party as such'; he added that 'the Party are exceedingly thankful that the Moscow aspect was kept fairly dark'. All sides wished to protect the susceptibilities of Stalin's Russia.[34]

In addressing the court, Somervell listed Glading as the chief instigator, Williams next in culpability and Whomack third. The prosecution did not compromise secret sources by revealing that Whomack had been put under surveillance by Special Branch in 1927, when he was chairman of Bexley communist party, or that his denial to Woolwich Arsenal authorities in 1929 that he was a communist had been discounted at the time by MI5. Somervell's speech concentrated on the material supplied to Glading by Williams, although these documents were not classified as secret, and indeed had not been sought by Moscow. The only classified secret document had been the naval gun mounting plan which had been photographed by 'Mrs Stevens' on her Leica. It could have been proved that the supplier of the blueprint, Whomack, had had direct dealings with her and her husband, who were obvious foreign agents. Yet, in answer to a direct question from the judge, Somervell stated that the naval gun was less important or secret than the pressure bar apparatus. This absolute misdirection was intended to dupe court reporters. Pritt assured the court that the defendants' actions were 'almost ludicrously unimportant'.[35]

Mr Justice Hawke was the senior judge of the King's Bench Division, a former Conservative MP and trusted with delicate cases. It was in his court at Ipswich Assizes two years earlier that Mrs Wallis Simpson had been granted the divorce that prefigured King Edward VIII's abdication (Stalin at the time wondered why she was not liquidated: as a law officer Somervell had worked to limit the repercussions of that court hearing). Hawke believed in differentiating between right and wrong, and in public service. It was not humbug, but a sincere expression of the values of their generation, when Lord Caldecote, the Lord Chancellor in Chamberlain's Cabinet, said of Hawke: 'No mere technicality appealed to him if it stood in the way of justice, and he sought at all times to carry out his duties in the sight of God and of men.'[36]

Hawke followed Somervell in minimizing the truthful technicalities. Both men underplayed the Moscow connection and the communist affiliations of Glading and Whomack, which were the factors that Pritt and Collard had been briefed to suppress too. In sentencing Glading to six years' imprisonment Hawke said: 'I am satisfied that this was done with the sole and vulgar motive of obtaining money.' The monetary pickings of his work for Moscow were welcome to Glading, but he had begun as an ideologue in the 1920s and had found fulfilling self-importance in his secretive wire-pulling during the 1930s. When sentencing Williams to four years Hawke declared, 'I do not see a great deal of difference between you and Glading. You obviously made great preparations to help him, and took a greater part in the matter than the other man in the dock.' Whomack was a worse culprit than Williams, but received a sentence of three years. 'You are the only one about whom I feel in difficulty, having regard to the comparatively small part you took in this case,' Hawke told him. The light sentences given to Glading, Williams and Whomack may have been rewards for pleading guilty, and thus keeping the secrets of Moscow and London from revelation in open court. Newspaper readers received an inaccurate sense of Glading's activities. Journalists were steered so that their reports avoided public accusations of Russian involvement.[37]

Investigations into the network continued. Special Branch officers visited Edith Tudor-Hart in June asking about the Leica camera which she had left at Holland Road. But MI5 had only twenty-six officers in 1938, and was too stretched to discover the illegals' connections to Melita Norwood or to the Cambridge penetration agents. Jane Archer visited Glading in Maidstone prison in October 1939, pursuing information from the Soviet defector Walter Krivitsky about agents in Whitehall run by Maly. 'When interviewed Glading was rather stuffy at first but gradually, under a good deal of flattery, his own conceit got the better of him,' noted Liddell. 'He did not say anything very useful.'[38]

As to Somervell, he admired Neville Chamberlain ('He can build up a bomb-proof argumentative structure with no fuss') and remained staunch in upholding his government's appeasement of Nazi Germany. When Chamberlain flew to Munich in September 1938 in an attempt to prolong peace with Hitler, Somervell was one of millions of British applauders. He was not forgiven for this by Churchill who, when forming his first peacetime Cabinet in 1951, defied expectations and did not appoint him to the supreme legal post of Lord Chancellor. Somervell took this grumpy retribution with crisp stoicism, and said a true thing: 'Better to be a man of Munich than a man of Yalta.'[39]

PART TWO

Asking for Trouble

Chapter 7

The Little Clans

School influences stronger than parental examples

'England', wrote Sir David Kelly, who was British Ambassador in Moscow in the year that Burgess and Maclean absconded, was the only country in the world in which 'the privileged classes asked of a young man not, "Who was his father?" but "Where was he at?"' Boarding schools placed a boy more definitively than his paternity. They were intended to be character-building: they institutionalized their pupils' loyalties, they sought to harden boys' feelings and to minimize the softening influences of home. The answer to the question 'Where was he at?' told the exact means whereby the boy's temperament had been disciplined and remade. When the teenaged Julian Amery went to Spain as a nationalist sympathizer in 1938, and jumping into a ditch to escape gunfire found himself crouched beside an effete-looking youth in the uniform of a monarchist volunteer, he greeted the stranger in French, German and Spanish without getting any response. Then the young officer amazed him by saying: 'Kemp. Wellington and Trinity. How d'you do?' Amery replied: 'How d'you do? Amery. Eton and Balliol.' They did not think of parents or family status: they did not say, 'Peter Kemp, my father is Legal Adviser at the India Office, we live in Wimbledon' or 'Julian Amery, my father is Secretary of State for India, we live in Eaton Square.'[1]

The conventional wisdom about the formative influences on the Cambridge traitors needs adjustment. Blunt, Burgess, Maclean and Philby grew to maturity surrounded by a Stonehenge circle of frowning, stony faces: headmasters, housemasters, clergymen and family solicitors. These non-parental elders shaped the youths' priorities, choices and resolve. Institutional influences – the boarding schools in which three of the quartet lived from the age of seven – counted for more than home in developing their characters. It was a commonplace that pupils should be hardened at school if they were to achieve anything memorable. The Victorians had, after all, redevised the English public schools to breed men who, as Cardinal Manning told the Irish, 'have made England what it is, – able to subdue the earth'. As Derek Walker-Smith, afterwards a Conservative government minister and Lord Broxbourne, ex-pupil at a Victorian-foundation school called Rossall, said in 1931, the public schools were 'based on the assumption that anything sufficiently unpleasant is sure to be good for a boy'.[2]

Each year boys isolated together at these boarding schools formed little clans. There were distinct fraternities for athletes, swots, clowns, duffers, arty types, devout Christians and those who knew themselves to be irredeemably average. The clansmen made defensive pacts together, scorned other clans and were primed for pre-emptive aggression. Fellow clansmen avoided solemn exchanges of innermost thoughts, recalled David Footman of SIS, who attended Marlborough a few years before Anthony Blunt; 'but we liked each other, we were allies, united in our impatience of the nonsense that seemed to make so much of school life'. All children are susceptible to the influence of their school-fellows: none more so than teenagers, and few teenagers more than English public schoolboys of the 1920s.[3]

The disappearance of Burgess and Maclean aroused a storm of publicity in 1951. Their reappearance in 1956, and accusations about the treachery of Philby, renewed the commotion. These squalls broke over an epoch when Marx and Freud were the two totems of the western intelligentsia. The Marxist misdirection reduced all explanations to class struggle and class guilt. The Freudian misdirection, in which the treachery of four of the Cambridge ring of five was infantilized by interpretations based on supposed familial psychodramas, stemmed from a painful historical context. Nazi ideology had categorized people by their bloodlines and family stock, and used imaginary racial traits as the justification for genocide. As a reaction, the western intelligentsia after 1945 preferred to explain human character and to understand adult choices according to psychological theories about parental nurturing, childhood environment, feelings and emotions. More than ever, in the 1960s, when American and west European students were rebelling against their parents, the treason of Burgess, Maclean and

Philby (for Blunt remained publicly unidentified until 1979) was attributed to defects in their parental upbringing. Family dynamics from half a century earlier were imagined and interpreted by commentators who were uninhibited by the fact that they had never met any of the family concerned.

The litterateur Cyril Connolly belonged to a generation that treated Freudianism as a faith. 'Politics begins in the nursery; no one is born patriotic or unpatriotic, right-wing or left-wing,' he asserted in 1952 in his pamphlet about Burgess and Maclean. 'It is the child whose craving for love is unsatisfied, whose desire for power is thwarted or whose innate sense of justice is warped that eventually may try to become a revolutionary or a dictator.' The subversive rebellion of the Cambridge spies expressed their hostility to their early paternal experiences, Connolly affirmed: 'Before we can hurt the fatherland, we must hate the father.'[4]

Fantasies about hateful fathers and fables of nursery politics more than ever clouded understanding after the intervention in 1968 of David Cornwell, who after serving in both MI5 and SIS had taken the pen-name John le Carré. It was under this fictive identity that he contributed a prefatory essay for a pioneering biography by *Sunday Times* journalists, *Philby: The Spy Who Betrayed a Generation*. Burgess and Maclean are 'psychiatric misfits' in le Carré's depiction (ten years later Andrew Boyle followed le Carré's misdirection, and with reductive inaccuracy entitled the chapter in *The Climate of Treason* on the boyhoods of Burgess, Maclean and Philby 'The Young Misfits'). Among other suppositions, le Carré wrote of Philby's father, who spent most of his working life abroad: 'Kim loved the absent parent best; and even though he had marked down the parent authority of England as his lifelong enemy, Kim Philby never quite absolved it from its parental duty to protect.' In le Carré's view, Philby used women 'as a consolation for a manhood haunted by his father's ghost. When they came too close, he punished them or sent them away, either as unsatisfactory mother-figures or as the spent instruments of his expression.' Philby's four wives and serial mistresses, le Carré continued, were always secondary to the symbolic woman to whom he gave most: 'Mother Russia was the boy's absolute.' Such fancies were shared by Leo Abse, who arranged for his fellow Labour MP Will Owen to receive immunity from prosecution in return for undergoing MI5 interrogation about

his spying for communist Czechoslovakia. Abse attended the questioning, and knew the extent of his colleague's avarice, but nevertheless
gave an absurd explanation that treachery was a version of incest: 'Owen
certainly did his puny best to rape his motherland.'[5]

The ideas of Connolly, Abse and their ilk are obsolete, but their
baneful influence persists. We now understand that DNA is as influential in character-formation as parenting. It has, for example, been
evident since 1993 that chromosomes have a stronger influence in
creating a disposition towards male homosexuality than psychoanalytical notions about aloof fathers or suffocating mothers. Yet writers
continue to fret over the remoteness of the fathers of Blunt, Burgess
and Maclean, as if most English fathers of the 1920s were not aloof
and inexpressive by twenty-first-century standards. More cruelly, they
indict – sometimes with harsh misogyny – the spies' mothers for various
contradictory defects: possessiveness, indifference, coddling, neglect,
over-indulgence, lack of sympathy.

Undeniably parents are formative influences on their children.
Miranda Carter in her biography of Blunt depicts his parents as 'pious,
austere, fiercely teetotal, anti-gambling and keen on charitable works'.
Blunt, she says, was a dutiful son, who imbibed their missionary zeal
for good causes, which he diverted from Christianity to Marxism.
Maclean's upbringing in a frugal, teetotal and Sabbatarian household
disposed him, judged his friend and biographer Robert Cecil, to substitute the *Communist Manifesto* for the Bible as holy writ. Such judgements
are tenable; but to exceed the evidence by attributing the mainsprings
of treachery to parental influence seems banal and suppositional. The
assertions of Connolly and le Carré cannot be proved, and prove
nothing.[6]

Debased Freudian interpretations have not been imposed upon the
fifth Cambridge spy, John Cairncross @ MOLIÈRE. He was born in
1913, in a cottage at Lesmahagow, a small town in Lanarkshire where
his father was an ironmonger. His mother had been a schoolteacher.
There is no reason, other than their relative poverty, why Cairncross's
parents have been protected from the punishing hypotheses levelled at
the Blunt, Burgess, Maclean and Philby parents. Arnold Deutsch, the
illegal in London who engineered Cairncross's recruitment in 1937,
wrote a psychological profile of him: 'MOLIÈRE comes from a Scottish
lower-middle-class family – religious people who because of the diffi-

cult life they lead are very hard-working . . . He is pedantic, industrious, zealous and thrifty. He knows the value of money and how to handle it.' A taxi-ride with Deutsch had been the first time in his life that he had travelled by motor-cab. Deutsch found him 'naïve and rather provincial', but 'very trusting'.[7]

To reiterate, Philby was a well-travelled married man of twenty-two, with recent experience of revolutionary street-fighting, when in 1934 he was enlisted as a penetration agent by Deutsch on a bench in the Regent's Park. Burgess was a worldly adventurer of twenty-three when Deutsch recruited him six months later. Blunt was in his thirtieth year when in 1937 Burgess introduced him to Deutsch, who recruited him as a Comintern talent-spotter. Cairncross was twenty-three when on Blunt's recommendation he was taken to meet Deutsch. Only Maclean could be thought callow, having turned twenty-one at about the time that he was enrolled. The ring of five took adult decisions, in an adult environment. It infantilizes the significance of their ideas, their acts and their consequences to treat them as programmed by defective parenting.

Kim Philby at Westminster

Philby was born in the Punjab on 1 January 1912. He was given the forenames Harold Adrian Russell, but was universally known as Kim. He was the only son and eldest child of St John Philby, then an official in the Indian civil service. St John had obtained a first-class degree in modern languages at Trinity College, Cambridge, where he spent an extra year studying Hindustani, Persian and Indian civil law before going to India in 1908. Valentine Vivian, the Indian Army officer who became chief of MI6's Section V, met St John Philby at this time. 'As a bullet-headed young Assistant Commissioner in Shahpur in the Punjab, he was singularly devoid of manners and always up against his superiors,' Vivian reported to Guy Liddell in 1940. 'He was strongly self-opinionated and expressed himself, often extremely capably and accurately, with such arrogance that no one had a good word for him.' He was not unlike his irrepressibly vain cousin Bernard Montgomery, later a field marshal and the victorious commander at the battle of Alamein, who was best man at his wedding in 1910 to Dora Johnston. Her father was a railway engineer in the Indian Public Works Department.[8]

May Philby, Kim's paternal grandmother, had been deserted by her drunken Ceylon coffee-planter husband, and averted poverty by opening a boarding-house in the military town of Camberley. She travelled from England to the Punjab in order to attend her grandchild's birth. Although she returned to Surrey during his infancy, she was installed as the primary figure in his boyhood when in 1915 he was sent to live with her at Camberley. One of her three sons had been killed at Ypres in 1914, and another was killed there in 1916. She brought up her grandson from the age of three, provided his home, felt consoled by his presence and had a closer influence than his parents.

Kim Philby saw little of his father in 1912–15, and nothing of him from 1915 until 1919. In 1921 the father succeeded T. E. Lawrence as chief British representative in Transjordan, and immediately proved cantankerous: as Reader Bullard, the British Consul in Jeddah, said, 'Any scheme that someone else puts up he disagrees with. His great phrase is, "I join issue with you", and he spends his life joining issue with someone.' In 1923 May Philby took her eleven-year-old grandson to visit Damascus, Baalbek, Tyre, Nazareth and Jerusalem with his father. It was only on this trip, and during the year that St John Philby spent in London after resigning as High Commissioner in Transjordan in 1924, that he had the possibility of exerting direct influence on his son. His resignation was ostensibly on a point of principle, but Bullard computed that it left him with an annual pension of £700 when his age was not yet forty.[9]

With the security of a pension St John Philby bought his first home in England, at 18 Acol Road, in what was euphemistically called West Hampstead although it bordered the far eastern reaches of Kilburn. This was a humdrum middling district: its one distinction was a bridge club where the world-famous Acol bidding conventions were devised. Kim Philby continued to spend much time at Crossways, his grandmother's villa in Middle Gordon Road, Camberley. The ordinariness of these houses and the shortage of ready money make nonsense of historians of espionage who write, as Oleg Tsarev and John Costello did, 'He hailed from a background of privilege and was schooled in the establishment of Britain's ruling class,' before adducing as supporting evidence that in Moscow he enjoyed Worcestershire sauce and *The Times* crossword.[10]

In boyhood Philby had a convulsive stammer which blocked any

tendency to his father's fatal vehemence. He spent five years at a preparatory school near Eastbourne before election as a King's Scholar at
Westminster School in 1924, when he was aged only twelve. The school
had been founded by Queen Elizabeth I in 1560 in buildings which
had been the monastery of Westminster before the Reformation. It
abutted Westminster Abbey, and was across the road from the Palace
of Westminster. With only about 360 pupils, two-thirds of whom were
day-boys, it was an atypical public school: most of the boarders returned
home at weekends to families living, like Philby's, in the London conurbation. In competitive sports, academic results and social cachet the
school was not in the top bracket with Eton, Winchester and Harrow,
but in the next grade with Charterhouse, Rugby and Shrewsbury. Its
ethos was not barbaric. Ian ('Tim') Milne, Philby's contemporary,
remembered its urbanity. 'There was room for a hundred flowers, if
not to bloom, at least not to be trampled on. Eccentrics were prized,
particularly if they made you laugh.' There was minimal bullying: 'the
small boys tended to take advantage of this by taunting the larger ones,
as a puppy might an Alsatian'.[11]

As a King's Scholar, Philby will have received preliminary instructions
before reaching Westminster. These included the rules for wearing the
five stipulated types of headgear (mortarboard, top hat, trilby for week-
ends, straw boater and sports cap of green and blue). School slang had
to be memorized: King's Scholars were tested on arrival, and threatened
with a beating if they did not know that 'greaze' meant crowd or scrum,
'shagged' meant tired, and 'pitch' meant apprehensive. All male servants
were addressed as 'John', and all female servants (regardless of age) as
'nymph'. Masters' nicknames had to be learnt by rote too: Chuff, Preedy,
Coot, Cissy, Puppy, Poon, Tubby, Beaker. One annual school tradition
was the 'pancake greaze' on Shrove Tuesday, when a cook tossed a
pancake high over a beam in the Monk's Dormitory, and the boy who
emerged from the brawl with the biggest piece of pancake was rewarded
with Maundy money (coins specially minted for the monarch to use
as alms). The King's Scholars had a more lethal ceremony, 'Declams',
in which four tables were piled atop one another: each junior boy had
to clamber to the top of this tottering edifice and there declaim a four-
line Latin epigram of his own composition while being pelted with
tennis balls. Shortly after Philby left Westminster, 'pancake greaze' and
'Declams' were abolished as too violent.[12]

Philby was a polite, neat, private, self-reliant, fastidious pupil. He won school prizes and scored high marks without cutting a figure in the school. His enthusiasms were for Beethoven, Arsenal football club and Tallulah Bankhead. Milne, who was caned only once at Westminster, doubted if Philby ever was. Philby was not forced to join the Officer Training Corps (OTC) or to play sports in his final year (previously he had boxed for the school, and fielded at cricket: 'I wish I could report that his regular position there was third man, but I think he was more usually to be found at deep extra cover,' recalled Milne). The lurid tale that at school Philby had 'buggered and been buggered' is a nasty invention. Overall he had scant reason for resentment. When he fled to Russia in 1963, he left his wife in Beirut but took his Westminster scarf with him. Nor did the school repudiate Philby entirely: when a new boarding-house was founded in 1997, pupils were consulted about which famous Old Boy should be commemorated in its name. Many voted for Philby: the school authorities however preferred the name of Milne's House, after Tim Milne's uncle A. A. Milne, the creator of *Winnie the Pooh*.[13]

Attendance was compulsory for daily morning prayers in Westminster Abbey and two services on Sunday: Philby, like other pupils, will have sat through up to 1,500 services during his time at the school. The sermons by the headmaster, the Reverend Harold Costley-White, were remembered as 'foggy and elliptical'. In his sing-song voice, Costley-White accentuated syllables in an arbitrary way in the forlorn hope of making his commonplaces sound pensive and sincere. His mellifluous remarks were often thoughtless contradictions. When asked about the Book of Kings, he replied: 'It *is amazi*ngly interesting, my friends, and perhaps what you *might* call extre*me*ly boring.' Compulsory chapel attendance was the rule at all similar schools during this period, although it receded in Cambridge colleges during the 1920s (partly because, with the rise in student numbers, few college chapels were large enough to accommodate all members of the college).[14]

The future philosopher of aesthetics Richard Wollheim and the future diplomat Brian Urquhart, who were King's Scholars at Westminster in the mid-1930s, recalled the opportunities for bracing political discussions: debates in the back seats of the coach taking them to football, in which Peter Ustinov, son of the MI5 agent known as 'Klop', and Rudolf von Ribbentrop, son of the Nazi Ambassador in London, disputed the justice of the treaty of Brest-Litovsk. Anti-militarist pupils formed a school society, the United Front of Progressive Forces, known as Uffpuff. Rudolf von Ribbentrop used to be driven to school every morning in a plum-coloured Mercedes-Benz limousine. On arrival, the chauffeur would alight, give the Nazi salute and shout 'Heil Hitler!' as he strutted through the medieval arch into Little Dean's Yard. Urquhart organized an ever-swelling group of boys who gathered each morning to laugh and jeer. The German embassy protested to Costley-White, who summoned Urquhart and said he would be expelled for 'insults to a friendly power'. Urquhart saved himself by remembering the head-master's talent for missing the point. He told Costley-White that the Mercedes-Benz was plum-coloured (plum being the colour reserved in England for the royal family's Daimlers). 'My dear boy,' the headmaster replied, 'why didn't you tell me this before?' The diplomatic protest was rejected, and Ribbentrop was told to arrive at school on foot.[15]

Political activism was unknown in the Westminster School of Philby's time, although there were many lessons in the power games of adult-hood. The masters, like their pupils, were embroiled in feuds, jealousies, alliances and stratagems. Wollheim recalled John Bowle interrupting a history lesson when he saw the French master walking outside in the yard. 'There goes Claridge,' he said, as he opened the mullioned class-room window. 'Spit whenever you see him, boys, like this!' And Bowle expectorated across Little Dean's Yard. Bowle's political hero was Frederick II, the thirteenth-century Holy Roman Emperor who was excommunicated by the Pope. Philby may have absorbed his taste for excommunicants from Bowle.[16]

Mutual antipathy flourished between Philby and the Reverend Kenneth Luce, who was housemaster of the King's Scholars. Admirers thought Luce was a fine earnest Christian, while his detractors sneered at his sanctimony. Philby evaded confirmation by telling Luce that he had not been baptized. He cannot have been impervious to the annual Armistice Day ceremony when the King's Scholars gathered at the Tomb of the Unknown Soldier. But he was always indifferent to beauties of English landscape and architecture: the Abbey seemed a remnant of Gothic barbarity, and the services like the entrails of disembowelled superstition. Dreary, complacent preaching made him receptive to Marx's view that Christianity was a futile sham which upheld class privilege. A quarter of a century after leaving Westminster, when Philby had children of his own, he showed an invincible hostility to them learning the abracadabra of religious dogma.[17]

English Christianity after 1918 had the spiritual equivalent of a vitamin deficiency: parishioners were numbed in their reflexes, and enfeebled in belief. Ninety thousand people panting for the kick-off at the Wembley cup final might sing 'I need Thy presence every passing hour', but they did not mean it. Churchgoing declined. There were 28 million baptized, 8 million confirmed and 2.75 million communicant members of the Church of England in 1927. Baldwin was the only inter-war Prime Minister with conventional religious faith. Lloyd George and Bonar Law were agnostics, Chamberlain was a Unitarian and MacDonald belonged to the Union of Ethical Societies. 'As we move away from the War, we are able to see its real magnitude', reflected Hensley Henson, the Bishop of Durham, on Armistice Day of 1922. 'What a full-flowing spring of malediction it was! All our present perplexities seem to run back to it. We are at our wit's end [sic] to know how to regain the positions from which it swept us . . . the War has given the *coup de grâce* to the Church of England.'[18]

Fewer people found the Incarnation and the Resurrection credible. 'We shall never get over Christianity, yet not two in a hundred of my acquaintances thought a future life worth discussing', Vansittart recalled of 'the early post-Christian era' of the 1920s. Polite agnosticism characterized the decade as much as muscular Christianity or evangelicalism had been the orthodoxy of previous generations. 'Sin' became a joke-word for many. Hell and theories of eternal punishment were dismissed as inventions to frighten people into behaving well. Prophecies and miracles were treated as if they were fungoid hallucinations. 'Our Lord Jesus Christ' became merely the supreme example of a good man. This change in attitude was as momentous as any event in English history since the conversion of the Anglo-Saxons to Christianity. It resulted from the convergence of several influences: eighteenth-century scepticism; nineteenth-century Darwinism; disbelief in the verbal inspiration of the Bible; a new materialism which discredited ideals of personal service; and the bellicosity of many clerics during the 1914–18 war which seemed to deny the gospel of the Prince of Peace.[19]

Equal to all these influences was the blatancy of Christian sexual hypocrisy. How else can one explain the success of two bestsellers of 1921, Robert Keable's novel *Simon Called Peter* and Somerset Maugham's

story 'Rain'? Keable was a Cambridge graduate who had resigned holy
orders to write his autobiographical novel. It describes a prudish army
chaplain who loses his faith in the carnage of trench warfare, visits a
brothel and eventually goes to bed with a nurse who gives renewed
meaning to his life. The book sold 600,000 copies during the 1920s,
and had over sixty reprints. Arthur Winnington-Ingram, the peevish
Bishop of London, prevented its dramatization on stage in 1925. The
novel 'scandalised the clergy' by depicting a fornicating parson questioning his faith, and devalued 'all we have ever taught about
self-control [and] chastity', the Bishop complained to the theatrical
censors. He imagined taking friends to see a production: 'any nice girl
would, I think, be sick at seeing any man and a woman emerge from
the bedroom where they had spent the night, in their night-dresses'.
Comparably, Maugham's 'Rain' offers an unforgiving picture of what
was to become a stock type, a sexually repressed, punitive Protestant
clergyman. In this case, a self-deluding vicar cuts his own throat after
raping the prostitute whom he has been persecuting with callous moral-
izing. The story resonated with readers, for it inspired three Hollywood
film versions between 1928 and 1953, with Gloria Swanson, Joan
Crawford and Rita Hayworth cast as Sadie Thompson.[20]

If clergy in the pulpit had preached against cant, national pride,
social injustice, economic disparity and backward thinking they would
have done their duty better than in urging submission to the status
quo. They fussed about 'necking' in shadowy 'cinema palaces' or fulminated over mixed swimming in the Serpentine, but from the great issues
of the time they fled. The puritans ensured that Sunday in every town
and city, even London, resembled a neat and hushed cemetery, in which
one met only flitting ghosts. The prudery was such that Wollheim was
threatened with expulsion from Westminster after he had painted the
naked breasts of women in watercolours for an art competition: the
trigger for righteous rebuke was the ink dots at the centre of the breasts;
these scant acknowledgements of nipples could only excite hateful
salacity, groused the headmaster. The efforts at sex education of the
muscular Christian who in 1929 succeeded Luce as housemaster of the
King's Scholars were touchingly inept. 'I say, fellows,' he would say after
evening prayers, 'are you troubled by dirty thoughts?' Hearty public
school chaplains keeping a straight bat in the pulpit bored dull pupils
and infuriated the clever boys. 'Religion played little part in our lives,

and the average sermon in chapel was stuff for ribald comment,' recalled David Footman. In 1936 he published a novel about a soldier with the Victoria Cross who becomes a confidence trickster because of the post-war spiritual dearth: the tragedy of bishops and schoolmasters, Footman felt, was that they lacked the moral courage to give a better lead.[21]

After his London furlough year of 1924, St John Philby settled at the port of Jeddah, where he held the local sales agencies for Marconi, Unilever and the Ford motor company. In 1930 he converted to Islam as a way of ingratiating himself as an unofficial adviser to the king, Ibn Saud. His real religion, judged Reader Bullard, was 'a simple dualism in which the spirit of darkness is represented by His Majesty's Government'. By 1940 Ibn Saud recognized that the scorn which Philby heaped on British war efforts against Hitler was 'mentally deranged'. Lord Lloyd told Harker that Philby was 'a brilliant lunatic', Sir Alexander Cadogan thought him 'a crank', and Guy Liddell, having been advised by a diplomat that Philby was 'a nasty piece of work', summarized the FO view as: 'in Mr Philby's world there is only Mr Philby. Loyalty and disloyalty are only words to him.'[22]

An otherwise helpful biography published in 1973 opens with the declaration: 'Kim Philby grew up in a climate of moral arrogance which armour-plated him for life against the assaults of doubts.' Its authors claim that his every major adult decision 'betrays the imprint of the father'. St John's rumbustiousness overshadowed 'the childhood of his gentle-natured son, and it is questionable whether Kim ever fully emerged from it'. The months in 1924 between twelve-year-old Kim's departure from his Eastbourne school and his arrival at Westminster were 'a summer of intense indoctrination', they wrote. 'St John took this promising child and pumped him full of his special brand of self-righteousness,' which was the making of a traitor.[23]

These assertions are wrong. Any paternal influence was spasmodic and remote. The spiritual vacuum of the 1920s influenced Philby's mentality more than the rowdy nonconformity of his father. He was not a pliable character who could be stamped with someone else's impression. As an adult he enjoyed deceit. A successful betrayal gratified him. He liked covert work, arcane influence and equivocation. In all this he was the opposite of his father, who never shied away from truth-telling in its most aggressive, open, implacable and arrogant forms.

The older man relished publicity, courted controversy and sprang head-long into confrontation. The younger man's undercover life was the antithesis.

Donald Maclean at Gresham's

The second of the Cambridge spies, Donald Maclean, was born in May 1913. He was the third of four sons of Donald Maclean, a Cardiff solicitor who had been secretary of the city's Chamber of Commerce before his election as a Liberal MP in 1906. The records of the Registrar General provide social statistics to place – in general and limited terms – the Philby, Maclean and other families of the Cambridge spies. The sealed files of the Inland Revenue yield none of the more significant data on their money. The distinctions of attitudes and prospects between the hereditary ruling orders, the gentry, the official and officer classes, the learned classes of lawyers and clergy, the expanding professional classes, and the varieties of business families were sharp and at variance with one another. It is bad enough to blur them, but worse to forget that these semi-defunct conventions were a less vital force than family income, which was what kept both individuals and families alive. To give total attention to class stratification when assessing the Cambridge spies is like trying to understand foxes by studying a dead mask and brush hung on a wall as a trophy. To understand the living creatures one must go to a fox's den and spy on the vixen sheltering, feeding and frolicking at home with her cubs.

Maclean's boyhood home was at 6 Southwick Place close to Paddington station. It was a better address than Acol Road, but unfash-ionably north of Hyde Park. 'Paddington wasn't smart, but the street had an independent air,' the youngest Maclean son, Alan, recalled. The father served temporarily as leader of the parliamentary Liberal party in 1919–20, after a general election in which most of its frontbench leaders had lost their parliamentary seats. There was not a single ex-Cabinet minister available to take the post, which went by default to Sir Donald Maclean. He could neither dominate nor inspire colleagues, but he kept liberalism alive in parliament during the hectic illiberal opportunism of the Lloyd George premiership. Opponents recognized that he was dutiful and plucky: his manners were unassuming but a trifle smug. Robert Vansittart called him 'prosaic'. He died of a heart attack, induced by overwork as Minister of Education in the National Government, in 1932. The newly widowed Lady Maclean opened a jolly little shop called the Bee in Church Walk, a winding alley off Kensington High Street. There she sold pretty and comfortable wool garments made by amateur knitters, and stylish straw hats, and had a hundred different jigsaw puzzles which customers could borrow like books from a lending library. Donald Maclean helped to scrub and redecorate the Bee before its opening.[24]

In 1926 Maclean went as a pupil to Gresham's School at Holt, on the Norfolk coast. This was a school with rare liberal credentials. Science had priority on the curriculum; Greek was ignored; there was minimal fagging and beating; there were neither privileges for senior boys nor colourful caps to distinguish successful games-players; few bounds were set on pupils roaming outside the school grounds. Gresham's headmaster James Eccles was a prude who bustled about the school in a pompous way carrying an armful of books. He interviewed every pupil after his arrival, adjured each of them to promise to avoid indecency or swearing, and to report any other boy who transgressed. Pupils resented this system of informants and developed an easy facility in evading surveillance.

What was the public school code which nature's rebels strove to defy or subvert? Governors, headmasters and housemasters saw the task of these boarding schools as preparing boys for the hierarchies of adult life. Pupils were trained to obey rules without complaint. Sir John Masterman, a crucial figure in MI5 during the 1940s, recalled of his Edwardian boyhood: 'My own school-days were not mournful, for I shunned eccentricities – indeed I was almost obsessively anxious to conform to expected standards and to do the right thing.' A housemaster at Eton, writing a reference in 1919 for his pupil Arthur Reade, whose adult life was to be dogged by the suspicions of MI5, gave him 'a perfectly honest testimonial of moral character' but warned of unamenable opinions. 'Here he was not popular among his fellows, for he was undoubtedly a prig, crude in his views and more than crude in his readiness to air them. And they were not the views that recommended themselves to conservative schoolboys. He thought it his business and privilege to be a "free-thinker" in the midst of a society that thought, if at all, in fetters.'[25]

If loyal conformity to school rules conduced to group satisfaction,

individual self-assertion did not. The imaginative vitality of a few inspirational schoolmasters enriched their pupils' lives, but the majority
were sententious men who kept anxious control of their pupils by virtue
of a regime based on mindless regulations and violence. Few boys were
fools, especially about the pointless school ideal of manliness isolated
from sexual activity. Pupils could look solemn, and mock inwardly, at
schoolmasters whose idea of sex education was to tell pupils: 'If a man
takes a man into a corner of the room and talks to a man, a man
shouldn't listen.'[26]

Maclean's clan chief at Gresham's was a pupil called James Klugmann.
His father was a London merchant dealing in rope and twine, who had
been born in Bavaria and had married the daughter of an importer of
tea and coffee named Rosenheim. 'Kluggers', a year older than Maclean,
was chubby, bespectacled and bookish; he won school prizes, but was
a dud at games; his tone was quiet, observant and amusing. He felt
isolated at Gresham's as 'the clever oddity', and provoked the school
authorities by calling himself communist. He had scant notion of what
communists believed or did, but started reading texts so as to be
convincing in his new role.[27]

Klugmann and Maclean thrived in earnest, intense schoolboy discussions about the purpose of life, and contributed argumentative pieces
to school magazines. Maclean's family creed respected penance and
martyrdom, and deprecated the indulgence of personal pleasures and
desires; but under Eccles's insipid, fretful preaching the boy lost all
reverence for biblical teachings. He left the school primed by Klugmann
to accept new doctrinal authority. It is unlikely that, outside school,
the two friends saw much of one another. The benefits of compartmen-
talizing what is important, and keeping it remote from home life, was
a valuable lesson of boarding school existence. To reveal one's closest
friends to one's family, like confiding one's secret ambitions, was to
court the possibility of humiliation. Neither boy exposed at home what
mattered to him most. Despite the distance kept between them outside
Gresham's, the ideas which were swapped there shaped Maclean's political direction.

Another early influence on Maclean, Burgess and Blunt proved as
formative of their temperament as Marxist writings. From early
manhood Maclean had a favourite book: Wilfrid Scawen Blunt's *Diaries
1888–1914*. His wife described it as his 'bible', and took a volume in

her luggage during her clandestine flight to join him in Russia in 1953. Burgess, too, as an adolescent was smitten by the diaries and inspired by the diarist's riotous path to perdition. Anthony Blunt was a first cousin twice removed of Scawen Blunt (not, as is often repeated, his great-nephew). He was attracted by the avant-garde dissidence of which his parents disapproved.[28]

Wilfrid Scawen Blunt was a landowner, poetaster, philanderer and self-obsessed hedonist. He championed anti-colonialism, loathed industrial capitalism and wrote in a retort to Rudyard Kipling that the white man's burden was the burden of his cash. His hostility to the British military occupation of India, Ireland and Egypt led to his short-term imprisonment. He impressed Burgess and Blunt, and inspired Maclean, by repudiating the sham-history that assumed the uniqueness and even genius of the British Empire. Patriots averred that this empire had distinctive origins, nobler purposes and a superior destiny to those of the European imperial forerunners, Spain and Portugal. They discounted the way that English colonialism had emulated the sixteenth-century conquistadors and seventeenth-century Dutch licensed trading companies in their administrative methods and repressive rule. They treated English expeditions to the East Indies, to the Caribbean and South America as heroic and beneficent rather than as, in twenty-first-century terms, the forays of neo-liberal bio-prospectors using slavery and violence to seize precious resources from indigenous peoples. Scawen Blunt's writings and actions made Maclean, Blunt and Burgess into insurrectionary adolescent anti-colonialists years before undergraduate study-groups drew them in early manhood to communism. The trio tended, in their rejection of English nationalism and exceptionalism, towards the conclusion of Kenneth Andrews, the great historian of maritime trade and exploration, that 'the involvement of England in the process of European overseas expansion was a natural consequence of her integral role in the commercial, political and cultural life of Europe'.[29]

In the first quarter of the twentieth century the public schoolboys' code, instilled by their masters, became petrified as sacred tribal custom: ostracism became the penalty for the slightest deviation in voice, manner, clothes or ideas. Maclean's outward respect for the cult leaders was convincing. 'He was a boy of the best type, and his moral character and conduct were exceptionally good', reported Gresham's acting headmaster when asked by the Foreign Office Selection Board for a character reference. 'I always found him entirely trustworthy, reliable and thoroughly sound.' After eleven years of boarding school, Maclean was camouflaged in amenability.[30]

Guy Burgess at Eton and Dartmouth

Guy Burgess was the most privileged of the Cambridge spies. He was born in April 1911 at Devonport, where his naval officer father was stationed. There was money on his mother's side from a small family bank in Portsmouth, and from investments in the utility companies that supplied gas and water to that naval port. Burgess was the only one of the Cambridge ring of five to have a rural childhood, for in 1922 his family settled at West Lodge, in the pretty Hampshire village of West Meon. West Lodge was the home of rentiers, not gentry. It was a low, square Georgian villa with five bedrooms and eight acres of pleasances – flowerbeds, shrubberies, a walled kitchen garden, paddocks and woodland. There were neither hunters in the stables nor shooting-parties in the coveys. The Burgesses were not the people for county committees or the magistrates' bench.

Burgess started as a pupil at Eton in 1924. His housemaster, Frank Dobbs, was cryptic in speech, but tolerant and cultivated: he went to the trouble of resuming contact with his most notorious pupil after Burgess had re-emerged in Russia in 1956, and sent terse, sympathetic letters for the solace of an exile. Other Eton housemasters, too, created enclaves of spacious civilized inquiry; but generally the school's inmates, like most people, exaggerated the importance of whatever was local or national. Modern European history was considered a hopeless subject for schools, with the result that nothing was taught about Europe except for patriotic accounts of wars with France and Spain, and of the struggle to protect other liberties from the influence of the Bishop of Rome. The demotion of modern European ideas is conveyed by an Etonian's remark that French language and literature were so meanly valued in the school that their teaching was entrusted to Frenchmen. Popularity was the chief ambition of boys at any boarding school. To achieve this, so Cyril Connolly argued in his memoir of Eton, they needed nonchalance, charm, fortitude and moral cowardice, and to hide their intelligence as 'a good tailor hides a paunch or a hump'. Deceptive powers were requisite for popularity. While conforming to the assumptions of their little clan, uttering its war-cries and skirmishing with its enemies, boys like Burgess mastered the craft of silent dissent from the group voice.[31]

Burgess's father, who died in September 1924, had intended him for the Royal Navy. Three months after his father's death he left Eton for Dartmouth Naval College, where he was to train as a naval officer. Dartmouth cadets in the 1920s endured martinet rules, constant shouting and perpetual menaces. Everything was done at top speed, by the clock, and in strict time with everyone else. Cadets were forbidden to address a cadet in a year above or below them. 'Everyone was forced into a mould; there was a discipline of iron, and a requirement of absolute efficiency, which pardoned no faults and forgot no weaknesses,' according to Masterman, who was a Dartmouth cadet some years before Burgess. Threats of violence ruled the place. There were savage beatings for minor infractions, such as talking after lights out.[32]

Although Burgess was an incorrigible scamp, he learnt at Dartmouth to accept discipline and to dissemble his feelings. His dependable punctuality, so essential for a spy keeping rendezvous and the one orderly element in his chaotic adulthood, may have been instilled by the naval college's obsession with drill and timing. He began to learn how to lead colleagues. The *Daily Mail*'s claim in 1956 that he had been expelled for theft was an easy slur that the newspaper knew would be hard to disprove. The likeliest reason for Burgess leaving Dartmouth in 1927 is that he decided against a naval career, convinced his mother that he should leave and engineered his departure by persuading a medical officer that his eyesight was too weak for navigation.

He returned to Dobbs's house at Eton, where he prospered. Some contemporaries remembered him as self-confident: others as insecure, and therefore too ingratiating. At Eton, if not Dartmouth, he will have enjoyed his first sexual experiences, which involved, in the phrase of his fellow Etonian Anthony Powell, 'a lot of manual labour'. His name was linked with that of David Hedley, a tall, sturdy blond, who was a King's Scholar, an able classicist, who won his colours playing rugby in the first XV, was a captain in the Eton Wall Game, a tennis champion and rower, edited the *Eton College Chronicle* and was elected a member of the most privileged and select of the Eton societies, Pop (from which Burgess had been excluded when he was proposed as a candidate). In addition to sexual tussles with Burgess, this sporting and academic prodigy had a romantic attachment to the young Citroën motor-car heir A. J. ('Freddie') Ayer; but when Hedley embraced Ayer and told him that he loved him, Ayer felt embarrassed and could not respond physically. Hedley had later importance in the development of the Cambridge spies: it seems that the hooligan ransacking of his undergraduate rooms in Cambridge by Hawks' Club hearties was a factor in Maclean joining the CPGB.[33]

During Burgess's last year at Eton, his widowed mother Evelyn ('Eve') Burgess married John Bassett, a lieutenant colonel in the Royal Berkshire Regiment, who had been awarded the Distinguished Service Order and Légion d'honneur during the European war. Bassett's position as man-of-the-house at West Lodge was recognized with an entry in Who's Who, which he retained when the Bassetts moved to Ascot in 1932. As further confirmation that Burgess's background was notable, but not consequential, Bassett was deleted from Who's Who after 1941 when, because of paper shortages, a quarter of the less significant entries were deaccessioned and never restored. The Bassetts had by then moved to a villa, Oakhurst, at East Woodhay in Berkshire.

Burgess excelled in history, which was taught at Eton with stress on the personalities, powers and foibles of great men. He treated the subject as if it was a gigantic gossip column in which everyone was somehow related and many had sonorous names. Rebellious radicalism was combined with nostalgic Toryism. Knight errantry and squalor were opposing attractions for him. He later told Murray Gladstone, a camp Etonian employed in the duty-free department of Selfridge's, to whom he sub-let his Old Bond Street flat in 1950, that when young he had faced a momentous decision: 'whether to be a great Christian or a communist'.[34]

Anthony Blunt at Marlborough

Anthony Blunt was born in a Bournemouth vicarage in September 1907. The prevailing temper of his parents' household was of puritanical piety, social duty, missionary zeal and good works. His father was a Church of England clergyman whose undoubtable intelligence was cramped by his narrow emotional outlook. His mother's family had generations of service in the administration of India. At home her skimping made life unnecessarily spartan. Fires were kept low, lightbulbs had dim wattage, chairs were hard. She scolded her sons if they showed signs of softness. The eldest of the Blunt sons said that their family was 'emotional, sentimental, gullible'.[35]

In 1912, when Blunt was aged four, his father was appointed chaplain of the Anglican community in Paris. St Michael's Church stood a few yards from the British embassy, and the Ambassador Lord Bertie of Thame attended services, but Stanley Blunt was not adjunct to the embassy and ministered to a diverse group of English residents in the French capital and its suburbs. Like many clergy, he had a theatrical vanity, and played to the diplomats and smart visitors in his congregation, but the claims of some writers that Blunt's family had moved in an exclusive Parisian set were fantasy. The family lacked the money, style and inclination for smartness. For two years Blunt attended a Paris day school, where he became proficient in French. In 1921 his parents returned to London, where his father was given the cure of souls in the parish of St John the Evangelist, Paddington. This was a small but prosperous parish, which included Southwick Place, where the Maclean family lived (although they were Presbyterians rather than members of the Church of England).[36]

Some months previously Blunt had gone as a prize scholar to Marlborough College. The school, which had been founded in 1843 to educate the sons of clergymen, was 'not a rich man's school', said the old Marlburian Footman. Classrooms were icy cold. Beds were stiff. Boys were kept hungry, with stale bread, watery bread-and-milk and perhaps a small kipper or sausage for breakfast; the only warm meal was at lunchtime, when the food was scanty and foul. Footman suspected that the 'low diet' was intended to reduce the sexual libido of pupils. He listed two benefits from his four years at Marlborough. 'My tendency to show off was quickly and drastically trimmed. It was good for me to have my self-confidence lopped: I could so easily have become over-pleased with myself.' Marlborough also taught him to doubt the pompous pronouncements of higher authorities. For the rest of his life he was an ironist about leadership. Like other Marlburians, Footman left the school still a 'muddled adolescent with little sense of purpose, little capacity for sustained effort, little self-confidence and a bundle of inhibitions'.[37]

Marlborough's headmaster Cyril Norwood was a profuse writer on

English boarding school management. He insisted that caning was not felt to be a degradation by his pupils, and provided a quick, effective way for prefects and house captains to quash 'uppishness' and insub- ordination. He was blind to senior boys' abuse of their powers to thrash other pupils. The shrill anxiety expressed in Norwood's writings about adolescent sexuality was as unpleasant as that of the clergyman in Maugham's story 'Rain'. Footman found that his Marlborough masters were divisible into two categories: 'potential enemies, to be evaded and outwitted, and potential figures of fun, to be warily exploited'. One housemaster's idea of sex education was to tell pupils: 'You might find some white matter exuding from your private parts. Don't worry about it. It's only a sort of disease like measles.'[38]

Blunt did not have a hot bath for five years, which may explain his adult need to take two hot baths a day. Instead, he had to wash in a 'tolly', the school name for a hip-bath. A school custom required that pupils had to upend and pour the dirty water over their heads when they had finished washing. The sight of Blunt's white skin and skinny body reminded boys of a candle: hence his school nickname 'the Taper'. Until the age of sixteen Marlburians spent their days, when not toiling in classrooms or competing on sports fields, in a vast barbarous barn known as Upper School. It had a hoodlum culture overseen by six prefects chosen for their sporting prowess and armed with canes which they swished on the backsides of smaller boys. 'The only law was a jungle law of force,' recalled one victim, 'and the special sufferers were the individualists.' For three years Blunt lived in fear that he would have to undergo the ordeal of 'basketing' in Upper School, although it appears that he never did. This involved an unpopular boy being stripped almost naked, having ink and treacle poured over his head, being shoved into a big wicker basket heaped with filthy rubbish and then hoisted with ropes to the ceiling beams. The master-in-charge was always forewarned of an imminent basketing so that he did not commit the solecism of inadvertently interrupting the fun.[39]

Blunt, who was hopeless at sports, had two miserable years at Marlborough before he began to devise avocations and find affinities. Another clergyman's son, with whom he shared a study, recalled: 'I don't think he was physically beaten up, but certainly he was made to feel a misfit, a pansy, and so on.' His housemaster Hugh Guillebaud mistrusted boys who preferred books and ideas to sports and actions, and deplored the reproductions of paintings by Matisse and Rouault hanging in Blunt's study as indecent. He liked it even less when, in 1924, Blunt and two other pupils founded the Marlburian magazine *The Heretick*. In it they railed against the patriotic teaching of history, competitive games, the OTC and philistinism.[40]

Just as Maclean forged a defensive pact with Klugmann, so Blunt was allied in an *entente cordiale* with Louis MacNeice (the son of a bishop). Both youths rejected military heroics, colonial pioneers and the 'divine mission' of the British Empire. They decried Kipling and Elgar. They tried to be subversive in every way, Blunt recalled, 'but we were rebels within the law, and we were careful enough and clever enough to carry out our crusade without ever infringing the rules of the school'. This taught him lessons of subterfuge for the future. MacNeice in his memoirs described Blunt as 'the dominant intellectual' of Guillebaud's boarding-house, with 'a precocious knowledge of art and habitual contempt for conservative authorities. He was very tall and very thin and drooping, with deadly sharp elbows and the ribs of a famished saint; he had cold blue eyes, a cutaway mouth and a wave of soft brown hair falling over his forehead . . .' He preferred objects to people. He thought it low to talk politics.[41]

The two friends spent interminable hours in Socratic disputes, gossip and ribaldry. They parroted the fashionable highbrow idiom, such as 'too *devastatingly* baroque', and aped the camping of Oxford aesthetes by bowling a hoop around the school, and playing catch with a huge painted rubber ball on the hallowed playing-fields. During their last term in the summer of 1926, they cavorted on the Wiltshire downs, with a blue silk handkerchief floating from the strap of Blunt's wrist-watch, and returned to school with their arms full of stolen azaleas to eat an iced walnut cake or bananas and cream in their study. On hotter afternoons they lazed away afternoons lying naked on the grassy banks of the school's bathing place, eating strawberries and cherries and reciting Latin poetry.[42]

The regimes at Gresham's, Marlborough and other boarding schools taught pupils a smooth-mannered duplicity. Boys prospered by giving outward deference to teachers and housemasters for whom they felt inward scorn. They learnt to give pleasant smiles while seeming to conform to rules which they intended to break. Institutional life, not parental influence, made Blunt, Burgess, Maclean and Philby what they were. They disliked the bullying, discomfort, injustice and surveillance of their schooling. Like their contemporary Kenneth Clark at Winchester they accepted these hardships as 'the invariable condition of growing up' rather than as personal attacks upon themselves. Boarding school life honed their cunning. It imbued each of them with a dislike of small-islander tribalism. Like Clark, they were emphatically not upper class in their backgrounds, allegiances, ambitions or habits. Kilburn and Paddington, or West Hampstead and Hyde Park as their families preferred to say, were not top-floor places any more than they were basement. The Cambridge spies came from the mezzanine class.[43]

CHAPTER 8

The Cambridge Cell

Undergraduates in the 1920s

'Our Secret Service reports of course do not deal with the better classes,' the Prime Minister Lloyd George was told in 1919 at a time when trade union militancy and egalitarian fervour seemed to threaten civil unrest. His Cabinet nevertheless received a few warnings of well-bred trouble to come. In 1920 the Home Office's Directorate of Intelligence reported in its weekly intelligence summary that letters had been intercepted in which communists urged that government offices, the army, postal and telegraph services, radio broadcasting and journalism should be infiltrated. An intelligence summary in 1921 reported that an Oxford university undergraduate, Arthur Reade, hoped to organize 'a Communist nucleus among the Varsity men, who will be going out as schoolmasters, scientific workers, literary men and professional and "intellectual" workers'. A further warning that Moscow sought to penetrate institutions with communist converts from the universities reached the Cabinet in 1922.[1]

'Bolshevism', declared a future Conservative MP Edward Marjoribanks in an Oxford Union debate of 1919, 'is non-representative, destructive of education, subversive of property, anarchical in legislation, a check upon industry, a scandal in food-distribution and the epitome of arbitrary cruelty.' This reflected the view of the vast majority of Oxford and Cambridge undergraduates during the 1920s: the intelligence services were right to focus their limited resources on monitoring working-class unrest rather than middle-class renegades. Only the tiniest sect of undergraduates would have agreed with Maurice Dobb, who joined the CPGB in 1922, that bourgeois culture and capitalist societies were 'decadent and sterile', that revolutionary communism would dwarf the

Renaissance, that 'non-Marxists [were] as silly as pre-Darwinian biol-ogists; & anyone who teaches a defence of capitalism [is] wicked & dangerous'. University communism made little headway in the 1920s when, as Cyril Connolly expressed it in 'Where Engels Fears to Tread', undergraduates parroted monosyllables, 'words like Freud, Death, War, Peace, Love, Sex, Glands, and above all, Damn, Damn, Damn!' It was only after the financial crisis of 1931 and the formation of the coalition National Government that, in a new mood of earnest salvationism, undergraduates began to chant big, new polysyllables such as 'The Workers' Revolution for the Classless Society through the Dictatorship of the Proletariat!' A tetchy young communist of the 1930s complained that sex had been the 'all-absorbing topic' of his elders in the previous decade: 'Weakness sought compensation in subjective self-assertion; Bloomsbury warmed its sterile soul in the artificial rays of aesthetic snobbery.' W. H. Auden agreed: the young intelligentsia of the 1920s were obsessed with the Freudian Bed and those of the 1930s with the Marxist Board, so he said in 1944.[2]

Valéry believed that young people learn best to form judgements when they are in 'an elegant, superficial, fickle and futile milieu'. Lady Maclean explained to MI5 that her son's undergraduate curiosity about 'this newish creed, Communism' was merely a phase of intellectual experiment: 'he was at a university for the purpose of finding his own mind'; Marxism had been a transient interest of his. 'The most valuable thing about college life is the infection of ideas which takes place,' according to Kenneth Clark, whose Oxford undergraduate years began in 1922. 'It is like a rapid series of inoculations. People who have not been to college catch ideas late in life, and are made ill by them.'[3]

In the process of inoculation and recovery, Arthur Reade was a path-breaker. Born in 1902, he was educated at Eton before spending seven months at the University of Strasbourg and matriculating at Oxford in 1920. He had his own carefully chosen furniture in his rooms at Worcester College, together with portraits of Marx and Lenin. It was mob vandalism by Worcester rugby hearties, who ransacked his rooms and broke the furniture and pictures by defenestrating them, that embittered him. 'Oxford's lovely city is defiled by the presence of the horde of social parasites from Mayfair, and paragons of bourgeois smugness from the provinces,' Reade complained in Eights Week of 1921: 'they bow down before the altar of the false gods of athleticism and salmon mayonnaise.'[4]

Reade began publishing a student magazine, which was entitled *Free Oxford* rather than *Red Oxford* because it favoured 'free love' as much as any political creed: mixed nude bathing was one of its early causes. Lewis Farnell, the university's Vice-Chancellor, was shocked that such 'obscene licentiousness' was being 'pushed into the hands of ladies coming out of church'. After publishing an editorial declaring 'By TERROR we shall destroy the domination of the bourgeoisie – by TERROR we shall establish the rule of the workers,' Reade was expelled from the university in December 1921. Farnell condemned *Free Oxford* for preaching 'extreme theories of Russian Bolshevism, the "Red Terror" . . . and the bitterest class-hatred: gross insults against all authorities were scattered through the pages. There was nothing of boyish fooling in it.' He suspected that the magazine had Soviet money behind it. 'No university where any discipline remained could', Farnell said, 'allow such filth to be flung in its face by its own students.'[5]

There were reports that Reade had visited army camps distributing pamphlets which were said to suborn military discipline. His member-ship of the CPGB was confirmed by an MI5 informant in Oxford. Political work in Greece and Albania disillusioned him with Bolshevism during 1924–5. In 1930, writing in an intercepted letter to Ewer, Reade deplored 'the transformation of Marxist thought into a religious faith complete with saint in the mummified person of Lenin – horribly reminiscent of the Patron Saint of Corfu whose embalmed body is paraded round the town in a Sedan chair'. He loathed the hunting and punishment of doctrinal heretics. 'The whole philosophy of the C.P. leaves no room for personal friendship – only loyalty to the Church. Independence – individualism – opportunism – desertion – renegacy – Siberia. The logic is perfect and intolerable.'[6]

Reade was a rarity in the Oxford of the 1920s. 'We were avid for experience, and did not care overmuch if some of it turned out to be wasted,' his contemporary Edward Sackville-West recalled, 'for the twen-ties was the last great period of Privilege.' The writers who most influenced this Oxford generation were Gide, Proust, Freud, D. H. Lawrence and Norman Douglas, the latter with his cult novel of cynical sensuality, *South Wind*. There was a 'general reversal of values' among the young literary intelligentsia: 'private life took place in public, and public life in private', according to Sackville-West, who in middle age claimed that he had been to bed with the youthful Donald Maclean.[7]

During the 1920s the CPGB attitude to Oxford and Cambridge universities was ambivalent. An editorial in *The Plebs*, a Marxist magazine edited for a time by Dobb, denounced the provision by Oxford's Extra-Mural Department of a two-year course of study free of charge for selected trade unionists: 'the policy of Oxford in making this offer is to endeavour to deprive the trade union movement of its most promising brains'. *The Plebs* objected to class fluidity. Workers who had attended university would 'fight violently against going back to factory or mine'. An Oxford education guaranteed that they would betray their class by finding 'remunerative occupation amongst the under-strappers of the employing-class'.[8]

Turning communist became fashionable in Cambridge colleges because of Maurice Dobb. Dobb was a north London draper's son and a Leninist who thrived on crisis. Marxism became his imperative faith. 'It is largely true', he told a Cambridge meeting in 1920, 'that man is not ultimately influenced by reason, but in the main finds reasons for what he wants to believe.' Dobb was an ideologue on a quest for coherent ethical laws, true definitions and unselfish ruling principles; a class warrior, too, who wanted a dictatorship of the proletariat in which the bourgeoisie were cured of their 'old psychology'. To the detriment of his academic career, he gave his best energies to promoting the cause of socialist equity for almost thirty years. The intellectual dishonesty and coercion of Lysenkoism, whereby thousands of Soviet biologists were dismissed, imprisoned and even executed for questioning the nonsensical Stalinist orthodoxy on genetics, finally disillusioned him in the late 1940s. Dobb formed the first communist cell in Cambridge University in June 1931. Without his leadership it is doubtful that communism would have been so influential in his college, Trinity, or in the wider university. He was crucial in creating Cambridge's ring of five by setting Philby on the course that led to his recruitment by the NKVD.[9]

Dobb's account of his visit to Russia in 1925, which he compiled as a retort to Keynes's criticisms of Soviet tyranny, is basic to understanding the development of the Cambridge communist mentality after 1931. Comparisons between capitalist individuality and Marxist collectivism were all to the latter's advantage.

Trains run on the main lines in Soviet Russia efficiently & to time
– in fact on the Moscow–Leningrad line they have brand new
wagons-lit which are the very acme of luxurious travelling. The
telephones work, if anything, better than in London. The Nevsky in
Leningrad – perhaps the most wonderful street in Europe – is gay
with arc-lamps & lighted shops at night, thronged with people in &
out of cafés, or the gardens of former palaces, where orchestras play
Tchaikovsky, Rimsky-Korsakov & Scriabin, with trams racing down
at a terrifying speed merrily ringing their bells. In Moscow the streets
are as clean as is compatible with cobbled surfaces; new Leyland
motor buses rival the crowded tram-cars.

Dobb admired the public parks, 'with their cleverly worked Soviet
designs in flowers, but disregard for the lawn-mower'. The performing
arts were as good as those in Vienna. 'Compared with anything in
Western Europe, of course, standards of efficiency are exceedingly low.
The Russian, with a temperament much like the Irish, is a charming
and kindly creature who will promise one anything on earth in order
not to seem unkind . . . but of elementary ideas of time, neatness,
thoroughness . . . he seemed to me woefully devoid.'

Leningrad and Moscow throbbed with zeal, Dobb continued.
'There's a hope in men's eyes, and a sturdy determination among the
young men and women who march in demonstrations.' Factory
workers knew that the unstoppable power of collective ownership was
preordaining communist supremacy over capitalism. Echoing *The
Plebs* editorial that deplored workers getting privileged Oxford experience and bettering themselves, Dobb admired the class immobility
that he found in the Soviet system. Russians who sought to use
education as a means to abandon their class, or regarded job promotion 'as a reason for dressing-up in a stiff white collar & assuming
the dignity of a "superior" person' were despicable: 'all one's qualities
as a "gentleman" which command respect, if not servility, in the
bourgeois West, count in Russia for nothing, except for laughter &
contempt'. At the frontier, where his train halted on his departure
from Russia, Dobb disdained the Latvian customs official, 'dressed as
in a comic opera to show you that he was an officer & a gentleman,
[who] displayed deference for my British passport & my bourgeois
manner'. His disgust swelled on the journey from Riga to Berlin at

'the fat, perfumed, wanton prosperity of a trans-continental restaurant car!'

Dobb admitted that freedom was curtailed in Russia. 'Members of the old régime are spied upon & watched. The Cheka, now the [O.] G.P.U., uses many of the weapons of the old Okhrana – spies in private households, offer of pardons to political prisoners if they will engage in espionage for the Government. There is a severe censorship, often like all censorships undiscriminating & stupid.' Political prisoners in the Siberian Arctic were said to die of exposure or hunger, Dobb conceded, but there were extenuating circumstances. 'One must preserve that sense of proportion which the intellectual so notoriously lacks. Russia emerged from invasion & civil war, is not only surrounded by foes, but has foes inside her boundaries, even in her Government offices.' The oppression of the security forces was excusable because it bore 'almost entirely on the bourgeois alone. The things which are forbidden to the worker are for the most part things which he does not want, or at least in Western Europe cannot usually afford. For him there is fairly free expression of opinion, because the whole essence of Communist theory is that Soviet rule should base itself on the consent of the masses & interpret their desires, & hence if the masses have a grumble, authority prefers it to be voiced aloud.'[10]

Marxist converts after the 1931 crisis

The hypothesis of capitalist equilibrium, which posited the impossibility of over-production, was refuted by the industrial rationalization movement of the late 1920s: Whitehall and the Bank of England induced competing steelworks, shipyards and cotton-spinners to merge and shut surplus factories, which aggravated regional unemployment. The Wall Street crash in 1929 and the abandonment in 1931 of the cherished idol of British capitalism, the gold standard that backed sterling, suggested to Dobb's disciples that capitalism was decomposing. The electorate's preference for reducing unemployment rather than lowering prices killed another sanctified emblem of British capitalism, free trade.

A trigger was set on Easter Sunday of 1931. A fierce, single-minded Trinity undergraduate, David Guest, son of a former Labour MP, had gone to study mathematical philosophy at the University of Göttingen. He was detained at an anti-Nazi youth demonstration, was kept incommunicado and alone in a cell for a fortnight, and returned to England as a convinced communist. Together with a youth called Maurice Cornforth he joined the CPGB and henceforth sported a hammer-and-sickle badge on his jacket in Trinity. After this dual recruitment, Clemens Palme Dutt – a CPGB activist like his younger brother Rajani – visited the university to consult Dobb, who in June 1931 began organizing a proselytizing cell. The 1930s were the decade of conversion: in Britain 12,000 a year were received into the Catholic Church; communist and Catholic recruiting drives among Cambridge and Oxford undergraduates often had the same targets. Philip Toynbee, who joined the Oxford University communist party in 1935 and became its recruiting officer, visited the rooms of potential recruits only to find a famous Roman Catholic proselytizer, Father Martin D'Arcy, already ensconced in them. Both creeds hoped to find a similar doctrinal amenability in the youths whom they approached.[11]

Energetic younger dons recommended dialectical materialism to thoughtful undergraduates. Patrick Gordon Walker (one of the stalwarts of the Oxford Labour Club) invited undergraduate historians into his rooms at Christ Church in order to convince them that Marxism provided 'objective laws of historical change' that were both scientific and infallible. The young Hugh Trevor-Roper, who was told that 'everything falls into place' once the Marxist philosophy of history was accepted, felt in the mid-1930s, as he embarked on adult life, that 'the vast pageant of history, hitherto so indeterminate, so formless, so mysterious, now had, as it seemed, a beautiful mechanic regularity'. Similarly, in Cambridge, Burgess became infatuated by historical determinism, which gave him the comforts of a requited lover. 'The Marxist testaments explained all that had ever happened, all that was happening, and all that would happen, and what each person should do to help it all along,' according to Michael ('Micky') Burn, who was one of Burgess's boyfriends. 'Nations, empires, epochs, fell into place as predictable stages in a *perpetuum mobile* of scene-changes.'[12]

Some people's education merely gives a fixed direction to their stupidity, as Lord Cromer said. Misogyny was rampant in Cambridge colleges. Male undergraduates broke down the gates of the women's college Newnham in order to celebrate the vote in 1921 to exclude women from admission to the university. 'This is a man's University, and I can see no reason whatever why women should not form a

University of their own,' declared a graduate of Pembroke, Lord Portsea, in 1923. 'There is no question that the sexes do not work well together in the University sense of work. There is the human animal, and the other animal.' A writer in 1940 conceded that such women as the fourteenth-century Countess of Pembroke had been valuable as 'pious Foundresses' of segregated all-male colleges, but denied that there could be benefits in treating twentieth-century women as equal members of the university: 'The most serious indictment of the women students, apart from the fearsomeness of the women which those students nearly always become unless they marry quickly and forget it all, is the complete pointlessness of their being there.' Women were not admitted to full membership of the university until 1948.[13]

Despite the brilliant reputations of Keynes and his colleagues at King's, of the mathematicians, philosophers and scientists of Trinity and of Lord Rutherford's team at the Cavendish Laboratory, insular complacence provided the keynote at many Cambridge colleges. The Senior Proctor of the university, an economist named Claude Guillebaud, wrote in 1934 with Anglocentric condescension of middle-class dicta- torships in Italy and Germany, 'and the picturesque personalities of Mussolini and Hitler'. This sort of sour put-down passed for clever wit in senior common rooms. John Bull smugness was unshaken by the arrival in the 1930s of such émigrés as the Budapest-born economist Péter Bauer, the Berlin-born biochemist Ernst Chain, the Freiburg-born scholar of Roman law and rabbinical studies David Daube, the Viennese- born molecular biologist Max Perutz, the Kiev-educated historian Michael ('Munia') Postan and the Austrian jurist and medieval historian Walter Ullmann. 'The bulk of the dons I have met are dull and provin- cial,' Postan reported to an anthropologist friend in 1935. 'They read little, know less and are smug and conservative in the worst Edwardian manner. They sneer at "fellows with ideas" or tell funny stories about Americans . . . It is all very painful and explains why so many of the young scientists here turn communist.'[14]

Lord David Cecil, the Oxford literary critic, whose family had lived in Hatfield House for 350 years, said after visiting dons in Cambridge colleges, 'One feels that they have accidentally inherited the place and haven't yet learnt how to live in it.' Hugh Trevor-Roper mused about 'the curiously unsympathetic, strained, correct, unintellectual atmos- phere of the university there, compared with the Oxford atmosphere

which, though often boring and even coarse, is at least alive'. Maurice
Cranston who visited Cambridge to give a lecture which he had spent
three weeks preparing was shocked by his reception: 'Cambridge *isn't*
Oxford; I was treated with a mixture of crude lifemanship [competi-
tiveness] and plain rudeness,' he wrote in 1954. 'Trinity high table
turned out to be a workhouse board, and the dinner was gastronomic-
ally lower than Lyons' [Corner House], but there was plenty of wine,
and I just gulped it down. For two hours before I had been sitting with
my host, he offering no sherry, no conversation and no response to my
increasingly nervous efforts to make it.'[15]

Young Marxists of the 1930s were intolerant of constrictive policing
in the British Isles but acquiesced in the murderous political policing
of the Soviet Union. Party members in Cambridge were indignant at
the authorities' treatment of the aged trade union leader Tom Mann,
who spent two months in Brixton prison for refusing in 1932 to be
bound over to keep the peace after calling for a day of action against
unemployment. Two years later, their ire was renewed when Mann and
Harry Pollitt of the CPGB were prevented from addressing a mass
demonstration against unemployment in Hyde Park, by being arrested
under Lord Sidmouth's Seditious Meetings Act of 1817 for speeches
they had made in Wales. Notes of Mann's speech, taken by two constables named Onions and Fudge, had him denouncing 'the rotten ruling
class' responsible for this 'tyrannical age': 'now is time for . . . class
action. We must take control of the points of government – railways,
dockyards, shipyards, telephones, wireless stations and use them for
our cause. The workers are our weapons.' Mann and Pollitt certainly
thought in these terms; but the constables had taken notes only on
passages in the speech that they considered 'strong', and had not
recorded all that was said. Denis Pritt, representing Mann, played
court-room tricks to discredit their abilities as note-takers. His humiliation of the police witnesses ensured Mann's acquittal to the delight
of CPGB members in Cambridge, who were indignant about Onions
and Fudge, but indifferent to the enormities of the Gulag.[16]

Cambridge undergraduate communists were similarly riled by Lord
Trenchard, the Commissioner of Metropolitan Police, proposing in
1933 that Scotland Yard should undergo technological modernization,
with patrol cars linked by radio to a central communications room.
Trenchard recommended forming an officer corps of university-

educated men, who would be excluded from membership of the Police Federation to ensure that they did not share the outlook of the rank and file or be at risk of imbibing the Federation's milk-and-water trade unionism. Constables were to be given police housing and recreational facilities that would distance them from their working-class neighbours. The left found these plans sinister and oppressive – indeed fascistic. George Lansbury, the Labour party leader, speaking in a Commons debate, called Trenchard's proposals 'a downright piece of class legislation'. The sequel, he predicted, would be that Trenchard, who was a marshal of the Royal Air Force, would organize police aerial bombing raids on working-class protesters: 'Yes, a couple of aeroplanes did fly over a body of men at Coventry and we were threatened with what would happen.' Echoing the complaints of Jack Hayes against General Macready in 1919, Lansbury warned that the Metropolitan Police was being turned into a 'semi-military' force. 'Trenchard's proposals', David Guest concluded in an agitprop magazine called *The Student's Vanguard*, 'illustrate almost every point in the Marxist theory of the capitalist state.'[17]

Guest, like Dobb, was a member of Trinity College, as were Blunt, Philby, Burgess and Cairncross. Some of the greatest minds of early twentieth-century England were Fellows of Trinity: the mathematician G. H. Hardy, the philosophers Moore, Russell, Whitehead and Wittgenstein; the classicist A. E. Housman; the historian George Macaulay Trevelyan. The Master until his death in 1940 was the Nobel physics laureate J. J. Thomson, 'who, by virtue of his knowledge of the smallest particles, attained the Mastership of the greatest college in either university', as A. S. F. ('Granny') Gow (a Fellow of Trinity) wrote in his Latin epitaph. 'Loud-mouthed, toothless and unkempt, he married an unpleasant wife, thanks to whose money he was able to leave eighty thousand pounds sterling to his heirs, a house filthier than a pig-sty to the college, and to posterity an unforgettable model of avarice.' College life fostered spiteful resentments among those Fellows who were not working hard enough.[18]

The first of the Cambridge spies to reach Trinity was Anthony Blunt, who entered the college in 1926 and originally studied mathematics. In his first year, he was shy, disheartened, relatively poor and ill-dressed. In 1927 he changed his course from mathematics to modern languages: he already had perfect French and excellent Italian, but now turned to

master German, which was the primary language of art scholarship.
His first real love affair was with Peter Montgomery, the scion of Ulster
military gentry. Sexual exchanges relaxed him, he dropped his defensive
pose of sardonic misanthropy and evinced a dry sense of humour. In
1929 he became the lover of Virginia Woolf's nephew Julian Bell, a
rumpled, rumbustious and sturdy youth, who pursued Blunt for a quick
inquisitive trial of a new sensation: his sexual energies were otherwise
always directed at women. Blunt's other undergraduate squeezes
included Claud Phillimore, subsequently an architect who specialized
in reducing extraneous wings of over-sized country houses during the
cash-strapped 1950s. Phillimore's father Lord Phillimore campaigned
against Stalinist slave-labour tactics, and in 1931 sponsored legislation
attempting to ban imports of timber and other commodities from penal
colonies in the Gulag. He later commended Marshal Pétain for making
a truce with Hitler in 1940 and decamped to South Africa in disgust
at socialist post-war England.

Kim Philby reached Trinity three years after Blunt, at the early age of
seventeen, in 1929. During his first Cambridge terms his chief avocation
was music: he listened to Beethoven records, and played the French horn.
Scores of his college contemporaries were strenuous outdoor types who
ran with the Trinity Foot Beagles, competed in point-to-points at
Cottenham and raced at Newmarket. Philby developed a hardy wander-
lust which showed that he was tougher than the swaggerers. For three
successive years he forayed into the defunct Austro-Hungarian Empire
and its Balkan hinterlands. In 1930 he bought a second-hand motorcycle
with side-car, and visited Budapest and Vienna with Tim Milne and
another friend Michael Stewart (British Ambassador in Athens, 1967–71).
Bosnia in 1931 and Croatia, Montenegro, Albania and Serbia in 1932
were added to his tally. He chose the worst hovels to sleep in overnight,
and bought the cheapest train tickets (he supposedly made his passage
through Bosnia in the cattle trucks). He became proficient in German,
and gained passable knowledge of Hungarian and Serbo-Croat.

Ignoring the reservations of *The Plebs*, Cambridge had taken half a
dozen former coal-miners on scholarships from the Workers' Education
Association, including Harry Dawes and Jim Lees. In both these men
Philby found a rare and invigorating authenticity. It was possibly under
the influence of Dawes that Philby switched from history to economics
in his third academic year. Years later Lees recalled Philby as dour,

austere and abstemious about alcohol. Other contemporaries remembered him as earnest, virtuous and unassuming.

Guy Burgess entered Trinity as a scholar in 1930. James Klugmann followed him there a year later. Klugmann's Gresham's clansman Maclean went in the same month to Trinity Hall – a pretty college wedged into a small site adjacent to the much grander Trinity. During the summer vacation of 1931, Ramsay MacDonald's Labour government disintegrated in financial crisis, and was replaced by a coalition government. In October, as Klugmann and Maclean settled into their colleges, the Labour party was annihilated at the polls in the general election by an alliance of Tories, Liberals and the rump of MacDonald's supporters. The omens of convulsive breakdown seemed unprecedented to Klugmann, Maclean and Burgess, and the possibilities of change looked illimitable. 'Life seemed to demonstrate', said Klugmann over forty years later, 'the total bankruptcy of the capitalist system and shouted aloud for some sort of quick, rational, simple alternative. There was in this period a very strong feeling of doom, doom that was not very far off.'[19]

Philby was a strenuous Labour canvasser in that general election in the rural constituency of Cambridgeshire. He was joined on the rounds by Denis 'Jakes' Ewer, the only son of Norman Ewer and afterwards an invertebrate zoologist; but their activism was unavailing. The Conservative candidate in Cambridgeshire, Captain Richard Briscoe, trounced his Labour opponent, and later told the *Birmingham Post* that if only Hitler and Mussolini could relax with a good game of bowls once a week, European peace would be untroubled.

The triumph of the National Government over socialism aroused bitter fury among the radical intelligentsia, who felt betrayed by the Labour old guard and by social democracy. The Cambridge University Labour Club collapsed. Dawes then organized the Cambridge University Socialist Society as its radical new replacement. Philby joined CUSS at the instigation of Dawes, attended its meetings, became more politicized and finally served as its treasurer in 1932–3. Another CUSS activist recalled Philby at this time: 'you would not have picked him out for distinction. He seemed then a useful bureaucrat, the sort who would have made a good career in Unilever.'[20]

Around the time of the 1931 election Maurice Cornforth married Klugmann's sister Kitty, a Girton graduate and communist. In the

Cornforths' rented rooms above a pawnbroker's shop, or at tables in the Lyons Corner House tea-shop, Guest, Cornforth and their acolytes plotted their revolutionary work. Guest had a puritan's dislike of what Dobb called perfumed, wanton prosperity. He would have preferred a paper bag of prunes to a glass bowl of ripe peaches. In his Trinity room, which was bare except for a bookcase, a piano and a picture of Lenin, Guest instilled a select group of susceptible acquaintances with iron, Marxist discipline and held tireless tactical planning sessions. He insisted that it was the duty of communist students to excel at their work in the university just as much as if they were communist prole-tarians working in factories. Disciples had to read *Das Kapital* chapter by chapter. Marxist jargon such as 'the negation of the negation' or 'the transmutation of quantity into quality' was bandied during sessions which might last all night. 'We did not understand half what was said, but were stimulated to go on reading,' one of the study-group recalled. Members of the cell sold copies of the *Daily Worker* on street corners and canvassed support in working-class districts. The Cambridge Marxists were as puffed up with spiritual pride as the Weimar commu-nist Leonhard Frank, who had coined the slogan 'Left, where the heart is'. Their embrace of virtuous causes, such as 'humanity', 'peace' and 'progress', inflated them with the exhilarant gas of their own rectitude. If they were always right, others must be wrong.[21]

Guest's group – many of them Dobb's disciples – hailed the Soviet Union as a great socialist nation, albeit flawed by Russian national character. The cruelty of Stalin's dictatorship – its enforced agricultural collectivization, its liquidation of the intelligentsia – was treated as a necessity to protect the great socialist experiment. Guest's friend M. Y. Lang recalled the prevalent mood:

> The philosophy student, led by the sophistry of a Whitehead or Wittgenstein to despair of the possibility of even *interpreting* reality, was electrified by the discovery that over in Russia they were actually applying a philosophy which claimed to *change* the world. The thrill of discovery gave way to the white heat of indignation. We felt ourselves surrounded by a wall of intellectual dishonesty, ivory-tower escapism, and apologetic accommodation. We felt in duty bound to smash that wall . . . we became inspired missionaries for a new integration of thought and action, a new science of life.[22]

Party members ambushed targets in Trinity Great Court or took them captive by unheralded visits at tea-time. They indicated their disposition by code-phrases such as 'Old Herrick was a status quo poet' or by saying of the film *The Private Life of Henry VIII*, 'Propaganda for the National Government, isn't it?' Then they could nudge conversation towards their eternal subject, class-struggle, and the victorious inevitability of proletarian dictatorship. The creed that class war was the motor and throttle of progress was irreconcilable with belief in government by consent. Devout communist undergraduates upheld the mechanical fallacy that twentieth-century beauty inhered in immensity and functionalism: towering grain silos, hydro-electric dams, airship hangars, gasometers were the new abbeys. To renegade communists, Guest and his comrades were no better than political pimps. 'The Comintern', as Arthur Koestler said, 'carried on a white-slave traffic whose victims were young idealists flirting with violence.'[23]

Philby tried to convert some unlikely men to Marxism. He approached his Trinity tutor John Burnaby, who had survived grim military service in Gallipoli and Flanders, and was Europe's leading expert on the theology of St Augustine. Burnaby had an officer's trim moustache, an ascetic's stern lines, and was an eloquent Christian preacher, who later took holy orders and became Regius Professor of Divinity. Philby tried to convert this upright man – the author of such works as *Amor Dei* and *The Belief of Christendom* – to dialectical materialism. Interviewed by Courtenay Young of MI5 in 1951, Burnaby called Philby 'a militant Communist' who had in his view converted Burgess to Marxism. Young reported, using the codename PEACH for Philby, that of the pair, Burnaby 'regarded PEACH as the dominant factor'. Philby did not apply for membership of the CPGB until 1934, a year after his graduation from Cambridge, and never received a party card; but Burnaby assumed that his pupil was a card-carrying partisan. 'I would be surprised', he told Young, 'if PEACH had not been a Party member as his Communism was so deep-seated that it would be inconsistent with the sincerity of his character if he were not also a Party member.' Burnaby's account of Philby's impact on Burgess is convincing. Burgess in turn told Harold Nicolson that he had been primed for the anti-colonial struggle by reading William Shuster's *The Strangling of Persia* (1912), an account of Edwardian English and tsarist Russian diplomatic intrigues which had 'a seminal effect' on him as an undergraduate.[24]

Oxford compared to Cambridge

On the extreme left, there was no one in Oxford as fervent, patient, timely and well placed as Dobb was in Cambridge in 1931–2. Philip Toynbee, who was a CPGB activist in Oxford, said that his comrades there showed 'ruinous insensitivity' in trying to convert undergraduates. Their proselytizers appeared in college rooms 'grinning and rinsing their hands like very bad salesmen'. The Oxford party's ruling cohort were dishonest almost as a principle, Toynbee added. Robert Conquest, who read politics, philosophy and economics (PPE) at Magdalen from 1937 and like many of his friends joined the CPGB from motives that were compassionate and unselfish, later estimated that there were about 30 overt and 170 clandestine party members in the university. 'But', he added, 'when you have a party that was headed by Philip Toynbee, it's not very serious.'[25]

A weightier figure was Arthur Wynn. The son of a professor of medicine, Wynn had read mathematics and natural sciences at Trinity College, Cambridge, joined the CPGB and was living in Germany when the Nazis took power in 1933. There he married Lieschen Ostrowski in order to give her the protection of a British passport. After bringing his bride to England, they were watched and evaluated by the NKVD talent-spotter Edith Tudor-Hart, who had recently approached Philby to spy for Moscow. Similarly, in October 1934, Tudor-Hart and Maly recruited Wynn as agent SCOTT. Wynn pursued postgraduate studies in Oxford, where he became a busy NKVD recruiter in 1935–8. There he met a fellow party member Margaret ('Peggy') Moxon whom, after divorcing Ostrowski, he married in 1938. In the same year, using the joint alias of Simon Haxey, the couple published an influential book, *Tory M.P.*, arguing that parliament was dominated by employers who oppressed the workers, suggesting that bank directors and arms manufacturers should be ineligible as parliamentary candidates, reiterating that there was a capitalist conspiracy to foment war for the profit of munitions makers, and noting that Conservative leaders by their investments were financially benefiting from rearmament. This bestselling polemic by Wynn and Moxon was an indignant and oddly pompous piece of class warfare, which drew innuendoes from a mass of conscientiously researched facts.[26]

Wynn entered the recruiting-grounds some seven years after Dobb's cell was formed. His contacts were less entrenched in their party commitment by the time of the Nazi–Soviet non-aggression pact in August 1939, after which their activism mostly ceased. Toynbee renounced communism in December 1939 following Russia's invasion of Finland. The Oxford-undergraduate communism of Denis Healey did not prevent him from becoming a major in the Royal Engineers, Secretary of State for Defence in 1964 and deputy leader of the Labour party. Wynn's tally of short-term recruits included a future Labour politician Bernard Floud and a future colonial governor Andrew Cohen, but they did not amount to a ring of Oxford spies. The young Americans who came to Oxford as Rhodes scholars however did.[27]

Crane Brinton, who was a Rhodes scholar at Oxford in the late 1920s, and later did wartime service as chief of research and analysis at the London outpost of the Office of Strategic Services (OSS), forerunner of the CIA, said that most American Rhodes scholars were 'disappointed with Oxford and disappointed with their achievement after their return'. They were, explained Brinton, 'horrified by its preciousness, by the free and easy habits of the undergraduates, and especially by their intellectual and moral irreverence'. One event changed all this: the Oxford Union debate of 1933 which resolved by 275 votes to 123 that the house would in no circumstances fight for its King and Country. Most of those voting were loyal citizens of a country that was then committed by the Kellogg–Briand pact of 1928 to the outlawing of war: few of them were, as Beaverbrook's *Daily Express* fulminated, 'woozy-minded Communists and sexual indeterminates'. The Oxford undergraduate memory moves in cycles of three years: its enthusiasms are ephemeral; the King and Country vote did not matter long in Oxford. But in the United States 'the Oxford Oath' became the focal point of a student peace movement. Thereafter, on Armistice Days, hundreds of thousands of American students boycotted classes and attended anti-war meetings. Inspired by the Union's pacifist vote, the brightest of them applied for Rhodes scholarships at England's oldest university. By 1936 the Warden of Rhodes House, Carleton Allen, was lamenting that an increasing number of American Rhodes scholars were communist sympathizers: 'It is not a circumstance which is palatable to oneself, but clearly we can do nothing and ought to do nothing about it.' He accepted that many of the best youngsters of their generation wanted to prove their social conscience, modernity and capacity for faith by communist displays, and trusted that this might prove, like most Oxford trends, transient.[28]

Mary McCarthy wrote of a Yale graduate in the early years of the New Deal, 'Marxism was to become for Jim's generation what an actress had been for the youths of the Gilded Age': an exciting, furtive rite of passage into manhood. American Rhodes scholars who took to Marxism in the mid-1930s included Daniel Boorstin, Duncan Lee, Peter Rhodes and Donald Wheeler. Boorstin and Lee were hoodwinked by their experiences on a visit to Soviet Russia organized by the Stalinist barrister Dudley Collard in 1937, but neither sought party membership in Oxford. Boorstin joined the CPUSA after returning to Harvard in 1938, and Lee on his return to Yale in 1939. Boorstin left the CPUSA following the Nazi–Soviet pact, and became an eminent opponent of doctrinaire politics and the historian of American consensus. Lee, however, became the best-placed communist agent to infiltrate wartime American intelligence in the form of the OSS. In a memoir later prepared for the NKGB in 1945, Wheeler described himself as a member of the agrarian proletariat, born on a primitive farm in Washington state, and as having joined the CPGB while at Oxford in 1935. After leaving Oxford, he worked for communist-front bodies involved in the Spanish civil war, then returned to the USA as a union organizer in government agencies. He joined the OSS on its formation, and was immediately an important Soviet source.[29]

Rhodes, who had been born in Manila with the patronymic of Beutinger, had taken a new surname after his mother shot and killed his father at Caldwell, New Jersey in 1916. This name-change long predated his arrival as a Rhodes scholar at Oriel College, Oxford. He joined the CPGB, and organized a proselytizing summer camp for the unemployed at the Thames village of Clifton Hampden in 1935. Gordon Fagg, landlord of the village's Barley Mow pub, complained to the police that the campers sang 'The Red Flag' in his bar and spoke disloyally of the royal family. In 1936 Oxford police questioned Rhodes after he had shouted abuse at a fascist meeting. Although he was obviously a middle-class American, Rhodes claimed to the police that he was an English proletarian who worked as an assembler at the Pressed Steel works at Cowley. After the expiry of his Rhodes scholarship, he became a Paris-based journalist, visited Spain in 1937 (ostensibly to investigate the plight of refugee children) and returned to London in 1941 as a member of the Foreign Monitoring Service, with a desk in the US embassy.

Aside from the Rhodes scholars, one of Wynn's recruits – Jenifer Williams, who read history at Somerville – needs attention. Her father was a former Liberal parliamentary candidate for Oxford and a judge at the Permanent Court of Arbitration in The Hague. Rebelling against the high-minded and salubrious idealism of her parents, she volunteered to work in Rhodes's communist-front summer camp for the unemployed in 1935. Her experiences there, including an affair with an unemployed milkman, induced her to join the CPGB. In doing so, she replaced the ample latitudinarianism of north Oxford with the rigid, cramping doctrines of Marxism. Her feelings in 1935–6 were conditioned by erotic pleasure and the fact that every party member was assigned a role and made to feel significant. Her first assignment, which was given to her by the Balliol historian Christopher Hill, was to recruit her friend Isaiah Berlin to the CPGB; but she knew this to be impossible. Like her friends Floud and Toynbee, she was exasperated by the ineptitude of the Labour party, and its hapless responses to regional unemployment and to the rise of fascism in Italy, Germany and Spain. She was aware of the cruelties of Stalinism, but took comfort from a letter sent to her in 1936 by an intellectual Englishman who had just returned from Russia: 'all the things that one is inclined to be worried about, restrictions on liberty, a failure to reach our standards of taste in something or other – all the things, in fact, which don't fit in with our oh so well-educated lives – simply don't seem to a genuine worker as sources of trouble'. Her rationalization in old age of her party membership was based on the balance of evil: 'Hitler's march into Austria in March 1938 seemed more important than Bukharin's execution three days later.'[30]

Williams was placed third out of 493 civil service candidates in 1936 and entered the Home Office, which was the recommendation of both the Civil Service Commission and her CPGB contacts. She was handled by Arnold Deutsch @ OTTO, who groomed her as a penetration agent. One of the attractions of party membership had been the camaraderie, but she was deprived of this as a secret member, from whom even a party card was withheld. Her Home Office work on juvenile delinquency, children's homes and reformatories held little interest for Moscow. Under the influence of Herbert Hart, whom she married, she

turned against Stalinist totalitarianism and towards Labour constitutionalism. Her party activism had petered out, she said, by 1939.

Some of the American Rhodes scholars shed their communist sympathies after the Nazi–Soviet pact of August 1939. Many of Wynn's recruits
similarly proved too fastidiously bourgeois to forgive either the pact or
the Soviet invasions of Poland and Finland. Oxford, however, seems to
have been more fallow ground than Cambridge. Cambridge was generally reckoned to be the more scientific university, and the supposed
scientific nature of Marxism attracted scientists to the CPGB in the
1930s, but none of the ring of five was a scientist. So what were the
other institutional, geographic and temperamental factors?

In the seventeenth century Cambridge had been a Roundhead city
and Oxford a stronghold of the Cavaliers. Puritanism persisted in the
Fenlands university throughout the twentieth century: in Oxford people
were more comfortable with personal fulfilment and less pleased by
self-mortification. The countryside surrounding Oxford abounded with
hosts and hostesses who encouraged the politically ambitious young
and introduced them to political sponsors. The Churchills at Blenheim,
Lady Desborough at Taplow, Lady Astor at Cliveden, Margot, Countess
of Oxford and Asquith at Sutton Courtenay, Lord Birkenhead at
Charlton and Lord Tweedsmuir at Elsfield were among the political
patrons and power-houses within easy reach of Oxford. Visiting young-
sters there were allured by the possibilities of serving powerful interests.
There were no comparable houses near Cambridge: Kipling's reclusive
daughter at Wimpole and the *enfant gâté* Lord Fairhaven at Anglesey
Abbey had no interest in running political salons. Few tourists visited
Cambridge in the 1930s: it was not on the road towards Shakespeare's
Stratford-upon-Avon, and its chief London rail terminus, Liverpool
Street station, was a grim deterrent to tourists in ways that Oxford's
Paddington was not. 'Oxford in vacation is as crowded and noisy as
Hammersmith Broadway, which much of it resembles,' wrote a graduate
of King's in 1940, 'while Cambridge in vacation just lives quietly from
one market-day to the next.'[31]

Cambridge was the more insular university, in which undergraduates
tended to be unnerved by the risks to their personal integrity of mainstream political commitment, but calmer about joining the outer
margins. Undergraduate politics were overt in Oxford: there was less
shame in conventional party ambitions and engagement; there were

fewer jibes about political careerism among the young. The Oxford Union debating society in Frewin Court was a better nursery of political leaders than its Cambridge counterpart in Bridge Street. Of prime ministers since 1900, only three graduated from Cambridge: Balfour, Campbell-Bannerman and Baldwin, all Trinity men, and all in power in the century's earliest three decades. By contrast, Asquith, Attlee, Eden, Macmillan, Douglas-Home, Wilson, Heath, Thatcher, Blair, Cameron and May were graduates of Oxford. Between 1920 and 1970 some 77 of the 161 permanent under secretaries who attended university were Oxford graduates: Cambridge lagged far behind from the 1940s. This is indicative of where the mainstream current flowed, and where the stagnant backwaters stood. The Oxford don Richard Crossman, on a visit to Cambridge in 1953, noted of the 'keen Socialists' who entertained him at King's, 'somehow they are detached from practical politics': Oxford's difference from Cambridge, he decided, was that in his university 'life is public affairs, not private affairs'. Two years later E. H. Carr, moving fellowships from Balliol to the former college of Blunt, Burgess, Cairncross and Philby, reported: 'Cambridge is infinitely more remote from the world than Oxford.'[32]

Another possible deterrent to Oxford communism were MI5 agents. Two Oxford undergraduate communists of the 1920s – Tom Driberg and Graham Pollard – are known to have been reporting communist activities within the university. There were probably others in the 1930s of whom we as yet know nothing. Driberg, whose serpentine activities recur throughout this book, was a shifty, squalid, over-publicized character (known as M/8 in MI5 files). Pollard was the more significant agent, as witnessed by his designation of M/1.

Graham Pollard, son of the great Tudor historian A. F. Pollard, won the senior history scholarship to Jesus College, Oxford in 1922. He was known among his contemporaries as a bibliophile and aesthete: he joined the decadent Hypocrites Club, and beat his fellow Hypocrite Evelyn Waugh in a spitting contest. To the dismay of his father he got only a third-class degree. Pollard had been a pupil at Willington preparatory school in Putney in 1909–16 – the school where Maxwell Knight was sports master in 1921 before embarking on his strange career which included being MI5's most successful agent-runner. The Pollards lived in Erpingham Road, close to the school, and near Knight's Putney flat. Knight's biographer Henry Hemming suggests that the twenty-one-year-old sports master and his eighteen-year-old neighbour met in 1921, and that it was at Knight's instigation that the undergraduate Pollard proclaimed himself (to the surprise of his fellow Hypocrites) to be a communist. After graduating, Pollard became junior partner in a Bloomsbury bookshop, ran the St Pancras branch of the Amalgamated Union of Shop Assistants, Warehousemen and Clerks, edited the magazine *Distributive Worker* and in 1924 married a communist called Kathleen ('Kay') Beauchamp. He and his wife joined the staff of the *Daily Worker*. Throughout he remained Knight's highly valued informant. His commitment continued despite his wife's imprisonment in 1933 for publishing an article criticizing the conviction of a communist called Wal Hannington. His resolve and utility began to diminish only in the mid-1930s after he had separated from his wife. He had long since left Oxford activism behind, but it is doubtful that he was MI5's last agent inside the Oxford University cell of the CPGB who weakened or betrayed its work.[33]

Whereas the Cambridge Labour Club collapsed after the National Government victory in the general election of 1931 leaving a vacuum in socialist organization, Oxford's Labour Club survived. This was partly because Oxford – unlike Cambridge – was ringed by factories, notably the Morris motor-car plant and its associated Pressed Steel works at Cowley. The strikes and other activism at Cowley in the 1930s influenced left-wing thinking in the university. Abraham ('Abe') Lazarus, a CPGB organizer in the south Midlands, was a charismatic force in both Cowley and the university: Jenifer Williams was one of his acolytes. But Lazarus's influence was countered by David Lewis (né Losz), who had lived in a Jewish *shtetl* in Belorussia from his birth in 1909 until his family moved to Canada in 1921. Lewis was a native Yiddish-speaker, who learnt English by reading *The Old Curiosity Shop* with a Yiddish–English dictionary beside him. From McGill University he went to Lincoln College, Oxford as a Rhodes scholar in 1932. He was a committed socialist, whose Marxism was modified by his family's experiences of Bolshevism. In university debates and on public platforms he put the case for 'parliamentary Marxism' with vigorous éclat. His brand of Marxist socio-economic analysis and constitutionalism, his rejection of revolutionary means and proletarian dictatorships, tripled the Labour party membership in the university in 1932–4 and stopped the communists from making headway.[34]

Above the level of student activism, Labour leadership was provided by several dons. Richard Crossman was elected to Oxford City Council in 1934. Gordon Walker contested the Oxford City parliamentary constituency at the general election of 1935. Both men were driven to socialist activism by first-hand experiences of Nazism during prolonged visits to Hitler's Germany. Like others of their political bent at Oxford, they upheld social democracy under the influence of two luminaries, A. D. Lindsay and G. D. H. Cole. 'Sandy' Lindsay had been instrumental in inaugurating Oxford's honours school of modern humanities (known as modern Greats, or PPE) in 1920, and was a progressive Master of Balliol in the years 1924–49. He was anti-totalitarian, not just anti-fascist, and gave hours each week to frank dialogues with the politically earnest young. With his engaging stammer, his social conscience and his deprecation of ideology, he influenced such undergraduate politicians as Denis Healey, Edward Heath and Roy Jenkins. Lindsay was 'a big man with a profoundly religious spirit', said an admiring colleague: 'there was nothing namby-pamby about his kind of democracy'. He mustered impressive support as the Popular Front candidate at the famous Oxford City by-election of 1938.[35]

Second only to Lindsay among the Oxford social democrats was G. D. H. Cole, Ewer's former *Daily Herald* colleague and university reader in economics from 1925. During the inter-war period, at moments of political crisis and economic stress, Cole made excitable remarks about the need for dictatorial socialism, and the redundancy of the capitalist conception of individual liberty; but his wife said that he was a Tory in everything except politics, and he proclaimed himself a pluralist. 'I was repelled', he explained in 1958, 'by the Bolsheviks' conception of a social philosophy based on rigidly determinist principles and involving the unquestionable class-correctness of a single, unified body of doctrine, regardless of considerations of time and place.' Although he admired Bolshevik leaders for emancipating Russia from monarchical feudalism, he had realized by the Kronstadt revolt of 1921 that those leaders believed 'that "class-enemies" had no human rights at all and could be killed or maltreated without any source of compunction'. Although this summary of his position depends upon selective amnesia, it is true that Cole's general influence in the 1930s was anti-totalitarian, not just anti-fascist, and that he did not proselytize for the Soviet Union. He had, thought his Oxford pupil Royden Harrison, 'a deep distrust of power, and was dismayed to find that those who exercised it repeatedly confused expediency with principle, and personal ambition with service to the good cause'.[36]

After a talk by Cole at an Oxford socialist Pink Lunch in 1932, Gordon Walker set out his credo – which diverged far from Cambridge notions. He rejected the Soviet model, and insisted upon English particularity: 'abstracts and fundamentals must be allowed', he conceded, 'but we are politicians and we are Englishmen' and so 'our particular concern is English socialism for England'. There was little resemblance between the history of England and that of Russia: 'even if the Marxist inevitable end is a true reading of history, England has half-escaped its applicability to her'. Gordon Walker disbelieved in long-term tactical planning ('he goes furthest who knows not where he is going'), rejected 'socialism imposed and maintained by force', and wanted 'no running after a vague equality. The ideal will be very near to the Medieval Church: of men chosen and promoted for their subservience to the main end.'[37]

There was another divergence between the two ancient universities. Male homosexuality was practised with some openness and reasonable acceptance in Oxford. The undergraduate letters and diaries of Evelyn Waugh, like the careers of Harold Acton, Brian Howard, Wystan Auden and Stephen Spender, show overt and fulfilled sex lives. Maurice Bowra coined the neologism Homintern, and described himself in the 1930s as a leader of the 69th International and a member of the Immoral Front. Men with sexual preferences that were criminal under the law of 1885 were elected as heads of houses in Oxford: some perhaps sexually abeyant, such as Cruttwell of Hertford in 1930, Stallybrass of Brasenose in 1936 and Smith of New College in 1944; but others – Bowra at Wadham in 1938, T. S. R. Boase at Magdalen in 1947, John Kelly at St Edmund Hall in 1951 and John Sparrow at All Souls in 1952 – demonstrably less so. In puritanical Cambridge, despite the exceptions of Maynard Keynes and his circle, male homosexuality was more culpable and repressed. Among heads of houses, Arthur Benson, who was Master of Magdalene until 1925, was virginal, while John Sheppard, elected Provost of King's in 1933, became an absurd gibbering wreck. Predilections were supposed to be sublimated in Cambridge: Anthony Blunt's research fellowship at Trinity was not converted into a full fellowship because of objections to his sexual activity, although there were plenty of bachelor dons in the college. The sexual climate was more clandestine, seething, tortuous and potentially dismal for men in the Cambridge colleges. Perhaps these uncomfortable local twists and frustrating deformities of erotic activity were a factor in young men's choices of political expression and allegiance.

Stamping out the bourgeoisie

Owen Wansbrough-Jones, the senior tutor at Trinity Hall when Maclean was an undergraduate, described him to MI5 in 1951 as 'not the kind of man to accept other people's ways of thinking, without having thought them out for himself and studied all the relevant authorities'. He recalled Maclean as 'a good athlete when it suited him to play games', but generally as 'the cat that walked alone'. Intellectually, he was outstanding, Wansbrough-Jones said. 'Everything came easily to him . . . He would be inclined to feel – more often than not correctly – that in dealing with any of his contemporaries, he was dealing – relatively – with a fool.' Wansbrough-Jones thought him of a type liable to join the CPGB.[38]

One of Maclean's contemporaries at Trinity Hall was Jocelyn ('Jack') Simon, later Lord Simon of Glaisdale and a law lord. His father was Unitarian by religion and a stockbroker by profession: his mother's maiden name was Mamelsdorf (anglicized in 1914 to Morland) and his maternal grandmother was a Rosenheim. Simon was thus a cousin of Klugmann and Kitty Cornforth, and was born in Belsize Park, where numerous Rosenheim cousins (including the Klugmanns) lived in affectionate proximity. These Jewish kinsmen were not mentioned when he was interviewed by Roger Hollis in 1956 about his early friendship with Maclean. By then he was a QC and Tory MP. He told how his parents had been friends of Sir Donald and Lady Maclean, and how he had attended Gresham's with Maclean as well as Trinity Hall. He and Maclean played cricket together in the holidays, and skated on the Holland Park rink. Maclean made no secret of joining the CPGB in the winter of 1932–3, recalled Simon, who thought his friend's conversion followed Hawks' Club rowdies wrecking the rooms of Burgess's Eton boyfriend David Hedley, then reading classics at King's and a convert to communism. If Simon remembered correctly, the anti-Hedley hooliganism was a trigger event reminiscent of the smashing of Arthur Reade's cherished possessions in Oxford eleven years earlier.

Maclean made a show of his communism, said Simon, 'by selling his wardrobe and replacing it with a rather scruffy set of reach-me-downs, and filling his bookshelves with Communist books'.[39]

Another of Maclean's contemporaries at Trinity Hall was Alan Nunn May. He was typical of most Cambridge undergraduate communists of the 1930s in being a grammar school boy rather than a public school man. Born in Birmingham in 1911, Nunn May was the son of a prosperous brass-founder who was reduced to working as a salesman when his business failed after a fire. Paternal humiliation and anxiety status dominated Nunn May's adolescence. As a pupil at Birmingham's leading grammar school, he was influenced by Erich Maria Remarque's novel *All Quiet on the Western Front* and Robert Sherriff's play *Journey's End*. He decided that his generation had been 'conned' by the governing classes about the war of 1914, the 'Hang the Kaiser' election of 1918, the Versailles peace treaty of 1919, the bogus Zinoviev letter of 1924 and above all the capitalist crisis after 1929. From the backwashes of Birmingham he saw 'deliberate deception' by the authorities on all sides: as he said, in self-justificatory old age, 'this feeling that the Establishment was not to be trusted, that any officially sponsored line of thought had to be critically examined, grew on me. I felt that the ruling class had lost all claims to trust.'[40]

Nunn May won a scholarship to Trinity Hall, where he gained a first in physics. His academic mentor there was the fellow-traveller Patrick Blackett. Communist propaganda in 1933–6 against the private manufacture of armaments aroused Nunn May, who became convinced that capitalists fomented war to increase their profits from munitions. After leaving Cambridge he joined the CPGB and visited Russia in 1936. His party commitment was dormant from the German–Russian pact of August 1939 until the German invasion of Russia in June 1941. He then began supplying atomic secrets to the Soviet Union: his unmasking in 1945–6 was to destabilize the other Cambridge spies.

Francis and Roualeyn ('Spider') Hovell-Thurlow-Cumming-Bruce came under the Marxist sway at Trinity. They were the identical twin sons of Lord Thurlow, an Anglican clergyman who specialized in missionary work among merchant seamen. During the 1920s their father had been chaplain to the Merseyside seamen's mission, with the quaint title of Rural Dean of North Liverpool, and during the 1930s he was rector of a parish in the vicinity of Durham collieries. Like

Blunt and Maclean, the Cumming-Bruce brothers were reared in an atmosphere of self-sacrificing Christianity, with added exposure to social deprivation. Deciding that the Church of England gave no solution to the perplexities of their time, they found a new faith in dialectical materialism, which they studied under the aegis of Dobb and Cornforth. They enjoyed the cloak-and-dagger way in which they were given their little green CPGB membership cards. Their party membership, so Roualeyn Cumming-Bruce said in 1953, 'was a mark of grace extended through Maurice DOBB only apparently when students had reached a certain state of political education'. The twins left the CPGB about the time that they graduated from Cambridge: their observations convinced them that 'an Engels-world upside-down offered no future at all, and both reverted . . . to a more sober Labour Party line'. Francis Cumming-Bruce, on furlough in England after five years in the high commission in New Zealand and before his posting to its counterpart in Ottawa, was still sufficiently keen to attend the Labour party conference at Blackpool in 1944: he admired the party executive's adroit management of the proceedings. He ended his official career as Governor of the Bahamas and a hereditary member of the House of Lords.[41]

Philby went to Berlin with his friend Tim Milne in March 1933 three months after Hitler's accession to power. The German capital was festooned with Nazi flags and anti-Jewish notices: the German communist party, which had failed to halt the advance of Hitler's political forces, was demonstrably in decline. Milne in old age suspected that this diverted Philby, 'always a believer in the realities of power, away from international communism and towards the Soviet Union as a mainspring of resistance to fascism'. Philby graduated in June 1933 with upper-second-class honours in economics. On his last day in college, he asked Dobb's advice on how to fulfil his commitment to combat fascism. 'Ach,' Dobb had said in exasperation in 1930, 'these conventional intellectuals without any spunk!' (He was talking about his failure to get Trinity colleagues to protest against the deportation of Edith Suschitzky, a Viennese communist who later took the surname of Tudor-Hart.) Dobb thought Philby had spunk: he gave him a letter of introduction to a Paris group, almost certainly Willi Münzenberg's newly formed World Committee for the Relief of Victims of German Fascism. In doing so, he launched Philby on the course which led to his first meeting with Suschitzky and her initiation of his recruitment as a spy. It must be stressed that although Dobb recruited young men into the party, he had no direct hand in inveigling them into working for Moscow.[42]

One such youth was John Cornford, who became a ruling force in Cambridge communism during 1933. Reared by cultivated, tolerant, liberal and inquisitive parents, he rejected their values with righteous irritation, joined the CPGB, visited Russia and used masterful aggression to achieve his ends. 'Keep Culture out of Cambridge' was a slogan coined by him. In the magazine *Cambridge Left* he quoted some lines of Louis Aragon as a rallying-cry for students and intellectuals:

I am the witness to the crushing of a world out of date.
I am a witness drunkenly to the stamping-out of the bourgeois.
Was there ever a finer chase than the chase we give
To that vermin which flattens itself in every nook of the cities?
I sing the violent domination of the bourgeoisie by the proletariat
For the annihilation of that bourgeoisie
For the total annihilation of that bourgeoisie.

A Darwin great-aunt described Cornford as 'poisoned by communism', thinking 'of nothing else but his political religion', rude to his elders, dirty and scruffy. Steven Runciman, who knew him at Trinity, judged him 'forceful, merciless, rather inhuman'. Runciman's biographer Minoo Dinshaw pictures Cornford as one of the best-looking undergraduates of his generation, 'with thick black curls and etched cheekbones worthy of some melancholy Russian princess'. He notes that Cornford, 'a cold, narcissistic and unavailable heterosexual youth', knew how to entice Blunt and other sexually susceptible youths into ideological havoc.[43]

Cornford and Klugmann transformed student politics in their university in 1933–4. They recruited a strong cohort within Trinity. Their acolytes then carried their disputatious propaganda into other colleges, forming undergraduate Marxist study-groups and mustering anti-war feeling in a period when Moscow rather than Berlin was thought by good communists to be London's target. They held open meetings throughout the university, and distributed leaflets. Above all they waged a campaign of ruthlessly tactical conversations to influence, convert and recruit undergraduates. Their group was as insistent as Christian evangelicals, and knocked on doors with the zeal of Jehovah's

Witnesses. Klugmann had a canny sense of which Cambridge under-graduates were worth fostering and which university organizations were worth penetrating. The Cornford–Klugmann cell set out to arouse a robust anti-fascist temper among students, and to organize loyal groups of student revolutionaries. Marxism gave their acolytes the notion that all of literature, the visual arts and the learned professions (law, medi-cine) had to be studied anew, weighed again and relabelled. The belief in the absolute iniquity of their capitalist, colonialist and fascist oppo-nents made them sure of their own invincible rectitude. Theirs was a total system to change the world.

One such acolyte was Egerton Herbert Norman, who had been born in Japan, where his Canadian father was a Methodist missionary, and arrived at Trinity with a history scholarship in 1933. He had lost his family's exacting Christian faith and was ripe for conversion by Klugmann and Cornford: it was under the latter's mentorship that he joined the CPGB. After holding a Rockefeller fellowship at Harvard, Norman joined the Canadian Department of External Affairs in 1939 and rose to ambassadorial rank while still, it seems, loyal to Moscow. The burden of his divided loyalties became so onerous that he finally killed himself.[44]

Charles Rycroft, the younger son of a fox-hunting baronet, was another acolyte. Before entering Trinity in 1933, he spent six months in Germany in order to learn the language. He found teenage excitement in attending Nazi rallies, watching street fights and distributing banned copies of *The Times*, which his brother sent wrapped in copies of *Tatler*. Arriving at Trinity, he discovered that only extreme left-wingers were interested in Nazi enormities. He joined the Society for Cultural Relations with the Soviet Union. 'My conversion, however, had surpris-ingly little effect on my daily life, which continued to be that of a young man who is treating the university as a finishing-school first and as a seat of learning second. I went to sherry parties, May-week balls and point-to-points, and considered it bad form actually to be seen working.' He did his necessary reading at home in the vacations so effectively that he got a first in the first part of the economics tripos, and was elected an exhibitioner. He took a 2.1 in the modern history tripos at the end of his third year. He was then elected to a studentship, which enabled him to remain at Trinity for a fourth year of perfunctory research. From his comrades Rycroft learnt:

that intensity, which I had previously thought a vice, was really a virtue, and also that I, poor thing, was decadent, a dilettante, a member of a dying class, precluded from the dialectic of history from ever having any understanding of the modern world or from playing any significant role in it. I was too young and innocent then to realize that passionate intensity is a sign of doubt rather than certainty, or to appreciate that envy and vanity lay behind their attitude towards me. Nor did I cotton on to the fact that their theories led to the conclusion that they, the educated cadres of the proletariat, would form the ruling class of the future.

Klugmann's rooms were on the next staircase to Rycroft's at Trinity. 'He seemed to need little sleep, and I joined the Party after a marathon series of indoctrination sessions lasting far into the night. It had become a choice between joining and exhaustion.' It became fashionable in Trinity, said Rycroft, to join the CPGB – 'a recognized form of social climbing'. The undergraduate communist cell was sub-divided by party headquarters. 'Nominally, "A" was the privileged cell; its members were supposedly the *crème de la crème* of the liberal intelligentsia, too original and gifted to be subjected to Party discipline.' Their revolutionary duty was to infiltrate universities, government departments and metropolitan elites, and to hold themselves ready to restore cultural life after the chaos of revolution. The deceived innocents of 'A' cell, who thought themselves exclusive and privileged, had in reality been quarantined in order to protect simple-minded proletarians from contamination: so far from being admired or envied by the rank and file, they were disparaged as 'social pansies'.[45]

On every Armistice Day (11 November) during the 1930s intimidating mobs of drunken undergraduates roamed through Cambridge requiring passers-by to fill the collecting boxes of the British Legion. Most dons kept inside their colleges during the afternoon and evening to avoid this patriotic thuggery. In order to exploit the justified resentment of this bullying, Dobb (abetted by Cornford and Klugmann) formed the Cambridge Anti-War Council, a communist front which helped to organize a march to the town's war memorial on Armistice Day of 1933. There were counter-demonstrations from rowing and rugger hearties, who blocked the road near Peterhouse and bombarded demonstrators with flour, eggs, tomatoes and white feathers (some of which were worn with pride as trophies). The hooliganism was so rowdy that the police drew their truncheons. Fingers and noses were broken. Burgess clambered into a car piled with mattresses, which Julian Bell drove on the edge of the march to block counter-demonstrators and to deflect their missiles. This confrontation invigorated undergraduate resistance to established authority. Even apolitical youths such as Alan Turing were impressed by the anti-war marchers. Anthony Blunt recalled this street skirmish as the moment when the Marxist lightning-strike hit Cambridge. 'We simply *knew*, all of us, that the revolution was at hand,' Klugmann recalled in old age. 'If anyone had suggested that it wouldn't happen in Britain, for say thirty years, I'd have laughed myself sick.'[46]

Maclean wrote some fighting verses, entitled 'Dare Doggerel. Nov 11', which were published in the Trinity Hall undergraduate magazine *The Silver Crescent*, extolling undergraduate dissidents who:

> Dared to think war-causes out,
> Dared to know what they're shouting about,
> Dared to leave a herd they hate,
> Dared to question the church and state;
> Dared to ask what poppies are for,
> Dared to say we'll fight no more,
> Unless it be for a cause we know
> And not for the sake of status quo.
> Not for the sake of Armstrong Vickers,
> Not for the sake of khaki knickers,
> But for the sake of the class which bled,
> But for the sake of daily bread.
> Rugger toughs and boat club guys
> Panic-herd with frightened eyes,
> Sodden straws on a rising tide,
> They know they've chosen the losing side.[47]

In the winter of 1933 Maclean complained in *Cambridge Left*, of 'the obscurity and the thin-bloodedness of modern writing', which was, he thought, serving as 'the unconscious propaganda of ruling-class culture' because it was divorced from contemporary reality. By 'reality' he meant 'the economic situation, the unemployed, vulgarity in the cinema, rubbish on the bookstalls, the public schools, snobbery in the suburbs, more battleships, lower wages, the genus undergraduate, and, above all, the rising tide of opinion which is going to sweep away the whole crack-brained criminal mess'.[48]

The National Unemployed Workers' Movement, which had support from neither the Labour party nor the Trades Union Congress, organized the Hunger March which headed for a Congress of Action at Bermondsey in February 1934. The Cambridge University Solidarity Committee (chaired by Cornforth) arranged buses to take student sympathizers to Royston, where they marched for some miles in solidarity with the Hunger Marchers. Some undergraduates felt like impostors in a proletarian march and worried if it would be patronizing to buy packets of cigarettes for unemployed men. Their self-consciousness abated as they marched along singing 'Pie in the Sky' and 'Solidarity Forever' or chanting 'Down with the Means Test!' Maclean was glimpsed there by his friend Robert Cecil, striding arm in arm with an unemployed worker and his face suffused with ardour. 'We believed', Cecil recalled half a century later, 'that if we could lose ourselves in dedication to a cause, this would solve our personal problems, to say nothing of the problems of the world around us. Commitment, we thought, like falling in love, would lift our hearts and minds above the complexities and frustrations of day-to-day existence.'[49]

Given the lurid and probably invented stories that began to circulate in the 1950s about Maclean's sexuality, it is noteworthy that Cecil recalled: 'he was handsome in an effeminate way, but was not regarded by his friends as a homosexual'. In July 1934, with his friends Roualeyn Cumming-Bruce and Anthony Blake, Maclean rented a holiday cottage at Saint Jacut de la Mer in Brittany. Cumming-Bruce had 'a holiday diversion' with a villager named Francine, while Maclean began 'a passionate alliance' with Francine's sister Marie, who was older than him and married to a member of the Garde Mobile stationed elsewhere. 'MACLEAN was seriously in love with the married sister,' said Cumming-Bruce. The young men and women drank cider together, lazed on the beach and in the evenings joined villagers fishing for lobsters and crabs. Maclean and Marie would disappear behind rocks while Cumming-Bruce with Francine found another place where they could make love. This idyll ended when Marie's irate husband returned to Saint Jacut seeking explanations, and the English boys decided that it was prudent to make a night-time getaway. For some months, recalled Cumming-Bruce, Maclean was pursued by amorous letters from Marie.[50]

Blunt returned to Cambridge briefly in January 1934 from a year's sabbatical in Italy and Germany. According to his manuscript memoir, he noticed then that most of his friends had joined the communist party or were allied to it. In June of that year Klugmann graduated with a double first in French and German: in the autumn he returned to Trinity for postgraduate work on Balzac under the supervision of Henry Ashton, the Molière expert. Ashton was also the tutor of John Cairncross, whom he introduced to Klugmann. Cairncross had previously studied at the Sorbonne, and had been appalled by what he had seen on bicycling tours of Austria and Nazi Germany during his vacations. At Trinity Cairncross soon succumbed to Klugmann's dialectic wooing: he became convinced that communism was the only force that could overpower fascism. In these same months Blunt, who had returned permanently to Trinity in September 1934, was converted to communism by Burgess, whose command of the Marxist dialectic of history impressed him, and by Klugmann's long night-time exegesis.

Another new arrival at Trinity in October 1934 was to have a major impact on Blunt's ultimate destiny. Michael Straight was a rich young American *marxisant* who studied economics under Dobb. Soon he was held by Klugmann and Cornford in nightly dialectical discussions. Their foxy and remorseless logic-chopping caught him for the Trinity cell. 'I'm filled with a violent, uncontrollable love for them; an extraordinary sense of comradeship,' he told his mother of Dobb, Klugmann and Cornford in 1935. He found in party activism, to use a line from Cornford's poem about Kirov, his only constant certainty. In his college rooms he hosted late-night doctrinal discussions which ended with the participants standing in a circle and singing 'The Internationale' with booming confidence. The noise, Straight liked to say, hastened the death of the ailing Trinity Fellow A. E. Housman, but in truth Housman was already in a nursing-home. Even in disobliging details, members of the Cambridge cell liked to misdirect.[51]

John Maynard Keynes epitomized the liberalism, rationality, altruism and progressive faith of Cambridge in the 1930s. He visited Leninist and Stalinist Russia in company with his wife, who had been born in St Petersburg and many of whose family remained stuck there: his detestation of Bolshevist collectivization was inveterate; he upheld instead the creativity of competitive individual initiative. Always Keynes distinguished between the Comintern's Bolshevization and native communist thinkers. 'There is no one in politics today worth sixpence outside the ranks of liberals except the post-war generation of intellectual Communists, under thirty five,' he told *New Statesman* readers in 1939. 'In their feelings and instincts they are the nearest things we now have to the typical nervous nonconformist English gentleman who went to the Crusades, made the Reformation, fought the Great Rebellion, won us our civil and religious liberties and humanised the working classes.' Perhaps it was so.[52]

CHAPTER 9

The Vienna Comrades

Red Vienna

After 1918, in every capital city of the defeated European powers, there were spivs dealing in currency, weapons, medicines, orphans, heirlooms, contraband and fake passports. 'Vienna, the lost city of Europe', wrote George Slocombe in 1921, is 'the prey of disease, hunger and death, and of worse than these, the greedy men, the traders of all nations who have descended upon it to exploit'. Thirteen years later, after a process of constructive renewal and violent relapse, it became the crucible that made the Cambridge spies. Treason in London had class warfare in Vienna as its provocation.[1]

The election in 1923 of Karl Seitz as mayor inaugurated the period of 'Red Vienna', during which, in the words of the Foreign Office's Soviet expert Don Gregory, the city became 'a Socialist Mecca, second only to the Kremlin'. Seitz's planners aimed to turn the former imperial capital into a model city for the urban proletariat. They built salubrious housing, parks and amenities, health and welfare institutions, co-operative shops, workmen's banks and adult educational facilities. Karl-Marx-Hof, erected in 1927–30, was a block of flats two-thirds of a mile long containing some 5,000 occupants, with laundromats, nurseries, doctors' surgeries and a library. These schemes were financed by onerous property taxes, which eliminated the rental income of private landlords and aroused vengeful resentment. 'One day,' an Austrian general promised, 'we are going to stop that business in Vienna by fair means or foul. Parquet-floors and shower-baths for workers, indeed! You might as well put Persian carpets in a pigsty and feed the sow on caviar.'[2]

About one-third of Austria's population lived in Vienna. Politically the nation was divided between the Social Democrats, who held an unassailable majority in the city, and the Christian Socialists, who commanded unshakeable support among the devout, conservative peasantry. Don Gregory, a stalwart Catholic, abhorred Vienna's socialists, whom he dismissed as 'non-Christian by heredity' and 'middle-class talmudists', for corrupting the workers with 'Marxian secularism' and the 'pagan squalor' of divorce, birth-control and cremation.[3]

After a crisis in 1927, in which scores of people were killed in street-fighting, Austria remained riven by violent tension. The bankruptcy of the leading Austrian bank in 1931 brought economic dislocation. A year later, in 1932, Engelbert Dollfuss, a dwarfish man nicknamed 'the Pocket Chancellor' or 'Millimetternich', formed a Christian Socialist government with a majority of only one vote. His party was pinioned between two vehement ideological enemies, the Marxists and the Nazis, with the latter intensifying their propaganda for the annexation of Austria by Germany. Politically Dollfuss was devious and agile, with the ecclesiastical nature that combines vanity with selflessness. In Slocombe's estimate, 'he felt himself quite honestly to be a servant of God and of God's church. The nation came next, and himself a very long way after.'[4]

Early in 1933 a socialist leader named Koloman Wallisch revealed that truckloads of weapons, comprising up to 50,000 rifles and 200 machine guns, falsely documented as scrap metal, had been shipped from fascist Italy to the Hirtenberger munitions works. The leader of the reactionary Heimwehr (home defence force), Prince Starhemberg, a brainless swashbuckler with eighteen castles and countless millions, was complicit in this illegal consignment. After international protests, Dollfuss conceded that the trucks must return to Italy; but when they reached Innsbruck on their journey south, their contents were seized in a Heimwehr ambush. The exposure by Wallisch and fellow socialists of Italy's illegal arms traffic to Austria convinced the Heimwehr that their conspiracies would always be foiled by the existence of the Social Democratic party backed by a free press.

A month later, in March 1933, Dollfuss extinguished the parliamentary system. His pretext was a procedural row caused by the disallowing of a card vote left by a socialist deputy who hurried to the lavatory before a crucial division. On Dollfuss's orders, the boulevard outside the parliament was blocked by barbed wire, the surrounding area was packed by mounted police armed with carbines, and stormtroopers prevented deputies from entering the building. In the ensuing months Dollfuss enacted decrees that restored the death penalty, deprived the urban proletariat of benefits, protected landlords, enriched his peasant followers, curbed the right to trial by jury, regulated the free press and put private letters under surveillance. Beginning in June (the month when Philby consulted Maurice Dobb about his future political duty), the Nazis waged a campaign of assassination, bombing, arson, sabotage and booby-traps aimed at individuals, bridges and telegraph and telephone systems. The British were indifferent to these preliminaries for a German seizure of Austria. In Room 22 George Antrobus considered Austria to be 'a ridiculous petty state' with 'no chance of ultimate survival'. English newspapers mostly ignored the Nazi terrorism: when Naomi Mitchison, a cousin of the MI5 officer Maldwyn Haldane, heard Austrian atrocity stories, she thought, 'Oh, it's only the *Manchester Guardian* again.'5

Slocombe concluded from his talk with Dollfuss in June 1933 that the Pocket Chancellor wished to establish 'a semi-dictatorship, a mild, paternal, Catholic version of the dictatorship of Mussolini'. In August Dollfuss secured Mussolini's promise that Italy would protect Austrian sovereignty; but in return he was required to give the Heimwehr liberty to extirpate the Social Democratic party. On 11 September Dollfuss held a huge rally to mark his adoption of Italian-model fascism. 'I announce the death of Parliament,' he declared. 'The liberal-capitalist economic system' and 'socialist materialism' were, he promised, finished. Social Democrats were 'the modern anti-Christ'. His 100,000 followers made a pretty sight as they cheered: Heimwehr fascists in green uniforms, Tyrolese national guards in snow-white stockings, black-and-red jackets and sugar-loaf hats topped by quivering osprey plumes, blue-and-yellow scout battalions and peasant irregulars in a variety of picturesque Alpine costumes. Dollfuss believed that Catholic fascism could defeat both German national socialism and revolutionary Marxism. 'Hitler is Jesus Christ for the whole of Europe,' Austrian Nazis told George Earle, the US Minister in Vienna, at this time. 'If the Jews continue resisting in Austria, the greatest pogrom in history will be executed.'6

Anti-fascist activism

It was around the time of the Dollfuss–Mussolini pact that Philby arrived in Vienna, at the instigation of Dobb's Paris contacts, to work for the International Workers Relief Organization. He rented a bedroom in a pleasant apartment belonging to Israel Kohlman, a civil servant of Polish origins who was active in Jewish welfare work. It was probably in the month of Dollfuss's public avowal of an Austrian fascist future that Philby became the lover of Kohlman's daughter, an intense, exciting divorcee named Alice ('Litzi') Friedmann. She was two years older than Philby. Previously she had been recruited by Gábor Péter, a hunch-backed, limping Hungarian tailor and Stalinist tough, into Vienna's illegal communist underground resistance. An MI5 source who had known 'Litzi' in Vienna described her in 1951 as 'an out-and-out Communist, [who] enjoys good living and is certainly not the self-sacrificing type . . . she was obviously above the level of card-holding Communists and never seemed to want for money'.[7]

Under her influence Philby deplored the moderate, temporizing response of Social Democrats to Dollfuss's 'Fatherland Front'. He raised money for Friedmann's group, which used him as a courier delivering sealed packets (containing money and political instructions) to communists both in Austria and abroad. His British passport and general bearing ensured that he was unhindered on five trips to Prague and two to Budapest.

In Vienna, on 12 February 1934, the Heimwehr seized control of official buildings, railway and radio stations, strategic roads and telephone and telegraph bureaux. Their thugs attacked the offices of trade unions and newspapers. Socialist leaders (including Vienna's mayor, Seitz) were detained in lightning swoops. Viennese social housing, notably Karl-Marx-Hof, suffered heavy bombardment as hateful symbols of progressive ideals. The victors were so proud of their destruction that afterwards they sold picture-postcards showing battle-scarred workers' flats. The Heimwehr's Social Democrat counterpart, the Republikanischer Schutzbund (Republican Defence Association), was fatally punctilious. Its paramilitary forces did not defend Friedshof station because they lacked platform tickets. A detachment surrendered in a park because their retreat from the advancing Heimwehr was marked with signs forbidding anyone to walk on the grass. An estimated

5,000 Social Democrats were wounded and up to 2,000 killed. Koloman Wallisch, who had revealed the previous year's arms scandal, was caught in the snows near the Slovenian border and garrotted. Numerous Viennese were arrested after denunciation to the police by their neighbours, sometimes for pay, but mainly so as to avoid arrest themselves.

Philby learnt enduring lessons in the need for ruthlessness during the Vienna fighting. Julius Deutsch, commander of the Schutzbund there, was proud that his militia had never plundered a single shop. There was a sardonic riposte when Deutsch's boast was repeated to a communist revolutionary turned diplomat *en poste* in Vienna:

> very nice, to be able to say that throughout the resistance to a brutal counter-revolution my men always behaved like perfect gentlemen. But had I been in command, I would rather have been able to say that my men had behaved like scientific revolutionaries. Very pretty, that nobody plundered . . . But if those not organized or armed for fighting had started to revenge themselves for this attack on their liberties by breaking open shops, things might have been very different. If every minute and from every quarter of the city had come a telephone call to the Chancellor: 'Mr Dollfuss, they are stealing my shoes – Mr Dollfuss, send police, they are stealing my cheese – Mr Dollfuss, quick with the police – bad men are stealing my motor-car' – police would have been running here, running there, and back again to arrest plunderers, and my poor troops would have had a chance to defend themselves against less terrible odds.[8]

For ten days Philby distributed money, food and clothes to stricken comrades. Many of the vanquished socialists took refuge in Vienna's sewers. Wounded men were tended there for weeks by selfless physicians, mostly Jewish, at the risk of their careers. An underground network smuggled the comrades to safety once they could be moved: Hungary returned all refugees, the Czech border was almost impassable, but hundreds got away – some to Soviet Russia. Philby was not directly involved with the sewer escapees, but collected respectable, inconspicuous clothes for them to travel in. He begged five suits from Eric Gedye, the *Daily Telegraph* correspondent in Vienna. 'Good God, man,' he cried to Gedye, 'I have six wounded men in the sewers in danger of the gallows.'[9]

The future Labour leader Hugh Gaitskell was visiting Viennese socialists when the sound of machine-gun fire started in the streets. The
cannonading of Karl-Marx-Hof and the murder of Wallisch were his
first experiences of fascist action. Similarly, the Vienna street violence
was 'a watershed' in the political career of the future Labour jurist
Elwyn Jones who, after returning to England, appealed in the *Cambridge
Review* for funds to aid destitute Viennese families. By contrast, Leo
Amery, a former Cabinet minister who sat on the boards of German
metallurgical companies and had a Hungarian Jewish mother, assured
his fellow Birmingham Conservatives that there had been an attempted
socialist 'revolution' in Vienna, that the bombarded housing blocks had
been designed as 'fortresses' and that Dollfuss exhibited 'wise and
generous clemency except in the summary punishment of the few
ringleaders'. In a single week nine men were hanged, three sentenced
to life imprisonment and sentences totalling 400 years imposed on
thirty-one prisoners. Vanquished socialists decided that the anti-fascist
resistance had been hobbled by social democratic scruples, and that
the future lay with the dictatorship of the proletariat. Austrian communist party membership, which had been negligible, rose tenfold after
February 1934.[10]

In the aftermath of the fighting, Philby joined Marxist reading-groups
and studied international press reaction. Litzi Friedmann was vulnerable
as a communist from a Jewish family. In order to bestow the protection
of British citizenship, Philby married her on 24 February in Vienna
town hall. This was more than a marriage of convenience, because it
rested on mutual sexual attraction, loving affection and shared political
excitement. Once Friedmann's British passport had been obtained in
April, they left for London, where they joined Philby's mother in Acol
Road.

Philby's recruitment as an agent

Philby's initial idea to join the civil service was frustrated when his
economics tutor at Trinity declined to give him a reference that did
not mention his political allegiance. He was also rebuffed when he went
to CPGB offices to try to join the party. He was interviewed by a party
functionary who disliked Cambridge-educated middle-class men, and
left the office without the promise of a green party card.

At this moment there was a decisive intervention by a woman who had been known in Vienna as Edith Suschitzky. Under that maiden name, she has already been mentioned as someone with whom Maurice Dobb was in sympathy. Under her anglicized married name of Tudor-Hart, she has already been named as the supplier of a Leica camera to Percy Glading's spy ring and as the NKVD recruiter who enlisted Arthur Wynn at Oxford. She was a photographer, who had run a shop that served as cover for the courier network for which Philby had visited Prague and Budapest. Born in 1908, the daughter of a Viennese social democrat bookseller, she first came to England in 1925 as a governess. She became the lover of Alexander Tudor-Hart, a Cambridge-trained physician and communist. He fathered children by different women, and dismissed sexual exclusivity as 'puritanical & sentimental', 'mid-victorian' and 'historically doomed'. After attending a workers' demonstration in Trafalgar Square, Suschitzky was ordered to leave Britain in 1930. 'I am terribly sorry to hear about the police & Edith,' Dobb wrote from Trinity to Tudor-Hart. 'I have fumed with quite useless anger since I heard of it.'[11]

During 1932–3 Suschitzky worked for Russian intelligence in Italy and Austria, in tandem with a Hungarian called Árpád Haaz, with a photographic studio as her cover. She was briefly detained after their activities had been discovered. Like Litzi Friedmann with Philby, she married Alexander Tudor-Hart in order to obtain a British passport: both marriages were a combination of political pragmatism and sexual attraction. Under the name of Edith Tudor-Hart she began cover work as a photographer and undercover work as a talent-spotter for the London illegals. Knowing of Philby's recent Viennese courier work, she invited him and Litzi Friedmann to tea in May 1934. Their stories of the street-fighting, and Philby's communist ardour, impressed her. Would Philby care to meet someone of unspecified interest? she asked. He did not hesitate in answering 'yes'.

Tudor-Hart stopped Philby from spoiling his cover by joining CPGB: his future lay as a conspiratorial worker rather than as an open activist. On a June morning she led him on an intricate journey designed to lose shadowers. They took a taxi, descended to an Underground train, walked the streets, hailed another taxi, changed to a third – a process lasting several hours. Eventually she brought him to a bench in the Regent's Park, where a handsome, blue-eyed, curly-haired man was sitting. This was Arnold Deutsch, whom Philby knew only by the codename OTTO (and who was also Glading's handler). During a relaxed conversation, mainly in German, Philby agreed to work for the anti-fascist cause. It is improbable that any organization was mentioned at this preliminary meeting. Tudor-Hart and Deutsch doubtless spoke of representing international Marxist interests without specifying any nation or communist front. This was certainly the practice of Ignace Reiss, Deutsch's Paris counterpart. But there can have been no doubt that Deutsch was acting for Soviet communism after he recommended that Philby should enhance his general utility to the cause by taking a language course in Russian (Philby never achieved proficiency).

In 1985, three years before his death, Philby gave an account of the Regent's Park meeting to the Russian television presenter Genrikh Borovik. 'You're a brave fellow, I was told how you behaved in Austria,' Deutsch reportedly told him. 'The Party doesn't play a big part in British life,' Deutsch continued. Rather than helping the anti-fascist movement by touting the *Daily Worker* in working-class districts, he should make the bolder decision to become an infiltrator of bourgeois authority. The bigger the risk, the larger the potential dividends, as capitalists knew. Philby was enticed by Deutsch's suggestion because he was too inexperienced to know what it entailed. In 1934, so he told Borovik, he could not imagine the reality of his future: 'the difficult, exhausting and often very ordinary, even boring, work that required enormous patience, will-power and control'. Hitherto he had dreaded trying to reconcile his revolutionary yearnings with the conformist drudgery of a bourgeois career; but now he was empowered with a secret, romantic purpose. He found his talks with Deutsch inspirational. At every meeting Deutsch made a show of his empathy by asking about Philby's plans, difficulties, pleasures and animosities. The young man felt valued, and responded with grateful admiration for his handler's composure, clarity and fixed commitment. He gave OTTO the highest compliment payable by an Englishman of his generation to a foreigner: 'he had a marvellous sense of humour'.[12]

It seems possible that, until Deutsch met Philby, Moscow's espionage services misunderstood the ranking of English universities. The greatest universities in Austria, Czechoslovakia, France, Ireland, Scotland and other European nations were in their capital cities: Vienna, Prague, Paris, Dublin, Edinburgh. Apparently Moscow's agents assumed that

London University mattered more than Oxford or Cambridge. It was perhaps under this illusion that Deutsch had enrolled in a psychology department there. But with the advent of Philby, Deutsch and his group belatedly noticed the possibilities in the older universities.

Philby's one eccentricity was his aversion to the sight, the smell, even the mention of apples. He was also scared of horses. Otherwise he had a hardy masculinity: he was indifferent to personal possessions, unobservant about rooms and their contents, and bored by gossip, archness, pretension and snobbery. After years of resentful adolescent attendance at Westminster Abbey, he disparaged institutions of which the conventional English were proud, never supported England during international sporting tournaments, yawned at English landscape and mocked complacent middle-class stereotypes. Philby was given the Russian codename of SYNOK and the German codename of SÖHNCHEN (London illegals preferred to use German codenames to disguise their Russian connection in case of interception).

Deutsch remitted to Moscow a character-sketch which depicted the young recruit as shy, irresolute, mild, solitary and emotionally awkward. He thought him a bad liar, sentimental in outlook and a pessimist who would need encouraging praise to keep him steady. Deutsch neither mentioned Philby's handsomeness nor predicted that masculine vanity would motivate Philby's undercover career. Once enrolled in a secret, exclusive and powerful cohort which survived by subterfuge and misdirection, Philby discovered that successful deception felt empowering. He became imbued with purposive ambition. The words of his contemporary Philip Jordan apply to the young man who became SYNOK: 'ambition, if you have it, consumes your whole being, and should be as secret and precious as your sexual organs; for if you have none, you are without the ability to create – impotent, castrate, pitiable'. Once Philby became a man of secrets, with plans and rules which could not be shared, his isolation was intense, but he never felt like a political eunuch. As Glading had also found, an intricate, risky clandestine life brought a unique perspective on world events and swelled feelings of secret importance. By enlisting with the communist cause, Philby chose to live in a constant state of emergency.[13]

Two years earlier Whittaker Chambers had begun work as a Soviet spy in Washington DC. 'Underground work is one test of a communist,' he wrote twenty years later in his repentant memoirs. 'Few other party activities make such insistent demands upon his devotion, discipline, resourcefulness, and courage, because few others require him to demonstrate daily, in action, his revolutionary faith beyond all appeals of country, family, friendship, and personal interest.' Although Chambers found the stealthy tradecraft of his work to be a nuisance, he felt pride in working for world revolution and proletarian dictatorship. Once the 'startling novelty' of underground work has gone, 'and in my case that happened within the first few months', wrote Chambers, 'revolutionary purpose alone makes it bearable'.[14]

As to Austria, in July 1934, three months after Philby and Friedmann had left Vienna, local Nazis seized Dollfuss's office, mortally wounded him and denied him the comforts of a priest while he bled slowly to death. 'We must keep out of trouble in central Europe at all costs', the Foreign Secretary Sir John Simon wrote two days later: 'of course I abstained entirely from any hint of *action*.' Nearly four years later, in March 1938, Germany annexed Austria. The communist view of the British ruling class was hardened by the House of Lords foreign policy debate a few days later. Ivan Maisky, Moscow's Ambassador in London, sat aghast listening to the legislators' wishful thinking. The veteran Marquess of Crewe, who had been Viceroy of Ireland during the 1890s, called for Czechoslovakia to give Gladstonian 'Home Rule' to Sudeten Germans who lived within its borders. Germany's union with Austria had been 'inevitable', said Cosmo Lang, the Archbishop of Canterbury. 'If the division had continued much longer it might have been a continuing sore spreading infection to other nations.' Lord Redesdale claimed that the *Anschluss* had prevented the outbreak of a central European version of the Spanish civil war: 'the gratitude of Europe and of the whole world was due to Herr Hitler for averting a catastrophe of such staggering magnitude without shedding one drop of blood'. Lord Stonehaven, reported Maisky, 'called for the publication in English of an unabridged translation of Hitler's *Mein Kampf* at the price of no more than a shilling a copy – so impressed was he by the profundity and foresight of the Führer's writings'. The Labour spokesman Lord Ponsonby of Shulbrede insisted that it would be against English interests to intervene in central Europe. 'There could not be one person in a 100 who knew where Czechoslovakia was,' he said to the sound of laughter. 'Other countries might commit crimes . . . but the attitude of getting on a pedestal and lecturing other people would not bring peace to Europe.' After sitting through the debate Maisky commented: 'The men sitting on these red benches are historically blind, like moles, and are ready to lick the Nazi dictator's boots like a beaten dog. They'll pay for this, and I'll see it happen!' It was similar loathing of complacent, reactionary defeatism that drove young Philby to treachery.[15]

Seven years after the *Anschluss*, in the spring of 1945, Vienna was again occupied: this time by ravaging Russian troops, who kept the eastern, southernmost and westerly districts of Austria's capital under Soviet domination until 1955. In the Baroque expanse of Schwarzenbergplatz, on which the occupiers tried to foist the name of Stalin Square, they erected the Heroes Monument of the Red Army, a semi-circular colonnade commemorating Soviet 'liberation' of the city and proclaiming the coming dictatorship of the proletariat. Atop a red-stone pedestal at the centre of the colonnade stood the black-and-gold figure of a proud hero of the Russian military with a machine gun strapped to his chest. This robotic-looking sentinel still keeps vigil over the city. Vladimir Putin laid flowers at the Red Army monument in 2007. The Viennese called the statue *der unbekannte Plünderer* – the unknown looter.[16]

CHAPTER 10

The Ring of Five

The induction of Philby, Maclean and Burgess

Litzi Friedmann had a Viennese friend named Peter Smolka. He had been born in Vienna in 1912, the son of the owner of a prosperous metallurgical business, and caused his first security scare when at the age of seventeen he was detained as a suspected Italian spy and expelled from France after taking photographs inside a fortress at Marseille. A month later, in September 1930, he arrived at Dover with a press pass from the Austrian newspaper *Der Tag* to report a conference on the future rule of India. Special Branch watched as he filed poignant English true-crime stories and photographed dismal-looking sandwich-board men in Trafalgar Square. He moved from a Bloomsbury hotel to Bayswater lodgings, and thence to rooms off Finchley Road and finally to a flat in Wembley. Special Branch suspected 'communist tendencies' and found him 'arrogant', but had no evidence that he was engaged in espionage.[1]

Smolka returned to England in May 1934, accompanied by his wife Lotty Jackl, as the London correspondent of a Viennese Catholic monarchist newspaper, *Neue Freie Presse*. To English eyes he seemed a podgy-faced, solemn-looking, bespectacled chump. 'Smolka is a Jew, rather a bore but decent,' Sir Arthur Willert of the FO's Press Department told Harker of MI5. In the autumn of 1934, probably at Edith Tudor-Hart's instigation and with Arnold Deutsch's approval, Smolka provided Philby with his first cover job. Together they formed a press agency called London Continental News. The idea of running such agencies as propaganda outlets was not new: the armaments manufacturer and former Intelligence Division officer Sir Vincent Caillard had, for example, sought financial aid from the Asquith government in 1916 for his projected Pronto Agency which would have been anti-German and pro-capitalist. All news agencies started in the 1930s were propaganda rackets: Associated Press, Havas, Reuters and United Press were so well entrenched that no younger rivals could compete without a subsidy from a right-wing millionaire or communist front organization. London Continental was intended to disseminate reports from central Europe, and to feed stories that purveyed the Moscow line, but it was still-born. Perhaps Moscow judged that Philby's potential would be wasted if he showed his communist affiliations. He later had other journalistic jobs; but London Continental News is the most significant in showing the ruthless dishonesty of Philby's new allies.[2]

Smolka established his London reputation with a series of articles in *The Times* about his travels in the Soviet Arctic. These were expanded into a bestselling book, *Forty Thousand against the Arctic: Russia's Polar Empire*. It was a beguiling work of propaganda with no hint that Soviet Russia was an empire based on mass murder and cruel deception. Smolka extolled Stalinist plans to extract coal, oil, gold, silver, platinum and nickel from the Arctic regions. He eulogized the factories, meteorological stations and aerodromes which one day would serve passengers flying, via Arctic Siberia, from London to Tokyo or New York to Shanghai. The handsome young aviator who piloted Smolka in a hydroplane was idealized as a hero of the people, 'tall and broad-shouldered, with a forehead firm and clear like a warrior's shield'. Smolka rhapsodized over the explorers, physicians, teachers, engineers and 'Red Missionaries' whom he met. He depicted the Gulag as a social reformatory for murderers, thieves, peasants and Trotskyites. Its prisoners had reviled Stalin as 'an opportunist traitor and wanted to smash him'. By their extremism, including a foreign policy that must bring Russia into conflict with the capitalist powers, 'they were jeopardizing success at home and courting a Fascist attack'. Death or exile were the only antidotes to their venom. 'They are the victims of history. Pitiable perhaps as individuals. But we had to sacrifice them to save the country.'[3]

In addition to Smolka, Philby was introduced by Deutsch to the newly arrived head of the Russian illegals in London, Alexander Orlov. Born Leiba Lazarevich Feldbin in Belorussia in 1895, Orlov had joined the Cheka in 1920 and had worked in Paris, under cover of the Soviet trade mission, using the alias of Leon Nikolayev until 1928. Then, under the name of Lev Feldel, he engaged in industrial espionage as a member

of a Soviet trade delegation in Berlin during 1928–31. After obtaining
a US passport in the name of William Goldbin in 1932, he served in
Vienna and Copenhagen. In London, he had the cover of running the
American Refrigerator Company in offices on the edge of Soho shared
with Hollywood's Central Casting Bureau and the Duckerfield School
of Dancing. Orlov took over the running of the station's active agents
and candidates for recruitment after a scare that Deutsch had come
under MI5 surveillance. The solicitude that he and Deutsch showed
Philby strengthened their agent's commitment to working for them.
Philby admired Orlov as 'a desperately energetic character', who liked
to sleep with a sub-machine gun beside him in bed.[4]

Philby compiled for Deutsch a list of seven young Cambridge men
who might be recruited as penetration agents. Topmost was Maclean,
who had just graduated from Trinity with first-class honours in modern
languages and was too earnest in his communism to favour his mother's
ambition for him to enter the Diplomatic Service, which would have
made him complicit in the abuses of the governing authorities. In a
recent contribution to *The Student's Vanguard*, David Guest had given
their cell's analysis of Whitehall. 'The higher posts in the State departments are almost exclusively recruited from the upper classes,' he falsely
declared. 'Among the lower officials habits of discipline and unthinking
obedience are inculcated. This makes the State machine not only an
instrument for ruling the society of today in the interests of capitalism,
but a handle to counter-revolution to prevent the system of society
being changed in any way.'[5]

Maclean thought like Guest until, in mid-August 1934, Philby invited
him to Acol Road and, after conversational feints, suggested that if he
was installed in the Foreign Office he could help communism by
supplying material from confidential diplomatic sources. According to
Philby, when Maclean asked if he would be working for Soviet intelligence or the Comintern, he replied that he did not know, but that
Maclean could be sure that it was a serious anti-fascist network tied to
Moscow. He forbade Maclean to consult Klugmann, who was too
embedded in the CPGB to be safe. After two days of thought, Maclean
agreed. Maclean was given the codename WAISE, meaning Orphan in
German. London's reports of these developments were photographed,
and then sent to Copenhagen in rolls of undeveloped film concealed
in boxes of women's face-powder. In cultivating potential recruits on

Philby's list of seven, Orlov and Deutsch were flouting Moscow's rule that agents who knew one another well should not be employed in the same network.

Other versions of Philby's approach to Maclean must be discounted. John Costello and Oleg Tsarev, for example, used the clichés of class warriors to caricature events. 'Like the sinister uninvited fairy at a royal christening party, he arrived during the first week of June when, even at the height of the Great Depression, the university was *en fête*,' they wrote with puritan disapproval. (June 1934 marked neither the height nor the depth of the Depression, but the beginning of recovery.) 'The spectacle of revellers still at midday in evening attire swaggering along King's Parade would have been a powerful inducement to Philby in his secret mission to undermine the British Establishment,' they imagined. 'Cambridge during May Week was nothing but a prolonged "coming-out party" for the sons and daughters of Britain's ruling class. During a time of mass unemployment, their hedonism confidently celebrated their accession to their appointed places . . . [in] the ruling elites.'[6]

Maclean prepared for the Foreign Office examination as part of a scheme to penetrate bourgeois institutions. Orlov doubted that a youth who was known for communist affiliations would pass the selection process, and urged him to collect letters of recommendation from his parents' influential friends. 'Donald is much more progressive than his dear father,' Lady Maclean admitted to people. Ignaty Reif, an illegal who was using a stolen Austrian passport giving him the alias of Max Wolisch, saw a letter (purloined or borrowed by Donald Maclean) from the Prime Minister Stanley Baldwin assuring Lady Maclean that he would exert influence to get her son into the Diplomatic Service. Maclean expected the Interview Board to ask about his communist past and had an answer pat: 'I did have such views, and I haven't entirely shaken them off.' His candour seemed attractive: he was one of half a dozen successful candidates. The Foreign Secretary, Sir John Simon, a former colleague of Maclean's father, sent the new recruit a letter of congratulation, which Orlov forwarded to Moscow.[7]

A nimbus of prestige radiated over the Diplomatic Service in the 1930s. It was an exclusively masculine domain, which was described in the manly similes of the hunter of wild animals and beautiful women. Sir Owen O'Malley, whose official career spanned 1911–47, revelled in the 'delicious atmosphere of secrecy, excitement and importance' in his work: 'the conduct of foreign affairs compared with internal affairs as big-game hunting compares with deerstalking or a covert shoot'. Lord Inverchapel, in whose Washington embassy Maclean was later Head of Mission, likened the diplomatist's role to that of an inconstant lover 'who moves from love to love taking on the new almost before the embraces of the old one are cold'. The Office environment was spartan, without feminizing touches. Valentine Lawford, who had a Cambridge double first in modern languages and studied at the Sorbonne and in Vienna, was in the same batch of recruits as Maclean. He was astounded by the charmless surroundings: 'the mahogany Office of Works hat-stand hung with unclaimed umbrellas and unattractive "office coats" with *glacé* [worn] elbows, the screen with its gruesome pin-ups of Himmler, Streicher and Roehm, the jaundice-coloured distempered walls, hanging light-bulbs under china shades, and threadbare, grey-blue-bistre carpet of the kind that one had dismissed at one's private school as probably made by convicts out of coconut fibre in the Andaman islands'.[8]

Maclean was put to work as a Third Secretary in the Western Department, which was responsible for Belgium, the Netherlands, Luxembourg, Spain, Portugal and Switzerland. The documents that reached his desk were enclosed in different coloured folders. 'White jackets' contained confidential material, 'green jackets' contained secret material, 'red jackets' contained SIS reports and 'blue jackets' contained the intercepted, deciphered messages of foreign powers. There were no restrictions on the papers seen by a newly recruited Third Secretary: Maclean was able to snitch material – mainly from folders with green or red bands on their covers, containing secret or SIS documents – which was copied overnight and returned. Blue-banded folders containing signals intelligence were high-security items which it was impossibly risky to smuggle out overnight; although Maclean was accordingly provided with a roll film reflex camera to photograph the contents of blue folders, this was seldom possible without detection. The films were smuggled by courier to Copenhagen, and went thence to Moscow. Maclean provided diplomatic dispatches and memoranda, reports from military attachés, appraisals by SIS and secret material from the Committee of Imperial Defence on British military, naval and aerial preparedness, the productive capacities and output of European munitions works, the mobilization plans of the European powers, and war plans against both Germany and the Soviet Union. He also supplied counter-intelligence material, such as the existence of an English informant in the People's Commissariat of Foreign Affairs, the penetration of Münzenberg's entourage and the plain texts of dispatches to Moscow at a time when King was providing enciphered versions of them. Comparisons enabled Soviet cryptanalysts to continue intercepting and eavesdropping on British secret radio traffic. Maclean also betrayed an ingenious GC&CS scheme of 1936 to break the Soviet embassy's cipher.

NKVD archives contain forty-five boxes of material supplied by Maclean @ WAISE between 1935 and June 1940. Each box contained over 300 documents. Little wonder that Maly warned Moscow in 1936 that the abundant material supplied by Maclean was overwhelming his resources. 'He came to us out of sincere motivation, namely that the intellectual emptiness and aimlessness of the bourgeois class to which he belonged antagonized him,' Deutsch wrote in an early appraisal of Maclean. 'He dresses carelessly like SYNOK [Philby], and is involved in the same Bohemian lifestyle. He takes an interest in painting and music. Like SYNOK, he is reserved and secretive, seldom displaying his enthusiasms.' Maclean explained to Deutsch that he was unmarried because he felt averse to girls of his own class, and would only live with a woman who was 'a comrade'. This seems true enough, for his first important lover and his choice of wife were female comrades whom he could trust. Contrary to later unsubstantiated tales about Maclean's sexuality, Deutsch gives no hint that WAISE was attracted by his own sex or differed in his tastes from SYNOK. Both these new recruits, 'and our other agents in England, have grown up in a climate in which the legality of our Party is upheld in an atmosphere of democratic illusions', Deutsch continued. For this reason they were sometimes careless about security. Overall, despite this bourgeois laxity, Deutsch was sure that 'our revolutionary cause has an absolute hold and authority over them'.[9]

In the Western Department Maclean's ashtray was always full of cigarette ash and butts. The typing-pool nicknamed him 'Fancy-Pants' because he dressed with sober conformity. Cyril Connolly recalled him as 'sandy-haired, tall, with great latent physical strength, but fat and rather flabby' when he joined the Office in 1934. Connolly, who was a shrewd judge of his contemporaries' sex lives, saw the young man as eager for experiences with women: 'an outsize Cherubino intent on amorous experience but too shy and clumsy to succeed'; and, perhaps because of his frustration in this area, 'given to sudden outbursts of aggression'. A few years of Whitehall responsibilities changed Maclean, who became 'painstaking, logical and resolute in argument, judicious and even-tempered', continued Connolly. After Maclean had vanished in 1951, Vansittart remembered him as an Office junior: 'I thought him a pleasant, although not an outstanding, young man, who might have had a respectable, though not a brilliant, career.'[10]

Maclean's boon drinking companion Humphrey Slater, who repudiated communism during the war, published a novel in 1948, *The Conspirator*, about a handsome, well-connected young man who is enlisted as a Soviet spy by an Oxford don while at university and lives in Sussex Square round the corner from Maclean's boyhood home in Bayswater. The Maclean-like anti-hero, Desmond Lightfoot, describes himself as 'a loyal supporter of the greatest social experiment in the history of mankind' and as having voluntarily submitted to 'para-military discipline'. His success as a spy imbues him with 'proud self-assurance' as European politics develop 'inexorably towards . . . the dictatorship of the proletariat'. He feels that 'there was absolutely no position in the world to which it would not be quite reasonable for someone of his age, ability and record to aspire. He walked across Sussex Square with an intensely strong sense of belonging to the future and of being a trusted and integral part of a massively invincible historic movement. He enjoyed the absolute discipline required and the rewarding consciousness of being valued.' Slater might have been describing his friend Maclean.[11]

After their recruitment, both Philby and Maclean were instructed to cease left-wing activism and make a somersault in their politics. Philby joined the Anglo-German Fellowship, and began reporting to Moscow on British capitalists who were lobbying for conciliation with Nazi Germany and for resistance to Soviet Russia. Maclean emulated Philby's pretend-conversion, but failed to convince Guy Burgess. 'Burgess would not have been Burgess', Philby told Borovik, 'if he had believed Maclean's switch.' Burgess pursued the neophyte diplomat with outrageous persistence. 'Do you think that I believe even for one jot that you have stopped being a Communist?' he would demand in front of other people. 'You're simply up to something! I know you, you old liar and sneak. You expect me to believe that you would betray yourself? Never in your life!' This mockery jeopardized Maclean's cover as well as exasperating him: finally he erupted when they were alone together, 'Listen, shut up, damn you! All right, I am still who I was. But I can say no more, I don't have the right.' Philby and Maclean agreed with Deutsch that it was essential to stop Burgess yacking among fellow communists. They could imagine Burgess showing off, averring with winks and nudges that Maclean was not lost to the party and confiding in trusted friends until everyone knew.[12]

Burgess was the seventh man – with '????' marked against his name – on the list of potential Cambridge recruits that Philby had given to Deutsch. Only a few months earlier, in March 1934, male homosexuality had been criminalized in Russia, with a penalty of three to five years in a correctional labour camp, mainly because the Stalinist authorities feared that same-sex parties were a cloak for politically malcontent talk. Nikolai Krylenko, the People's Commissar of Justice who believed that socialist judges should convict prisoners in accordance with political priorities rather than footling individual guilt or innocence, warned a party congress that male homosexuality was seditious: 'under this cover, in the foul dens and dives, another sort of activity takes place – counter-revolutionary activity'. Orlov believed that men 'tainted with homosexual perversion' were 'unstable individuals', but in December 1934, when Maclean arranged for him to meet Burgess, Deutsch had the imagination to see that the louche name-dropper might be an asset as a contacts-man.[13]

Orlov compiled a psychological portrait of Burgess @ MÄDCHEN in 1939, by which time his agent was working for SIS. It contains some misjudgements, such as that Burgess's homosexuality had been instilled by experiences at Eton where, Orlov falsely stated, pupils slept together in dormitories and were seduced by masters. Altogether Orlov's assessment reflected Burgess's own strenuously promoted myth-image and was less acute than those of Philby and Maclean. 'He grew up in an atmosphere of cynicism, opulence, hypocrisy and superficiality,' Orlov reported. 'The Party was for him a saviour. It gave him above all an opportunity to satisfy his intellectual needs.' Burgess's 'abhorrence of bourgeois morality' and pleasure in feeling estranged from conventional society led him to cultivate a wide network of sexual outsiders 'ranging from the famous liberal economist Keynes and extending to the very trash of society'. Another interpretation of Burgess would be as an adventurer who liked to pit himself against the odds, and enjoyed the thrill of pushing his luck. He had an appetite for aberrations that needed to be fed in increasing doses. Deutsch's assessment of Burgess differed from Orlov's: 'MÄDCHEN has imagination and is full of plans and initiative, but he has no internal brakes. He is, therefore, prone to panic easily and he is also prone to desperation. He takes up any task willingly, but he is too unstable to take it to its conclusion. His will is often paralysed by the most insignificant of difficulties. Sometimes he lies, not maliciously, but because of fear of admitting some minor error.' Over the course of time, Deutsch reported, as Burgess realized that he was trusted as a comrade, his self-confidence improved. He repeatedly told Deutsch that he thought his handlers were 'his saviours'.[14]

The Marxist ideology of Philby, Maclean and Burgess was a mixture of quasi-religious faith with quasi-scientific certainty. Religions deal in prophecy rather than reliable predictions: the historical determinism of Marxism delivers misplaced conviction. As a consequence, ideologues like these three young Cambridge graduates were hopeless at predicting the consequences of their decisions and actions. Like other spies, they were most vulnerable in the months after their recruitment, because they were not at first taught how to evade watchers. As Krivitsky told Jane Archer during his debriefing in 1940: 'the greatest care was taken not to impress upon a new recruit the dangers of what he was doing. As time went on and the recruit became more hardened, then he would be given the fullest instructions.' Krivitsky thought that it was only in the first weeks after enlistment that an agent might be monitored effectively by counter-espionage. Trained Soviet agents were, he said, so adept at evading surveillance that little or nothing could be gained by watching them. Only recently recruited novices were vulnerable to tracking and monitoring.[15]

Philby learnt that when he met new contacts, he should not ask personal questions, but should memorize faces and voices. When he was introduced in 1937 to a new handler, he asked her to walk about, so that he could memorize her gait. The instructions for making first contact with Maclean, which were given to Grigory Grafpen, the legal NKVD *rezident* who took over the networks of Deutsch and Maly after their recall to Moscow, show the precautionary complexities of trade-craft. He was to telephone Maclean at home, before 9.30 a.m. or after 10.30 p.m., saying: 'Hello, it's Bill here, wouldn't you like to go to the theatre?' This meant that they would meet at a prearranged time next day at Charing Cross Underground station. Grafpen, carrying a copy of the *Manchester Guardian*, would say, 'I have not seen you for a long time, Donald.' Maclean, armed with a copy of *Esquire*, would reply, 'Have you got any news of Theodore?'[16]

The Spanish civil war veteran Alexander Foote was surprised when asked in 1938 to work under cover in Switzerland: 'Speaking only inferior French, a little kitchen Spanish, and elementary German, I was not exactly qualified for work on the Continent.' He had no training in wireless transmission, microphotography, secret inks or sabotage, and did not know which organization was using him. His instructions to meet his handler Ursula ('Ruth') Kuczynski @ SONYA were elaborate. He was to loiter at the General Post Office in Geneva wearing a white scarf and holding a leather belt in his right hand. At noon he would be approached by a woman carrying a string shopping-bag containing a green parcel, and holding an orange in her hand. The woman would ask in English where Foote had bought the belt. After replying that it came from a Paris ironmonger's shop, he would inquire where he might buy an orange and she would answer that he could have hers for a penny. Half a century later she recalled their rendezvous: 'I took note of everything, every word, cadence, gesture, facial expression.'[17]

The Cambridge spies focused on the feeble response of English parliamentarians to right-wing totalitarianism. 'Fascism is naked capitalism,' J. D. Bernal had pronounced in *Cambridge Left*. The ring of five were riled by class prejudice, regional unemployment and the funk of the Labour leaders who had betrayed socialism in 1931. It was less obvious in 1934 than in 1945 that communism was the ideology deployed by the Stalinist nation state to make its push to become a world super-power. The quintet comforted themselves with the notion that they were aiding the Comintern's underground war against fascism, and that the Comintern was merely an international link between national communist parties, rather than serving Stalin's Russia. The ring may have believed that when the dictatorship of the proletariat took control in other European countries, without Russia's cruel despotic traditions, it would be less degrading of its citizens. In any case, they had not been immunized against the infectious belief of the 1930s vanguard that the Soviet Union constituted one of the wonders of the age. Progressive clergymen, pacifists and town planners visited Russia, and revered its atheism, the tanks in Red Square and the slums. Above all, Dobb, Guest and Cornford had instilled in young Cambridge communists the belief that, in Bernal's words, 'the whole tradition of the intellectual is to do nothing until it is too late'.[18]

Philby, Maclean, Blunt and Cairncross were priggish about commerce and consumers. Burgess disliked American culture, voices and influence. Living in London in the mid-1930s they found reasons enough to feel alienated. The capital of the British Empire seemed every year to pay closer cultural obeisance to Hollywood and more to resemble Chicago. On his release from Parkhurst prison in 1935, Wilfred Macartney was overwhelmed by the changes in eight years: 'everything was speeded up . . . Whitehall, Regent Street, Piccadilly, Baker Street – new, new, new, new, all new! Hard lines where soft curves had shown; sheer walls; huge blocks of flats.' He baulked at neon signs flashing from the front of buildings, gaudy snack-bars, movie palaces and new super-luxury hotels. He was astounded by the change in men's appearances: 'all wearing straight-striped patterns, loud shirts, and hectic ties. I got an impression of general pansification from the men.' His greatest shock was when he visited the once fusty offices of his solicitors in Lincoln's Inn Fields, and found that they had adapted to the brash new competitive environment. Brisk youngsters had replaced the Dickensian clerks. Modern office-machinery meant that 'everything went with a click'. Traditions had yielded to capitalist imperatives: peers from historic families were turning their agricultural and urban estates into limited companies so as to minimize taxation and maximize income. After returning to London after years in the Balkans, David Footman in 1935 felt equally estranged from the encroaching materialism which increased the tempo of the times: 'What we want now is salesmanship, energy, machine-made idealism directed with an eye on practicalities, and that form of public-school spirit which finds its practical expression in the insincere bonhomie of a Rotarian Congress.'[19]

London was the traitors' terrain. Ewer's network made Fleet Street, Holborn and the Temple their sector of secret operations. Oldham lived south of Kensington High Street while Glading rented his photographic lair just north. The illegals leased flats in Marylebone. Pieck's business front was near Victoria station. The drinking-clubs of Soho and bottle-parties in Chelsea were pleasure resorts for Burgess and Maclean. Another compact historic district was added to the spy topography: St James's, bounded by Piccadilly to the north, Haymarket to the east, St

James's Park to the south, Green Park to the west. Systematically, after their enlistment to work for Moscow in 1934, and doubtless under instruction, Burgess, Maclean, Philby and Blunt sought election to clubs in St James's: moreover, to adjacent clubs, with frontage side by side along Pall Mall and with rear access to the private gardens of Carlton House Terrace. Maclean was elected to the Travellers at 106 Pall Mall in 1936. The following year, at the nomination of Dennis Proctor, Burgess and Blunt were both elected to the Reform next door at 104–105 Pall Mall: Burgess thereafter had his personal letters sent to the Reform, and was a devoted, conspicuous member. Philby also became a clubman in 1937, with his election to the third club in the row, the Athenaeum, at 107 Pall Mall. This club vicinity was not by chance. It gave the quartet parallel but unduplicated ranges of contact; they saw and heard different men, and collated opinions; they had easy, casual access to one another in adjacent premises.

Philip Jordan, who was a devoted member of the Travellers, wrote a novel in 1939 in which the narrator gives a malcontented account of his fellow members: 'I used to despise their narrow, class outlook; their failure, particularly that of the diplomats, to go out into the world beyond their little circle and discover what was happening and what was important; their belief in their own infallibility and their unuttered hope of ultimate honours from the hands of a puppet king who did as they told him.' One can fancy that Maclean's inner thoughts were similar. Jordan's narrator was heading for the Spanish civil war, and felt abject in relation to the Travellers' diplomats: 'they and their rolled umbrellas and their spare-time academic hobbies were now far above me . . . they seemed to me to dwell in heaven and to have earned the right to do so'.[20]

Francis Graham-Harrison, who was described by one Home Secretary addressing the House of Commons as having a Rolls-Royce brain, told an MI5 interviewer in 1963 that it had been impossible to move among the London intelligentsia of the late 1930s without meeting Burgess. Rosamond Lehmann, who first met Burgess about the time of his enlistment by Moscow, was sixteen years later to describe him to Skardon of MI5 as 'an avid, belligerent and bawling left-winger', 'a noisy drunkard . . . with extremely shocking conversation', and 'ambitious . . . to be a power behind the throne'. Her husband Wogan Philipps (later, as Lord Milford, the first CPGB member in the House of Lords) 'despised BURGESS, and wrote him off as no value to man or beast'.[21]

In 1935, on Orlov's instructions, Burgess took a Russian-language course at the School of Slavonic Studies in London, where SIS officers were taught foreign languages. He failed however in his object of making SIS contacts or inveigling his way into the trust of its officers. He was personal secretary for some months to a Tory MP who had once been detained for spying in Tunisia and whose German sympathies owed something to his pleasure in embracing young Aryan manhood. In 1936 Burgess hooked a job in the Talks Department of the BBC. He secured this post with help from an impressive referee, the Trinity historian G. M. Trevelyan, who offered reassurance: 'he has passed through the communist measles that so many of our clever young men go through'. Burgess commissioned and produced radio talks: he got the Comintern agent Ernst Henri on the airwaves as well as Blunt and less subversive speakers. The National Labour MP Harold Nicolson became his patron: Nicolson's sexual partner James Lees-Milne recalled that Burgess 'had the look of an inquisitive rodent emerging into daylight from a drain'.[22]

David Footman and Dick White

In July 1937 Burgess was instructed to cultivate David Footman. The only child of a country clergyman, and describing himself as an Anglo-Catholic in the 1930s, Footman survived combat as a teenage army officer on the Western Front. In 1927 he married his twenty-year-old cousin Jane Footman, who was an aspiring actress under the stage-name Joan Clement-Scott, but there have been hints of unknown reliability that he was bisexual. After consular postings in Egypt and Macedonia, he left the Consular Service in 1929 to manage a gramophone company in Vienna (he later wrote a story about a man who leaves his job in the Balkans to manage a gramophone company in Vienna in an attempt to revive a failing marriage). Footman moved in 1932 to Belgrade (then 'the boom town of the Balkans') as representative of the London bank Glyn Mills. He was the sort of self-sufficient, ironical Englishman who, when he toured Albania, packed an odd volume of Gibbon's Decline and Fall, Wyss's Swiss Family Robinson and two packs of patience cards. Yugoslavia he described as 'the land of unlimited impossibilities'. One of his haunts was Kalemegdan Park, beside the Belgrade fortress, with its maze of paths and underground passages popular with loving couples after dark. It was at a rendezvous in Kalemegdan Park that Footman was recruited to SIS in 1935 by Edwin ('Eddy') Boxshall, the Vickers agent in Bucharest. Footman took the cover of a passport control officer, in which he cannot have been convincing: he was an animal-lover who found human faces harder to recognize individually than those of dumb beasts. Government service taught him 'that vested interests are very important, and that little personal vanities are even more so'. He measured a country's political sophistication by its efficiency in handling its card-indexes of suspicious foreigners.[23]

In 1935 – as well as joining SIS – Footman published a volume of short stories about seedy English expatriates in the Balkans, *Half-Way East*, reminiscent of Somerset Maugham's stories, but with a playful touch of Hemingway. A few months later there came an acclaimed travel book, *Balkan Holiday*, which provoked the jealousy of Rebecca West. In 1936 Footman published his first novel, *Pig and Pepper*, with a Balkan diplomatic setting. His next volume of stories, *Better Forgotten*, evinced 'an urbane scepticism, a gentlemanly doubt' about human significance, judged *The Times* reviewer, and was 'modern, in the cool, concise style'. Burgess, as a member of the BBC Talks Department, invited Footman to dinner in 1937 and convinced him (although a man on SIS payroll) to give a broadcast talk, 'Albania, Fish and a Motor-Car', in August. A second broadcast talk followed in November. Thereafter the two men met occasionally. Footman found Burgess 'a highly entertaining partner for a drink or a meal', whose harangues on dialectical materialism seemed no more significant than an intellectual parlour game.[24]

In May 1938 Konrad Henlein, the Nazi leader of the Sudeten Germans, stayed at the Goring Hotel on a visit to London. Burgess convinced his boyfriend Jack Hewit, who was a telephone switchboard operator at the Goring, to eavesdrop on Henlein's calls and report the scraps that he heard for Footman's benefit. Burgess undertook other freelance SIS work for Footman, who recommended him to an SIS colleague as someone who might report on Mussolini's responses to Franco's recent victories in Spain. While the possibility of sending Burgess to Italy was under consideration, he mentioned in a casual way to Footman that he had been a communist at Cambridge. In that case, Footman responded trustingly, Burgess might be useful to the anti-communist section of SIS, and he took Burgess to lunch with Valentine Vivian, chief of Section V. The three men had a frank talk. Burgess later reported to Moscow that neither SIS man seemed to suspect him. 'Why? Class blinkers – Eton, my family, an intellectual . . . people like me are beyond suspicion.' Although Vivian is often represented as obtuse, crabbed and blimpish (certainly as a result of stomach ulcers he looked dyspeptic), he impressed Burgess with his understanding of Comintern operations and Marxist dialectic. Vivian's *obiter dicta* to Burgess at this lunch were canny. 'Theory is necessary for action,' he reportedly said. 'Legal Party members are not dangerous.'[25]

During the 1930s two Jewish comedians from the East End of London, calling themselves the Western Brothers, raised their laughs by wearing Old Harrovian ties, sporting monocles and singing such satirical ditties as 'We're Frightfully BBC' and 'Play the Game, You Cads'. Above all they mocked traditional deference in 'The Old School Tie', with its feebly rhymed refrain 'Don't forget Marlborough, remember St Paul's and Dulwich and Harrow and how! /And Wormwood and Dartmoor and Pentonville too and Doctor Barnado's says thou.' Despite Burgess's stereotypically Marxist assurances to Moscow about class blinkers, eyes were opening wider, the public school spirit was increasingly seen as risible and institutions were becoming more socially diverse.

The appointment in 1935 of MI5's thirtieth officer, Dick White, was an indicator of change. His father was an ironmonger with a shop in Tonbridge High Street, who deserted his family and became a hopeless drunk. His mother was able to send him to a boarding school at Bishops Stortford with a nonconformist religious tradition. White's athletics prowess, intelligence and conservatism (his reaction to his disturbed childhood) made him a thorough success reading history at Christ Church, Oxford, where he became a protégé of Masterman. In early manhood he hankered after being a novelist in the Proustian mould. In 1932, after extensive travels, he got a job teaching history, English, French and German at a school in Croydon. At Easter of 1935 he escorted fifteen pupils from his school on a Mediterranean cruise aboard a White Star liner. He struck up a shipboard friendship with a young soldier, Malcolm Cumming, who unknown to him had been sent on the cruise by MI5 to assess his suitability for recruitment (Masterman having recommended him for secret service). In July White was called for interview by Liddell, who offered him a tax-free salary of £350 a year, which was half his pay as a schoolmaster. He was intrigued by his exchanges with Liddell, but affronted by the money. 'They were rather secretive, so I wasn't quite sure what they were trying to say,' he recalled to his biographer Tom Bower. 'Everything was by way of hints. I left it that they would have to say something direct.' In praising White ('He did not talk too much . . . he looked and sounded a good committee man'), Bower also slurred his colleagues with catchy alliteration: 'Unlike other intelligence officers, White was neither fruity nor florid.'[26]

The officers of MI5 in the mid-1930s – Holt-Wilson, Haldane, Harker, Boddington, Robertson, Cumming, Miller and Liddell – had hetero-geneous backgrounds, thoughtful opinions and versatile minds. They were neither infallible nor (as sometimes caricatured) snobbish, insular, smug and prejudiced. Although at the end of the working day they might gather for fireside drinks together in a collegiate way, as a group they were neither fruity nor florid. They were shrewd, patient, watchful, self-sufficient and empathetic: it is wrong to depict them as wooden-tops just because they respected military discipline and felt patriotic.[27]

With the exception of Rebecca West, the formative commentators on British espionage and counter-espionage were all men, and were imbued with their generations' unquestioned assumptions. Among later scholars of intelligence history, Gill Bennett has shining rarity as a woman. They have been blind to a more important discrimination than class in Whitehall – gender. What united the officers as they gathered in collegiate fashion for a fireside drink was not their class prejudices and allegiances, which were mixed, but their gender, which was unmixed. When Vivian was introduced by Footman to Burgess, he appraised the young man, and enlisted him as an SIS freelance, on the basis of affirmative manly recognition, confidence in the tight bonds of right-thinking men and the secure comforts that came from the caparison of regular office life. What mattered was not that Vivian had been educated at St Paul's, Footman at Marlborough and Burgess at Eton, with fathers who were an artist, a vicar and a naval officer. The dynamic was of three men together, reacting as men, with little thought of women beyond domestic settings. The great government depart-ments, the Foreign Office, SIS and MI5 were masculine in their controls and procedures. With few exceptions, women were underlings, who had low influence in or out of the workplace.

The recruitment of Blunt and Cairncross

In January 1937 Burgess introduced Deutsch to Anthony Blunt. Blunt then held a research fellowship at Trinity and was a member of the French department of the university: his postgraduate thesis had investigated Italian literary influences on Poussin's art, he was converting himself into an art historian, and he was due to leave Trinity in June 1937 for a post at the Warburg Institute in London to pursue his studies of French and Italian art of the Renaissance and seventeenth century. He had been a theoretical Marxist since 1934, but the Spanish civil war, which raged from July 1936 and in which his ex-lover Julian Bell was killed in July 1937, was (as he told his Courtauld colleague Peter Kidson in 1962), 'the moment of truth' for him. Kidson, in a shrewd essay on Blunt, depicts the art historian changing from a scholar who used Marxist ideas as a provocation and discipline in art criticism to a politically aroused citizen who thought that Britain's status as a world power was unsustainable, that its foreign policy was 'pussy-footing with pious hopes', that its leaders were philistine capitalists who thought only of protecting their investment dividends and that 'the only great power with the will and the means to take on the fascists was Soviet Russia'. Kidson speculates that in the late 1930s Blunt may have imagined the possibility of becoming Commissar of Culture if ever a Marxist government was installed in London. Whatever the truth of this, Blunt agreed to talent-spot for Deutsch during his remaining six months in Cambridge. Deutsch found Blunt super-intelligent, high-flown in his spoken English, self-controlled, and effeminate.[28]

Two undergraduates, Leo Long and Michael Straight, were recruited by Blunt for Deutsch in his last months working in Cambridge. Long was a carpenter's son, had been educated at Holloway County School in north London and was a Trinity linguist. Straight was an American banking heir whose mother and stepfather ran the experimental Dartington Hall School in Devonshire. He was 'very melodramatic', the poet Gavin Ewart told Miranda Carter. 'You felt he was in a deep conspiracy all the time.' Charles Rycroft, who went to Russia with Straight, judged him 'an attitudinizer'. In Moscow Straight bought some local clothes, and asked, 'Do I look like a proletarian?' Rycroft answered: 'No, you look like a millionaire pretending to be a proletarian.'[29]

By 1937 Deutsch needed to induct another Cambridge spy inside the Foreign Office: the Office posted all third secretaries to overseas embassies after two years' experience of Whitehall; and Deutsch knew that Maclean was due to leave London. Blunt was therefore asked by Burgess to approach John Cairncross, whom he had supervised in French literature at Trinity. After graduating with first-class honours at Cambridge, Cairncross had passed head of the list in the civil service examinations, and had joined the American Department of the Foreign Office in October 1936.[30]

Blunt invited Cairncross to spend the last weekend of February 1937 as his guest at Trinity: Burgess came by arrangement to meet the possible recruit there on the Sunday. 'He comes from a lower middle class family,' Burgess reported, 'he speaks with a strong Scottish accent and one cannot call him a gentleman.' Although he professed theoretical Marxism, Cairncross was not a partisan in the class war, Burgess continued, but a 'petit bourgeois who is intoxicated with his own success, with the fact that he could raise himself to the level of the British ruling class and has the possibility of enjoying the luxury and delights of bourgeois life'. Cairncross had worked for six years without holidays or leisure: 'it was his dream to get into the Foreign Office at any price'. Burgess concluded that it might be possible to enlist Cairncross if he could be convinced that he could combine careers in both the party and the Foreign Office. (It is notable – given the later false emphasis put on the homosexuality of the Cambridge spies – that Cairncross and Long were exclusively attracted to women. Straight was, like Cairncross, highly sexed, and it is beyond doubt that his predominant interest was always for women. It has been suggested that when his hormones were raging at Cambridge he had some pleasures *faute de mieux* with another man – said to be Blunt. This is easy to say, impossible to prove or disprove and on balance doubtful.)[31]

There was concern that the illegals might be exposed if Cairncross rejected the NKVD's overtures. Accordingly the first approach was delegated to Klugmann, who was then working in Paris for the International Students' Organization against War and Fascism. Klugmann would not agree to meet Maly and Deutsch until they had been endorsed by a CPGB member whom he trusted, Percy Glading. Thus reassured, Klugmann persuaded Cairncross to work for the two Soviet spies. As a linguist Cairncross was faultless in French, German,

Spanish and Italian: he later acquired a reading knowledge of Russian, Norwegian and Swedish. Yet his workplace skills proved defective: Office colleagues found him verbose and graceless. During his two years there he was shunted through the American, League of Nations, Western and Central departments. Shortly after providing documents during the Munich crisis of September 1938 (the material was delivered through Klugmann), Cairncross was transferred to a section in the Treasury supervising the Post Office and Stationery Office. Although this sounds humdrum, he sometimes had access to important material. In June 1939, for example, when his departmental head was on leave, he supplied reports on Germany circulated by the Committee of Imperial Defence, and material on wartime propaganda plans including the creation of a Ministry of Information. In July he provided documents on SIS, MI5, GC&CS and a chain of secret radio interception stations. In August he supplied documents needing nine rolls of film to be photographed, including minutes of the Committee of Imperial Defence, documents on raw material reserves and wartime evacuation plans.

One key to understanding Cairncross is that he was an expert on Molière, and was indeed given the codename MOLIÈRE. His chosen subject was the most protean of playwrights, a comic genius, a satirical moralist, a flatterer of bourgeois values, a toady to the nobility. Cairncross was equally loath to hold any line or to conform to any orthodoxy. His dissident nature was both political and personal: he had an inner pride which needed praise and craved status, but his prickly, conceited and resentful temperament discouraged people from giving him what he wanted. He was proud of the powerful analytical orderliness of his mind, but got into scrapes, had a reputation for untidiness and disorganization and made himself unpopular. His scrutiny of human foibles was sometimes sour and condescending: of Maclean @ WAISE he told Maly, 'He knows from his Cambridge days that WAISE also was a Party member and he says that although WAISE has become a complete snob, he nevertheless maintains a "healthy line" in his work which shows that he has retained Marxist principles in his subconscious.' Deutsch in parallel reported Maclean's view of Cairncross: 'intelligent, but works badly and is careless . . . because he considers himself cleverer and better than all the others'.[32]

Maclean in Paris

Maly, who remained London *rezident* until August 1937, wished his prize source to have a handler of his own. Accordingly, in 1937, Maclean was allotted to a dark, attractive NKVD officer, Kitty Harris @ GYPSY @ NORMA @ ADA @ Elizabeth Dreyfus @ Alice Read @ Elizaveta Stein. A Jewess who had been born in Belorussia in 1899, she lived in Winnipeg in 1908–23 before moving to Chicago. In 1926 she married the communist Earl Browder, with whom she undertook secret work in Asia. After they had separated in 1931, Browder became leader of the Communist Party of the USA (CPUSA), with the NKVD codenames of HELMSMAN and SHAMAN, until dethroned from his position on Moscow's orders in 1945. Harris meanwhile returned to Europe, where she served as a courier of undeveloped films obtained by the *vorón* Fyodor Paparov from the Foreign Ministry in Berlin and was trained to run agents. In 1937 she was transferred to London, where at her first rendezvous with the London *rezident* in a Leicester Square cinema she carried a copy of A. J. Cronin's novel *The Citadel* for identification. Harris photographed the documents that Maclean had brought overnight from the Office: he had been hoping for some years to find a woman comrade; she was headstrong and oddly gullible; and despite the difference in their age, they soon became lovers.

When Maclean was posted as Third Secretary to the Paris embassy in September 1938, Harris followed him to the French capital. After a few months there, still his lover as well as his handler, she reported to Moscow: 'While in London he could act as he liked. He had his friends and lots of time to read.' But in Paris he was constricted by formal responsibilities. 'He must attend dinners and receptions. His whole life is centred on the embassy. He hates this atmosphere, but at the same time must work in it.' There were few chances to scout in bookshops or loiter beside the news kiosks in the boulevards. He seldom had the time to go drinking and smoking in Left Bank bars frequented by writers, artists and the left intelligentsia.[33]

Maclean did not appreciate Sir Eric Phipps, the Paris Ambassador under whom he served. Phipps was a shrewd opportunist and cynical wit, although inwardly a man of conviction. He had been schooled in Dresden and Vienna, and after a year at King's College, Cambridge had graduated *bachelier ès lettres* at the University of Paris. As Ambassador in Dollfuss's Vienna he had been popular, but in Berlin he was more refractory: 'a complete thug, Sir Phipps', Hitler called him. 'The rapidly growing monster of German militarism will not be placated by mere cooings', Phipps warned in 1935: Hitler could be charming, 'but there *is* the other side – the tiger side – and when it shows itself, oh Weh!' He offered no hope that the overthrow or death of Hitler would bring 'the emergence of a benevolent, carpet-slipper régime'. He was exasperated by the unrealism of 'England's bleating pacifists', and from 1936 onwards advocated rearmament. When appointed to the Paris embassy in 1937, he said that he regarded 'the *Ville Lumière* as the hub of civilization'. After the Nazi annexation of Austria in March 1938, he felt sure that war would come.[34]

Whereas Maclean was appalled in 1938 by the Anglo-French capitulation to Hitler at Munich, which freed the Nazis to annex part of Czechoslovakia, Phipps supported Chamberlain's policy of appeasement as prolonging peace and providing an opportunity for rearmament before the inevitable war. Maclean was disgusted by his reading of secret messages that passed between Chamberlain and Daladier, and it is likely that he saw Phipps's telegram of 24 September upholding capitulation. 'Unless German aggression were so brutal, bloody and prolonged (through the gallantry of Czechoslovak resistance) as to infuriate French public opinion to the extent of making it lose its reason, war would now be most unpopular in France', he telegraphed. 'All that is best in France is against war, *almost* at any price (hence the deep and really pathetic gratitude shown to our Prime Minister).' For good measure Phipps characterized French opponents of German belligerence as a 'small, but noisy & corrupt war group'. Two months later Phipps wrote that 'Bolshevism' remained just 'a bogey in our still relatively happy island', whereas on the European mainland it posed a substantial threat. Soviet Russia had been fomenting strikes to disable France since 1936. 'In Spain thousands of people have been murdered, in Russia millions. In Italy Fascism would seem to have been directly due to Communism. In Germany Naziism was certainly due to Communism.' It was incomprehensible to Phipps 'why, if we hate all these horrors that Communism has caused or produced, we should imagine that an alliance with it is going to benefit us in any way'.[35]

Con O'Neill, a young law Fellow at All Souls, resigned as Third Secretary at the Berlin embassy in 1939 because he found unbearable the propitiating of the Nazis by his Ambassador, Sir Nevile Henderson: it was eight years before he could resume his diplomatic career. Maclean, by contrast, remained in the Phipps embassy, chafed at his circumstances, felt sorry for himself, drew his salary, rose in the hierarchy and betrayed his colleagues' trust.

Maclean and his fellow Third Secretary in the Paris embassy, Valentine Lawford, saw incoming and outgoing telegrams and dispatches as well as Phipps's personal letters to Cadogan and Sir Orme ('Moley') Sargent at the Foreign Office. The two young men shared a Chancery office, swapped quips about their work and bonded by laughing together. Maclean pleased Lawford by undertaking the duller tasks and by staying late in the office to finish their duties singlehandedly, when Lawford, a charmer who enjoyed a glamorous social life in the French capital, had divertissements to attend. Lawford, who later renounced his diplomatic career to become the life partner of the German-American photographer Horst P. Horst (they adopted a son together), seems not to have thought of Maclean as sharing his sexual preferences. He enjoyed Maclean's company, and never suspected that he was being used to facilitate espionage for Moscow. Maclean said that he missed the laughter when Lawford was replaced by the dour Henry Hankey in 1940, but he must have missed Lawford's carefree way with papers and office hours more.

Philby in Spain: Burgess in Section D

Early in 1937 Maly gave Philby instructions from Moscow to proceed to the area of Spain controlled by the Nationalists, under cover of a freelance journalist, both to collect political and military intelligence from Franco's forces and to build a legend as an intrepid right-wing reporter on the Spanish battlefields. When he was interrogated by Dick White of MI5 in 1951, he was stumped by one direct question: who paid for his trip to Spain in 1937? The answer, which he could not give with impunity, was that the Spanish assignment was set up and financed by Moscow. The NKVD instructed him to penetrate Franco's entourage, report on the habits, schedules, affinities and vulnerability of his staff and guards, and thus facilitate the General's assassination. Moscow indeed ordered Philby to kill Franco himself, but the youngster had no aptitude as a hitman. After inundating *The Times* with unsolicited reports, he was appointed in May 1937 as one of that newspaper's two correspondents attached to Franco's armies. His accounts of Nationalist victories over the Republicans solaced those readers of *The Times* who admired Franco's crusade against Bolshevism.

Philby had to present Franco's victories positively, but without crude bias, while inwardly more committed than ever to communism as an anti-fascist resistance. His task was far harder than that of Peter Rhodes, the American who had become a communist while a Rhodes scholar at Oriel College, Oxford: Rhodes, who had the alias of Johan Kazer, was free as a war correspondent for the United Press in Spain during 1937 to file reports that did not dissemble his sympathies. He extolled the Americans fighting with the International Brigades in Spain, and had the comfort of being able to work openly for international agencies providing aid to Spanish Republicans. English journalists covering the Spanish civil war were biased partisans. 'Men of the extreme left', wrote Philip Jordan (who covered the war for the *News Chronicle*), 'were unscrupulous, and cared little for the humanities'; but the anti-totalitarian cause was so precious for Europe that 'it seemed right and proper to put aside all doubts, to conceal the truth from oneself at all costs, so that in the end one came to believe what one had always known to be nothing but a lie'.[36]

In December 1937 Philby was travelling with three other journalists to the battlefield at Teruel when their motor-car was hit by an artillery shell. He sustained light head injuries, but his companions died. As a result, in March 1938, Franco personally pinned the Red Cross of Military Merit to Philby's chest. Franco's officers had hitherto suspected British journalists, because so many of their compatriots were fighting in the International Brigades that they thought the whole nation must be rotten; but after being decorated by their Generalissimo, Philby became acceptable to the Nationalist forces.

In the autumn of 1938, Philby returned to London on furlough. Jordan, describing a similar return from reporting the Spanish war, enjoyed listing what he found good in his native land: 'small fields, duck and green peas, some measure of personal liberty for those with decent incomes, walnut trees, the kindness of poor people, Rolls-Royce motor-cars, Bath, comfortable beds for those who could afford them'. Philby, though, had no time for savouring softness: Litzi Friedmann mentioned that she had heard of a scientist who was researching a new form of energy with a power equivalent of one lump of coal fuelling a train for the 4,000 miles from Vladivostok to Moscow. He arranged for her to report this rumour to a Soviet contact of Burgess's. Later he suspected that the physicist was Klaus Fuchs, but never knew if he and his wife were the means of Moscow's introduction to the atomic physicist who was to give Russia vital secrets about the atomic bomb.[37]

Meanwhile Burgess had been introduced by Footman to Laurence Grand, a major in the Royal Engineers who in 1938 was seconded to SIS as chief of its new D Section (charged with planning wartime 'dirty tricks' and non-military attacks). Grand, who was scouting for men who might be adept at creating misdirection, asked Burgess to help D Section – while continuing his work as a BBC talks producer – in preparing anti-Hitler radio propaganda which was broadcast to Germany from Luxembourg and Lichtenstein. Burgess signed the Official Secrets Act before gaining access to Foreign Office material. Moscow received all that he learnt.

Grand was a *beau sabreur* with an imperious manner but erratic abilities who came to be regarded inside the Foreign Office as a mountebank. 'His judgement is almost always wrong,' Gladwyn Jebb advised Cadogan, 'his knowledge wide but alarmingly superficial, his organisation in many respects a laughing-stock, & he is a consistent, fluent & unmitigated liar.' His leading positive trait was generosity to his staff, who responded with loyalty. 'But to pit such a man', continued Jebb, 'against . . . German Military Intelligence Service is like arranging an attack on a Panzer division by an actor mounted on a donkey.' In 1940 Grand was shunted to the remote sidings of GHQ in New Delhi: in 1945 he was the unsuccessful Conservative candidate in Nancy Astor's former Plymouth constituency.[38]

Grand's deputy, Montagu ('Monty') Chidson, was more effective. At the age of twenty-one he was the first British pilot to claim the destruction of a German aircraft, which he shot down off the Kent coast on Christmas Day of 1914. He was taken prisoner when his aircraft crashed behind German lines in 1915 while he was on aerial photographic reconnaissance. Subsequently he organized secret message routes out of prisoner-of-war camps as well as several escape attempts. He spent the 1920s in the Military Intelligence Directorate, and the 1930s as an SIS officer in Vienna, Budapest and Bucharest. He had a Dutch wife, spoke Dutch and French like a native, and was PCO in The Hague when in 1938 he was recalled to London as Grand's deputy. During the battle of the Netherlands in 1940 Chidson spirited industrial diamonds worth well over a million pounds out of Amsterdam in a backpack and brought them to safety in England. When questioned about Burgess in the 1950s, he was amnesiac, apparently as the result of incipient dementia. An SIS insider extolled his 'integrity and fervent patriotism', and said that he was admired by 'people in all walks of life in this country and abroad for his quality of infectious gaiety and wit'. These were the terms which showed the best service ethos of SIS.[39]

Goronwy Rees at All Souls

Burgess weakened the security of the ring of five by his recruitment of an Oxonian named Goronwy Rees. Andrew Boyle in *The Climate of Treason* presented Rees as 'a scholarship boy from a pious, lower-mid-dle-class home in Wales'. Cliché-ridden journalists followed this misdirection by describing his father, the Reverend Richard Rees, as a 'humble minister'. All clergy should be humble, no doubt, but the implication of 'humble' was absurd here. His father had a first-class degree from Oxford and charge of one of the largest Presbyterian churches in Wales; his brother had a first-class degree from Cambridge and became a circuit judge; his sister went to university and married a leading solicitor. He attended the best school in the Welsh capital, Cardiff High School, where he was a spotty and charmless adolescent. The glamour of Oxford University transformed him as an undergrad-uate. The Oxford don Maurice Bowra aptly described him as 'a normally sexed pansy', which meant that he was a *coureur de femmes* who felt at ease in the company of gay members of the intelligentsia, liked to tease and bemuse them, and attracted some of them by his moodiness.[40]

Rees was the lover of two eminent novelists, Elizabeth Bowen and Rosamond Lehmann. 'He was like a bright little cracker that, pulled hard enough, goes off with a loud bang,' Bowen wrote of the character based on him in *Death of the Heart*. Politically he seemed an extremist without fixed bearings. The philosopher Stuart Hampshire, who like him was a young pre-war Fellow of All Souls, saw him as a roving insurgent who liked to lay dynamite charges under hypocrisy. 'Rees', he told Isaiah Berlin in 1936, 'sees himself as a marauding Fascist power, in league with the have-nots against the haves, and persecuted by status quo interests who talk of public law and international morality, and succeed in making even bilateral agreements and regional alliances seem immoral.' Rees's intelligence was emulative rather than original, and too unsystematic for scholarship. 'Goronwy was very quick at picking things up,' said Hampshire, 'and he was very sensitive and observant, but he never had an intellectual outlook which gave him a mission to do something he thought important.' His social charm exceeded his intellectual stability, Hampshire judged, and in the 1930s (despite being a novelist, a *Spectator* editor and a seducer of exciting women) he was scared of becoming a 'boring plod'.[41]

Hampshire said that his proximity and Rees's to some of the leading appeasers of Hitler – Fellows of All Souls such as Lord Halifax (the Foreign Secretary), Sir John Simon (the former Foreign Secretary) and Geoffrey Dawson (editor of *The Times*) – enabled them to observe the 'servility of Conservatives in the face of Fascism at first-hand'. The young Fellows felt that the Conservative fixation on the rights of private ownership swamped any other moral considerations: 'they were ready to tolerate Fascist outrages and threats, and even to curry favour with Fascists, for the sake of protecting private property, which was threatened by the anticipated spread of Communism and of Socialism throughout Europe'. The sordidness of Conservative expedience, Hampshire felt, reinforced Rees's tendency to take the left's side with fatally vehement over-simplification. Louis MacNeice recalled an evening when Rees addressed a meeting of some fifty members of the intelligentsia opposed to fascism. 'Goronwy', he wrote, '. . . spoke like a revivalist, flashed his eyes, quivered with emotion, led with his Left and followed with his Left, punch on punch, dogma on dogma, over and over-statement, washed in the blood of – well, nobody asked of whom, but it certainly made you stop thinking.' Rees hymned the proletariat as the only progressive class: writers, he said, had to repress their own personalities, obey orders from the workers and serve as the microphones of the plebs. After the meeting, he went for oysters at Prunier's.[42]

Burgess made his recruitment approach to Rees after reading a review by him in November 1937 of a book about unemployment, malnutrition and slum hovels in South Wales. They sank a bottle of whisky together, and were in an alcoholic haze when Burgess declared, 'I am a Comintern agent, and have been ever since I came down from

Cambridge.' He volunteered the information that Blunt was collaborating with him, flattered Rees by soliciting his help, and urged him to
give purpose to his life by aiding the communist resistance to the
Nazis.[43]

Under the codenames of GROSS and FLIT, Rees reported political
talk at high table, and in the smoking-room and coffee-room, from All
Souls grandees such as Halifax, Simon, Dawson, Sir Donald Somervell
(the Attorney General), Sir Eric Beckett (the Foreign Office's legal
adviser), Leo Amery (former Secretary of State for the Colonies), Cosmo
Lang, Archbishop of Canterbury and Hensley Henson, Bishop of
Durham. Younger Fellows in the 1930s, who were probably less regular
in attendance, included the diplomats Roger Makins, Con O'Neill and
Patrick Reilly. Visitors airing their opinions included Churchill, the
German Chancellor Brüning, the Czech leader Beneš and Whitehall's
arch-exponent of appeasement Sir Horace Wilson. All Souls discussions
were privileged under the Chatham House Rule, which meant that
confidential remarks should not be attributed when quoted to outsiders.
Exchanges were highly informative: another college Fellow, A. L. Rowse,
used to say that if he was away from All Souls for a fortnight, he could
no longer interpret the news in the papers.[44]

Hearsay from a discussion-group that met at All Souls may also have
been reported by Rees. Named after its convener Sir Arthur Salter, who
was MP for Oxford University and a Fellow of the college, 'Salter's
Soviet' included the military strategist Basil Liddell Hart, Arnold
Toynbee of the Royal Institute of International Affairs, the Nobel peace
prize winner Sir Norman Angell, the MPs Harold Macmillan and Harold
Nicolson and a former director of Ewer's *Daily Herald*, Lord Allen of
Hurtwood. Rees may have reported Allen's desire to conciliate Nazi
Germany and his view that Czechoslovakia had 'a monstrous record'
in its dealings with Germany: Allen described the beleaguered republic
in May 1938 as 'a geographical area distraught with the ambitions of
several competing nationalities'; he thought it wrong 'to insist that
British youth shall be killed and Europe involved in a ghastly catastrophe'
merely to sustain Czechoslovak territorial integrity; the personal dictatorships of Hitler and Stalin were a 'neurosis' which had 'revived
primitive emotions of cruelty'. Rees stopped acting as the All Souls nark
after the Nazi–Soviet non-aggression pact of August 1939. Burgess lied
to him that he, too, was going to stop work for the comrades, and

thereafter avoided Rees. 'The crisis has shown', Burgess reported to Moscow, 'that he was no Marxist at all.'[45]

The Marxism of Burgess, though, was unassailable. Blunt told Liddell that Burgess had defended the Moscow show-trials of 1936–8. Burgess condemned Chamberlain's government, Blunt said, for sending to Moscow in August 1939 low-level negotiators, lacking plenipotentiary powers and led by Admiral Sir Reginald Drax rather than a statesman, to discuss a tripartite military agreement between France, Russia and Britain against Germany. Drax's ability was undeniable, but his delegation was made to seem dilatory and insincere by penny-pinchers at the Board of Trade, which chartered a slow steamer to carry Drax's team to Leningrad when a train or air journey would have taken no more than two days. 'Incredible!' exclaimed Ambassador Maisky when he heard that the ship had a maximum speed of 13 knots. 'This comes at a time when the ground in Europe is beginning to burn beneath our feet!' Maisky suspected Chamberlain of insulting deviousness: 'it's not a tripartite pact that he needs, but talks about a pact, as a trump card for cutting a deal with Hitler'. Burgess at this time sent three crucial reports to Moscow. The first attributed to Chamberlain's intimate adviser Sir Horace Wilson the statement that the Chiefs of Staff believed that Britain could beat Germany in a war without signing a defensive pact with Soviet Russia. In mid-August Burgess reported to Moscow a conversation with 'Monty' Chidson of SIS Section D. 'It is a fundamental aim of British policy to work with Germany whatever happens, and, in the end, against the USSR,' Chidson supposedly said. 'But it is impossible to conduct this policy openly: one must manoeuvre every which way.' German eastwards expansion would not be resisted by Britain, Chidson putatively assured Burgess. Finally, Burgess reported that Hermann Göring was expected to reach London on a secret mission on 23 August. Instead, on 23 August, the Nazi–Soviet mutual non-aggression pact was promulgated: its provisions for the partition of Poland between Germany and Russia, and for Russian annexation of Latvia and Estonia, were kept secret. On 1 September Germany invaded Poland. Soviet troops advanced from the east on 17 September.[46]

The Chamberlain government was attuned to the majority public mood in its policy of appeasing Germany, but its handling of Stalin's Russia was less in accord with voters' preferences. In a pioneer British opinion poll taken in December 1938, of respondents who were asked if they would prefer a German or a Soviet victory in a war between the two nations, 59 per cent favoured the Russians and only 10 per cent supported the Germans. In answer to a poll question in January 1939, requiring a forced choice between fascism and communism, 63 per cent opted for communism and 21 per cent for fascism.[47]

Nothing was sure in the advancing world crisis, despite the confidence of dialectical materialists that ultimate victory was theirs. In May 1939 the German Air Attaché in Spain unfurled a map of Europe before the British Ambassador, Sir Maurice Peterson. 'Only see', he cried, pointing with his finger, 'what gains the Führer has brought about without firing a shot!' Peterson asked what would happen when the shooting began. 'Ah,' replied the Attaché turning away, 'that is just the doubtful point.'[48]

CHAPTER 11

The People's War

Emergency recruitment

'If the balloon goes up, can you lay on a few chaps?' was a question asked during the summer of 1939. The phraseology was flippant, for the speakers came from a generation that disliked grandstanding: as Crane Brinton, wartime chief of research and analysis in the London outpost of the US Office of Strategic Services, reported, 'British self-assurance takes the (to us) odd form of an incurable addiction to understatement.' The slang conveyed the certainty that Whitehall on a war footing needed to recruit active-minded men (women were not considered) who would take responsibility, appraise situations and suggest initiatives in the expanded government apparatus needed to wage war against Nazi Germany. Haste and wartime volatility brought topsy-turvy recruitment, affiliations, promotions and demotions. The Oxford don Maurice Bowra, who shirked official work, said in 1940: 'War is a) very dull and b) brings all the crooks to the top.' The motley backgrounds of the emergency recruits brought a perception that the People's War, in Evelyn Waugh's words, filled government ministries with 'experts, charlatans, plain lunatics and every unemployed member of the British Communist Party'. How reasonable are these evaluations?[1]

The government budgeted £93,000 to fund MI5 in 1939–40. The service was chronically understaffed, with 83 officers (almost entirely men), 253 support staff (almost entirely women) and only 36 watchers in Harry Hunter's B6 surveillance section. Subsequently Jasper Harker and Guy Liddell recruited another 570 officers and staff. In June 1940 Churchill sacked the Service's Director, Sir Vernon Kell, and his deputy Eric Holt-Wilson: Kell's successor, Sir David Petrie, who used the title Director General, had been a police chief in India. 'No Security Service could have had . . . a better chief,' J. C. Masterman believed. 'He was a rock of integrity, the type of Scot whose reliability in all conditions was beyond question, with strong and independent judgement, but ready and willing to delegate and trust.' Petrie erred by being too considerate. Unlike Sir Stewart Menzies, his counterpart at SIS, he decided not to trouble Churchill with briefings on the Security Service's wartime work. Not only would the Prime Minister have enjoyed Petrie's briefings: they might have proofed him against the views of Sir Desmond Morton, his confidential security adviser, who as a former SIS officer felt antipathy to MI5.[2]

In September 1939, when Germany and Russia invaded Poland, Maclean was a member of the Paris embassy and Cairncross already a government official. Burgess was employed by the BBC, but had an anomalous involvement with an SIS section that was the forerunner of SOE. The subsequent admission of Blunt, Philby and Burgess into MI5, SIS and the Foreign Office respectively has led to unforgiving criticism of lax security. The trio's easy absorption into secret intelligence systems has been contrasted with the objections raised against, for example, Douglas Jay, the City editor of the *Daily Herald*, before his appointment to the Ministry of Supply. Jay's blacklisting in 1939–40 was apparently because he had once attended a communist meeting in Paris, and believed that confiscation of inherited personal income was a better form of socialism than the nationalization of the means of production. Temporary recruits to MI5, with education and experience of the world, thought that Special Branch was unreasonable in treating attendance at fringe meetings as suspicious. They chortled when they investigated old files and found absurd misappraisals expressed in Special Branch's costive, stilted reports. In free-spirited reaction to the obtuse alarmism of Special Branch, MI5 officers tended to imprudence in some of the recruits whom they accepted on trust. Jay's MI5 file was destroyed by a friend who read it and found it unfair.

'Before the war there were no resources with which to check on undergraduate activities,' Dick White recalled forty years later. 'Consequently I guess there were quite a number of former Communists & Marxists around in the wartime Int[elligence] services including Bletchley . . . but my equally strong guess is that few of these were spies & that for many of them the war brought enlightenment. On balance it was not such a bad bet to fight the war as a united front.' The debit, he told Hugh Trevor-Roper in 1980, was to have Blunt inside MI5, Philby in MI6 and Burgess and Maclean in the FO, but on the credit side there was 'a massive intake of brains & abilities from the Universities which set entirely new standards of intellectual achievement. What I am getting at is you can't expect to understand individual cases or events of thirty years ago without being fully aware of *how* we fought the war.' The purpose of this chapter is to give a fuller context of how the war of 1939–45 was fought.[3]

Castigators of the recruitment of Blunt, Burgess and Philby rely on the benefits of hindsight. They treat Britain as distinctive from other western democracies, overlook the reality that no government apparatus on either side of the Atlantic had yet introduced the costly, time-consuming system of positive vetting, and discount the simple truth that MI5's advice to exclude suspect individuals from certain posts was routinely rejected by its political masters. It was impossible to appraise people with consistency in the conditions of 1939–40: some traits that are regrettable in peacetime civilians become useful in wartime; ethical criteria and risk assessment change in times of war; permanent mental transformations may occur in combatants whether they are fighting on battlefields or sitting at desks. 'There are degrees of moral obliquity,' wrote Masterman: 'it is sometimes hard to determine when shrewdness and the ability to make the most of an opportunity end, and when the commission of crime and pursuit of evil begin.' Critics such as Andrew Boyle, who described wartime MI5 officers as 'often mediocre', under-value the prowess of many emergency wartime recruits. A quartet plucked from a sample of dozens – the circus master Cyril Mills, the lawyer Herbert Hart, the banking heir Victor Rothschild and the art dealer Tomás Harris – make the point.[4]

Cyril Mills's father Bertram Mills was the son of an undertaker, embalmer and pioneer of cremation: Bertram's work with funeral cortèges, and love of thoroughbred horses, led him to start a coach-building and harness business. With its profits he gentrified his elder son Cyril (born in 1902) by sending him to Harrow School. Cyril was one of the first post-war generation of undergraduates at Corpus Christi College, Cambridge. After obtaining an engineering degree, he worked in the oilfields of Burma: he survived an explosion in which he was drenched in burning oil, and saved himself by rolling in filth to extinguish the flames. As a substitute for the declining coach-building business, Bertram Mills began importing American automobiles, opened a circus in 1920 and diversified into dance halls. After Cyril Mills's return from Burma in 1925, he became assistant manager of his father's Covent Garden dance hall, and then assistant manager of the Christmas circus at Olympia. His first challenge was to transport a pride of seventy lions from Paris to London in 1926. As a good linguist and keen aviator he flew himself across Europe seeking talented new performers, especially from the big German circuses. He hired a female 'fakir' who hypnotized crocodiles, jugglers, clowns, trick unicyclists, high-wire walkers, human cannonballs, wall-of-death motorcyclists, 'Borra', King of the Pickpockets and a trapeze family called the Flying Gaonas. His side-show amusements included a Burmese troupe of giraffe-necked women and Major Horace Ridler @ the Great Omi, the most tattooed man in the world. Mills was embarrassed when in old age, on the television programme *This is Your Life*, an American admirer called him 'a typical English aristocrat'. He was as bourgeois as Philby or Burgess.

In his eighties Mills confided some of his memories to a former MI5 colleague. 'At this stage there is no harm in my telling you, although I do not tell anyone else, that for 21 years I had a single engine aircraft and from 1933 onwards I did all my talent-spotting in Europe flying myself and this involved going to Germany eight or ten times every year,' he informed Hugh Trevor-Roper in 1985. Flying over Germany in his De Havilland Hornet Moth in 1936, Mills noticed a railway disappearing into remote mountains, which suggested to him a covert installation. On returning to England, he asked the passport officer at Lympne aerodrome to put him in touch with someone to whom he could describe his observations. He was contacted by MI5, which introduced him to Frederick Winterbotham, head of the Air Section of SIS, who used him as a source for the next three years. On aerial trips over Germany Mills flew off course, near factories or aerodromes, used his circus man's eye for subterfuge and reported what he saw: 'when working for Winterbotham before the war I was not paid a cent even for expenses'. He provided the first reports of the existence of the Messerschmitt 110 fighter-bomber, constructed in a secret new factory which he found by flying over a prohibited area near Ravensburg. In September 1939 he tried to enlist in the RAF, but at thirty-eight years of age was wanted only as ground staff; so he telephoned his MI5 contact and started work a week later at MI5's wartime headquarters in Wormwood Scrubs prison. He was night duty officer on 29 September 1940 when the prison was bombed. Later, Mills and Richard ('Dick') Brooman-White advised the Special Operations Executive (SOE) on improvements in subterfuge. Mills's office nickname was 'the old dog'. He controlled the double-cross agent Juan Pujol Garcia @ GARBO, and was crucial in turning a colleague's idea for deceiving the Germans about allied plans for the invasion of France in 1944 into the practical reality of Operation MINCEMEAT. 'Perhaps,' he mused to Trevor-Roper, 'it was because I had taken a few risks in a difficult business that I adapted to the XX game.' Mills was shrewd, amusing, urbane and proud; a tough disciplinarian; capable of either plain-speaking or careful discretion as necessary; a sharp-eyed showman with plenty of initiative, adaptive ingenuity and energy.[5]

Herbert Hart, son of a Jewish tailor and furrier in Harrogate, had been mortified at failing to gain a Prize Fellowship at All Souls in 1930 and took up practice at the Chancery bar. 'His great quality', in the estimate of his intimate friend Richard Wilberforce, 'was intense curiosity about all varieties of life – the more special, or even comic, the better – and he was wonderfully good at getting specialists and "characters" to talk about their niches.' He had 'vast tenacity in pursuit of the truth', judged Wilberforce, who became one of the great law lords of their generation. Hart was chaotic in desk-work, but superb at mental synthesis. Having failed on medical grounds to join the Military Police after the outbreak of war, he was brought into MI5 at the instigation of his future wife, the Home Office high-flier Jenifer Williams, who claimed to have left the CPGB by 1939. Williams had several meetings with Harker about her lover's recruitment into MI5: at one of them, Harker asked, 'you were a communist, weren't you?', and seemed satisfied by her quick response, 'Oh, we were all red in our youth.' Hart's introduction to MI5 by his ex-communist wife excited hostile newspaper coverage when it emerged in 1983. There is not a jot of evidence that he betrayed his employers. 'Everybody in the world of intelligence adored Herbert: he was the perfect intelligence officer,' recalled his colleague Stuart Hampshire. 'He was absolutely accurate and reliable, but not very intuitive. He was also very sensible in a crazy world: he was perpetually amazed at . . . human folly.'[6]

In 1941 Hart was put in charge of MI5's B1B Division, which (writes

his biographer Nicola Lacey) 'amassed a treasure-trove of highly sensitive intelligence material', and thus gained masterful knowledge of
German intelligence's attack on Britain. 'His lawyer's capacity to assimilate and master a brief, his ancient historian's skill in marshalling and
evaluating evidence, and his philosopher's taste for precision' enabled
Hart, when in charge of B1B, 'to assimilate, interpret, and organize this
information so that it could be used to maximum effect by . . . double
agents, police forces, immigration authorities, coast guards, military
personnel'. Isaiah Berlin remembered his friend in terms that might be
wished on all counter-espionage officers: 'always moderate, just, understanding, sane . . . he was a man who could not tolerate obscurantism,
oppression, injustice, all that he regarded as reactionary'.[7]

Victor Rothschild was brought into MI5 by Liddell. A banking
millionaire, a member from the age of twenty-six of the House of Lords
(where for a time he sat on the Labour benches), a zoologist, jazz
pianist, cricketer, art collector and bibliophile, Rothschild was a man
of intellect, wealth and taste, with a mind that liked to classify and rule.
He was as autocratic as any spoilt child, but too disciplined and productive to waste time. He had a taste for going incognito, wore an
open-necked shirt and carried a workman's satchel so as to be mistaken
for a plumber. In Cambridge during the 1930s he knew Burgess, Maclean
and especially Blunt, whom he considered saintly. Rothschild ran MI5's
first counter-sabotage department (B1C). Using skills that he had learnt
when dissecting frogs' spawn and sea urchins, he proved his courage
in defusing German bombs. He was exceptional in describing his every
bomb-disposal move into a field telephone as he worked, so that if he
was blown up other bomb-disposal men would learn from his mistake.
Churchill nominated him for the George Medal after he had defused
a device secreted in a crate of Spanish onions and timed to explode in
an English seaport. As Churchill's poison-taster, he smoked Havana
cigars, ate Virginia hams and drank vintage Armagnac. Indeed, he was
a consumer with gusto. 'I like him very much and admire his physical
energy and more-than-life-size qualities, and an enormous appetite for
self-improvement,' Stuart Hampshire wrote after several months of
official work in Paris with Rothschild in 1945. William Waldegrave, a
Fellow of All Souls who was recruited by Rothschild into the Cabinet
Office's Central Policy Review Staff in 1971, described him as 'one of
the most complex and difficult men of his age'. The fable that he was

a Soviet spy – trying perhaps to protect his wealth by conciliating Stalinists – depends, says Waldegrave, on wishful thinking, envy and anti-semitic conspiracy fantasies. This delusion has been refuted by Dick White, Oleg Gordievsky and Vasili Mitrokhin, but still festers in some minds.[8]

Another MI5 recruit was Tomás Harris. Born in 1908, he was the son of Lionel Harris, Jewish owner of the Spanish Art Gallery in Mayfair, and his Spanish wife, Enriqueta Rodríguez. In 1923, at the age of fifteen, he won a scholarship to the Slade School of Fine Art. He was a pianist, saxophonist, sculptor, engraver and ceramicist, and a culinary artist, too. During the 1930s, from his gallery in Bruton Street, he sold the works of El Greco, Velázquez and Goya, medieval tapestries, oriental carpets, Renaissance jewellery and other artefacts acquired from Spanish palaces and religious houses. Harris was thought illiterate by Philby: certainly his abilities were visual, tactile and sensual; he had subtle, astute intuitions when reading people as well as images. Harris's knack for discovering lost works of art in unlikely places was admired by Blunt, who appreciated his exuberant generosity of spirit. After the outbreak of war, Harris and his wife Hilda Webb became the cook-housekeepers at Brickendonbury Hall, the SOE training school in Hertfordshire. Later he handled the double agent Pujol @ GARBO. The Germans, he believed, could be duped by elaborate deception operations because their minds rejected the irrational: rationalists were easier to mislead. Harris was an enthusiast in his connoisseurship, in his hospitality and (like many of his generation) in his drinking. His death in a car smash in 1964 was due to drunk driving: the innuendoes that he was killed by the security services, midway between Philby's defection and Blunt's confession, are silly fancies.

Mills and Harris were brought into full-time secret service after showing their suitability in other roles; Hart and Rothschild came on recommendation; none of the quartet underwent vetting. The difficulties in being just and consistent in this process were shown by the cases of Arthur Reade, Dudley Collard, Wilfrid Vernon and Peter Smolka. The fact that Britain and Russia were allies from June 1941, and were bound by a treaty of May 1942 that was a primary guide to London's subsequent wartime decisions, provides the ruling context for all that happened.

Reade had been sent packing from his Oxford college in 1921 for sedition, but gave convincing signs of being disillusioned with communism by the late 1920s. He became a barrister, was elected to the Travellers Club and stood as a Labour parliamentary candidate. When, in October 1939, he sought a job in military intelligence, MI5 blocked him. Ten months later, when MI5 discovered that he was a lance-corporal in the Field Security Police at Belfast, they had him dismissed. The Deputy Director of Military Intelligence at the War Office, who interviewed Reade in 1940, 'considered him a he-man and just the sort of fellow they want'. Harold Nicolson, Under Secretary at the Ministry of Information ('futile and self-satisfied' as Cuthbert Headlam called him), provided a further testimonial for Reade. MI5 relented, but in 1942 Reade was repatriated to England from the Intelligence Corps in Cairo following a complaint of drunken verbal indiscretions. Loftus Browne of MI5, who met Reade during the war, thought him 'an insufferably self-important ass', but Dick White expressed unease about the case in 1948. The adverse vetting reports had not been evaluated, he minuted. On the basis of untested information, 'outside bodies were ten times warned against READE. What makes it much worse is that there are in this file ten testimonials in favour of READE . . . our obstinacy in this case must have gained us a bad reputation in many different quarters.'[9]

Similarly Dudley Collard, the communist barrister who had defended Percy Glading in 1938, found his way blocked. His applications were spurned for an intelligence job ('I can speak almost perfect French, reasonably good German and Russian, and I can read with ease Swedish, Norwegian, Danish and Spanish, and to some extent also Italian and Dutch'). The Ministry of Information declined his overture. Collard finally became an ordinary seaman in the Royal Navy in 1941, and next year was commissioned as a naval officer despite MI5 telling the Naval Intelligence Department that it was 'strongly opposed' to Collard's 'particularly dangerous' type of communist becoming officers: 'well-educated men of good social position, frequently members of the legal profession, who place their services at the disposal of the Executive of the Communist Party, and work for the latter secretly, so far as possible without disclosing their membership'. Once a man of this type succeeds in joining one of the armed forces, they refrain from 'subversive propaganda amongst their fellows, or, at any rate, are so careful and clever over it that it is extremely difficult as a C.O. [commanding officer] to detect them. Their aim is to behave well outwardly in order to qualify for commissions, and after that to continue satisfactory outward behaviour.' In this ploy educated communist servicemen were aiding 'the long-term policy of the Communist Party, which is directed to turning National War into Civil War when the right moment arrives – probably during the demobilisation period, when they hope to reproduce what happened in 1919 with much greater chances of success'.[10]

Wilfrid Vernon, who had escaped so lightly when prosecuted without much earnest in 1937 for stealing aviation secrets, was vetoed by MI5 for any form of employment at the Air Ministry in 1939. The Security Service ensured that he was refused a commission in 1941, and withheld his vetting certificate in 1943. Together with Tom Wintringham, who had been expelled from the CPGB in 1938 on the grounds that his wife was a Trotskyite spy, he ran the wartime Home Guard in Osterley Park.

Where Reade, Collard and Vernon were sieved out, Philby's former partner in the London Continental News Agency, Peter Smolka, squeezed in. Smolka had anglicized his surname to Smollett in 1938, and was naturalized as a British subject with the sponsorship of Sir Harry Brittain, founder of the Empire Press Union and former Tory MP, and Iverach McDonald of *The Times*. He ingratiated himself with Lord Astor (who considered installing him as editor of the *Observer*). At the time of the Nazi–Soviet pact, MI5 opposed Smolka's appointment to the Ministry of Information; but their qualms were allayed by the Foreign Office's Rex Leeper, and Smolka/Smollett took charge of the ministry's propaganda news service to Switzerland, the Netherlands and Belgium on 1 September 1939. The Directorate of Military Intelligence soon complained to Kell of the scandal that Smolka/Smollett had access to secret material. An MI5 report of February 1940 depicted him as 'an unpleasant but brilliantly clever little Jew'. Dick White attributed the hostile tales about Smolka to temperamental failings: 'he has a most unattractive personality and is a pushing type'. Roger Hollis of MI5, after reading Smolka's burgeoning files, concluded that he was 'too closely concerned with his own prosperity to commit himself to any side until he is sure that is the winning side'. In sum, the justified doubts raised against Smolka were couched in anti-semitic terms which provoked other officials who read his file to compensate for the racial prejudice against him by under-evaluating his suitability for confidential work. Smolka penetrated the Ministry of Information without needing a slot in the English class system.[11]

Despite the prevalent mistrust of Smolka, he took charge of the Soviet Section of the Ministry of Information in 1941. His influence and tentacles were extensive. He was not merely a Soviet informer, but a master at misdirection by hints, distractions, suppressions and diversions. He had his part in the toadying of official information and propaganda, and hence in inducing unofficial civilian obsequiousness, towards Stalinism. The Ambassador in Moscow, Sir Archie Clark Kerr, wished that there was franker criticism of Soviet policy in Britain. 'We should put a stop to the gush of propaganda at home,' he urged in March 1945, 'in praise not only of the Soviet war effort, but also of the whole Soviet system, which can only have convinced the realists at the Kremlin that there is a complex of fear and inferiority in Great Britain where the Soviet Union is concerned.'[12]

MI5 continued to hold Smolka in suspicion after Russia had joined the western allies to fight the Axis powers, and its officer Roger Fulford asked Brooman-White to consult the latter's SIS colleague Philby about the London Continental News Agency which he and Smolka had formed together. Philby characterized Smolka as 'extremely clever', Brooman-White reported. 'Commercially he is rather a pusher but has nevertheless rather a timid character and a feeling of inferiority largely due to his somewhat repulsive appearance. He is a physical coward and was petrified when the air-raids began. Philby considered his politics to be mildly left-wing but had no knowledge of the C.P. link-up. His personal opinion is that SMOLLETT is clever and harmless. He adds that in any case the man would be far too scared to become involved in anything really sinister.' Philby's comments fed the racial prejudice against his former associate: his suggestion that Smolka, who had gone by aircraft to the North Pole and explored the freezing wastes of Siberia, was too self-concerned and nervy for risks worked with Brooman-White and Fulford only because of general assumptions about Jewish milksops.[13]

The United States

Evaluations must have a supra-national comparative element if they are not to be hopelessly insular. How did Britain's chief western ally perform in the wartime rush to recruit expert advisers and versatile freelances? Were the choices of recruits, the security checks and the receptivity to warning signs better or worse in Washington than in London?

The United States had not been a primary adversary of Moscow in the 1930s. The Federal Bureau of Investigation (FBI) was excitable about communist infiltration of factory workers, but otherwise Washington was lax in its attitude to Soviet agents. Perhaps the most significant operative was the journalist Whittaker Chambers, who had been instructed to break overt contact with CPUSA in 1932, went to Moscow for intelligence-training in 1933 and thereafter acted as a courier between underground cells and Soviet intelligence. The leading figure among the Washington officials run by Chambers was Alger Hiss, who progressed from harrying armaments manufacturers as legal assistant to Senator Gerald Nye's investigation to posts at the Justice Department and State Department. In 1935 Chambers told Hiss to start another intelligence apparatus, which was joined by further well-placed Washington officials including Harry Dexter White @ JURIST of the Treasury Department. By the late 1930s Washington was riddled with penetration agents in the Treasury, State Department, Justice Department, Labor Department and other federal bodies. The infiltration was more extensive than in Whitehall.

In 1937 Moscow threatened the security of its penetration agents in Washington by summoning Chambers to Moscow. He realized that he had been targeted for purging, prevaricated about making the journey and in 1938 broke with the NKVD and went into hiding. After meeting Krivitsky in 1939, he tried to denounce the Soviet penetration of Washington, but the FBI took no interest in his stories, which were also discounted by the Roosevelt administration. Every democratic state had grave security failures caused by inexperience rather than by complacence. Washington was exposed to security breaches after it entered the war in 1941, alongside Russia and Britain, against Germany and Japan, because of the hectic, urgent improvisations of wartime recruitment and by the traditional assumptions of trust that were integral to the departmental culture of democracies.

Until 1938 the CPUSA ran a secret apparatus for procuring phoney American passports for the use of American communists travelling abroad and for Soviet espionage agents. US passports were prized by

Moscow's illegals because the heavy migration to America from central and eastern Europe and from tsarist Russia meant that a US citizen with broken English or an obtrusive accent was not necessarily suspect. The former Oxford communist Peter Rhodes lent his US passport to a fugitive German, who had fought with the International Brigades in Spain and was on Nazi death-lists, so as to enable him to gain safety by entering the USA illegally. Rhodes was a war correspondent in Norway during 1940, and then served as an officer of the Foreign Broadcasting Monitoring Service in Washington. This brought a posting to London, where he had a desk in the US embassy and liaised with the BBC. He was a regular contact of Jacob Golos @ Yakov Raisin @ ZVUK @ SOUND, a Ukrainian who had been naturalized as a US citizen in 1915 and was the NKVD's chief contact at the CPUSA; but, among Rhodes's falsehoods when interviewed by the FBI in 1947, he denied having met him. Rhodes remained a sufficiently loyal Stalinist to give a stout defence of the Nazi–Soviet pact during this interrogation. There were strong suspicions, including references to him in intercepted and deciphered Soviet wireless messages, but no evidence that was usable in court.[14]

In July 1941 President Roosevelt – alias CAPTAIN in NKVD secret messages – appointed William ('Bill') Donovan, a Wall Street attorney who had been a military hero in the European fighting of 1917–18, to head the Office of Co-ordination of Information (COI) with the remit to bring order and qualitative consistency to the chaos of American intelligence-gathering, subversive activities and political warfare. In June 1942 the COI was renamed the Office of Strategic Services (OSS). Donovan was forbidden to poach staff from the FBI, the Military Intelligence Division and the Office of Naval Intelligence, but this did not incommode him, for he preferred to fill his department from unofficial sources. He approached men whom he knew and trusted, or who had been recommended by people whom he knew and trusted. Lawyers, bankers, manufacturers, amateur sportsmen, university professors and the former commander of the Abraham Lincoln Battalion, which had fought for the Reds in the Spanish civil war, joined COI and then OSS. Donovan's approach seemed admirably direct, informal and pragmatic at the time, but with hindsight resembles careless innocence. David Bruce, wartime chief of OSS in London, later said of Donovan: 'His country right or wrong was his primary impulse, but his boys right or wrong came a close second.'[15]

It was inconceivable to Donovan that White Anglo-Saxon Protestants, from prosperous and socially secure backgrounds, would choose to betray the United States. 'He built his new organization on trust,' in the summary of a later CIA intelligence officer Mark Bradley, who quotes him saying, 'I'd put Stalin on the OSS payroll if I thought it would defeat Hitler.' Donovan thus kept Donald Wheeler (the NKGB agent IZRA) at OSS, despite an FBI warning in 1942 that the former Oxford Rhodes scholar was at best a communist sympathizer, because three OSS officers vouched for Wheeler's assiduity in monitoring German manpower. The leading Soviet illegal in the USA, Iskhak Abdulovich Akhmerov @ Michael Greene @ Michael Adamec @ Bill Greinke @ YUNG @ MER @ ALBERT, who worked under cover as a New York furrier and had married Earl Browder's niece, reported of Wheeler in 1944: 'He says it makes no sense to be afraid: a man only dies once.' Wheeler despised his OSS colleagues, Akhmerov continued, and regarded them as vacuous. Donovan similarly promised protection to his subordinate Maurice ('Maury') Halperin, who had been fired from an academic job on suspicions of communism. 'You're a brave soldier,' Donovan told Halperin in 1942, 'and if ever you get into trouble, remember that you've got one of the top lawyers of Wall Street to defend you.' There was a nonchalance about departmental security in wartime Washington.[16]

COI and OSS were not complacent, clannish, self-protecting outposts of Ivy League fraternity. Woodrow Borah, an eminent historian of Mexico who served in OSS in 1942–7, was shocked by the personal and jurisdictional in-fighting within Donovan's agency, and between Washington government agencies. The 'Harvard-Yale-Princeton people' were ruthless in their mutual disloyalty, Borah recalled; they played football together, but were smilers with knives under their cloaks, who 'would cut each other's throat . . . without a moment's hesitation. A Harvard man would knife another Harvard man, his own bosom pal, for a little advantage. I came from California, and was really startled by it.'[17]

There were over fifty and perhaps as many as a hundred members of CPUSA within OSS. At least twenty-two of these supplied secrets to Moscow. Foremost among them was Duncan Lee, a young lawyer in Donovan's firm Donovan, Leisure, Newton and Lumbard. Born in 1913 in an American church mission in a remote port on the Yangtse river, Lee proved his academic and sporting prowess as a student at Yale. A testimonial from a professor there affirmed that he was a 'thorough gentleman, earnest, high-minded, tactful, clean, and honorable'. He seemed politically quiescent, but may have been misled by the Oxford Union 'King and Country' vote of 1933 into thinking Oxford to be a hotbed of anti-militarism. He went as a Rhodes scholar to Christ Church, Oxford in 1935–8. At Oxford Lee began to doubt his Christian missionary upbringing, and like Blunt and Maclean sought a substitute secular faith. During 1936 he was moved by reports from the Spanish civil war, but above all was radicalized after meeting Ishbel Gibb, the daughter of a Scottish official in India, a history graduate from Somerville College, Oxford, who was then working in Selfridge's department store in London. They became lovers, and in euphoric gratitude for sexual pleasure he emulated her radical activism. In August 1937 they went on a group tour to Russia led by Dudley Collard. The communist MP Willie Gallacher was another member of the touring party.[18]

Gibb and Lee married in 1938, and after leaving Europe joined the CPUSA in 1939. In Lee's final year at Yale Law School, a New Haven neighbour denounced the couple to the FBI as communists; but at that time in 1940 the FBI was deluged with reports of suspected fifth columnists, whether communist or Nazis, and the brief report on this obscure law student was filed away. After the Nazi invasion of Russia in June 1941, he became legal adviser to Russian War Relief, and in 1942 joined the executive board of the communistic China Aid Council. In 1942 he was also recruited to OSS, where he became one of Donovan's closest aides, and began spying for Moscow, after an approach from Mary Price @ DIR, an NKVD agent who was personal secretary to the pontifical Washington newspaper columnist Walter Lippmann and adept at rifling Lippmann's desk for confidential material.

KOCH, as Lee was codenamed, controlled the risks that he took in ways that the ring of five never sought to impose on their handlers. He refused to purloin secret material overnight or photograph it in the office, but recited from memory the gist of documents to Price, who became his lover rather as Kitty Harris had become Maclean's. He would give material only to US citizens, in the feeble self-deception that it would be passed to Earl Browder of CPUSA and not to Soviet Russia. Early in 1943 Lee was Donovan's representative at secret meetings in

Geneva and Berne between Prince Max Egon Hohenlohe-Langenburg, Himmler's peace emissary, and the local OSS chief, Allen Dulles. As assistant chief of the OSS secretariat from 1943, and chief of OSS's Japan–China section from 1944, Lee gained access to material of utmost secrecy. When Price broke down under the strain of her duplicity, she was replaced as Lee's handler by Elizabeth Bentley @ Elizabeth Sherman @ CLEVER GIRL @ MISS WISE @ MYRNA.

Elizabeth Bentley deserves a corrective digression. She was an individual of considerable abilities, intelligence, initiative and courage who has been disparaged by most writers on espionage history with sexist condescension. They cannot agree whether she was a slut or a neurotic spinster, a dummy or an arch-manipulator, a confused incompetent or a wily Mata Hari. The earliest vilification came from liberals who were her contemporaries, and could not forgive her unsettling testimony about American communist organization, but later generations, unfettered by ideological alliances, have proved equally unsympathetic. Bentley's supposed inadequacy and ineptitude are belied by her success in managing a busy travel agency, and in running a large Washington spy ring. She showed courage in turning FBI informant, and was an impressively self-possessed witness, under great pressure, when she testified to HUAC. The substance of what she said was true, although in some matters she dramatized or misled. Her fear that Soviet agents wished to murder her was accurate, not fantastic. She suffered astounding abuse after becoming a public figure, she was ostracized and found herself unemployable. It is time to salute her brains, fortitude and resilience rather than to repeat demeaning clichés.[19]

Bentley won a scholarship to Vassar College aged eighteen in 1926. After graduating in English, French and Italian, she studied at the University of Perugia, and in 1933 won a fellowship at the University of Florence. She became a member of the Columbia University cell of CPUSA in 1935, and an underground agent in 1938. She reported to Golos, who became her lover. After the outbreak of the European war in 1939, the US authorities seized the records of a travel agency named World Tourists run by Golos, and convicted Browder for his part in the procurement of false American passports. When World Tourists had been ruined as a cover, Golos opened a new front, the US Service and Shipping Corporation, with Bentley as office manager. She took over managing his Washington spy rings when he had a fatal heart attack while taking an after-dinner nap on the sofa of her Brooklyn apartment in 1943. Initially she answered to Akhmerov.

One of the sources from whom Bentley collected material was the academic turned Washington functionary named Maurice Halperin @ HARE. Halperin had been born in Boston in 1906 to Jewish parents who had emigrated a few years earlier from a *shtetl* on the Polish–Ukrainian border. The family were supported by a small store selling cigars. He studied Romance languages at Harvard in 1923–6, married at the age of twenty, got a job teaching French and Spanish in Ranger, Texas and then moved to Norman, Oklahoma, where he worked in the modern languages department of the university. He gained a doctorate from the Sorbonne during a long sabbatical. *Das Kapital* proved incomprehensible when he tried to read it, but he understood and was attracted by commentaries on Marxist historical dialectic. He came to see the communist front as the best resistance to the Nazis, and was by 1936–7 at least a fellow-traveller. In 1941 Halperin was fired from his academic post in Oklahoma on the supposition that he was a communist. A few months later, days before the Pearl Harbor attack, he was recruited by the Harvard historian William Langer to work in COI. By 1943 Halperin was head of the Latin America Division of OSS. According to Bentley, he was a secret CPUSA member and, under the alias of HARE, an assiduous supplier of material to her and Mary Price until 1945. After the war he gained a post in the State Department, despite having been named by Bentley to the FBI.[20]

Another notable source for Bentley was Gregory Silvermaster @ Nathan Masters @ PAL @ ROBERT, who had been born in Odessa in 1898. He became fluent in English while living with his Jewish parents in China. He moved to the USA in 1914, gained a doctorate at the University of California, Berkeley with a thesis on Lenin's early economic thought, became a US citizen in 1926, and from 1935 worked as a labour economist for a succession of New Deal government agencies. Silvermaster was an early member of the CPUSA who, after the Nazi attack on Russia in 1941, developed an important Washington espionage network with some two dozen informants in government offices. Using clandestine communist influence he obtained an appointment at the Board of Economic Warfare in 1942. Both the Office of Naval Intelligence and the War Department considered him to be a potential security risk, and tried to block this appointment. Both agencies held back from accusing him without evidence of espionage: neither had been trusted by the FBI with the knowledge of Silvermaster's contacts with Soviet spy networks in the US. To counter the military and naval intelligence veto on him, Silvermaster mustered support from senior government officials, Harry Dexter White @ LAWYER @ REED, Lauchlin Currie @ PAGE and Calvin Baldwin, who lobbied the Under Secretary of War, Robert Patterson, insisting that an injustice was being done. Patterson trusted and wished to accommodate his colleagues in other departments, and therefore nullified military intelligence's ban on Silvermaster. Patterson had no way of knowing that White and Currie were Soviet spies, and Baldwin a secret communist sympathizer. His naive susceptibility to their approaches was typical of both London and Washington at this time. After a year with the Board of Economic Warfare Silvermaster gained a transfer to the War Production Board, where he remained until 1946. He provided Moscow with classified material on US armaments output, which was collected from him in microfilm form by Bentley.[21]

Despite being denounced by Bentley and others, Silvermaster was never prosecuted. Like scores of other communist infiltrators he escaped prosecution for lack of evidence that could be used in court. He flourished after the war as a building contractor in New Jersey. His chief coadjutor, William Ullmann @ DONALD, a graduate of Harvard Business School and sometime assistant to Harry Dexter White in the Treasury Department, lived in Silvermaster's Washington home, ran a basement darkroom there to photograph the network's secret material, became the lover of Silvermaster's wife and from 1942 supplied secret material on the United States Army Air Force which he obtained while working in the Pentagon. Ullmann, too, was never prosecuted, became a New Jersey real-estate developer and was a multi-millionaire when he died in 1993. Rhodes prospered as a public relations consultant, dividing his time between a Kensington flat and a Paris apartment until his death in 1966. Halperin lost his job at Boston University in 1953, after pleading the Fifth Amendment before a Senate inquiry into espionage, and thereafter had a peripatetic life in Mexico City, Moscow, Havana and Vancouver.

As the feeble federal response to the CPUSA–Soviet passport frauds showed, the experience and techniques of American counter-intelligence were rudimentary. There was a random element in the definition of official secrets and in the rules to protect them. Washington officials engaged in endless vitiating skirmishes that failed to settle which agencies held responsibility for the protection of such material. The security criteria for Washington personnel with access to sensitive information were indistinct: there was little or no vetting of pre-war or wartime appointees. Warnings about such appointees, whether from neighbours, the FBI or high-quality informants such as Chambers and Bentley, were discounted. There was excessive trust not only in personal recommendations, but in personal exonerations. Suspicious characters were protected by powerful mentors who explained away their defects. Sometimes these mentors were playing great inter-agency power games, with little responsible consideration of national security. Inter-departmental rivalries, notably between the FBI, service intelligence officers and OSS, made US counter-espionage ill concerted. The USA failed to exclude doubtful individuals such as Akhmerov, secured few convictions for passport fraud, and for political reasons commuted Browder's prison sentence for passport crimes. Though overwhelming suspicions and evidence were in time accumulated against Moscow's agents in Washington, there was a lack of evidence that could be used in court.

Security Service vetting

During the war MI5 gave priority to catching German parachutists, Nazi sympathizers and fifth-column subversives, but its efforts to enhance national security were hindered by powerful challengers. In the 1950s Lord Beaverbrook's *Daily Express* was (like its proprietor) furiously indignant about MI5's previous failure to vet officials and catch spies. As Minister of Aircraft Production in 1940–1, however, Beaverbrook was equally angry with MI5 for using what he called Gestapo techniques to limit his access to expert manpower. On one occasion, in August 1940, Victor Rothschild was summoned to Beaverbrook's ministerial room. The outer office resembled the antechamber of a capricious sultan, with a dozen supplicants and aides talking in undertones in separate huddles, while Beaverbrook left them waiting. Sir Cuthbert Headlam noted of Beaverbrook in 1941, 'money is a great asset to success in this world – money, cheek, cunning and bounce': the press lord was resentful that in the matter of millions Rothschild was the bigger man, and set out to cut him down to size.[22]

After keeping the MI5 officer waiting for more than an hour, he commandeered Rothschild to accompany him to 10 Downing Street, where he left his millionaire appanage waiting outside in the car for another ninety minutes. Once Beaverbrook had returned from seeing Churchill, he spent ten minutes browbeating Rothschild about some Germans, employed in a factory of strategic importance, whom MI5 had interned as possible Nazi informants or saboteurs. Beaverbrook repeatedly claimed that the eight detainees were Jews who deserved consideration. 'They are not,' Rothschild answered each time, 'they are what is known as Aryan.' Beaverbrook insisted, however, that he knew better than Rothschild in matters of Judaism. They also discussed John Archer of MI5: 'I fired him because he said a terrible thing to me,' declared Beaverbrook. 'He said that if those poor Jews [the suspect Aryan businessmen] were let out, the public would hang them on every lamp-post. Anybody who says that to me gets fired at once.' Beaverbrook told Rothschild, 'you should not be involved in this persecution and you should not be in MI5 witch-hunting. You should be leading your people out of the concentration camps.' He presented himself as the protector of Jewry: 'I have not always been pro-Semitic, but . . . I am the only liberal member of the Cabinet, and I am sticking up for them everywhere.' MI5, he told Rothschild, 'ought to be abolished. I do not think there is any danger from Nazi spies in this country. I do not think it matters if they are at large.'[23]

Sir Alan Brooke, who was Chief of the Imperial General Staff from 1941 and head of the Chiefs of Staff Committee, reflected in 1943, 'Running a war seems to consist in making plans and then ensuring that all those destined to carry it out don't quarrel with each other instead of the enemy.' Hardy Amies, who continued to design dresses for his Mayfair couturier shop while an officer in the Intelligence Corps and in the Belgian Section of SOE, said that by the end of the war he realized that 'there was no more intriguing, cunning and touchy person than a high-ranking officer' in 'the more secret departments' of the government. The dissensions and rivalries between MI5 and SIS are undeniable; but they have been given undue prominence, either by vocal retired officers with embittered memories or by historian-journalists trying to make a good story. There was a reasonable level of respect and cooperation, despite the distracting snipers on both sides.[24]

On 11 May 1940 the Home Office declined to act on MI5's recommendation that 500 members of the British Union of Fascists should be detained, but a fortnight later, as Operation DYNAMO (the evacuation of the British Expeditionary Force from the Dunkirk beaches) got under way, there was panic reaching from xenophobic newspapers and chief constables upwards to the Cabinet about German women masquerading as Czech refugees, Jewish exiles succumbing to bribes or threats, and alien fifth columnists ready to welcome German parachutists and to begin work as saboteurs. 'The essence of sound security policy is wise discrimination,' insisted the Home Office under its remarkable PUS, Sir Alexander Maxwell. 'A violent policy fitfully administered is not nearly as effective as a more moderate policy firmly and consistently applied.' The Home Office warned that the general internment of aliens would gratify public opinion in the short run, but would soon bring misgivings.[25]

This sane approach was overwhelmed after Italy had entered the war on Germany's side on 11 June 1940. There was large-scale internment of Austrians, Germans and Italians while the CPGB and its sympathizers were largely left alone. As early as mid-July, after interrogating internees and other intensive inquiries, MI5 accepted that there was no evidence of a fifth column of Nazi sympathizers primed for sabotage or espionage. Given the Russian Oil Products organization for which thousands of CPGB members worked, it is likely that a different conclusion would have emerged from investigations of communist sympathizers. MI5 advised that anti-communist measures would arouse the resentment of non-Marxist factory workers and trade unionists, and thus impair social cohesion and armaments production. 'The Communist problem', MI5 advised, 'will be as urgent, or even more urgent, at the end of the War, and suppressive action now would sow the seeds of future ill-feeling.'[26]

Defence Regulation 18B suspended the right of suspected Nazi sympathizers to test the evidence against them before a judge and jury. Instead detainees could appeal to a Home Office advisory committee chaired by the eminent barrister Norman Birkett (afterwards Lord Birkett). According to this committee's secretary, Jenifer Hart, Birkett regarded MI5 as 'illiberal, disorganized and incompetent'. To Lord Hankey, a Cabinet minister inquiring into the wartime security services, he complained of MI5's 'pathological stupidities'. To MI5 it seemed that

Birkett's approach was sometimes contemptible, with MI5 witnesses being browbeaten as if they were petty criminals. The other committee members were the barrister John Morris (afterwards Lord Morris of Borth-y-Gest), whom Hart described as 'patient, humane and vigilant to protect the freedom of the individual', and a common-sense land-owner and committee man Sir Arthur Hazlerigg (afterwards Lord Hazlerigg). Liddell thought that Birkett's committee induced the Home Office to think of MI5 as unbalanced and narrow in its views.[27]

'MI5', Churchill's adviser Desmond Morton said in 1943, 'tends to see dangerous men too freely and to lack that knowledge of the world and sense of perspective which the Home Secretary rightly considers essential.' This comment followed the assembly by MI5 officers of evidence that fifty-seven members of the CPGB were working in secret installations, actually or potentially remitting to Moscow secret material on armaments, aircraft production, anti-radar devices, jet engines and other strategic matters. The Home Office recommended that the fifty-seven should be moved to non-classified work, but Morton convinced Churchill to establish a Whitehall panel to consider on a case-by-case basis reports tendered by MI5 on communists in confidential positions. This panel had nugatory effect.[28]

At MI5 White and Liddell developed a plan to run double agents by letting Germans land in Britain, detaining them and turning them so that they supplied misdirection to Germany. The German agents who reached Britain after September 1940 were recognized by the Security Service as potential assets who could be used to deceive and manipulate their controllers in Germany. The politicians, however, wanted to make propaganda by publicizing the capture and execution of German agents. In October 1940 Churchill badgered Lord Swinton, the ex-Cabinet minister whom he had recently appointed as head of the wartime Home Defence (Security) Executive and who regarded himself as head of MI5 and to some extent of SIS, to explain why more captured German spies had not been shot. Liddell advised Swinton that painstaking interrogation and turning of such agents should be MI5's priority. In Dick White's words, 'Intelligence should have precedence over blood-letting.'[29]

The Security Service strove – in its home territories, at least – never to stoop to Nazi or Stalinist methods: colonial field operations were another matter. Liddell's comment was pragmatic and principled when, in 1940, a colonel from military intelligence was found punching a German parachutist who was under interrogation and being appraised for turning as a double agent: 'we cannot have this sort of thing going on in our establishment. Apart from the moral aspect of the whole thing, I am quite convinced that these Gestapo methods do not pay in the long run.' He was keen in 1942 to avoid embedding an informant in the War Registry to watch for possible leakages of information: 'we should be laying ourselves open to accusation that we were employing Gestapo methods in the civil service'. The Home Office had strong objections to the use by MI5 of agents provocateurs.[30]

In 1942 Helenus ('Buster') Milmo, a barrister seconded to MI5, consulted Philby about Juan Gómez de Lecube, a Spanish footballer, greyhound-breeder and Abwehr agent, who had been arrested earlier that year in Trinidad on his way from Spain to Panama and been brought to MI5's wartime interrogation centre, Camp 020, at Latchmere House in Surrey. At the time, London and other cities were recovering from an aerial bombing campaign that had killed 42,000 civilians and destroyed 130,000 houses. About fifty British merchant ships were being sunk each month. Millions of civilians were being subjugated, slaughtered or enslaved in mainland Europe. The British had no certainty of winning the war. But Camp 020 did not torture or psychologically disorientate its suspected adversaries, as in the twenty-first century was done at Guantánamo and Abu Ghraib. Milmo devised a delicate scheme, 'Plan Squealer', whereby Lecube was told that another informant had betrayed him and that it was better to make a full disclosure. 'This ingenious plan to trap LECUBE', Philby agreed, 'is undoubtedly worth trying.' Lecube did not fall for 'Plan Squealer'; but he was never subjected to what his captors called Gestapo methods. As Robin ('Tin-Eye') Stephens, the polyglot who ran Camp 020, wrote in his internal manual for running detention centres, 'Violence is taboo, for not only does it produce answers to please, but it lowers the standard of information.' He forbade the hitting of prisoners. 'For one thing it is the act of a coward. For another, it is unintelligent, for the spy will give an answer to please, an answer to escape punishment. And having given a false answer, all else depends upon the false premise.' He preferred to apply pressure rather than to punch. 'Pressure is attained by personality, tone, and rapidity of question,' Stephens said: it allowed 'no respite, no time to recover, no time to plan'.[31]

Wartime London

After Churchill became Prime Minister in May 1940, he was given the alias of BOAR in NKVD wireless traffic. Whitehall was converted into a war zone, with barbed-wire entanglements and machine-gun posts to prevent ministries being raided by enemy parachutists. The camouflage of one machine-gun redoubt in Parliament Square as a newspaper kiosk was compromised by the vendor, who was not the usual runt with a fag in the corner of his mouth and a muffler round his neck, but a spruce, erect young Hercules primed for armed combat. Sandbags were piled high in front of buildings, shops and monuments. Bomb-shelters and anti-aircraft batteries filled parks and squares. Anti-aircraft balloons, resembling fat porpoises with silver scales that sparkled in sunlight, floated in the sky. The evacuation of the British army from Dunkirk began on 26 May. 'If we lose our empire, we shall become not a second-rank, but a tenth-rank power,' the new Prime Minister's son Randolph Churchill told Maisky. 'We have nothing . . . So, there is nothing for it but to fight to the end.' Maisky however thought that many Conservative leaders still hoped to divert Germany to attack Russia. This group was, he recognized, 'scared stiff about the social and political consequences of the war, and is ready to conclude a "rotten peace" . . . in order to retain its capitalist privileges'. Soviet penetration agents in Whitehall could not relent in their espionage.[32]

German aerial bombing raids, known in England as the Blitz, began in London on 7 September 1940. Officers of the security services, like other Londoners, were placed under maddening strain on bombing-nights, and took daytime decisions when enervated by sleep deprivation. Norman Mott, who was head of security at the London headquarters of wartime SOE and peacetime SIS, kept his colleagues sane during bad air-raids with his imitations of Donald Duck. 'Mott was a much liked, laconic pipe-smoker who was never seen to be anything less than cool and controlled,' wrote an SIS colleague, before mentioning that prized virtue of Whitehall officials of his generation: 'his sense of humour was always capable of relieving tension.'[33]

The clubs of St James's Street and Pall Mall were so close to the prime targets of Whitehall, the Palace of Westminster and Buckingham Palace that bombs rained down on them. Late at night on 24 September Liddell left the Reform Club in Pall Mall, where he had dined with Burgess and Blunt, just after 'a Molotov breadbasket' (a high-explosive bomb, which scattered a cluster of incendiary bombs as it fell) dispersed its fiery load around him: 'people were rushing about in dressing-gowns with bags of sand. When I got into the Mall the whole of St James's Park was lit up as if by Roman candles.' Malcolm Muggeridge and Graham Greene, both wartime SIS operatives, sometimes ventured out in the Blitz together. 'This was not out of bravado or a wish to be killed; just an instinctive movement towards where the noise was loudest, as people on a seaside beach gather where the throng is greatest,' Muggeridge recalled. 'There was something rather wonderful about London in the Blitz, with no street lights, no traffic and no pedestrians to speak of; just an empty, dark city, torn with great explosions, racked with ack-ack fire, lit with lurid flames, acrid smoke, its air full of the dust of fallen buildings.'[34]

Hostile voices have long protested that the secret services were recruited to an excessive extent from the privileged class who were members of such clubs as White's, Brooks's, Boodle's, the Athenaeum and the Travellers. Criticism focuses on the class exclusivity of the clubs, not on their gender exclusivity (the Reform first admitted women members in 1981, while the Oxford and Cambridge Club delayed admitting women graduates until 1996). In fact, many of the wartime recruits to SOE, SIS and MI5 were encouraged to join such clubs after their enlistment precisely because (unlike restaurants or public houses) it was impossible for outsiders to keep watch inside a club, and much harder to be overheard in a compromising way. Even so, Hugh Dalton, successively Minister of Economic Warfare and head of SOE, was 'appalled at the amount of quack quack which goes on in West End Clubs', he said in 1940. 'Some tell me . . . that the Athenaeum is a little safer than some other Clubs, but I doubt even this. It is always observed, I say, who is with whom, and intelligent guesses are then made as to why they are together.' This was also the view of Dick White who, as Chief of SIS in 1967 invited Hugh Trevor-Roper to lunch at the Garrick Club to discuss recent publicity about Philby, but then changed the venue to a French restaurant in Northumberland Avenue, off Whitehall. If they were seen together in the Garrick, White explained, speculation would be rife.[35]

Dennis Wheatley, the novelist of black magic who was recruited in 1941 to Whitehall's efforts to deceive the German enemy, gave a rollicking account of lunching with intelligence officers in a St James's club. With a novelist's imagination, he claimed – and others believed – that the officers consumed two or three glasses of Pimm's in the club bar, a shot of spirits laced with absinthe, then a meal of smoked salmon or potted shrimps, Dover sole, jugged hare or game, ending with a Welsh rarebit savoury, washed down by red and white wines, finished with port or Kümmel. The drab reality is that rich, lengthy lunches were rarities preserved by Victor Rothschild. A major in the Intelligence Corps, Rupert Speir, when he lunched with MI5 colleagues at his club Brooks's, had hasty meals: 'I merely flash in and out.' At Philby's club, the Athenaeum, there was no cocktail bar serving Pimm's or absinthe. The rationed meals comprised snoek, whale-meat, frozen cod-fish, processed tinned meat, powdered potatoes and margarine. On three days every week no wines were served at meals. On other days there was a limit of one glass of sherry before the meal and one glass of port after. The wine served had the alarming description of 'Algerian burgundy'. Sir John Sinclair, post-war head of SIS and like Speir a member of Brooks's, had an identical lunch every day: a grilled herring and a glass of water.[36]

'Better Communism than Nazism'

In the opening months of the war Churchill (newly appointed as First Lord of the Admiralty) had several talks with Stalin's Ambassador, Maisky. 'Your non-aggression pact with Germany triggered the war, but I bear you no grudge,' Churchill told him. The jolt had been necessary to get the fighting started. 'I'm all for war to the end,' Churchill declared. 'Let Germany become Bolshevik . . . Better Communism than Nazism.' (This contrasted with Beaverbrook's message to Maisky. 'What concerns me is the fate of the British Empire!' he exclaimed. 'To hell with that man Hitler! If the Germans want him, I happily concede them this treasure and make my bow. Poland? Czechoslovakia? What are they to do with us?')[37]

For most of September 1939 the CPGB supported, in an equivocal way, the war against Germany. Early in October, however, under Comintern directions, and at the remorseless urging of the Marxist-Leninist theoretician Rajani Palme Dutt, it resolved to treat the fighting as an imperialist war waged in the interests of the ruling classes rather than a proletarian anti-fascist war. The three leading opponents of Moscow's line, Harry Pollitt, Willie Gallacher and J. R. Campbell, subsequently recanted, and submitted to party discipline. The CPGB abased itself in repentance of its 'vulgar liberal democrat conceptions' in September 1939, and 'blurring of the distinction between the national interest of the British people and the imperial interest of the British ruling-class'. The Home Office successfully opposed the suppression of the CPGB in 1940 when the *Daily Worker* was shut on government orders. Palme Dutt's orthodoxy imposed after the Nazi–Soviet non-aggression pact led to over a quarter of CPGB members leaving the party. Membership was at a low of 15,000 when Germany launched Operation BARBAROSSA against the Soviet Union in June 1941.[38]

Throughout 1941 Blunt was running his sub-agent Leo Long, who supplied sound British military intelligence analyses of German intentions towards the Soviet Union. Vladimir Dekanozov, Stalin's Ambassador in Berlin, sent confirmatory reports on the tendency of events. When Philby also supplied early warnings of German divisions being mustered near the Russian frontier, the chief of Soviet military intelligence speculated that with the Luftwaffe daily blitzing London, the English secret services were using Philby to deceive the Kremlin. In April 1941 Sir Stafford Cripps, Ambassador in Moscow, made an unauthorized threat to Stalin that if the Anglo-German war was protracted by Soviet supplies to Germany, 'we might be tempted to make peace with Germany at Russian expense'. The crazy peace mission of Rudolf Hess, who flew to Scotland in May, intensified Stalin's distrust of perfidious Albion. Fearing an Anglo-German united front against Russia, he dismissed as 'disinformation' more than a hundred warnings of Hitler's preparations for Operation BARBAROSSA as an English conspiracy to jockey Russia into war with Germany. Then, in Jonathan Haslam's words, 'Beria, utterly inexperienced but inebriated by overweening self-confidence, proved [himself] to be the most disastrous head of intelligence the Soviet Union ever had.' On 21 June, the eve of BARBAROSSA, he toadied to Stalin by demanding Dekanozov's recall from Berlin and punishment for bombarding Moscow with misdirection about German invasion plans: 'surely the nadir of Moscow's intelligence assessment', says Haslam.[39]

Once Russia had joined the war on Nazi Germany, Lord Swinton of the Security Executive ordained that MI5 must concentrate all its efforts on Nazis and their fifth columnists. The Soviet Union became an ally rather than an adversary, and was reduced more than ever as a counter-espionage priority. The CPGB adjusted its criterion so that an unjust imperialist war became a righteous People's War. As Swinton observed in October 1941, 'the Communist game is still the same, but it is being played on a much better wicket'. CPGB membership revived to about 50,000 by December 1942. Registered membership settled at about 46,000 for most of 1944–5.[40]

Visitors from London began to arrive in the beleaguered Soviet Union. The earliest journalist to arrive there, Philip Jordan, who spent seven months reporting the Eastern Front fighting from July 1941, assured English readers that the Russian army was a stronger fighting force for having been 'purged of its incompetents and its traitors', although he conceded that the purges may have 'sheared a little too closely to the bone'. He only wished that generals had been purged in other armies. 'Had the Spanish Government behaved as drastically as the Russian Government did in the middle thirties, there would have been no civil war in Spain; for the traitors would have been dead. Had we applied a purge to our own Army, it would have been a more effi-cient fighting force when this war broke out.' Moscow had jettisoned the Trotskyite theory of world revolution, he reported. In Stalin's entou-rage the Comintern was considered 'one of the great historic failures of our age'.[41]

In December that year Anthony Eden, the Foreign Secretary, visited Moscow to confer with Stalin at a time when German troops were only 20 miles from the city. He travelled by destroyer to Murmansk, where Maisky visited his cabin clutching a black bag packed with rubles which he asked Eden to feel free to use without reservation. 'I was agape at so much wealth,' said Eden, who did not pocket the bribe. Stalin impressed Eden in conference as prudent, well informed and an unex-pectedly good listener. At the final banquet of caviar, sturgeon and suckling pig, after swilling vodka, champagne and Georgian wines, Marshal K. Y. Voroshilov fell across Stalin's knees in a stupor. The feasting was a morbid and grotesque experience for Eden because, he said, 'where one man rules all others fear'.[42]

The Anglo-Soviet alliance agreed in May 1942 committed both signa-tories to safeguarding and strengthening the economic and political independence of all European nations, and disavowed future territorial aggrandizement by either party. It had no more value than earlier scraps of paper. In the month of the treaty's signature the English diplomat Roger Makins noted that the Soviet aim was 'exclusive Russian influence over the whole of Eastern Europe, to be effected by the occupation of Finland, the Baltic States and Romania, the closest possible association with Czechoslovakia and Yugoslavia, the crushing of Hungary and the encirclement of Poland'. The future PUS William Strang minuted on Makins's comments: 'I do not think that we can counter the establishment of Russian predominance in Eastern Europe if Germany is crushed and disarmed and Russia participates in the final victory.' Sir Archie Clark Kerr, Cripps's successor as Ambassador in Moscow, expected the Soviet Union to make post-war territorial claims in the Baltic and Bessarabia, and to assert a protectorate over the Slav nations of Europe, but did not expect the spirit of the Anglo-Soviet treaty to be broken. 'One thing can be said: Soviet Russia, after the war, will probably be prepared to take things quietly for a considerable period of time. There will . . . be a general desire for a greater degree of comfort and happiness than was granted them before the war.' Articles by E. H. Carr in *The Times* urged that Britain should resile from central Europe and the Balkans, and accept those parts of the continent as Russia's exclusive sphere of interest.[43]

In April 1943, shortly before the first anniversary of the Anglo-Soviet treaty, central European leaders exiled in London tried to rouse British resistance to Stalin by invoking the spurious arguments of national exceptionalism. 'We are immensely powerful, and may be more powerful at the conclusion of the war,' argued O'Malley, who was the British Ambassador to the Polish government-in-exile. 'We shall have the opportunity to exert moral authority on the continent of Europe, because we are the only European Great Power that has no wish to annex or dominate or even create a new "sphere of influence", because we alone are feared by none except those with whom we are at war, because we alone can hold the balance between despotism and chaos, and because, without us, nothing can ensure freedom, justice and security to all.' Commenting on O'Malley's attempt to rally Britain against Soviet intrigues, Strang wrote: 'Unless the 80,000,000 aggressive Germans can be contained or tamed, our very existence, not only as a world power, but as an independent state, will again be threatened. In order to contain Germany we need Russian collaboration. The conclusion of the Anglo-Soviet treaty last year marks our decision that this must be our policy now and after the war . . . There is a respectable and well-informed opinion that Russia will not, either now or for some years after the war, aim at the Bolshevisation of Eastern and Central Europe.' Even if it did, 'I should not like to say that this would be to our disadvantage,' Strang admitted. 'It is better that Russia should dominate Eastern Europe than that Germany should dominate Western Europe.'[44]

London believed that it was working in concert with Moscow, and showing its trust of Soviet intentions. It had meagre intelligence sources on the intentions of the Kremlin, and was following hunches based more or less on optimism. Moscow, however, had no trust in London. It knew from its various spies that the British were not sharing either their progress with the Americans in developing nuclear weaponry nor their success in deciphering the Abwehr's wireless traffic. The British intervention in the Russian civil war of 1918, the anti-Bolshevik propaganda of the inter-war period, the exaggerated fear of British spies, the slowness of Anglo-American armies to open a second front in the west, and suspicions that the Americans and British would make a separate peace with Germany were all reasons for Soviet hostility. 'Spectacular Russian victories continue,' noted the Foreign Office's Oliver Harvey in February 1943. 'The Russians are very tiresome allies, importunate, graceless, ungrateful, secretive, suspicious, ever asking for more, but they are delivering the goods.' Churchill, meanwhile, gave policy guidance to Clark Kerr in Moscow: 'I don't mind kissing Stalin's bum, but I'm damned if I'll lick his arse.'[45]

Inside SIS, among its younger officers, there was a feeling that the pre-war service had been obsessed by Bolsheviks but insufficiently concerned by Nazis. They began thinking of the Russians as allies after June 1941. 'Chapman Pincher is quite wrong to see Oxbridge intellectuals as responsible for this sort of view,' a retired SIS officer told Anthony Glees in the 1980s. 'The *Daily Mirror* and [its columnist] Cassandra were far more significant: it was an anti-upper-class populism that made us so pro-Russian. Everybody who was intelligent and powerful underestimated Soviet long-term plans in the intelligence sphere.'[46]

In an episode that would have astounded the pre-war anti-Bolshevik Conservative leaders – Churchill himself, Curzon, Birkenhead, Joynson-Hicks – the twenty-fifth anniversary of the creation of the Red

Army was celebrated with mass enthusiasm across England on 21 February 1943. William Temple, Archbishop of Canterbury appointed the date as a day for special prayer for Russia and Soviet comrades. Eden addressed a 'Red Army' demonstration in the Royal Albert Hall, Kensington. There a gigantic hammer-and-sickle flag was raised above the stage, whereon stood a solitary Red Army soldier with his rifle. Government ministers spoke at solidarity meetings in twelve industrial cities. Attlee in Cardiff compared the Red Army overthrowing the corrupt tsarist regime to Cromwell's New Model Army defeating the obsolete Royalist forces of the 1640s. Sir Stafford Cripps in Sheffield extolled the Red Army and 'the unruffled steel-like purpose of their supreme commander, Stalin', to whom 'the world owe[d] the deepest debt of gratitude. In the dark days of retreat his leadership of the Soviet Union was as inspiring as was that of our own Prime Minister in the days of Dunkirk. I could pay no higher tribute than that to any man.' At the demonstration in Newcastle City Hall, Sir Charles Trevelyan, a former Labour Minister of Education, assured the audience that every second man in the Red Army had received a secondary education. 'On the platform were all the swells – generals, admirals, air marshals, M.P.s, the nobility and gentry,' reported Sir Cuthbert Headlam. 'The audience was mainly composed of sailors, merchant seamen, soldiers, airmen, representatives of trades and industries, A.R.P., Fire Service, etc. with of course a large attendance of extremists in the galleries for whom the whole thing was a political demonstration.'[47]

London became gripped by pro-Soviet enthusiasm. The Red Flag was flown over Selfridge's. Young women emulated by the cut of their clothes the Soviet comrade type. Russian songs and films came into vogue. Seventy thousand copies of a booklet of the war speeches of Stalin and Molotov were sold in a few weeks. Beaverbrook kept a photograph of Stalin on his mantelpiece. The Athenaeum and St James's clubs both elected Maisky to membership; the mayor of Kensington gave a reception in his honour with 500 eminent guests. The Hollywood film of Joseph Davies's ambassadorial memoirs, *Mission to Moscow*, was released in England: with its deceptive documentary format and rousing music, it hailed Soviet military prowess, upheld the integrity of Kremlin statesmanship, belauded the efficiency of state planning and shamed those who had residual doubts about Russia's recent pact with Germany. The defendants in the show-trials of the Great Terror were portrayed as fifth columnists serving Germany and Japan. Sir Robert Bruce Lockhart, Director General of the Political Warfare Executive in 1942–5, warned that press adulation might convince Stalin that British public opinion was so pro-Soviet that he could do what he liked in Europe. 'Moreover,' warned Bruce Lockhart, who had been imprisoned in the Kremlin in 1918 while on a mission to Trotsky, 'to Bolsheviks hardened in the school, first of revolution and then of social ostracism, *bourgeois* flattery is a certain sign of *bourgeois* weakness.'[48]

There was unstinted admiration for the Red Army in England, noted Maisky: 'Everywhere – among the masses and in the army. To fight this wave would have been dangerous.' As part of the ideological capitulation, King George VI announced a gift to Stalinist Russia, the Sword of Stalingrad. This was a ceremonial sword 4 feet long, with a steel blade sharp enough to behead a man and sufficiently ductile to bend into a crescent moon. When finished it was exhibited at Goldsmiths' Hall and the Victoria & Albert Museum, and then taken on a triumphal tour of provincial cities, where it attracted huge, appreciative crowds. Evelyn Waugh, in *Unconditional Surrender*, described the scenes in October 1943 when the Sword reached Westminster Abbey, where it was displayed near the shrine of Edward the Confessor. There were long queues outside the abbey, where Philby as a schoolboy had spent so many frustrating hours at services. The populace shuffled forward in a mood of devotion, said Waugh, every civilian looking shabby and grubby, each carrying a respirator against a gas attack, some munching Woolton pies while others sucked on cigarettes pieced together from the sweepings of butts on canteen floors. 'Every day the wireless announced great Russian victories while the British advance in Italy was coming to a halt. The people were suffused with gratitude to their remote allies . . . They knew no formal act of veneration. They paused, gazed, breathed and passed on.' Any member of the crowd who tried to linger in front of the Sword was pressed forward, Waugh wrote, 'not jostled resentfully, but silently conscribed into the unseeing, inarticulate procession who were asserting their right to the fair share of everything which they believed the weapon symbolized'. Churchill presented the Sword to Stalin during the Tehran conference in November 1943, and toasted the Generalissimo as 'Stalin the Great'.[49]

This atmosphere of Anglo-Russian unity gladdened the Cambridge spies, and helped the atomic spies Alan Nunn May and Klaus Fuchs to feel that they were doing right by giving official secrets to Britain's Soviet allies. Similarly, Ormond Uren saw no harm in his meetings with Douglas Springhall of the CPGB. Uren, a young Australian-born, Quaker-educated and intellectually powerful SOE officer, who was fluent in French, Spanish, Hungarian and Russian, met Springhall in order to expedite his application for party membership. Among other indiscretions, he provided a written account of SOE activities, which he did not think betrayed any useful secrets. For this misjudgement, Uren was sentenced to seven years' penal servitude in October 1943: after his release in 1947 he was blacklisted from academic posts for years before finally receiving a lectureship in linguistics at the University of London.

Stalin was sacrosanct. In 1944 London publishers refused to handle George Orwell's new novel, *Animal Farm*, after being warned by Smolka that it insulted Stalin and would afflict Anglo-Soviet relations. Orwell was told that the novel might seem less offensive in an age of Stalin-worship if a species other than pigs was used. He later included Smolka in a list of crypto-communists with the comment: 'some kind of Russian agent. Very slimy.' Churchill, though, had another animal in mind when two months after the Tehran conference *Pravda* claimed that England was negotiating a separate peace with Germany. 'Trying to maintain good relations with a communist is like wooing a crocodile,' he told the Cabinet, 'you do not know whether to tickle it under the chin or to beat it on the head. When it opens its mouth you cannot tell whether it is trying to smile, or preparing to eat you up.'[50]

'Softening the oaken heart of England'

From the 1920s the Czech leader Edvard Beneš worked for the 'Europeanization' of the Soviet Union and urged western governments to accommodate it among the comity of European nations. In 1948, during the final months of his life, as the Stalinists took control in Prague and wrecked his hopes, he could only curse them: 'Liars! Frauds! Scum!' The Beneš-like hope that Stalinists might be made into good social democratic Europeans underlay the tactics of Churchill and Roosevelt when they conferred with Stalin at Yalta and Potsdam in 1944–5. By courtesy of the Cambridge spies Stalin knew in advance the contents of British policy papers. Roosevelt was a dying man while

Churchill was often verbose or contrary at this stage of the war. 'P.M. still pursuing savage vendetta against France,' Oliver Harvey recorded in April 1945. 'He is now very definitely on the side of fallen royalty: Hapsburgs, Hohenzollerns or Glücksburgs.'[51]

Russia was kept as an ally against Germany with the bribe of a free run in eastern Europe. The English-speaking allies gambled that if Stalin was enabled to recover the territories of tsarist Russia in Bessarabia, eastern Poland, Finnish Karelia and the Baltic states, his forces would refrain from communist militancy and territorial aggression elsewhere. Churchill's conciliation of his ally Stalin, to whom he was bound by the Anglo-Russian treaty of 1942, was required by Britain's diminishing international power. 'Make no mistake, all the Balkans, except Greece, are going to be Bolshevised; and there is nothing I can do to prevent it,' Churchill told his private secretary in January 1945. 'There is nothing I can do for poor Poland either.'[52]

Some opinion-formers in London felt that Chamberlain's insularity had lost Britain the trust of mainland Europe. 'Englishmen do not yet realize the intense and enduring bitterness, hatred and mistrust that Chamberlain sowed in Europe,' Philip Jordan, who was appointed First Secretary at the Washington embassy in 1946, wrote in the year of the Anglo-Russian treaty. 'Europe attributes, and rightly, her own present miseries to the British Conservative Party. Until we can oust that party from its place of power, Europe will not trust us again – whatever the Ministry of Information may tell us about the success of our broadcasts.' Some of Churchill's finest hours were spent in reducing Europe's mistrust of the offshore kingdom where he was the paramount war leader.[53]

In 1945 Russia won its first victory in a major war since 1812. This triumph put the federated socialist republics in a 'rough and boisterous mood', reported Clark Kerr from Moscow. 'The Soviet Union tends to disport itself like a wet retriever puppy in someone else's drawing-room, shaking herself and swishing her tail in adolescent disregard for all except herself. We must expect her thus to rampage until she feels that she is secure from any unpleasant surprises in neighbouring countries.' Only then would the Soviet Union 'settle down to the serious and respectable business of . . . her relationship with Great Britain under the Anglo-Soviet Treaty, a commitment by which she sets great store.'[54]

Rather as the Bolshevik revolution of 1917 arose from Russian participation in the European war and not from a Marxian crisis of capitalism, so the continent-wide destruction of 1939–45 enabled Stalinist Russia to impose communism in eastern and central Europe. It was by the conquests of Soviet troops that Estonia, Latvia, Lithuania, Finnish Karelia, Carpathian Ruthenia, a quarter of Austria and one-third of Germany were swallowed in the Soviet maw by the end of the European fighting. The decision of the supreme allied commander General Dwight Eisenhower not to push eastwards hard and fast had momentous and enduring consequences. The settlement at Yalta signified less than the demarcation lines between east and west on VE Day in May 1945, and the brute fact of Soviet armies of occupation. The Russians' military advances westward in the spring of 1945 were the necessary precursor to the political scheming and constitutional malpractices whereby, during the next few years, Albania, Bulgaria, Czechoslovakia, Hungary, Poland, Romania and Yugoslavia became Soviet satellite states. The solidarity of the Soviet bloc was ensured by the Warsaw Pact of 1955, which was not dissolved until 1991.

Owen O'Malley, as ambassador to the Polish government-in-exile, was aghast at the concessions made to Stalinist domination of Europe. His Polish contacts understood that 'British public opinion needed tactful handling, having been misled for many years into wishfully thinking that Stalin & Co., though a bit rough in their methods, were not bad fellows at bottom.' The Poles were however astounded by Churchill's courting of Stalin at the Tehran and Yalta conferences, and by the false hopes that led the western powers to yield to Russian pretensions. O'Malley's contacts were shocked that government ministries, newspapers, the BBC, the Army Education Department and the Political Warfare Executive had all expressed trust in Soviet intentions. The Poles were dismayed, he said, that these bodies employed foreigners, some like Smolka/Smollett with anglicized surnames, 'of multiple allegiances, self-appointed saviours of society, bitter little Messiahs, do-gooders, cranky professors, recognizable fellow-travellers and numberless camp-followers from among the frustrated and ambitious intellectual proletariat – all burrowing like wood-beetles, corrupting and softening with their saliva and excrement the oaken heart of England'. The Soviet occupation of Poland was brutal. 'The Russians really control nearly everything,' the young diplomat Robert Hankey reported from Warsaw in August 1945. 'People disappear (in driblets not masses) all the time, and the police have a foul habit of sitting in a house and picking up anyone who comes to it.' The captives taken in these household 'blockades' were kept starving in cellars for weeks. 'This is essentially a *polizeistaat*,' Hankey informed the FO of Stalinist Poland. He found common ground, though, in the gender of the outright Polish leaders who avowed their communism: 'They are real men, and one can get on with them.'[55]

Bill Cavendish-Bentinck, newly installed as Ambassador in Warsaw, summarized a speech by the communist Vice-Minister of Justice complaining that the Polish judiciary was defying the will of the people. 'The courts of justice must state decisively on whose side they will be in their everyday work,' declared the minister. 'They must understand that there is no room for courts of justice that have regard for formal truth.' If judges did not support 'the interests of the vital matters of the nation, then Polish democracy will be compelled to establish new forms of courts of law at the cost of resigning from the worship of the professional skill of Polish courts of justice'. This was the reality of the Soviet bloc.[56]

Until the publication in 1998 of Sir Antony Beevor's *Stalingrad*, the patriotic, indoctrinating bias of Anglophone history focused attention on Anglo-American campaigns in Italy, France, the Low Countries and Germany. It discounted the fact that the principal theatre of war in Europe had been in the east, where the Red Army had bested the Nazis. Losses in the region were appalling: 6 million Jews were exterminated there; Poland lost 17 per cent of its population (5.7 million people), Lithuania 14 per cent (370,000) and Yugoslavia 11 per cent (1.7 million). England was largely indifferent to the national oppression, local barbarities and individual cruelty visited by Red forces on the European mainland. Just two instances need be given of the nature of the new enemy. In 1945 a German field hospital, which had been installed in a school at Gorizia, an elegant town on the Italian–Slovenian border, was captured by communist partisans. The sixty-four patients were tied to their beds, with a detonator taped in their mouths. Slow fuses attached to the detonators were wound over chairs so that all could watch the progress of their deaths. When the Grenadier Guards reached the hospital later, sixty-three of the Germans were dead in bed without their lower jaws. One wounded German had survived because the detonator in his mouth failed to explode. Count István Bethlen, the elderly Transylvanian liberal who had kept fascism from power in Hungary when he was Prime Minister, was seized at this time, and soon perished in a Moscow prison. His widow was bound to a post and used as a living scarecrow on a Hungarian farm, with branches tied to her arms and feathers stuck in her hair.[57]

The truth of the times was enunciated by Sir Victor Wellesley in 1944: 'Europe can be saved only if the nations which compose it can free themselves from pre-war prejudices and conceptions and bring themselves to think on broader lines than in terms of nationalism and sovereignty. They must come to visualize the continent and not the nation as the economic unit of the future.' Wellesley included his own country in the continental revisionism: 'We must all begin by being good Europeans rather than good nationalists, and then follow on by being good world citizens.' It was in a similar temper that Labour's Ernest Bevin started as the first post-war Foreign Secretary. He proved one of the greatest holders of that office. The primary objective of his foreign policy, he declared in 1945, was to be able to go down to Victoria station for the boat train and buy a ticket to where the hell he liked without a passport.[58]

CHAPTER 12

The Desk Officers

Modrzhinskaya in Moscow

If a trusting office culture in London and Washington facilitated security failures, the Stalinist environment of distrust was disabling to Soviet espionage. Of all the available sources for Russia's global intelligence during the People's War, the Cambridge ring of five – as desk officers in the intelligence services or the Foreign Office – were the best. Yet the purges of 1936–8 had degraded intelligence analysis in Moscow and disrupted the running of foreign agents. The first-class material provided by the Cambridge spies did not seem threatening enough to convince Stalinist paranoiacs. Moscow's analysts mistook intelligence of unparalleled quality received from London as cunning misdirection by British intelligence. They rejected the evidence supplied by Philby that SIS had no agent network in Russia. They refused to believe that SIS had not possessed a pre-war Moscow station. They never accepted that the Soviet Union was a far lower intelligence priority for London than Britain was for Moscow. (The paranoia of Stalin's bureaucracy similarly led Moscow intelligence analysts to mistrust Duncan Lee, the most highly placed Soviet informant within OSS. Given his traceable communist sympathies, it seemed incomprehensible to Moscow that he had first been hired in Washington, and then heavily promoted within OSS; they suspected him of being a double agent duping them with misdirections.)

The morbidly suspicious young head of the NKVD's British department Elena Modrzhinskaya was a doctrinaire who so little understood England, although she spoke English, that she thought the ring of five were 'aristocrats'. Her obstinate misjudgement and repeated bad decisions exemplified Robert Conquest's observation that every organization behaves as if it is run by the secret agents of its opponents. Her paranoid doubts put an onerous burden on Anatoli Gorsky, né Gromov @ HENRI @ KAP @ VADIM, a dour, rigid, irritable Stalinist who had come to London in 1936 as assistant to the *rezident* and as cipher clerk. One after another his chiefs were recalled for liquidation or purging, so that in the critical eighteen months from September 1938 until March 1940 he had to run, as a solo operation, fourteen agents (including the Cambridge spies), take his own photographs, encrypt or decrypt messages, translate and type. In February 1940 he was abruptly recalled to Moscow because the NKVD, and particularly Modrzhinskaya, feared that it was receiving misinformation. Not until November that year did Gorsky return to London, where he remained until 1942, when Boris Kreshin @ BOB replaced him. During the ten months of 1940 when the Cambridge spies lost contact with Gorsky and the *rezidentura*, Philby, Burgess and Blunt (but not Cairncross or Maclean) gave their material to Edith Tudor-Hart, who ensured that it reached Moscow through Bob Stewart of the CPGB. Talking of Russian spy rings in 1943, Stewart boasted: 'I know more about this bloody job than most people. For years I saw every bloody man that come on the job . . . I might have been caught quite easy, because I carried the stuff.'[1]

Modrzhinskaya and her colleagues felt sure that the ring of five could have exposed British agents in the Soviet Union or in the Soviet embassy in London if they had been sincere; and thus thought them falsifiers and shams. She also attacked the ring of five for trying to recruit Footman of SIS and other dubious candidates. In October 1943 Moscow reiterated to Kreshin that, after analysis of the voluminous intelligence received, they were sure that the five were double agents, working on the instructions of SIS and MI5. As far back as their years at Cambridge, Philby, Maclean and Burgess had probably been acting on instructions from British counter-espionage to infiltrate socialist or communist activism in Cambridge. This was the only possible explanation for why both SIS and MI5 were employing known Cambridge communists in confidential positions in the secret state. Modrzhinskaya thought herself hyper-vigilant, and reiterated a nagging question: why had no British agent been exposed in Russia?

The Great Patriotic War was the Soviet Union's title for the conflict that from a different perspective Americans and western Europeans called the Second World War. The ring of five were active on Moscow's behalf throughout the conflict, taking fearful risks, seizing initiatives and enduring secret tensions that could not be shared or mitigated by alcohol. Yet (with the partial exception of Maclean) they were ill-appreciated, and were handled with a maladroitness that was inherent under Stalinism. The similar obtuseness in the NKGB's mishandling of Elizabeth Bentley in New York and Washington had immensely damaging repercussions on all sides: the NKGB network in the USA was compromised and for a time defunct; agents' lives were ruined; some were convicted of perjury, although there was generally insufficient evidence for treason charges. Vice-President Henry Wallace, whom Maclean admired, had recently proclaimed the Century of the Common Man, and brutal, thoughtless populism gained political legitimacy in the republic. In turn better modulated voices opposed Stalinist-like purges or Gestapo-type round-ups in the government departments of the English-speaking powers.

In 1944 Anatoli Gorsky was transferred from London to serve as NKGB chief in the USA with legal cover at the Washington embassy. He disliked Bentley's recalcitrant independence and lack of formal indoctrination in tradecraft, and was worried by the potential for incriminating discoveries by the FBI because many of her sources knew one another or worked together. Over the course of a year Gorsky supplanted her in running the Washington networks, isolated her from her friends, kept her in solitude in a hotel bedroom, where her alcoholism deteriorated, and urged her to embark for the Soviet Union without legal documentation. She rightly saw this plan as the preliminary to her liquidation, and felt mounting fears for her life (Juliet Poyntz, the Nebraska-born communist responsible for recruiting Bentley, had been abducted in New York in 1937 and was never seen again).

There is little doubt that Gorsky urged that she should be killed. Her life was threatened to her face by Lement ('Lem') Harris, disinherited heir to a fortune derived from Texaco oil, Chicago commodity-dealing and Wall Street brokerage, who had joined the CPUSA in order to champion the cause of poor agricultural workers. Feeling thoroughly endangered, Bentley went on 8 November 1945 to FBI offices in New York, where she volunteered a long statement with names. Hoover's agency gave a summary of her accusations to Sir William Stephenson, the shady Canadian financier who was the liaison between SIS and the

FBI. Stephenson's report to SIS in London was soon seen by Philby, who warned Moscow of what was pending. Gorsky, who left the US once it was known that Bentley had compromised him, urged that she should be poisoned or shoved under a subway train.

Philby at SIS

In 1940 Philby began living with Aileen Furse, a store detective in Marks and Spencer's Oxford Street branch. They had three children before he divorced Litzi Friedmann and married Furse in September 1946: Josephine (1941); John (1942); Dudley (1943). Two further children were born after the marriage, Miranda (1946) and Harry (1950). Philby reported on his common-law wife to Moscow: 'Her political views are socialistic, but like the majority of the wealthy middle class, she has an almost ineradicable tendency towards a definite form of philistinism (petite bourgeoise), namely: she believes in upbringing, the British navy, personal freedom, democracy, the constitutional system, honour, etc.' He assured the NKVD that he could 'cure her of these confusions, although of course I haven't yet attempted to do so; I hope the revolutionary situation will give her the necessary shake-up, and cause a correct revolutionary response.'[2]

Philby was in France as a war correspondent of *The Times* when the French armies surrendered and the Third Republic fell in 1940. During the ensuing evacuation of British subjects, Philby met Hester Marsden-Smedley, who worked for SIS under the cover of the *Daily Express* correspondent in Belgium and Luxembourg. On her recommendation he was invited to meet Leslie Sheridan, former night-editor of the *Daily Mirror*, who ran an SIS section disseminating false rumours and black propaganda, and had perhaps been given Philby's name by Burgess. Both Marsden-Smedley and Sheridan recommended Philby to Marjorie Maxse, formerly a propaganda organizer at Conservative Central Office, who was wartime chief of staff of SIS Section D charged with sabotage and covert activities. Valentine Vivian recalled in old age that during lunch with St John Philby, whom he had first met before 1914, he asked about Kim, who was on a list of potential SIS recruits. 'He was a bit of a Communist at Cambridge, wasn't he?' asked Vivian. 'Oh,' replied St John Philby, 'that was all schoolboy nonsense. He's a reformed character now.' This senescent reminiscence should be treated charily. There is no evidence that any SIS officer involved in Kim Philby's recruitment in 1940 knew of his allegiances at Trinity or his activities in Vienna. What got him into 'the pool' – the list of potential SIS recruits – was that he was an active and ambitious young man, who had shown courage under bombardment in Spain, who had been decorated with a medal by Generalissimo Franco and who had won acceptance at fascist military headquarters. There had been palpable bias against the left in his reports on the civil war for *The Times*. During the French collapse he had shown self-mastery and self-reliance. Vivian admitted that he had given a vague security endorsement to the young Philby: 'I was asked about him, and I said I knew his people.' But it was not family connections or the Westminster School tie that got Philby into SIS: it was his stupendously convincing cover story from Spain.[3]

Some junior intelligence officers, who knew of Philby's communist past, were 'rather cheered than depressed by this unusual recruitment', according to Hugh Trevor-Roper, who was one of them. 'My own view, like that of most of my contemporaries, was that our superiors were lunatic in their anti-communism. Many of our friends had been, or had thought themselves, communists in the 1930s; and we were shocked that such persons should be debarred from public service on account of mere juvenile illusions which anyway they had now shed: for such illusions could not survive the shattering impact of Stalin's pact with Hitler in 1939.'[4]

When Philby joined SIS in June 1940, the memory of its late Chief Admiral Sinclair was omnipresent, not least because his successor Sir Stewart Menzies and other pre-war staff kept photographs of 'Quex' in their rooms. There was little for Philby to do at his desk in Section D. After SOE had absorbed Section D, Philby was sent in the autumn of 1940 to instil techniques of underground propaganda into the trainee saboteurs of many nationalities who were billeted by SOE on Lord Montagu of Beaulieu's estate in Hampshire. With his Beaulieu pupils he developed the idea of the 'subversive rumour', which had to be plausible if it was to undermine morale: subversive rumours were to abound in post-war England, for the benefit of Soviet Russia, after the defections of Burgess, Maclean and himself. 'Truth is a technical advantage,' he told his students while instructing in the composition of convincing subversive leaflets. Many of his pupils, especially those from Poland, Mitteleuropa and the Balkans, were adamant anti-communists.

'Gentlemen, I have no wish to stop you blowing up the Russians, but I would beg you, for the sake of the Allied war effort, to blow up the Germans first.' Moscow's agent inside Beaulieu coined an effective slogan for his trainees: 'Germany is the *main* enemy.'[5]

With much of Europe occupied by Nazi forces, the neutral capitals of the continent – Stockholm, Madrid and Lisbon – were the only common ground on which the Abwehr and SIS vied on equal terms. In the summer of 1941 Tómas ('Tommy') Harris and Dick Brooman-White, head of SIS operations in Iberia, both cognizant of Philby's previous experiences in Spain, recommended him as the head of the new, expanded SIS Sub-section 5d covering Spain and Portugal. Philby in his memoirs *My Secret War* attributed this opportunity to 'the Old Boy network', and harped on the 'mental block which stubbornly resisted the belief that respected members of the Establishment could do such things' as spy for Russia. *My Secret War* is an exercise in spreading Philby's old speciality, subversive rumours. He wrote it under Soviet direction, with the purpose of damaging confidence in SIS – partly by deploying the language of class suspicion and antagonism. Trust was not the exclusive frailty of the supposed ruling class: the success of confidence-tricksters in cheating people at every social level shows that individuals seldom expect to be told lies, to hear falsified personal histories or for cruel betrayals to be meticulously planned.[6]

Philby began his new Iberian work in September 1941. His efficiency, his patience, his calm under pressure, his inordinately long working hours were immediately distinctive, and soon made him seem near-indispensable. Favourable judgements of him owe nothing to 'the Old Boy network': everything to the fact that he was superb at his job. 'Kim was not an intellectual in the All Souls sense; he was not drawn to abstract ideas at a high level of generality,' began an assessment of 1973 drawing on numerous off-the-record sources. 'The aptitude required for counter-espionage is a minute study of the subject on which one is working. His desk was deluged with telegrams from his men in the field, with pressing requests for tip-offs from MI5, with situation reports on Abwehr strength . . . and . . . the vital raw material of the radio intercepts from GC&CS.' To clarify this mass of material, to trace the significant patterns in it and to keep its ingredients in due proportion required a kind of all-absorbing scholarship. Ever since 1934 he had been training his brain and his emotions to compartmentalize his activities. He disallowed any room for overlapping mental clutter. At his desk he dictated lucid reports, gave clear briefings and wrote minutes in a small, neat, legible handwriting which seemed to signify all his virtues.[7]

In a novel by J. C. Masterman published in 1956, one of the chief protagonists is a blackmailer who spent the war as an SIS double agent in Portugal and has since betrayed his closest friends. Masterman never said or did anything by chance: it is hard to believe that the resemblance of the fictional Evelyn Bannister to the real-life Kim Philby is accidental. 'Lisbon became a kind of international clearing-ground, a busy ant-heap of spies and agents, where political and military secrets and information – true and false, but mainly false – were bought and sold, and where men's brains were pitted against each other', Masterman wrote of Bannister @ Philby. 'I believe that if he had dined with the Borgias and been faced with two glasses of wine one of which was probably poisoned, he could have lifted and drained one of them without a tremor of the hand. I believe, too, that he would have been quicker than any other man to note the smallest indication which might suggest that one glass was more likely to be safe than the other. And the very risks of his life were meat and drink to him.' His further description of Bannister applies equally to Philby. 'Calculated, steel-cold courage he had, and yet he shrank from physical violence, and that, I fancy, was his heel of Achilles.' Masterman's character could order, without a tremor, the killing of an inconvenient agent, 'but if, as an officer, it had been his duty to draw his revolver and shoot, let us say, a man for cowardice, I can see him flinching and going to any lengths to escape the task'.[8]

Philby's staff appreciated him. 'If one made an error of judgement he was sure to minimize it and cover it up, without criticism, with a halting stammered witticism', recalled Graham Greene in his foreword to *My Silent War*. 'He had all the small loyalties to his colleagues, and of course his big loyalty was unknown to us.' His super-efficiency was ubiquitous. He did not fawn on the chiefs of SIS: nor did he chafe with impatience at their methods or allow himself disrespectful jokes. In 1943 Trevor-Roper predicted that the organizational problems of SIS would solve themselves. 'As each area becomes really important, it will have to be given to Philby, and thus, in the end, he will control all, and Cowgill and Vivian and the rest will drop uselessly from the tree, like over-ripe plums.' Philby received his extra energy and motivation from what Trevor-Roper later called 'the exquisite relish of ruthless, treach-erous, private power'.[9]

Trevor-Roper, who was told in 1952 by White of MI5 about the suspicions of Philby, grew fascinated by the psychological problem of his former SIS colleague. After lunching with White in 1967, Trevor-Roper asked himself apropos Philby: 'How can any man, being an intelligent man, devote his whole life to so negative a satisfaction as the secret destruction not merely of the impersonal system around him, but of all the personal relations – relations of friendship, dependence, trust – which have been built up, in good faith, around him?' But then Trevor-Roper wondered about the degree of Philby's intelligence. 'Sharp, shrewd, superficially sophisticated – yes; but is (or was) he in any sense intellectual? By contrast with the other members of the Firm he did of course seem to be an intellectual; but did he in fact read, could he in fact think?' He never mentioned a book to Trevor-Roper, except a single reference to Marx. 'Nor could I ever get him to talk on serious topics: he would always keep conversation on a superficial plane, in ironic, Aesopian language, as if he knew of the differences which would divide us should we break the surface on which, till then, we could happily and elegantly skate.'[10]

Philby resumed contact with the Viennese Marxist with whom he had collaborated in 1934–5, Peter Smolka @ Smollett. After Smolka had been put in charge of the Russian Section of the Ministry of Information, Philby asked him to provide items of interest for remittance to Moscow. They agreed that when Smolka wished to convey material, he would take two cigarettes from a pack, holding them in the shape of the letter 'V', and give Philby one while he smoked the other. Under the codename ABO, Smolka funnelled good material to Philby and was introduced by him to Burgess. When Gorsky forbade further use of ABO in 1941, Blunt, Burgess and Philby privately agreed that Blunt would check Smolka's MI5 file, that Burgess would handle him and pass his material to the *rezidentura* as his own. Gorsky was infuriated when in 1943 he discovered from Burgess's indiscretions and Blunt's admission that his instructions to drop ABO had been ignored. He went so far as to recommend that Moscow Centre should break contact with the Cambridge trio.

Some of Smolka's secret notes, which he passed to Burgess with the intention that they go to Moscow, were later found by MI5 secreted in

Burgess's belongings. From the Ministry of Information he peddled the line to officials in other departments that the Soviet Union had no need of territorial expansion for economic strength, was less interested in ideological expansion than it had been in the 1920s and would only seize buffer zones necessary for its strategic defence. Smolka recommended a passive British policy towards the Soviet Union. Freed from military dangers, its citizens would develop a taste for the comforts of bourgeois consumerism, and Russia accordingly drift from communism to capitalism. He advised his fellow Whitehall officials that they should 'persuade our high-ups' to try pursuing policies that gave the Russians no cause for feeling insecure. Given the possibility of Soviet communism evolving towards democracy, 'The ruling class of Russia must therefore be free of fear from foreign intervention. In order to free the Russians from this fear and allow them to become democratic, we must show them that we intend to leave them alone and trust them. In fact, we want to initiate a virtuous circle.' Amid other material, Smolka provided Burgess in May 1942 with a résumé of remarks by William Ridsdale, the waspish but trusting head of the Foreign Office's News Department. 'The talks with Molotov are one long sweat,' 'Rids' said of the Anglo-Soviet treaty negotiations. 'These bastards are absolute shits to deal with. The trouble is they know they are shits, they know we know they are shits, and they don't seem to care a damn what we think of them . . . You make a little concession to them and being an English gentleman you instinctively expect that the other fellow will make some decent countermove or at least acknowledge that you have been trying to be decent to him – not pushing, they go straight on to their next demand.'[11]

Patrick Reilly became the Foreign Office liaison in SIS in 1942: his influence was resented by Valentine Vivian, who spoke of 'the unfair advantage of the All Souls style'. Reilly acknowledged that the Service had been underfunded and understaffed before 1939, and that some of its officers were intellectually nondescript. He however spurned the fashion for discounting the pre-war SIS as a collection of retired Indian Army officers and Anglo-Indian policemen jumbled with '"metropolitan young gentlemen whose education had been more expensive than profound", rich playboys recruited from White's and Boodle's, failed stockbrokers and the like'. This myth confused the pre-war Service with the wartime recruits, and relied on excessive generalization taken from a few examples of St James's Street clubmen. Reilly emphasized that SIS officers were in aggregate 'a devoted body of men, loyal, discreet, with a strong *esprit de corps*, content to work hard in obscurity for little reward'.[12]

The wartime masterstroke of Philby was to jockey his way to promotion in 1944 to be head of SIS Section IX, which was charged with collecting and analysing material on communist espionage and subversion. In his memoirs, he dates the preliminaries for the reactivation of Section IX as occurring in 1943, so as to mislead readers into believing that SIS, with Foreign Office connivance, was preparing to turn against the Soviet Union two years before the Hitler war had been won. Felix Cowgill had joined SIS as an anti-communist expert, in the expectation that he would be put in charge of an expanded Section IX. Instead, his wartime efforts had been directed against the Nazis. He made many enemies, especially among temporary wartime recruits to the intelligence community. These included the classicist Denys Page and the historian Trevor-Roper, both Christ Church associates of Masterman, and the Bletchley Park code-breaker Leonard Palmer, an academic philologist who after the war became a Fellow of Worcester College, Oxford, where Masterman was Provost. This trio were outspoken critics of Cowgill's mismanagement and hogging of deciphered radio traffic.

Cowgill returned to London after establishing Special Counter-Intelligence Units in liberated Europe to find that in his absence Philby had been named to take charge of Section IX with effect from November 1944. Section V was taken over by Philby's friend, nominee and semi-stooge Tim Milne – a fact that is notable for its omission from Philby's memoirs. In usurping Cowgill, Philby got rid of a staunch anti-communist and ensured that Britain's counter-communist efforts would be accessible to Moscow. His mischievous claim in his memoirs that the Foreign Office helped the intrigue by which he ousted Cowgill was denied by Reilly. Philby's appointment to lead Section IX convinced Trevor-Roper and others that he was being groomed to succeed as 'C', the Chief of SIS, some time in the 1950s.

Maclean in London and Washington

Maclean was confronted in January 1940 by his NKVD handler in Paris, Kitty Harris, who was his illicit lover, about changes in his behaviour. He admitted to her that he was in love with a young American,

Melinda Marling, to whom he had confided his communist allegiance and espionage activities. He had been compelled to these indiscretions, he explained, after Marling had halted their affair with the explanation that she found him intolerably evasive and erratic. When he explained that he had a double life, as a communist penetration agent, she made the capital mistake of reconciling with him. On 10 May 1940 Germany invaded France. Just over a fortnight later the British Expeditionary Force began its evacuation from Dunkirk. Marshal Pétain set out on his quest to save France from what he called 'Polonization', meaning ultra-brutal Nazi occupation. On 10 June, the French government declared Paris an open city, Italy declared war on Britain, and Maclean married Melinda Marling in a hasty ceremony in a *mairie* in Paris. Owen Wansbrough-Jones, Maclean's senior tutor at Trinity Hall, later volunteered to MI5 that having met her, he thought her a typical 'intellectual Communist'.[13]

Back in London, Maclean worked in the Foreign Office's prosaic General Department, where he handled shipping and contraband matters. The Canadian diplomat Charles Ritchie recorded a visit to the Office in the week that France fell to find 'three or four pleasantly satirical and studiedly casual young [diplomats] draped about the room drinking their tea and eating strawberry shortcake'. These men knew as well as anyone what was at stake for Europe: their afternoon tea and ironic jokes were their deliberated response to totalitarianism, said Ritchie, and a symbolic expression of 'What We Are Fighting For.' Maclean was more earnest and perhaps more self-obsessed than these sane, amusing youngsters. In December 1940, he assured Moscow Centre of his relentless commitment to espionage: 'it is my life', he told them, 'I live for it'. He undertook not to endanger his position. 'I can't say that I like my work. But I admit that it is one of the uses in our great struggle to which I am most suited, and I intend to stand by it until I am relieved of it.' This zealotry and subterfuge set him apart from his contemporaries in the Office, who upheld and epitomized a gentler system. He fostered an impression that his fellow-travelling sympathies had been jettisoned, but he did not convince all of his contemporaries. To Fitzroy Maclean, who was no relation but had read history and classics at Cambridge and joined the Diplomatic Service a year ahead of him, he admitted being a communist in 1935. When they met again four years later, possibly in a Foreign Office corridor, Fitzroy

Maclean challenged him to say if he was still a communist and received a feeble reply, but did not report his suspicions. Nor did the author Christopher Sykes, when Maclean admitted being a communist to him around 1943.[14]

In April 1944 Maclean was transferred to the Washington embassy. His eldest son Fergus was born there in September of that year. A second son Donald followed in 1946. His daughter Melinda was born soon after his defection in 1951. Maclean's reaction to his new surroundings doubtless resembled those of the diplomat-politician David Eccles on an official mission to Washington in 1941: 'I was stupefied by the number and size of the cars, four lanes on each road bowling along head to tail at 40 m.p.h. For the first time I realized we were not the richest people. This revelation gives a new edge to patriotism, it is better and purer to love the second-rate.' Eccles found American officials 'frisky and foolish', because they were too impatient to listen to the answers to their own questions. 'They love themselves ecstatically, and gape at the world in a trance of self-satisfaction . . . with a million Buicks on the road and the President going to church.'[15]

Lord Halifax was the Ambassador under whom Maclean initially served in the Washington embassy. In 1946 Halifax was succeeded by the newly created Lord Inverchapel, who as Archie Clark Kerr had been many things, including Harold Nicolson's Edwardian lover and Ambassador in Moscow during 1942–6. Since the 1980s Inverchapel's success in handling Stalin has been used not as evidence of his diplomatic aptitude, but as a reason to blackguard him as a traitor. As his biographer Donald Gillies declares, 'These baseless smears are invariably encountered in the more sensational and hysterical outpourings of right-wing molehunters, whose methods too often involve exaggeration and misrepresentation.' Inverchapel was a complicated man. In Guatemala, early in his career, he had been supervising the erection of a marquee for a garden party to mark George V's birthday when some urchins, mistaking the tent for a circus, asked when the animals were arriving: thereafter he referred to diplomatic colleagues as 'the zoo'. He was witty, expressive and fearlessly candid, as shown by his description of Churchill's visit to Moscow in 1942: he envied, so he wrote, Churchill's 'ability to transform his face from the rosiest, happiest, the most laughing, dimpled and mischievous baby's bottom into the face of an angry and outraged bullfrog!'[16]

Inverchapel was a raunchy bisexual. When he received his peerage, he took three heraldic mottoes: 'Blast!'; 'Late but Hungry'; and 'Concussus Surgo', meaning 'Having been shaken, I rise', which was given its meaning by the heraldic supporters, two naked, full-frontal and promisingly unaroused male athletes. He was attracted to cheerful, straightforward young men, but married a beautiful Chilean heiress in 1929, was divorced by her in 1945 and remarried her three years later. On relinquishing the Moscow embassy he was presented by Stalin with an inscribed photograph, two bottles of brandy, a huge pot of caviar, a panther-skin rug and (what was far rarer than any of these) an exit visa and valid passport for a Volga German youth named Evgeni Yost. The visa had been his special request to Stalin: Yost, a former embassy footman promoted to be the Ambassador's valet-masseur, had been accused of 'hooliganism' and was at risk of hard labour or execution. Stalin had released Yost in the manner of a tsar liberating a serf, and in Washington Inverchapel liked to tease po-faced Americans by saying, 'I have a Russian slave at the embassy given to me by Stalin.' Maclean first met Yost when he arrived in Washington with Inverchapel, and showed his disapproval by hostile glares. Possibly he suspected that Yost was a watchdog set on him by the NKVD. Probably he feared that the interloper Yost would bring American surveillance on the embassy and therefore complicate his own arrangements. Inverchapel used to lie in hot baths reading telegrams and official papers, and hand each item, when he had finished his scrutiny, to Yost, who was standing by. Yost would then carry them to the Ambassador's private secretary. There would have been ample chances for chicanery if Yost was a spy; but he was an abused Volga German, not a Russian, and hated the Soviet system. He remained with his saviour until Inverchapel's death.[17]

The prudes in the FBI were also appalled by Inverchapel going to stay in Eagle Grove, Iowa with Roger Newburn, an energetic, dark-haired, twenty-year-old farm-boy whom he had met at a Washington bus stop. 'I have to confess to a vast natural capacity for love,' Inverchapel admitted complacently in 1948. 'It has always been my trouble and here and there it has got me into trouble.'[18]

In Washington Maclean drank too much, but never let his work suffer from hangovers. There was never a hint of sexual interest in other men. His Washington colleague Jock Balfour said that no one in the embassy had any reason to suspect Maclean. 'To all appearances he

was the pattern, the almost too-perfect pattern, of the trained diplomatist – efficient and conscientious at his work, amiable to meet,
imperturbably good-tempered, elegant, exceedingly self-possessed, and
with a rather cynical outlook which betrayed no particular ideological
bias.' Throughout his four years in Washington, Maclean reported regularly to his 'control' in the Russian consulate general in New York,
providing intelligence intended to ensure Soviet communist hegemony
rather than US capitalist victory in the post-war era. This included
material on Anglo-American atomic research. His Washington embassy
colleagues trusted him. 'I always considered Maclean to be a particularly
good example of the public-minded, educated, selfless person this
country so often produces,' George Middleton stated in 1952. 'He was
patient, even-tempered, sometimes rather sleepy and lack-a-daisical in
manner.' To Middleton, Maclean's politics seemed '"liberal", i.e.
social-democratic or labour or whatever one cares to call it'.[19]

He kept his guard with close embassy colleagues such as Balfour and
Middleton. Those who worked at a distance from him saw a more
difficult, tense and excitable man. After he had asked Isaiah Berlin to
introduce him to some New Dealers, the two men went for dinner at
the house of Katharine ('Kay') Graham, whose family owned the
Washington Post. The evening proved disastrous. Berlin's appreciative
remarks about the shrewd and funny Republican hostess Alice Roosevelt
Longworth made Maclean erupt. 'He said that persons who called
themselves liberals had no business knowing reactionaries of her type,'
Berlin recorded. 'All life was a battle, and one . . . must be clear which
side of the barricades one was on: relations with the enemy were not
permissible – at this point he became exceedingly abusive.' Thirty years
later Berlin reflected that he should have realized from this outburst
that Maclean was 'some sort of a political extremist, e.g. a Communist
. . . but the thought never entered my head'.[20]

Burgess desk-hopping

As to Burgess, he spent the early months of the war in the Foreign
Division Directorate of the Ministry of Information, working alongside
Smolka, producing a propaganda bulletin for BBC broadcast overseas.
When Philby returned to London after the Fall of France, Burgess, who
was by then working for Laurence Grand in SIS, recommended his

recruitment to the Service. He also resolved to make direct contact in Moscow with the NKVD. As cover for his journey to Russia, he concocted a scheme in June 1940 for Isaiah Berlin of All Souls, a Russian-speaker, to be posted to Moscow as Press Attaché, and for himself to accompany Berlin as an induction courier. Burgess mustered some official support for this scheme, and embarked with Berlin on a tortuous journey via Washington DC and Vladivostok towards Moscow. They had reached the US capital when informal protests from Miriam Rothschild, who deplored Burgess's influence on her brother Victor and their mother, and from John Foster, an All Souls lawyer who was temporarily First Secretary at the British embassy in Washington, raised doubts about the project, which was quashed after further objections from Fitzroy Maclean at the Foreign Office. Burgess was ordered back to England.

Burgess, like Philby, then became an instructor in an SOE training camp. The two spies gave their foreknowledge of future SOE operations to Soviet Russia, which was then still party to a non-aggression pact with Nazi Germany and therefore may have remitted details of Burgess and Philby's material to the Germans. Burgess's career as an SIS officer petered out in 1941 after a corporal on one of his courses complained that he tried 'to muck about with him'. He had another spell at the BBC, where he achieved the remarkable coup of arranging a radio broadcast by the NKVD agent Ernst Henri. He also arranged for broadcasts by the communist MP Willie Gallacher and by Clark Kerr, who praised Stalin's Russia. Despite Burgess's dismissal from SIS for importuning the corporal, Blunt convinced Liddell to recruit him as an agent (not an officer) codenamed VAUXHALL running two informants, Eric Kessler (Press Attaché in the Swiss embassy) and Andrew Revai (a journalist, and president of the Free Hungarian Association in London). Both Kessler and Revai were possibly intermittent sexual partners of Burgess. Liddell accepted from Blunt the line that had earlier fooled Footman and Vivian: that Burgess's Cambridge dalliance with communism gave him an insider's understanding of the CPGB. MI5's counter-subversion expert John ('Jack') Curry was unconvinced of the sincerity of Burgess's renunciation, and declined to employ him in F Division. When Curry was seconded in 1943 to an SIS unit monitoring communist penetration in foreign countries, he was unfairly mocked: sending telegrams to Curry, the Oxford don and wartime intelligence officer Gilbert Ryle told Trevor-Roper, was like 'posting love letters up the arse-hole of a camel'. Yet Curry was right about Burgess, when cleverer men were not.[21]

By July 1943 Burgess was so anxious about his error in recruiting Goronwy Rees as a pre-war All Souls informant, and fearful of a denunciation by Rees of him and Blunt, that he suggested Rees's liquidation, and offered to commit the murder himself. Moscow and the London *rezidentura* suspected this might be a provocation devised by MI5 or SIS. This was not the only threat of violence. James Pope-Hennessy was introduced to Burgess by Harold Nicolson in 1940. Pope-Hennessy became besotted during an affair lasting a year or eighteen months: after stormy rows, he threatened to shoot Burgess. Thirteen years later he claimed that he had broken with Burgess 'because he was destroying . . . all one's beliefs in life', as Skardon summarized it after an interview in 1954, 'though I suspect that he was thinking more in terms of moral destruction'. Pope-Hennessy understood that Burgess was a communist, and told Skardon that Burgess's associates – he named Blunt, and Victor and Tess Rothschild – behaved like communists. Subsequently Pope-Hennessy became a lover of James Lees-Milne. One night in 1943 Pope-Hennessy, Lees-Milne, Burgess and Charles Fletcher-Cooke (an officer in naval intelligence who had been on a tour of Russia arranged for Cambridge undergraduate communists in 1935) embarked together on urban black-out adventures. They met at the Ritz bar, moved on to the smart, louche Gargoyle Club in Soho, dined at the White Tower restaurant in Fitzrovia, visited sleazy pubs and drank beer and gin. The party was joined by the Prime Minister's daughter Mary Churchill: 'Guy and Mary got on a treat, which was a relief, & very bizarre,' said Fletcher-Cooke, who noted Burgess's ineradicable name-dropping about Beneš and other European leaders. Burgess struck Lees-Milne as a truculent drunk, dangerously indiscreet, and boring in his 'depravity'.[22]

During 1943 the News Department of the Foreign Office, under Sir William Ridsdale, had begun trying to moderate the pro-Soviet material issued by the Ministry of Information, where Smolka headed the Russian Section. Moscow decided to graft Burgess on to the News Department to resist this tendency. After various manoeuvres, and with support from Harold Nicolson, Burgess left the BBC and started full-time work at the FO in June 1944. Ridsdale, who had his career ruined by employing Burgess and speaking unguardedly to Smolka, later said of

Burgess: 'He was slovenly and irresponsible, and it was never possible to assign to him any task of importance.' When he rebuked Burgess, as he did on several occasions, for his soiled appearance and poor manners, Burgess's reaction was 'to cringe and be most apologetic'. His undesirable traits had to be weighed against the fact that 'he was a Double First at Cambridge and could be amusing at times'.[23]

Both in the News Department and in his later Foreign Office activities Burgess was suspected of leakages to Freddy Kuh, the communistic London correspondent of violently anti-English Chicago newspapers and renowned for his scoops and mischief-making. Kuh began one of his destructive reports, 'A Foreign Office spokesman gazed dreamily out of the windows across Horse Guards Parade and murmured, "Of course, one of the troubles with America is that it has no government."' Burgess was the official in question. The ensuing rumpus added 'new lustre to his reputation as an *enfant terrible*', wrote Alan Maclean, who joined the News Department in 1945. 'Guy took both pride and pleasure in annoying establishments . . . and "being in trouble" was a matter for glee.'[24]

The opportunities for espionage were immense. Burgess provided the Soviets with over 4,000 documents in the last year of the war alone. 'It really was very challenging to one's sanity', Dick White recalled in 1985, 'to suppose that a man of Burgess's type could be a secret agent of anybody's.' His alcoholism, his scruffy, stained clothes, his bad breath, his filthy fingernails, his boastful indiscretions and his unbuttoned sexuality made a perfect cover, as was doubtless intended by the arch-deceiver of Soho and Fitzrovia.[25]

Blunt in MI5

Blunt had been dormant as a Soviet helpmate since June 1937, but Gorsky resumed contact in August 1939 and urged Blunt, with his proficiency in French, German and Italian, to apply to join the Intelligence Corps. After the outbreak of war, the Director of Military Operations and Intelligence at the War Office ordered him to report on 16 September to Minley Manor, near Camberley in Surrey, for an intelligence course. After little more than a week, Blunt was peremptorily withdrawn from the course on security grounds and summoned for interview by Kevin Martin, former Military Attaché in Warsaw and

Deputy Director of Military Intelligence at the War Office. 'I want you to realize that we have to be very careful indeed in intelligence,' Brigadier Martin told him. 'What has been done was probably done in excessive zeal, and I hope therefore that you will not feel that you have a grievance.' They discussed Marxist doctrine and the Nazi–Soviet pact. Blunt let drop that his father had been chaplain at 'the embassy church' in Paris for ten years. 'I am sure', Martin said, 'he would turn in his grave if he thought you were doing subversive work or perhaps I am a little traditional in this way, I mean about respect for one's forebears.' Martin closed the interview on a note of friendly caution: 'I should like a little time to think over the impressions of you I have formed, which I may say are favourable, and I hope you won't mind perhaps coming here again for another talk.' Burgess arranged for Dennis Proctor to call on Martin and convince him that 'all decent people have if not left-wing views, then at least left-wing friends'.[26]

Blunt was reinstated on the intelligence course at Minley Manor in mid-October 1939. He was able to compile a report on the structure of British military intelligence, dated 17 November, for an appreciative Moscow Centre. Subsequently, his Cambridge admirer Victor Rothschild (by then the Security Service's head of counter-sabotage) recommended him to Liddell, who appointed him in June 1940 to a job in MI5's St James's Street office. Liddell was not the sole target of Blunt's charm. He seems to have cultivated MI5 officers with responsibilities for Russia or communism. He began to sit with Dick White in the canteen, discussing art and advising White on contemplated purchases of prints. White, who was working at full pelt on matters of higher policy, cannot be expected to have read Blunt's file or to have known of his earlier suspension from the Minley Manor course. Blunt at this time shared an office with the secretary of Courtenay Young. 'My God, he was a charmer!' she recalled. 'We were all a bit in love with Anthony . . . He used to wander around with his cod-liver oil and malt, saying "That's what Tiggers like for breakfast." He knew *Winnie the Pooh* very well. He had a Leslie Howard face – a matinée idol.' When she was informed in the mid-1960s that Blunt had admitted spying, 'It was exactly like being . . . on a quicksand, I couldn't believe it. I really, truly, couldn't believe it . . . You started thinking, "Who else? What about me? Was I one too?"'[27]

Modrzhinskaya was suspicious when Blunt reported that MI5 took little interest in Soviet citizens in Britain. She and her Moscow colleagues could not believe the assurances of Blunt in MI5 and Philby in SIS that no serious anti-Soviet operations were under way. The fact that the surveillance material supplied by Blunt never once included any Soviet intelligence officer, his report that MI5 had no agents inside the Soviet embassy and that surveillance of visitors to the embassy had halted – all this was enough to discredit his authenticity. Blunt reported that only telephone tapping and penetration of the CPGB were continued. For most of 1940 Blunt received no guidance from the NKVD, because Modrzhinskaya's mistrust had caused the closure of the London *rezidentura* and Gorsky's recall to Moscow. Among the first tranche of papers supplied to him by Blunt in January 1941, after the resumption of the two men's contacts, was Jane Archer's report on debriefing the defector Walter Krivitsky. He may have been the source inside MI5 who warned the CPGB in 1941 that Tom Driberg was Maxwell Knight's prized agent M/8 informing on party activities: a denunciation that resulted in Driberg's expulsion from the party. Modrzhinskaya complained in 1943 that Blunt, in addition to supplying 327 rolls of film in the last year, had brought about a hundred documents to each weekly meeting, which she found unforgivable for compromising security.[28]

Blunt's Sub-division B2 distributed deciphered diplomatic telegrams, analysed intercepted diplomatic correspondence and telephone intercepts, monitored the movements of foreign diplomats, separated couriers from their diplomatic bags for just long enough to scrutinize their contents and worked with Mrs Gladstone, who ran the Ellen Hunt employment agency in Marylebone High Street, which was controlled by the security services and placed domestic spies in foreign diplomatic buildings. Blunt supplied Boris Kreshin, who succeeded Gorsky in 1942, with MI5 internal documents, files on people targeted for cultivation, GC&CS intercepts, diplomatic telegrams, German intelligence reports, copies of illicitly opened diplomatic mail, weekly summaries of German intelligence radio intercepts, telephone intercepts and surveillance reports. In 1941–5, according to KGB records, Blunt supplied a total of 1,771 documents (compared with Burgess supplying over 4,000 documents in the last twelve months of the war). 'Usually at meetings TONY is very apathetic, he comes very tired and forgetful,' Kreshin reported in 1943. 'When he is nervous, he drinks.'[29]

Blunt was involved in the surveillance of the diplomatic missions in

London of neutral states. He proved deft in the tricky, speedy work of receiving and assessing material, and disseminating his conclusions to colleagues. He attended a few meetings of the Joint Intelligence Committee. He also ran his former pupil Leo Long, who was working in military intelligence, as a sub-agent betraying official secrets to Moscow. When diplomatic privileges were suspended in April 1944, ahead of the Normandy landings, Blunt was assigned to Supreme HQ Allied Expeditionary Force (SHAEF), where he worked on deception. In May 1944 Blunt provided a complete copy of the deception plan for the D-Day landings, Operation OVERLORD, scheduled for June 1944. Thereafter, Moscow Centre accepted the honesty of material supplied by Philby and the others. This was because it was being corroborated by material from other sources: probably the American OSS.

The Blitz affected MI5 officers and their families as much as it did other Londoners. Roger Hollis, who had been recruited to MI5 in 1938, lived at 18 Elsham Road, Kensington, close to Glading's former safe-house in Holland Road and within easy reach of MI5's temporary headquarters at Wormwood Scrubs. His pregnant wife left London in 1940 for the safety of rural Somerset. Similarly Victor Rothschild, whose wife was also pregnant, decided that they should take refuge from the Blitz in Cambridge. He leased their home at 5 Bentinck Street, Marylebone – a minute's walk from the Langham Hotel, where Krivitsky had been debriefed earlier that year – to two young women, Teresa ('Tess') Mayor and Patricia Rawdon-Smith, who had just been blitzed out of their shared flat. Mayor was his secretary at MI5 and future second wife. Blunt joined the women to help with the rent, and six months later Burgess took the remaining bedroom after the lease of his flat had expired.

Distorted legends have flourished about this household. Malcolm Muggeridge, who visited Bentinck Street once, left an artful account of Burgess manipulating the political and cultural notabilities grouped there around him. 'There was not so much a conspiracy gathered around him as just decay and dissolution. It was the end of a class, of a way of life; something that would be written about in history books, like Gibbon on Heliogabalus, with wonder and perhaps hilarity.' The force of Muggeridge's dramatization set the tone for subsequent comment. Dick White has been faulted for being neither suspicious nor disapproving when he visited 'Bentinck Street's den of decay and dissolution'.

John Costello memorably described the household as 'a homosexual bordello serving as a viperous nest for Soviet spies', before showing in more forgettable language that this was not the reality. Stephen Koch claimed that in Bentinck Street 'Burgess gathered the homosexual underworld of London together with some of the most devious and despicable operatives then at work.'[30]

Anthony Blunt resented these lurid descriptions of the Bentinck Street arrangements as 'an alternation of sexual orgies and conspiratorial conversations designed to hinder the war effort'. It is true that he probably had a sexual affair with Rawdon-Smith, that Burgess claimed less reliably to have gone to bed with her, and that both men were involved with Jack Hewit, a sparky working-class man who had previously been Christopher Isherwood's boyfriend; but there is nothing remarkable about this bedroom-hopping among young people in a flat-share. Blunt maintained that he and his co-tenants were working too hard on onerous jobs to spend their nights disporting riotously. London was a beleaguered city: there was little chance of a hotel bedroom unless it had been booked weeks in advance. The Bentinck Street tenants therefore sheltered friends who visited London on leave or were stranded there overnight by train cancellations. People who did not live in London during the Blitz had no idea, said Blunt, how casually sleeping-arrangements were improvised. Flats became dormitories, and on nights of heavy bombing so did basements, in which people bedded down together on lilos and mattresses on the floor. There were many such communal households in wartime London. Blunt's MI5 colleague Herbert Hart lived in an Oxford-orientated group with his ex-communist wife Jenifer, Douglas Jay, the Balliol economist Thomas Balogh, Patrick Reilly of the Foreign Office and Francis Graham-Harrison of the Home Office. Hugh Gaitskell of the Ministry of Economic Warfare and his wife Dora lived with Evan Durbin of the War Cabinet secretariat's economic section, the moral philosopher Oliver Franks of the Ministry of Supply and the music critic William Glock.[31]

Goronwy Rees was an occasional overnight visitor to Mayor and Rawdon-Smith's rented home: he was notable for being drunk at breakfast. In his memoirs he described Burgess filling Bentinck Street with 'a series of boys, young men, soldiers, sailors, airmen, whom he had picked up among the thousands who thronged the streets of London at that time'. Strenuous couplings and political mysteries abounded, he suggested. 'Bedroom doors opened and shut; strange faces appeared and disappeared down the stairs, where they passed some new visitor on his way up; civil servants, politicians, visitors to London, friends and colleagues of Guy's, popped in and out of bed, and then continued some absorbing discussion of political intrigue [or] the progress of the war.' Blunt counters – convincingly – that there was a house rule in Bentinck Street forbidding the bringing home of any 'casual pick-up' for the night: they were too unpredictable, and might be noisy or disruptive when other tenants needed their sleep; Burgess had lovers who spent the night, including James Pope-Hennessy, Peter Pollock and Jack Hewit, but no 'boys' or 'rent'. Rees said that the only subject on which he believed that Burgess told the invariable truth was on the subject of his sexual conquests; but Burgess would be unique among men if his sexual brags were true, and we know that his mendacity on other matters was appalling. The only reason to believe Burgess's accounts of his performances with other men is a desire for lubricious sensationalism.[32]

Cairncross hooks BOSS

Early in the war Cairncross was instructed to seek work with Lord Hankey, who had been brought into the War Cabinet in September 1939 as Minister without Portfolio and was pursuing a roving strategic brief. As Cabinet Secretary and Secretary of the Committee of Imperial Defence in the 1930s, Hankey had been conspicuously security-conscious: he ordered that papers must never be left on desks overnight, prowled round the offices in Whitehall Gardens to check that his rule was being kept, and was unforgiving when in 1933 he spotted 'a sheet from THE most secret of documents which had just been issued to THE most secret of committees' lying in a fire-grate, where it had been placed as a grate-screen by a charwoman. Yet even Hankey was vulnerable. He was a devout vegetarian, who often ate at the Vega restaurant near Leicester Square. Cairncross made a show of becoming vegetarian, sat demurely by himself at a table in the Vega when Hankey was there, and was finally introduced to the great man by his son Henry Hankey, who had been one of the few colleagues who liked Cairncross at the Foreign Office. In due course, Lord Hankey asked the Treasury to release Cairncross to act as his private secretary.[33]

All official papers and much personal correspondence came to Cairncross's desk before they reached Hankey's. His job was to skim and assess them, and order them on the minister's desk with the most urgent files on top. He monitored Hankey's telephone calls, was sometimes expected to listen on an extension, controlled the minister's visitors and held the keys to his safe. BOSS was the codename bestowed on Hankey by Moscow. When Chamberlain's government fell in May 1940, the new Prime Minister Churchill demoted Hankey from the War Cabinet, but gave him the solace of a ministerial post, Chancellor of the Duchy of Lancaster, which had Cabinet rank outside the War Cabinet and came with offices off the Strand. In July 1941 Hankey was shifted again, to the post of Paymaster General, with rooms in the Privy Council Office. Churchill finally shunted him out of the government in March 1942. This progressive loss of favour owed much to the bitter antipathy between him and the more powerful minister, Beaverbrook; something also to the fact that from 1941 onwards Hankey engaged in open but ineffective intrigues against Churchill's exuberant and idiosyncratic leadership.[34]

Cairncross claimed in his memoirs that between the Nazi–Soviet pact of 1939 and the German invasion of Russia in 1941, he supplied no documents to Moscow. In truth, the London *rezidentura* complained that the secret material supplied by him in that period was too profuse to encipher for telegrams to Moscow. Hankey prepared authoritative 'War Appreciations' at six-monthly intervals, which summarized such matters as the strategic views of the Chiefs of Staff, enemy strategy, problems of inter-allied cooperation and likely developments in the actual fighting. Hankey was involved in preparations for biological warfare, in disrupting the supply of Romanian oil to Germany and in planning military assistance to Turkey in the event of an attack by Russia. As the supervising minister for SIS, MI5 and GC&CS, Hankey prepared two elaborate reports on the secret services in the spring of 1940: Cairncross duly supplied copies to Moscow. Cairncross remitted 3,449 intelligence items during 1941 (a figure exceeded only by Maclean's 4,419). These included secret Cabinet papers, Foreign Office cryptograms, weekly bulletins from SIS, the FO and the Imperial General Staff and Scientific Advisory Committee documents.

As chairman of the Scientific Advisory Committee, Hankey had a leading part in the atomic-bomb programme in 1940–1. Although, after his public naming by Oleg Gordievsky as 'the Fifth Man' in 1990, Cairncross denied that he had supplied atomic intelligence to the Soviet Union, there is no doubt from the Moscow archives that he was the first of Britain's atomic spies. In September 1941 he reported that the so-called Uranium Committee, chaired by Hankey, had endorsed an Anglo-American cooperative project to build an atom bomb. In October he provided the text of a crucial policy memorandum prepared by Hankey. Stalin was thus informed from the outset of the Anglo-American work to develop a super-weapon, and knew that the Soviet Union was excluded by its ostensible allies from any knowledge of the project. Cairncross's first-rate material was nevertheless mistrusted as possible disinformation, especially by Modrzhinskaya, who had no insight into Whitehall procedure. The NKVD could not understand why Hankey, after his removal from ministerial office by Churchill in 1942, continued to receive secret documents: dismissed ministers in Stalin's Russia were ostracized if they were lucky, liquidated if they were not, and certainly not kept on circulation lists of top secrets.

Following Hankey's political retirement, Cairncross went to work at GC&CS as an editor and translator in the section handling Luftwaffe decrypts. He continued to supply material to his Russian handlers. Although in 1943 he transmitted only ninety-four documents, these included Enigma decrypts from Bletchley Park, which were crucial in Russia's victory in the battle of Kursk. Using decrypts supplied by Cairncross, and backed by other sources, the Red Air Force bombed German airfields and destroyed over 500 Luftwaffe aircraft on the ground. Although this was a turning point in Russia's war against Germany, the NKVD continued to suspect Cairncross of supplying disinformation. In August 1944 he was transferred to the political branch of SIS. The 794 documents that he sent to Moscow that year included a new SIS survey of Soviet intentions; but fears of British disinformation and inadequate analysis and appraisal of his material meant that it was put to limited use. Altogether, from his several desks, Cairncross supplied 5,832 documents to Moscow during 1941–5.

It is not surprising that none of the ring of five was suspected or caught, for there are worlds of difference between detecting a murderer and detecting a spy. The murderer, usually acting alone, kills his victim; the body is found, the crime is known, and law-abiding people come forward with their accidental knowledge of the crime. A railway clerk

remembers selling an incriminating ticket, a postmistress hears everyone's gossip, a gardener glances over a fence, a dog-walker notices a
smashed headlight, a barmaid recalls a stained overcoat: all these innocent witnesses understand from newspaper headlines that they are
needed to contribute their little piece to the jigsaw of truth. The spy,
though, acts in secret, and keeps his crime unknown except from an
equally clandestine accomplice. There is no outcry for justice to be
done. Various individuals may hold incriminating knowledge of the
traitor, but probably are unaware that treason has been committed. No
one expects their colleagues to be secret outlaws. It is never easy to
accept that a dangerous minority of people make promises for the
satisfaction of breaking their word and humiliating their dupes; that
setting snares to catch clever men is exciting, and the pride feels almighty
when the trap springs on the prey; and that deception-artists and
confidence-tricksters enjoy the havoc that they stir up.

CHAPTER 13

The Atomic Spies

Alan Nunn May

'Fear is a demoralising emotion,' as David Footman knew. The cruel, bloodthirsty hunt for imaginary traitors during the Stalinist purges of 1936–8 daunted the next generation of Soviet intelligence officers. They used cloddish methods, shrank from responsibilities, wanted quick results in order to deflect criticism from Moscow and violated simple precautions. Ivan Ilichyov, who took effective control of Soviet military intelligence in 1942, had made his career on pre-emptive denunciations of colleagues: he regarded all established intelligence officers as potential 'enemies of the people', said another member of the GRU directorate, 'and the agent network created by them as wholly hostile and therefore subject to liquidation'. All Soviet officials sought authority from Moscow before taking even minor decisions, Alan Roger, MI5's Defence Security Officer (DSO) in Tehran, reported in 1944 during wartime cooperation with them. 'Throughout our dealings so far we have found a complete unwillingness on the part of any Soviet department or authority to act in concert with another locally, even when some of the persons live inside the same Embassy compound.' Instead of the Poles, Latvians and Germans who had predominated in successful Soviet espionage before the purges, Moscow in the 1940s sent Russians, who were functionaries rather than ideologues, and had been chosen because they left families in the Soviet Union who were hostage-guarantors of their mindless loyalty. They knew few foreigners, and were untutored in western languages, attitudes and practices.[1]

Sometimes, in a literal sense, they did not know where they were going. Igor Gouzenko, the young Ukrainian who was posted as a cipher clerk at the Soviet embassy in Ottawa in 1943, thought, when he was sent abroad, that he was destined for south-east Asia until he arrived in Canada. Two years later, grateful for western comforts and resentful of his boorish bosses, he decided to defect. The Cold War began on 5 September 1945, when Gouzenko stashed 109 documents on Soviet espionage in Europe and America and fled. His defection nearly failed, for embassy thugs tried to snatch him with his wife and baby from their apartment; but Canadian neighbours showed unshakeable decency in protecting them from abduction.

By the time that Canadian politicians had agreed to Gouzenko being protected and debriefed, Cyril Mills, who had been (in his words) 'a sort of one-man miniature MI5 in Canada' since 1942, had embarked on a trans-Atlantic ship with two members of the royal family, the Earl and Countess of Athlone, on their return to England after the Earl's five years as Governor General of Canada. Unknown to Mills, the Royal Canadian Mounted Police wished to recall the ship to Canada, so that he could disembark and handle Gouzenko; but the rank and priority of the Athlones made this impossible. It was only when Mills reached London that he heard about Gouzenko. Hollis had meanwhile been flown to Canada to manage the debriefing that would otherwise have been Mills's responsibility. Mills regretted missing the excitement.[2]

Gouzenko was codenamed CORBY. He revealed wartime Soviet espionage, spies in the atomic-bomb programme and a Soviet spy codenamed ELLI in London counter-espionage headquarters. Attlee and Bevin, Labour's Prime Minister and Foreign Secretary since July 1945, wanted an immediate confrontation with Moscow on these espionage activities, but the need to conciliate the Americans, and to concert a united Anglo-American response, slowed this process. Menzies passed the ELLI warning to his chief of security, Vivian, who delegated it to the chief of SIS counter-espionage and real-life ELLI, Philby. Moscow was therefore kept informed of CORBY developments throughout. Tim Milne, whom Philby asked to handle ELLI inquiries, decided with Menzies that ELLI was inside MI5 rather than in SIS.[3]

Among the ring of five the CORBY ramifications had most impact on John Cairncross, who had in June 1945 been appointed Principal in the Treasury section handling War Office estimates. This gave him access to confidential material, and made him the recipient of indiscretions: 'Biffy' Dunderdale of SIS told him, for example, that the Soviet air force ciphers had been broken by exiled Poles, and that the British knew of the Soviets' atom-bomb testing-site north of Yakutsk. But this flow of information halted after three months: following Gouzenko's defection, Moscow severed all contact with Cairncross until 1948.

The Canadian government appointed a Royal Commission to investigate the betrayal of state secrets to foreign agents by persons in positions of trust. Its interim report in March 1946, and final report in August, were highly informative about Soviet espionage, which had been running a member of the Canadian parliament and nearly twenty officials as informants or agents. Sir Peter Clutterbuck, the High Commissioner in Ottawa, reported that sixteen members of the Soviet embassy in Ottawa had been withdrawn at Canada's request, while the Ambassador and Military Attaché were summoned to Moscow, where the latter was believed to have been liquidated. 'Many people see little difference between the Russian methods of today and the German methods we have fought two wars to eradicate,' Clutterbuck continued. 'Though there is a general hope that the Russians merely want educating and will settle down in time, a deep disquiet inevitably remains.' When Cabinet ministers in London mooted giving official publicity to the Royal Commission's findings, including Gouzenko's statement that the Soviet Union was preparing for a third world war, Denis Healey, the pre-war Oxford communist who was running the International Department of the Labour party, gave decisive advice that 'it would be damaging to the Party' for the government to criticize Russia 'at a moment when for the first time the Russians appear to the public to be making concessions'. Healey recoiled from offending public opinion by correcting its ignorance.[4]

'All communists, from the top to the bottom, have a conception of the outside world based upon the works of Marx, Lenin and Stalin,' Sir Frank Roberts wrote from the Moscow embassy at this time. Inconvenient incidents were squeezed into orthodox ideological interpretations. In an international crisis such as the Gouzenko case, 'a small group of high communists or N.K.V.D. officials might cover up their own clumsiness by convincing Stalin that what appeared like Soviet espionage was in fact only a further example of the determination of the outside capitalist world to stage a major anti-Soviet demonstration'.[5]

Gouzenko's material revealed that Soviet intelligence had received atomic secrets from Maclean's Trinity Hall communist contemporary Alan Nunn May. Nunn May had in 1942 joined the Cambridge-based,

French-led team of Hans von Halban and Lew Kowarski, which had shipped 185 kilograms of heavy water from France to England ahead of the German invaders. Halban had been born in Leipzig; his ancestors were Polish Jews, Vienna civil servants and Bohemian soldiers; his doctorate was from Zurich; and he was a French citizen. Kowarski had been born in St Petersburg, spent his adolescence in Vilnius (the Lithuanian capital, which was then in Poland), had his scientific training in Paris and was also a naturalized French citizen. 'Too many damned foreigners', Sir George Thomson, the Nobel laureate physicist, barked as he contemplated this research team. Nunn May was supposed to keep a patriotic watch on them as well as developing measurement techniques and improving the handling of experimental errors.[6]

Sir James Chadwick, a Nobel laureate physicist who had discovered the neutron in 1932, was leading research and development in England's secret atomic-bomb project, which was codenamed TUBE ALLOYS. Once, in 1942, Chadwick put an abrupt question to Nunn May: 'Do you know Nahum?' Ephraim ('Ram') Nahum, who was killed that year by one of the few German bombs that fell on Cambridge, was the son of a rich textile merchant from Manchester: Eric Hobsbawm called him 'a squat, dark natural scientist with a big nose, radiating physical strength, energy and authority . . . and . . . the ablest of all communist student leaders of my generation'. At the Cavendish Laboratory in Cambridge (where Chadwick had worked until he obtained the chair of physics at Liverpool) everyone knew Nahum as the CPGB organizer of science students. When Nunn May admitted to knowing Nahum, Chadwick continued: 'We tried to get him for work on the project, but the security people made objections, on very silly grounds.' He then gave Nunn May a pointed look. Chadwick was indicating that he knew Nunn May, like other Cavendish scientists, to have been a party member, and did not regard this as a bar to recruitment to the Halban–Kowarski project; but as security officers were unlikely to show latitude, Nunn May should be discreet about his past or present beliefs. 'Chadwick's attitude was at the time perfectly normal,' Nunn May judged. 'This was a war against Fascism in which Russia was our ally, so a history of resisting Fascism and of support for Russia was no bar to recruitment, [it was] even a positive recommendation.' There were few suitable scientists available for the work: if Chadwick had followed the security officers' criteria he would have been chronically short-staffed. It is also arguable that MI5 were keener to keep communists out of development work on such important projects as radar that promised imminent tangible success. Atomic weapons at this stage were a remote and less understood possibility.[7]

After joining Halban's project, Nunn May had an unheralded visit from CPGB members whom he had known as a research student. They urged him to revive his party contacts, which he had let lapse after the Nazi–Soviet pact. Nunn May was told to attend weekly meetings of a secretive cell of government employees who studied party literature and undertook non-subversive work. By this time Chadwick was sleepless with the knowledge that atomic bombs would be used in war and would proliferate among nation states. He was said by his university Vice-Chancellor to have 'plumbed such depths of moral decision as more fortunate men are never called upon even to peer into': Chadwick, he continued, suffered 'almost insupportable agonies of responsibility arising from his scientific work'. Thinking in similar terms, but acting differently, Nunn May decided in the autumn of 1942 that it would be criminally irresponsible to leave the Russians unaware of the possible dangers of nuclear-bomb or radioactive-poison attacks. He wrote a summary of the project and of Anglo-American intentions, so far as he knew them, which he handed across the table in a seedy café after an apparently casual encounter in the street. He and his contact sat at a window table in the café, and afterwards Nunn May worried that the handover had been photographed for blackmail purposes.[8]

Later Nunn May was instructed by his party group leader to accompany Halban's team when it relocated to Montreal as the English equivalent of the American MANHATTAN PROJECT. Once settled in Canada in 1945, Nunn May was visited by a man who uttered the agreed recognition signal, 'Greetings from Alex'. This was Pavel Angelov, codenamed GRANT, from the Russian embassy in Ottawa. Nunn May determined to help the Russians because, or so he afterwards maintained, his American colleagues were explicit that Leslie Groves, the US General who ran the MANHATTAN PROJECT in 1942–7, intended to use atomic weaponry to ensure post-war American domination. Nunn May felt 'loyalty as a socialist to what was then the only socialist country in the world', and judged that Stalin's Russia would be a stronger bulwark against American domination than any London-based parliamentary democracy.[9]

Nunn May provided uranium samples and laboratory reports as well as material on the chemistry and metallurgy of uranium and plutonium, the design of the American graphite piles, xenon poisoning and the Wigner effect (the displacement of atoms by neutron radiation). He informed on the organization of the MANHATTAN PROJECT, and provided secret information on its successor organization at Oak Ridge, Tennessee. He spied on the experimental nuclear pile at Argonne, Illinois and reported on the vast Hanford installation in Washington state. Natural uranium is comprised of two isotopes, U-238 (which accounts for about 99 per cent of the substance) and the much rarer U-235, which is highly radioactive and best for atomic explosions. On the day that the US dropped its second atomic bomb on Nagasaki (9 August 1945), Nunn May stole a platinum foil coated with U-235 from the Montreal laboratory. Within hours it had been flown to Moscow. Angelov so little understood the motivation of Nunn May that he tried to ensnare him with paltry gifts of whisky and 200 Canadian dollars (which Nunn May claimed to have burnt).

Gouzenko's evidence of Nunn May's treachery was accepted within days in Whitehall, where the traitor became known by the codename PRIMROSE. As early as mid-September, about a week after Gouzenko's defection, the British Ambassador in Washington, Lord Halifax, informed General Groves of the security breach. Groves was enraged, because a year earlier he had raised his concerns about Nunn May's repeated, prying visits to Argonne, where nuclear-pile technology was being developed. Chadwick had assured Groves that Nunn May was 'exceptionally reliable and close-mouthed'; but Groves in October 1944 had forbidden further visits by Nunn May to Argonne. After Halifax's admission to Groves, American trust in Britain dived.[10]

The Danish physicist Niels Bohr had earlier urged Roosevelt and Churchill to prevent a nuclear arms race by sharing atomic secrets with the Soviet Union. Halifax now raised with Groves and recommended to London that the Anglo-American powers should consider pooling their atomic secrets with their Soviet wartime allies in return for free facilities for inspection and assurances of peaceful intent. 'Perhaps I should apologize for inflicting such superficial thinking on you, who are so much more deeply steeped in all this baffling business, and I may be dead wrong,' Halifax wrote in a top-secret message to London on 20 September. But in the aftermath of his discussions with Groves about Nunn May, two facts were revolving in his head: '(i) that the Russians are going to get the secret anyway; (ii) that, if Groves is right, they are long years off being able to translate knowledge into practice'. Halifax was not alone in hoping that a policy of cooperative trust of the Russians in nuclear matters might reduce risks. A few days later President Truman told him that he feared 'the impossibility of keeping scientific secrets secret for more than a very short time' and was reflecting whether it might be possible to reach a nuclear agreement with the Soviet Union by 'passing on scientific knowledge which they would probably get anyway pretty soon', together with development expertise. Groves was insistent that the Russians would cheat and betray any undertakings along these lines. The Foreign Office, too, thought that the Soviets would find 'specious excuses' to break any such agreement when they had got all that they wanted from it. A tripartite nuclear treaty, placing trust in Stalin's intentions, would be reviled: 'Opposition would be raised in many quarters of these much blitzed islands, and by friendly nations in Western Europe and indeed all over the world, if a gift were made to the country which attacked Finland in 1939 and Poland . . . of facilities for blitzing us and others out of existence.'[11]

The advice of Bohr, and the hopes of Halifax and Truman, to attempt to establish mutual nuclear trust were remote from Nunn May's outright betrayal of his colleagues' scientific results to Moscow. Nunn May, though, considered that his actions were not dissimilar to those of the atomic appeasers. A few days later, oblivious of Gouzenko's denunciation of him, he walked along a corridor at the Montreal laboratory to collect the documents for his return flight from Canada to England. Ahead of him were two unmistakably English civil servants holding standard-issue Whitehall briefcases. They were greeted by the senior British administrator who shook their hands and then spotting his approach, said: 'Why, here *is* Dr Nunn May!' The two visitors swivelled round, looking as shocked as if the administrator had said, 'Why, here *is* Josef Stalin!' Nunn May was rattled by this incident. Soon afterwards, back in London, in the coffee-room of the Royal Society, Sir George Thomson cut him dead. Patrick Blackett, who was to be awarded the Nobel prize for physics in 1948, was beckoned away by Thomson while talking with Nunn May, and hurried off after Thomson had whispered to him. When MI5 warned that it was too short-staffed to keep Nunn May under surveillance, the Minister at the British embassy in

Washington, Roger Makins, who was bearing the brunt of American fury, protested to the PUS, Sir Alexander Cadogan, about MI5's handling of what the few British officials privy to Gouzenko's material called the TUBE ALLOY leakage. 'Apparently our people are now saying they can't guarantee to watch or control the bird who has come over here,' noted Cadogan. 'This [is] ridiculous, & I sent for Liddell.'[12]

Nunn May was due to meet his new Russian handler on 7 October in Great Russell Street, Bloomsbury and was primed with a new recognition signal, with 'Greetings from Mikel' replacing 'Greetings from Alex'. A colleague at King's College, London said to him casually, 'you will find this an interesting topic' and passed a slip of paper on which was written: 'Do not keep your appointment.' This warning may have originated from Philby. A few days later Nunn May met a former colleague from the Halban team, who asked: 'What have you been up to? We have all been told not to talk to you.' He realized that he was being followed and that his telephone was bugged. On 27 October, in a Bloomsbury street, he met by chance an ex-colleague from the Cavendish whom he had not seen for years. They went into a nearby tea-room to exchange news. Two other men followed them into the tea-room, and sat at the next table, although the other tables were all vacant.[13]

On 15 February 1946 Nunn May was unexpectedly confronted by two men in military uniform, Commander Leonard Burt of Special Branch and his colleague Reg Spooner. 'Burt opened the proceedings by greeting me using the ultra-secret password which had been assigned to me ("Greetings from Mikel") while looking me straight in the eyes for my reaction.' Nunn May claimed to have put on a successful show of calm, and to have parried their questions with nonchalance. The MI5 report of the interrogation gives a more convincing account of Nunn May turning pale at hearing 'Greetings from Mikel', looking distressed, pausing for two or three minutes before answering questions and almost always limiting his responses to 'yes' or 'no'. When asked if he would volunteer information – that is, to become an MI5 informant – Nunn May claimed to have replied, 'Not if it is going to be used for counter-espionage.' Burt regarded his refusal to admit anything as a sure sign of guilt. Although Burt dwelt on 'Greetings from Mikel', neither he nor MI5 colleagues challenged Nunn May about the password 'Greetings from Alex', which indicated illicit contacts before Nunn May went to Canada. MI5 wanted a clean, clear case to bring to court, and eliminated complications. It was only after Nunn May's conviction, when he was in prison, that they interrogated him about pre-1945, pre-Canadian espionage. Nunn May was determined not to incriminate himself further, admitted nothing and yielded no information. Indeed, he remained anxious about a further prosecution on pre-Canadian leakages to the end of his life.[14]

There was insufficient evidence to convict Nunn May without a confession: this was extracted by William ('Jim') Skardon, whose working life had begun as a clerk in the household of Prince Arthur, Duke of Connaught and who had been, as a detective sergeant in the Metropolitan Police, seconded to MI5 in 1940. The investigation of the Nazi propagandist William Joyce ('Lord Haw-Haw') in 1945 had shown his abilities as an interrogator. Skardon's easy manner disguised his purposive ruthlessness. He graded people's susceptibility to treason by categorizing their hobbies as 'constitutional' and 'non-constitutional' – that is to say to connoting safe, trustworthy and stable social values, or insecure characteristics and risky attitudes. Gardening he reckoned was 'very constitutional', skiing 'doubtful' and motor-racing 'very suspect'. Skardon won Nunn May's trust, told him that the British had proof of his treason and bluffed him into a full confession of his guilt in February 1946. Writing of him afterwards, in a book sponsored by MI5, Alan Moorehead declared that Nunn May was 'an entirely new sort of traitor: a man who gave away secrets not for money or for power or through fear or hatred or the perverse attraction of the act of spying, or even because he believed in a political faith. He betrayed because he found himself in possession of information of the utmost value and with an Olympian confidence decided that he should pass it on for the good of mankind.' He was, said Moorehead, 'a self-appointed world saver'.[15]

Nunn May faced an Old Bailey trial on 1 May 1946 with the Attorney General, Sir Hartley Shawcross, prosecuting and Gerald Gardiner defending. 'My Lord,' Shawcross told the judge, 'I ought to make it abundantly clear that there is no kind of suggestion that the Russians are enemies or potential enemies.' He stressed that the charge concerned communicating information to unauthorized (and unspecified) persons, and emphasized that Nunn May had received $200, as if his motives were mercenary. Sir Roland Oliver, the High Court Judge who sentenced Nunn May to ten years' imprisonment, reiterated Shawcross's point about this paltry sum as if it mattered. Spy trials are show-cases of misdirection.[16]

Klaus Fuchs

Unbeknown to the security services, there was another atomic spy, Klaus Fuchs. Fuchs had been born in Germany in 1911. His father was a Lutheran pastor who became a Quaker. He suffered traumatic losses during his early manhood: his grandmother committed suicide, he saw his mother die after taking hydrochloric acid in 1931, one sister threw herself under a train in 1938 and the other was schizophrenic. For years after these tragedies he would be subdued by sudden involuntary bouts of mourning during which he lay for hours, or even days, with his face turned to the wall, starving himself, mute, unresponsive, as if in a trance. He was myopic, cackhanded, preternaturally precise, physically frail, but with formidable self-command. He chain-smoked cigarettes, was a mighty drinker of spirits and drove cars at top speed because he loved the thrill of skids and the excitement of controlling them.

Fuchs had degrees in mathematics and physics from the universities of Leipzig and Kiel. He joined the German communist party in 1932, and was once beaten up by Brownshirt students at Kiel and chucked into a river. On 28 February 1933, the day after the Reichstag fire, a warrant was issued to arrest him. By chance he left home early that morning, before the police arrived to detain him, in order to meet student communists in Berlin. Seeing newspaper reports of the arson, as he sat on the train to Berlin, he took the hammer-and-sickle badge from his lapel and from that moment went underground. He hastened on party orders to Paris, where he registered with the Quaker Bureau. His entry into England in September 1933 was sponsored by Ronald Gunn, an executive of the Imperial Tobacco Company living near Bristol, who knew of his Quaker affiliations and (perhaps significantly) had visited the Soviet Union a year earlier. It was with Gunn's help that Fuchs obtained a post in the laboratory of Nevill Mott, Professor of Theoretical Physics at Bristol University. In Bristol, Fuchs frequented meetings of the Friends of Soviet Russia and of Münzenberg's front organization, the Society for Cultural Relations with the Soviet Union. It seemed innocuous to Mott for a refugee from Nazism to evince communist sympathies.

Fuchs, who was awarded his PhD in 1936, continued to live with the Gunn family until 1937, when he went to work for his DSc in Max Born's laboratory at the University of Edinburgh. Born spoke of him as 'a brilliant young fellow', a sad and lonely refugee, 'likeable, kind, harmless', and 'passionately pro-Russian'. Fuchs reconciled himself to the Nazi–Soviet pact of August 1939 by persuading himself that Stalin was buying time to gather strength against Hitler rather as Chamberlain had done by means of the Munich agreement of 1938. His German passport having been revoked by the Nazis, he applied for British citizenship in 1939. This had not yet been granted when war broke out: he was interned as an enemy alien in May 1940 and shipped to a primitive internment camp in Quebec, where he gave classes in theoretical physics. One of the internees who attended his brilliant lectures was Max Perutz, a molecular biologist at the Cavendish Laboratory, who was later awarded the Nobel prize and the Order of Merit. 'Fuchs is a brilliant mathematician and physicist; he also has an accurate memory and a remarkable ability to explain difficult concepts lucidly,' Perutz said; but 'I had no human contact with that pale, narrow-faced, thin-lipped, austere-looking man.' After eight months of internment, both Fuchs and Perutz were released in January 1941 following representations by the Royal Society.[17]

Two refugee scientists in Birmingham, Otto Frisch and Rudolf Peierls, had in March 1940 circulated a memorandum showing that only a few kilograms of the fissile uranium isotope 235 were needed to detonate an atomic weapon. Their exposition set in train the development of atomic bombs under the codename of the TUBE ALLOYS project. Forces of incredible violence began to be harnessed by men of mild looks and unassuming manners. Peierls recruited Fuchs to investigate the gaseous diffusion process involved in separating uranium isotopes. When Fuchs joined TUBE ALLOYS in June 1941, he signed the Official Secrets Act. There was no interview or investigation of him by MI5 officers, who were over-stretched on other urgent matters. Jane Archer did comment, after reading inconclusive entries on his file about communist affiliations, 'Fuchs is more likely to betray secrets to Russians than the enemy.' She recommended that he should not be shown more secret material than necessary, but, as Peierls commented, in a project like his 'there was no half-way house'. Everything was hurried in the wartime emergency. Frisch was pleased when Chadwick told him in

1943 that he would have to become a British subject if he was to follow
the project to America. Within a few days a Special Branch officer
visited Frisch to establish his antecedents, personal details and character
references as the preliminaries to naturalization. 'You must be a pretty
big shot,' the policeman mused. 'I have been told to get everything done
in a week!'[18]

Fuchs joined TUBE ALLOYS in the month that Nazi Germany
attacked Soviet Russia. He soon contacted the NKGB/NKVD organizer
in London, Jürgen Kuczynski, was accepted as a source in August 1941
and provided his first tranche of scientific secrets in the following
month. His subsequent codenames included REST, BRAS and
CHARLES. He became a British subject in 1942. His first Soviet handler
Simon Kremer @ BARCH did not build an affinity with him. In 1942,
after he had complained of BARCH to Kuczynski, the latter's sister
Ursula was (by Moscow's decision) put in charge of running him. Best
known by her codename SONYA, she was Ursula Kuczynski @ Ruth
Kuczynski @ Ruth Werner @ Ursula Beurton @ Ursula Hamburger.
Born in 1907, the daughter of an eminent Jewish statistical economist
in Berlin, she joined the German communist party at the age of eighteen.
During the early 1930s she worked for Red Army intelligence in
Shanghai, Peking and Mukden: Mao Tse-tung's victory in 1949 was 'the
most important milestone in the history of the Labour movement since
the October Revolution of 1917', she wrote in her eighties. 'For me
personally, it was one of the happiest events of my life.' After returning
from undercover work in Switzerland in 1941, she had handled the
atomic spy Melita Norwood. She was ruthless in promoting her cause.
Noël Coward's account of his breakdown in the Artists Rifle Corps,
which led to his hospitalization in a ward for shell-shock patients in
Camberwell in 1918, excited her contempt in 1941: 'His reactions as a
soldier in the First World War are exactly the reaction of a liberal
intellectual incapable of disciplining himself, incapable of renouncing
his individualism, of subordinating himself and withstanding physical
effort.'[19]

Her first meeting with Fuchs was in Banbury, midway between his
base in Birmingham and her wartime home in Oxford. At this inaugural
rendezvous they walked arm in arm together, according to an established practice of illicit meetings, discussing books and films as a way
of gaining mutual trust. No one mentioned espionage; she found Fuchs

sensitive, reserved, donnish and clumsy. Their next half-dozen meetings were also in the countryside, because it was harder for watchers to shadow them in open rural areas. She pedalled to their assignations on a bicycle with a wicker child's seat cushioned by a cheerful green pillow embellished with pictures of daisies. They could conduct their business in two minutes, but it looked less suspicious if they took a pleasant walk together for up to half an hour. Fuchs supplied SONYA with numerous blueprints, copies of all the reports he had written, and data on the gaseous diffusion method of separating the uranium isotope U-235 and on the mathematics used to evaluate the size and efficiency of atomic bombs. By December 1943, when Fuchs crossed the Atlantic with Peierls to work on the MANHATTAN PROJECT, he had confirmed to the Russians that the Americans and British were building plants to produce atomic weaponry and that Germany's equivalent projects had stalled.

The MANHATTAN PROJECT was based in New York and Los Alamos, New Mexico. In February 1944 Fuchs had his first rendezvous with his new American handler, Harry Gold @ GOOSE @ ARNO @ MAD @ RAYMOND, who was a chemist by training and son of an anti-Romanov radical who had fled tsarist Russia in 1903 to avoid military conscription. The two conspirators met at the entrance to the Henry Street Settlement, which provided health care and social services to the needy in Manhattan's Lower East Side, and identified one another by holding gloves, a green-covered book, a handball and other paraphernalia. Thereafter Fuchs supplied Gold with material on the design and assembly of the atomic bomb, which proved of utmost value in advancing Soviet atomic expertise. Under the Soviet system, with its reliance on denial and deception, the Kremlin's scant public references to the bombing of Hiroshima and Nagasaki in August 1945 were an index of the importance attached by Stalin to atomic nuclear weaponry. 'It has never been admitted that the atomic bomb had any real influence on the Japanese capitulation and Stalin did not refer to it in his final victory broadcast,' Clark Kerr, the Ambassador in Moscow, reported in September that year. Ignorant of the espionage by Nunn May and Fuchs, Clark Kerr was encouraged by the Kremlin's mild reaction to Anglo-American duplicity: there had been no denunciation of 'our failure to impart to them the formula of the atomic bomb which can imply nothing but a lack of confidence in our Soviet allies'.[20]

A fortnight after the destruction of the two Japanese cities, the Prime Minister Clement Attlee circulated a memorandum on the atomic bomb. 'No Government has ever been placed in such a position as is ours today. The Governments of the U.K. and the U.S.A. are responsible as never before for the future of the human race.' Attlee saw no hope of restricting the spread of nuclear weapons. 'Any attempt to keep this as a secret in the hands of the U.S.A. and U.K. is useless. Scientists in other countries are certain in time to hit upon the secret.' The experience of recent years had convinced him that the necessary response to saturation bombing was retaliatory raids. 'Berlin & Magdeburg were the answer to London and Coventry. Both derive from Guernica. The answer to an atomic bomb on London is an atomic bomb on another great city.' This was the hard, hostile new terrain through which Fuchs, as well as Attlee's government, had to find a safe path.[21]

In the summer of 1946 Fuchs was appointed head of theoretical physics at the new Atomic Research Establishment at Harwell (then a bleak encampment around an empty airfield). From the technical questions asked of him by the Russians, Fuchs deduced the existence of another atomic spy: this, unknown to him, was Melita Norwood. Once installed at Harwell, he tried to contact Jürgen Kuczynski, who however had worked for US military intelligence in 1944–5, reached the rank of lieutenant colonel while attached to the US army of occupation in Berlin, and declined to cooperate with the local NKGB station. In September 1947 Fuchs had his first rendezvous with his new handler, Alexander Feklissov @ KALISTRAT, at the drab Nag's Head public house in Wood Green. For mutual confirmation of identity, Feklissov said, 'Stout is not so good: I generally take lager,' and Fuchs replied, 'I think Guinness is the best.'[22]

Fuchs resumed the supply of official secrets, which had been suspended when he left the USA a year earlier. Hydrogen-bomb plans, English and American atomic stockpiles, processes for isolating plutonium, and theoretical calculations of explosion were among the material that he betrayed. 'I used my Marxist philosophy to establish in my mind two separate compartments,' Fuchs explained, with acute self-analysis, to his MI5 interrogator in 1950. In one compartment he allowed himself:

to make friendships, to have personal relations, to help people and to be in all personal ways the kind of man I wanted to be . . . I could be free and easy and happy with other people without fear of disclosing myself because I knew that the other compartment would step in if I approached the danger point. I could forget the other compartment and still rely on it. It appeared to me at the time that I had become a 'free man' because I had succeeded in the other compartment to establish myself completely independent of the surrounding forces of society. Looking back at it now the best way of expressing it seems to be to call it a controlled schizophrenia.[23]

Feklissov told Fuchs that if he had to defer a rendezvous or needed an emergency meeting, he should go to Richmond, Surrey and throw a copy of the magazine *Men Only* over the wall of 166 Kew Road, with a message on page 10 supplying a new place and date. He then had to make a chalk mark on a wall in nearby Holmsdale Road. The garden in Kew Road belonged to a former CPGB activist, Charles Moody, who had become an outwardly conventional Attlee supporter: nominated by the Labour party to the bench of Richmond magistrates in 1945, this former dustman was eventually a respected chairman of the juvenile bench. He had been the husband since 1927 of Gerty or Gerda Isaacs, daughter of a rabbi named Moses Isaacs (described in the 1901 census as Russian-born, but a subject of the Sultan of Turkey). The Moodys lived at 166 Kew Road with three sons and Gerty's sister Clara Isaacs. The two women were not open CPGB members but, as an MI5 report noted in 1954, 'Mrs MOODY often refers to people who are merely sympathisers with a pro-Russian or Communist organisation as being "the unconverted".'[24]

There were tens of thousands of Soviet sympathizers like the Moodys, who wished to believe that Stalin wanted world peace. When the Atomic Energy Bill was debated in the Commons in 1946, its provisions for safeguarding official secrets were resisted by the Labour MP Wilfrid Vernon, the member of the aviation spy ring at the Royal Aircraft Establishment whose activities had been compromised by the bungling Blackshirt raid on his shack. Vernon lacked subtlety. He advocated open, unrestricted collaboration between nuclear physicists of all nations. Official secrecy, he said, was a hindrance to scientific advances. If the purity of scientific exchanges was polluted by considerations of national security, able graduates would be scared of entering atomic research lest they make an inadvertent slip and land themselves in prison. Scientists working on nuclear weaponry would moreover be prevented from consulting those interested in nuclear energy, and vice versa. The world shortage of fuel was taking the planet back to 'the Stone Age', Vernon feared. Instead of maximizing the effort to develop new power to replace coal and oil, 'we are letting our military madness clamp down on this vital possibility for the future of mankind'. Such ebullitions confirmed the judgement of a former Farnborough colleague that Vernon was 'a second-rate man with a second-rate mind . . . an idealist and a type who would die on the barricades'.[25]

Alexander Foote, Ursula Kuczynski's former associate in Switzerland-based espionage, defected in Berlin in 1946 and gave full information on her to MI5. As a result of Foote's defection, Moscow broke contact with her. For several months she cycled on allotted days to her dead drop in the hollow root of the fourth tree on the left after a railway tunnel on the Oxford–Banbury road, but never found a message. MI5 began to test Foote's account. SONYA was found to be living in a house called The Firs in the Oxfordshire village of Great Rollright. Effective surveillance was impossible: she was too careful to post incriminating letters; the local telephone exchange was too small for the monitoring of her calls to pass unnoticed; in a village watchers would be spotted within a day.

On a summer day in 1947, Skardon and Michael Serpell arrived without warning at The Firs. (Serpell was the favoured personal assistant of the then Director General of the Security Service, Sir Percy Sillitoe, who later said after rewarding him with a hoist in the office hierarchy, 'if I don't promote him nobody else will'.) They walked into the room and said without pausing, 'You were a Russian agent for a long time, before the Finnish war disillusioned you. We know that you haven't been active in England. We haven't come to arrest you, but to ask your cooperation.' She almost laughed at what seemed a clownish attempt to throw her off balance. They asked about incidents in Switzerland, which made her suspect that her activities had been betrayed by Foote, but stressed that they considered her a loyal British subject, who had been disillusioned with communism by the Russian invasion of Finland. She admitted to her marriage ten years earlier to an active communist in China, but refused to answer questions about her experiences before she got a British passport. Her interrogators professed astonishment at this obstinate attitude from someone who had been guiltless since settling in England.[26]

Harwell and Semipalatinsk

Code-breakers posed as great a threat as defectors to Moscow's espionage apparatus. During 1944–5 the Soviets were careless enough to reissue some one-time pads, which made their cipher system for high-grade diplomatic and intelligence communications vulnerable to American and British code-breakers. In 1946 Meredith Gardner of the US Army Security Agency (ASA), who knew German, Sanskrit, Lithuanian, Spanish, French, Japanese and Russian, began decrypting messages exchanged between Moscow Centre and its American agencies. His team of code-breakers, who were mostly young women, embarked on a momentous project which received the codename VENONA. They collected evidence of massive Soviet espionage, which was not reported by ASA to the FBI until 1948. (The CIA was, however, not informed about VENONA until 1952: partly because of bitter inter-agency rivalry; but also because its decrypts revealed that Moscow's agents had infested the CIA's predecessor body, the OSS, and Hoover feared that the CIA was equally pest-ridden.)

Moscow Centre heard about VENONA five years before the CIA. William Weisband, a Russian linguist in ASA, codenamed ZHORA and RUPERT by his chiefs in Moscow, was a prowling snooper who peered over Meredith Gardner's shoulder at the moment when the cryptanalyst was decrypting an NKGB telegram which revealed that Los Alamos had been penetrated by Soviet agents. Weisband was never prosecuted for betraying VENONA to Moscow, because the US authorities shrank from court disclosures about VENONA. He did, however, serve a prison sentence in 1950–1 for contempt of court after refusing a grand jury subpoena: he thereafter worked as an insurance salesman. Moscow was thrown into uncertainty by Weisband's revelations, for it was impossible to predict which NKVD telegrams would be decrypted or which Soviet agents would be compromised. Its perturbation was increased in July 1948, when Elizabeth Bentley testified in public to the House Un-American Activities Committee. Whittaker Chambers named Alger Hiss, Harry Dexter White and others in evidence to HUAC a month later. Moscow Centre expected these revelations to lead to a series of show-trials.[27]

In September 1949, just before leaving for Washington, Philby warned Burgess that VENONA was close to identifying a major atomic spy, who had been active in the United States (Philby did not know the spy's identity as Fuchs). Burgess's information from Philby was included in three rolls of microfilm received from Blunt by the new Soviet contact, Yuri Modin, on 11 October 1949. The microfilms had, however, been over-exposed and were unusable. When 168 recopied documents, totalling 660 pages, were delivered to Modin on 7 December, Burgess forgot to repeat his warning about the Anglo-American decryption effort and the atomic spy. If Blunt had not photographed the early batch of material badly, or if Burgess had remembered to repeat his warning note, Moscow could have exfiltrated Fuchs in November or December, or at least briefed him on handling MI5 interrogators. Instead, when Fuchs was arrested, they became obsessed with the idea that he had been betrayed by his former American handler, Harry Gold.

Fuchs underwent repeated vetting in 1946–9 as he took charge of the mathematical work needed to develop nuclear power, and was promoted to be deputy chief scientific officer at Harwell: Roger Hollis had cleared his file for the sixth time. Then VENONA decrypts identified a Soviet agent codenamed CHARLES as a supplier of vital intelligence on the MANHATTAN PROJECT. There were three prime suspects for the part of CHARLES: Fuchs, Peierls and Frank Kearton. A bricklayer's son with a first-class degree in chemistry from Oxford, Kearton had shared an office with Fuchs in America, never doubted him and treated him as a friend. Kearton, who became one of post-war England's most formidable industrialists and received a barony in 1970, said the worst time of his life was when he was under MI5's suspicion. It did not last long. By careful study of all the references to CHARLES, MI5 cleared first Kearton and then Peierls, which left only Fuchs. MI5's Arthur Martin and John Marriott interviewed Kearton in mid-November. 'KEARTON could not believe that FUCHS was a spy, although it did not seem from anything KEARTON said that this could be ruled out,' noted Liddell. In fact, he added, Kearton had been just as incredulous as Nunn May's colleagues when security doubts were raised about him.[28]

From July 1949 Fuchs was subject to tapped telephones and intercepted mail, but nothing incriminatory was found. An intensive investigation by MI5's B Division could find no incriminating evidence because he had by then renounced espionage. MI5 could not use the highly classified secret VENONA decrypts or any SIGINT intercepted material as evidence against Fuchs in a criminal trial. Skardon – the man who had failed to shake Ursula Kuczynski two years earlier – was sent to interview Fuchs at Harwell on 21 September 1949 without being told of the VENONA decrypts. He saw no signs of guilt, as he reported after two interviews. Arthur Martin and Evelyn McBarnet found no suspicious inconsistencies or incriminating contradictions in the interview transcripts. The cover for MI5's sudden interest in Fuchs was that his father had recently moved to Leipzig, in communist-controlled Germany, and that this raised security concerns which might require Fuchs to leave the Harwell establishment. Dick White coached Skardon like a schoolmaster preparing a star pupil for an examination, and sent him on further visits to Harwell, where Skardon simulated a trusting affinity with Fuchs.

In mid-January 1950, with an air of relaxed sincerity, Skardon suggested that there was still a chance that Fuchs could become Director of Harwell if he told his story fully. Fuchs could not have been incriminated if he had said nothing, but he relented as lonely men under sympathetic questioning sometimes do. He volunteered his story – although, as Skardon did not have a high enough security-clearance, he refused to give technical details of the official secrets that he had given the Russians. There was then a nerve-racking hiatus for Fuchs lasting more than a week. Finally he was asked to come to London, where he gave and signed a full confession on 27 January. Breaking Fuchs was the acme of Skardon's career. It vindicated his technique of formidably ruthless sympathy. 'My name is Skardon,' he would say by way of introduction to someone whom he was about to interview. 'I was the man who persuaded Klaus Fuchs to confess. A dear man.'[29]

Edward Teller, the Budapest-born deviser of hydrogen bombs, who had complained that Fuchs was 'taciturn to an almost pathological degree', exclaimed on hearing of Fuchs's arrest: 'So that's what it was!' Fuchs's trial at the Old Bailey on 1 March took a total of ninety minutes: Skardon was the only witness; no jury was needed, for Fuchs pleaded guilty; he was given a sentence of fourteen years. There was as much official misdirection as there had been in the trials of Glading and Nunn May. The indictment referred to four specific acts of espionage in 1943, 1944, 1945 and 1947 without revealing that Fuchs had confessed to starting his betrayal of atomic secrets in 1942 and continuing until 1949.[30]

Ursula Kuczynski left England with her young children, whom she was rearing as anti-fascists, days before the start of Fuchs's trial. She was unsure whether MI5 had failed to connect her with Fuchs or had preferred her to escape like Glading's handlers: her arrest might have complicated the case, brought awkward public disclosures about a decade of Soviet espionage and perhaps provoked the punitive ire of the FBI. She was living in East Germany when Stalin died in 1953: 'every communist I met considered it as I did – a great loss'. Skardon interviewed Charles and Gerty Moody on several occasions; their associates were investigated; Home Office warrants for telephone and postal interception were issued; their file was revisited periodically for years. Evelyn McBarnet of MI5 concluded, 'I am left with the *impression* that MOODY must, almost certainly, have been the person concerned with retrieving the magazine thrown over the wall by FUCHS, that he was possibly not aware of the precise significance of his action, and that he had probably never heard of FUCHS before the story of his arrest appeared in the press.'[31]

Graham Greene, who had joined SIS in 1941 and worked in the Iberian Section under Philby in 1943–4, concluded from his experiences that Soviet espionage was 'a branch of psychological warfare' in which the object was to destroy trust between the allied powers that were its adversaries. He remained an SIS Friend, received funding from the Service for his inveterate travelling and reported to it from Russia, Poland, Vietnam and China during the 1950s and 1960s: the virulent anti-Americanism of his public statements about the Vietnam War may have been a cover for his continuing SIS allegiance. It was as an SIS trusty that he gave his conclusion that Russia had been enabled by Nunn May and Fuchs to advance its manufacture of atomic bombs by a few years, but would have soon reached parity in its ability to destroy the world even without their help. 'The real value of the two scientists to the Soviet Union', he wrote, 'was not the benefit they received from their scientific information, but from their capture, and the breakdown in Anglo-American relations which followed. A spy allowed to continue his work without interference is far less dangerous than the spy who is caught.'[32]

In Wakefield prison Fuchs shared a cell with Edouard-Jean Johnston @ 'Count' John Edward Johnston-Noad, a Mayfair *bon vivant* who had been disbarred as a solicitor after his conviction for keeping a brothel near Burgess's flat in Old Bond Street, who posed as a member of the Montenegrin royal family, who was married to a Hatton Garden diamond thief known as 'Black Orchid', and who was described by his own counsel, at his fraud trial in 1952, as 'a vain, egotistical megalomaniac'. This incompatible pair, who were the least rough cellmates in the prison, were both released in 1959. Fuchs soon moved to Dresden. There, suspected by the KGB of having given the names of its agents to MI5 under interrogation, he was forbidden to give interviews, prepare his memoirs or contact his former handlers. This treatment was a torment to him. Markus Wolf, head of the Foreign Intelligence Division of the Ministry of State Security in communist East Germany, encountered him during the 1980s and ranked him as a master-spy comparable to Philby. He tried to assuage his enemies by hard-line loyalty, which made him tell western visitors that the dissident nuclear physicist Andrei Sakharov deserved more condign punishment than compulsory exile in Gorky (Nizhny Novgorod). Yet the KGB shunned Fuchs, never honoured his self-sacrificing achievements and perhaps blamed him for getting caught. 'This silence from a country that he had served purely out of conscience and at great cost to his liberty and scientific career, weighed on him like a daily burden,' wrote Wolf.[33]

It is interesting to compare Fuchs's fate with that of Theodore Hall @ MLAD. Born in 1925, son of a New York furrier named Holtzberg, he anglicized his surname before going to study physics at Harvard, from which he graduated in 1944. He and his Harvard room-mate Saville Sax @ STAR, who was another New Yorker of Russian Jewish ancestry, shared communist ideals. After Hall had been assigned to a Los Alamos team investigating the physics of implosion for plutonium-bomb development, he and Sax agreed that his secrets should be shared with America's ally, the Soviet Union. Sax tried to approach Earl Browder, head of the CPUSA and ex-husband of Maclean's handler Kitty Harris. After rebuffs, Sax finally contacted the NKGB agent Sergey Kurnakov @ BECK, whom he introduced to Hall. Kurnakov agreed to receive Hall's material, if it was brought to him in secret batches from New Mexico by Sax. Hall was far junior to Fuchs as a scientist, but was well placed at Los Alamos to gain access to useful secrets. 'His English is highly cultured,' wrote Kurnakov in a pen-portrait of 1944 for Moscow Centre. 'He answers quickly and very fluently, especially to scientific questions. Eyes are set closely together; evidently, neurasthenic. Perhaps because of premature mental development, he is witty and somewhat sarcastic, but without a shadow of undue familiarity.' His family were Jewish, continued Kurnakov, 'but [he] doesn't look like a Jew'. Hall, who moved to scientific work in Chicago after the war, fell under suspicion with Sax in 1949, when VENONA decrypts showed their names in plain text, before they had been allotted cover names. They denied contacts with Soviet intelligence when interrogated by the FBI in 1951; and given the decision not to bring VENONA evidence to open court, and in the absence of other incriminating material, they were not prosecuted. Hall moved to England, where he worked in Cambridge University's electron microscopy research laboratory before his death in 1999. Sax taught 'values clarification' in an educational programme of the mid-1960s, is said to have become a drug-experimenting hippy and died in 1980.[34]

American witch-hunts intensified after (with help from the espionage of Nunn May, Fuchs and others) the Soviet Union had exploded its 'First Lightning' plutonium implosion bomb at Semipalatinsk in Kazakhstan in August 1949. The project was run by the nuclear physicist Igor Kurchatov, but was under the control of the fearsome Beria. With characteristic Stalinist paranoia, Beria both suspected the Anglo-American atomic secrets as disinformation and used the same espionage material as a check on Soviet atomic scientists whom he equally distrusted. The test-site was a stony, sparsely covered expanse where the heat was oppressive by early morning. It had been arrayed with locomotives, railway-stock, tanks, artillery, animals and homesteads so that the effects of irradiation could be studied. After Beria's arrival at Semipalatinsk, the device was detonated in its tower. A mushroom cloud rose 5 miles into the sky. At ground level everything was annihilated.

'Molten lumps flew about in all directions like small pieces of shrapnel and radiated invisible alpha, beta and gamma rays,' noted the chief of the Radiation Protection Service. 'The steel girders of a bridge were twisted into ram's horns.' Beria was mistrustful of what he had seen. 'Haven't we slipped up?' he asked. 'Doesn't Kurchatov humbug us?' He telephoned Stalin and said, 'Everything went right.' Stalin, who had been asleep, was confused by drowsiness and old age. 'I know already,' he replied untruthfully, and put down the telephone receiver. Beria erupted into paranoid rage at his companions at Semipalatinsk. 'Who told him? You are letting me down! Even here you spy on me! I'll grind you to dust!'[35]

CHAPTER 14

The Cold War

Dictaphones behind the wainscots?

'The British as a people are still self-assured, serene in their national sense of superiority' and did not yet understand that they were no longer 'top nation', OSS's Crane Brinton wrote in an assessment of the future of Anglo-American relations in 1945. This complacence proved unsustainable in a country where income tax averaged 50 per cent of earnings, where the top earners paid 97.5 per cent (19½ shillings in a currency when 20 shillings equalled a pound) and where it seemed impossible to save enough money to retire on. Despite the victory over Germany, domestic demoralization began within months, and soon saw the onset of four decades of national inferiority complex. In 1948 Angela Thirkell, the chronicler of mid-twentieth-century English county society, recorded the state of the nation in her novel *Love among the Ruins*. She pictured a nation burdened by dead glories and reduced to meagre hope by its manifest international disempowerment: 'people who had taken six years of war with uncomplaining courage and were now being starved, regimented and ground down by their present rulers, besides the deep hidden shame of feeling that England's name had been lowered in the eyes of all lesser breeds'. Sleepless nights did not refresh the English. They queued for unpalatable food, plain clothes and scarce fuel, their savings depreciated, they chain-smoked to kill time, they were squashed on overcrowded trains, they were annoyed by inquisitorial officials and prying questionnaires, and they felt shouldered aside by surging crowds of foreigners everywhere: 'the lesser breeds, who although by their own account penniless expatriates, mysteriously had huge sums of money'. In *Love among the Ruins* these privations are lamented by the organizers of a charity garden-party until a naval officer half jokes: 'I daresay there is a dictaphone behind the wainscot, and whoever is in charge of liquidating land-owners taking it all down in shorthand.' The secret services were neither understood nor trusted.[1]

Only a few political leaders and officials, who had been indoctrinated into Masterman's Double-Cross System, knew that the Security Service had perpetrated the most successful wartime deception since the Trojan horse. Masterman's historical monograph, *The Double-Cross System in the War of 1939–45*, was suppressed until 1972 in compliance with the wishes of the security services, the Cabinet Office and other stakeholders. These departments feared that counter-espionage revelations would 'boomerang', in the words of Lord Normanbrook, Cabinet Secretary from 1947 until 1962. They expected journalists to stress that Masterman was an Oxford historian, who had been temporarily engaged in wartime counter-espionage, and that full-time career Security Service staff were of lower calibre. Dick White in 1967 thought it would be detrimental to public trust of the two security services to know that the XX System had relied on 'an immense amount of talent [seconded] from the outside world, particularly the Universities, during the war'. Both Normanbrook and White were advising in the context of press stories which had besmirched Whitehall and the security services as incompetent and untrustworthy after the defections of Burgess and Maclean in 1951, and of Philby in 1963.[2]

Not a hint of XX was heard by the public or by hundreds of new MPs who were elected in the Labour landslide at the general election in 1945. Socialist parliamentarians knew nothing of the pre-war Vigilance spy network manned by the nominees of their former whip Jack Hayes. Instead they blamed MI5 for the spurious Zinoviev letter, which had lost their party the general election of 1924. Many of them mistrusted Special Branch. The former SIS officer 'Rex' Fletcher, who had been created Lord Winster, was ousted from his post as Labour's Minister of Civil Aviation in 1946, because socialist MPs suspected his antecedents. At least a dozen Labour MPs were either secret CPGB members or pro-Soviet crypto-communists. In addition to Driberg, at least one had spied for Russia: Wilfrid Vernon, after being elected MP for Dulwich in 1945, acted as parliamentary spokesman of the far-left Association of Scientific Workers and was included on a list compiled by the general secretary of the Labour party of fifteen subversively pro-Soviet MPs. Two of his closer parliamentary associates, John Platts-Mills and Konni Zilliacus, were expelled from the parliamentary party in 1948. Some socialist leaders vied to excuse past excesses. Cecil L'Estrange Malone, who had sat in turn as a Liberal, Leninist and Labour MP, was recommended by socialist friends for a peerage in 1945. After losing his Commons seat in 1931, he had become Tokyo's paid lackey during the Sino-Japanese war, and ran the propagandist East Asia News Service until Pearl Harbor in 1941. Attlee dismissed the suggestion that Malone should receive a barony with one of his crisp understatements: 'hardly suitable'.[3]

The incoming Labour government wanted to curb MI5's powers of surveillance. Proposals in the autumn of 1945 either to bring the Security Service under the Home Secretary's direct control or to subordinate it to SIS were defeated by Sir David Petrie, who was due to retire early in 1946. Petrie's preferred successor, Guy Liddell, was discounted by Labour ministers who had doubted the political impartiality of MI5 insiders since the Zinoviev and ARCOS incidents in 1924–7. An impressive shortlist was drawn up, including two major generals, Sir Ronald Penney, recently retired as Director of Military Intelligence in south-east Asia, and Eisenhower's intelligence chief Sir Kenneth Strong. 'Latter the better, but didn't much plunge for either of them,' noted Cadogan. The selection process demonstrated that the candidate who shines at interview may not be the best person for the job. Sir Percy Sillitoe, the Chief Constable of Kent, who made a strong show before the appointment board, was unanimously chosen. 'He certainly seemed v. good' to Cadogan; Attlee liked him as 'an honest policeman'; but MI5 officers complained that he never understood that the security services differ from the police, not least because their best evidence cannot be aired in court. In the constabulary Sillitoe had received automatic obedience to rules and unquestioning subordination to discipline, but he complained that in MI5 he met evasion and insolence.[4]

Labour's suspicions of MI5, and ingratitude for its achievements, were ill timed. The Joint Intelligence Committee (JIC) reported in September 1946 that the global spread of communism under Moscow's direction was the primary threat to the British Isles, British colonies, western democracies, eastern Europe and eastern Asia. 'The appeal of Communism is based on an all-embracing ideology, to which Communists adhere with religious fervour, and on the promise of a better world free from exploitation and war. The Communist Parties are led by nuclei of able, experienced and devoted men, capable of directing mass movements, and firm in the belief that they are assisting in an inexorable historical process.' Under direction from Moscow, 'Communists will use any instrument in any way, provided that the cause of Communism is furthered thereby, and are prepared to execute sudden and complete reversals of policy to meet a changed situation.' In one respect the JIC analysis was misguided. It emphasized the role of the CPGB, and communist parties in other parliamentary democracies, in providing from their membership individuals willing to spy and subvert. Open party members, rather than penetration agents without current party allegiances, were put in the foreground of concern.[5]

At the Foreign Office, from which the security officers William Codrington and Sir John Dashwood retired with the coming of peace, a former RAF group captain, George Carey-Foster, was appointed to head a Security Department in October 1946. Harold Caccia, the quick and able Chief Clerk, rejected Carey-Foster's recommendation that all members of the Diplomatic Service should undergo positive vetting – not just new entrants. Officials felt that positive vetting (particularly of existing staff) sapped the tradition of trust upon which department loyalty had hitherto relied. It was too similar to the raucous injustice of loyalty testing in the USA and to barbarous purges in Soviet Russia. Yet positive vetting was little more than a systematic, comprehensive version of the checks that had been in place in the intelligence agencies for years: when someone was contemplated for a confidential appointment, their associates had long been asked about their family, their affiliations, their character and their frailties. The principle did not change, even if the methodical intensity increased. Carey-Foster installed regional security officers in New York, Cairo and a few other cities, but found successive heads of the FO's Personnel Department to be obstructive. He was hugely overworked: it took three years for funds to be allotted for him to have an assistant, in the elegant form of Milo Talbot, who had recently inherited the Irish barony of Talbot de Malahide.

The Office's Personnel Department was described as 'the most paper-logged Department in this paper-logged office!' It was understaffed and sometimes overwhelmed, but found time to obstruct Carey-Foster by maintaining that the purview of the Security Department was limited to buildings, safes, locks and couriers' bags, with human insecurity excluded. This resistance continued until Burgess and Maclean absconded in 1951.[6]

As successor to Sir Stewart Menzies, 'C' at SIS, Cadogan wished to appoint a civilian, Victor ('Bill') Cavendish-Bentinck, who had been wartime chairman of the JIC and first post-war Ambassador to Poland. Cavendish-Bentinck had been rejected on medical grounds for military service in the first European war in which many of his contemporaries had died, and in expiation worked with formidable concentration, beyond the strength of most people, to master immense quantities of paperwork. He was sceptical, unprejudiced and amid tragedy could savour the human comedy. From the 'eerie and awesome' ruins of war-devastated Warsaw in August 1945, Cavendish-Bentinck relished the challenge: 'Despite squalor etc., this is more amusing and interesting than the JIC . . . now that the war is over.' Cadogan's plan was however baulked when his candidate became embroiled in a squalid divorce, and was ejected from the Diplomatic Service, with loss of pension rights, on the personal decision of the Foreign Secretary, ex-trade union leader Ernest Bevin, who knew that Cavendish-Bentinck was heir-in-line to the dukedom of Portland (which he inherited at the age of eighty-two some thirty years later). 'I could have saved him if his name had been Smith,' Bevin said.[7]

Once Cadogan's excellent candidate had fallen, Menzies, who opposed SIS being led by a civilian, obtained the appointment as his successor-designate of Major General John ('Sinbad') Sinclair, former Director of Military Intelligence at the War Office. Menzies's friend General Sir James Marshall-Cornwall, whom he had appointed as Assistant Chief of SIS in 1943, retired in 1945. Philby in his untrustworthy memoirs is slyly misleading about many MI5 and SIS personnel, including Marshall-Cornwall (whom Reilly thought 'brought to Broadway long experience in Intelligence and a much needed intellectual distinction'). His estimate of Sinclair, however, was fair: 'Sinclair, though not overloaded with mental gifts (he never claimed them), was humane, energetic and so obviously upright that it was impossible to withhold admiration.'[8]

George Blake, who served SIS in The Hague and Hamburg before his posting to Seoul in 1948, felt that the pre-war service had resembled a club of amateur enthusiasts, ruled by an autocratic Chief who hired, fired and paid them as he wished, without regard to civil service rules. But in the first months of peace Cadogan instigated a committee to settle the post-war future of SIS, and Menzies soon reorganized the Service into, said Blake, 'a properly established Government Department with a personnel department, grading, regular promotions, pension schemes and annual increments'.[9]

A further point must be stressed about Whitehall after 1945. It was appallingly overworked. Its officials at every level were exhausted by the extra duties, the heavy responsibilities, the emergency pressure, insomnia, the meagre rations and the accumulative stress of the war years. With the exception of the end of night-time bombing, there was little peacetime alleviation. Indeed, the continuing shortages and inefficiencies of peacetime seemed more frustrating. When Sir James Chadwick, the atomic physicist whose trust had been betrayed by Nunn May, returned from his planet-transformative work in the United States in 1946, he and his wife were met at Southampton docks by a driver and car from the Ministry of Supply. The car ran out of petrol before they reached London. The chauffeur had no petrol coupons with which to refuel. Lugging their suitcases on a hot summer's day the Chadwicks finished their journey to the capital on a series of jolting buses.

Overwork caused the death in 1946 of the master-negotiator and trans-Atlantic commuter Lord Keynes, and devitalized almost everyone in government administration. There was a grave shortage of competence for all the big tasks that needed to be done. Having failed to become chief of MI5, Penney was appointed Director of the London Communications Security Agency, which advised on cipher security and was the forerunner of GCHQ's Communications Electronic Security Group. Churchill's man in SIS, Desmond Morton, proved unwelcome there to Bevin, but was soon redeployed as the Treasury's representative on the Inter-Allied Reparation Agency, and on the Tripartite Gold Commission in Brussels. Everywhere tired, hungry, uncomfortable officials were doing two simultaneous jobs. During 1950, as the VENONA-inspired investigations into the Foreign Office espionage intensified, Reilly was too busy to participate in inquiries for which he was specially fitted. With the continuing freeze of the Cold War, and especially after North Korea's surprise attack on South Korea in June

1950, Reilly gave priority to preparing JIC advice for the Chiefs of Staff and government ministers on the danger of a new world war.[10]

Contending priorities for MI5

Hostility to the British Empire was the common ground of the United States and Soviet Russia before and after the defeat of Germany and Japan. 'Traditional American dislike and suspicion of anything that savours of selfish British imperialism coincides with one of the major themes of Soviet anti-British propaganda,' Jock Balfour and Archie Inverchapel (who had both served in the wartime Moscow embassy) reported from the Washington embassy in 1946. Yet until the 1970s MI5 was deeply, necessarily committed to activities that bore the stamp, or at least the residual marks, of the British Empire. This hindered good relations between London and Washington, and at MI5 entailed over-work and information overload.[11]

'Intelligence requirements: prune these vigorously as no service can cover every subject' – so Brian Stewart of SIS urged in his handbook for security agencies. The demands on MI5 were insupportable during the late 1940s: there was no surplus growth that could be trimmed, even if there had been time to wield the secateurs. Throughout the Cold War, MI5 bore heavy responsibilities for security and counter-espionage in Britain's colonies as well as in the homeland. Intelligence was crucial to the process of decolonization in several territories. MI5 officers reformed local security procedure, trained colonial intelligence officials and posted security liaison officers (SLOs) in all the major colonies and dependencies that were given independence. Newly inde-pendent governments, without major exception, asked these SLOs to stay in place and continue to act as advisers. Intelligence was crucial to the decolonization programme of the 1950s and 1960s.[12]

Attlee's decision in 1946 that Britain should resume its rule in Hong Kong after the Japanese occupation, rather than relinquish control to the Chinese, had far-reaching consequences. The colony became the sentinel outpost of the western powers in a communist-dominated region. Sillitoe visited Hong Kong in 1948 and advised on its security. Wilfrid Vernon was a mouthpiece of the communist-front China Campaign Committee, and was vocal in support of Mao Tse-tung's 'efficient, humane and democratic' forces in what he called 'the Liberated

Area' of China: whereas Russia had 'refrained most meticulously from interfering in China', the US had (in Vernon's view) intervened with 'absolute shamelessness'. After Mao's victory in 1949, the encircled colony of Hong Kong became Asia's equivalent of Berlin.[13]

Britain's decision to cede independence to India, Burma and Ceylon was an unmatched devolution of imperial power. Three-quarters of the British Empire's subjects were removed with the loss of the Raj, which took place at midnight on 14–15 August 1947. Nine months later, in May 1948, the British began to withdraw their forces from the Palestine mandate. Despite these withdrawals, 7.1 per cent of gross national product was spent on the euphemism of 'defence spending' in 1948; the figure grew to 9.8 per cent in 1952 (during the Korean war) and still exceeded 6 per cent in 1963.[14]

The British commitment in Greece was an important part of the resistance to communism. Sir Daniel Lascelles summarized the position, as seen from the Athens embassy, in November 1945. 'During the occupation period we officially backed an unpopular and ostentatiously non-Greek monarch,' King George II of the Hellenes, 'who made no secret of the fact that he disliked the Greeks and preferred to live in England.' This preference was intensified by his devotion to his gentle and intelligent mistress, Joyce Brittain-Jones, who later married Eddy Boxshall, the former SIS officer in Bucharest. 'What was still more unfortunate', continued Lascelles, 'was the fact that, simultaneously, certain British organizations which were grossly ill-informed about Greece and which ought to have been under the control of the Foreign Office but notoriously were not, backed and armed the King's bitterest enemies of the extreme Left, whose resistance included the attempted liquidation, *more sovietico*, of all their internal political opponents.' The Greek National Liberation Front, 'loudly encouraged by that contempt-ible section of public opinion which believes any group labelled "Left" to be incapable of sin, committed a long series of really ghastly atroc-ities in the name of democracy', Lascelles reported. These London-based groups included the League for Democracy in Greece, which had the support of eighty-six Labour MPs, including Driberg, Platts-Mills, Vernon and the winner of the Stalin peace prize, Pritt.[15]

In January 1947 Attlee proposed the assuagement of competitive tensions with Stalinist Russia by offering Moscow the economizing policy of withdrawing costly British forces stationed in the Balkans and

Middle East. His plan was quashed by the Foreign Office. 'It would be Munich over again, only on a world scale, with Greece, Turkey and Persia as the first victims in place of Czechoslovakia,' Bevin warned. 'Russia would certainly fill the gap we leave empty, whatever her promises.' Middle Eastern regimes might seem unsavoury, but they all valued their national independence. 'If we speak to Stalin as you propose, he is as likely to respect their independence as Hitler was to respect Czechoslovakia's, and we should get as much of Stalin's goodwill as we got of Hitler's after Munich.' The world would see retreat from the Middle East 'after our abandonment of India and Burma . . . as the abdication of our position as a world power'.[16]

The following month, in February 1947, the Attlee government informed Washington that it could no longer afford to give financial aid to Greece or to maintain troops there. Britain had intervened there by force of arms, so as to prevent 'the establishment by terrorism of a Communist minority regime which would have turned Greece, like the other Balkan states, into another Soviet Satellite State'. But the cost was no longer supportable. This renunciation gave a violent jolt to Washington. Within days President Truman had declared his resolve that the US would uphold the integrity of free states against armed minorities or outside intervention. The Truman Doctrine, which was adopted with rare unanimity in Washington, proved as momentous as the nineteenth-century Monroe Doctrine: it ended American isolationism for seventy years, and led to the formation of the North Atlantic Treaty Organization (NATO) in 1949. 'The missionary strain in the character of Americans', reported Inverchapel, 'leads many of them to feel that they have now received a call to extend to other countries the blessings with which the Almighty has endowed their own.'[17]

A dominant fear in Whitehall was that Britain's withdrawals from its colonies would leave a power vacuum that the Soviet Union would hasten to fill: that, in Calder Walton's phrase, 'the red on British imperial maps would be replaced by the red of communism'. In response to these concerns, the Security Service formed its Overseas Department in 1948. During 1946–50 Sillitoe made twelve major tours of British overseas territories: Canada, Palestine, Egypt, Kenya, Rhodesia, South Africa, Singapore, Hong Kong, Malaya, Australia and New Zealand were inspected and assessed by him. Sir Roger Hollis, MI5's Director

General during 1956–65, was also an inveterate traveller, who made a priority of security in the colonies as much as in the British Isles.[18]

The primary threat to British internal security in 1946–7 came not from the Soviet Union but from a radicalized Middle Eastern minority. In July 1946 the Zionist group Irgun, led by Menachem Begin, a future prime minister of Israel and co-winner of the Nobel peace prize, arranged for six men disguised as Arabs to carry milk-churns containing 500 pounds of explosives into La Régence, the basement restaurant of the King David Hotel in Jerusalem. The secretariat of the British mandatory authority for Palestine as well as the MI5 and SIS stations were housed immediately above La Régence. The explosives were a combination of gelignite and TNT designed by the Irgun's bomb expert, Isser Nathanson @ Gideon, later a physicist at the Hebrew University of Jerusalem. The detonated churns killed ninety-one people. A photograph from the scene shows a typewriter atop some rubble with severed fingers still resting on the keys. A day after the blast a corporal heard a faint voice from deep in the rubble. He knelt and shouted, 'Is that a wog down there?' A dying man who had kept his humour called back, 'Yes, a wog named Thompson, Assistant Secretary.'[19]

The terror campaign was then taken to the capitals of Europe. In August 1946 Sillitoe briefed Attlee that he and all his Cabinet were targets of Zionist terrorist cells operating in London. In October two suitcases left by the Irgun wrecked the British embassy in Rome, where Francesco Constantini @ DUNCAN had stolen pre-war secrets for Moscow. British military headquarters in Vienna were bombed. In March 1947 the British Colonial Club, used by servicemen and students from the West Indies, off St Martin's Lane in London, was bombed. In April Betty Knouth @ Gilberte Lazarus walked into the Colonial Office, which shared the same block in Whitehall as the Foreign Office, and asked a guard for a moment's respite from the cold outside. She then went to a basement lavatory, where she left twenty-four sticks of dynamite wrapped in newspapers. The timer on the bomb broke, but if the device had exploded it would have caused carnage on the scale of the King David massacre. Knouth, who had received the dynamite from a Frenchman who smuggled it into England inside his prosthetic leg, subsequently opened a nightclub in Beersheba.

In June 1947 twenty-one lethal packages containing letter-bombs were posted from Italy to politicians in London. Sir Stafford Cripps was saved by a secretary who put the fizzing packet in a bucket of water. The shadow Foreign Secretary, Anthony Eden, carried a letter-bomb in his briefcase all day, thinking that it was a boring circular that he could wait to read in the evening. A death threat was issued against Hugh Trevor-Roper for his qualified magnanimity about Germans in *The Last Days of Hitler*. Yaacov Eliav, who ran the Colonial Office plot, planned to contaminate London's water supplies with cholera cultures procured from Zionist sympathizers in the Pasteur Institute in Paris. Attlee's decision to withdraw from the Palestine mandate and to pass responsibility to the United Nations averted the execution of this attack.

Sillitoe, Liddell and their senior staff were too busy with crisis inter-ventions to refresh old training procedures or revitalize organizational management. Observation rather than new initiatives was the order of the day. MI5 watchers followed Soviet officials through London streets, surreptitious photographs were taken, old files were reread, and reams of transcripts of bugged telephone calls were translated by elderly émigrés. Surveillance of suspects in secret installations and blacklisting were forbidden by the Attlee government until 1948, when the commu-nists seized power in Czechoslovakia, fomented unrest in Italy and France and blockaded Berlin. Then the numbers of watchers were increased, but they were inexperienced, and their reports of plodding about London had limited value.

The United States had extended a massive loan, with onerous condi-tions attached, to save Attlee's Britain from economic ruin. This enabled the Labour government to introduce the welfare state, to persist in its global pretensions and to embark on its misguided nationalization of coal-mines, railways, civil aviation, road haulage, canals, electricity and gas supplies, the Bank of England, Cable and Wireless and steel manu-facturing. Washington's money did more than pay for deleterious socialism. 'The American loan opened the way to a silent infiltration of American influence into almost every walk of British public life,' E. H. Carr noted in 1948. It became obligatory for anyone appointed to an important official post, whether civilian or military, to be accept-able to their US counterparts. 'To be known as anti-American is a bar to promotion to a responsible position in any walk of life.'[20]

By an agreement of 1947, SIS and MI5 sent liaison officers to work in the Washington embassy. A London liaison office for the FBI and CIA was opened at 71 Grosvenor Street above a shop selling beds and mattresses. Every morning SIS delivered summary reports and analyses to Grosvenor Street, and received a deciphered message from Washington containing equivalent material. The 'scrambler' telephone at Grosvenor Street was linked to MI5's headquarters, Leconfield House in nearby Curzon Street, and to SIS's Broadway Buildings.

Attlee wrote in March 1947 to Inverchapel of the feeling that the Special Relationship was one-sided, and that Britain was being used by Washington as 'a mere breakwater between the United States and Russia'. Three months later, in June, the FO's Sir Oliver Harvey speculated that if required 'to choose between Communist Russia and Capitalist America the Western Europeans might hesitate, for Western Europe has now quite outlived capitalism and free enterprise in the United States sense, which is but 19th century Liberalism. The Western democracies, including Great Britain, now stand for progressive Socialism and controlled economy.' Mass opinion in Britain was 'mildly Left', Harvey judged. 'Some may have doubts about Socialist planning, but all have greater doubt, if not complete disbelief, in the United States system, with its total lack of plan, its primitive labour laws and tariffs and above all its congressional government.' Harvey warned that if Americans pressed unregulated capitalism too hard on Europe and Britain, they would lose influence on the corporatist-minded continent.[21]

Anglo-American attitudes

Mass opinion in the United States was not veering towards Europe's regulated capitalism. Instead it was being whipped up against Red enemies in the nation's midst. Extensive investigations of Elizabeth Bentley's denunciations began in 1945–6, but made limited headway in obtaining evidence of espionage that could be used in court to obtain convictions. Bentley and Whittaker Chambers might name their former associates, but their assertions were a long way from clinching incrimination. When evaluating allegations of espionage cover-ups by the London government, and accompanying complaints that traitors were not brought to trial, one must compare the record of MI5 with that of the FBI. Bringing spies to book was tricky on both sides of the Atlantic.

When interviewed by the FBI, Gregory Silvermaster @ PAL @

ROBERT, Helen Silvermaster @ DORA, William Ullmann @ POLO @ PILOT, Mary Price @ DIR, Ishbel and Duncan Lee, and Peter Rhodes (all of whom had been named by Bentley) stalled rather than cracked. An FBI lawyer who analysed the evidence collected as of January 1947 concluded: 'What we know to be true in this case is a far cry from what we are in a position to prove beyond a reasonable doubt.' A Grand Jury, which heard forty-seven witnesses between June 1947 and April 1948, failed to indict Lee for treason or perjury. To protect the FBI from accusations of incompetence, Hoover determined to give Bentley's material to HUAC. He did this against the advice of Milton ('Mickey') Ladd, head of the Bureau's Domestic Intelligence Division: 'I doubt whether it could be handled without them playing a great deal of politics, and resulting in its being grief for everybody involved.'[22]

On 30 July 1948 Bentley, who had sunk to a secretarial job with the Pacific Molasses Company of New York, testified to legislators who were more interested in embarrassing President Truman than in eliciting her full story. In terms that might have been used by Cairncross or Nunn May, she declared that her sources were 'a bunch of misguided idealists' who felt that the Russians were America's allies, believed 'that Russia was bearing the brunt of the war' and resented the fact that Washington was not sharing with Moscow all the information and material support with which it provided London. 'They felt it was their duty, actually, to get this stuff to Russia, because she was hard-pressed and weakening.' Bentley called Browder and his CPUSA associates 'cheap little men pulled on strings from Moscow'.[23]

In December 1948, as the VENONA decrypts accumulated and Chambers and Bentley testified to HUAC, the FBI interviewed Laurence ('Larry') Duggan, an official of the State Department in 1930–44, at his suburban home. Duggan was an optimist, an altruist and a constructive idealist who believed in taking action on his own responsibility and knew that he was more intelligent than most people. In a cocksure mood, with the encouragement of his wife Helen Boyd, he had started supplying official secrets to Soviet Russia in 1936. The couple were just two of the 'bonanza of anti-fascist romantics' who started working at this time for the NKVD. He nearly broke off contact in dismay at the Moscow purges of 1937, but continued to supply material until he received a semi-official State Department warning after Chambers, in September 1939, named him as a Soviet source. Despite believing that

FBI investigators were like 'boys lost in a forest', Duggan insisted that the risks were too high for his spy work to continue. The NKVD forcefully renewed contact during 1942, and pressed him to divulge further official secrets at a time when State Department security officials were also giving him renewed trouble. He solved this double bind by leaving the State Department in July 1944 to become diplomatic adviser to the United Nations Relief and Rehabilitation Administration. On 11 December 1948, under FBI questioning, he denied espionage, looked uneasy and cut short the interview. Four days later, by coincidence, he was telephoned by a Soviet operative codenamed SAUSHKIN seeking to convince him to resume work for Moscow. Duggan must have felt beset on both sides. During the early evening of 20 December, he fell to his death from the window of his sixteenth-floor Manhattan office. It is likely that he jumped, conceivable that he fell in a weird accident while trying to put on a snow-boot, but some prefer to think that he was pushed.[24]

Hearing of Duggan's death, Karl Mundt, a Republican congressman from South Dakota who was acting head of HUAC (its chairman being under indictment for fraud), rushed into action. A few years earlier the Foreign Office had received a character sketch of Mundt from the Washington embassy. 'An ignorant man, gifted with a somewhat slow intelligence, but sincere and constantly baffled by problems largely outside his mental scope,' Isaiah Berlin had reported. 'His appetite for facts is, unfortunately, much greater than his ability to grasp and evaluate them. (Until quite recently, he was under the impression that Canada "paid tribute" to Britain!)' Mundt rushed to convene a press conference before midnight. Flanked by another HUAC member, Richard Nixon, he revealed Isaac Don Levine's testimony that Duggan's name had been among those given in 1939 by Chambers as a member of the communist apparatus within the State Department. Mundt regaled journalists with loose hearsay, and made a cheap wisecrack that the identity of other State Department communists would be disclosed when they jumped from high windows. The *Washington Post, New York Times, Christian Science Monitor* and radio broadcasters criticized Mundt for publicizing unverified hearsay. Eleanor Roosevelt writing in a New York newspaper on Christmas Eve denounced Mundt for an 'irresponsible, cruel' publicity stunt perpetrated 'without real proof in his hands'.[25]

In a memorial volume to Duggan published in 1949, the Under Secretary of State Sumner Welles referred to Mundt and Nixon as 'fanatical or unscrupulous slanderers'. He honoured Duggan 'as one of the very first to instill an element of social conscience into United States foreign policy'. He deplored 'the wave of hysteria that had swept over the United States as the result of the tactics employed by the Soviet Union since the end of the Second World War'. From London, Harold Laski praised Duggan as 'one of the most upright and devoted people I had ever known, with a mind vividly conscious of public obligation'. A memorial to 'dear Larry Duggan' was read at the annual general meeting of his New York club, the Century, after his death: 'a sensitive, sincere and good man, loyal in all his bones to our country and to the principles of democracy in which live the hope of the world. Those of us who wept at his passing, wept of course from deep sorrow, but we also wept from cold anger.'[26]

These were patrician voices, speaking on behalf of justice, unimpaired legal process and the objective testing of truth by calm and honest rationalists rather than by fanatics and opportunists. They saw the value in resisting snap populist judgements engineered by crooked editors and self-seeking politicians. 'Personally, I am going to believe in Alger Hiss' integrity until he is proved guilty,' Eleanor Roosevelt told a New York newspaper after Duggan's death. 'I know only too well how circumstantial evidence can be built up, and it is my conviction that the word of a man who for many years has had a good record of service to his government should not be too quickly disbelieved.' She feared that as a result of the prevalent search for spies, 'the great gift of curiosity, which makes men safe and secure in a really democratic society, is going to be shortly discredited among us. There would be no development, there would be no people who understood what had built the Communist movement in this country, unless there were among us some few who were interested enough to find out how other young people think, and, in addition, to study opposing regimes.' American liberty, continued Eleanor Roosevelt, rested on the principle that citizens must be presumed innocent until proven guilty. 'Insinuations should not be made unless proof is in hand. A man's job may be jeopardized and his whole life may be wrecked before his innocence is proved.'[27]

Eleanor Roosevelt's principles seemed right for her generation: not least her belief in trusting people until they were proven to have betrayed their colleagues or their country. Her grounding and values were similar to those of Whitehall during the 1940s. The dominant mood was against political tests of officials or policing of their ideas. Responsible men detested the mentality of the lynch-mob. They disliked alarmism, bans, black-lists, snoopers and scapegoating. The possibilities for malicious denunciations were shown in 1949 when a postal intercept revealed an application to join the CPGB from the zoologist Solly Zuckerman, afterwards Lord Zuckerman, an authority on the effects of bomb-blast, who was in line to become the government's Chief Scientific Adviser. Investigations suggested that the application was a mischievous forgery by a jealous, hard-drinking colleague of Zuckerman's named Lancelot Hogben. Generally there were qualms at building an apparatus of suspicion and risk-assessment. Mistrust was known to be politically contaminating. Trust was one of the elements that distinguished liberal democracies from despotisms. All this was understandable in the state of security knowledge in the 1940s, although men's confidence in their colleagues let Alger Hiss, Harry Dexter White, Duncan Lee and the Cambridge ring of five leach official secrets from their different spheres.[28]

Roger Hollis of MI5 noted in 1945 that the civil service had hitherto 'shown an extreme and understandable reluctance to have its intake vetted by us'. One reason for this is implied in a passage – perhaps intended to disarm interrogators, but also sincere – in Klaus Fuchs's confession of 1950. 'Since coming to Harwell, I have met English people of all kinds,' Fuchs said. 'I have come to see in many of them a deep-rooted firmness which enables them to lead a decent way of life. I do not know where this springs from, and I don't think they do, but it is there.' Trust and self-respect were obvious and integral parts of this deep-rooted firmness: the notion of vetting seemed to poison those springs.[29]

The resistance to positive vetting was helped by the dismay among intelligent people at the stupidity both of the headline-stealing witch-hunts in America and of the most vocal English proponent of 'loyalty tests', Sir Waldron Smithers, Tory MP for a constituency of commuters and market gardeners in Kent. Smithers was a lugubrious, boneheaded stockbroker with a love of figuring in newspaper headlines, and neither a man of marked ability nor one insensitive to the consoling effect of alcohol. Once in the Commons he challenged the Attlee government to prove the sincerity of its anti-communism by prosecuting Hewlett

Johnson, the 'Red Dean' of Canterbury. He further demanded that, if and when Johnson was convicted, the government should ensure that his hanging was public. Smithers's advocacy of a 'Civil Service Purge', 'Security Tests for Ministers' and the institution of a House of Commons Select Committee on Un-British Activities aroused contemptuous distaste.[30]

Gouzenko's revelations and the Nunn May trial reinforced MI5's growing suspicions that the greatest threat to official secrets did not lie with open CPGB members. On the contrary, the NKVD (and its successor agencies) discouraged its major informants from joining the party, partly to avert mistrust of their political views among their colleagues, but also to foster an exciting air of conspiracy which would accentuate their self-importance and make them amenable to performing special tasks. In May 1947, as a delayed response to the Canadian analysis and under pressure from Washington, Attlee formed a secret Cabinet committee on subversion known as GEN-183. Its members included Cabinet ministers, high officials and Sillitoe. Committee papers reporting their deliberations always referred to 'subversives', not 'communists', although communists were their target. In March 1948 Attlee announced procedures to purge government departments of both communists and fascists with access to sensitive material. This was to be done by negative vetting: checking Security Service card-indexes against the names of those with access to official secrets and confidential material.

MI5 was unhappy with these developments. It would have preferred to keep the current informal vetting system, while making it more systematically targeted; it was appalled by the extra workload. It feared that a purge based on negative vetting would complicate or spoil its interaction with secret sources within the CPGB: it worried about its effect on such a case as Graham Pollard's. By 1948 Pollard was a senior official at the Board of Trade, where he specialized in reorganizing the machinery of government, dismantling wartime controls and revising tariff regulations. He was known to many people as a former member of the CPGB; but no MI5 index-card will have existed to explain that he had joined the party at the prompting of Maxwell Knight and had been an invaluable long-term informant on the CPGB for MI5. Liddell and other senior Security Service officers resented the way that Labour ministers, who had instigated the extension of the vetting system, deflected blame from their supporters and civil libertarians by implying that the impetus for the civil service 'purge' came from MI5. Liddell remonstrated with Attlee as Prime Minister and Herbert Morrison as Deputy Prime Minister, protesting that the Security Service was being used as a scapegoat for political decisions: MI5 appeared to the press and the public as 'a bunch of irresponsible autocrats' and 'black reactionaries' who were engrossing powers 'to victimise unfortunate Civil Servants'.[31]

GEN-183 (and Whitehall generally) dismissed Smithers and his kind. The US Federal Employee Loyalty Program, whereby the FBI made far from perfunctory, although not necessarily efficient, security checks on some four million government staff, was thought disproportionate. The Westminster parliament resisted pressure from Washington to emulate HUAC tactics. The political settlement that had been enshrined in the fulfilment of parliamentary democracy in 1929 rested on trust and attempted inclusiveness, not paranoia and exclusion; but the detonation at Semipalatinsk in August and Mao Tse-tung's victory in September 1949 increased tensions and risks immeasurably.

In April 1950, after the Fuchs case had discredited reliance on negative vetting, Attlee appointed a committee on positive vetting (PV) which comprised John Winnifrith of the Treasury, Roger Hollis of MI5 and Graham Mitchell, who had joined MI5 at Philby's recommendation soon after the war. Hard on the appointment of Winnifrith's committee came the unexpected outbreak of war in Korea in June 1950, and alarms about Harwell security breaches involving the nuclear scientists Bruno Pontecorvo and Boris Davison. In November the Cabinet committee on subversion recommended the adoption of PV. The Attlee government's precarious parliamentary position meant that it did not wish to alienate its more liberty-loving supporters by a public announcement of the new policy. The practice of PV was implemented – slowly and secretly – during the early months of 1951 before receiving massive propulsion from the defection of Burgess and Maclean. A much expanded PV programme was agreed in principle in July 1951 in the hope of appeasing American anger at the Fuchs, Burgess and Maclean cases; but the Attlee government felt too weak to implement this decision, which was not announced until January 1952, when a more confident Tory government, under Churchill, was in power. MI5 and GEN-183 preferred to move suspects in a discreet way to less delicate posts rather than expel them. In the Home Civil Service between 1948 and 1982, twenty-five officials were dismissed for security reasons, twenty-five resigned, eighty-three were shifted to non-sensitive work and thirty-three were reinstated after further investigation. None was publicly named. In the USA over a comparable period, 9,500 federal civil servants had been purged, another 15,000 resigned while under investigation as communists, and all were named.

A seizure in Istanbul

In the same month – September 1945 – that Gouzenko defected in Ottawa and supplied the chilling disclosures that began the Cold War, a Soviet official called Konstantin Volkov, who had recently been transferred from NKGB headquarters in Moscow to a post under consular cover in Istanbul, made contact with John Reed, acting Head of Chancery at the British embassy in Ankara, which transplanted itself during the summer heat to the Istanbul consulate. Reed, who had been a Cambridge undergraduate at the same time as Philby, entered the Foreign Office in the same batch as Maclean, and served in Bucharest, Washington and Moscow. As a Russian-speaker, he interpreted at secret meetings with Volkov, who sought political asylum for himself and his wife, as well as £27,500, and offered in return to tell all that he knew of NKGB headquarters and overseas networks, and to name Soviet agents in the Middle East and elsewhere.

Volkov, who provided a selection of his wares for transmission to London, insisted that a handwritten account of his offer must be sent as a personal letter, by diplomatic bag, to a senior official at the Foreign Office. Nothing could be trusted to radio signals or typists, because two Soviet agents were embedded in the Foreign Office, while another headed a counter-espionage organization in London. Reed reported Volkov's walk-in to Sir Maurice Peterson, an ambassador who regretted secret service activities. 'No one's going to turn my embassy into a nest of spies,' Peterson told Reed: 'if you must go ahead with this business, do it through London.' Peterson's decision excluded the SIS head of station from involvement. Peterson reluctantly forwarded the Volkov papers to the Foreign Office, signing a covering letter to Sir Orme Sargent, who was also chary of intelligence work, rather than to Cadogan, who was responsible for FO liaison with SIS.[32]

'Moley' Sargent referred the Volkov material to Menzies, who passed the dossier to Philby and told him to handle the Russian's defection and debriefing. Within hours of reading Volkov's offer, on 20 September 1945, Philby breached tradecraft by hastening to see Burgess at the Foreign Office and pressing on him an envelope with instructions to give it to his Soviet handler that same evening. Burgess did so. The envelope contained Philby's news of Volkov's intended defection. The Radio Security Service, which monitored London–Moscow wireless traffic, noticed that on 20 September there was a sharp rise in wireless traffic from the Soviet embassy in London to the Moscow headquarters of the NKGB. The length of such traffic could be measured in milliseconds, and it was found that there had been an identical upsurge of wireless traffic between Moscow and Istanbul of precisely the same duration as the London–Moscow messages. The London–Moscow messages had been repeated to Istanbul. It was a dead certainty that the Volkov leak had happened in London.

Philby knew that once SIS in London accepted Volkov's offer and agreed to exfiltrate him, the operation would be run by the SIS station head in Istanbul. He therefore tarried for three weeks before flying to Turkey. During that interval Volkov vanished: strapped to a stretcher and swaddled in facial bandages to hide his identity, he was hustled aboard a Soviet military aircraft and flown to his doom. When Reed asked why someone from SIS had not come from London sooner, Philby gave the irritating reply, 'Sorry, old man, it would have interfered with leave arrangements.' Philby broke his return journey to London in Rome, where he visited James Angleton, the US chief of counter-espionage there. He recounted the story of Volkov's disappearance with a show of candour intended to disarm any later suspicions about the case. SIS surmised that an unguarded telephone call between British officials in Istanbul and Ankara might have betrayed Volkov's intentions. Philby was not blamed for his inexplicable dilatoriness – except by Reed, who retired from the Diplomatic Service in 1948, after marrying the daughter of the director of the *champ de courses* at Nice. When interviewed in 1967, by then High Sheriff-designate of Shropshire, Reed said that he had long before settled in his mind 'that either Philby was criminally incompetent or he was a Soviet agent'.[33]

In October 1946, following the Gouzenko and Volkov cases, Sargent circularized heads of missions in Ankara, Tehran, Nanking, Athens,

Rome, Berne, Paris, eastern Europe and South America with instructions on the handling of renegade members of Soviet missions seeking asylum in exchange for betraying secrets. Such defectors 'have reached a state of depression in which their life and work seemed intolerable, and the possibility of escape, at whatever cost, became the only prospect of relief'. Perhaps mindful of the mistrust with which Agabekov, Bessedovsky and Krivitsky had been treated before 1939, Sargent stressed that recent defectors had been 'sincere': in one case (Gouzenko was not named) the material yielded had been of utmost value. Without specifying Volkov's abduction, Sargent warned that Soviet missions were 'ready to act with speed and ruthlessness as soon as any propensity to disloyalty is observed'. Overtures from a renegade must be handled speedily, 'as even a short delay will almost certainly involve the removal of the official concerned and the loss of the information which he is able to provide'. Contrary to Peterson's decision in Volkov's case, the SIS representative attached to the mission should be involved. Reports should be sent by telegram marked 'personal for Sir O. Sargent to be deciphered by Private Secretary'. Lessons had been learnt from the Volkov bungle, although Philby's basic betrayal was unknown.[34]

Around the time of the Volkov episode, Philby sought a personal interview with Vivian, gave a sanitized account of his marriage to Litzi Friedmann, described his involvement with Aileen Furse and explained the bastardy of their three children. Vivian approved his intention of seeking a divorce, asked MI5 to check on Friedmann and was soon told that she was a suspected Soviet agent, living in East Berlin with Georg Honigmann, who was known as a definite Soviet agent. About a year later, on 25 September 1946, at Chelsea Registry Office, Philby married Furse: their two witnesses were Tomás Harris and a businesswoman named Flora Solomon (who had introduced the couple, knew that Philby had been working under Moscow's orders in the 1930s, but did not denounce him until 1962). In the year of his second marriage, Philby was transferred from Soviet counter-espionage to be head of the SIS station in Istanbul, with the rank of First Secretary. Given the tension between Turkey and the USSR, this was an understandable posting for a former head of Section IX. It also accorded with a new SIS policy of encouraging officers to circulate between both Service sections and overseas postings so as to prevent narrow specialization.

Disquiet over the Friedmann–Honigmann connection may also have contributed to the decision to shift him from headquarters.

Blunt left MI5 soon after the war to become Surveyor of the King's Pictures (in charge of the royal art collection) and in 1947 was installed as Director of the Courtauld Institute of Art in Portman Square. He acted as an intermediary between Burgess and Philby for a period after the Volkov affair, and again from June to October 1947, and took photographs for them. Philby had no regular controller while he was head of station in Turkey, and used Burgess to communicate with Moscow. SIS developed a strategy of training exiled Armenians and Georgians from outlying districts on the edge of the Russian empire, and sending them over the frontier as spies or fomenters of unrest. Philby was involved in organizing several such ventures, including Operation CLIMBER of 1948, whereby two men were sent over the border from north-eastern Turkey into a mountainous district of Georgia with orders to infiltrate local communities. They vanished immediately: it is beyond doubt that Philby had betrayed them.

The true index of a man's character, Cyril Connolly used to say, was the state of his wife's health. During Philby's posting in Istanbul, his wife began to harm herself. On one occasion she claimed to have been ambushed by a robber who hit her on the head with a rock. Her wounds, whether self-inflicted or the work of a real assailant, were certainly reinfected by her during her hospitalization. For the remaining ten years of her life, she was a recurrent self-injurer. The consequent domestic strain aggravated Philby's drinking, which had intensified after the Volkov crisis.

Philby's trail also began to be stalked by Maurice Oldfield. Like many effective intelligence officers, Oldfield had a historian's mentality. He had envisaged a career as an academic historian before his mentor at Manchester University, Sir Lewis Namier, got him involved in intelligence work in European university cities during 1937–8. Installed from 1947 as deputy head of R5 counter-espionage section at SIS headquarters, Oldfield began studying a case that had disturbed him when he was in wartime Cairo with Security Intelligence Middle East (SIME). It concerned Alexander Rado, a cartographer who had joined the Hungarian communist party in 1918 and been recruited by the GRU while a refugee in Geneva in 1935. Rado was short, stout and foxy as well as fluent in six languages. Under the anagrammatic codename of

DORA, and with the cover of a map business called Geopress, he ran a network spying on Germany. Alexander Foote was its radio operator. After the network had been compromised, Rado and Foote underwent separate tribulations before converging on Paris in November 1944. On 6 January 1945 they were both passengers on the first Soviet aircraft to leave the French capital since its liberation. Rado had been lured on to the flight with the promise of $80,000 and a guarantee that he would be permitted to return to Paris after a fortnight. But when the aircraft halted in Cairo, Rado fled from his hotel after an alarming night-time talk with Foote. He appealed to the British authorities for asylum and was interviewed by Oldfield, who saw that his defection could yield useful material.

When the Russians requested Rado's extradition (as he was Hungarian it could not be called repatriation), his Cairo internment camp sought guidance from SIS. An unsigned reply came promptly from Broadway: 'Release the subject to Egyptian police for onward transit to Moscow.' When Rado heard this news, he cut his throat and resisted the guards who saved his life: 'Let me die! Let me die!' he cried. Meanwhile Foote, who was undergoing harsh debriefing in Moscow, was assured that Rado would be returned to Moscow by force. 'Very soon there will be no place in the world where it will be possible to hide from the Centre,' Foote was told. Oldfield and the camp commandant repeatedly queried the instructions from London, but always received the unsigned response: 'Release the subject to Egyptian police for onward transit to Moscow.' As late as June 1945 Cairo received an inquiry from London: 'Please telegraph present position RADO case. Is he still in hands of Egyptian police?' Rado was returned to Moscow, where he was condemned without trial to ten years in Siberia for negligence in allowing his cipher to be taken by the Swiss police. He went, said Foote, 'to the living death of an NKVD [NKGB] labour camp'. (Foote was sent to the Soviet sector of Berlin under the alias of Granatov with instructions to establish a new identity as a German called Albert Müller; but conditions were so objectionable that in 1947 he defected to the British sector.)[35]

In rescrutinizing Rado's case and while evaluating leakages about Erich Vermehren, an Abwehr agent in Istanbul who had defected in 1944, Oldfield noted that Philby had been a desk officer on duty at SIS at the time of the anonymous telegrams dismissing Rado and that

Vermehren had been lodged in London in the flat of Philby's mother. He recalled the Volkov debacle. By 1949, at the latest, Oldfield suspected Philby, although he had not a jot of evidence to support a denunciation. Indeed, it would have wrecked his career to attack a man with a golden reputation who was in line to become Chief of SIS. 'Nowadays it is not what you do that counts,' as Evelyn Waugh wrote in *Scott-King's Modern Europe* (1947), 'but who informs against you.'[36]

CHAPTER 15

The Alcoholic Panic

Philby's dry martinis

Shortly before the Semipalatinsk detonation in August 1949, it was decided to move Philby from Istanbul to Washington, where he was to serve as SIS representative and chief contact with the Central Intelligence Agency (CIA) which had replaced OSS two years earlier. This was such a plum job that Philby did not consult Moscow before accepting it. Soon he was meeting the agency's officers on a daily basis and betraying its activities to Moscow. His reports on the agency's personnel, developing ideas, tactical plans and preconceptions enabled Moscow's deception planners to incorporate existing CIA assumptions into their misdirections and thus make misinformation more credible.

In September, shortly before Philby's departure to Washington, the CIA informed SIS that recent VENONA decryption had established that there had been intelligence leakages from the British embassy in Washington in 1944–5. Maurice Oldfield knew the advantages of fostering insecurity in a suspect against whom nothing could be proved, and was expert in turning agents after catching them. Just before Philby embarked for the United States, Oldfield gave him a counter-espionage briefing in which he described the VENONA material. This information, as Philby later admitted, worried him. It was obvious to him that the leaks which had been revealed by VENONA and were under active investigation had emanated from Maclean, whom he had recommended for communist recruitment as a penetration agent fifteen years earlier. Once he reached Washington, he saw each new batch of VENONA decrypts and reported to Moscow the encroaching threat to the security of the ring of five.

The progressive VENONA advances put pressure on Philby, Maclean

and Burgess, and to a lesser extent Blunt, that sent them lurching into
alcoholic debauches that were intended to quieten their anxiety and
fear. (Cairncross was the exception in this, as in much else.) After the
identification of Klaus Fuchs as an atomic spy in 1949, there was an
intensifying effort to identify a Soviet spy who had been active in the
British embassy in Washington under the codename HOMER and
whom Philby knew to be Maclean. Philby learnt in June 1950 that
VENONA decrypts mentioned an important spy – codenamed
STANLEY – working for the Russians in 1945: he knew that he was
STANLEY. More than ever, during 1949–51, Burgess spoke and behaved
with destructive alcoholic bravado. Maclean tried to quell conscience
and worry by drinking himself insensate. Philby had heavy binges.
Blunt drank steadily, especially when under stress, although his behaviour and efficiency were unimpaired. This was the impalpable
background to Philby's posting in Washington.

The mounting menace did not disempower his ability to do harm.
His baneful duplicity reached as far as the Adriatic. In November 1945
the governments in London, Moscow and Washington had recognized
Enver Hoxha's communist government of the most impoverished and
vulnerable of Balkan states, Albania. As Hoxha owed his position to
the support provided by Britain in the closing stages of the war, it
seemed irrational to deny recognition to his regime. Four years later,
however, London and Washington were keen to shake the communist
hold on Albania. Joint operations were therefore devised in 1949 with
the aims of inciting insurgency against Hoxha's regime, of detaching
Albania from Moscow's orbit and of helping the CIA and SIS to bond
by running a joint project. The idea was to recruit exiled Albanians,
who were marooned in displaced-persons camps in Italy, Greece and
Turkey, and train them in Malta and later Heidelberg to act as infiltration agents to provoke local uprisings. A joint Anglo-American group,
the Special Policy Committee, was formed in Washington with oversight
of the enterprise; but divergences between the approaches of Washington
and London were soon evident. The Americans spent freely, prepared
intricate organizational charts and made formal presentations to large
planning meetings as if they were launching a foreign sales drive for a
mass-market consumer product. They seldom used the word 'Albania'
or considered local conditions and susceptibilities. Menzies at SIS was
unenthusiastic about the Albanian scheme, but agreed to participate

as a way of gratifying ex-SOE 'stinks and bangs people' who knew the country from earlier operations. One participant recalled a planning session at SIS headquarters which remained desultory until someone said, 'I say, why don't we get old Henry up here? He knows about this.' A day or two later 'old Henry' arrived from Sussex, and when the challenge was put to him, agreed with the right touch of self-deprecation to meet it. 'This will wreak havoc with the garden,' he said. 'Just getting it into trim.'[1]

The FO representative on the Special Policy Committee was a dashing young veteran of SOE operations in Greece, Lord Jellicoe, while SIS was represented by Philby. 'Kim was the one who made all the operational decisions,' Jellicoe recalled. 'He was intelligent, professional and hard-working. How on earth he found time to do a job for the Russians, I just don't know.' Philby exercised the secret ruthlessness that he had first learnt in Vienna in 1934 was essential to achieve the dictatorship of the proletariat. The numbers, movements, instructions and timings of the guerrilla landings were all betrayed by him. The twenty-four men in the first British contingent went ashore at night, in small groups, along the southern Albanian coast and were ambushed by Albanian troops when they went inland: four of the raiders were killed, while the others escaped to Greece. The Americans' infiltration agents, dropped by parachute in northern Albania, were caught by waiting security police, who either put them before a firing-squad or subjected them to show-trials that were broadcast by Radio Tirana.[2]

Philby, in his later public account written in Moscow, exaggerated the importance of his betrayal as a way of denigrating the Anglo-American authorities. The poverty of the Albanian peasantry, rather than his treachery or indiscretions from ex-King Zog of Albania's entourage, was the chief cause of failure. Very poor people are sharp risk-assessors and disinclined to risk losing what little they possess. In remote districts of Albania, the impoverished peasantry would not jeopardize their lives and property, or endanger their neighbours by provoking reprisal raids, without definite proof that the men inciting them were supported by the wealth and might of the USA rather than optimistic freelances or worst of all Hoxha agents trying to entrap them. As the US was committed to 'plausible deniability', this proof could not be given.[3]

Washington ran on dry martinis at this time. Philby and Angleton of the CIA's Office of Special Operations had a weekly liaison lunch either at Harvey's Seafood House or at the Army and Navy Club. They had cocktails before lunch, wine with the food and brandy afterwards. Philby had a strong head for alcohol, and lured Angleton into shattering and calamitous indiscretions as they sat boozing. Philby kept a clear enough head to report what he heard to Moscow. Philby is described by Angleton's biographer as 'a product of the privileged old-boy system, one of the foundations of the self-protecting world of the British upper-class'. Angleton succumbed to Philby's 'upper-class plausibility', it is said, 'as did nearly everyone else in the Washington and London intelligence communities'. This is to miss all the points. Philby duped his fellow spooks because he was infallibly and unostentatiously efficient: he seemed to do his duties exceptionally well; his plausibility derived from his super-competence; it had nothing to do with upper-class manners, for Philby was a representative of the middle classes, disavowed the old school tie, refused to look spruce in or out of the office, despised church-going, was a militant atheist and was known to have lived with the mother of his children for years before marrying her.[4]

Philby was involved in settling the terms of CIA–SIS cooperation in the event of the Atlantic powers going to war with Russia. He helped Soviet deception planners by reporting CIA responses to the misdirection that he helped to fashion. All the time he seemed to his SIS chiefs to be an excellent officer. He had no enemies to obstruct him. He never showed impatience or disrespect towards slower but senior minds. His successive responsibilities had given him a wide understanding of SIS's varied branches, and equipped him well to take command of it. Few people noticed that he was drinking too much, or knew of his grievous marital troubles with a wife who felt rejected and contrived physical injuries to gain his attention. Maurice Oldfield had kept his doubts to himself. John Reed had resigned from the Diplomatic Service in 1948, and was engaged in forestry in Shropshire. In the summer of 1950 Menzies and his designated successor 'Sinbad' Sinclair agreed that they must fix the SIS succession so as to exclude the appointment of an unsympathetic or blundering outsider, as had happened with Sillitoe at MI5. Menzies's apprehensions were well judged, because the government indeed forced an unwelcome outsider, Dick White of MI5, on SIS when Sinclair was replaced in 1956 well before his sixtieth birthday. In the succession plan envisaged by Menzies and Sinclair, James ('Jack')

Easton was the front runner. Easton was a former air commodore who had succeeded General Marshall-Cornwall as Assistant Chief of SIS in 1945. His assumed air of fumbling haziness masked a shrewd, subtle and decisive mind which Philby, at least, reckoned hard to fool. Philby was identified as a conscientious and effective officer who should be groomed to follow in the Sinclair–Easton sequence.

Menzies and Sinclair explained their plan to the Foreign Office, which had oversight of SIS. Reilly, as the Office's liaison with SIS, was asked to interview and assess Philby. 'I just did not like the smell,' as he later told William Waldegrave (both men were Fellows of All Souls). After his near-exposure by Volkov, Philby had become a heavier social drinker: the VENONA threat had him swilling more booze than ever. Yet it was not only that Philby's suffused and bleary face convinced Reilly that he was a drunkard. In other ways he made a poor impression on the FO's intelligence expert. 'There was something about the whole man which made me think that . . . he had gone completely to pieces,' recalled Reilly. 'The impression was overwhelming. I had never experienced anything like it in my life.' The FO vetoed the Philby succession plan ostensibly on the grounds of his alcoholism.[5]

Although SIS officers later shuddered to think that – without Reilly's veto – Philby might have become 'C', his friend Tim Milne disagreed that the higher Philby rose in the Service, the greater his value to the Russians in misdirecting its actions to serve Soviet interests. Milne thought that Philby as Chief of SIS would have lost close contact with detail. He would have known the broad lines but not the operational details of current or future operations, because he would always be working through and relying on subordinates. His actions would be accountable to Whitehall committees, to the Prime Minister and to Cabinet ministers. It would have been impossible for him to take zigzag journeys by bus, tube trains and taxi to rendezvous. To signal the need for an emergency meeting, he could not amble through Kew and chuck a copy of Men Only into Charles Moody's front garden. Nor could he – without observation – make chalk marks on walls or lamp-posts under cover of stooping to tie a shoelace or halting to light a cigarette. Moreover, how could Moscow act on information from such a highly placed source without betraying him? The only advantage for Moscow in having Philby as 'C' would have been if the communists took power in Britain or western Europe.

Burgess's *dégringolade*

In December 1946 Burgess was appointed personal assistant to the Minister of State at the Foreign Office, Hector McNeil. He thus became an established member of the Diplomatic Service: it should be emphasized that he was not absorbed into the permanent government machinery through the influence of his family, fellow Etonians, sexual partners, members of the Reform or mandarin officialdom; straightforward political influence, exerted by a Labour MP, who was the son of a journeyman shipwright, did it. The Service's Personnel Department refused to admit him into the senior branch A, but kept him in the secondary branch B. McNeil had been a journalist on Beaverbrook's Scottish newspapers before his election as a Labour MP in a by-election of 1941. His recent promotion to be Minister of State was in the place of his former mentor Francis Noel-Baker, who bored the Cabinet (''E talks too much, this chap', said Ernie Bevin) and infuriated Cadogan, who thought him a 'silly baby'. McNeil had earlier proven himself by going to Athens during a constitutional crisis: 'he found himself landed in a position', wrote the British Ambassador, 'which would have been perplexing and discouraging even to the most hardened and experienced. He was in a strange land amongst very strange people at a very strange time. His quick grasp of essentials, his initiative and resourcefulness saved the situation.' McNeil, it was said, 'worshipped the ground Bevin trod'. His generous spirit, respect for justice and trenchant vocabulary were exemplified by an incident at a session of the United Nations. When Vyshinsky made a vitriolic attack on Churchill, McNeil replied with unstinting praise of the Conservative leader: 'it was not in his nature to keep silent when Sir Winston was traduced', commented the *Manchester Guardian*, 'and by a Russian, too. It was handsome and British.'[6]

Liddell thought Burgess unsuitable for posting in the Minister of State's private office, and Footman had misgivings; but the appointment proceeded. Burgess imagined himself on his way to high-altitude influence, for he predicted that McNeil would be the next Prime Minister but two. Like Cairncross when he had been Hankey's private secretary, Burgess saw policy memoranda, telegrams, Cabinet papers and private correspondence with ambassadors. He monitored telephone calls and visitors. At night he took away documents in his briefcase, either surreptitiously or with Office consent, on the implausible pretext that he would work on them at home. In time, Burgess's alcoholism, seediness, disruptions and indiscretion determined McNeil to transfer him to the Office's new Information Research Department (IRD).

This propaganda unit had originated with a memorandum of April 1946 circulated by Christopher Warner, who was then in charge of the Foreign Office's Northern and Southern departments, and entitled 'The Soviet campaign against this country'. Recent speeches by Stalin and other Soviet leaders signalled 'the return to the pure doctrine of Marx-Lenin-Stalinism', 'the glorification of Communism as the inevitable religion of the future' and 'the revival of the bogey of external danger to the Soviet Union', Warner cautioned. 'We should be very unwise not to take the Russians at their word, just as we should have been wise to take *Mein Kampf* at its face value.' In the eleven months since the collapse of Nazi Germany, Russia had been 'despoiling foreign countries in her sphere' – in eastern Europe, the Balkans and the communist zone of Germany – 'harnessing them to the Soviet system, and at the same time posing as their only benefactors'. Communism must be treated, Warner argued, 'not merely as a political creed, but as a religious dogma and faith which can inspire such fanaticism and self-sacrifice as we associate with the early Christians and the rise of Islam, and which in the minds of believers transcends all lesser loyalties to family, class or even country'. He urged the need to attack and expose the myths which the Soviets were generating to justify their actions: 'the myth of the encirclement of Russia by the capitalist powers, the myth that a new Germany is to be built up for use against Russia, the myth that Russia alone gives disinterested support to subject races against their continued enslavement and exploitation by the colonial and capitalist powers'. Warner's close arguments resulted in the formation of the Information Research Department, headed by a Labour MP, Christopher Mayhew, who had previously been an outstanding administrator in SOE and had in 1935 visited Russia in a travelling party including Blunt, Michael Straight, Charles Fletcher-Cooke, Charles Rycroft and Michael Young. Mayhew's new outfit was charged with providing factual briefings about communism to overseas embassies and legations. McNeil tried to stow Burgess in the hold of the IRD, but Burgess proved an unstable weight during a trial period of employment, and Mayhew would not confirm his appointment. He would have been invaluable to Moscow in the IRD if only he had controlled his behaviour.[7]

In November 1948 Burgess – a counterfeit coin in the circulating currency of the Foreign Office – was slotted into the Far Eastern Department. He told his Soviet handler that he intended to provide bigger bundles than hitherto, and asked to be given a suitcase for this purpose. Dennis Proctor, who had known him since Cambridge days and had proposed him for membership of the Reform Club, had watched his operations in pre-war Pall Mall and wartime Whitehall with amused toleration: 'he had a profound love of intrigue, of being in the know and of dabbling in cloak-and-dagger projects'. But after 1945 Burgess grew 'more and more intolerable with drink . . . drugs and general degeneration', Proctor later told MI5: 'his conduct was so disreputable' that their meetings 'became fewer and less welcome'. Yet Burgess remained efficient for Moscow's purposes: on 7 December 1949, for example, he gave 168 documents, totalling 660 pages, to his Soviet handler Yuri Modin.[8]

Burgess's former sexual partners, including Harold Nicolson and Micky Burn, were dismayed by his messy appearance, diminished charm, intellectual enfeeblement and reckless impulses. Burn had been captured during the Commando raid on Saint Nazaire in 1942, and then incarcerated in Colditz. One night, back in post-war London, he saw Burgess looking conspicuous in a camelhair coat, cruising the 'meat-rack' under the archways of the County Insurance office at Piccadilly Circus. It was notorious that police agents provocateurs entrapped men there, so Burn accosted his friend, saying, 'Don't be such a fool.' Burgess let Burn lead him away: they went to the Reform Club for triple sherbets. By then Burn was a foreign correspondent of *The Times*, roaming in Austria, Hungary and Yugoslavia (Victor Rothschild's insinuation that he had been a Nazi sympathizer was nonsense). In 1947 he married a remarkable divorcee named Mary Booker, who was twice his age. When Burgess visited the newly married couple, he suddenly told Burn, 'I want to speak to you alone,' took him into a corridor, tried to kiss him and importuned him to resume their affair. 'You don't understand, I'm married,' Burn protested, at which Burgess snapped back, 'Don't be so pompous.' Burgess then said, as a way to keep some control over the man who had spurned him, that if ever Burn wanted a room for sexual assignations, he could use one in

Burgess's flat in Old Bond Street. 'I remember thinking', Burn later said, 'that if I ever did, and I did now and then, it would not be anywhere of his. I had ceased to trust him.'⁹

Blunt continued to collect titbits from friendly conversation with ex-colleagues at MI5. He was able, for example, to warn Moscow in March 1948 that MI5 had increased its surveillance of Soviet officials in London: a microphone had been inserted into the Military Attaché's telephone; other handsets were bugged. Some MI5 officers were more unbending and impermeable than others. 'Dick White is too correct in his manner, and will never gossip on matters connected with work like Guy Liddell,' Blunt reported. 'Hollis is also correct and almost hostile. John Marriott sometimes talks, but he isn't overfond of me.' In fact Hollis had the distinction of being the only MI5 officer to show suspicion of Blunt, whom he disliked. He teased him in 1945 by calling him ELLI, the codename of a Soviet spy revealed by Gouzenko and only many years later identified as Blunt's sub-agent Leo Long.¹⁰

Cairncross returned to the Treasury a month after the end of the war. Moscow severed contact with him after Gouzenko's defection. Under the codename KAREL he resumed passing documents in July 1948. He was in a department authorizing expenditure on research in atomic weapons, guided missiles, microbiology and chemical and underwater warfare. His job gave him legitimate reasons to collect research data from aviation, radar, submarine detection, signals intelligence and eavesdropping. His utility for Moscow increased in 1950 with the development of NATO, the outbreak of the Korean war and increased expenditure on armaments and personnel.

In 1949 Burgess and his mother went for winter sun in Gibraltar and Tangier. He carried letters of introduction from David Footman and from a more recent figure in his life, Robin Maugham. The latter was a decorated young army officer who had saved the lives of a score of soldiers trapped in burning tanks, and joked that a head wound sustained in North Africa qualified him for a job in intelligence. He was already an eminent travel-writer and was beginning to publish interesting novels: Somerset Maugham was his uncle. He was candid about his sexual preference for men, which led him to live abroad, and to become a barfly who drifted into alcoholism because of the sexual environment in which he lived. As a member of the House of Lords, Maugham was later a pioneer campaigner against human trafficking.

These were the sort of well-placed men whose goodwill Burgess exploited.

In Gibraltar Burgess went on a prolonged binge, irritated officials by importuning them to cash his travellers' cheques, boasted of his friendships with Footman, Philby and Dick White, and committed fearful indiscretions. Kenneth Mills of MI5, who had broken a journey from Tanganyika in Gibraltar, and Teddy Dunlop, the local SIS head of station, were outraged by his misconduct and complained to London. In Tangier Burgess continued to pester British officials, gatecrashed drinks parties and luncheons, made himself unpopular by stealing the boyfriend of a popular expatriate and talked airily of secret services. Burgess's prosecution under the Official Secrets Act was considered for his loose talk about SIS, but this idea was dropped, perhaps because it was feared that his defence in court would reveal his earlier work for MI5 and SIS. After Burgess's return to London, Footman warned him that Vivian of SIS was gunning for him, but in fact Vivian gave his qualified approval in a report to the FO's Security Department in January 1950. 'His knowledge both of MI5 and S.I.S., where he has numerous friends, is, though perfectly legitimate, quite extensive,' Vivian told Carey-Foster. 'He has influential friends on high levels in the Foreign Office. His unnatural proclivities are, I understand, well known, but are not regarded as having caused any anxiety in official matters, and, as far as his friends are concerned, are more than balanced by his quick and alert mind, his other obvious intellectual qualities and a certain charm of conversation.'[11]

On 4 June 1950 Burgess had a long talk in a suburban London park with Nikolai Korovin. He conveyed his worries, and those of Philby and Blunt, about the VENONA decryptions. They had an idea that Litzi Friedmann, Philby's ex-wife, was involved with Fuchs, and that he might compromise her under interrogation. It would be easy to trace her connections to her Viennese contemporary Edith Tudor-Hart, who had instigated Philby's recruitment in 1934 and handled the Cambridge ring's material when Gorsky was absent in Moscow for ten months of 1940. Korovin's attempts to allay the Cambridge men's fears were unsuccessful.

In August 1950 Burgess was confirmed as Second Secretary at the Washington embassy. As he was known to want to remain in London, it may be that the Personnel Department wished to provoke him into resignation. The Minister in Washington, Derick Hoyer Millar (Lord Inchyra), the Head of Chancery, Bernard Burrows, and the Security Officer all knew his bad reputation and resisted his appointment, but never suspected him of being a spy. Before his departure Burgess likened himself at a London party to Sir Roger Casement, the Irish nationalist who had been hanged for treason in 1916. He was so haphazard that when he vacated his room in the Office to leave for Washington, he emptied the entire contents of his desk into a briefcase without any sorting. In the Washington embassy he was foisted on Denis Greenhill, afterwards Lord Greenhill of Harrow.[12]

Greenhill found Burgess unprepossessing. 'Deep nicotine stains on his fingers and a cigarette drooping from his lips,' Greenhill recalled. 'Ash dropped everywhere. I took an instant dislike, and made up my mind that he would play no part in my official duties. It took little longer to find out that he was a drunken name-dropper, and totally useless to me in my work.' He was open about his homosexuality, 'but', said Greenhill, 'at that time there was no link in official minds with security'. Greenhill refused when Burgess asked to see classified telegrams that were not his concern, because he expected that his boastful subordinate would show off by talking about their contents; but had no inkling that he might be a spy.[13]

Philby was doubtless aghast at Burgess's posting to Washington. Burgess invited himself to stay in Philby's family home at 4110 Nebraska Avenue. It was against procedure for two Soviet spies to share accommodation in a foreign city, but Philby probably accepted Burgess as a house-guest in the hope of restraining his alcoholic delinquency and reckless chatter. It was a grievous mistake, which soon compromised his standing with Washington officials and visitors. When Lord Cairns, a listener at GCHQ (as GC&CS had become after the war), visited Washington to consult with the National Security Agency, the Philbys invited him to dinner: Cairns was 'very annoyed' by Burgess quizzing him in 'the most searching and unpleasant manner . . . about GCHQ stuff'. In January 1951 Philby and his wife held a dinner party for James Angleton of the CIA, the FBI's Robert Lamphere, the ex-FBI man William King Harvey, who was now a CIA man investigating Soviet spy rings, and Wilfrid Mann, the liaison with the CIA on atomic matters. The four guests came with their wives. Sir Robert Mackenzie, an SIS baronet in the Washington embassy, was also present. Late in the evening, when everyone was rat-arsed, Burgess blundered in drunk. Libby Harvey knew of his talents as a caricaturist and asked him to draw a sketch of her. He retaliated with an insulting cartoon which showed her dress hitched up to her waist and her chin resembling a warship's jutting underwater battering-ram. Her husband tried to punch Burgess, Aileen Philby wept in mortification, and the party ended in furious disarray. This fiasco occurred three days after Fuchs had confessed to Skardon, and a few hours before Alger Hiss was convicted of perjury. The simmering heat was moving closer to boiling point.[14]

Maclean's breakdowns

As to Maclean, his Washington colleague Nicholas Henderson believed that his manner changed, and he began drinking more heavily, after Alger Hiss had been unmasked in the midsummer of 1948. Patrick Reilly thought that the Hiss case had intensified anxieties which began a slow escalation after the conviction of Nunn May. Another Washington colleague, Jock Balfour, dated the deterioration to the months after Maclean had been posted to Cairo as counsellor and Head of Chancery in September 1948. For a man whose hero was Wilfrid Scawen Blunt, the anti-imperialist campaigner against the British military occupation of Egypt, the post was an ideological strain. For the past seventy years no British diplomatic mission had wielded more brute imperial force than the British embassy in Cairo. The Egyptian proconsuls Lord Cromer, Lord Allenby, Lord Lloyd and Lord Killearn were great figures of imperial history. During the recent war, Cairo had been the military capital of the British Empire with up to 120,000 British and Dominion troops garrisoned there at one time. Chic visitors from Mayfair, imposing grandees from Belgravia and racy members of the Chelsea set enlivened the most densely populated city in Africa, with its degraded *fellahin* and epidemic disease. Ten years earlier it had been visited by Burgess's friends W. H. Auden and Christopher Isherwood. 'Cairo,' they wrote, 'that immense and sinister Woolworth's, where everything is for sale – love, lottery tickets, clothes hangers, honor, justice, indecent postcards, bootlaces, disease – as much and as cheap as you like, till the buyer goes mad with boredom and guilt.'[15]

The Ambassador-Plenipotentiary at Cairo, Sir Ronald Campbell, had been Minister at the Washington embassy during Maclean's time there, and expected well of him. Maclean's unease in Cairo was obvious, though. His embassy colleague Lees Mayall saw that the discrepancies between the standards of living of Europeans and of Egyptians distressed him. Maclean expressed 'great sympathy for the working man and indeed for any under-dog', and supported the Jewish side in the Palestine troubles. Mayall regarded him at the time (not unsympathetically) as 'a Left-wing intellectual' and only with hindsight realized that he was 'exactly the sort of person who could be a communist'. Maclean was bold in excusing traitors. He shocked the wife of a Dutch diplomat in Cairo by saying at dinner: 'If Alger Hiss felt as he did about communism, he was quite right to betray his country.'[16]

In Cairo, Maclean drank deep. He broke Mayall's leg in a drunken fracas. It has been repeatedly said that when drunk, and to alleviate stress, Maclean started having rough, perfunctory sex with male pick-ups. His wife Melinda is the one person who definitely stated this: she did so to another diplomatic wife, Kathleen Cecil, whose husband had succeeded Patrick Reilly as the FO's liaison with SIS; she uttered the confidence only after her husband's disappearance, during a period when she was giving misdirection so that his tracks could be lost and his activities misunderstood. There is not a jot of evidence of this in the official archives or from contemporary eyewitness accounts in other sources. A former military attaché in Cairo is said to have reported that Maclean was 'carousing openly with promiscuous young men he picked up while cruising through town'; but these oft-repeated, unsubstantiated tales are suspect. The interest lies in the purpose of these sexual anecdotes. The intention of the nuclear scientist Wilfrid Mann's story, that he found Burgess and Philby in bed together in Washington, drinking champagne, at ten in the morning, was to distract attention from the fact that Mann had also supplied Moscow with classified material, although he was later turned and run against the Russians.[17]

In December 1949 Maclean included a note asking to be relieved of Soviet intelligence work in a bundle of classified documents which he gave to the Soviet *rezident* in Cairo. This individual did not read this plea before forwarding it to Moscow Centre, where it was also unread. It was noticed by his controllers only in April 1950, when Maclean sent a renewed request for release from his obligation to spy for them. Meanwhile his disintegration continued apace. Robin Hooper, newly installed as head of the FO's Personnel Department, minuted on

8 January 1950 that at a recent drunken party, during a 'rather silly alcoholic argument, Donald Maclean stung to fury by some very silly remarks of [an] ex-Communist, said "of course you know I'm a party member – have been for years!"' Hooper commented, in a minute that went to MI5, 'Obviously this is not to be taken seriously, but it is evidence that D. is still hitting it up and that he is apt to be irresponsible in his cups.'[18]

The disaffected communist was the painter and novelist Humphrey Slater, who had fought with the International Brigades in Spain, but turned against communism and took up the bottle instead. On a later occasion, in November 1950, Slater and his second wife Moyra met Maclean by chance in a Soho street, had dinner with him, went to the Gargoyle Club afterwards and ended in a drinking session in Mark Culme-Seymour's flat: as Maclean got drunker, he spouted 'the Party line' with diminishing inhibition. Humphrey Slater told several people at the Office that he thought Maclean was a party member. His novel about a Soviet spy, *The Conspirator* (published in 1948 by Sir Ronald Campbell's cousin John Lehmann), was made into a film starring Elizabeth Taylor. In the novel Slater depicted the quandary of an intelligent young woman who has been told by her favourite cousin, under a solemn vow of secrecy, that the cousin's husband is spying for Soviet Russia. She feels that she should warn the authorities of his treason: 'but then, she thought, one of the most disgustingly unpleasant things about communist regimes was the obligation they put upon people to betray their dissident friends or relatives'. She decides that if she were to break her promise of secrecy, 'she would be behaving in exactly the same inhuman way as any contemptible informer of the Gestapo or the Soviet secret police. Decent human relations were impossible, she thought, unless individual friends could trust one another and promises given as seriously as she had given hers could be expected to be honestly kept.' Moyra Slater, talking at a drinks party with John Lehmann's sister Rosamond Lehmann in 1950, agreed that Maclean had been a communist for years, was probably a spy and was so indiscreet that the security services must already know. The two women decided that it was not their job to denounce Maclean to the authorities explicitly, but decided to gossip widely so as to ensure that his communist allegiance was known to everybody, including the authorities.[19]

Maclean's position deteriorated after his friend Philip Toynbee, a repentant ex-member of CPGB, arrived in Cairo in April 1950. They went on a succession of violent binges: Maclean struck his wife, hit an effete English aristocrat called Edward Gathorne-Hardy, threw glasses against walls and raved. As Toynbee wrote from Cairo on 9 May to Julia Mount, who fifteen years earlier had gone skiing with Maclean, 'Poor Donald has engaged in a wild crescendo of drunken, self-destructive, plain destructive episodes.' Melinda Maclean blamed Toynbee's influence but, as he protested, 'actually, I've done my honest best to control him'. A diplomatic incident had occurred when the two English drunks 'smashed to pieces the flat of the American ambassador's secretary (God knows why)'.[20]

It does not need God to give explanations. Maclean had twice besought Moscow to be released from his spying commitment, but had received no response. As a result of smashing the American's apartment, he was returned post-haste to England for detoxification, which accomplished his object of escaping the immediate stress of his double life in Cairo. It is further possible that, in attacking American property, he hoped that the outcry raised by US officials would be such that Moscow would decide that his cover had been impaired and would therefore release him, as he had twice requested, from the intolerable strain of his Cairo duplicity. But the US protest was unexpectedly muted, and Sir Ronald Campbell was determined not to ruin the career of a member of his staff. Campbell had a record of feeling responsible for people in difficulty. When Yugoslavia had been overrun by the Italians in 1941, the Belgrade legation staff, under his unruffled leadership, made a cross-country trek to Kotor, where Campbell's persuasive tenacity enabled 100 vulnerable people, not only the legation staff, to leave Yugoslavia and escape Italian clutches. His protective empathy during Maclean's disgrace may have been influenced by another matter. Campbell was a bachelor who was accompanied in his overseas postings by a devoted manservant whom Campbell had in the past defended from prurient criticisms. Like anyone of sense and experience, he disliked people's private habits being held against them if they were good at their work.

Edwin Chapman-Andrews of the Cairo embassy reported Maclean's breakdown to the FO's Personnel Department on 10 May 1950 in gendered language: 'He is a very good man, fundamentally, and well worth making a very special effort for.' Melinda Maclean was blamed for her husband's collapse. 'She is a vivacious and no doubt attractive person and the whole build-up of her character is so definitely American and can never become anything else that I think there has been some maladjustment.' Through her hard-drinking compatriots on the US embassy staff her husband had fallen in with 'a fast set keen on sitting up late at night or all night and assing about a bit'. This had brought him to an alcoholic breakdown. 'He has become thoroughly ashamed and disgusted with himself,' reported Chapman-Andrews. 'What he needs is quietness and green fields and a little good companionship.' He recommended Maclean's transfer to the Foreign Office, 'where his wife would at least have a chance to become a little anglicized'.[21]

For Campbell and Chapman-Andrews, as for any able diplomat, tolerance was a hallmark of civilization. 'The British upper-class code encourages variation,' reported Crane Brinton of OSS, 'once a few essentials are complied with.' When in 1948 it had been reported to Sir Alexander Cadogan, head of the British delegation at the United Nations General Assembly in Paris, that Burgess had provoked outrage by attending a meeting of the Balkan sub-committee drunk with cosmetics on his face, Cadogan replied 'that the Foreign Office traditionally tolerated innocent eccentricity'.[22]

In London Maclean lived first in the Mascot Hotel, off Baker Street, and later moved to 41 York Street, Marylebone. He declined to go for treatment by the Office's Harley Street physician and insisted on becoming the patient of Dr Erna Rosenbaum in Wimpole Street. Her consulting-rooms were a few minutes' walk from the Mascot Hotel and York Street. It is unclear how he knew of Rosenbaum after seven years abroad in Washington and Cairo; unclear, too, why the Office agreed to his insistence. Middleton and Carey-Foster became suspicious of Rosenbaum after her patient absconded, but MI5 could find no material against her. Any chance of success for her treatment was dashed when, in August 1950, Mark Culme-Seymour (who had introduced Maclean to Melinda Marling and had been best man at their wedding) arranged for him to become a member of the Gargoyle Club at 69 Dean Street, Soho. The Gargoyle was open to members only, and thus circumvented the regulations, first introduced under the Defence of the Realm Act during the First World War, which limited the hours when licensed premises could serve the public with alcohol from noon to 2.40 p.m. and 6.30 to 9.30 p.m.

Maclean had for sixteen years kept a cordon sanitaire between him and the other two Cambridge spies recruited in 1934, but this was breached by joining the Gargoyle. Philby had been a pre-war regular, and Burgess a habitué since 1943. Maclean, who kept control of himself at the Office, could discard all inhibitions at the Gargoyle, which was blasé about rowdy scenes. He got hugely drunk night after night, accosting other Gargoyle habitués with admissions such as 'I work for Uncle Joe' or 'I'm the Hiss of England, you know that!' One night, seeing Goronwy Rees in the Gargoyle, he snarled, 'I know all about you, you bastard: you used to be one of us, but you ratted!' Culme-Seymour considered whether to report Maclean's startling avowals to the Foreign Office, but decided that as they were being broadcast to all and sundry at the Gargoyle, the authorities would already have heard. It was not only in the Gargoyle that Maclean had furious outbursts. Over lunch in the Travellers with his colleague Sir Anthony Rumbold he became so vehement in denouncing American policy in Korea that Rumbold had to work hard to avoid a dining-room scene.[23]

Maclean resumed work in November 1950 as head of the FO's American Department. He commuted from the family home, a modern house called Beacon Shaw, on the edge of the village of Tatsfield, near Sevenoaks in Kent. During the intensified freeze in the Cold War, which followed China's intervention in the Korean war in October, he continued to purvey valuable material for Moscow. In December that year Attlee hastened to Washington to discourage President Truman from deploying atomic bombs in Korea. A copy of the Prime Minister's report to the Cabinet on his visit to Washington lay among the secret papers found in Maclean's steel filing cabinet at the Office after his disappearance. Another copy will have gone to Moscow. Neither Burgess nor Maclean had access to operational decisions, however: the claim of General Douglas MacArthur, commander-in-chief of US forces in the Far East and of UN forces in Korea, that his strategy had been foiled by their forewarning of the enemy is a self-serving absurdity. Cyril Connolly, who encountered Maclean at the Gargoyle in this period, thought his appearance was frightening. 'His hands would tremble, his face was usually a vivid yellow, and he looked as if he had spent the night sitting up in a tunnel.' One evening a man got into a taxi outside a nightclub only to find Maclean asleep in the back with a rug and furious at being woken: he had hired the cab for the night as his bedroom. 'Though he remained detached and amiable as ever, it was clear to us that he was miserable,' wrote Connolly. 'In conversation a kind of shutter would fall as if he had returned to some basic and incommunicable anxiety.'[24]

On 18 March 1951 the *Observer* published Toynbee's article 'Alger Hiss and his Friends' in which he criticized liberals who wanted to whitewash Hiss by blackguarding Whittaker Chambers (he did not deign to mention Elizabeth Bentley). Correctly but unfashionably Toynbee called Chambers's conduct 'reasonable and decent', before declaring: 'It is now established beyond reasonable doubt that Alger Hiss had at one time divulged State Department secrets to the Communists. And this must surely have given them an unbreakable hold on him.' Talk of unbreakable holds upset Maclean, who had failed in Cairo to break free from Moscow's grip. He may have convinced himself that world peace depended upon preserving an even balance between the United States and the Soviet Union, which required him to supply Moscow with material on, for example, Anglo-American policy towards Korea; but most of all he felt semi-captive to the MGB, which held the means to compel him. A few nights later, blind-drunk in the Gargoyle, he chanced upon Toynbee. 'You are a Judas, and I am the English Alger Hiss,' he proclaimed before shoving Toynbee backwards into the band.[25]

The VENONA crisis

In March 1951 a new VENONA decrypt of a message to Moscow in 1944 stated that HOMER had visited New York to see his pregnant American wife. It was easily established that Maclean had done just this. He was put under close investigation by MI5, which gave him the codename CURZON. The Security Service advised the Foreign Office that in order to obtain a confession from Maclean, it was better to muster and collate evidence before interrogating him. The cryptographic evidence against him was conclusive, but could not be used in an open criminal trial or even in the questioning of him. MI5's aims were twofold: to extract the evidence for a prosecution from the sort of confessional debriefing that had cornered Nunn May and Fuchs; and also to collect information and understand the background far beyond Maclean's individual case. This could not be achieved hurriedly. Sillitoe was anxious to conciliate Hoover, who had been enraged by the Nunn May and Fuchs cases. He informed and consulted the FBI at every stage after HOMER had been identified as Maclean; but every message to Hoover crossed Philby's desk.

The Foreign Office did not expect the MI5 investigation, which was run by Arthur Martin, to last nearly three months. Special Branch and the MI5 watchers decided that it would be impossible to keep the isolated Tatsfield house under surveillance without being spotted. Maclean seems to have chosen the house with care: it stood on its own, back from the road; he could leave it in four different directions; any car waiting near the house for more than a few hours would be conspicuous. Watchers followed him in London only as far as the ticket barrier at Charing Cross station, but said that they lacked the resources to cover him beyond there. Carey-Foster once glimpsed him in Pall Mall, near the Travellers, with the watchers following too closely behind. Patrick Reilly, too, saw him returning to the Office after lunch, crossing from St James's Park to the Clive Steps, walking fast with his head down and looking disarrayed. The man following him was obvious. Maclean's face was ravaged by drink, Reilly recalled, yet his office work remained impeccable. In mid-April he lunched at the Travellers with Wayland Young, a young diplomat who was chafing at Office life and asked the older man in all innocence how to cope with frustration. Maclean may have thought that he was being tested, or enticed towards admissions, for his responses were stolid and cagey. His meetings with his Soviet control, Yuri Modin, will have been halted as soon as Philby's reports on HOMER reached Moscow or whenever Maclean spotted his watchers – whichever was sooner.

Every update from MI5 to the FBI crossed Philby's Washington desk. Hitherto he had used Burgess as his courier to the illegal *rezident* in New York, Valerii Makayev, but the threat to Maclean was so grave that Philby took the risk of meeting Makayev to give a face-to-face report. Of all the Cambridge spies, Maclean was held in the highest esteem by the Soviets: his reports were reliable and his loyalty seemed unimpeachable, despite his requests to be released from his onerous Cairo duties. They also understood that his nerves were too frail to withstand interrogation, and feared that he would reveal Philby's part in his recruitment.

There were many ways to forewarn Maclean in London, where he had an effective handler in the person of Modin. There was no need to involve Burgess in alerting Maclean to his looming danger of inter-rogation. But Burgess's situation in the United States rapidly became untenable. On 28 February he drove at headlong pace from Washington to Charleston and picked up a young black hitchhiker and gas-station loafer, James Turck, whose appearance may have suggested his exciting history. Turck had been arrested by police in Richmond, Virginia, under puritanical morality laws, for living with a married woman, was later sentenced to a year's probation for aggravated sexual assault and was suspected of petty theft. The FBI later interviewed him in an intimi-dating way, and got the responses that they wanted: Turck said that Burgess had made sexual overtures to him during the journey to Charleston and renewed his advances during the night that they spent in a motel. Probably Turck was not as averse to such advances on the right terms as he claimed to the FBI.

Burgess's car was stopped for excessive speeding three times within a few hours. He was obstreperous with policemen, claimed diplomatic immunity and was disgracefully provocative. In Charleston, where he was due to speak at a military academy, he was drunk and contentious. On 16 March, at a cocktail party given by Kermit Roosevelt of the CIA, he rowed with his host about the Korean war, and other guests had to intervene to stop a brawl. In early April, at the time when the atom spies Julius and Ethel Rosenberg were sentenced to death by electro-cution, Burgess went on holiday with his mother Eve Bassett to Charleston. On 18 April, after returning to Washington, Burgess was rebuked by the Ambassador, Sir Oliver Franks, for his motoring offences, for his rudeness at the military academy and for the Roosevelt scrim-mage. He was ordered to return in disgrace to England.

Burgess reached London on 7 May, and returned to his flat in Old Bond Street which he continued to share with Jack Hewit, the working-class former boyfriend of Christopher Isherwood. In the three weeks that followed he combined colossal alcohol intake with Nembutal (barbiturates) at night to sleep and Benzedrine (amphetamines) to revive his daytime mind. The Benzedrine will have rendered him prone to making ingenious, quasi-paranoid connections between incidents and people that were in truth unconnected. References to an Old Bond Street flat suggest Mayfair luxury, which was belied by the dirty brick-work, tired pointing and chipped and faded paint on the window-frames of the building. Burgess's roof-top rooms, with their poky, grimy dormer windows, were far from a penthouse. The downstairs premises were occupied by a textiles and garments merchant.

Burgess conferred with Blunt, and then visited Rees. He repented trusting the latter as a source on All Souls appeasers in 1938–9, and wanted to assess if Rees was likely to inform MI5 of what he knew of the activities of Burgess and Blunt for the NKVD. Next he lunched at the Royal Automobile Club with Maclean, whom he had not seen for years. Maclean had already spotted that he was being watched, had noticed that since 17 April files with high-security classification had been withheld from him, assumed that his mail and telephone communications were being intercepted and expected that there were bugging devices inside Beacon Shaw. Maclean was reluctant to defect, however, as his wife was scheduled for a Caesarean birth in mid-June. Perhaps as a fumbled misdirection to MI5, which did not hear of the incident until later, Burgess visited Victor Rothschild's sister Miriam and said that he wished to lease her expensive Mayfair flat. He consulted the Eton headmaster, Robert Birley, about a project to write a biography of the Victorian statesman Lord Salisbury, and discussed the same idea with Quentin Bell, whom he met at the Reform, and James Pope-Hennessy. He telephoned the poet Stephen Spender in the hope of reaching W. H. Auden, who was visiting London from New York. Tomás Harris's wife had barred Burgess from their house; but two or so days before his disappearance he was allowed a visit. When Harris asked after Philby, Burgess put his head in his hands, said, 'Don't speak to me of Kim – nobody could have been more wonderful to me,' and burst into tears.[26]

On 19 May he attended the Apostles' annual dinner in Cambridge, where the youngest guest was Peter Marris, who had read philosophy and psychology at Cambridge, served as a soldier in the British occupying forces in Japan shortly after the dropping of the nuclear bombs and then spent two years as a colonial district officer in Kenya: he resigned because he decided that sound administration was no substitute for self-government, and had been ashamed at his inaction when a policeman shot dead an unarmed schoolboy standing a yard from him. Marris represented a new generation, both hardened and compassionate, which felt moral disgust about colonial injustice and cruelty, but was averse to political theories that proclaimed their historical inevitability and excused the mass murders of Stalinism. Burgess pressed

Marris to accept a lift back to London, and then treated the ex-colonial district officer as if he was indistinguishable from the American drifter James Turck: he was so 'aggressive and insinuating' in the car that Marris asked to be let out when it reached Whitestone Pond atop Hampstead Heath.[27]

Accounts of the next few days by its chief protagonists are confusing: people later lied in self-defence, misremembered in wishful thinking, were too upset to be consistent, enjoyed a chance for malice or were inherently untrustworthy. Many of the details of this phase hold biographical but not general historical interest. The important points are these.

Andrew Boyle stated in 1979 that Herbert Morrison, Bevin's successor as Foreign Secretary, 'quashed the delaying tactics of his senior officials' and upheld MI5's proposal for an immediate interrogation of Maclean. This untruth is particularly objectionable, because it fosters the suspicion that diplomats were trying to protect a fellow member of the old-boy network. There was no advantage for the Foreign Office in delay: indeed, it was positively awkward to ensure that ultra-sensitive material did not go to the American Department where Maclean might see it. Some officials, notably the Deputy Under Secretary of State, Roger Makins, were impatient for a confrontation after months of insecurity. Strang, PUS, found the Security Service slow-moving, and in particular faulted its delay in interrogating Maclean once it was certain that he was a traitor. On 25 May Morrison was asked for authorization to interrogate Maclean on Monday 28 May and gave it. The interrogation was set for the Monday because, in accordance with the undertaking given to the FBI, Hoover had first to be told.[28]

Much about the running of agents and incriminating of spies is a matter of fine timing. 'Think of all this Burgess and Maclean stuff we're always reading about,' J. C. Masterman wrote in 1956. 'They were allowed to run on after suspicion had been aroused, and a fine mess everyone made of it. Of course if they'd not got away, but had been quietly picked up at a convenient moment, everyone would have said how efficient our security was and how skilfully it worked; but as things turned out it proved a blunder.'[29]

In the light of warnings from Philby in Washington, the MGB's man in London, Yuri Modin, urged both Blunt and Maclean to defect. Reared in a culture of torture, purges and executions, it was unthinkable for him that a traitor might take the risk of exposure and arrest: yet Blunt refused outright, while Maclean prevaricated because of his wife's difficult pregnancy. Finally a plan was concocted (possibly by Blunt) for Burgess to accompany Maclean on to a ship, the *Falaise*, which was leaving Southampton late on the Friday night of 25 May for a weekend pleasure cruise to French seaside towns. Maclean's name was on a border control checklist, and a Southampton passport officer telephoned MI5 in London to report his departure for France. SIS officers in western European capitals were immediately alerted, but the Sûreté in Paris was not informed, for fear of leakages to journalists: a well-founded fear, since the *Daily Express* bureau in Paris received a tip-off after the French counter-espionage service, known as the SDECE, became involved. At Saint Malo, after breakfast on Saturday morning, Burgess and Maclean went ashore, leaving their luggage behind, and fled to Berne, where they collected false passports. On Sunday 27 May they reached safety behind the Iron Curtain in Prague.

For an Eton and Cambridge man of his generation, Burgess was a poor letter-writer. His incoherent, rambling screeds, with their self-contradictions and diffuse irrelevancies, show that he seldom stopped to think before starting to write a sentence, never knew what he was going to say in it or how he would finish it. His pen skimmed across the paper in a spree of ink without thought of consequences or endings. One example is a letter to Liddell of February 1950 after his disgrace in Gibraltar and Tangier:

> my career appears ruined on present form. However I feel like Foch (my left retreats, my right ceded, my centre crumbles, *j'attaque*) and Churchill (Disaster? Unutterable. I feel 20 years younger) combined and am meditating a gigantic spring campaign, but don't yet know whether to launch it in the political stratosphere or the official heavy side layer. Or whether to resign, or not launch it at all. The whole balloon really is Robinson Vivian plus whoever is the Heath of your office. Sorry to waste time – tho' when the campaign opens I fear I'll waste more (but not yours).[30]

The thinking behind Burgess's jaunt on the *Falaise* seems equally confused. The MGB, via Modin, may have misled him into thinking that he would be free to return to England from Switzerland, but their intention was probably always to retain him. Although he was not yet suspected in London of treachery, he would certainly be interviewed, for he had been seen in London recently with Maclean, had previously lived with Philby, who was one of the few people indoctrinated into the HOMER investigation, and was therefore in a position to forewarn Maclean; and the trio had been contemporaries at Cambridge. Once Burgess came under scrutiny, he was too rackety to survive questions about his undeniable, inexplicable and incriminating associations.

One sure sign of the hectic events in London, after the Southampton passport officer's report, is that Guy Liddell's office diary went out of kilter. The entry for Sunday is entirely redacted, but misdated as if it was Monday. The Monday entry is dated for Tuesday. MI5 and SIS were working at full pelt to find Maclean. All the SIS officers in Berlin were summoned to their headquarters in the Olympic stadium on Saturday 26 May, given photographs and spent a sleepless weekend scrutinizing everyone passing the security checkpoints into the Soviet sector of the city. One of these officers, Anthony Cavendish, recalled being handed photographs of both Burgess and Maclean, although it is often stated that Burgess's disappearance was not realized until the Monday, 28 May.[31]

Certainly it was not until after the weekend of 26–27 May that William Manser, a trade attaché at the legation in Berne who knew Burgess by sight, was visited by 'the resident cloak-and-dagger man' in Berne. The SIS station head told him that Burgess and Maclean were 'defecting' and, when Manser showed that he didn't grasp the meaning of the word, half shouted in exasperation, 'They're going to Russia!' Manser was told to hurry to Ascona on the shores of Lake Maggiore, where intelligence reports suggested the absconders now were. 'Pick a fight,' ordered the SIS man. 'Get yourselves arrested. The Swiss police are *au fait*. Do anything!' Manser found these instructions hard to take seriously ('members of the Foreign Office', he mused, 'did not betray their country'), and asked: 'Do you want me to kill him?' The head of station stayed mute. Manser spent some days searching Ascona for Burgess: by then the fugitives were far away.[32]

When Burgess did not return on Sunday evening to Old Bond Street, a puzzled Hewit telephoned Blunt, who advised him not to worry. Hewit, against Blunt's advice, next telephoned Rees. Blunt and Footman were then contacted by Rees saying that he suspected that Burgess had debunked to Moscow. At about eleven on Monday morning Footman reported Burgess's absence to Liddell. On Monday afternoon, Melinda Maclean (having waited the weekend, as arranged) reported to Carey-Foster that her husband was missing. It seems that neither SIS nor MI5 had informed the Office of this fact which the security services had known all weekend. Carey-Foster and Reilly informed Strang, and were joined by Sillitoe and White from MI5. Blunt meanwhile visited Rees to try to persuade him to keep quiet. He also searched the Old Bond Street flat for incriminating material, but missed a guitar case containing, among other documents, letters from Blunt, a postcard from Philby and a bundle of Treasury documents which were identified by MI5's Evelyn McBarnet and Churchill's private secretary John ('Jock') Colville as prepared by John Cairncross. Liddell tried to contact Blunt during the day, but could reach him only in the evening. White flew to Paris to try to concert action: he and Liddell were dismayed by the way that the Sûreté and SDECE turned every particle of French intelligence work into ammunition for the crossfire in their skirmishing for primacy. MI5 officers began interviewing the men and women who they hoped had crucial evidence. Blunt was regularly consulted by Liddell. Tommy Harris, Goronwy Rees, Victor and Tess Rothschild and others were asked what they knew or could suggest. It is impossible to overstate how shocked and incredulous every official was.

The two defectors had months of arduous debriefing. In October 1951 they were granted Soviet citizenship, awarded hefty salaries and allotted spacious apartments in distant Kuibishev (this Stalinist substitution for the old place-name of Samara commemorated a communist engineer). As an industrial conurbation, full of munitions works and strategic factories, Kuibishev was a 'closed city' which no one could legally visit without authorization – still less could anyone stay overnight. Burgess and Maclean were thus, in effect, kept in a cordoned area. The inability to stay quiet, and the fidgety need to act, were two of Burgess's conspicuous failings. Maclean's sense of his own dignity depended upon showing his efficiency at work: inactivity and aimless time-filling were for him akin to suspended animation. Maclean briskly learnt Russian, and was given work teaching English to apparatchiks: Burgess, who never gained more than a rudimentary knowledge of key Russian words, prowled and drank and smoked. The two Englishmen's anonymity was safe in Kuibishev, standing on a bend of the River Volga, with its drab modern buildings rising from the surrounding plain like a cluster of stalagmites; but the lack of purpose made for burdensome days. They were not seen by westerners for more than five years: yet during their durance as non-persons in Kuibishev, they were never forgotten. The 'missing diplomats' were a pervasive cultural force in the 1950s, who had disappeared but never went away.[33]

PART THREE

Settling the Score

CHAPTER 16

The Missing Diplomats

'All agog about the two Missing Diplomats'

Lady Maclean tried to convince Skardon that her son had disappeared because he was dreading the arrival in England of his brash American mother-in-law. Nigel Burgess thought his brother had gone on a deliberately mystifying holiday so that he could pretend when he returned that he had been on a secret mission for Churchill. The story spread in White's that Burgess and Maclean had gone to France to bugger one another, that Burgess had murdered Maclean during a tiff and had dumped the corpse in a river. At All Souls the story was that the pair had absconded with an unnamed MP. Humphrey Slater suggested that the Russians feared that Maclean was backsliding from his creed and might denounce ex-comrades as Bentley and Chambers had done, and had exfiltrated him with the object of liquidation. David Footman convinced himself that Maclean was being blackmailed in *une affaire de moeurs* in Paris, that Burgess tried to help in extracting him from the imbroglio and that the extortionists had murdered them in the French capital. Many people suggested that in a quixotic gesture the two diplomats were 'trying to do a Hess' – making a unilateral peace mission to Russia comparable to the flight by Hitler's deputy to Scotland in 1941. Bob Stewart of the CPGB suggested that the missing diplomats were pretending to be hunted refugees so that they could reach Moscow and spy there for London. The chairman of the Wine Society, Edmund Penning-Rowsell, on whom MI5 kept a file and who was known as 'the Bollinger Bolshevist' because of his politics, told Nigel Burgess that the missing diplomats had been kidnapped by American agents for interrogation so as to give the State Department an edge over the Foreign Office in security matters. When Nigel Burgess demurred, Penning-

Rowsell shook his head sagely and said such things happened all the time. As late as August, T. S. Eliot believed what he read in the *News of the World*: 'the mystery of Maclean and Burgess, the missing diplomats, will soon be solved. The *dénouement* will be undramatic and quite unconnected with anything to do with Communism or the Iron Curtain.'[1]

MI5's apprehensions about the leakiness of the French police were confirmed on 6 June by the Paris office of the *Daily Express* receiving a telephone tip-off from a police source that two British diplomats had vanished. Next day Beaverbrook's newspaper broke the story on its front page. 'The news of their disappearance exploded with megaton impact in Whitehall,' one of its journalists later crowed. Over the next ten years Beaverbrook's nationalistic newspaper spent nearly £100,000 chasing 'missing diplomat' stories. Like its rivals, it offered bribes for catchy quotes or vivid stories that could be passed off as true. A young babysitter was offered £100 to purloin Maclean family photographs from Beacon Shaw. Jack Hewit was taken to Paris by the *Express* in a stunt to search for the missing diplomats, and was remunerated for making various sensational but useless remarks. The financial rewards were such that Hewit even forged an incriminating letter from the young diplomat Fred Warner to Burgess. Scores of people with connections to Burgess or Maclean were pestered by *Daily Express* reporters protesting 'we are only doing our job'. Its editor sent handsome young Don Seaman to Ischia to interview W. H. Auden, who had known Burgess in New York: Seaman (best known as a racetrack sprinter) was an inexperienced interviewer who garbled what he heard and reported that Burgess knew Nunn May (in fact it was Maclean who had been at Trinity Hall with the atomic spy). Journalists' cars blocked Rees's driveway so that he could not leave home; the doorbell and telephone rang without cease; his children were tempted with chocolates and half-crowns to make quotable remarks; one reporter tried to lure Margaret Rees into admissions with the disarming remark, 'It's all right to talk to me, Mrs Rees, I'm bisexual myself.'[2]

On 11 June Sillitoe flew to Washington, where he was to placate and update Hoover. The trip was meant to be secret, but the *Daily Express* published a photograph of Sillitoe emplaning – a security breach that prolonged American displeasure with MI5. Beaverbrook's hacks took the line that Burgess, like Maclean, came from a rich, privileged family and that accordingly the authorities were trying 'to paper over the scandal'. The *Daily Express* was proud that its tenacity in pursuing the missing diplomats, and in investigating their social sets, discomfited Whitehall and aroused official displeasure. The newspaper was so strenuous and noisy that for a few days MI5's Courtenay Young was able to pooh-pooh the rumours by saying 'the whole thing was an *Express* scare'.[3]

The animosity of Beaverbrook's newspapers was such that Sillitoe sought an off-the-record lunch, on 24 July, with E. J. ('Robbie') Robertson, editor-in-chief of the group, John Gordon, the harsh bigot who edited the *Sunday Express*, and Percy Elland, editor of the *Evening Standard*. Robertson had first come to Beaverbrook's attention as a Toronto hotel bellhop carrying the future press lord's suitcases. He continued to do his master's bidding, and was a master of po-faced humbug, as when he testified to the Royal Commission on the Press in 1948 that the walls of the *Daily Express* news-room were plastered with notices insisting to staff that accuracy was indispensable. 'We cannot look anywhere without seeing them,' he said, without adding that they were there as a reminder not to get caught in inaccuracies or inventions. Sillitoe complained that the Beaverbrook press had blackguarded the authorities for not preventing the defection to Russia of the Harwell atomic scientist Bruno Pontecorvo in September 1950, but denounced 'Star Chamber' tyranny when the same authorities withdrew the passport of Eric Burhop, a nuclear physicist who wanted to visit Moscow. 'Was their policy to pick up any old stick and beat the Government?' Sillitoe asked. Robertson, Gordon and Elland gave evasive replies. Sillitoe then objected to the onslaught on MI5, which he suspected was on orders from 'the Beaver'. Sillitoe reminded the three editors that these attacks 'did not come very well from that quarter, seeing that it was Beaverbrook who was raking the internment camps during the war and filling up our research with people of the type of FUCHS. Moreover, in doing so he was going directly against the advice of the Security authorities.'[4]

Beaverbrook's editors took revenge on Sillitoe for criticizing their boss. As a signal that they would damage him personally if he continued to censure the Beaver, the *Daily Express* soon splashed a rancorous story headlined, 'M.I.5 SILLITOE TAKES A (Burgess–Maclean) HOLIDAY'. It reported that the Director General and his seventeen-year-old son were staying at the Hôtel Cécil in the French seaside resort of La Baule. 'Sir Percy insists that he is on holiday, that all he is hunting is sunshine,' the newspaper reported with another disrespectful photograph. 'Sir Percy also insisted that he knew nothing new about the missing diplomats. The place to look for them, he said, was behind the Iron Curtain.' Sillitoe was travelling without a bodyguard, they added: 'the local police are a little peeved with Sir Percy', as they had not been forewarned of his arrival. Given the semi-Stalinist tradition of vindictive character attacks in the *Express* newspapers, it is understandable that the modernist Fleet Street building that housed their offices was nicknamed the Black Lubianka.[5]

The information reaching Whitehall from Washington, from European capitals, from Gargoyle habitués and from other social sources was too confused, disturbing and anomalous to be absorbed, ordered and publicly acknowledged. On the night that Beaverbrook's presses rolled with the first public reports of the missing diplomats there came the first fatality: Philip Jordan, Attlee's press secretary, died of a heart attack aged forty-eight. He was an exceptional man, educated at the Royal Naval College with the intention of becoming an officer, but had swerved into journalism after being hired as the *Chicago Tribune*'s tennis correspondent on the French Riviera. He was converted to militant socialism in 1927 when he saw the brutality of the Paris police in dealing with marchers protesting at the frying of the Italian-American anarchists Sacco and Vanzetti in the electric chair. He at once set up a first-aid station in the lobby of the Paris office of the *Daily Mail*. The *Mail*'s chief correspondent in Paris, who had just sent a telegram to the London paper declaring that the French capital was overrun by 'Asiatic Jews' making razor attacks on gendarmes, started yelling from a staircase about 'Bolsheviks' and kept shrieking 'bastards' at the wounded. 'I decided that I would never buy the *Mail* again,' recalled Jordan, 'and it is one of the few good resolutions that I have ever kept.'[6]

Jordan was intrepid, with superb connections across the world. With a beautiful Swedish wife (who had managed a beauty parlour on the Champs-Elysées) and a house overlooking the Regent's Park, and as someone who believed with a passion in 'fair deals for extremists', Jordan was the sort of man whom populists and conspiracy theorists like to denigrate. The facts that he had published a book entitled *Russian Glory* in 1942, that he had served as press secretary at the Washington embassy when Maclean was also working there, that like Maclean he was a member of the Travellers, that Francis Meynell the *Daily Herald* jewels-smuggler wrote his obituary tribute in *The Times*, and that the government did not grant a pension to his widow were adduced, after the publication in 1979 of Andrew Boyle's *The Climate of Treason*, as signs that he too was a suspected spy. Malcolm Muggeridge gained publicity in 1979 by claiming to Andrew Boyle that he had organized Jordan's Fleet Street memorial service and that Attlee had refused to attend. The truth is that Mr and Mrs Attlee headed the list of those attending the church.[7]

MI5's treatment of Melinda Maclean was gentler than Fleet Street's. When Skardon first interviewed her on 30 May, he found her calm and self-contained. Knowing that she was due for a Caesarean birth within a fortnight, he was solicitous in not adding to her stress. By contrast, the press showed no mercy in besieging Beacon Shaw. The driveway gates had to be padlocked and the curtains drawn so as to deter the journalists shouting boorish questions and the photographers snapping intrusive shots. In retrospect, there is no doubt that Melinda Maclean knew about her husband's secret work for Moscow before they married in 1940. She was aware of his continuing commitment in Washington, Cairo and the Office. She was complicit in his weekend dash for safety, understood what was planned with Burgess and delayed reporting that he was missing until he was far away. Her children were overheard making such remarks as 'My Daddy works to stop all wars.' Yet MI5 were considerate, attentive and even fatherly in protecting her. Skardon, who worked to keep the trust of all the Maclean family, determined to treat her account as credible until he had evidence that it was false. Ronnie Reed of MI5, who interviewed her with her mother on 10 August, regretted that she was still being vexed by 'newspaper hounds'. At the Foreign Office Patrick Reilly believed that 'the Maclean family have every motive to help us' if they could be protected from the 'hullaballoo' of press stunts. 'I wish something cd be done to stop Mrs Maclean from being molested,' minuted the Foreign Secretary, Herbert Morrison, after a *Daily Mirror* story in September. 'She is having a rough time.'[8]

For many people the strain after the *Daily Express* broke the story was intolerable. Inverchapel's death on 5 July was hastened by his devastation at the betrayal that had occurred in his Washington embassy.

June and July of 1951 passed in 'a nightmarish blur' for Reilly. One evening he read a minute in which Carey-Foster urged him to implement a recommendation over which he had been hesitating. 'This entirely justified reproach touched off a violent nerve storm,' Reilly recorded. 'Within seconds I demolished the solid wooden chair in which I had been sitting. I stood for a long time looking aghast at its ruins. Then I collected the debris together, put my papers away in my safe, and went off to bed, deeply shaken and ashamed.'[9]

In Whitehall there was extreme concern about Washington reactions to these defections, which came so soon after Fuchs's trial and Pontecorvo's defection. On 5 June Milo Talbot de Malahide forwarded to Dick White an emphatic message from the Washington Ambassador, Sir Oliver Franks, to the effect that 'our best chance of securing co-operation and secrecy on the American side is that we keep them continually informed and never let them feel that we are holding back from them. If this latter feeling ever grew up I should fear efforts of public self-defence by Hoover of the FBI who can be, and sometimes is, very unreasonable.' Whitehall did not dare to follow this good counsel. All the training and habits of the security services were against following a precept of Churchill's. 'In politics,' said the war leader, 'if you have something good to give, give a little at a time, but if you have something bad to get rid of, give it all together and brace the recipients to receive it.' MI5 and SIS did not dare to tell their American counterparts that Maclean had been under observation at the time of his disappearance. Whitehall press officers were told to keep their mouths clenched shut, which made journalists suspect that the missing diplomats were being protected by ex-colleagues, whereas it was confidential sources of top-grade information – such as VENONA – that were being protected. On 9 June a watch list including the names of Goronwy Rees, James Klugmann, Philip Toynbee and Anthony Blunt was issued to passport officers at ports. By the end of June Philby, Footman and Blunt were under intense investigations. Acquaintances of the missing men were methodically interviewed. None of these developments could be briefed off the record to any Fleet Street journalist.[10]

The veteran statesman Lord Simon interrupted work on his memoirs on 11 June to prepare a memorandum 'The Mystery of Maclean and Burgess'. As Foreign Secretary, and as a friend of his parents, he had welcomed Maclean into the Diplomatic Service in 1934. He suspected that the two diplomats had been kidnapped at Saint Malo by Soviet agents in order to arouse tensions and intensify mistrust between the United States and the United Kingdom. 'What better means', Simon asked, of bringing Whitehall, and especially the Office, 'under sharp reproach from the other side of the Atlantic' than by engineering 'another instance of apparent slackness plus treachery à la Fuchs'? He supposed that Burgess and Maclean had already been killed. 'The men would be of no value to the Government in Moscow, for I do not suppose they have any material secrets to disclose. They are not like a man of science who possesses the secret of our atom-bomb experiments. The value of their capture is merely that it creates a mystery which will prompt many people on both sides of the Atlantic to think that this is another case of inadequate screening and of cold-blooded treachery.'[11]

Alan Maclean, then personal secretary to Gladwyn Jebb at the United Nations, was summoned back from New York. When his aircraft landed at Prestwick, the passport inspectors at border control isolated him in a small room, where they questioned him with insolent contempt before permitting him to continue to London. There he was whisked by Daimler to the Foreign Office's Personnel Department in Carlton House Terrace. On the drive he was treated with such ominous civility that he thought, 'they're not arresting me: they're going to kill me'. In the event, he received blandishments rather than threats when he began his series of interviews with Skardon, whom he likened to a convivial stoat. 'We became friends of a working sort. He was a nice, unpretentious and even cosy man, who got on famously with my mother. They made each other laugh, and he never said a nasty thing about Donald to her – or to me for that matter. He was considerate in many small ways, and made her path through the woods less thorny.' The defections meant, so Harold Nicolson predicted on 11 June, that 'the old easygoing confidence of the FO . . . will be destroyed and henceforth everybody with begin to distrust everybody else. I do hate that. It is the loss of one more element of civilization. We used to trust our colleagues absolutely. Now we cannot any more.' The truth of this prophecy was soon shown. Herbert Morrison, as Foreign Secretary, judged Alan Maclean guilty by fraternity, and insisted that he must leave his United Nations post and resign from the Diplomatic Service. This was not the only such travesty: in the same month, after Morrison removed the semi-retired 'Old China hand' Sir John Pratt from an official committee because of his sympathies with North Korea, the *Daily Mail*, supporting Pratt's dismissal, traduced him as villainous on the basis that his younger brother was Boris Karloff, the Hollywood actor who played evil monsters.[12]

'We are all agog about the two Missing Diplomats,' the novelist Rose Macaulay told an American friend. Literary London was intrigued by their escapade, she said, as 'most of us knew them'. Her fellow novelist Nancy Mitford was Parisian by adoption. 'We eat & drink & breathe Burgess & nobody thinks of anything else,' she wrote from the French capital on 11 June. 'The frog papers are quite sure it is sex,' although she supposed that 'if they were just bouncing about on some double bed they would have been found by now. *Oh* the fascination.' She had discussed the missing diplomats with her brother-in-law Sir Oswald Mosley, who suspected that 'Burgess was probably always *communisant* & Maclean horrified by the trend towards war, & both together thought out some Hess-like mission.' Another novelist, Rosamond Lehmann, Rees's ex-lover who knew of Burgess's recruitment approach to him, telephoned Stewart Menzies of SIS, who showed no interest in her information. She was then put in touch with MI5 by Harold Nicolson, with whom Burgess had almost certainly had vanilla sex during 1936. It was, however, not until October that she was interviewed by Skardon in a safe-house in Mayfair.[13]

Goronwy Rees's reaction to the disappearance was tragic for himself and destructive for others. He was in a funk: afraid of being unmasked as a Soviet informer on All Souls opinion before the Nazi–Soviet non-aggression pact of 1939; fearful, too, of jeopardizing his relations with the college and SIS (for which he did part-time work at headquarters). Apart from the possibility of criminal prosecution, he was married with small children and short of money. He was drinking heavily, excitable and fuddled, and harmed himself by his agitated and unconvincing behaviour. He gave an absurd interview about Burgess to the *Daily Mail*. 'He was in some ways one of the most patriotic Englishmen I have ever known and was entirely free from the kind of denigration of British social life and political policy which is typical of most Communists. He was absurdly sentimental about England.'[14]

Rees was interviewed by both Liddell and White, and gave a garbled account of Burgess's recruitment overtures which he claimed to have resisted. He implicated Blunt, towards whom he evinced a strong and burgeoning antipathy. Sensing the dislike of him by White and Liddell, he became panicky and widened his denunciations of Burgess and Blunt into accusations against innocent men, notably Robin Zaehner and Stuart Hampshire. Zaehner had run SIS counter-intelligence operations in Iran in 1943–5, had served as Press Attaché and SIS representative in the Tehran embassy until 1947, had trained anti-communist Albanians who were later betrayed by Philby in 1949, and was to be elected alongside Rees as a Fellow of All Souls in 1952. 'The idea of Zaehner as a Soviet agent was grotesque,' Isaiah Berlin judged. Rees's accusations against Zaehner were all the sadder because the ex-SIS man's 'loyalty to him was beyond words': when Rees became ostracized in Oxford, and suffered crushing misfortunes in his career, Zaehner 'stood by him through thick and thin'.[15]

Rees's other wrong-headed Oxford target was the philosopher Stuart Hampshire, who had been a wartime intelligence officer and later conducted a security review at GCHQ. MI5 investigations discredited both accusations. 'Goronwy is an utterly changed character,' Hampshire wrote of him early in 1952, 'he seems invalid, uncertain, almost apologetic and somehow broken . . . the physical basis of his vitality has collapsed, and he simply asks for kindness.' In time Rees began to besmirch Liddell, who had tried to persuade him to keep quiet and minimize disturbance. He aroused doubts that harmed Liddell's standing in his lifetime and posthumously. White was incensed that it had taken Rees thirteen years to tell MI5 that he knew Burgess to be working for Moscow. 'I thought he was a four-letter man. If he knew these things, why hadn't he come forward? Then he went into this spiel that he assumed we knew it all. So I said, "You assumed we knew! Burgess was working for the Russians, and we did nothing about it! What can you mean?"'[16]

Other denunciations were made: Rebecca West told Sir Toby Mathew, the Director of Public Prosecutions, that Footman was a Soviet spy, and later spoke of Inverchapel as a communist. She suspected that the missing diplomats had been spirited to Moscow 'simply to weaken public confidence and make mischief between America and England'. She also badgered her publisher Harold Macmillan, who was a Conservative frontbencher in the Commons, with her suspicions. Lists of names, which might become suspect names, were accumulated day by day. Tomás Harris's telephone was tapped as the result of a stray

remark by Aileen Philby to Nicholas Elliott of SIS. Doubts about
Footman were pervasive: talking with Dick White, Robert Cecil asked,
'What about David Footman? He is not necessarily in the clear.' White
replied: 'You can say that again.' Hector McNeil, who regarded the
missing diplomats as 'two sad unbalanced creatures who took a hysterical jump', named Burgess's 'chief friends' as Blunt, Footman and Philby.
His political career was ruined by his association with Burgess. He lost
favour with his party's leader Attlee, put his energies into promoting
the *Encyclopaedia Britannica* in Britain and died at the age of forty-eight
after suffering a stroke on an Atlantic liner taking him to New York.[17]

Under instructions from Moscow, Yuri Modin of the MGB urged
Blunt to follow Burgess and Maclean in defecting. Modin was dumbfounded when Blunt refused. For Blunt the intellectual fulfilment of
directing the Courtauld Institute would not be matched by the dour
ideological confinement of Soviet cultural bureaucracy. He was confident that there was no evidence that could be brought against him in
court, and perhaps little evidence altogether. He may have been buoyed
by his tacit standing with Liddell and White. They and Roger Hollis
used him as an informal consultant. He explained the milieux of the
missing men, provided guidance on personal histories and connections
between Cambridge and London, and helped MI5 to manage Burgess's
bewildered mother. To distance himself from past associates and
previous convictions, Blunt resigned from the Reform Club, which he
had joined together with Burgess in 1937. Miranda Carter reported a
tentative notion of Stuart Hampshire's that Blunt made limited, informal
admissions to Liddell and White in June 1951, and thereafter was
accepted by them, without explicit discussion, as someone who had
made a limited transfer of allegiance to their side. It is curious that
although White was soon convinced of Philby's guilt, and obtained his
recall to London in July, he made no move against Blunt. When MI5
turned to question Blunt, it was done gently, first by Courtenay Young
and then by Skardon.

Skardon found grim amusement in his dealings with the Burgess
and Maclean families. Eve Bassett, Burgess's doting mother, was, he
reported, 'a very stupid woman, and made a great many suggestions to
account for his disappearance, most of them being slightly comic. These
suggestions were greeted by her spouse with derogatory snorts.' Later
Skardon showed his sardonic humour by arranging a charade at

Waterloo station. 'One morning Jim rang up very jolly, to say that I could now collect Donald's belongings which he had left on the cross-Channel ferry,' as Alan Maclean recalled. 'He mentioned, a shade too casually, that as all their belongings were mixed up, it would be sensible if Colonel Bassett, Guy's step-father, and I went together to Waterloo Station and picked out our respective family treasures.' An official car collected both men. 'The Colonel was dressed for war – impeccably pin-striped, complete with bowler and rolled umbrella and just a whiff of expensive aftershave.' Skardon joined them, 'silent and smiling . . . bent on enjoying the outing'. They were met at Waterloo by an imposing station master in top hat and tails who, seeming both excited and embarrassed, led the trio to his gloomy office where sad-looking objects and clothes were piled. 'You go first, Colonel,' young Maclean said respectfully. 'No,' the Colonel replied. 'We'll do it fair. Turn and turn about.' Both men decided to get the business over at top speed. They chose items entirely at random, without a moment's thought, one after another, until only two items remained: a pair of filthy, torn black pyjamas and a revolting pair of socks which were stiff with dried sweat and had holes in heels and toes. Alan Maclean felt sure that they were both Burgess's, and said so. The Colonel disagreed, and snorted, 'Your chap's.' Maclean had an inspired reply. 'Donald never wore pyjamas,' he said. 'A sin against Nature, he once told me.' The Colonel paused for a moment, shut his eyes, tried to find an excuse, opened them and accepted defeat. 'Right,' he said, hooking the pyjamas into his bag with the handle of his umbrella, 'but you're having those bloody socks.' As they crossed the station concourse, Maclean saw a big, wire-meshed rubbish bin. 'Colonel,' he said, 'look!' 'Good man,' he said, and both pyjamas and socks were binned. MI5's car dropped Bassett at the United Services Club ('the Senior') in Pall Mall. He shook hands with Alan Maclean, nearly smiled, but thought better of it. 'I hope you've enjoyed your morning, Jim,' Maclean told his remaining companion. Skardon sighed: 'I've had a *lovely* time.'[18]

In the weeks immediately after the two men had vanished, White kept insisting to MI5 officers: 'We must trust everyone unless there is proof to the contrary.' He knew how mistrust can damage organizations. Everybody of sense and responsibility understood the destructiveness of paranoid accusations. When the defections came to be debated in the House of Commons in 1955, it is noticeable that two Tory MPs with intelligence backgrounds, Dick Brooman-White and Rupert Speir, both supported positive vetting, but decried any outbreak of McCarthy-style witch-hunts in England. There had once been too much reliance on 'the old-boy network' in vetting intelligence officers, White told an SIS conference in 1961, 'but we can't tolerate Gestapo-style coverage'.[19]

Sir David Kelly, Ambassador in Moscow, struggled to save Fred Warner, his First Secretary in the embassy, from having his career wrecked by the associative guilt of his friendship with Burgess. Warner was 'sincerely horrified' by the turn of events, Kelly reported; but he strove in vain to protect Warner, who was soon posted from the fast lane of Moscow to the dead-end of Rangoon. At Kelly's suggestion, Warner submitted a long handwritten report on his knowledge of Burgess, which was passed by Carey-Foster to MI5. He listed Burgess's respectable circle as comprising himself, Hector McNeil and his wife, Kenneth Younger, 'Isaiah Berlin of All Souls', Charles Fletcher-Cooke, 'Mr David Footman of Broadway', Arthur Marshall, a camp and comic housemaster at Oundle School, the Cambridge don Noël Annan, Goronwy Rees, Ellis Waterhouse, Director of the National Gallery of Scotland, Harold Nicolson and his son Benedict, and Hester Marsden-Smedley, who eleven years earlier had first recommended Philby to her colleagues in SIS as a possible recruit. 'His best friend', Warner judged, 'was Professor Blunt, the Keeper of the King's Pictures. On all these people he would rely for support, and he was such a loyal friend in intention that they generally felt ashamed of withholding it, although his friendship might have become only burdensome.' This list of friends, commented Kelly to Carey-Foster, 'is as impressive as it is to me astonishing'.[20]

Warner was targeted for attention by the *Daily Express*. In August 1952 its prize reporter Sefton ('Tom') Delmer obtained Hollis's private telephone number from Bill Cavendish-Bentinck and sought a meeting with an MI5 officer. When J. C. Robertson saw him at the Lansdowne Club, he said that he was handling Burgess–Maclean investigations for Beaverbrook's newspaper, which intended to shadow Warner during his upcoming summer holiday in mainland Europe. When Delmer hinted at the possibility of his paper collaborating with MI5, Robertson replied that if the *Daily Express* chose to 'trail' Warner abroad, this would not be harmful, and that MI5 would be glad to hear of any results. 'He is a worldly, shrewd, suave individual with considerable charm,' Robertson reported of Delmer. 'Treated cautiously, I think he might on occasion prove a very useful contact for the office.'[21]

The first anniversary of the disappearances revived press interest in June 1952. Press photographers took shots of the Maclean children at their school, made a mob at the Beacon Shaw gateway and on 6 June Ernest Ashwick @ Ascheri filed a false *Daily Express* story from Zurich that Maclean was living in Prague sustained by illicit Swiss bank accounts. MI5's Anthony Simkins minuted on 10 July: 'many people (and perhaps most women) would say that the Security Services have taken a very naïve attitude to Melinda MACLEAN'. She must have heard versions of the drunken admissions that her husband had thrown at Culme-Seymour, Slater, Toynbee and others at the Gargoyle: more-over, Simkins argued, 'even if she was not a party to Donald's escape, she knew at once what was behind it.'[22]

Melinda Maclean was helped in her purposes by official distaste for Beaverbrook's vendetta. A *Daily Express* story of 16 July contained quotes from her, which she could prove were fabricated. Lady Violet Bonham Carter complained in *The Times* on 21 July about the harass-ment of this lone woman stuck at Beacon Shaw with her small children. Sympathy for her intensified: with the prior consent of MI5, she took her children to live in the relative anonymity of Geneva in September 1952. There she misled friends by saying that she was contemplating divorce. Nora Beloff, the Paris correspondent of the *Observer*, was sent by her editor David Astor to report the harassment to which Melinda Maclean had been subjected by reporters and photographers. 'She was dishonestly demure,' Beloff recalled, 'behaving like a bereaved widow who knew nothing of how, why or where her husband had vanished.' A year later, in September 1953, newspaper headlines blazoned Melinda Maclean's disappearance with her children behind the Iron Curtain to join her husband. 'The *Express* is especially enjoying it!' noted Harold Macmillan. 'She may have been in it from the beginning,' Aileen Philby told Moyra Slater in a bugged telephone call after the news had broken. 'She was very Red at one period . . . but on the other hand, she swore she knew nothing about it.'[23]

There remained in London another Maclean woman to harass. Some years later the spitefulness of journalists was such that they prompted the porter of Lady Maclean's block of flats in Kensington to report her to the ground landlords for taking a paying-guest against the terms of her flat's lease. She needed the money of her lodger and, as an old woman living alone, welcomed the companionship. But it was thought that there was the making of a good story if the spy's aged titled mother was put out on the street. The landlords had more sense.

'As if evidence were the test of truth!'

It took only a few days for MI5 to suspect Philby and give him the codename PEACH. He rejected the possibility of emulating Maclean's desperate flight. In mid-June an SIS expert in the fabrication of deception material arrived in Washington bearing a handwritten letter from Jack Easton of SIS forewarning him to expect 'a most immediate, personal, decipher-yourself telegram from the Chief' summoning him to London. 'Why should Easton warn me of the impending summons and why in his own handwriting if the order was to reach me through the normal telegraphic channels anyway?' Philby wondered. He concluded that Easton's letter was intended to prompt him to flee, if he was guilty, and thus to save SIS from the awkwardness of confronting a traitor.[24]

According to Philby, Easton was surprised when he appeared at SIS headquarters in Broadway. They proceeded together to MI5 headquarters at Leconfield House, where (with Easton in attendance) Philby underwent the first of two interrogations by White. His published account of these interviews was prepared in 1967–8, when White was still Chief of SIS, and was designed to diminish White and damage SIS. It is clever but untrustworthy. White, who was hampered in his questioning by his inability to use confidentially obtained incriminating material, had no doubt of Philby's guilt. The Volkov affair, viewed in retrospect from 1951, convinced him. Reilly and Carey-Foster at the Foreign Office were of the same mind as White. What they felt sure to be true, and what they could prove, were far apart: they might have exclaimed 'As if evidence were the test of truth!', Cardinal Newman's indignant retort when someone expressed doubt about reports that St Winifred had walked about after her decapitation. Philby's friends and colleagues in SIS were however loath to believe the calumnies spread by non-SIS men such as White of MI5 and Reilly and Carey-Foster of the FO. This has been represented – notably by John le Carré – as a matter of class bias; but it is understandable that any department would doubt that one of its most efficient, successful and admired officers had been working all along for the enemy. The loyalty of colleagues working together should preclude such a thought.

Washington meanwhile declared Philby *persona non grata*. He went to see Menzies, 'C', to whom his opening remark was reportedly: 'I'm no good to you now, and never will be again. I'll put in my resignation. I think you'd better let me go.' This manly self-sacrifice was thought admirably unselfish at SIS, although of course it meant that he resigned before any question of dismissal was raised. Philby, however, maintained that he had been dismissed, and instead of a pension was given a gratuity of £2,000 with another £2,000 coming in instalments over two years. An unconvincing gang of workmen began many weeks' digging the road outside his temporary English home, The Sun Box, at Rickmansworth. On 10 July an incoming call to The Sun Box, from 'Bunny' in Rugby, was recorded. Aileen Philby was alone in The Sun Box with the children, who were 'making a hell of a row'. She railed against Burgess. 'You know our escapist lived in our house in Washington?' she asked. 'This is absolutely on the Q.T. [hush-hush] . . . It's mucked Kim. It's the most wicked thing that ever happened.' She avoided naming Burgess on the telephone: 'one of Kim's oldest friends', she called him, 'the unmarried one . . . you've met him, ducky.' Aileen Philby told 'Bunny' that they had twice asked him to vacate his room in their Washington house, but he did not leave until Franks ordered his return to London. After he had left, Aileen Philby asked, 'Kim, have I really got to have him back in my house?' and was reassured by the reply: 'No, he's worn out all the friendship I ever had.' It was 'an absolute stinker' that 'the Americans won't play as far as Kim is concerned'. Although his colleagues, she said, 'backed him 100% . . . it was impossible to fight the crazy outlook which the Americans had on things. The individuals with whom he had worked were all for him and she knew of one who was fighting like mad for him . . . It had all been rather a pity because Kim was being coached for a big job.'[25]

In November, after careful preparation, the barrister and wartime MI5 officer Helenus Milmo (flanked by Arthur Martin) interrogated Philby. Like White, Milmo was handicapped by having intelligent conjecture, but not evidence, to arm his attack on Philby. All Philby needed to do was to avoid contradicting what he had said previously, and to concede nothing in answering Milmo's questions and accusations.

There was no need for cleverness or subtlety: exaggerating his stutter so as to pace his responses carefully, it was easy to evade awkward questions from a team that had no evidence. It did not matter that he was unconvincing. So long as he continued his denials, however implausible, he could not be touched. Accounts of this interrogation by Milmo are partisan and contradictory: 'some felt that he was perhaps too much of a gentleman for that daunting task – though a first-class cross-examiner'. Others say that, after failing to lure Philby into inconsistencies or admissions, Milmo resorted to bluster and shouted accusations without intimidating or ruffling Philby.[26]

Skardon accompanied Philby to The Sun Box, after the final Milmo interview, to collect the suspect's passport, which was temporarily impounded. During the journey to Hertfordshire, 'Skardon wasted his breath sermonizing on the Advisability of Co-operating with the Authorities,' recalled Philby, who was too relieved at surviving the Milmo ordeal to listen. Skardon continued interrogations at intervals over several weeks. 'He was scrupulously courteous, his manner verging on the exquisite,' said Philby: 'nothing could have been more flattering than the cosy warmth of his interest in my views and actions'; yet he had no more success than White or Milmo.[27]

Denial is part of what it means to be human. Individuals, households and institutions all require 'a blind zone of blocked attention and self-deception', as the South African-born sociologist Stan Cohen has shown. The preservative silences, false alibis and 'vital lies' inside families about violence, sexual abuse, emotional deformity, bullying, adultery, alcoholism, gambling addiction and disappointment have their equivalents in official life. 'Government bureaucracies, political parties, professional associations, religions, armies and police all have their own forms of cover-up,' says Cohen. 'Such collective denial results from professional ethics, traditions of loyalty and secrecy, mutual reciprocity and codes of silence.' Denial may not be intentional lying: individuals, groups and societies can reach states of mind in which they simultaneously know a situation and don't know it.[28]

Philby's allies in SIS were in fervent denial of his guilt. White and others in MI5 were equally set on denial of his innocence. SIS opinion preferred to suspect Liddell: after years of hard work and shrewd service in Special Branch and MI5, he became a dubious object whose hopes of succeeding Sillitoe as Director General were dashed by the protracted sequels to the defections of 1951. Liddell was slow to accept the possibility of Burgess's guilt, and was friendly with Blunt. His tolerant urbanity, which meant that he was on easy terms with gay men without feeling a need to avoid their company or make a show of repudiating their behaviour, made him suddenly suspect among unimaginative he-men. Quite apart from the personal issues involving Philby and Liddell, the friction between SIS and MI5 over suspicions and culpability in the case of the missing diplomats, the shock and wider departmental skirmishing within Whitehall, Washington's exasperation and London's discomfiture were bonuses for the MGB.

Only one member of the ring of five had a clean cut-loose. Weeks before Burgess and Maclean decamped Cairncross had once again undergone an inter-departmental transfer after alienating his superior: in May he had been shifted from the Treasury to the Ministry of Supply. He had been recruited to spy by Blunt and Burgess, and had known Maclean remotely at the Foreign Office and the Travellers, but it is unclear how well he knew Philby. On 23 June Modin advised that the defections should not endanger his position, but that he should leave England if he seemed close to arrest. Modin also primed him on handling counter-intelligence interrogations, which the NKGB/MGB had failed to do with Nunn May and Fuchs. On 23 June, and at a later meeting in July, Cairncross supplied parcels of secret documents totalling 1,339 pages. Material about weaponry, military equipment and rearmament was considered so important that it was reported direct to Stalin. Cairncross brought further documents to a meeting on 20 August.

After Evelyn McBarnet and Jock Colville had identified Cairncross as the author of the unsigned aides-memoires describing confidential Whitehall discussions, he was put under surveillance. A telephone tap revealed that he had arranged to meet Modin in Gunnersbury Park; but Modin spotted the watchers. In September Cairncross was summoned for interrogation by Arthur Martin, whose aggressive questions were along expected lines and for which Cairncross had rehearsed answers. He said that he had known Burgess somewhat, but had not seen him since 1943. He and Maclean knew one another slightly, as fellow members of the Travellers, but had never eaten a meal together there. He conceded that he had sympathized with communist views on Nazi Germany, but insisted that he had never joined the CPGB. He was suspended from the civil service, required to resign and encouraged to live overseas.

States of denial

Philby's other contacts were pursued by MI5. The discovery in Burgess's papers of detailed and revealing summaries made by Peter Smolka of informal discussions among wartime officials led to a round of interviews with people who had known Philby's former business partner. Alan Roger was asked for his memories of Smolka's journey from Russia through the Caucasus to Tehran in 1944. Roger recalled him as 'filled with open admiration for Russia and things Russian, but many people were then'. Nothing was said or done to make Roger suspect his visitor of being a communist. Investigation by Skardon and others led to a re-evaluation of Smolka. The earlier view, which Philby had helped to form, that Smolka was too cowardly and lazy to be a sincere communist or an effective agent changed. It was realized that he had always been a bold and irredeemable believer in Marxist doctrine: indeed in 1952 he had been an active member of the Vienna communist party. By then he was out of reach in the Soviet sector of Vienna, where he lived in a comfortable villa and ran his father's factory making metal kitchenware, buckles, locks, shoehorns and shoe-trees.[29]

Another historic contact of Philby's, Edith Tudor-Hart, had been suspect for years. As a young Viennese visitor she had joined the CPGB in 1927, and had been expelled from Britain soon afterwards. She had been enabled to return by a marriage that entitled her to a British passport. Unknown to MI5, she had made the first recruitment approach to Philby in 1934. A year later MI5 watchers saw her being visited by the London illegals' courier Brian Goold-Verschoyle. She was known to have sought contact in 1937 with Wilfred Macartney, who had previously been imprisoned for attempted RAF espionage. It was established in 1938 that she had supplied Percy Glading with a Leica camera and other photographic equipment. In 1946 she was heard soliciting work as a CPGB courier at a bugged meeting in a London hotel with Bob Stewart and Willie Gallacher, the communist MP for West Fife.

In 1951 Tudor-Hart still held a CPGB membership card under the alias of Betty Grey. She was evidently alarmed by the Burgess–Maclean defections, for in August 1951 (speaking to a friend who was an MI5 informant) she expressed anxiety about a police raid on her flat, and destroyed photographic negatives which might harm her if found by the police. These included posed portraits of Glading's barrister Denis Pritt and of Philby, whom she called 'an ace man in MI5' (sic). An MI5 officer prepared an evaluation in advance of her interview: a 'rather typical emotional, introspective and somewhat intellectual Viennese Jewess', he called her, with 'a morbid interest in psychology and psychiatry'. In October 1951 she was heard to say in a bugged conversation that party membership was of paramount importance to her; if she lost faith in the party, she would have nothing left. An MI5 source described her that autumn as 'a sick woman, highly neurotic and suffering from a persecution mania'.[30]

MI5 watchers were set on her, preparatory to the interrogation of Philby, but it was found that efficient observation of her flat at 12 Grove End Court in St John's Wood could not be maintained by fewer than eight men. Tudor-Hart had a mentally impaired son, Tommy, who was boarded at the Rudolf Steiner School in Aberdeen. The boy had previously been treated by the paediatrician and psychoanalyst Donald Winnicott, who was eminent for his work on true and false selves. MI5 understood that Winnicott and Tudor-Hart were or had been lovers. If so, she will have been stricken by Winnicott's curt typewritten letter of 2 January 1952, acknowledging one from her about Tommy's treatment, with the handwritten postscript reading, 'I think that you would like to know from me that I have remarried.'[31]

Certainly she was prostrate when Skardon and his colleague A. F. Burbidge, calling himself Mr Burlington, went unannounced to her flat on 8 January 1952. 'A woman came to the door in response to our ring,' Skardon reported: 'we had some difficulty in penetrating to the bedroom and having got there even more difficulty in getting rid of the unwanted woman before starting the interrogation of Mrs TUDOR-HART. The latter was lying in bed, a low divan, and proved for various reasons to be a difficult person to interview.' In answer to their questions about Litzi Friedmann and her family, Tudor-Hart 'sheltered not only behind a faulty memory but also behind the fact that for some years she has been much distracted by caring for an invalid boy . . . She was quite indecisive in her replies and always unhelpful.' For an hour Tudor-Hart prevaricated with Skardon and Burbidge: 'she was completely composed and answered questions in the manner of a person well trained to resist an interrogation'. But in the days that followed she became paranoid, and had to be hospitalized at Epsom.[32]

Skardon made a sweep of old cases. The extent of the espionage by Frederick Meredith and Major Wilfrid Vernon, who had been run by Ernst Weiss and HARRY II, had become clearer to MI5 after 1945. They gained Meredith's cooperation, but did not approach Vernon, who was by then a Labour MP, so as not to embarrass Attlee's socialist government: the Security Service was as chary of seeming to attack Labour politicians as it had been with Jack Hayes in 1929. This inhibition was released after Vernon's defeat in the general election of October 1951. Skardon reread the files and prepared tactics before interviewing Vernon at his Beckenham house in February 1952.

The interview began by Skardon telling the Major that the Security Service knew that he had worked for Moscow's agents, Weiss and HARRY II, in association with Meredith. 'VERNON was completely deflated,' Skardon reported. 'He had commenced the interview by taking a seat at his table and adopting something of an "elder statesman" pose. There was no doubt at all that he was completely shattered by the allegations I had made, and for a time was unable to orientate his thoughts.' Skardon stressed that neither Weiss nor Meredith had been detained despite MI5's knowledge of the conspiracy. 'I asked him to assume from these facts that I was not there in an offensive or belligerent way, and told him that the authorities were not anxious to embark upon a prosecution. We desired to fill in gaps in our knowledge and since this particular conspiracy had existed undetected for three years, we were concerned to-day to find out as much about it as possible, simply so that we might arm ourselves against present enemies of the Service.' Vernon temporized. He talked with anxious flummery about the Left Book Club, Chamberlain's coquetting with Hitler and his duty to his country, but told Skardon nothing that he did not already know. 'Over and over again he would bring himself to the point of telling me exactly what he had done in his illicit association with MEREDITH, WEISS and HARRY II, but would check himself before making the actual disclosures,' Skardon reported. His overall assessment shows a generosity which one cannot imagine in an FBI or KGB interrogator. 'VERNON is a straightforward and upright person according to the dictates of his own conscience,' about which he was somewhat vain. 'It is unlikely that he would be guilty of any petty meanness': he was not a liar, and preferred evasive silence to deceit. He had almost the 'simplicity' of a Russian holy fool: 'not particularly intelligent'; 'he has probably been a pretty honest but not very brilliant Member of Parliament'.[33]

Smolka was out of reach of interrogators. Tudor-Hart's fearful disintegration was conclusive evidence of her guilt. The undertaking not to prosecute Meredith or Vernon – the preference to collect precise knowledge of their activities and connections rather than to put defunct spies in the dock – left the Major free to continue as a figure of ineffectual conscientiousness on Camberwell borough council. But as the next two chapters will show, that most destructive of maelstroms, a moral panic, had been gathering apace from the moment in June 1951 that the diplomats disappeared. The phrase 'moral panic' was not coined until 1972, when Stan Cohen used it in his sociological study of the Mods v. Rockers culture clashes. Cohen defined such a panic as occurring when an episode, an individual or group of people suddenly become defined as weakening society's aims and values and as threatening prevailing statuses, interests, ideologies and values. The nature of the threat is presented in a stylized and stereotypical fashion by the mass media so as to raise alarm and dread. Moral barricades are manned by editors, columnists, politicians, public moralists, accredited experts and unlicensed mischief-makers. When Burgess and Maclean vanished from the *Falaise* at Saint Malo, they started an inextinguishable moral panic about the arcane mysteries of the class system and the instabilities of sexuality. From this public consternation ensued the follies, abasements and fanaticism of their compatriots' deepening obsession with spy rings. In 1951 the defecting diplomats launched a new national hobby of taunting and debasing government service. Their most enduring damage was just begun.[34]

CHAPTER 17

The Establishment

Subversive rumours

The inquest on the missing diplomats turned into a frontal attack on the governing cadre in Whitehall, on metropolitan elites, on trained expertise and on the Foreign Office in particular. The heavy guns used in this onslaught were the problems of social exclusion and class divisions. While teaching underground propaganda to SOE's trainee saboteurs in 1940–1, Philby and Burgess had both studied the craft of spreading stories intended to arouse divisive suspicion among one's opponents and to lower their morale. This chapter shows the successful deployment, after Burgess and Maclean had absconded, of injurious and subversive half-truths which destabilized the London government and are still reverberating more than sixty-five years later. The rhetoric against 'the Establishment' that overwhelmed Britain in 2016, and overturned its place in the world order, first began as a Moscow-serving refrain after the two diplomats had vanished behind the Iron Curtain.

The Foreign Office had been a Marxist target since the 1920s. It typified and represented 'the British ruling-class', and was therefore inimical to the dictatorship of the proletariat, as Norman Ewer wrote in *Labour Monthly* in 1927. 'Hard fact forbids peace between a caste determined to cling to its privileges and to its power of exploitation, and an aroused working class determined to abolish that privilege and to free itself from that exploitation.' Maisky, as Ambassador in London, took a similar line in moments of party orthodoxy. Vansittart, he said, was 'flesh of the flesh of the ruling class of Great Britain' and hell-bent on 'resisting the forces of historical progress'.[1]

After September 1939, the Office was blamed by some for failing to avert war. When the Labour MP Hugh Dalton told *Daily Herald* readers that British diplomats were 'tired and elderly, too traditional and too gentlemanly to be a match for Hitler's gangsters', no one asked if Dalton wanted a civil service that was the equal of the Nazis. The 'Red Clydesider' MP David Kirkwood denounced 'the old school tie' predominance in the Diplomatic Service and denied the benefits of having an elite of carefully chosen men. Morgan Price, Labour MP for a mining constituency, decried the Diplomatic Service as 'a closed caste' of privileged, out-of-touch idlers, and insisted that 'there is a greater air of reality in the atmosphere of a Consulate than that of an Embassy' as if commercial travellers, wayward tourists and stamped visas were more important in the world than bilateral negotiations, confidential talks, the sifting of opinion among traders, soldiers and newspaper prophets, the measurement of popular moods and movements, and official *démenti*. W. J. ('Bill') Brown, the trade unionist MP for Rugby, objected that staffing reforms introduced in 1943 assumed 'a necessary connection between education and diplomatic ability'. These reforms, said Brown, were 'undemocratic' because they excluded non-university men: they failed to make 'the Diplomatic Service safe for democracy', but instead ensured that 'the Diplomatic Service [stayed] safe for the old gang . . . safe for the boys of the governing class of this country'.[2]

Sir Eric Phipps, Maclean's former chief in the Paris embassy, posed the right question in this controversy: 'Diplomatists are being accused of living too sheltered lives; but was it not rather the public that was allowed to live in a sheltered world of illusions while HM representatives abroad struggled with grim realities?' The fatal errors of the 1930s had arisen from politicians pandering to an electorate with strong but uninformed views rather than giving corrective leadership. Without politicians who were trusted by voters when they told unwelcome truths, Phipps continued, 'no great results will come from merely divesting the diplomat of his old school tie'. Self-seeking politicians who misrepresented the national interests to gullible or scared voters did more danger than the envoys and plenipotentiaries, patriots but not small-islander nationalists, murmuring cautions or delivering protests in the *coulisses* of power.[3]

Burgess liked to report to Moscow that he was surrounded in the Office by Etonians, who wrapped him in tendrils of trust on the basis of his OE tie; but his class analysis was stereotypically Marxist rather than accurate. Small independent schools in the smaller provincial cities gave the educational grounding of many of them. William Ridsdale, his chief in the News Department, had been educated at Sir Thomas Rich's School, also known as the Blue Coat School, in Gloucester. Ridsdale's deputy Norman Nash originated in Geelong, Australia. Another member of the department, William ('Bertie') Hesmondhalgh, had been a pupil at St Edward's School in the Oxford suburb of Summertown. Burgess's closest colleague in the Far Eastern Department, Frank ('Tommy') Tomlinson, had been educated at High Pavement School in Nottingham. What united such men was a dislike of closed systems and totalitarian states.

The Foreign Office was no more of a closed caste than the Quai d'Orsay in Paris or equivalent ministries in European capitals. In 1949, for example, the Italian Ambassador to the Court of St James's was Duca Tommaso Gallarati Scotti, the Portuguese Ambassador was the Duque de Palmela, the acting Spanish Ambassador was the Duque de Sanlúcar la Mayor, the Danish Ambassador was Count Eduard Reventlow, the Belgian Ambassador in London was Vicomte Alain Obert de Thieusies, and the Dutch Ambassador was Jonkheer Michiels van Verduynen. Baron Geoffroy Chodron de Courcel, French Ambassador in London during 1962–72, was the grandson of Baron Alphonse Chodron de Courcel, who had held the same post during the 1890s. Courcel's successor in 1972 was Jacques Delarüe-Caron de Beaumarchais, descendant of the diplomat used by Louis XVI of France to supply munitions to the rebel colonialists in the American War of Independence. Patricians like Carel-Godfried ('Pim'), Baron van Boetzelaer van Oosterhout, successively Dutch diplomatic representative in London, Ambassador in Washington and Minister of Foreign Affairs in The Hague, suggest that most western European countries found advantages in using adaptive survivors of *anciens régimes* to represent them internationally. Many organizations are strengthened by evolving an aristocratic cadre. 'The carefully nurtured feeling of belonging to a nobility in the KGB' was a source of strength, judged the East German Stasi's spymaster Markus Wolf.[4]

The Burgess and Maclean scandal broke at a time when England's traditional ruling classes were experiencing unprecedented domestic misfortune. Sir Alexander Cadogan had been brought up on a Suffolk estate, Culford, with 400 acres of parkland amid an additional 11,000 acres: his father, who also owned Chelsea House in London, had enlarged Culford to contain fifty-one bedrooms, fifteen bathrooms and eleven reception rooms; there was indoor and outdoor staff in abundance. Cadogan's diaries, which during his five years as British representative at the United Nations Security Council in New York had chronicled the *va et vient, poste et riposte* of world statesmanship, degenerated after his return to London in 1951 into a lament about workshy cleaners, a 'Swiss slut cook . . . on the verge of a nervous breakdown', 'a lazy liar' of a housemaid, 'the useless old daily hag', forty-five-minute queues to buy groceries, and a brand new Rootes motor-car that kept breaking down. For the first time in his life Cadogan lacked a reliable supply of clean shirts, attempted housework and made breakfasts for himself and his wife. 'These domestic crises are really a curse,' he noted in 1951. 'I don't know what will happen to civilisation if all educated people are condemned to spend the *whole* of their time in domestic chores.' Similarly when Harold Macmillan and his wife went on a summer holiday in Scotland in 1953, visiting aristocratic in-laws and cousins, they found Cabinet ministers' wives cooking for their own dinner parties. The Macmillans stayed in hotels so as to avoid 'putting too much strain on them. One can only *stay* nowadays in the few remaining houses of the very rich.' It is easy to overlook the sapping of energy and confidence that these social changes brought on England, a depletion that persisted until the 1980s. Before leaving for Whitehall each morning, senior officials had, in Zola's phrase, to swallow their daily toad of failure and disgust.[5]

Lord Inverchapel, while Ambassador in Moscow, had described British journalists as 'obscure people without honour in their own country'. During the 1950s, particularly after the advent of commercial television in 1955, sales of mass-circulation newspapers fell, and advertising revenues followed. Editors and proprietors felt commercial pressure to grab attention. They hoped to profit by belittling their targets. Stories became more aggressive, more irresponsible, more unforgiving, more careless of accuracy and more unfair to individuals. Privileges were attacked, but also weakness. 'The humblest and poorest names in the land often feel the scourge of the whip of the gutter press,' as Randolph Churchill noted in 1958. If a plumber's daughter in Balham killed herself, or a Birmingham carpenter's wife was raped, their homes were besieged by a horde of reporters trying to bully or bribe the family into providing 'human-interest stories', and faced a battery of photographers, who did not scruple to set ladders against walls and snap pictures through upstairs windows. Fleet Street exploited the squalid recesses of tragic stories, and fought reader apathy by conjuring outbursts of rabid hostility.[6]

The Foreign Office was believed by Fleet Street to be stonewalling. It would neither confirm nor deny major leads or irrelevant titbits obtained by reporters. There was a sound but unavowable reason and strong prompting for these sealed lips: Maclean had been identified and put under surveillance entirely because of the ultra-secret VENONA decrypts (known in the Office as BRIDE). 'It is most important to conceal from the Russians our knowledge of Bride material,' was Milo Talbot de Malahide's summary in 1953. 'This is really an MI5 point, but we have felt bound to accept it and our policy of silence is built upon it.' If the Russians knew that London was extracting material from their encrypted wireless traffic of the mid-1940s, 'they could take defensive action, which would probably ruin any chance we still have of making use of the knowledge we obtain this way'. In reality, both Philby and Soviet agents in the United States had given early alerts to Moscow of the ongoing decryptions, but this betrayal was not known in London for many years. It was to protect the intelligence advantage bestowed by VENONA, as Talbot de Malahide explained, that the Office concealed the fact that Maclean had been under investigation before he disappeared. 'I know that MI5 attach very great importance to our doing so.'[7]

The existence of SIS was not officially admitted until the Intelligence Services Act of 1994, and much of its activities were subject to the D-notice security system and could not be reported. The Foreign Office was therefore a massive, visible target for snipers, while SIS was not. The obscure people without honour, in Inverchapel's formulation, who ran Beaverbrook's newspapers led the way in maligning the Office. Nancy Mitford, in her novel about the Paris embassy, fictionalized the *Daily Express* as a rag 'once considered suitable for schoolroom reading' called the *Daily Post*, which 'fed on scandal, grief and all forms of human misery, exposing them with a sort of spiteful glee which the public evidently relished, since the more cruelly the *Daily Post* tortured its victims the higher its circulation rose. Its policy, if it could be said to have one, was to be against foreign countries, cultural bodies and . . . above all it abominated the Foreign Office.'[8]

Rebecca West wrote in 1954 to Charles Curran, a journalist who had worked on Beaverbrook's *Evening Standard*: 'more and more do I feel that the Old Man is under the influence of someone who presses the Communist line on him'. West, who had been Beaverbrook's mistress, thought 'few people realize quite how stupid the Old Man is about anything and everything except making money'. He could master a balance sheet in a trice, but was easily duped on other matters. His anti-German obsession, 'mania about Burgess and Maclean' and 'passionate desire to go on hounding the F.O. about them' suited Soviet purposes.[9]

In her complaint to Curran, West mentioned Sefton ('Tom') Delmer, the *Daily Express* chief foreign reporter. Delmer had been a correspondent in Berlin during the Weimar and Hitler years. In 1939 he made a failed attempt to join MI5, found work in the BBC, and then ran SOE's subversive political warfare section spreading destructive rumours and false stories in war propaganda directed against Nazi Germany. Delmer showed ruthless hostility to those surviving leaders of the German Social Democratic party who were exiled in wartime London and were anathema to Moscow. He had projected a clandestine European Revolutionary Radio Station, which was to beam messages of revolutionary socialism at the German proletariat, but emasculated his scheme once German democratic socialists offered to help. He prevented them from broadcasting under their own names, and gave Moscow a monopoly of effective broadcasts to German workers. He seemed almost to discourage the German internal opposition to Hitler. Views of him were mixed. The German writer and broadcaster Karl Otten despised him as a cynic who mocked ideals, a coward who toadied to bullies, and a hoaxer who cared for snappy headlines rather than truth; but Peter Ramsbotham, a wartime intelligence officer and future Ambassador in Washington, who was usually a sound judge, trusted him. Of Delmer's two closest collaborators in PWE, Wolfgang zu Putlitz, who had been a crucial source of German diplomatic secrets to SIS in 1935–9, became a British subject in 1948, but defected to Soviet bloc Germany in 1952. Delmer's other nearest coadjutor, Otto John, was inveigled into East Berlin in 1954, where his detention enabled the Russians to spread propaganda that he had defected too. Despite the self-promotion of his memoirs, Delmer failed on many fronts to make hard-hitting subversive propaganda. To his many enemies, this sinister, self-important, selectively ingratiating man seemed to act as if to please Moscow.[10]

The Truman administration in the USA had in 1950 urged that West Germany should be permitted to rearm so as to help meet the increasing threat to Europe from the Soviet Union and its satellite states. This resulted in the signature in 1952 of a treaty whereby West Germany, Belgium, France, Italy and the Netherlands agreed to form the European Defence Community (EDC) in parallel with the nascent European Economic Community. This plan foundered in 1954, when it was rejected by French legislators – some of whom dismissed it in accordance with Moscow's line, some of whom feared German remilitarization and some of whom held out for British participation in the EDC. This impediment to the formation of the EDC led to West Germany's admission into NATO in 1955. Communist parties in Europe, nationalists and xenophobes in Britain and notably the Beaverbrook newspapers opposed German membership of both the EDC and NATO. Scare stories, for Delmer and his *Express* colleagues, were what their contemporary black-market spivs called nice little earners.

Beaverbrook's journalists included Ian Colvin, whose unauthorized book *The Unknown Courier*, published in 1953, first publicly told the story of Operation MINCEMEAT. Colvin had previously written a biography of Admiral Canaris, chief of the Abwehr until deposed and killed on Hitler's orders after the Vermehren leak (which Oldfield attributed to Philby). In March 1954 Colvin filed a *Sunday Express* story based on an interview with 'a mystery man of Harwell' warning that West Germany was starting atomic research and development. 'Within the foreseeable future she will have the means and knowledge for making the atom bomb – if allowed,' Colvin wrote: West Germany might even become Europe's leading atomic nation. He doubted if the Bonn government's intentions were peaceable: 'Germany's atomic plans should be known to the people of Britain.' Michael Palliser, one of the rising talents in the Foreign Office, linked Colvin's report with recent *Pravda* attacks on resurgent German militarism and atomic research: 'This is not the first time that we have been struck by the picture of Communist propagandists and Lord Beaverbrook walking hand in hand down the primrose path towards a neutralized Germany.'[11]

Delmer visited Germany at the same time as Colvin to gather material for stories suggesting that Bonn militarists were preparing for future wars. In Cologne he interviewed Putlitz, who told *Express* readers that he had 'decided to get out [of West Germany] and go over to the Russians' because only the Soviet Union had sound policies to enforce Germany's demilitarization and deNazification. The Putlitz–Delmer exchanges included mischief-making about the missing diplomats. In Delmer's words, 'The baron is quite ready to chat. "You know," he said to me, pensively sipping his Moselle, "I *may* have been the indirect inspiration of Guy Burgess's decision to come over to us." He smiled and quickly added: "Of course I cannot be certain that Maclean and Burgess are with us . . . such things are secret." Putlitz told Delmer that he had been 'an intimate friend' of Burgess since 1934. 'He was immensely impressed with what I had done. He kept telling everyone we met he thought I was the bravest man he ever met. It was most embarrassing. Probably he made up his mind to follow my example.' Their last meeting had been at a party in the Old Bond Street flat before Burgess left for Washington. 'It was a terribly wild evening,' said Putlitz. 'Everyone was there. Even Guy Liddle [sic] and Blunt of M.I.5.'[12]

Michael Palliser was roused by Delmer's hotchpotch of denial, misdirection and propaganda as he had been by Colvin's tale of resurgent German militarists assembling atomic weaponry. 'One is struck once again by the almost unbelievably naïve – or unscrupulous – way in which the Beaverbrook Press follows the Communist line on Germany,' Palliser commented. The main source for Delmer's warnings on the rebirth of German militarism was a communist pamphlet. As to the Putlitz interview, Delmer 'admits that an avowed Communist has come to the West to preach what he describes as "the propaganda line". He does not point out that this communist "propaganda line" is identical with the Beaverbrook "propaganda line". A senior colleague endorsed Palliser's minute: 'Exactly. One is sometimes tempted to wonder if some Communist moles are not at work in the Express office.'[13]

In September 1954 Jock Colville, Churchill's private secretary, lunched with the newly appointed editor of the *Sunday Express*, John Junor. In answer to a question about Delmer, Junor admitted that he had been worried by evidence suggesting that 'Delmer was Left-wing to an extent that might perhaps even be dangerous'. Churchill endorsed 'Yes' in red ink to Colville's recommendation that 'C's organisation might ask M.I.5 to keep a close watch on Sefton Delmer and see whether he has any Communist affiliations.' Downing Street was informed that neither SIS nor MI5 could substantiate rumours of Delmer's covert Marxism. Anthony Eden, as Foreign Secretary, was relieved when Churchill abandoned his notion of bearding Beaverbrook about Delmer over lunch.[14]

In March 1955 Delmer launched a new scarifying series for *Daily Express* readers under such headlines as 'How Dead is Hitler?' and 'Jobs for the Gestapo Boys – They're Back at the Old Game'. 'The rush to re-arm Germany, prompted by the war in Korea, has already given back enormous clandestine power to the same militarists' and industrialists' clan that was behind the disastrous wars of aggression of Bismarck, the Kaiser and Hitler,' Delmer reported. 'These men, despite their smooth protestations of "Europeanism" and devotion to the western ideals of democracy, are out for themselves and their clique only.' Their object was control of Europe. Delmer presaged 'the revival of Hitlerism', for 'the Nazi type of officer' was ascendant in the new German army, 'the old terroristic herd discipline' was reviving among civilians, and 'the germs of democratic freedom are already being extinguished'. In the Foreign Office Delmer's reporting was deplored. Sir Frank Roberts, a future Ambassador in Moscow and Bonn, noted the damage inflicted on the cause of democracy in Germany by such untruths: 'That however would hardly weigh with Lord Beaverbrook.' Sir Anthony Nutting, Minister of State, minuted: 'From such a scurrilous source I shd not have expected anything different . . . the more Delmers, the more Hitlers & the fewer Adenauers.' There was an urgent need, wrote Nutting, to get the EDC operating with West Germany as a member, and to 'give German democracy a chance to prove itself free of the suspicions sown so liberally and joyously by Mr Delmer and his unscrupulous boss'.[15]

William Marshall

This spirit of class suspicion aroused after June 1951 crystallized in the Marshall case of June 1952. William Marshall had been born in 1927. His father drove a bus, his mother worked in a newspaper shop and they lived together in Wandsworth. He trained at the British School of Telegraphy before attesting for military service in 1945. After military service in Palestine and Egypt, he was released from the army in 1948 and joined the Diplomatic Wireless Service, which posted him to SIS's wireless station at the strategic Suez Canal port of Ismailia. It is likely that in Ismailia he was solicited by the Russians, who flattered him into believing that his low-grade leaks would be valued. After his Ismailia posting he made persistent applications (perhaps at the instigation of a Soviet handler) for transfer to the Moscow embassy, which he finally reached in 1950. Marshall proved so morose among his Moscow colleagues that after a year he was transferred to the SIS Communications Department at Hanslope in Buckinghamshire. There he had access only to low-grade secrets.[16]

In April 1952 MI5 watchers monitoring Pavel Kuznetsov, Second Secretary at the Soviet embassy, saw him meet a tall, pallid, graceless young man at a cinema in Kingston-upon-Thames. The pair lunched together in a restaurant with wide plate-glass windows opening on to the street, facilitating observation, and then strolled to a riverside park where in open view the youth showed papers and drew maps for Kuznetsov. The youth was soon identified as Marshall. Instead of designating dismal public houses and suburban parks as their meeting-places, Kuznetsov made assignations in smart restaurants in Mayfair and Chelsea, where Marshall's cheap tailoring was conspicuous. Kuznetsov evidently wanted to be seen and remembered with Marshall. His conduct makes sense if Moscow wished to provoke a public spy trial to capitalize on the embarrassments caused by Burgess and Maclean. On 13 June, Kuznetsov and Marshall were detained at an oddly visible rendezvous in Wandsworth. In a search of Marshall's billet after his arrest, a locked attaché case on top of his wardrobe was found to contain copies of *What is Marxism?* by the CPGB's Emile Burns, Klugmann's *From Trotsky to Tito* and *High Treason: A Plot against the People* by Albert Kahn, who had been named by Elizabeth Bentley as one of Jacob Golos's sources.

Marshall seems to have been primed by his Marxist handlers to express class grievances under interrogation. The British embassy in Moscow had been a snob-centre, he said. 'The people there were not in my class of people.' It is true that Lady Kelly, the Ambassador's wife, had excessive pride of caste, and used to recommend her sons to debutantes by saying that they had 'the blood of the de Vaux'; but for all Marshall's claims that the unkindliness, snobbery and pettiness of embassy life had made him appreciate the striving egalitarian ideals of the Russian people, the truth was that the embassy had some hundred staff, including technicians, typists, cipher clerks, radio operators and other clerical employees: the diplomatists –Ambassador, First Secretary and attachés – were in a minority.[17]

As Glading's trial demonstrated in 1938, the prosecuting and defence counsel in such cases like to agree a coherent and simplified narrative which the jury can understand and believe. Complicating facts are omitted by agreement, so that awkward questions are not raised in the minds of the jury or public, as Nunn May's trial had shown in 1946. There was scant mention during Marshall's trial of his contacts in Ismailia or of his duties at Hanslope. Instead, the case heard by the court depicted an anti-social introvert who felt estranged by the luxurious pride and icy haughtiness of embassy life, until in lonely humiliation he agreed to spy. This explanation, which exculpated the bus driver's son but incriminated the high-ups, came just a year after the initial Burgess–Maclean revelations had brought discredit on the Diplomatic Service. It made Marshall rare among traitors in receiving public sympathy. The jury convicted him, but recommended mercy in the sentencing. The judge sentenced him to five years' imprisonment, instead of the maximum possible of fourteen.

Sir Alvary ('Joe') Gascoigne, who succeeded Kelly as Ambassador soon after the Burgess–Maclean defections, reported that his predecessor had instructed senior staff that troubles in the embassy 'had nearly always been traceable to a lack of balance in the private life or judgement of the person concerned, and sometimes directly to the fact that he or she was unhappy or discontented, or a bad mixer, or even had an unhappy home background'. He and Kelly both insisted that the primary consideration in choosing members of the Moscow embassy staff, from the most senior to the most junior, must be stable character. Marshall's case had vindicated this standpoint: 'while Whitehall cannot be certain that they will never appoint a secret communist here, they can ensure that no one is sent here who is in any way abnormal'. When that case broke in 1952, Gascoigne stressed to his section heads that 'it was their duty to keep a sympathetic eye on their juniors. I equally insisted that they should avoid any appearance of spying: for the moral effect on the staff if they thought they were being suspected or watched would be deplorable.'[18]

Six months after Marshall's conviction Skardon interrogated him at Wormwood Scrubs prison. Again there was an outpouring of Marxist-instilled complaints of class discrimination. Skardon could not stem the 'flow of muddled abuse of the capitalist world, as Marshall sees it through the jaundiced eyes of an embittered young Communist. All the ideas to which he gave expression are heard from the lips of Communists at Spouter's Corner.' With a mass of collaborative detail Marshall inveighed against the conditions whereby 'the common people are oppressed by the middle and upper classes. The ideas simply tumbled from his lips in no sort of order.' Skardon showed sympathy in assessing the prisoner: 'There is no doubt that he suffers from an inferiority complex, and through a natural shyness has found difficulty in living with people, with the result that gradually he has formed the view that it is MARSHALL against the world.' He was sure that Marshall had discussed his job in general terms with Kuznetsov, but felt that he may have been arrested before he had disclosed any 'serious Top Secret information.'[19]

'The Third Man'

In April 1954 Vladimir Petrov, the KGB chief in Australia, who had a taste for the red-light districts of Australian cities and feared that as a protégé of Beria he was due for liquidation, defected. He had been drawn into doing this by Michael Bialoguski, a Polish-born physician and refugee from communism, who acted on his own initiative. There was minimal involvement from the Australian security services, which had stalled in the conventions of MI5 a quarter of a century earlier, when defectors were discounted as creeps ranking on the social scale between a pimp and a bookie's runner. The social status of the Cambridge spies had not yet transformed Canberra's perceptions.

Petrov hoped that his defection would permanently separate him from his wife Evdokia, another Soviet intelligence operative; but when the aircraft on which she was being forcibly returned to Russia halted for refuelling at Darwin, she was rescued by Australian police. The couple were granted political asylum: like Gouzenko nine years earlier, Petrov proved a rich source of intelligence revelations. A Royal Commission on Espionage was appointed by the Australian government and proved as informative as its Canadian predecessor, although it was misrepresented by Australia's Labor opposition as a conspiracy of the Zinoviev-letter type intended to bias the upcoming general election campaign. Yuri Modin made his first contact since 1951 with Blunt and Philby in order to reassure the latter that Petrov knew nothing about him, and that there was no danger of him being named in the Australian hearings. Modin also provided £5,000 in cash for Philby.

Sefton Delmer attended the Petrov hearings in Canberra. 'I've been getting', he informed *Daily Express* readers, 'an insight into the minds of Russia's rulers; the kind of orders they are giving their agents; the methods they use to build a Fifth Column network of spies, saboteurs and underground guerrillas; the grim professional humour of their code words; the psychology with which they woo their operatives, then terrorise them into obedience.' But where, he demanded, were Whitehall's spy hunters 'who are supposed to be following up the disappearance of Burgess and Maclean?' He affected to believe that the British security services were not monitoring the Canberra revelations.[20]

Dick White, now Chief of MI5, was set on another close interrogation of Philby. He proposed to seize the initiative by pre-emptive publication of Petrov's disclosures. 'It will undermine Philby,' he told the Foreign Secretary, Eden. 'We'll lure him into a new interview, and try again to get a confession.' But Churchill's retirement as Prime Minister was imminent, and Eden discountenanced any disturbance that might unsettle his succession. 'It'll look like a cover-up if it comes out in any other way,' White supposedly warned Eden. In April 1955, newly installed as Prime Minister, Eden appointed Macmillan to succeed him at the Foreign Office. White meanwhile heard that Eden had been advised by his officials that SIS felt that he was pursuing an inter-departmental vendetta against Philby. Indeed in July Sinclair of SIS stated in a letter to White that Milmo's hostile interrogation had victimized Philby whose enforced retirement from SIS had been unjust.[21]

The Australian Royal Commission's final report was published on 14 September 1955. Bialoguski's account of his dealings with Petrov had appeared in book form a few days earlier. Neither source mentioned Burgess or Maclean. But Petrov had sold his own revelations for simultaneous publication in Sydney, New York and London. On Sunday 18 September the *People* ran Petrov's story. In it he described the missing duo as 'long-term Soviet agents', recruited at Cambridge, who 'regularly supplied the Kremlin with all the information they could lay their hands on as trusted servants of the Foreign Office'. The Petrov exclusive – headlined 'Empire of Fear' in the *People* – made clear that Maclean but not Burgess had been under investigation when they absconded, and that a tip-off could be assumed. The Office's News Department knew what was coming, and confirmed to the Press Association that the *People* story was accurate. This marked the end of the Office's stonewalling, which had never convinced Fleet Street.[22]

Press comment was generally misleading. 'It was careless talk by Guy Burgess at Washington cocktail parties', opined Norman Ewer in the *Daily Herald* on 19 September, 'that first aroused suspicions of him and Donald Maclean. Until then they had played very cleverly.' Burgess was known to have been communistic at Cambridge, 'but everyone – including myself – who knew him thought he had been cured'. No one, Ewer continued with monstrous inaccuracy, had any suspicions about Maclean: 'Maclean, I believe but cannot be sure, was tipped off by a friend in the Foreign Office that he was under investigation.' Although both men 'knew that trouble was coming and that the game was up . . . they did *not* know that it had been decided not to prosecute'. But no such decision had been taken: far from it.[23]

Partly because of resentment at Whitehall's perceived earlier stonewalling, and partly in the spirit of class resentment, the lead story in the Labour-supporting *Daily Mirror* on 20 September 1955 was headlined 'Foreign Office Scandal':

The British public have been treated in a shabby manner by the British Foreign Office.

Officials in that particular department of the Government have always regarded themselves as far above the level of the intelligence of ordinary people.

But ordinary people now know that the behaviour of the Foreign Office over the traitors Burgess and Maclean is an example of monstrous stupidity.

Donald Maclean was allowed to continue working in the Foreign Office AFTER he was suspected of spying for Russia. That is stupid enough.

Even more stupid is the Foreign Office attempt to conceal their stupidity from the people who pay their wages – YOU – until the facts were revealed by a Russian renegade.

The British Foreign Office – crammed with intellectuals, the Old School Tie brigade, long-haired experts and the-people-who-know-the-best-people – have taken a mighty drop in the estimation of the very ordinary men and women of Britain.[24]

On 22 September Henry Fairlie published an article in the *Spectator* attacking 'the pattern of social relationships which so powerfully controls the exercise of power in this country' – which he called 'the Establishment'. Although the left-wing historian A. J. P. Taylor and the young diplomat Hugh Thomas had both previously used this phrase, it was Fairlie's article that popularized it. He specified that he was considering the exercise of power in England – Scotland and Wales were different cases – and that the Foreign Office stood at the centre of 'the whole matrix of official and social relations within which power is exercised'. The Office's traditions ensured that 'members of the Foreign Service will be men (and the Foreign Service is one of the bastions of masculine English society) who, to use a phrase which has been used a lot in the past few days, "know all the right people"'. All journalists interested in the Burgess–Maclean affair resented 'the subtle but powerful pressures which were brought to bear by those who belonged to the same stratum as the two missing men'. Fairlie indicted the two Astor newspapers as the leading practitioners of the 'Establishment' suppression. *The Times* – owned by Lord Astor of Hever – allowed only three references to Burgess–Maclean throughout 1951. There were hardly more (under the editorship of David Astor) in the *Observer*.[25]

On 25 September there was another development: Burgess and Maclean were discussed on British television for the first time. Until 1957 there was a universal ban on any matters that were to be discussed in parliament within the next fortnight being examined on radio or television, but as parliament was not then sitting the maverick Conservative MP Sir Robert Boothby, the left-wing Labour MP Michael Foot, the trade unionist ex-MP W. J. ('Bill') Brown and A. J. P. Taylor discussed the missing spies for the first time openly. Foot dismissed Petrov as 'a renegade' whose information was 'not worth the paper it was written on'. Boothby and Brown called for tightened security procedures. Taylor volunteered that he had met Maclean in 1950, thought him a dipsomaniac, and claimed 'it stuck out a mile' that he was a Soviet agent. He said that it was 'crazy' to introduce witch-hunt procedures 'just because some chap in Australia has said all this'. As a diplomatic historian he denied that the Foreign Office held any secrets worth having: 'It is a gigantic build-up for leaders of the aristocracy, so that they can go all over Europe and people will call them "Your Excellency"'. The four members of the panel began shouting interruptions at one another, and the discussion was terminated. Shortly afterwards Taylor was recruited as a highly paid Beaverbrook columnist, and began his career there by denouncing in vile terms the imminent state visit by the President of West Germany (who had spent the war years hiding for his life from the Nazis).[26]

Every more obnoxious than Taylor was George Brown. In the early 1950s Evelyn Shuckburgh, private secretary at the Office to Morrison and Eden, gave a small party in London to introduce FO officials to younger Labour MPs. Brown took the opportunity to tell the diploma-tists that both the Office and overseas embassies were redundant: individual ministries in Whitehall should each deal directly with the corresponding ministries in foreign capitals; he pooh-poohed warnings that this would create chaos. As a Labour frontbencher, he continued to take pride in being disruptive and unpleasant. 'This is the jet age. The era of moving damn fast,' Brown declared in a *Sunday Pictorial* onslaught on 25 September headlined 'FO Flops: Spies Are Not the Only Trouble'. Diplomats, Brown said, were 'cynical, long-haired young gentlemen toddling from one cocktail party to another, never meeting ordinary people, and proclaiming a belief in nothing at all'. It is odd that he thought cynicism and scepticism were undesirable traits in diplomacy: did he prefer naivety and credulity? Brown was frustrated by his experience of a Buenos Aires embassy dinner in 1954. 'Every attempt I made to discuss Argentina and British prospects there was met with levity' (possibly because he was drunk). 'The final curtain was pretty fine disorder, as I lost my temper and displayed how unsuit-able I would be for the appointment to the cynical, ineffectual, prattling body we call our diplomatic service.'[27]

The mood for guillotining aristocrats was abroad. Chapman Pincher of the *Daily Express* was memorably described by the historian E. P. Thompson as 'a kind of official urinal in which, side by side, high officials of MI5 and MI6, Sea Lords, Permanent Under-Secretaries, Lord George-Brown, Lord Wigg stand patiently leaking in the public interest'. Adapting his metaphor, Thompson presented Pincher's prolific jour-nalism and sensationalist books as 'excreta' of secrets sometimes 'still warm from the bowels of the State'. Pincher was 'too self-important' to notice how often he was manipulated by his sources, Thompson said, always saw himself in virile posture and used manly phrases about his deep penetration of departments. During a convivial lunch in September

1955 with the admiral in charge of the government's D-notice press censorship apparatus, Pincher mentioned that although he had originally been tipped off that Philby was the abettor of the missing diplomats, his newspaper no longer suspected Philby. Pincher, who was abstinent but never stinted on another bottle for his guests, had heard from a former Tory MP that Lord Talbot de Malahide had 'tipped the wink to BURGESS to tell MACLEAN to clear out'. Talbot had the attraction as a scapegoat for the Beaverbrook press of being a bachelor, a nobleman with an effete title, and a Cambridge graduate.[28]

Parliamentary democracy was tawdry in its handling of the Cambridge spies post-mortem. Blunt, Burgess and Philby had got their government jobs, and done their worst work, when the country was being ruled by a Tory–Labour–Liberal coalition government. No party was exempt from indirect responsibility. Yet when Burgess and Maclean disappeared in 1951 under a Labour government, Tory frontbenchers such as Duncan Sandys and backbenchers such as Waldron Smithers led a partisan attack. During the parliamentary exchanges about Philby in 1955, when the Tories were in power, Labour spokesmen exploited their chances without scruple. At no stage did any politician state that the Cambridge spies were relics of the special conditions and relaxed security of 1941–5, when the Soviet Union and British Empire were allied against Germany and Japan.

Anthony Eden, the Prime Minister who had spent so many years as Churchill's Foreign Secretary, and the current Foreign Secretary, Macmillan, were shaken by the Petrov publicity: to visitors arriving at Chequers, the Prime Minister's official country home, Clarissa Eden stage-whispered a warning, 'Don't mention Burgess or Maclean.' It was 'a terribly shaming story', Macmillan noted privately. 'The gutter press (esp. *Mirror* and *Sketch*) have violent attacks on me today', he noted on 19 September 1955. He minded this personal abuse less than 'the disgraceful interview' given by Herbert Morrison, Foreign Secretary when Burgess and Maclean deserted, to the *Daily Herald*. 'He has the impudence to say that when he was Foreign Minister (and the worst in history, except perhaps John Simon) he had a poor opinion of the Office.'[29]

Morrison was an envious, grudge-ridden egotist who objected to intellect. He was devoid of self-insight: when appointed Home Secretary in 1940, and asked by Sir Alexander Maxwell if there was anything that he particularly wished to learn about his new department's responsibilities, he affirmed that he would like to watch a woman being hanged for murder. Morrison's memoirs published in 1960 disavowed any wish for power or fame, but made clear that he felt cheated out of his right to succeed Attlee as leader of the Labour party. He attributed this mortification to his exclusion from 'the close-knit coterie of cocktail parties' in affluent homes 'and similar social delights so beloved of the intellectuals'. His antipathy to the Foreign Office was undisguised. 'High officials are prone to address one another by Christian name in the presence of their Minister,' which he thought deplorable. 'This easy-going familiarity . . . exists among all ranks, and crosses the usual barriers between seniors and juniors. Even Secretaries of State have been known to address Foreign Office civil servants by their Christian names.' Burgess, he wrote, was 'an intelligent and rather bumptious young man – a typical young career diplomat'.[30]

Macmillan resented Fleet Street's irresponsible approach to the tricky balance of national security and civil liberty. 'Almost all of the accusations of the Press against the laxity of the authorities are really demands for changing English Common Law,' he noted on 19 October. Newspaper editors and proprietors seemed to want to empower the government to arrest individuals without legal evidence, to suspend habeas corpus and to fire civil servants on the basis of their rumoured beliefs. Such procedures would have been arbitrary and unjust, although for sure the resultant outcry would have sold newspapers. It was against this background that Eden and Macmillan agreed to publish a white paper on the missing diplomats. This was drafted by Graham Mitchell of MI5, who worked under awkward constraints. Many of the most crucial facts were highly classified and could not be printed. Mitchell could not state that Maclean had been under investigation for months because of the ultra-secret VENONA deciphering, and therefore suggested that he had only come under suspicion shortly before he vanished. The white paper did not admit that Maclean had spotted the surveillance team, and understandably but ineffectually tried to minimize the importance of the official secrets that had been betrayed. The government was keen to reduce a raging tempest to the level of a local gusty squall: false accusations, innuendo, character assassination and McCarthy-style witch-hunts were to be discouraged. Unfortunately, the white paper was so opaque and bland that it intensified suspicions of a cover-up and provoked more questions.[31]

One needs to remember that the cult of official secrecy demanded stifling loyalty from its votaries. When the Foreign Secretary Selwyn Lloyd mentioned the wartime Special Operations Executive in the Commons in 1956, he described SOE as a body supplying wartime propaganda to neutral countries. When in 1966 the Home Secretary, Roy Jenkins, asked the Director General of MI5, Sir Martin Furnival Jones, for an information summary on the KGB defector Anatoli Golitsyn @ KAGO and for cognate material on the Cambridge ring of five, Furnival Jones asked that Jenkins did not share the secrets in his report with the Prime Minister, Wilson. The *Dictionary of National Biography* account of Alan Turing, which was published in 1971, limited itself to an obscure half-sentence which did not mention Bletchley or code-breaking: all that was permissible to say was that Turing's Cambridge research was interrupted during the war, when he worked for the Foreign Office's Communications Department.

In this publicity crisis Macmillan agreed that Philby should be reinterviewed by his ex-colleagues at SIS. The MI5 representative and transcribers who attended the three interrogations on 7, 10 and 11 October recorded on file that Philby was never pressed hard: indeed one of the SIS officers repeatedly fed him pat answers to awkward questions. To White's incredulity, and J. Edgar Hoover's fury, SIS concluded by exonerating Philby. The upshot was that the FBI leaked stories to Sunday newspapers in New York naming Philby as 'the Third Man'. These were published on 25 October 1955.

Marcus Lipton, a Labour MP who was a catspaw of Fleet Street newspapers, asked Eden in parliament whether the government was determined 'to cover up at all costs the dubious Third Man activities of Mr Harold Philby'. Macmillan as Foreign Secretary gave a formal answer on 7 November, after consulting Dick Brooman-White, a Tory MP who had served in SIS alongside Philby and was close to Nicholas Elliott and Philby's other SIS defenders. Macmillan admitted that 'Mr Philby had communist associates during and after his university days', but said with technical accuracy but disingenuously that there was no evidence that he had forewarned Burgess and Maclean. 'I have no reason to conclude that Mr Philby has at any time betrayed the interests of this country, or to identify him with the so-called "third man", if indeed there is one.' Macmillan had little choice other than to exonerate Philby in the Commons: there was no evidence on which to convict him, and it seemed wrong to make, under protection of parliamentary privilege, an unsubstantiated accusation in the House of Commons which he did not dare to repeat outside the Commons for fear of a defamation action. This public exoneration infuriated the CIA, which was convinced of Philby's guilt.

The Commons had a full debate on the missing spies on 7 November. There were no momentous revelations, but some significant premonitory signs of the mounting attack on Whitehall. The Oxford don turned Labour MP Richard Crossman made a notable onslaught. Back in 1945, when Herbert Hart had returned from MI5 to an Oxford fellowship at New College, Crossman had jeered at him, 'Still worrying about the truth, I suppose.' Hart retorted: 'I'm sure *you're* not.' Denying Crossman a ministerial appointment, Attlee had said: 'Nothing to do with your ability, Dick; strictly character.' The Cambridge fellow-traveller turned Tory MP Charles Fletcher-Cooke had described Crossman in 1952 as 'the biggest draw' among Labour backbench speakers in the Commons. 'Can it be because the House likes to be bullied?' Fletcher-Cooke wondered, 'for he is the School Bully *in excelsis*'. Crossman was a ruthless propagandist who would say anything for the main chance. He was to congratulate himself in 1963 on having spent twelve years, 'since the Burgess and Maclean episode, exposing the effects on the British ruling class of this deep inner laxity which is constantly mistaken for genuine freedom and tolerance'.[32]

As a *Daily Mirror* columnist Crossman had recently suggested that there had been 'a deliberate attempt to cover up the criminal activities of two young men who went to the right schools and knew far too many of the right people'. In the Commons, two months later, his language was more circumspect.

> Maclean belonged to the *élite* of the *élite*; he was one of the inner group of really gifted men, one of the half-dozen stars for top promotion; an intimate friend, a confidant, a man who spent long evenings with half-a-dozen people who are now in key positions. I am not blaming anyone. I am only saying that if a man has been desperately misjudged, if risks are taken for him – and, of course, risks were taken for Maclean; if a risk is taken and it does not come off, then certain people are not very anxious to have the extent of the risk they took on his behalf exposed.

As to Burgess, 'pushing his way up by means of somewhat unsavoury personal connections', his case showed the Office's toleration of eccentricity as 'curious perverted liberalism'. Crossman decried the Office's privileged character and assumptions of infallibility. 'The Foreign Office was too high and mighty. It was *infra dig* for the Foreign Office to abide by the common laws of security.' The real problem of the Office was not security, said Crossman, but the selectiveness of its recruits. The wartime recruitment reforms which had tried to draw 'boys from lesser grammar schools' and thus reduce the preponderance of major public schools had not brought democratization, because grammar school boys were often careerist toadies or social chameleons: 'a person who comes up from below and enters the Foreign Office, with its august position, in order to obtain the protective colouring required, becomes more Foreign Office than the rest'. Crossman's experience of visiting embassies had convinced him that 'the man from the smaller grammar school is even more Foreign Office than those who came from the kind of school from which I come'.[33]

Herbert Morrison, who had been Foreign Secretary when Burgess and Maclean fled, also intervened in the Commons debate: 'There have been some working-class cases [of espionage], but the funny thing about the middle and upper classes, the well-to-do class, is that if they go wrong in this fashion they are, if anything, worse than other people.' Morrison was mistrustful of the effects of higher education: 'I never studied at a university. I am a product of the elementary schools, and I am not ashamed of the fact. All sorts of things happen at the universities. Abnormal ideas are evolved.' He doubted if it was necessary or beneficial for the higher reaches of Whitehall, including the Foreign Office, to be peopled by 'largely university men'.[34]

On 8 November, the day after the debate, in his alcoholic mother's flat in Kensington, Philby gave a press conference to American and English newspaper and newsreel reporters. The film of this question-and-answer session is available on YouTube. Philby could not look more devious, smirking or unbelievable: he is the picture of a cornered liar; and yet his handler Modin, his SIS supporters and many commentators somehow find his curt denials sincere and effective. Even within MI5 the guilt of PEACH felt less sure.

Three weeks later Ronnie Reed circulated an MI5 discussion paper entitled 'The Disappearance of Burgess and Maclean'. He recalled that in May 1951, although the Security Service had considered that Maclean might try to leave England if he was alerted to its suspicions, no one thought this was likely, especially in the light of observation reports. 'None of us believed for one moment that Guy BURGESS would act as a prime mover in the escape.' During the shock of June 1951 it was agreed that Maclean and/or Burgess had been tipped off by someone privy to the investigation, and that Philby's evasions made him the natural suspect. But after the parliamentary debate and Philby's press conference, Reed thought it was time to re-examine settled assumptions about the tip-off. He listed five FO men who might have learnt that the security services were investigating Maclean and warned him: Ridsdale ('a high priority'), Lord Talbot de Malahide ('a close second'), Sir Michael Wright (then Ambassador in Iraq), George Middleton (the former head of the FO Personnel Department) and Nicholas Henderson. Reed recommended that they should be reinterviewed.[35]

After Christmas, on 29 December, Courtenay Young amplified: 'we have been perhaps turning and re-turning the PEACH stone, without pushing far enough down the various avenues available both in the Foreign Service, as regards a possible tip-off, or our own Service'. He recommended that Blunt should be reinterviewed 'fairly toughly' as 'the conscious source of the wartime leakage from the Security Service'. Young summarized the case against Blunt: 'He has been left fairly untouched since the early days of the enquiry, when for a variety of obvious reasons it was necessary to handle him, as indeed the whole enquiry, with kid gloves. If he is guilty, he should now have lulled himself into a state of comparative calm. He has hardly been contacted by the Office since 1951; various debates on B. and M. have left him unscathed; the various articles and books on the subject have also treated him with the utmost decorum.' A tough interview might jolt his self-control. Three fears must haunt him, Young suggested: 'the first, his guilt as a spy, if he is one; secondly his left-wing background before the war; and thirdly his private life. Any one of these, or any combination of these three, could, were they ever made public, ruin him. I am not, of course, suggesting that this proves a blackmail motive in the interrogation, but if the matter is put to him plainly and bluntly, it might show him that he is in a bigger pickle than he thought.'[36]

George Blake

In 1956 the Eden government's folly led it to collude with France and Israel in bombing and invading Egypt in a bid to retake control of the Suez Canal. The failure at Suez led to Eden's supersession as Prime Minister by Harold Macmillan, and to a mood of national demoralization. 'A people zealous in imposing themselves, their beliefs and their institutions upon others, as the British were in the last century, may lose heart when they can impose themselves no longer,' Michael Young wrote four years after the Suez affair. 'In such a situation a whole people may freeze into insularity, like a melancholic who has withdrawn into himself.' In the altered mood after 1956, Young recognized, 'Britain needs Europe even more than Europe needs Britain. It is out of the dialectic relationship between discontent in Britain, and union with Europe, that progress will come, towards a more lively country.' The preference of older generations, the less educated and the xenophobes for 'wooden-headed jingoism' seemed to Young 'suicidal as well as morally disgraceful'.[37]

It was against this national background that the case of the SIS turncoat George Blake @ Behar developed. The public narrative that was promoted at the time of his trial and reiterated in his memoirs tells how he was captured by the communists in North Korea in 1950 and spent three years in captivity, during which he was indoctrinated with Marxist theories and was shocked, he said, by the relentless bombing of Korean villages by American Flying Fortresses. He converted to communism, and worked as a Soviet spy after his return to SIS in 1953. For some two years he used a German miniature camera to take about 200 exposures of documents that crossed his desk. In 1955 he was posted to the SIS station in West Berlin. There he filched details of American, British and West German spy networks in East Germany. On the basis of his material some 500 agents in East Germany were detained in April 1955: some forty of them were killed as a result of Blake's betrayals. He had previously betrayed the Anglo-American tunnel in Berlin, which began tapping East German official telephone conversations in May of that year. Some 368,000 telephone conversations were recorded before the East Germans staged an accidental discovery of the tapping system in April 1956. It took until 1958 for all these recordings to be transcribed in offices at Clarence Gate in the

Regent's Park. In 1959 Blake was posted to an SIS section from where he recruited British businessmen, students and tourists travelling to the Soviet bloc, placed interpreters, microphones and bugged telephones in targeted situations and solicited diplomats from Warsaw Pact countries. All these activities he betrayed. Every document of significance that crossed his desk was photographed by him and sent onwards to Moscow.

A class-bound rigmarole was spun as an explanatory narrative for Blake. His memoirs, written in Russian retirement, put his objection to class distinctions foremost among the reasons that made him receptive to his reading of Marx's *Das Kapital* and Lenin's *The State and Revolution* while in captivity in Korea. He professed to loathe individual competitiveness, whether in sports or beauty contests, as well as the 'sheer snobbishness' of the English. His complaints about the 'class consciousness' of his official surroundings signify no more than the Marxist fixation with class analysis at all costs. It sounds as if Blake was parroting similar lines, learnt by rote, to those instilled into that infinitely less important spy, Marshall. Historians have followed his explanations too credulously, as if his professed discomfort with SIS's pride of caste excused his espionage and as if there was not comparable pride in counterpart Soviet organizations. Blake supposedly hoped to marry Iris Peake, daughter of the Minister of Pensions, Lord Ingleby, and granddaughter of the Earl of Essex. She is described as 'upper-crust', their relationship is said to have splintered when it hit 'the immovable British class-system', and Blake's rejection as a suitor 'sharpened his resentment of the British establishment'.[38]

Probably the true narrative is completely different. Born in Rotterdam in 1922, with a Dutch mother and an eminent Egyptian communist as an admired cousin, Blake worked for the Dutch resistance as a courier after the German invasion of the Netherlands in 1940. The Dutch resistance was riven with communists, and the likeliest story is that when he came to England in 1942 he had already discussed working for Moscow. In 1944 he became a junior member of the Dutch Section of SIS. Why and when he was activated by Moscow to spy on SIS is not yet clear. It is unlikely to be in the circumstances or at the date that have hitherto been given.

The Polish intelligence officer and triple agent Michael Goleniewski, codenamed SNIPER in Washington and LAVINIA in London, defected

to the USA in January 1961, and provided evidence that led to the
arrest in England of the Portland spy ring and of Blake. For five days
in April 1961 Blake was interrogated by a team of three: Harold ('Harry')
Shergold, Terence Lecky and a former police officer, Ben Johnson.
Shergold had been educated at St Edmund Hall, Oxford and Corpus
Christi College, Cambridge before working as an assistant master at
Cheltenham Grammar School in 1937–40. He had served as an officer
in SIME in 1941–6 and as an SIS officer in Germany monitoring Soviet
Russia in 1947–54. Lecky had been educated at Winchester and Clare
College, Cambridge (where he was a modern languages scholar) before
SIS postings in Germany, Switzerland and the Netherlands. These were
not the class-bound dunderheads or clubland boobies imagined by
Whitehall's critics.

Blake was allowed to return to his mother's flat at Radlett, when
the first day's interview was suspended at six in the evening, and asked
to return next morning at ten. His interrogation remained courteous
and unthreatening, but he had no doubt that SIS knew that he was
working for the Soviets. After lunch on the third day, Thursday 6 April,
Shergold's team told Blake that they believed that he had confessed
under torture, when he was a prisoner in Korea, to being a British
intelligence officer and had then been blackmailed into espionage. 'I
felt an upsurge of indignation,' Blake claimed in his memoirs. 'I wanted
my interrogators and everyone else to know that I had acted out of
conviction, out of a belief in communism, and not under duress or
for financial gain. This feeling was so strong that without thinking
what I was doing, I burst out, "No, nobody tortured me! No, nobody
blackmailed me! I myself approached the Soviets, and offered my
services to them!"' On Friday 7 April Blake was taken into informal
custody for the weekend. He was driven in a car with Ben Johnson
and John Quine, head of SIS counter-espionage (formerly posted in
Tokyo and Warsaw), with Shergold in a second car and police escort
cars before and aft, to a Hampshire village where Shergold's mother
had a cottage. Shergold's wife Bevis (who had been an intelligence
servicewoman in the war and competed as a shot-putter and discus-
thrower at the Olympic Games of 1948) received them. In the evening
Blake made pancakes for his Special Branch guards. He shared a
bedroom with Quine, the cottage was ringed by Special Branch officers,
and a police car drove slowly behind when he went for walks with

Alexander Foote – author of *A Handbook for Spies* – spied for Moscow before defecting to the British in Berlin and cooperating with MI5.

The revelations of Igor Gouzenko, the Russian cipher clerk who defected in 1945, signalled the start of the Cold War. Previous Soviet defectors had been killed on Moscow's orders, so when he met American reporters he had to make himself unrecognizable to Soviet informers.

Donald Maclean perched on Jock Balfour's desk at the Washington embassy, with Nicholas Henderson and Denis Greenhill.

Special Branch's Jim Skardon (left; on his way to testify at Klaus Fuchs's trial) was the prime interrogator of Soviet spies, and of their associates, office colleagues and families.

Lord Inverchapel, as ambassador in Washington, appreciating young American manhood.

A carefree family without a secret in the world: Melinda and Donald Maclean.

Dora Philby and her son in her Kensington flat after he had been exonerated in parliament from being the Third Man.

Many people fell for Philby's charm. None felt more betrayed or broken by his duplicity than his wife Aileen – here facing prying journalists at her front door.

The betrayer of atomic secrets Alan Nunn May, after his release from prison, enjoys the benefits of the Affluent Society.

The exiled Guy Burgess lies festering beside the Black Sea.

John Vassall was a pert, wily urban survivor whom the official story misrepresented as an inexperienced, vulnerable man open to blackmail.

George Blake returns from his incarceration in North Korea bursting with energy and primed to spy and betray within SIS.

Despite George Brown's scorn for diplomats, he was appointed Foreign Secretary. The job's burdens and refreshments made him stumble.

Although Richard Crossman was a master propagandist against the Establishment, he was not a populist at ease with the Common Man.

The *Daily Express* journalist Sefton Delmer was thought in the Foreign Office to be doing Moscow's dirty work.

Maurice Oldfield of SIS – here with his mother and sister outside Buckingham Palace – became in retirement the object of calumny.

Shergold or Quine. This bizarre situation struck the captive as 'endearingly English'.[39]

Dick White, who had been moved from Director General of MI5 to Chief of SIS in 1956, thought Blake's admissions to Shergold, Lecky and Quine showed instability and self-importance: he judged Blake to be more a 'Walter Mitty' fantasist than a master-spy. Quine, who had known Blake for years, thought him too unbalanced to merit prosecution. Nevertheless, on Sunday afternoon he was driven to an SIS safe-house at East Sheen, and on Monday 10 April he was taken to Scotland Yard for arrest. White was concerned that Blake might withdraw his admissions and force the open testing of the evidence against him. 'We can't go through the agony of our operations being presented in court,' he told his SIS staff. 'If he isn't prepared to plead guilty, we'll just put him on a plane to Moscow.'[40]

A month later Blake became the first SIS officer to be tried for treason. He appeared before Lord Parker of Waddington, the Lord Chief Justice, who had been privately told of the forty-odd executions attributed to Blake's betrayals. The public were shocked and uncomprehending when Parker passed what seemed a savage sentence of forty-two years in prison. 'Naturally, we can say nothing,' Harold Macmillan noted on 4 May. 'The public do not know & cannot be told that he belonged to MI6 – an organisation which does not technically exist. So I had rather a rough passage in the H of C.' He invited the leader of the opposition, Hugh Gaitskell, to a confidential briefing together with three Labour Privy Councillors, Earl Alexander of Hillsborough, Emanuel Shinwell and George Brown: 'I only hope the last one will not chatter too much in his cups.' Ten days later Macmillan noted of the Blake case, 'The Press has been terrible, without any sense of responsibility. They want sensation. Also, since the Press is tired of me & the Govt, and since I refuse to run after the Press Lords, they are all attacking me. We are said to be exhausted, ageing, & practically in articulo mortis.' At his meeting with Gaitskell and the Labour Privy Councillors, Brown 'was sober (it was 11.30 a.m.) but had clearly been pretty bad the night before. I told them the facts of the Blake case & that I intended to appoint a small committee to enquire into the whole question.'[41]

The committee appointed to report on security procedures and communist penetration in the civil service was chaired by the jurist Lord Radcliffe. After Radcliffe had submitted his final report to Downing

Street, but before its publication, Macmillan again briefed Alexander, Brown and Shinwell on terms of sworn Privy Council confidentiality on the established facts. Brown, who, noted Macmillan, 'was so rude that I could have kicked him out of the room', promptly broke his Privy Councillor's oath and leaked all he heard to Pincher of the *Daily Express*. He complained to Pincher of an Establishment 'cover-up' which had to be exposed, and added that his duty to the Labour party, which was using real or factitious security concerns to injure the Conservative government, overrode his duty as a Privy Councillor. Pincher however attributed Brown's betrayal to 'hunger for personal power'. The Labour party began calling for the appointment of a minister of security, regardless of the totalitarian connotations which other people heard in such a job title. The Tories countered privately that no politician of any ability would take such a benighted post: his only purpose would be to deflect the blame from the Prime Minister on to himself whenever a security scandal broke; he would be a lightning-conductor or fall-guy putting his hopes of political promotion at risk.[42]

The parliamentary performances of George Brown were bent on damaging the Office and diplomats against whom he nursed tormented prejudices. As Foreign Secretary in 1966–8, he evinced an obsessive resentment of the phrase 'Her Majesty's Ambassador' as applied to dignify people whom he regarded as his subordinates. 'He's my man,' Brown used to say both contemptuously and possessively of ambassadors. He was so sexually suggestive when drunk that Martine de Courcel, Claude Pompidou and Jacqueline Couve de Murville would not sit next to him at Paris banquets. One of Brown's nastiest traits was his public humiliation of his admirable wife Sophie Levene with such shouts as 'Shut up! You're nothing but an East End Yid.' In a generation of alcoholic frontbenchers he and the Tories' lazy, emollient Reginald Maudling were the most blatant. 'Man for man, most people would, I imagine, prefer to entrust the Foreign Office to, say, Maudling than George Brown,' Donald Maclean wrote in exile.[43]

After Radcliffe's report had been published in 1962, Burgess telephoned Driberg, who obligingly regaled the Moscow line to newspaper readers. 'All that I read of what is going on in England now and the letters that I get from friends *in the Establishment*' – Burgess emphasized these words to Driberg – 'make me delighted to be here. These letters show me what a ghastly state of collective neurosis people in Britain are living in.' He was discouraged from thoughts of returning to England, he told Driberg, by 'this new outbreak of McCarthyism in England – the Radcliffe Report and all that'.[44]

Blake was sprung from Wormwood Scrubs prison in 1966 with the help of a ladder made of knitting needles. The escape was organized by an alcoholic Irish labourer and two Committee of Nuclear Disarmament campaigners who thought his forty-two-year sentence was inhumane. The KGB had no part in the plot. According to Markus Wolf, Blake's peculiar sadness, which Maclean and Philby were spared, was to outlive the Soviet Union. After 1990 he was marooned in an adopted homeland which had discarded the cause to which – perhaps from the age of eighteen – he had dedicated his life.

Class McCarthyism

Philby in his insincere, scheming memoirs denigrated the security services as a posse of placemen, parasites, mediocrities, cretins and snobs. Other writers have been keen to follow him in depicting SIS as an 'upper-class preserve, effete, riddled with class prejudice, only too ready to cover up when one of their members came under suspicion'. Tim Milne commented on such caricatures, 'Well, it makes more inter-esting reading than the truth, which is that in Section V [of SIS] at any rate we were a mixed but mostly middle-class lot'. Overseas agents included journalists, commercial representatives of English businesses in foreign capitals, bank and shipping clerks: usually they had military or naval experience simply because most men of their generation did after the war of 1914–18. Often they were recruited because they were good linguists or had lived abroad and knew foreign countries.[45]

'The Old Boy Network came under heavier fire, following the Burgess and Philby affairs,' wrote David Footman. He conceded that the old system permitted abuses, 'but at least it gave to many of us a code which we valued' and 'enabled the British Empire to be run, on the whole successfully, for a great many years, with far less personnel and far less talent than would otherwise have been needed'. Such still, small voices of calm were not much heard in the 1960s. The excitable clamour of such men as John le Carré was all too audible (it was *always* men who raised the din against the Establishment: women knew that there were more basic structural prejudices, more offensive social and economic and legal inequities and more impenetrable workplace barriers than class). In 1968 le Carré, in an influential essay on Philby, depicted 'the Establishment' as 'stupid, credulous, smug and torpid', as behaving with 'grotesque ineptitude', and thus 'a microcosm of that "great capitalist class" now in the process of internal disintegration'. For him vain, murderous Philby was 'the spy and catalyst whom the Establishment deserved'.[46]

Moscow scored a huge success in the decades after 1951 in discrediting the government apparatus of London. Forty years of well-spun revelations about the Cambridge spies, the propaganda element in the Marshall, Vassall and Blake cases, contributed to a Marxist presentation of a ruling class in retreat, taking the wrong decisions, preferring the wrong people. This was accentuated in the Profumo affair. The Secretary of State for War had enjoyed a short affair in 1961 with a young woman named Christine Keeler. In January 1963 she was induced to say, by journalists who had bought her story and wanted value for money, that she had simultaneously been the lover of a naval attaché at the Soviet embassy named Eugene Ivanov. The sex with Ivanov was a male journalists' fantasy; but the story was virile enough to be used by Macmillan's political enemies to belabour his government and the civil service.[47]

Thus the Cabinet Secretary, Lord Normanbrook, 'a real old Establishment figure' standing at the acme of Whitehall, was the target of the *Sunday Mirror*'s front-page headline 'Who Runs This Country, Anyhow?' at the height of the Profumo press stunt in June 1963. It attacked 'Lord Normanbrook of Chelsea', as he had become earlier that year, for his supposed inadequacies in responding to the (non-existent) security risks of Profumo's involvement with Keeler. Normanbrook was damned for being accountable neither to parliament nor to the people. 'Is it safe for the Mandarins of Whitehall, who know so little of life outside their own narrow world, to wield such influence?' Elsewhere in the 'Who Runs This Country?' issue of the *Sunday Mirror* the ubiquitous Crossman claimed that the British people were stuck with 'an Establishment still dominated by the mandarin mind which despises the expert and the technician and relies on a genteel amateurism out of date even in Edwardian Britain'. This class-bound dilettantism was the cause of the successive 'security scandals which have disgraced Macmillan's regime'. The journalist and former SIS officer Malcolm Muggeridge, who loved making mischief, revelled in the Profumo affair.

He saw its indignities as the culmination of a series of episodes that had begun with Burgess and Maclean – 'all calculated to undermine the repute, not just of Upper Class individuals and circles, but of the class system'. Muggeridge was both puritanical and sexually vain: his middle age had been full of serial adulteries; his juices were now drying, and within a few years he became sexually abstinent, a Catholic convert and a shrill opponent of the Permissive Society. His disapproval of other people's pleasures was already evident by 1963: 'the Upper Classes', he told *Sunday Mirror* readers, 'have always been given to lying, fornication, corrupt practices and, doubtless as a result of the public school system, sodomy'. He had a particular dislike of male homosexuality, and on another occasion called Inverchapel 'a well-known paederast'.[48]

Diplomats were anti-democratic conspirators in the Century of the Common Man, the foreign correspondent James Cameron explained to *Sunday Mirror* readers. 'Every man jack of our Foreign Service abroad is a creature not of the Government of the day, but of the permanent staff of the Foreign Office, owing allegiance not to any popular administration but to the Machine.' Cameron wanted populism rather than non-partisanship from diplomats, and apparently valued bad manners and ill-education, for he faulted the present Diplomatic Service for employing 'gentlemen of impeccable tastes and great civility; they are always excellently educated, and usually well-born'. He recalled that in the 1940s there had been promises that the Service would 'be revolutionised, democratised, disinfected of its almost total adherence to the upper-class myth, purged of its insistence on the Public School and Oxbridge'. Instead Britain would be represented abroad by 'technicians, businessmen, trade unionists'. Instead, 'the great crushing irresistible weight of the Establishment overlaid the plan . . . and left the FO exactly as it was: the pasture of the public school, the grazing-ground of the upper-class intellectual, above all the haven of the play-safe'.[49]

This publicity offensive had a crucial part in the election of a Labour government, with Harold Wilson as Prime Minister, in 1964. Wilson affirmed that the fumbling, privileged *ancien régime* was retarding Britain, and that his new brand of managerial professionalism would be a panacea. He convinced his supporters that if only the government apparatus had efficient managers, with slide-rules in their pockets and technical jargon on their tongues, the country would be able to afford its global military burdens and its high defence expenditure as well as expanding social services, cutting unemployment and eradicating poverty. After his promises began to be broken in the years from 1967, the Labour party, as Nora Beloff of the *Observer* wrote in 1973, 'developed a mood of "anti-elitism" and "anti-intellectualism" repudiating any confidence in expertise or superior knowledge, and coming round to feeling that it was just as unfair for the clever as for the rich to have all the advantages'. A new stage in the undermining of experienced authority had begun. Young adherents to the Alternative Society, and the student revolts of 1968–72, received immense publicity in this period. They diverted attention from the more enduring and significant fact that it was becoming unacceptable, as the historian G. M. Young had earlier lamented, to tell voters that 'a man has no more right to an opinion for which he cannot account than to a pint of beer for which he cannot pay'.[50]

Donald McLachlan, a wartime naval intelligence officer, who had recently retired as editor of the *Sunday Telegraph* to write *Room 39: Naval Intelligence in Action, 1939–45*, published a convincing defence of the secret services in October 1967. 'The revival of the Philby affair has provoked a fresh wave of anti-gentleman, down-with-the-old-boy-ring, let's expose the Establishment fervour, of which the Labour Party has been in the past such a beneficiary. The implication is that the Secret Service is a closed circle which should be "exposed"; that it is probably decadent and inefficient; that it should be "cleaned up" and released from its "class loyalties". He regretted that most newspaper readers did not realize that this was 'one of the favourite lines of Communist propaganda', which had developed 'most conspicuously during the Burgess and Maclean episode'. A secret service had to be an exclusive body, which co-opted its officers, rather than openly recruited by competitive examination. 'Its members must be highly educated, loyal, intelligent, ruthless, secretive and ready to be lonely. The field is at once greatly restricted; it must, in fact, be an old-boy net, like its Soviet, French and American counterparts. If it has shown a partiality for gentlemen, that is on a par with the Soviet preference for good party members.' He reminded readers that Britain's record of defections, traitors and long-undetected spies was no worse than that of the United States. He gave a litany of American spies that sounded like a list of New York delicatessens: Hiss, Soble, Soblen, Gold, Rosenberg, Slack, Greenglass, Brothman, Moskowitz, Abel, Coplon, Haynahen, Scarbeck,

Bucar, Cascio, Verber, Dorey, Sobell, Boeckenhaupt, Martin and Mitchell. He overlooked Duggan, Halperin, Lee, Rhodes, Silvermaster and others.[51]

The Cambridge spies failed in their aim to achieve the dictatorship of the proletariat, but by the 1960s they had helped to discredit and destabilize the government apparatus of Russia's historic adversary. SIS, MI5 and the Foreign Office were all weakened. The wrecking of the Establishment was a gift to the Kremlin.

CHAPTER 18

The Brotherhood of Perverted Men

The Cadogan committee

Sir Rupert Grayson, who underwent four security vettings during his work as an Admiralty courier and Foreign Office King's Messenger, asked his interrogators on each occasion what weakness they considered to be the greatest security risk. He expected to be told homosexuality or alcoholic excess, and was surprised by the unanimity of their response: though the vetting interviews were years apart, 'they all four opted for vanity'. The conceit of Hayes, Ewer, Slocombe, Oldham, King, Glading, Vernon and other communist agents, and the self-regard with which they played their duplicitous roles, exemplify the power of vanity to draw men into treachery.[1]

The next greatest security risk was alcohol. Officers in SIS, MI5, the KGB and CIA, journalists employed by Fleet Street newspapers, many parliamentarians and some diplomatists shared one character-istic with the Cambridge ring of five: they drenched themselves in alcohol. Many protagonists in this book were often soused: lead characters such as Oldham, Goronwy Rees, Elizabeth Bentley and Duncan Lee; secondary players including Tomás Harris, James Pope-Hennessy, Philip Toynbee, Joseph McCarthy and James Angleton. Drunkenness was a ceaseless threat to security, judgement and discre-tion on every side. Blunt, Philby, Maclean and Burgess (but not Cairncross) were all alcoholics: Blunt controlled the outward signs of his drinking, and was seldom seen the worse for his lashings of gin; but the other three were problem drinkers. Yet dipsomania only bordered the narrative that was spun to explain the security lapses discovered in 1951. Too many of the men apportioning blame were themselves heavy drinkers, who were unlikely to start a campaign against the mistakes, omissions, truancy and hangovers associated with boozy colleagues.

Still less were officials likely to fault the joke-filled, masculine sociability which kept their departments working agreeably. Instead, after Burgess and Maclean's vanishing act, male homosexuality was brought to the fore of security assessments: same-sex contacts became more publicized, policed, politicized and punished; indeed they were treated as a national menace. The worst damage wrought by the missing diplomats was to the administrative leadership of the nation that they betrayed; but indirectly, through the official reactions to their treachery, they were the pretext for a sexual intolerance that marred hundreds of thousands of lives. The harmful repercussions of the security inquest of 1951 endured into the twenty-first century.

Sexual acts between men were criminal offences until 1967, when legal sanctions were partially repealed. These illegal pleasures were obnoxious to some people, but insignificant to others. The Departmental Committee on Sexual Offences had reported in 1926 that 'sometimes juries are loth to convict, even when the evidence is clear', and that this may be due to the fact that in some cases they find it hard to accept as true the shocking facts submitted for their verdict, or it may be due to an insufficient appreciation of the gravity of the offence'. A Liverpool wool-broker who sat on a jury which acquitted a man charged with sodomy explained afterwards that although the accused had been guilty, 'half the jury didn't think it was possible, and the rest of us didn't think it mattered'.[2]

Among diplomats opinion was divided between those who thought the subject too sordid for notice, those who reckoned it to be unimportant and a few like Vansittart who had a neurotic hatred of homosexuality, which he identified with Germans. Van's views were at odds with those of some of his colleagues. As young attachés Harold Nicolson and Archie Clark Kerr (the future Lord Inverchapel) had been lovers. 'Dear warm gentle Arch,' Nicolson wrote in 1911, 'either one dislikes you, or finds you a darling'; and in 1912, recommending a novel with 'an attractive bugger' and a woman 'rather like you' as central characters, he wrote, 'Dear Arch I want you so . . . How careless we were to let it slip away!' After dinner at the Carlton Grill in 1916, Gerald Villiers made advances to his departmental junior, Duff Cooper, in the misplaced hope that any man as highly sexed as Cooper, even though a womanizer, might lend a hand. 'I parried his advances as best I could,'

Cooper recorded, 'but as I was opening the front door to let him out, he caught hold of me and kissed me which was very unpleasant.' Sir Louis Mallet, after his retirement as Ambassador in Constantinople, lived in the inter-war years in Park Lane and Port Lympne, overlooking the Kent coast, with his fellow bachelor Sir Philip Sassoon.[3]

Jock Balfour, who spent four years interned in Ruhleben, the imperial trotting course at Spandau where thousands of British subjects were confined in 1914, accepted that the complete absence of women led many prisoners to join 'the gay brigade . . . on a temporary basis'. He served in two embassies, Moscow and Washington, where Inverchapel was Ambassador, and doubtless sensed his chief's vigorous bisexuality. It was no secret that Inverchapel left a big enough legacy to his valet Evgeni Yost for the young man to start a catering business on the Isle of Bute (Yost learnt to speak English with a Glasgow accent, made money from fish-and-chip shops, jukeboxes and ice-cream, fathered nine children, voted Conservative and admired Margaret Thatcher). When Sir Maurice Peterson, who joined the Diplomatic Service in 1913 and served as Ambassador in Baghdad, Madrid, Ankara and Moscow, came to write his memoirs, he dropped unmissable hints about the pugnacious, stealthy and insecure Lord Lloyd. 'His courage, both physical and moral, was of a high order: the very suggestion of a menace, from whatever quarter, was for him but an incentive to further effort,' Peterson wrote of Lloyd, who began as an unpaid attaché in the Constantinople embassy and ended as High Commissioner in Egypt. 'He had a keen, almost feminine intuition, which was a real asset in the East where most things happen underground . . . His mind was, above everything, suspicious. The hidden motive was what he always sought.'[4]

Perhaps the majority of members of the Diplomatic Service thought it silly and unpleasant to be prejudiced against an activity which might not attract them, but should not be illegal. Sir John Dashwood, the Office's wartime deputy adviser on security, welcomed gay men to his Buckinghamshire home. 'Staying there', Charles Ritchie noted in 1941, 'was one of these aesthetic intellectuals or intellectual aesthetes who leave their London flats, their left-wing politics and their rather common "boy-friends" at the week-ends for the more decorative and well-heated English country houses.' It may have been Burgess or Blunt described by Ritchie 'peering at old family letters in pillared libraries or adjudicating the origin of rugs . . . or else . . . simply sitting on the sofa before the fire with their legs curled up having a good gossip with the wife of their host'.[5]

Hardy Amies, the couturier who joined the Intelligence Corps in 1939 after completing an application form in which he claimed boxing and shooting as his hobbies, liked the joke that the Tudor-rose motif on the Intelligence Corps badge represented 'a pansy resting on his laurels'. Among some university-educated wartime officers there was a reflective curiosity about the range of sexual possibilities. 'I am not naturally monogamous, and slightly homosexual,' Stuart Hampshire wrote in a self-analysis of 1942; 'I wish I were more homosexual, because I very much prefer the society of men to the society of women.' On a walk Maurice Oldfield once asked his SIS colleague Anthony Cavendish if he had had any homosexual experiences. 'I admitted that I remembered one occasion with other boys in a shepherd's hut in the Swiss mountains,' Cavendish recalled. 'Maurice just nodded.'[6]

Patient, resourceful and perceptive men with criminalized sexual tastes undertook sterling intelligence work in every theatre of war. To give one example, Alan Roger, the notably successful Defence Security Officer (DSO) in Tehran, was a cheerful, comfortable and shrewd bachelor who after the war was posted to Hong Kong before becoming a director of Cable & Wireless. He lived in London with his Japanese majordomo, popularized bonsai gardening, operated as an SIS Friend and left much of his fortune to his companion's children. One of Roger's successful operations arose from an Iranian living in Berlin who had been allowed to return to his homeland on the understanding that he would remit wireless reports to the Abwehr and answer strategic questions. This Iranian, who was codenamed KISS, had no intention of spying for anyone. He was detained by the British after his return to Tehran, where he refused when asked to act as a double agent feeding misinformation on Iraq and Iran to the Abwehr. He would rather spend the war in custody, he said, than get involved in such dangerous duplicity. He was eventually released, and spent the next three years oblivious of the fact that during his detention his style on the Morse key was emulated to perfection, his misuse of German grammar and vocabulary were imitated and his mental traits were studied so that a counterfeit KISS could send wireless traffic. By this ruse, Berlin was misled on many crucial points. The British, in order to sustain the

deception, had to confide particulars of the KISS deception to their
Russian counterparts in Tehran and sought their help in providing
material on Russian troop movements. 'To work in contact with Russian
Intelligence with proper reserve and eyes well open seems to me to
afford far better opportunities for learning all about it than by peering
through key-holes or relying entirely on "delicate" and highly placed
sources which must not be compromised and which are therefore often
uncheckable,' reported Roger.[7]

Another intelligence officer with criminalized sexual tastes was
Roger's brilliant and brave SIS colleague in Iran, Robin Zaehner. In
appearance Zaehner was likened to one of Snow White's Seven Dwarfs,
with thick pebble spectacles to adjust his myopia: this made it hard for
him to find men who would reciprocate his lusts, which were vigorous
when young. He later had a succession of obsessive interests including
a Czech lover, Charles Manson (whom he believed to be the reincar-
nation of ancient savage gods), Californian hippies (whom he saw as
a prelapsarian race of angels) and motorcyclist Hell's Angels (who
thrilled him). He combined an esoteric brilliance of intellect with a
childish bent: on a visit in the 1950s to Goronwy Rees's seaside house
in Wales he consumed sherbet and lollipops galore, and was found
screaming with fear in the drawing-room after, he said, meeting a ghost
on the stairs. These eccentricities never compromised his work or
reduced his value. Sir Alistair Horne, who had been an intelligence
officer based in Cairo, noted that his two ablest bosses, Claude Dewhurst
and Maurice Oldfield, were both homosexual. The campaign to identify
and exclude such men, Horne reckoned, 'caused a loss of talent to the
secret services comparable to Louis XIV's ill-conceived expulsion of
the Huguenots from France'.[8]

In these matters newspapers, like church pulpits, were 'half a generation at least behind the times', admitted the editor of the *Sunday
Dispatch* (Rothermere's forerunner of the *Mail on Sunday*). 'Fleet Street
morality was that of the saloon bar,' recalled Peter Wildeblood who
was appointed diplomatic correspondent of the *Daily Mail* in 1953:
'every sexual excess was talked about and tolerated, provided it was
"normal"'. Otherwise pressmen shrank from the abnormal. The *Daily
Express* journalist Sefton Delmer recalled his first meeting with the
German master-spy Otto John, who became a valued source for him.
It occurred in 1944 at Delmer's old school, St Paul's in Hammersmith,

which was being used as an interrogation centre for incoming aliens. John had dyed his hair and eyebrows while hiding from the Gestapo in Spain: Delmer's first reaction to the resultant peroxide brightness was hostile. 'Good God,' he thought, 'I do hope he is not another one of those!'[9]

On 10 June 1951 – three days after the disappearance of Burgess and Maclean had been publicly admitted – a notable article appeared in the *Sunday Dispatch*. Its author, Alastair ('Ali') Forbes, was an American of bounding self-confidence and histrionically anglicized manners. He was also a gossip with a love of showing that he knew the inside dirt; a voluptuary who was censorious of other people's pleasures; and a provocateur who liked to embroil people in denunciations, calumny and feuds. Forbes claimed that he had long suspected that Burgess was a secret member of the CPGB: 'if he has defected now it must either be on superior orders or because he believes that war is imminent'. He said little about male homosexuality in the *Sunday Dispatch*, other than to enjoin that 'the case for weeding out [from the Foreign Office] both sexual and political perverts seems unanswerable'; but his dig was made clear by the headline to his article, 'Whitehall in Queer Street'. Next day, in the Commons, the Labour MP George Wigg asked Morrison, as Foreign Secretary, to investigate Forbes's account of 'widespread sexual perversion in the Foreign Office' (although 'Whitehall in Queer Street' had not made any such sweeping allegation). Wigg added the absurd suggestion that, if these allegations were disproved, Forbes and the newspaper's editor Charles Eade should be prosecuted by the Crown for criminal libel. Morrison did nothing to defend his officials from obloquy, but instead gave the shocking reply, 'I have not been long enough at the Foreign Office to express an opinion.' As Harold Macmillan noted of Morrison's speeches as Foreign Secretary, he appeared 'to know nothing whatever about matters of the highest importance'. Conscious that he was 'quite out of his depth', his reaction to parliamentary challenges was 'bad-tempered, rude & silly'.[10]

There were class distinctions in MI5's approach to interviewing Burgess's sexual partners after he had vanished. James Pope-Hennessy and Peter Pollock were treated perhaps as curiosities but certainly with courtesy. Maxwell Knight, on 12 June 1951, was politely condescending about working-class Jack Hewit ('the "cosy one of the two who does the cooking"'), but Skardon, who had interviewed him a week earlier, had begun his report with a single-sentence paragraph: 'He is a loathsome creature.' It ended just as tersely, 'I was glad when the interview was over.' When Commander Leonard Burt of Special Branch (the officer who had arrested Nunn May and Fuchs) was asked to interview Hewit, Sir Harold Scott, the Metropolitan Police Commissioner, enjoined upon him the extreme delicacy of the inquiries. Burt assumed from this that Hewit was of 'the same social class as the principals in this enquiry'. Skardon corrected this misunderstanding by recounting Hewit's 'immoral background'. In Skardon's words, once Burt understood that Hewit was 'just an unpleasant working-class man, he did not feel that there should be any particular difficulty in handling him'.[11]

On 29 June Sir William Strang, PUS of the FO, asked Sir Alexander Cadogan to chair an inquiry into the Diplomatic Service's security checks on staff: the Cabinet Secretary, Lord Normanbrook, and the retired Ambassador Sir Nevile Bland were the two other members of the committee. Cadogan would arrive less than a minute before the due time, and start organizing his papers for the meeting. Brook would hustle in a couple of minutes late with his papers neatly arranged in a folder. 'Ah, there you are, Norman,' Cadogan would say, as if they had been waiting for a long time. He enjoyed teasing Brook, whom he thought a zealot, and liked to pretend to miss the point of what Brook was saying. Andrew Boyle, in *The Climate of Treason*, stated that the committee was chaired by Brook and thought Cadogan was a peer. He aspersed it as part of 'the Whitehall "Club"' and as sitting as 'judge and jury in its own cause'. This suggests partiality in the committee's work and inadequacy in their findings: neither charge is justified.[12]

Because Cadogan's remit specified the Diplomatic Service, he did not seek evidence from other Whitehall ministries or from the Civil Service Commission. Over the course of thirteen meetings, Cadogan, Bland and Brook heard evidence from six members of the Office: the PUS, Strang; the Deputy Under Secretary, Ashley Clarke; the intelligence expert Patrick Reilly; Carey-Foster of Security; Roderick Barclay, former head of the Personnel Department; and his successor Robin Hooper. Four external officials were seen: John Winnifrith, the Treasury official who had been involved in the extension of positive vetting; Menzies of SIS; White of MI5; and Sir Ronald Howe, who was Assistant Commissioner of Metropolitan Police in charge of the Criminal

Investigation Department. The Cadogan report confirmed the policy of positive vetting, which had been instituted before Burgess and Maclean disappeared, but which, through manpower shortages, had not yet been applied to them. Its conclusions were calm and serviceable: if their lack of razzamatazz displeased men like Boyle and Chapman Pincher, it was apt for the circumstances.

The most notable part of the Cadogan deliberations concerned a memorandum submitted by the Office on the subject of homosexuality in the Diplomatic Service. It was based on the certainty that Burgess had been homosexual, and on the dubious assumption that Maclean had been bisexual, although there is no available evidence of the latter having male sexual partners after he left Cambridge. Maclean, it seems, was being lumped together with Burgess in this respect for tidiness's sake. Rather as happened in the trials of Glading, Nunn May and Fuchs, an explanatory narrative was being devised that seemed coherent and convincing, although in truth it was unsupported by evidence and probably untrue. This FO memorandum has not been fully quoted before, although its consequences were far reaching. Its preliminaries were fair and sound:

> Homosexual and heterosexual tendencies are present to a varying extent in all human beings. There is no hard and fast dividing line between normality and abnormality. Many people indulge in homo-sexual practices in adolescence who subsequently lead an entirely normal sexual life. Some authorities indeed would say that it was unsafe to diagnose permanent inversion in an individual until the age of 25. All that can be said is that an individual is abnormal when homosexual tendencies predominate . . . The propensity to homo-sexuality is innate. In cases of 'true inversion' there is nothing that the individual, the doctor or the psychiatrist can do to remove it. Marriage affords no guarantee that the homosexual will not relapse into his old ways. The individual can curb or sublimate his tenden-cies; but the attempt to do so inevitably sets up stresses and involves problems which are not those of the ordinary run of mankind . . . So far, very little evidence has come to light that homosexuality has caused disloyalty, though there may be some connection between the homosexual and the other aspects of the Maclean–Burgess case.

This summary was followed by some negative riders. A homosexual man was 'subject to greater psychological stresses than the normal individual, even if he sublimates or restrains his natural inclinations. Restraint may add to the psychological tension.' Moreover, 'abnormality in one direction is often symptomatic of instability in others; and it may be that homosexuals have a greater tendency to extreme and unbalanced political views than normal persons. Their feeling that they are different from others may lead to a feeling of rejection by society, and give them a grudge against it.' The Office posited 'a solidarity between homosexuals which may in certain circumstances override other loyalties'. Certainly this type of man was potentially 'open to blackmail' and to pressure by hostile intelligence agents.

Then the Office reached the crunch. 'By far the most important problem is that of the United States. American public opinion is strongly anti-homosexual: the American security authorities are convinced that homosexuals are a security risk; and the State Department are peculiarly sensitive to the charges that are sometimes levelled against them that the U.S. Foreign Service is a refuge for expatriates and perverts.' As the State Department was determined to purge itself of homosexuals, 'the relationship of mutual trust and confidence between ourselves and the State Department may be endangered if they get the impression that we are ignoring the problem'. Chiefly in order to satisfy the Americans, the Office concluded that 'our policy should aim at eliminating homosexuals from the Foreign Service'. Already, in a circular letter sent to all heads of missions by the PUS, Strang, on 10 July, 'sexual abnormality' had been described as a 'danger signal'. Henceforth heads of overseas missions or of Foreign Office departments should report 'whenever they have genuine reasons to suspect that a member of their staff is so afflicted'. The Office in its evidence to Cadogan nevertheless disavowed McCarthy-style methods. 'Anything in the nature of a witch-hunt would not only be repugnant to our traditions but, by breeding an atmosphere of delation [denunciation] and distrust, would seriously affect the morale of the Service.'[13]

The Cadogan report, dated 1 November, tempered the departmental advice to exclude male homosexuals. It recommended a policy of surveillance, with leeway for personal discretion and the judging of cases on individual merits. 'We are now living in a state of international tension when a deliberate and skilfully directed attack is being made upon the minds and loyalties of our people and in particular of public officials and those handling highly confidential matters,' Cadogan's committee reported. It therefore recommended that 'any member of the Foreign Service who is suspected of indulging homosexual tendencies should be carefully watched, even though his conduct has not occasioned any public scandal, and that his appointment within the service should take account of this risk'. The employment of such men should not be 'a matter for hard and fast rules: we think it preferable to leave it to the discretion of those responsible for the reputation and efficiency of the Service'. Colleagues needed to treat one another with trust and respect. 'It would be distasteful to encourage the notion that it is the duty of every member of the Service to watch the behaviour of his colleagues and, in school parlance, to "blab" about them to the "Head". Spying and delation would be contrary to all the traditions of the Service and would gravely jeopardise its morale and efficiency.'[14]

The question of blackmail was irrelevant in the case of Burgess. He was a man who, as it were, faced the world with his flies undone. As Valentine Vivian of SIS had noted in 1950, he was too open about his habits to need to hush anyone into keeping them secret. Similarly, a Balkans expert who had joined SIS's Section D under Burgess's sponsorship doubted that someone so 'blatant' would be vulnerable to blackmail. Yet there was a big prohibitive jump in the years after the Cadogan report. Milo Talbot de Malahide was appointed as Carey-Foster's successor as the Office's head of security in July 1953, but was prematurely retired from that post in January 1954 – probably because of American suspicions of his elegant bachelorhood. It took nine months to find him a new post, as Envoy Extraordinary in the Laotian capital, Vientiane; but despite the face-saving sop of promotion to the rank of ambassador there, he was marked *en disponibilité* on the Foreign Office list in August 1956. The likely reason for this early end to an interesting career is implicit in a statement by the Marquess of Reading, Foreign Office spokesman in the House of Lords, in 1955. Burgess had been 'addicted' to 'homosexual practices', declared Reading, and a lesson had been learnt in the Office: 'anybody who is thought to be disposed to homosexual practices is thereby laying himself open to blackmail to an extent which makes him an unacceptable security risk'. Reading did not mention Maclean in this context.[15]

Whitehall, which was already committed to introducing positive vetting, was thus set by the Cadogan committee on a policy of a calm compromise. The Americans were to be placated, but Office systems were to be flexible and porous rather than rigid and impermeable. Whitehall disclaimed any wish for Gestapo methods or McCarthy-style loyalty purges. They had not reckoned, however, with the moral panic and vindictive cruelty of a free press. The practice of positive vetting, as it developed in the second half of the century, grew increasingly severe: apparently intensifying *after* the partial decriminalization of male homosexuality in 1967. In particular, higher levels of security clearance were withheld.

Like many of his colleagues, Robert Cecil did not submit to the indiscriminate new sexual regime, but preferred to use his own judgement. After his appointment as Consul General in Hanover in 1955, he noticed that a colleague who had previously been *en poste* there was continuing to visit the city at intervals and to be seen in the company of a pretty, blonde German telephone operator who worked in the British mission. When he teased the girl about her admirer, she replied, 'Oh, it's not me he comes to see! It's my young brother.' Although the Englishman, who held an important post at a contact-point between western Europe and the Soviet bloc, would have been 'a valuable scalp for the KGB', Cecil thought him too level-headed to submit to blackmail and decided that he was therefore not a security risk. Cecil was glad that he took no action on his discovery, for the Englishman prospered in his career and eventually reached the rank of ambassador. Civilization rests on mutual trust.[16]

'Friends in high places'

Newspapers and Washington officials incited one another in voicing alarm at sexually based national insecurity. In August 1952, for example, Percy Hoskins of the *Daily Express* told John Cimperman of the FBI that his newspaper held letters from Burgess identifying homosexuals in the Foreign Office. If it did, these may have been forgeries, for it was known that the Beaverbrook press paid well for anything that might be represented as a new lead. Cimperman hastened to MI5, where he asked if there was evidence of serving diplomats having been sexual partners of Burgess. 'I am afraid', A. F. Burbidge noted, 'I was extremely non-committal to Cimperman throughout the interview.' (The FBI's inquisition against same-sex heretics was made demented by the fact that its Torquemada, J. Edgar Hoover, was a ferocious closet-case himself.)[17]

In England in 1938 there had been 134 prosecutions for sodomy, 822 for attempted sodomy and 320 for gross indecency – a low rate reflecting juries' reluctance to convict on such charges. In 1952, after the Burgess and Maclean publicity, these figures stood at 670, 3,087 and 1,686 respectively. The following year a police commander from Scotland Yard was sent for three months to the USA to learn FBI techniques for purging government departments of male homosexuals. There then followed the notorious trials of Lord Montagu of Beaulieu. During the August bank holiday weekend of 1953 a camera was stolen from his bathing hut on the Solent. When he complained to the police, the thief countered that he had been sexually assaulted by Montagu. The young peer's adamant denial was discounted by the police. 'While the Director of Public Prosecutions was dithering about whether or not to bring his case, his mind was made up for him', recalled Montagu, 'by a threat of exposure from the Beaverbrook press. I was always led to believe that this came from the top – from Lord Beaverbrook himself.' While Montagu was taking refuge in Paris, two men visited his hotel and offered to arrange for him to take the same route to Russia as Burgess and Maclean. He reported this overture to MI5, although he suspected that it was an attempted Fleet Street entrapment. His first prosecution at Winchester Assizes on charges of committing an unnatural offence and indecent assault was discredited when it became clear that the police had tampered with the evidence.[18]

In January 1954 the DPP launched a new prosecution on different charges. 'I see the police are determined to have Lord Montagu!' Hugh Trevor-Roper wrote. 'They are obviously piqued by their failure at Winchester. I suppose a new ripple of apprehension is now running through the upper-class Homintern.' In the second case, Montagu had two co-defendants, a Dorset landowner named Michael Pitt-Rivers and Peter Wildeblood of the *Daily Mail*. As a diplomatic correspondent Wildeblood was treated as a security risk, and had his telephone tapped: a 'routine watch' was reportedly kept on his line until 1957. The principal prosecution witnesses were two RAF conscripts, Edward McNally and John Reynolds – described by prosecuting counsel as 'perverts' who 'cheerfully accepted corruption' and committed 'unnatural offences

... under the seductive influence of lavish hospitality'. McNally's evidence was especially vague, but he had been schooled to repeat one solid affirmation whenever he became confused. 'Mr Wildeblood committed an offence against me,' he insisted, with wooden-top phraseology that showed his police coaching clearly enough. Montagu, Wildeblood and Pitt-Rivers were convicted and imprisoned.[19]

The Admiralty issued new Fleet Orders in 1954 stressing 'the horrible nature of unnatural vice' and instructing naval officers 'to stamp out the evil'. In grotesquely specific detail, officers were told how to inspect sailors' underwear for seminal or faecal stains, and jars of Vaseline or Brylcreem for pubic hairs. Fearing that these new initiatives would be a cause for mirth, the Admiralty ordered officers to enlist 'the help of the steadier and more reliable men on the Lower Deck' to quell the deplorable tendency 'to treat these matters with levity'. The War Office, frightened of the 'essentially secret nature' of male homosexuality and apprehensive of 'contamination by civilian sources', introduced new regulations. The Air Ministry, however, were sure that because aircrews were all 'selected individuals with a paramount interest in flying', they were immune to 'corrupting influence', and that male homosexuality was 'almost entirely confined to ground trades'.[20]

Vansittart's loathing of male homosexuality drove him to make a vehement speech in a House of Lords debate in May 1954. He referred to Burgess and Maclean without naming them:

on the day when the news broke, I met a man – healthy-minded, all fresh air and exercise, and happily married – who said to me that by an extraordinary coincidence he happened to know all about one of those involved, and he poured out a horrified tale. When he had finished, I said, 'But did you also suspect that there was any question of disloyalty?' And this was his answer, which I think it would pay us all to ponder. He was immediately smitten with the prevalent modern fear of going too far and said, 'Oh, no, no, no! I did not suspect anything of that kind. None of us did. We knew about the drink. We thought there was something else. But otherwise he seemed a decent enough fellow.' I think the 'otherwise' contains a tremendous lot of history. 'Otherwise this' and 'otherwise that' – half of it comes from the fear of seeming intolerant, which may in the end prove our undoing.[21]

In David Footman's favourite Belgrade bar of the 1930s there had been a sly, ignorant barman whom he nicknamed 'Rothermere', because the man knew nothing but had an answer for everything. The difference between the Rothermere Mail group and Beaverbrook's Express newspapers was pithily put by Harold Macmillan: 'Lord Rothermere . . . like all the Harmsworths . . . only care[s] about money . . . Ld B (to be fair) cares more for spite & mischief than money.' While the *Daily Mail* reported the Lords debate under the headline 'SEX VICE', John Gordon in the *Sunday Express* warned against enemies of the people who wished 'to legalize perversion, and even to sanctify perverts . . . STUFF AND NONSENSE. Perversion is very largely a practice of the too idle and too rich. It does not flourish in lands where men work hard and brows sweat with honest labour. It is a wicked mischief, destructive not only of men but of nations.' Arthur Christiansen, editor of the *Daily Express*, told Beaverbrook that he had identified a 'notorious homosexual' on the Foreign Office Selection Board.[22]

After Petrov's revelations about Burgess and Maclean in 1955, Fleet Street became strident. The front page of the *Sunday Pictorial* special 'EVIL MEN' issue of 25 September thundered that the 'sordid secret' and 'wretched, squalid truth about Burgess and Maclean is that they were sex perverts'. It asserted that 'there has for years existed inside the Foreign Office service a chain or clique of perverted men' who by their machinations had 'protected' the duo and were still 'hoodwinking' public morality. Under the headline 'Danger to Britain', the story continued: 'Homosexuals – men who indulge in "unnatural" love for one another – are known to be bad security risks. They are easily won over as traitors. Foreign agents seek them out as spies.' Seven years later, preening himself on the 'EVIL MEN' articles, Hugh Cudlipp of the *Sunday Pictorial* noted with satisfaction: 'doctors, social workers and the wretched homosexuals themselves recognized this as a sincere attempt to get at the root of a spreading fungus'; he regretted, though, 'that nothing practical was done to solve the worst aspect of the problem – the protection of children from the perverts'.[23]

A Tory MP called Captain Henry Kerby had been elected in a recent by-election. Kerby, who had been born in Russia, spoke its language so fluently that he translated for Khrushchev and Bulganin during their state visit to England, for dignitaries who visited the Commons and as a member of parliamentary delegations to the Soviet Union in 1957 and 1959. He was an utter snake, who leaked party confidences to the lobby correspondent of the *Daily Express*, and served as MI5's informant in the Commons. When an all-party Civil Liberties group was inaugurated by MPs, he insinuated himself into the post of vice-chairman and acted as MI5's mole. After being dropped by MI5 in 1966, he became a Labour party informant of confidential Tory discussions and sought a knighthood from his opponents. Kerby, who had served in wartime military intelligence, gave a front-page interview in the *Sunday Pictorial*'s 'EVIL MEN' issue under the headline 'Who is Hiding the Man Who Tipped Off These Sex Perverts?' He decried 'the "brotherhood" of perverted men' responsible for the cover-up of 'flagrant homosexuality' among diplomatists: 'there are still many people of this ilk today in the Foreign Service'. The will of the people was being frustrated by withholding 'the names of those Foreign Office officials who shielded both traitors during their service'. Kerby wanted politicians to provide their officials as the quarry in a witch-hunt: 'The archaic tradition of Ministers manfully shouldering and shielding Civil Servants at the Foreign Office is ABSURD and DANGEROUS.'[24]

Burgess and Maclean's public re-emergence in Moscow in February 1956 prepared the way for another onslaught. On 11 March the *People*, which had published the Petrov revelations six months earlier, began to run a series of weekly articles on the Burgess and Maclean scandal. The pieces were anonymous, but an influential minority knew the identity of the author. The young historian Keith Thomas had recently received a kind letter from Goronwy Rees congratulating him as a fellow Welshman on his election as a Fellow of All Souls. Sixty years later Thomas still remembered seeing a copy of the *People* article, illustrated by a pair of sinister, peering eyes, lying on the central table in the college coffee-room and being discussed. Everyone realized that Rees was the author. His decision to sell his story to a Sunday scandal-sheet, and to let its hacks sensationalize the more temperate memoir that he had prepared, was an act of tragic self-spoliation. Rees was finding himself, in George Herbert's phrase, 'no star, but a quick coal of mortal fire': a bright but unstable force, who was burning out, his judgement unbalanced by an alcoholic intake that was ruining his health as well as disappointing his hopes of himself. The articles were intended by him as pre-emptive of any damage that Burgess might do him by revelations of their association before 1939; but his complex character included a liability to harm his own interests.

Rees let the *People* journalists attribute destructive exaggerations to him. 'Guy Burgess is the greatest traitor in our history,' stated the opening article. 'He was a Communist of the deepest Red.' At the time Rees was the most compassionate and enlightened member of the government inquiry into homosexuality and prostitution under the chairmanship of Sir John Wolfenden, so it is extraordinary that he let himself be used as a ventriloquist's dummy mouthing populist bigotry. 'For 20 years one incredibly vicious man used blackmail and corruption on a colossal scale to worm out Britain's most precious secrets for the rulers of Russia. That is the truth . . . that even today the men whose duty is to protect us from foreign spies dare not admit.' The ersatz Rees in the *People* warned, 'men like Burgess are only able to escape detection because THEY HAVE FRIENDS IN HIGH PLACES'. Wolfenden and the Home Office agreed that Rees must retire from the committee after such utterances.[25]

A subsequent issue of the *People* reverted to this prurient theme:

THE MOST PAINFUL PART OF THE ENTIRE GUY BURGESS AFFAIR IS THE STORY OF HIS INCREDIBLY DEPRAVED PRIVATE LIFE.

For this man who was the greatest traitor Britain has ever known – and who for a long time was my closest friend – indulged in practices that repel all normal people.

Yet I must place the facts before you because they disclose a state of affairs in high places that remains to this day a terrible danger to Britain's security.

Guy Burgess was not only guilty of practising unnatural vices. He also had, among his numerous friends, many who shared his abnormal tastes.

And he was in a position to blackmail some of them – including men in influential positions – to get information for his Russian masters.

Without naming Hewit or Footman, Rees gave a garbled account of Burgess's help to SIS in monitoring Henlein's telephone conversations at the Goring Hotel: 'he made use of a young man he had corrupted.

He actually got this perverted lad installed as a telephone operator in Henlein's hotel.' Without naming Blunt, he referred to 'a distinguished academic' as 'ONE OF BURGESS' BOON SEX COMPANIONS AND HE HOLDS A HIGH POSITION IN PUBLIC LIFE TODAY'. At All Souls it was clear, as it was to the cognoscenti elsewhere, that Rees meant Blunt. Isaiah Berlin, an All Souls friend who remained devoted to Rees *malgré tout*, said that no one except fellow-travellers objected to the attack on Burgess, and few people minded 'the anti-homosexual tone of the piece'. What was found unforgivable was the 'hysterical McCarthyism' of the accusations that the Foreign Office was full of homosexual communists. Rees was ostracized by many friends: among former intelligence officers Hampshire sent him an indignant letter, but A. J. Ayer, F. W. Deakin, Footman and Zaehner did not waver in their affection for him.[26]

The prejudices of the *Sunday Pictorial*'s 'EVIL MEN' articles and of the *People*'s 'Guy Burgess Stripped Bare' series were assimilated by institutions that ought to have been wiser. Thus the memorandum of evidence submitted by the British Medical Association to the Wolfenden committee began by declaring: 'The proper use of sex, the primary purpose of which is procreative, is related to the individual's responsibility to himself and the nation.' Physicians were pained to 'observe their patients in an environment favourable to sexual indulgence, and surrounded by irresponsibility, selfishness and a preoccupation with immediate materialistic satisfaction'. The BMA deplored licentious advertisements, suggestive articles and photographs in Sunday newspapers, cheap novels with lurid covers and the eroticism of the cinema, all of which 'tends to increase heterosexual over-activity, while, for homosexuals, it fans the fire of resentment at the latitude allowed to heterosexual indulgence'. There was a national threat, the BMA judged. 'Homosexual practices tend to spread by contact, and from time to time they insidiously invade certain groups of the community.' Male homosexuals aroused public hostility by placing 'loyalty to one another above their loyalty to the institution or government they serve'. Such outcasts, when in positions of authority, gave preferential treatment to their kind or required 'homosexual subjection as an expedient for promotion. The existence of practising homosexuals in the Church, Parliament, Civil Service, Forces, Press, radio, stage and other institutions constitutes a special problem.' If the BMA words meant anything, the Association wanted a purge of sexual deviancy undreamt of by J. Edgar Hoover.[27]

The psychiatrists of the National Health Service's famous Tavistock Clinic in London also submitted evidence to Wolfenden. 'The staff of this Clinic are unanimously of the opinion that homosexuality is a disorder of the personality and as such to be regarded as an illness.' They discerned in the majority of homosexuals 'a lack of capacity to form lasting affectionate relationships (of a non-sexual character) towards any other persons, with a correlated morbid degree of self-centredness which may take the form of self-admiration or self-abasement.' Tavistock psychiatry deplored any sexual act 'which offends public decency or decorum, or which tends to flaunt or glorify this mental illness as if it were a superior social cult'. For this reason it favoured 'strict legislation in relation to the offences of importuning, corrupting, soliciting or the establishment and maintenance of clubs or "maisons de rendezvous" for homosexual purposes'. The Tavistock reiterated: 'abnormal sexual behaviour should be regarded basically as a public health problem. The homosexual should be thought of and proclaimed in the public mind as an immature, sick and potentially "infectious" person, and the whole subject divested of the glamour of wickedness as well as the aesthetic of superiority.'[28]

It is too much to say that the BMA and Tavistock prejudices were engendered by Burgess and Maclean; but certainly such views were escalated by them.

John Vassall

In Ian Fleming's novel *Goldfinger* (1959) James Bond meets a lesbian couple whose names, Pussy Galore and Tilly Masterson, indicate which of them plays the feminine role and which the butch. 'Pansies of both sexes were everywhere, not completely homosexual, but confused,' Bond reflects. 'He was sorry for them, but he had no time for them.' The fear that 'unhappy sexual misfits', as Bond called them, were growing ubiquitous had entered the national psyche since 1951. This anxiety was to be invigorated three years after *Goldfinger* by the Admiralty spy case.[29]

In April 1962 the Soviet defector Anatoli Golitsyn gave information which led to the detection of a junior Admiralty official who was a communist spy. John Vassall had been born in 1924, the son of an impecunious clergyman, and was educated at a boarding school in Monmouth, where his sex life began with his fellow pupils. After conscription into the Royal Air Force in 1943, he became expert at handling Leica cameras, developing pictures and making prints. Following demobilization in 1947, he became a clerical officer in the Admiralty. He was a sexually confident young Londoner who attracted prosperous and amusing men. 'He was very successful in this sphere,' wrote Rebecca West, and 'could hold his own in an outlaw world where tact, toughness and vigilance had to be constantly on the draw'.[30]

By his own account, Vassall applied on impulse for a post as a clerk on the Naval Attaché's staff at the British embassy in Moscow in 1954. The likelier truth – as in Marshall's case – is that he was induced by a prior Soviet contact to apply for a Moscow posting with espionage in mind. Like Marshall again, Vassall claimed that he had been driven to espionage by the snobbery of embassy life. He described, or invented, rebuffs and snubs supposedly delivered by the Ambassador and his wife, Sir William and Lady Hayter, by the Naval Attaché for whom he worked and by other diplomats. After his arrest in 1962, his fluent rigmarole of complaints about the aloofness of the Hayters, the rigidity of the embassy hierarchy and the inexorable protocol was uncannily like Marshall's. It seems to have been a KGB instruction for English spies, if caught, to parrot tales of class stigma and subjugation.[31]

Vassall claimed that one evening in Moscow he was dosed with a drug that made him extra-suggestible, and induced him to strip naked and disport with three men while being photographed under harsh lights. In later public self-exculpations Vassall spoke of crying out with pain; but at the age of thirty, after multiple experiences, he can hardly have been a novice at being buggered, and this is just one of several unbelievable flourishes in his account of his entrapment. According to his later narrative, he agreed to spy after being confronted by compromising photographs and threatened with gaol. Only an inexperienced, helpless man would have submitted to KGB threats of exposure, and Vassall was hardy, smart and resourceful. A man who had the nerves for years of high-level espionage would not have been so timid with blackmailers.

Vassall began taking documents from the Naval Attaché's office, giving them to Soviet agents for photographing and returning them. After resuming work in the Naval Intelligence Department in London in 1956, he regularly photographed material. After a year he was appointed assistant secretary in the private office of the Civil Lord of the Admiralty. In 1959 he was posted to the Fleet section, where he had access to secret documents. He suspended spying when the Portland spy scandal broke, but resumed in December 1961 and continued until his arrest in September 1962.

Vassall's Old Bailey trial in October was held partly in camera. The prosecution accepted his story of the compromising photographs as the reason for supplying his Soviet controllers with documents. It was no truer than the prosecution arguments at the trials of Glading, Nunn May and Marshall. The judge endorsed this tale in his summing-up. After Vassall had been sentenced to eighteen years' imprisonment, MPs debated his activities without anyone questioning the official line. A subsequent tribunal of investigation led by the law lord Lord Radcliffe did not challenge the legend. Radcliffe's report enforced the view that Vassall was flighty, malleable and submissive, which seemed less threatening than the reality that he was a resilient and abundant source of secrets for Moscow.

In order to pay for his defence, Vassall sold his memoirs to the *Sunday Pictorial* for £7,000. The first instalment appeared on the first weekend after his conviction, and was full of the archness and salacious guilt that the newspaper required for its money. The stifling class discrimination of the Moscow embassy and Vassall's bracing lack of snobbery were stressed. The front-page lead in that issue parroted the new conventional wisdom – unknown before the FBI's pressure on Whitehall in 1951 – that 'civil servants with homosexual tendencies were especially vulnerable as security risks'. Detectives were tracking such men and expunging them from influential government posts. A week later, the *Sunday Pictorial* reported Vassall urging the need for an inquiry into 'sex blackmail' of officials 'to weed out homosexuals and bisexuals in high office'. Many of them, Vassall was made to say, appeared to be 'respectable married men' beyond suspicion of 'abnormal sexual practices'. The *News of the World* had to vie with the *Sunday Pictorial* exclusive serialization as best it could. On 28 October it moved into its customary mode of scaremongering about 'twilight people working in places where they can betray their country to indulge their perverted pleasures'. It pretended that Burgess was the spymaster who had recruited and run Vassall: 'BURGESS

SITS IN MOSCOW LIKE A PATIENT TOAD AWAITING HIS NEXT WILLING VICTIM.'[32]

Vassall was paroled from prison in 1972, and three years later published his self-serving memoirs which made him, for a few months, a celebrity spy. Before publication of the memoirs he holidayed in Brighton with the former Labour MP Thomas Skeffington-Lodge, who (in the words of the novelist Francis King) took him incognito to a bar, where he introduced him to 'a male tart' who was brought back to the house and paid after giving satisfaction. Some time later, when Vassall's memoirs were being promoted by the publisher, an outraged rent boy returned to Skeffington-Lodge's front door. 'He had been watching the telly and had seen his former client on it. How dare S-L get him to go to bed with a spy?'[33]

Charles Fletcher-Cooke

The FBI's obsession with hunting perverts, the Cadogan committee's focus on male homosexuality rather than alcoholism as the primary 'danger signal', the misdirection about Maclean's sexual tastes, the spurious evidence of motives adduced at Vassall's trial, the prejudice of journalists and Fleet Street's appetite for personalizing issues and making scapegoats created an unpleasant national atmosphere.

One forgotten casualty is the politician-barrister Charles Fletcher-Cooke. Born in 1914, he was an undergraduate at Peterhouse, a small, reactionary Cambridge college containing few fellow-travellers. In the summer of 1935 he joined a group of young CPGB members or sympathizers which visited Russia. Apart from Fletcher-Cooke, these included Blunt, John Madge, Charles Rycroft, Brian Simon, Michael Straight and Michael Young, all of whom made dutiful visits to showpiece factories and collective farms. Fletcher-Cooke's special interest, however, was the Moscow theatre festival. 'We worried that we were squandering the resources of the Worker's State if we put two lumps of sugar in our tea,' recalled Straight. 'We tried not to see the poverty, the squalor, the primitiveness that surrounded us wherever we went.'[34]

Fletcher-Cooke edited *Granta*, was president of the Cambridge Union and got a first in his finals. He was called to the bar at Lincoln's Inn in 1938, entered the chambers of the Labour lawyer Sir William Jowitt, co-authored a textbook on monopolies and restrictive practices and later took silk. He joined naval intelligence in 1940, and was posted to Washington in 1943 with the rank of lieutenant commander charged with liaison with US naval intelligence. 'I am quite hopeless to fight our battles here,' he admitted to Noël Annan. 'I succumb to the charm of the American navy immediately. And it's very difficult to explain . . . when I come back having bartered our whole case for a smile!' His posting back to London, where he was to work on the Cabinet Office's Joint Intelligence staff, left him with 'a broken heart', he told Annan. On paper he left the gender of his lovers unspecified – 'they are so beautiful, so gentle, *so affectionate*' – but admitted that his experiences left him 'near tears continually. It's just as well to part.' Before leaving the US, Fletcher-Cooke had 'an eight cylinder orgy in New York – the Metropolitan, "Oklahoma", the Navy yards at Brooklyn, and some squandering of dollars in the stores'.[35]

At the general election of 1945 Fletcher-Cooke contested East Dorset as Labour candidate. He was legal adviser to the Foreign Office at the Danube River conference held at Belgrade in 1948. Vyshinsky's negotiating brutality – the Russians opposed unrestricted Danube navigation as they did any measure that smacked of the American pet project of internationalized European waterways, and refused compensation for nationalized property – led Fletcher-Cooke to resign from the Labour party. He had transferred his political allegiance by 1951, when he was elected as Conservative MP for the Lancashire cotton town of Darwen. Fred Warner listed him to MI5 in June 1951 as one of Burgess's closest friends.

Fletcher-Cooke noticed women's clothes but was deaf to their speech. 'Can anyone think of anything said by a Lady Member during this Session?' he asked after his first year in the Commons. 'I remember vividly what they look like, but not a word that they have said . . . First prize for turn-out is shared by Mrs Castle, whose dazzling yellows draw every eye, and by Lady Tweedsmuir, the exponent of that dying cult, Good Style.' He was a connoisseur of the performing arts: in 1946 he contributed an ironical yet stirring report in the *Observer* of the first post-war Salzburg Music Festival, at which the cast of *Der Rosenkavalier* threatened a sit-down strike between acts because they were so hungry, while other performers lamented the European-wide shortage of catgut; in 1953 he complained in parliament that a work permit had been refused to the New Jersey actress Yolande Donlan to enable her to take the part of Peter Pan in a Christmas run, a Ministry of Labour official having told the theatre management that the part was 'not suitable to be played by an American'.[36]

As a backbencher in the 1950s Fletcher-Cooke pressed for repeal of the criminal sanctions still visited so traumatically on people who survived suicide attempts. He had crisp nicknames for people, for example calling his bombastic ministerial colleague Lord Hailsham 'the Pathetic Fallacy'. In 1960 he was one of only twenty-two Tory MPs to vote in favour of the partial decriminalization of homosexuality (174 voted against): he was brave enough to denounce the vote publicly as a 'fiasco'. He grieved at the birth of a stillborn child from his short-lived marriage to an ex-actress. In 1961 he was appointed Parliamentary Under Secretary at the Home Office, where he proved adept at speaking strongly against crime while supporting less brutal treatment of criminals. He also achieved the passing of the Suicide Act. In the Commons his terse wit was an antidote to the Home Secretary, Henry Brooke, who (in Macmillan's description) 'answers questions with a portentous & often risible solemnity'.[37]

Then, in 1962, Burgess's tipsy friend Lord Maugham introduced Fletcher-Cooke to a teenager named Anthony Turner, who was both an ex-borstal inmate and a policeman's son. Early in 1963 Fleet Street reporters were tipped off that Turner was living in Fletcher-Cooke's flat in Great Peter Street, near the Palace of Westminster. Shortly afterwards Turner was stopped by Stepney police while exceeding the speed limit in Fletcher-Cooke's Austin Princess. 'I have had to deal with a sad case of Fletcher-Cooke (Under Sec. Home Office) who has got into trouble,' Harold Macmillan noted on 21 February. 'I fear he will have to resign.' (Macmillan was dealing at the time with the repercussions of Philby's disappearance from Beirut, and had Richard Llewellyn's Burgess-and-Maclean-inspired novel, *Mr Hamish Gleave*, as his bedtime reading.) Ten days later Turner was convicted at Bow Street magistrates' court of driving while unlicensed and uninsured. Fletcher-Cooke's ministerial career was over.[38]

Fletcher-Cooke's Darwen constituents supported him, so that he remained their MP until the constituency was abolished twenty years later. Within MI5, however, his Cambridge and recent friendships prompted the idea of giving renewed scrutiny to former contacts of Burgess who were or might be homosexuals. The object was to discover if any of them were vulnerable to blackmail while holding positions, as Fletcher-Cooke had done until recently, where they had access to classified information. 'We must reckon', urged an MI5 officer, 'that the Russians will have been interested in learning from BURGESS the names of his homosexual friends and that they will subsequently have made it their business to discover if any of these people were worth blackmailing.'[39]

The versatility, altruism, deprecating wit and sense of duty that characterized Fletcher-Cooke are always in short supply in parliament. Yet the whole nature of the man was now suspect. For the rest of the century there would be no respite in the official rejection of sexual variety that had been started as a sop to J. Edgar Hoover.

CHAPTER 19

The Exiles

Burgess and Maclean in Moscow

In exile the Cambridge spies continued to make trouble. After nearly five years of invisibility and silence, Burgess and Maclean reappeared on 11 February 1956 at a hastily improvised press conference held in a suite in Moscow's National Hotel. In a sitting-room dominated by a giant mirror framed in porcelain, with cupids and gold fittings, written statements were handed to the four journalists present. There was an uninformative question-and-answer session that lasted about five minutes. 'For a foreigner in the Soviet Union,' as a later Ambassador in Moscow, Sir Duncan Wilson, noted, 'there are no degrees of knowledge, only degrees of ignorance.'[1]

There were two reasons for the sudden disclosure of the missing diplomats. Anthony Eden had recently returned from a successful prime ministerial visit to Washington: any revival of the Burgess–Maclean story chafed Anglo-American unity at a sore spot. Moreover, the post-Stalinist Soviet leaders, Nikita Khrushchev and Nikolai Bulganin, were due to pay a state visit to the young Queen Elizabeth in April. The Kremlin had belatedly accepted that, unless doubts about the whereabouts of the missing diplomats were dispelled, the visit would be marred by endless distracting press questions. As it was, there were disharmonious passages during the state visit. At a dinner for the Soviet and Labour parliamentary leaders, George Brown cracked an ill-appreciated joke that the Soviet Union was a breakaway movement from the Transport & General Workers' Union. He later toasted Khrushchev with noisy semi-mockery, 'Here's to the big boss,' to which Khrushchev raised his glass in reply and said, 'You look like a little boss yourself.'[2]

The great fiasco of the visit occurred underwater. SIS sent a heavy-smoking, hard-drinking frogman named Lionel ('Buster') Crabb diving into Portsmouth waters to spy on the cruiser *Ordzhonikidze*, which had brought the Soviet leaders to England. He never resurfaced. Fleet Street ran amok speculating whether he had defected, been kidnapped or drowned by misadventure. Inevitably, given Fleet Street's lubricity, some hinted without evidence or relevance that he was bisexual. The speculation was not stilled when a headless corpse, wearing Crabb's diver's costume, appeared fourteen months later on a sandbank in Chichester harbour. This botched *Ordzhonikidze* venture resulted in the dismissal of 'Sinbad' Sinclair as 'C' of SIS and his replacement by Dick White, who had previously succeeded Sillitoe as Director General of MI5 in 1953.

The curt press conference in the National Hotel started a news storm raging across the English-speaking world. A few days later the *Sunday Express* asked Burgess to send a message for publication. He responded with a 789-word cable which resembled Delmer's Moscow-line reports in the *Daily Express* on the threat of German militarism. 'To give unlimited backing to, and to rearm, precisely the same expansionist social forces in Germany which have created two wars in this century, is a wild and dangerous gamble,' wrote Burgess. 'The Hitlers of the future, like the Hitlers of the past, can be easily dealt with if there is Anglo-Soviet collaboration.' He attacked US foreign policy while praising Mao Tse-tung's regime: 'The Chinese People's Government is a Government of the Chinese people by the Chinese people for the Chinese people.' His article was flanked by a *Sunday Express* editorial berating the Kremlin for 'putting up a drunken traitor like Burgess to soft-talk the people of Britain'. Beaverbrook's hirelings, who had sought Burgess's views, declared with their usual grace: 'Deeds will win friendship. Not the propaganda of a pervert.'[3]

On 25 February Driberg wrote to Burgess asking if he might interview him in Moscow and enclosing a column that he had contributed to that day's *Reynolds News*. Petrov (the source of the first sure confirmation that Burgess was a long-term Soviet spy rather than Maclean's impulsive, muddle-headed travel companion) was dismissed in Driberg's article as 'a paid nark'. Driberg praised Burgess as 'whimsical and erudite', decried 'the Morrison–Macmillan witch-hunt' against the defected diplomats and concluded, 'if it be true they have been advising the Kremlin on relations with the West, and so are to some extent responsible for easing

East–West tension, they may yet be hailed as benefactors of the human race'. Burgess replied on 15 March with standard KGB disinformation: 'what you say about Petrov is true – he was a "paid nark" . . . he gave his original information C.O.D. [cash on delivery] and subsequently added to it – in different and self-contradictory forms in England and America – on the hire-purchase system. They always do – and the Foreign Office and Intelligence services should know that perfectly well.' Defectors like Petrov and Krivitsky 'invent to earn their keep . . . but I don't want to go here into a long screed about not having been an agent. There is no evidence that I was: in fact I wasn't, and that's that.'[4]

Burgess's first visitor in July 1956 was his mother, with whom he spent a month's seaside holiday at Sochi. They stayed in an enclave for privileged members of the Soviet bureaucracy rather than in the prole-tarian resort where loudspeakers boomed martial music interspersed with propaganda about communist triumphs and capitalist villainy. The *Daily Express* falsely reported that Eve Bassett had travelled under an alias. Her return journey proved an ordeal that half killed her: aggres-sive journalists swarmed around the tired old lady during a stopover at Stockholm airport; 'I had an hour & a half of 3rd degree, no escape from them'; the *Daily Express* was so avid for Burgess relics that its reporter collected her cigarette stubs.[5]

Driberg was Burgess's next visitor from London. During his August fortnight in Moscow, he was photographed by the KGB fellating a man in a urinal, and was cajoled into becoming a KGB informant codenamed LEPAGE. LEPAGE reported on the dynamics of the Labour national executive and parliamentary Labour party, and retold gossip about the foibles and frailties of Labour leaders. Although the Soviets overesti-mated the influence that Driberg could exert as chairman of the Labour party in 1957, he peddled their line during the nuclear disarmament rows that rent the party. He cut contacts with the KGB in 1968 when they increased pressure on him while he was recovering from a heart attack. Driberg had been one of Maxwell Knight's MI5 sources inside the CPGB for nearly twenty years until 1941. He also supplied the Czech intelligence services with parliamentary assessments during the 1960s. MI5's relations with him remained cagey but cordial throughout.

Driberg's first task for the KGB was to write a hurried, obsequious book entitled *Guy Burgess: A Portrait with Background*. He netted £5,000 by selling its serialization rights to the *Daily Mail*, which ran his paltry pieces in October under the billing 'News that even MI5 could not get'. These represented Maclean as the dominant partner in the escape and as a devout communist; Burgess was treated as his subordinate, and painted as no worse than an extreme socialist. MI5 judged that Burgess hoped that this 'white-wash' would be the enabling preliminary to his return to London if the Labour party won the next general election: 'he might even hope to have a friend in Ministerial circles in the form of DRIBERG himself'.[6]

Driberg's book had the misfortune to be published in November 1956 when Europe was reeling from the ruthlessness with which the Soviet Union had suppressed the Hungarian uprising. His presentation of Burgess and Maclean as heralds of peaceful coexistence, with the moral equivalency of pacifist pro-Boer campaigners of 1899–1902, was belied by the nationalist aggression of Moscow's actions against Budapest. 'Hungary has put a new gloss on tales of individual conscience and loyalties above country,' declared a *Manchester Guardian* editorial. 'The Burgesses of this world . . . belong to the past. It is doubly unimportant whether they now strum the Eton boating song in Moscow or in Mayfair.' While members of the CPGB and other European communists recanted their faith, Burgess in Moscow could not forswear the old creed.[7]

Edward Crankshaw of the London School of Economics reviewed Driberg's corrupt propaganda in the *Observer* under the headline 'Unbelievable'. He later admitted to Patrick Reilly that he found the little book so ill-written that he could only skim its pages. His review identified its hub as the chapter giving Burgess's explanation of his flight in 1951: 'if one does not believe it, then the book has no value at all', Crankshaw judged. 'The actual account of the escape is an insult to the intelligence, full of improbabilities and inconsistencies.' *Portrait with Background* denied that Burgess had been a Soviet spy, and depicted him as a lofty idealist wrestling with his fine conscience. Alan Pryce-Jones, a reviewer who had known Burgess well, teased him as a mix between 'Meddlesome Matty', the irritating fidget in a Victorian nursery homily, and Lupin Pooter, the brash, silly chancer in *The Diary of a Nobody*. Burgess was quintessentially frivolous, wrote Pryce-Jones, 'for the essence of frivolity is to be unable to perceive any necessary connexion between cause and effect, to treat every act and every passing idea as though they could, at will, be made self-sufficient'. Driberg's book, despite the scornful reviews, showed the sales-value of Burgess and Maclean: thereafter journalists telephoned Burgess for topical quotes, or visited him in Moscow for headline-grabbing interviews, which pleased the Kremlin because constant references to him discomfited Whitehall.[8]

Besides Driberg's book, Burgess was eager to read acclaimed new biographies, histories and novels as they were published in London, and advised on English-language books that might safely be translated and circulated to the Soviet policy elite. He told Nora Beloff that the great aim of his life was to persuade the Russian authorities to commission a translation of Proust. He parroted Moscow's denigration of Pasternak's novel *Dr Zhivago*. 'I don't consider that the Soviet Government will penalise Pasternak,' he told an English journalist who telephoned him. 'I don't think there is any possibility of his losing his house or suffering any other penalty.' He had abandoned reading the book after ten pages, he claimed: 'There is no objection here to reading anti-Soviet literature, but I found it boring. I cannot understand why the quislings of the West have praised this book and compared it to *War and Peace*.'[9]

Anthony Blunt acted as an intermediary between MI5 and Eve Bassett, advised the old lady on parrying press attention, steered her contacts with her son and helped MI5 in quelling his hopes of returning to London. 'He enjoyed knowing that he could do something terribly well,' Neil MacGregor, one of Blunt's protégés and a future director of the National Gallery, told Miranda Carter. His success depended upon the impermeable compartmentalization of his connoisseurship and espionage so that neither could leak into the other. 'I suspect', said MacGregor, 'that he got a great deal of enjoyment out of keeping the two bits separate and not tripping up. You have to be terribly clever to carry it off, and he knew that he was terribly clever. There was a delight in the game, in being able to do it so completely, and to live completely differently in the two worlds must have been quite exhilarating. My hunch would be that that was what really kept it going: the intoxication of playing this wonderfully complex game.'[10]

There was little affinity between Burgess and Maclean, although they made similar jokes about the twinning of their names like those of department stores for middle-class Londoners. 'So awful and boring being chained to poor Donald like Marshall to Snelgrove,' Burgess complained to the actress Coral Browne. Maclean wrote to his fellow roisterer Philip Toynbee: 'Burgess and Maclean! We have become like Swan and Edgar, or Debenham and Freebody; yet I neither know Guy very well nor like him very much.'[11]

Maclean and his old boon companion Philip Toynbee tried to revive their old friendship, despite the orthodox Marxism-Leninism of the first and the other being a repentant communist who had grown to loathe totalitarianism. 'The central point is whether there would have been fascism in Hungary if the Soviet army had not intervened,' Maclean insisted to Toynbee after the Soviet aggression of 1956. Without Russian military occupation, would the Hungarian people 'have had a better life – freer, with more food, clothes, housing, schools, books, hospitals, holiday places – all the things that make the basis for the happiness of a man and his family? Or would they have had a worse one, ruled in effect by capitalists, the Church and the landlords, with some sort of fascist front and permanent witch-hunts to keep down the enemies of such people – in short a sort of Franco Spain?' Maclean argued that Hungary would have become a vassal state serving American capitalism if there had not been Russian armed intervention. 'We should have seen repeated in Europe, with European modifications, the sort of real horror which the Americans in rather similar circumstances have created in South Viet-Nam and South Korea.' He promised Toynbee that 'the nightmare' of Stalinist purges was over in the Soviet Union. 'The enemy you think you are fighting – Stalinism, brutality, firing-squads – isn't there any more.' The Maclean–Toynbee friendship foundered after this.[12]

Free to resume contact with his mother and brother, Maclean rhapsodized about the reality of a socialist state. 'It's neither a bronzed youth looking towards the sunrise nor a plain-clothes socialist official coldly ordering everybody about, but a great swarming mass of human beings going about the business of living,' he informed Lady Maclean in August 1956 in a letter that he knew would be intercepted and read by officials in Moscow and London. Under a dictatorship of the proletariat, 'it doesn't take long to realise that they are all going in a good direction, having burst the bonds of capitalism which hold everything back or, even worse, force whole peoples with [sic] war'. In private conversation he was more critical. The former Soviet spy inside OSS, Maurice

Halperin, settled in Moscow in 1958, and befriended an Englishman named Mark Frazer without realizing at first that this was the Moscow alias of Maclean. The men talked with reasonable openness about their disappointment with Khrushchev's regime. Maclean divided the Soviet leadership into two distinct camps, 'the Progressives and the Black Hundreds'. He abominated the latter die-hard group, and despised one of its leaders, Andrei Gromyko as, in his words, 'a jumped-up peasant'. Maclean was also said to be 'deeply wounded by his treatment in the Western press, and by his portrayal as a homosexual'.[13]

As a forcibly retired social networker Burgess was frustrated by the limited scope in Moscow for regenerative gossip. He longed for well-connected, informative visitors from London. 'You will have heard that I normally prefer boys,' he told Nora Beloff, 'but I will make an exception in your case.' He advised her on survival in Moscow: in negotiations with bureaucrats, bang fists on tables and shout them down; storm at hotel servants in order to get good service. Members of the British embassy were instructed to leave any gathering attended by Burgess or Maclean; but they had indirect contact through the many reports that English visitors to Moscow provided of Burgess, who craved meetings, and the scarcer accounts of Maclean, who avoided them.[14]

Patrick Reilly, who was Ambassador in Moscow in 1957–60, remitted to London an account received in 1959 from Edward Crankshaw of three recent meetings with Burgess. 'We exchanged some quite hard words, calling spades spades, but quietly and reasonably,' Crankshaw wrote in his invaluably unbiased appraisal. 'I had never known anyone who flaunted his homosexuality so openly: whether he did this in England others will know. But he neither bullied one nor bored one with it. And once I got accustomed to this strange atmosphere I liked him very much and finished up by being deeply sorry for him, although at no time did he exhibit self-pity.' Burgess, said Crankshaw, was avid 'for the opportunity to talk and talk and talk with someone who, sex apart, could speak his language'. Tonya, 'his "boy friend" who lives with him, is a young factory mechanic who plays the concertina beautifully, keeps up an incessant moan about living conditions and the regime, and is intelligent, unsqualid, and pleasant in a pansy way. B also has a "boy friend" who is a priest at the Novo Devichi church. Over 6 foot tall, youngish and wholly repellent – v. handsome in a horrible way – and corrupt to the core. B is quite obviously head over heels in love

with this monster.' Crankshaw watched Burgess gazing at the priest
during a service: 'B's face was radiant and he was clearly transported
with delight. One could have wept.' Crankshaw assessed Burgess's political views as at the level of 'intelligent junior Party members . . . He
said he could not live now anywhere but in the USSR, so long as the
cold war continued. His anti-Americanism is as strong as ever, and he
said he would be stifled in a non-socialist country, in spite of the many
sins and defaults of this one. At the same time he talked incessantly
and with delight of Eton and Oxford [sic] and mutual friends.'
Crankshaw's companion Doreen Marston asked Burgess to telephone
Maclean to arrange a meeting. 'Melinda wanted to meet us but Donald
would not hear of it. Burgess got angry and called him in effect a stuffed
shirt. Donald got angry back.' Burgess said that Maclean 'liked laughing
at himself, but could not bear it when others laughed at him', whereas
he, Burgess, 'found it almost impossible to laugh at himself, though he
tried very earnestly, but he did not mind being laughed at by others'.
Burgess agreed with Crankshaw's strictures on 'the atavistic methods
of repression and treachery' used to repress the Hungarian uprising of
1956, 'but insisted that, although there was a genuine and reasonable
revolt among the factory workers and the intelligentsia, the Soviet Govt.
had sufficient evidence of American efforts to support such a rising . . .
to make it necessary for them to use extreme measures'. As he talked,
Burgess paced incessantly up and down the room, and seemed 'full of
almost incoherent impulses'. He was desperate to visit his seventy-seven-
year-old mother: 'He expresses conviction that he cannot be nabbed
on an official secrets or treason charge, though he thinks M.I.5 might
nobble him and rig a trial in camera; he was a little lurid about that.
He also thought he might be taken on a charge of homosexual conduct
and put away for a bit and was interested in the workings of the statute
of limitations.' Crankshaw's conclusion was compassionate but fatalistic:
'The man is half dotty, not actively vicious'; trapped in 'the sort of
personal tragedy that can only be ended by death. It is a terrible waste,
but the waste is absolute.'[15]

The England to which Burgess wished to return was changing fast.
'Macmillan has captured the hearts of the great British public,' Harold
Nicolson warned him in 1959. 'The proletariat is becoming bourgeois,
or so close to the middle classes that they are beginning to feel themselves budding capitalists. Thus they regard extreme socialism as a relic

of their impoverished youth and aspire to be among those who stand by the established order.' Next year a writer in the *Spectator* mused on 'this fascinating, frightening, trembling moment of time' in which the working class was revelling in its new-found 'selfish solidarity, its mass-produced culture, its cheerful apathy'. The pool of potential Labour votes was notable for 'its reluctance to enrol in crusades, its obsession with trivial, sentimental injustices, its old-fashioned affection for capital punishment, bad food, derelict transport, hypocritical laws, hideous architecture, and sensational newspapers, its sudden outbursts of point-less and ineffectual violence'. Michael Young, the sociologist who had accompanied Blunt on his visit to the Soviet Union in 1935, wrote his seminal pamphlet *The Chipped White Cups of Dover* in 1960: 'More people than ever before recognise that Britain is *inferior* in many ways it should not be to other countries in Europe and America. More people than ever before recognise that in certain respects Britain is *superior* in many ways it should not be to other countries in Asia and Africa. Britain is too drab in relation to Europe, and too selfish in relation to Asia and Africa.' With the exception of the Iberian despotisms, Salazar's Portugal and Franco's Spain, almost every western European country excelled Britain in the quality of their public amenities: town planning, architecture, transport and the scope for enjoying leisure. Young found Britain's complacent insularity to be pitiful. 'We go on arrogantly refusing to learn the languages of Europe,' said Young, and 'go on making ourselves ridiculous by talking English a little louder when we get to Orly [airport]'.[16]

Macmillan described the Soviet Union in 1961 as 'this strange system, half Orwellite & half Byzantine', but its pioneering technological feats, notably the orbiting of the planet by the satellite Sputnik in 1957 and Yuri Gagarin's outer-space flight in 1961, increased anxieties that Britain was technologically retarded and economically failing. After two years of guerrilla warfare, Fidel Castro announced his seizure of power in Cuba on 1 January 1959, and was joined a day later in Havana by his deputy commander, a Marxist physician from Argentina named Ernesto ('Che') Guevara. Castro was an innovator in class warfare, who had the unprecedented notion of expelling the bourgeoisie from his nation, so the middle classes were sent packing to the United States. Guevara's advocacy of rural guerrilla warfare across Latin America incited a decade of revolutionary turbulence in that continent. A few weeks later, the Secretary of the Communist Party of the Soviet Union's central committee avowed to the 21st Party Congress: 'the ideas of communism have become the ruling ideas across the entire world, no borders or barriers impede them, they conquer peoples by their life-affirming strengths and truth'. Little wonder that, as the Foreign Secretary Michael Stewart was to write in the aftermath of the Soviet invasion of Czechoslovakia in 1968, 'The Soviet leaders continue to have a deep-rooted and dogmatic belief in the eventual universal triumph of their model of Marxist-Leninism.'[17]

Burgess kept rousing himself to sound grateful. 'I love living in this country,' he told Stephen Spender, who visited him in 1960. 'It's solid and expanding like England in 1860, my favourite time in history, and no one feels frightened.' Yet a few minutes later he gestured at the wall and said: 'I suppose they're listening to everything we're saying.' He seemed a figure of Whitehall *un peu passé*, with 'a seedy, slightly shame-faced air, and shambling walk: like some ex-consular official you meet in a bar at Singapore and who puzzles you by his references to the days when he knew the great, and helped determine policy'. Burgess gave no sign of reluctant allegiance to a lost cause when, having donned his Old Etonian tie, he met a *Daily Herald* interviewer in 1962. 'I like living in the Soviet Union under Socialism,' he insisted. 'I would not like to live in expense-account England.' He regarded Macmillan as an American stooge. 'He will do what he is told, just as he has always done. He would take out a warrant against me like a shot if Kennedy asked him.'[18]

Philby in Beirut

Philby's domestic life was destroyed in 1951. In the months after his abrupt recall from Washington, he would return home in the evenings sodden with drink, and demanding more alcohol. At a dinner party with neighbours he lost his temper with his wife, went outside in a fury, punched through the windscreen of their car and was left standing there when she sped off. He began an affair with a middle-aged civil servant. For the next few years he repeatedly went on alcoholic 'blinders'. Money from Aileen Philby's aunt enabled them to buy a spacious, gloomy, decrepit Edwardian house near the Sussex dormitory town of Crowborough. Aileen came to realize that he was a spy, and blurted out drunken, panicky remarks on the subject. She was horror-struck by her belated recognition of his deep, inscrutable secrecy. Mistrust of everyone and every surface appearance ruined her mind. He began to hate her, as someone to whom he had done irremediable harm, and to fear that she might betray him as he had done her. He seldom went to Crowborough except to see his children at weekends: when there he preferred to sleep in a tent in the garden; he discouraged potential visitors by telling them that she was mad and aggressive. Looking neglected, unwashed and frantic, she sank into alcoholic isolation, once crashed her car into a shop-window in Crowborough and more than once was hospitalized. In December 1957, after four years of increasingly secluded struggle, Aileen Philby was found by her young daughter dead in bed, aged forty-seven, having succumbed to heart failure (her heart was weakened by alcoholism), tuberculosis and a respiratory infection. Her mother-in-law, Dora Philby, had been drinking more than a bottle of gin a day before her death earlier that same year.[19]

As Chief of SIS Stewart Menzies remained non-committal about Philby's guilt or innocence. After his retirement in 1952 he suffered a recurrent nightmare in which a Russian defector was flown above the English Channel in a helicopter and given the choice to reveal what he knew of Philby or be chucked into the sea: the ordeal always ended with the defector being thrown to his death. Jack Easton, Deputy Director of SIS, felt sure of Philby's guilt and shunned approaches from Nicholas Elliott and other SIS officers seeking their friend's rehabilitation. In August 1956 Philby was enabled to escape from the morass of his life in Crowborough, when SIS, acting through the Foreign Office, arranged for him to go to Beirut as the correspondent of the *Observer* and the *Economist*. The compassionate wish to help an ex-employee who was down and out, and had been exonerated months earlier in the House of Commons, was mixed with continuing suspicion of him. His Beirut posting enabled SIS to preserve working contacts with him, and to monitor his working environment, in case – as happened in 1962 – new evidence emerged which would justify a renewed bout of close questioning. From Beirut Philby reported on developments in the Arab but not the communist world. The expenses claims that he submitted to his London employers were said to be 'staggering'.[20]

Hugh Trevor-Roper once asked Dick White why, when he became Chief of SIS in 1956, he left Philby on the strength in Beirut. White

replied that he had been dismayed to find that Philby had resumed
work for SIS, but decided on reflection that 'it was safest to leave him
there because if he were brought back to London it would be impossible
to convict him or to prevent him from seeing his old colleagues in SIS
and picking up old threads'. In his Middle East years Philby was wary
of official associations. Perhaps fearing a verbal ambush or tricky darting
questions, he exaggerated his stutter when he went to stay in Amman
with Julian and Margaret Bullard. This gave him time to think of the
best answer to any remark ventured in this quick-thinking diplomatic
household. During his Beirut evenings, he was helpless with drink: he
found a fellow drunkard – Eleanor Brewer, divorced wife of the Middle
East correspondent of the *New York Times* – whom he married in
London in 1959.[21]

Blake's arrest in April 1961 doubtless shook Philby. The defection in
December that year of Anatoli Golitsyn resulted in closer tracking of
him. Probably he heard that MI5 interviewing of his old associates had
been resumed. The most interesting approach was to his former news
agency partner, Peter Smolka. After the war Smolka had moved to
Vienna at a time when the conurbation was divided into four sectors
of occupation, Russian, American, French and British, with the inner
city administered by each power for a month at a time. Smolka chose
to live in the Russian sector. When E. H. Carr lectured in Vienna in
1947, he stayed with Smolka. Carr's lecture, with its denigration of US
capitalist imperialism and emphasis on British political and economic
decline, will have gratified Smolka, although it pained British officials.
A year later Graham Greene visited Vienna in search of ideas for a
film-script. As a former SIS officer and continuing SIS Friend, he
lunched with Charles Beauclerk, a colonel in the Intelligence Corps
based in Austria and afterwards Duke of St Albans. Beauclerk filled
Greene with lashings of pink champagne and gave him the idea of
putting the murderous trade in black-market penicillin at the centre
of the plot of *The Third Man*. After lunch, dressed in heavy boots and
mackintoshes, Beauclerk guided him through the extensive system of
Viennese sewers that also feature in the film. Smolka was also at hand
proffering advice. He persuaded the film director, Carol Reed, to cut a
scene from the shooting-script in which Russians kidnapped a woman:
he could not claim that the scene was unrealistic, but warned that it
smacked of facile anti-Soviet propaganda. Greene accordingly inserted

into the script a knowing joke in which a Beauclerk-figure offers a shot of vodka to an American visitor. The vodka is Russian, and its brand-name is Smolka.[22]

An intermittent watch was kept on Smolka in Vienna during the 1950s. He developed creeping paralysis, which deprived him of the use of his legs, and by 1958 depended on a wheelchair. He avoided London until September 1961, when he returned for the first time in fifteen years and took rooms in the Savoy Hotel. MI5's Arthur Martin arranged to interview him at the War Office on 2 October. He arrived in a wheelchair with a rucksack tied to the back, chain-smoked and exploited his disabilities. Whenever he needed time to think of the safe reply to a tricky question, he fumbled with lighting a new cigarette and some-times distracted Martin by asking him to hold the lighter. Loud street noises from pneumatic drills also put Martin at a disadvantage.

Smolka won most of the tricks in the interview. He was quick, wily and forceful. He claimed that after being introduced to Philby and opening a news agency with him in 1934–5, his business partner, as the son of the Arabist St John Philby, was 'anti-Jewish' and had shunned him. He called Burgess 'a colourful and attractive nut' and 'a very vain busybody', who asked him to supply reports on conversations and opinions that he heard. Believing, so he said, that Burgess was attached to MI5, he supplied notes on discussions with Ridsdale, Fletcher-Cooke and others, which were later found among Burgess's belongings. He admitted to having met Blunt in the Bentinck Street flat, and pretended to have forgotten whether it was owned by a Sassoon or a Rothschild. As to his own politics, he described himself as a fellow-traveller during his years as a Ministry of Information official, and as a member of the Vienna communist party from 1946 until the anti-semitic show-trial in 1952 of the Czech communist leader Rudolf Slánský and his asso-ciates who were accused of a Trotskyite–Titoist–Zionist conspiracy. Eleven men, including Slánský, were executed. Since 1952 Smolka, although he stayed in the Savoy Hotel, counted himself as a Titoist. Nothing that he said was demonstrably false, but most of his statements were untrue. He presented himself as an enfeebled man, near to death, but in fact survived until 1980.[23]

Philby was put in jeopardy by denunciation from an unexpected source. Flora Solomon was the Marks & Spencer executive who had introduced him to Aileen Furse in 1940 and had together with Tomás

Harris been a witness at their wedding in 1946. Solomon had known of his communist affiliations and services to Moscow since a lunch in 1938 when he tried to recruit her to the Soviet cause; but she took no action until October 1962. Then, irritated by what she considered to be the anti-Zionist tone of Philby's reports in the *Observer*, she told Victor Rothschild – at a meeting at the Weizmann Institute in Israel – that Philby had tried to enlist her as a Soviet agent. How could David Astor, she asked, employ at the *Observer* a known communist who had surely worked for Moscow? After Rothschild reported these remarks, she was interviewed by Martin in Rothschild's London flat, with Martin's MI5 ally Peter Wright listening. Wright thought her an untrustworthy, vindictive, screechy, rambling witness. 'I guessed from listening to her that she and Philby must have been lovers in the 1930s,' he later said. 'She was having her revenge for the rejection she felt when he moved into a new pair of sheets.' This is typical of Wright's false links: there is no evidence for it; she was sixteen years older than Philby.[24]

When Lord Carrington, First Lord of the Admiralty, first discussed Vassall's arrest with Macmillan in 1962, the Prime Minister supposedly exclaimed: 'Very bad news! You know, you should never catch a spy. Discover him and control him, but never catch him. A spy causes far more trouble when he's caught.' Already dismayed by the Portland, Blake and Vassall cases, Macmillan had indicated to White that it was preferable to avoid further sensational espionage publicity. It was agreed with Macmillan that Philby should be confronted in Beirut. Instead of Martin of MI5, Nicholas Elliott of SIS was sent to the Lebanese capital early in January 1963. Elliott had been Philby's stoutest defender within SIS, but was now convinced of his guilt. He was widely known to be 'a poop', but White thought that in Beirut, outside British jurisdiction, Philby might disclose in full his activities to his former ally in return for an offer of immunity from prosecution. There was no advantage for the intelligence services, or for any Whitehall department, in giving the Soviet Union the propaganda gift of another spectacular treason trial so soon after Blake and Vassall had rocked public opinion and shaken the Macmillan government. A meeting was arranged whereby Philby went to an embassy flat in Beirut, ostensibly to meet the SIS head of station Peter Lunn to discuss possible future work. When Elliott rather than the local man opened the flat door, Philby said, 'I rather thought it might be you.'[25]

In offering Philby immunity from prosecution, Elliott threatened that without a deal he would be harassed until his living arrangements became intolerable. It was apparently suggested that his bank account could be frozen, that the *Observer* and other potential employers would be warned against using his stories and that his residence permit in Beirut might be rescinded. It is likely that Philby was tempted by the immunity-from-prosecution deal. He admitted working for Soviet Russia from 1936 until 1946, and to tipping off Maclean in 1951, but did not admit to his Cold War activities. Transcripts of the taped and drunken talk between Elliott and Philby are not publicly available. We do not know whether Elliott said that London had new information that incriminated Philby. Did he mention Flora Solomon, or leave Philby to think that the source was Golitsyn or Blake? The accounts of these discussions given by Philby to the KGB were self-servingly inaccurate.

Hollis and White were relieved by Elliott's account of Philby's attitude, and reported to Edgar Hoover that the damage to US interests of Philby's espionage had been limited to the war years – for four of which the Soviet Union and the United States had been allies. The Nunn May precedent, in which the British security services had chosen to investigate spying over a truncated period, and had ignored a longer, more untidy time-span, was being followed. Philby, however, was either fooling Elliott when he seemed receptive to the immunity deal or had second thoughts. Perhaps there was also a calculation in London that if Philby was allowed to make an easy escape, Moscow Centre might suspect his loyalty, doubt his material and treat him as a disinformant. Elliott left Beirut, with responsibility for monitoring Philby devolved to Peter Lunn. On the night of 23 January 1963 Philby seems to have tramped through the streets of Beirut to check that he was not being tracked, to have donned the disguise of a Russian merchant seaman and then to have boarded the freighter *Dolmatova*, which unexpectedly weighed anchor without loading its cargo and steamed to a Soviet port. From Moscow he sent White a message: 'You have won this round, but I assure you that I will win the last.'[26]

White was exasperated by misrepresentations of this episode. Criticizing John le Carré's essay of 1968, for example, he wrote that the novelist showed 'his longing for Br. Intelligence to match the K.G.B. in ruthlessness & cunning – & ends to justify all means'. Le Carré had suggested that SIS should have kidnapped or murdered Philby in Beirut in 1962. 'But', wrote White, 'corpses of already famous 3rd men are more easily disposed of in novels than among Br. Diplomats & Home Office officials. Moreover in terms of legal evidence it could still quite easily have been said that the wrong man had been disposed of. Who in our democracy accepts responsibilities of this kind?'[27]

The handling of Philby's Beirut interrogation, and the ease with which he fled, convinced the paranoiacs – Angleton in the CIA, Wright and Martin in MI5 – that there had been betrayal within the British intelligence services. Angleton was traumatized by the defection of his once trusted friend. He felt humiliated and fractured by having been outwitted and out-drunk. He lost objectivity in assessing people as he developed a malignant obsession with conspiracies. One of Philby's greatest achievements was to tip Angleton into clinical paranoia after 1963. Angleton sat at his desk in Langley, Virginia, chain-smoking behind drawn curtains, scouring old files and spreading crazy, destructive suspicions within the CIA.[28]

For six months the fires of the story of Philby's disappearance were banked: Whitehall wished to avoid yet another scorching of the government and the civil service, and made no public admission; and journalists feared getting burnt in a libel action if they reported the defection and Philby then reappeared in the west. (SIS was known to encourage its agents, such as Greville Wynne, who was imprisoned for spying by the Soviets in 1963–4, to supplement their pensions by suing newspapers which called them spies: there was never any evidence that the newspapers could use in justification.) Then, on 1 July 1963, a Cabinet minister, Edward Heath, surprised the House of Commons with a statement that Philby had defected to Russia and was the Third Man in the Burgess–Maclean case. Once again the press went berserk. New fusillades were launched at the Establishment. As the *Daily Mirror* editorialized,

Hardly a day goes by without some fresh revelation of how the Old Boys work in high places to keep the Old Boys in high places.

Don't worry, Old Boy, if you're found out – there are buckets and buckets of surplus whitewash in Whitehall, and your friends will see you through . . .

Look at what happened to Maclean. Working for the Foreign Office in Cairo he was as soused as a herring, involved in wild and disgraceful episodes which no business concern would tolerate for a second in its messenger-boys.

Fired? Not on your life, Old Boy. Dear old Donald was given a rest until his hangovers cleared up, and then he was given another Foreign Office top job.

. . .

It is beginning to look as if the whole of the Tory Party approves of the cover-up, hush-up, keep-it-dark, Old Boys technique of getting in power and staying in power – and to hell with what the country thinks.[29]

Two months later, on 30 August, Burgess died of acute liver failure. Norman Ewer, under the byline 'Britain's most experienced diplomatic correspondent', wrote an assessment of his fellow Soviet spy for the *Daily Herald*. 'All his life he was a highly talented, deeply unhappy misfit. Whether a misfit because he was homosexual or homosexual because he was a misfit is a matter for psychologists.' Following Driberg's artful misdirection, Ewer doubted that Burgess had ever been a communist of Maclean's sincerity. He was a mere escapist whose disappearance had been no more significant than 'a flight from a society in which he could find no place'. Burgess's death terminated those mischievous, plausible, distorting press interviews which for seven years he had lobbed into the west as mini-projectiles of propaganda. But with Philby in Moscow a new phase of disinformation could begin. A weightier means than telephone calls to Driberg, namely the Anglophone world's hunger for spy stories and publishers' avidity for proven bestsellers, was available for KGB manipulation.[30]

Bestsellers

The era of the spy bestseller began in 1956 with the publication as a Pan cheap paperback of Ian Fleming's novel *Casino Royale*, which had received little attention when issued in hardback as the earliest James Bond adventure in 1953. Fiction prepared the way for the ostensibly non-fiction works that prolonged and loudened the impact of the Cambridge spies. Fleming's thrillers, Len Deighton's *The Ipcress File* (1962) and John le Carré's *The Spy Who Came in from the*

Cold (1963) and *The Looking Glass War* (1965) preceded the investigations by the *Sunday Times* researchers known as the Insight Team and Philby's memoirs. Their commercial success was an incentive for the works of Andrew Boyle, Anthony Cave Brown, John Costello, Richard Deacon and Chapman Pincher. Already in 1968 Dick White regretted that 'the rational aspects of the intelligence function [were] distorted as they so often are in the public mind by the melodramas of the fiction writers'. He nevertheless recommended to Hugh Trevor-Roper an American bestseller of 1967, *Topaz* by Leon Uris: 'a rather badly written novel', but 'worth reading because partly based on authentic inside information'. Generally, though, the smudged and crooked lines of fiction-writers and journalists made the truth ever more illegible.[31]

If the James Bond phenomenon was launched by the Pan paperback of *Casino Royale*, it was blasted skyward in 1957 when the *Daily Express* ran a comic serial adaptation of *From Russia with Love* and it became unstoppable after the film version of *Dr No* had been released in 1962. Fleming's James Bond, as distinct from the cinema version, had unimpeachable upper-middle-class antecedents. He was the son of a senior manager of the Vickers armaments company, an Old Etonian, honoured as a Commander of the Order of St Michael and St George, at ease in St James's clubs but disappointed in post-war England. He relished his privileges, drove a Bentley, bought groceries from Fortnum & Mason, drank coffee from a Queen Anne silver pot and impersonated a herald from the College of Arms. For readers, he fulfilled a reassuring fantasy of Britain's endurance as a world power by besting not only Soviet agents but foreigners such as the Albanian money-launderer known as Le Chiffre, the Polish-Greek master-criminal Ernst Stavro Blofeld, the Italian racketeer Emilio Largo, the Latvian metallurgist Auric Goldfinger and the Aryan supremacist Hugo Drax.

Fleming had little respect for the charades of parliamentary government. He attended a debate in the House of Commons only once, in 1938, when the Chamberlain government's policy towards Mussolini's Italy was under discussion. 'I found the hollowness and futility of the speeches degrading and infantile, and the well-fed, deep-throated "Hear Hears" for each mendacious platitude verging on the obscene,' he recalled in 1959. Asked what he would do if he was Prime Minister, he replied that he would try to 'stop people being ashamed of themselves' and to raise individual self-respect. 'The fact that taxation, controls and certain features of the Welfare State have turned the majority of us into petty criminals, liars and work-dodgers is . . . having a very bad effect on the psyche of the kingdom.' He understood that just as rationing created the opportunities for black-market spivs, and the prohibition of narcotics provided a profit incentive for drug-smuggling, so high taxation induced tax evasion. The psyche of the United Kingdom, Fleming thought, was increasingly banal, childishly petulant and (as he showed by his preoccupation with luxury brand names) pretentiously consumerist. 'You have not only lost a great Empire, you have seemed almost anxious to throw it away with both hands,' a Japanese master-spy says in *You Only Live Twice* (1964). 'When you apparently sought to arrest this slide into impotence at Suez, you succeeded only in stage-managing one of the most pitiful bungles in the history of the world.' Successive governments had ceded control of economic matters to collective bargaining and strikes. 'This feather-bedding, this shirking of an honest day's work, is sapping at ever-increasing speed the moral fibre of the British, a quality the world once so admired. In its place, we now see a vacuous, aimless horde of seekers after pleasure – gambling at the pools and bingo, whining at the weather and the declining fortunes of the country, and wallowing nostalgically in gossip about the doings of the Royal Family and of your so-called aristocracy in the pages of the most debased newspapers in the world.'[32]

The big profits from Deighton, Fleming and le Carré novels induced publishers to diversify into espionage memoirs and popular spy histories. This occurred at a time when respect for Whitehall was being weakened even as the mandarins' freedom to explain their decisions and recount their careers to the public was being circumscribed. Sir George Mallaby's memoirs *From My Level* (1965) provoked Sir Laurence Helsby, head of the civil service, to circularize permanent secretaries and heads of overseas missions insisting that ministers must have 'full confidence that they can speak their minds plainly in front of their official advisers without any fear that unguarded remarks may be stored up for publication.' Helsby condemned officials who abused positions of trust by keeping diaries or private records that could later be exploited 'for personal profit or acclaim.' Sir Evelyn Shuckburgh, UK representative to NATO, who twenty years later published his FO diary covering the Suez crisis, retorted to Helsby that this instruction marked 'a serious step in the downgrading and devitalisation of civil servants'. Ministers could not expect advisers of any intelligence to be nullities 'without memory or judgement, in whose presence the talk and behaviour of the Ministers are to be as if they had never been. A man is responsible for his acts and his statements wherever he makes them and must learn to judge what confidence he can place in others and to use discretion. Politicians surely cannot be given a kind of blanket exemption from this human condition. There is also History to consider and the claims of truth'. Shuckburgh concluded with a prescient warning for Helsby: 'If we are not careful we shall turn ourselves, the civil servants, into intellectual eunuchs and un-men, and create in our politicians a wholly erroneous idea of their immunity from the normal human responsibilities.'[33]

Shuckburgh's remark had sharper point in a period when officials were receiving abuse in a way that had previously been restricted to politicians. The *Sunday Times* Insight Team's compilation *Philby: The Spy Who Betrayed a Generation* was an unforgiving exercise which spared no one in Whitehall. 'The Philby stuff in the Sunday papers has been very tiresome,' Dick White wrote in October 1967 after the book's publication. 'My present service [SIS] is criticised in every possible way for their handling of the matter. My previous service [MI5] comes out of it fairly well.' The position taken by both the *Observer* and *Sunday Times* was, in White's words, that 'the brilliant work of the war was sacrificed and nullified in the years immediately after peace by the traitors in our entrails'. White particularly resented the Insight Team's accusation that 'successive British governments have allowed the public to believe that Philby was a defecting journalist of minor importance – and have tried to deny the state of grotesque dilapidation (now belatedly remedied) that allowed him to do what he did'. As J. C. Masterman commented of the Insight publicity, 'the generality of people do not discriminate between the work of different parts of the service. I doubt whether they have any idea of the difference in the function of M.I.5 and M.I.6. What they feel is a mistrust of the "Secret Service" – they feel this, I am sure, because the failures are broadcast everywhere & the successes entirely concealed.'[34]

Hugh Trevor-Roper, as a former intelligence officer, had been asked to provide an authoritative introduction to the *Sunday Times* book, but it was perhaps thought that his temperance, precision and irony were too selective a taste for commercial success. Trevor-Roper was usurped in this role by the suspense novelist le Carré. Writing in commiseration to Trevor-Roper, White averred that the 'high-pitched hysterical denunciations [in le Carré's introduction] are quite ridiculous & will merely cause laughter among the younger members of my service'. The blame was not entirely le Carré's, he thought. There was 'a substratum of truth' to the Insight Team's presentation of the Philby case, but overall it was 'full of misconceptions, gaps in knowledge & sheer prejudice'. The journalists were 'sickeningly self-righteous', procedurally flawed and factually incomplete. For them the story had to be presented as 'a public scandal, the revelation of which puts the authors into the role of knights in shining armour'. They seemed unaware 'that you cannot hope to write a sound historical piece about an event in the continuous secret struggle between intelligence services when both sides are only going to reveal the facts that suit them. In our case there is the need to live to fight another day'. The Insight Team never 'stopped to think that the background against which we had to handle the Philby case was very different from their own gleanings from published material. It was enriched from the study of many similar not less important cases in the western world & from the revelations of some 30 or so defectors from the K.G.B. The experience of the Philby case is of course a part & an important part of our knowledge of what the western world is faced by in the K.G.B.'[35]

A *Sunday Times* foreign correspondent, Murray Sayle, had several interviews with Philby during 1967. He concluded, in the summary of his colleague Bruce Page, that 'Philby was more Soviet loyalist than Communist', well grounded in Marxist-Leninist doctrines, but with attitudes to China, Africa and Latin America that were 'vehemently those of a Russian national Communist'. Philby expressed, for example, 'puzzled indignation about the Maoists. ("These people have got the sauce to say that *we* are in Asia as a colonial power!")'. Sayle found him polite, worldly and arrogant: 'although his allegiance to, and admiration for, the Soviet elite (of which he counts himself a member) is complete, it is accompanied by a certain genial contempt for the Russians'. 'Communism', Philby told Sayle, 'must be a pretty good system if even these Russians can run it.'[36]

In 1968, under KGB auspices, Philby published a memoir of the period before 1956 entitled *My Silent War*. It was a medley of fact and fiction, history and disinformation, intended to serve Soviet aims by damaging the British security services. It received an astonishing measure of credence from reviewers and journalists meeting deadlines: the fact is that it was the literary equivalent of a prisoner's evidence from the dock about his movements on the night of the crime. When a sound historian such as Angleton's biographer Michael Holzman refers to White as 'a man of impeccably bad judgment', it is under the influence of Philby's hostile memoirs.[37]

Moscow's negative propaganda about Whitehall was not countered by positive news about the successes of MI5 and SIS. Lord Normanbrook, the former Cabinet Secretary, told Masterman that it was impossible to permit publication of his historical treatise on the XX System because of the stories generated by or concerning the Cambridge spies and cognate scandals. 'Many people know that the Service was greatly strengthened during the war by the recruitment of people, like yourself, who would never be found within it in peace time,' wrote Normanbrook, 'and part of the newspaper case against the Service is that it is not now what it was: its glories have departed.' That being so, the Cabinet Office feared that readers of Masterman's book would doubt that MI5 was still as efficient as a counter-espionage organization as it had been in the war years. The secret services fully appreciated the importance of 'public image' and knew that they had a low rating with the public. 'The difficulty is to do something about it without damaging ourselves still further,' White explained to Masterman. 'We don't like getting into a public "answer back" position when we know that we can really only use a fraction of the evidence.'[38]

One instance when there was no official correction of a gross injustice concerns Donald McCormick @ Richard Deacon's *History of the British Secret Service* (1969). 'Very few Secret Service chiefs in modern times have been able to go against the Foreign Office,' Deacon proclaimed. 'Even if Menzies had wished to get rid of Philby, all the evidence suggests that the powerful pro-Philby body of opinion in the Foreign Office would still probably have overruled him and insisted on hushing the matter up and allowing Philby to continue in a minor role.' This is rubbish. Menzies did rid SIS of Philby, as early as July 1951. There was no 'pro-Philby body of opinion' in the Foreign Office, powerful or otherwise. Few people knew him in the Office. The official who knew him best was Reilly, who had recently prevented him from

being designated a future 'C'. It is untrue to say that SIS in any generation was domineered or overruled by the FO. It is doubtful that the
Office was consulted before Sinclair reattached Philby to SIS in 1956.[39]

Masterman was full of sympathy for the intelligence services' predic-
ament after 1967. The public were only interested in espionage 'when
any set-back or scandal crops up', he told White. 'Then books and
articles proliferate, and all, or nearly all, of these are dangerously slanted
against the two Services.' In consequence the public was misled into
believing that 'the "Secret Service" is and always has been inefficient
and out-matched by the Secret Services of other countries'. The partial
disclosures of the Philby books had 'undermine[d] British institutions',
as was their purpose, and this at a time when he was forbidden from
publishing his history of the XX System. 'To control the whole German
espionage system throughout the war, as we did, is surely a much greater
contribution to the credit side than Philby's treachery is to the debit.'
Masterman's book *The Double-Cross System in the War of 1939 to 45*,
when finally published in 1972, proved salutary. He stressed the obstacles to peacetime counter-espionage: 'it is immensely hard to secure
proof; it is impossible to act on suspicion however strong; the whole
tenor of life in this country is antagonistic to over-regimentation and
to rigid classification; it is better to let many spies "run" rather than to
risk one mistake.'[40]

Oleg Lyalin in London

Defection was not all on one side. The last section of this chapter
considers Soviet bloc activities in London, and gives a wider view than
that of Philby or journalistic mercenaries. Soviet Russia and the Warsaw
Pact countries seemed immutable and unchallengeable in the 1960s.
Neither policies nor rhetoric had moderated. The Bratislava Declaration
of August 1968, following a conference of the Bulgarian, Czech, East
German, Hungarian, Polish and Soviet communist parties, was
described by Sir William Barker, the Ambassador in Prague, as 'a hotchpotch of old-fashioned Soviet hate slogans combined with a re-pledging
of socialist solidarity'. Power in the USSR rested less with the Soviet
government and more with the Communist Party of the Soviet Union,
as the Foreign Secretary Sir Alec Douglas-Home summarized the position in 1970. The party leadership still regarded 'the foreign policy of

the Soviet Government as only one part, and neither the major nor the determining part, of a world-wide historical and political progress which follows the laws of the class-struggle as formulated by Marxism-Leninism'. The ruling generation of Soviet leaders were, according to the then Ambassador in Moscow, Sir Duncan Wilson, 'guilty men, guilty towards their own peoples and towards the world outside, who can best maintain their position by positing a Manichean world-struggle between good and evil'.[41]

To serve the cause of class struggle there was a large concentrated Soviet intelligence attack on Britain in the 1960s and 1970s. Over a hundred agents were at work, but their efforts were often ineffective, not least because the interpretation of the material they remitted to Moscow was poor: the top levels of bureaucracy were given analyses that fitted their presuppositions and did not challenge their expectations. Espionage by Soviet officials was the subject of occasional protests. Vladimir Drozdov, who had trained as a nuclear physicist, was expelled from Britain in 1968 after being caught collecting secret material from a dead drop. In December that year the PUS, Sir Paul Gore-Booth, remonstrated with the Soviet Ambassador, Mikhail Smirnovsky, about two embassy officials, I. A. Kulikov, whose expertise lay in chemical radiation, and Alexander Benyaminov, afterwards head of the Soviet delegation to the United Nations International Atomic Energy Agency, both of whom sought to collect confidential information by illicit means: Smirnovsky received this oral communication with half a minute's gloomy silence. In 1970 Sir Denis Greenhill (Gore-Booth's successor as PUS, and Burgess's former departmental chief in the Washington embassy) noted Britain's unwitting slide into a position where high levels of Soviet intelligence activity were accepted. 'This', Greenhill said, 'was not good enough.' But the Labour government led by Harold Wilson did not act on Greenhill's prompt. The parliamentary Labour party's mistrust of the security services, which had begun with the Zinoviev letter of 1924, was entrenched. Labour leaders had an ambivalent attitude to the Soviet leadership: they behaved, said Greenhill, 'as if they were nonconformists meeting the Pope'.[42]

A new phase began in the spring of 1971 when MI5 recruited a member of the London *rezidentura*, Oleg Lyalin, as an agent-in-place. First he was debriefed at a safe-house, 24 Collingham Gardens, in Earls Court. It was learnt that Lyalin, an expert in marksmanship and

unarmed combat, had previously been used to monitor shipping off
the Lithuanian coast. Now the KGB had installed him under the cover
of the director of a Russian import-export firm based in Regent Street:
among other tasks he ran a small spy network in London of Armenian
Cypriots. Ostensibly he served a KGB section preparing for the sabotage
of foreign public services, transport, communications and 'nerve
centres' in the event of war or crises short of war. Lyalin wanted to
start a new life with his Russian secretary-mistress, and began providing
information on Soviet sabotage plans in London, Washington, Paris,
Bonn and other European capitals, including the selection and monitoring of key individuals who would be targeted for assassination in a
crisis. The flooding of the London Underground system and the destruction of the missile early-warning system were among the sabotage plans
provided by Lyalin. Another was for Soviet agents posing as messengers
or couriers to drop in Whitehall corridors capsules containing deadly
toxins which would kill any official who trod on them.[43]

Probably as a result of Lyalin's revelations, an inter-departmental
conference was held on 25 May 1971 to discuss how best to counteract
Soviet clandestine activities. Julian Bullard was surprised at the number
of officials in attendance who seemed oblivious to the threat to national
security posed by the relentless intrigues of Soviet representatives in
London. Sir Antony Part of the Department of Trade and Industry
asked how much actual harm was done by the Russians. Sir Martin
Furnival Jones of MI5 replied that there was evidence of continuous
penetration of the Foreign and Commonwealth Office, the Ministry of
Defence, the army, navy and air force, the Labour party, trade unions
and the Board of Trade. 'It was difficult to say how much damage was
being done,' Furnival Jones said, 'but it was equally difficult to believe
that the Russians maintained such a large establishment for no profit.'
He estimated, and Sir John Rennie of SIS agreed, that thirty or forty
Soviet intelligence officers were running agents in government organizations or in technical industries concerned with the Concorde
supersonic jet aircraft, the Bristol Olympus 593 aero-engine, nuclear
energy and computer electronics. Sir Thomas Brimelow of the FCO
confirmed that recent cases differed from those of Philby and Blake,
'and involved the cultivation of commercial or defence officials'.[44]

Sir Alec Douglas-Home, Foreign Secretary in the Heath government
of 1970–4, ranks with Bevin as one of the great post-war holders of

that post. His steady, strong and shrewd approach was indicated by an axiom that he sent to Duncan Wilson in Moscow in 1971: 'A forthcoming style, accompanied by strict attention to our own self-interest on matters of substance, is a dictate of common sense.' His excellent manners hid his ruthlessness, which he had displayed most decisively in 1963 when he encouraged Harold Macmillan to resign as Prime Minister in a fit of morbid hypochondria about a non-existent cancer, hastened to announce the resignation before Macmillan's entourage could dissuade him and then positioned himself, with the killer determination of a usurping duke in the Wars of the Roses, to snatch Macmillan's crown. Home as Foreign Secretary took Greenhill's point that the blatancy of Soviet espionage was too insulting to be tolerated.[45]

For the previous quarter-century Britain had been the sick man of Europe, rather as Ottoman Turkey had been in the nineteenth century, but in the course of 1971 its institutions began a phase of invigorating renewal and rebounding confidence. In June the negotiations for Britain's entry into the European Economic Community (EEC) were concluded, and in October the terms were approved by parliament. Eight years earlier, as a dutiful Soviet citizen, Burgess had opposed European unity and regarded the EEC as a conspiratorial power bloc run by France and Germany. 'Pleased by collapse of menacing Common Market negotiations,' he wrote a few months before his death. He equated European economic strength with exploitation, poverty and 'frightful beastliness . . . for undeveloped countries'. Macmillan, Gladwyn Jebb and other British diplomatists involved in the European negotiations had all 'lied like an American division of marines'.[46]

That had been the Moscow line. The Kremlin had watched the dissolution of the British Empire and saw the rump of the United Kingdom as a medium-sized, developed European country possessing special, if diminishing, capabilities in international finance and some useful technology. Russian leaders felt apprehension that a European community including Britain might disrupt their plans. Among the pro-Europeans in Britain there were opposing apprehensions about the country staying out of the EEC. 'If', said the economist-businessman Lord Crowther in July 1971, 'we are left in isolation, then we shall get more and more inbred, and I have no doubt that we shall go on telling ourselves every day how British is best, how good we are, and how the world looks to our leadership, as we wait in the queue for our daily bread ration.' Three months later, as chairman of the Royal Commission on the Constitution, Crowther told the House of Lords: 'It is a great mistake to believe that there is only one level upon which sovereignty and decision-making can operate. We would never have slipped into this mistake if we did not live in such a compact island, and if we were not served by such an efficient civil service; we would never have slipped into the delusion that it is possible to take all important decisions in one place, here.' Old diplomatic prohibitions and political inhibitions were being jettisoned: there was a sense of abundant new possibilities.[47]

The confidence that came from imminent EEC membership embold-ened the British government's handling of Soviet espionage. On 30 July Douglas-Home and the Home Secretary, Reginald Maudling, briefed the Prime Minister, Edward Heath: between 120 and 200 Soviet spies were operating in Britain; altogether 517 Soviet officials had pretexts to operate in the country, including 189 members of the Soviet embassy, 121 members of the Soviet trade delegation, 73 contract inspectors and 134 individuals working for the Soviet press agency TASS, the state airline Aeroflot, the travel agency Intourist or the Moscow Narodny Bank. Although Maudling had treated previous MI5 reports of Soviet espionage as exaggerated, he joined Douglas-Home in convincing Heath that the numbers of Soviet officials were unacceptable. Heath was nervous of any incidents that might distract his government from his primary aim of gaining British admission to the EEC, but he was also rattled by Chapman Pincher's mischievous pieces in the *Daily Express* under such headlines as 'Give our spies cloaks and daggers again', claiming that SIS had been 'downgraded below the safe limit'. It was settled that the bulk of the Soviet agents must be booted out in Operation FOOT.[48]

Only the Cabinet Secretary, Sir Burke Trend, knew the extent to which resources were being diverted – in the paranoia engendered by the defection of three of the Cambridge spies – into internal 'mole' hunts for Soviet penetration agents within the Security Service. No Cabinet minister was aware of this consuming obsession indulged by Peter Wright and his fellow inquisitors. In accordance with the zealots' insistence, MI5 believed that there must be KGB moles within the Service, despite Lyalin's assurance that the KGB regarded it as impen-etrable. The Service therefore welcomed Douglas-Home's proposal of drastic action because it could not cope with all the Soviet agents in England while it was being undermined by internal mole hunts.[49]

Neither the Soviet embassy nor the KGB had any inkling of what was afoot. If there were Soviet penetration agents in government departments, they were either junior or in the wrong sections. On 30 August there were two coincidental events. A junior naval officer, David Bingham, admitted supplying material on submarines to the Soviets in order to raise money for his wife's shopping expeditions. That same day Lyalin was arrested for drunk driving in Tottenham Court Road by a police constable who had no idea of the events he was setting in train. Knowing that he would be repatriated in disgrace by his chiefs, Lyalin defected immediately and was hurried to an MI5 safe-house. Preparations for Operation FOOT were accelerated. On 24 September Greenhill, as PUS, informed the Soviet embassy that ninety named officials must leave the country within a fortnight, and that another fifteen with re-entry visas would not be let back within its borders. A rump of some forty intelligence officers was allowed to remain. 'Moscow Centre was stunned,' as Oleg Gordievsky recorded in the major history of the KGB of which he was co-author. 'In 1971 the golden age of KGB operations [in Britain] came to an end. The London residency never recovered from the expulsions. Contrary to the popular myths generated by the "media" revelations about Soviet moles, during the next fourteen years, up to Gordievsky's defection, the KGB found it more difficult to collect high-grade intelligence in London than in almost any other western capital.'[50]

Press analysis of Lyalin's defection and Operation FOOT was low-grade. Right-wing newspapers banged their hollow nationalist drums. The coverage by Patrick Keatley, diplomatic correspondent of the *Guardian*, veered into the slipstream of the Soviet embassy's propaganda counter-offensive. He traduced Lyalin as a 'playboy spy', indulging in 'a steady round of expense-account dinners', spending up to £100 a night on 'vodka and caviar' sessions. Whitehall was embarrassed, 'with officials silent on orders from 10 Downing Street', when Lyalin's drunk driving and statuesque girlfriend were publicized, because – according to Keatley – these infractions were enough to discredit him as a trustworthy source. Keatley predicted that Heath would 'come under fire' from MPs 'for his deliberate technique of a block expulsion of more than a hundred officials – the first time that this has been used by Britain against any Power'. Keatley's slant was that Lyalin had made the government vulnerable: 'the sharpest criticism is likely to centre on the character of the KGB defector', who had been the informant in preparing the expulsion lists and 'is now seen as a person of considerable instability'. This character assassination was a tried Stalinist technique. As a KGB diversionary tactic during Operation FOOT, Philby in Moscow named SIS officers in the Arab world and accused Britain of espionage and disinformation against the Brandt government in West Germany.[51]

In view of the resounding success of Operation FOOT, the reaction of some MPs was shocking. The Labour MP Arthur Lewis used an adjournment debate to vilify Lyalin as 'a traitor', 'a member of a murder-squad', 'a self-confessed spy and saboteur', 'having some liaison with a beautiful Russian blonde' and soiled by 'escapades in night-clubs'. Lyalin had not been prosecuted for drunk driving because the security services claimed that a court appearance would endanger his life. 'The general public do not believe it,' Lewis protested. If Lyalin's life was truly at risk, 'he would not need a driving licence because he cannot travel around'. How unjust that this scandal-ridden foreigner should escape scot-free when 'many fine British citizens, with fine records in the Services and medals for gallantry, are sometimes pulled up after military reunions for driving under the influence of drink'![52]

The Soviet bloc had realized that it would be easier to extract confidences from politicians and other informants if they were approached by representatives of supposedly Soviet satellite states such as Czechoslovakia: sources could salve their uneasy consciences by saying that they were not actually helping the Russians. The Czechs in 1971 had four Labour MPs on their payroll, the money-grubbing Will Owen @ LEE (who was nicknamed 'Greedy Bastard' by his Czech handlers), the fantasist John Stonehouse (subsequently imprisoned for fraud), the delinquent Tom Driberg @ CROCODILE, and another codenamed GUSTAV, whose identity has not been settled. They also used and paid Ray Mawby, who had made a short-term stir when, as a state-educated electrician, he had been elected in 1955 as Tory MP for the safe seat of Totnes. Mawby was a bovine, inarticulate drudge, who appreciated the low prices in the Commons bars and liked gambling in glitzy casinos. For some ten years he provided the Czechs with information on Commons security, informed on his fellow MPs and leaked documents, at £100 a meeting, but contacts were broken after the expulsions of 1971. Mawby appeared on television in 1967, while he was on the Czech payroll, with the false claim that most British spies who had spied for the communists were homosexual, and urging that homosexual acts should remain illegal for people covered by the Official Secrets Act even if such acts were partially decriminalized for the civilian population of England and Wales. (Men serving in the army, navy, RAF and merchant navy, or living in Scotland and Northern Ireland, were exempt from the Sexual Offences Act of 1967.)

The KGB was humiliated that none of its sources had given forewarning of Operation FOOT. 'For all their resources and efficiency,' Wilson's successor as Ambassador in Moscow, Sir John Killick, reported in November 1971, the KGB leadership were 'out of their minds' with anger and frustration that the Kremlin did not retaliate against Britain to anything like the extent that Moscow Centre wanted. The Soviet system ossified in the late 1970s, at a time when British admission to the EEC and Thatcher's election victory in 1979 were renewing the influence and confidence of the London government. Sir Curtis Keeble (the product of Clacton County High School, and the son of a clerk on Bethnal Green Council), who was Ambassador in Moscow in 1976–82, surveyed the condition of the Soviet people as seen in that period. 'They have inflicted upon themselves a governmental system which combines lofty principle with evil application and monumental dullness. They have built themselves a military superpower. To run it, they have a group of old men, mediocre in spirit, who view the Western World with a malevolence, sometimes timorous, sometimes vengeful, always suspicious.' The Soviet Union was no longer 'a revolutionary power bent on world domination', confident that capitalism would crumble under the inexorable logic of Marxism-Leninism, but a sclerotic administration of diverse territories held together by force.[53]

CHAPTER 20

The Mole Hunts

Colonel Grace-Groundling-Marchpole

In his *Sword of Honour* trilogy Evelyn Waugh devised a character named Colonel Grace-Groundling-Marchpole. This laughable, damnable spook sits at his desk amassing and scouring files reporting garbled hearsay, spurious facts and ludicrous suspicions of subversion or treachery. With rapturous self-importance he sets out to find the hidden connections between individuals and sects, to discover the arcane sense inside random jumbles and to unravel the conspiracies that no one else has the courage to face. Grace-Groundling-Marchpole's dossiers were, Waugh recounts, 'micro-filmed and multiplied and dispersed into a dozen indexes in all the Counter-Espionage Headquarters of the Free World and became a permanent part of the Most Secret archives of the Second World War'. The conspiracy-hunter becomes one of England's great conspirators: he hoards his information; he operates in such sacrosanct isolation that government ministers know nothing of him; to his relief, they never ask to see his material. 'Premature examination of his files might ruin his private, undefined Plan. Somewhere in the ultimate curlicues of his mind, there was a Plan. Given time, given enough confidential material, he would succeed in knitting the entire quarrelsome world into a single net of conspiracy in which there were no antagonists, merely millions of men working, unknown to one another, for the same end; and there would be no more war.'[1]

Graham Greene, a sometime SIS officer and longer-term SIS Friend, understood that Philby's defection in 1963 stimulated a new generation of Grace-Groundling-Marchpoles with fantasies of intricate conspiracies. 'How right SIS was to defend Philby and how wrong MI5 to force him into the open,' wrote Greene. 'The West suffered more from his

flight than from his espionage.' Institutional caution developed into
fierce suspicions of ramified conspiracy, and then into rampant paranoia. The MI5 officers Arthur Martin and Peter Wright began a
lamentable hunt for non-existent traitors: leaks about their activities
induced an equally deplorable outburst of bad books. The United States,
too, had its Grace-Groundling-Marchpole in the form of James Angleton
of the CIA. Angleton never recovered the balance of his judgement
after discovering that he had been hoodwinked by Philby in Washington
during 1949–51. The embroidered intricacy of Angleton's counter-
espionage notions grew increasingly unreal. He became so obsessed by
Soviet penetration and disinformation that he was duped by the delu-
sional Soviet defector Anatoli Golitsyn into affirming that the Sino-Soviet
ideological split of 1960 was a stunt intended to fool the capitalist
powers. The curlicues of Angleton's mind filled with certainty that the
Soviet Union and the People's Republic of China had agreed a plot
whereby they faked hostility while conspiring together in underhand
alliance. Angleton's absurdities were the ultimate travesty of intelligence
analysis.[2]

The last-recruited of Philby's ring of five had been John Cairncross.
He was teaching at the Western Reserve University in Cleveland, Ohio
when, after an approach from Arthur Martin in 1964, he admitted that
he been a Soviet spy until 1951. Over the next few years he underwent
a series of MI5 interviews, during which his replies were often vague
or inconclusive. As Cairncross had an exact and clarifying intelligence,
with a scholar's neat and retentive memory, it is likely that he was
bamboozling his interrogators. Certainly his memoirs contain defensive
untruths and a lot of fudge.

Blunt had been interviewed eleven times by MI5 before the clinching
moment came in April 1964. Arthur Martin visited his flat atop the
Courtauld Institute and asked what he knew about Michael Straight.
This was the American banking heir whom Blunt had recruited at
Cambridge, and who had recently divulged his espionage history while
undergoing vetting in the US for a cultural post to which he had been
nominated by the Kennedy administration. Martin assured Blunt that
no action would be taken against him if he now told the truth. Blunt
sat gazing at him in silence for a minute. Martin told him that this
silence told all that he needed to know. He added that he had been
through a similar scene a few weeks earlier with Cairncross, who had

said afterwards that he felt eased by his confession. Blunt fixed himself a stiff gin, and stood for several minutes, with his back to the room, gazing into the darkness of Portman Square. Then he sat in a chair, and began the first of many informative interviews which he gave to MI5. He remained as Surveyor of the Queen's Pictures at Buckingham Palace until 1972, when he turned sixty-five, for an early retirement would have been seen in Moscow as a sign that his guilt had been established.[3]

Because Straight's evidence could not be used in open court, Blunt was given immunity from prosecution in return for his full cooperation. The Prime Minister, Sir Alec Douglas-Home, was not apprised of these events, although Queen Elizabeth was told in general terms of the position. Among other ex-associates Blunt mentioned Leo Long, whom he had recruited for Arnold Deutsch in 1937. After Long had been investigated, and his connections traced, he was interviewed by MI5 officers, to whom he gave a full statement later in 1964. Long admitted supplying Soviet Russia with GC&CS's decryptions of German communications – the high-quality SIGINT codenamed ULTRA – and other military secrets both during the war and after the Nazi defeat, when he was deputy head of intelligence at the British Control Commission in Germany. He had remained active as a Soviet agent until 1952, but in return for his cooperation he was neither arrested nor charged.

An officer inside one secret service who betrays its secrets to another 'appals and enthrals' his colleagues, according to Markus Wolf of the East German Stasi. 'The psychological culture of an espionage service resembles that of a clan or tribe, in which individuals are united by some greater goal and a shared sense of identity,' Wolf explained. A defection or the discovery of long-term treachery resembled a septic wound which spreads the poison of distrust throughout the body system. Even field agents who were unconnected to the sphere of work where the betrayal occurred felt more vulnerable when next they approached a dead drop. It became harder to recruit new agents following a major defection.[4]

Toxic distrust spread in MI5 after Philby's disappearance from Beirut in 1963. The Service received reports that in the preceding summer he had begun drinking even more heavily than usual to assuage his nerves. The obvious conclusion that he had been alarmed by the dangers posed to him by Golitsyn's debriefings was discounted. 'Conspiracy theory,' as Christopher Andrew writes, 'triumphed over common sense in explaining Philby's anxiety.' There developed in some MI5 minds the suspicion that a member of the Security Service had warned him of revived interest in him and of the imminent resumption of his interrogation. Five members of the Service knew of these plans: only two of them, the Director General Sir Roger Hollis and his deputy Graham Mitchell, 'had long enough service and good enough access to classified information to fit the profile of a long-term penetration agent'. A tortuously complicated interpretation of a simply explained fact thus started the most harrowing and unnecessary phase of the Service's Cold War history of 1945–91. Its initiator was the head of MI5's Soviet counter-espionage section Arthur Martin, who had been brought into the Service on Philby's recommendation in 1946. An internal assessment of him, made by John Marriott, had noted that despite 'his undeniable critical and analytical gifts and powers of lucid expression on paper', he was 'a rather small-minded man, and I doubt he will much increase in stature as he grows older'. By 1963 he was ominously under the sway of Golitsyn, whose paranoid ebullitions were increasingly unsettling American and British intelligence agencies.[5]

In March 1963, two months after Philby had vanished from Beirut, Martin took his concerns about Mitchell to Hollis, although he did not voice his related doubts about Hollis himself. Hollis had joined MI5 in 1938 after being invalided home with tuberculosis following eight years working for the British American Tobacco Company in China. In the Security Service his desk-work was calm, fair-minded, equable and conscientious. He specialized in monitoring international communism. Even in 1941–5, when MI5 was under political direction to treat the Soviet Union as an ally, he husbanded small resources to ensure that threatening trends in Soviet Russian policy were evaluated and understood. He was thus centrally placed in the Security Service when what the Soviets called the Great Patriotic War was followed by the Cold War. He succeeded White as Director General in 1956.

In May 1963, in a mood of hysterical suspicion, Mitchell was put under surveillance. Following the admissions of Blunt and Cairncross in 1964, Martin began to consult a colleague in MI5's Science Directorate named Peter Wright about his mistrust of Mitchell and Hollis. Wright, too, was susceptible to Golitsyn's unreliable material, and therefore prone to weak thinking and false deductions about

high-level penetration of the Service. During 1964 Martin became so
disruptive an influence that he was transferred from the Soviet counter-espionage section to other responsibilities. It was 'tragic', to use
Christopher Andrew's words, that the lead roles as Blunt's interviewer
and as the Security Service 'witch-finder general' then passed to
Wright, whose conspiracy theories soon proved a worse menace than
Martin's and ultimately damaged the Service as much as Blunt's
treachery. After Mitchell's planned retirement in September 1964,
attention shifted to Hollis. In November a joint Security Service–SIS
working party codenamed FLUENCY was established with Wright in
the chair to investigate the suspicions generated by Martin. It is easier
to propose that a conspiracy may exist than to disprove its existence:
imaginary suspicions, like primitive fears, have an irrational tenacity
that is hard to eradicate. When, in May 1965, FLUENCY reported
that both Services had been penetrated, Hollis was confronted with
the accusations against him. He retired, as previously agreed, at the
time of his sixtieth birthday in December 1965, but the case against
him was pursued by Wright until 1971 (Mitchell had been cleared of
Wright's suspicions a year earlier). By then the 'witch-finder general'
was shunned within the Security Service, where his poor judgement
and snaky methods were compared to those of the Gestapo. He did
not retire until 1976, however, and continued with an ally to make
trouble. As a result of their agitation, Lord Trend, who as Burke Trend
had been Cabinet Secretary until 1973, reviewed the investigation
and reported in 1975 that he found no evidence that either Mitchell
or Hollis had been a Soviet penetration agent.[6]

Wright was an unfortunate. In boyhood he had rickets and a disabling
stutter. As a pupil at Bishop's Stortford College, he expected to go to
an ancient university, but instead left school at fifteen when his father
was sacked by Marconi's Wireless Telegraph Company in 1931 and
descended into alcoholism. He became a farm-worker in Scotland and
then spent fourteen years as an Admiralty scientist before his recruitment in 1949 as external scientific adviser to MI5. His technical
cleverness and mechanical improvisations misled him into feeling that
he was equally sharp in understanding human affinities. He was stubborn, prosaic and self-satisfied, and cherished grudges: one influence
on his obsessive mole-hunting was his grouch that 'the well-born
Englishmen who had become addicted to communism in the 1930s

. . . had enjoyed to the full the privileged background and education denied to me'.[7]

In 1964 the Security Service realized neither that Blunt was the Fourth Man nor Cairncross the Fifth in the Cambridge ring of five. This was one reason for assuring Blunt that he would not be prosecuted: MI5 officers had no wish for criminal trials and press storms that might hinder their search for associates of Philby and Maclean who were not yet apprehended. A dire mistake was made in taking literally Golitsyn's report that all of the group had been at Cambridge together. Neither Blunt nor Cairncross fitted Golitsyn's loose impression of the ring of five as exact Cambridge contemporaries. Blunt was seven or so years older than the others, and had not been recruited by Burgess until after Philby and Maclean had left Cambridge. Cairncross was discounted because he had reached Trinity two years after Philby left. MI5 began to accept that Blunt was the Fourth Man in 1974. Oleg Gordievsky, the KGB *rezident* in the Soviet embassy in London in 1982–5, who had been working for SIS since 1974, identified Cairncross as the last of the ring of five in 1982, and publicly named him in 1990. Although Cairncross surpassed Blunt in importance as a spy, English newspapers were little interested in a shopkeeper's son, who was a gangly-looking swot. Cairncross could not be made into a crowd-pleasing hate-figure, for he was untitled, looked drab rather than patrician, and was neither a connoisseur nor bisexual.

In the quarter-century between Cairncross's confession to Martin and public identification by Gordievsky there were expensive distractions. The FBI in 1966 gave Michael Straight a list of eighty-five US citizens who had attended Cambridge University in 1930–4, from which he identified two or three men who had seemed fellow-travellers or been members of the Trinity cell. Subsequently the FBI shouldered the burden of investigating nearly 600 Americans who had attended the two ancient English universities during the 1930s. In 1967 MI5 started the University Research Group, which worked to identify CPGB members and communist sympathizers at all English universities between 1929 and 1954, and to establish their employment history. Five years of investigations yielded not a single Soviet spy.

Many journalist-commentators wanted levels of relentless persecution and brutal threats that MI5 knew to be unproductive of worthwhile material. Fleet Street sought the good copy that came from the rough methods and dramatic outcomes associated with the interrogation of two Canadian ambassadors, Herbert Norman and John Watkins. Norman had been recruited to the Cambridge communist cell by John Cornford and James Klugmann around 1934. After being named by Elizabeth Bentley in testimony to the US Senate sub-committee on internal security, and despite his admission under interrogation by the Royal Canadian Mounted Police that he had been a communist at Cambridge, he was protected by Canada's Secretary of State for External Affairs, Lester Pearson, who suppressed investigations into his affiliations and possible espionage. The interventions on Norman's behalf by Pearson, who was awarded the Nobel peace prize in 1957 and became Prime Minister of the dominion in 1963, seem startling in retrospect. Norman was appointed High Commissioner in New Zealand and then Ambassador to Egypt. When the US Senate sub-committee renewed its accusatory investigations of him, he jumped to his death from the top of a Swedish embassy building in Cairo in 1957. John Watkins, Canadian Ambassador to the Soviet Union in 1954–6, suffered similar treatment. In 1964 he died in a Montreal hotel bedroom where he was being questioned by the CIA and Royal Canadian Mounted Police about accusations that he had acted as a Soviet agent of influence. These were good press stories with minimal intelligence yield.

After decades of anti-Establishment rhetoric, and in an epoch when respect for the duties and attainments of public intellectuals was being quenched by angry populism, journalists gratified the mass appetite for discrediting highbrows. Innocent Cambridge dons, notably Donald Beves and A.S.F. Gow of Trinity, and Frank Birch and Arthur Pigou of King's, were brought under public suspicion as Soviet spies. There was a competitive scramble to identify an Oxford ring: three eminent academics – Jenifer Hart, Stuart Hampshire and Robin Zaehner – were among those investigated. Isaiah Berlin told Hart, after she had been caught in a *Sunday Times* sting in 1983, that newspapers in the 1980s wanted to 'throw intellectuals to the lions of the political pornography-hunger public'. Men who had died years earlier, notably Guy Liddell and Tomás Harris, were grabbed in the maw of suspicion. Dick White characterized this epoch as that of 'the spy torment'.[8]

Around 1962 MI5 officers had interviewed Jenifer Hart, who had been an official at the Home Office and CPGB member in the 1930s, about her party contacts. She was candid in her replies, because she felt that she had nothing to hide. She was reinterviewed in 1966 by Wright. By her account, their meeting was 'a long and rather nasty affair', during which she was quizzed about a long list of friends and acquaintances (none of whom she knew to be communists). 'Jennifer [sic] Hart', Wright wrote in his ghosted memoirs *Spycatcher*, 'was a fussy, middle-class woman, too old, I thought, for the fashionably short skirt and white net stockings she was wearing.' Hart was a Fellow of St Anne's College, Oxford, where she was tutor in modern history and in politics, philosophy and economics, and thus unusually a member of two university faculties; she had written a path-breaking treatise, *The British Police*; and yet Wright saw her as a post-menopausal woman who ought to accept desexualization. He admitted that she was straightforward in her replies, but did not feel that she was sufficiently impressed by his questions: she had, he complained, 'a condescending, disapproving manner, as if she equated my interest in the left-wing politics of the 1930s with looking up ladies' skirts. To her, it was rather vulgar and ungentlemanly.'[9]

Wright pursued targets connected to Hart, notably Bernard Floud, Phoebe Pool and Andrew Cohen. Floud had attended the universities of Oxford, Berlin, Grenoble and Toronto. He served in the Intelligence Corps in 1939–42 and then the Ministry of Information. In peacetime he farmed in Essex before becoming personnel manager at Granada Television and his election as a Labour MP in 1964. When Harold Wilson nominated him for junior ministerial office, MI5 registered a security objection, and Floud was called for an interview with Wright on Monday 9 October 1967. To his children on the preceding Sunday he had seemed downcast, and Wright at the Monday interview found him as off-hand as Hart. He appeared uninterested in Wright's questions, to many of which he replied that he had no memory of the answers – no doubt truly as he was badly depressed. 'I was tough on him,' Wright boasted. 'I knew that his wife, an agoraphobic depressive, had recently committed suicide . . . I explained to him in unmistakable terms that, since it was my responsibility to advise on his security clearance, I could not possibly clear him until he gave a satisfactory explanation of the Hart story.' Wright asked him to attend a second interview next day: Floud returned to his home in the Regent's Park in a distressed state. He was a teetotaller, but that evening took a large amount of alcohol, swallowed barbiturates and went to his children's playroom in the basement where he locked the door, turned on but did not light the gas fire and swaddled his head in a blanket. Wright's victim was fifty-two.[10]

Sir Andrew Cohen was described by Wright in *Spycatcher* as a diplomat, but in fact he had been an official in the Colonial Office, where he had proven indispensable in managing British political withdrawal from Africa. He served as Governor of Uganda in 1952–7, and was known in Whitehall as the sturdy advocate of financial aid to ex-colonial developing economies. As such he was selected as the first PUS of the Ministry of Overseas Development on its inauguration by the incoming Labour government in 1964. He was imposing in his outlook, ambitions and physical bulk: he died of a heart attack, apparently before Wright could interview him, in 1968.

Phoebe Pool, whose father was a meat-trader in Smithfield market, had phenomenal intellect and artistic discrimination, but from childhood was an insomniac depressive. She was a long-term associate of Blunt's at the Courtauld Institute, collaborated with him in a book about Picasso and acted as his courier during the 1930s. When Wright turned his attention to her, she was a patient in the psychiatric wing of Middlesex Hospital: accordingly Wright instructed Blunt to manipulate another Courtauld scholar, Anita Brookner, to act as an unwitting cut-out providing material from Pool. Pool hurled herself under a tube train in 1971. 'All these suicides,' his boss Martin Furnival Jones supposedly told Wright, 'they'll ruin our image. We're just not that sort of Service.' Wright compressed his account of these events: in fact there were four years between the deaths of Floud and Pool; the chronology and detail of his widely quoted recollections cannot be right. His procedure throughout these investigations typified his method: putting together broken shards of knowledge in the wrong contiguities and producing perversely misshapen intelligence.[11]

Another object of suspicion was the ex-MI5 officer Tomás Harris, who had been killed in a drunken car smash some years earlier. After the bruiting of his name in 1979, his reputation was defended by Ewen Montagu, on behalf of Harris's surviving sisters: 'they are all most distressed and feel alone and helpless as they all worshipped Tommy – one has become almost hysterical'. Montagu could not forgive 'the crooked (and the stupid) writers . . . cashing in to get publicity for their books . . . by flinging accusations against safely dead men', he told Hugh Trevor-Roper in 1980. Dick White also gave his judgement to Trevor-

Roper. 'I do not believe Tomás Harris was a Soviet spy but my conviction is not of the hand in the fire type. He was an international art dealer with contacts on both sides during the Civil War. If he got caught up in anything it would have been in these circumstances & would not connect him with the Cambridge conspirators. He has been closely investigated & I believe cleared.'[12]

Robin Zaehner and Stuart Hampshire

The cases of Robin Zaehner and Stuart Hampshire show the stupidity of Wright's fixations. Goronwy Rees had suggested to MI5 in 1951 that both men had been Soviet spies. One oddity of this accusation was that all three of them were associated with the same Oxford college. Rees had won a fellowship at All Souls in 1931, and was appointed the college's estates bursar in 1951. Hampshire was elected Fellow in 1936, and re-elected in 1955 with the additional post of domestic bursar. Zaehner became a Fellow of the college in 1952, on his appointment as Oxford's Spalding Professor of Eastern Religions and Ethics. 'The idea of Zaehner as a Soviet agent was grotesque,' said Rees's stalwart friend and All Souls colleague Isaiah Berlin. 'Similarly Stuart Hampshire . . . was perfectly innocent, and a perfect patriot.'[13]

Rees's accusation against Zaehner matched the story of the Russian defector betrayed by Philby in 1945, Konstantin Volkov, who had spoken of a Soviet spy embedded in SIS operations in the Middle East. By Wright's account, Zaehner had run MI6's wartime counter-intelligence operations in Iran. His initial task was to protect the railways into Russia, on which vital military supplies were transported, from German sabotage. Later, when the Russians were striving for control of the railway, he had to work to defeat their aims. Zaehner, who spoke local dialects fluently, first worked undercover, 'operating in the murky and cut-throat world of counter-sabotage' to borrow a cliché from Wright, and latterly behind Russian lines. In the first phase he was at constant risk of betrayal and murder by pro-German Arabs and in the second phase by pro-Russian Arabs. 'On the face of it,' declared Wright, 'the very fact that Zaehner survived gave a touch of credibility to Rees' allegations.' After the war, Zaehner served for two years as Press Attaché in the Tehran embassy bribing editors and trying to alter public opinion to favour English interests. Then he returned to academic work in

Oxford, although this was twice interrupted by affairs of state. In 1949 he was seconded to Malta, where he trained the Albanian insurgents whose part in the Anglo-American operation against Enver Hoxha's regime was betrayed by Philby. It took Zaehner only three months to master the Albanian language. He accompanied some of his trainees on their fatal journey to their homeland. In 1951–2 he returned to Tehran as acting Counsellor in the embassy trying to foment opposition to the Iranian Prime Minister Musaddiq after his nationalization of the Anglo-Iranian Oil Company. Zaehner wrote in 1970 that he was relieved to be elected to a chair at Oxford in 1952, because pure scholarship was 'a single-minded search for truth', and he was weary after ten years abroad in a branch of government service 'in which truth is seen as the last of the virtues, and to lie comes to be second nature'.[14]

Zaehner's inaugural lecture as Spalding Professor of Eastern Religions and Ethics was ferocious, witty and deliberately offensive to its audience. He was a Catholic convert who complained of Anglicans that, 'rather than be thought unfashionable or even "reactionary" – titles of which they might well have been proud – they have progressively abandoned the mysteries of their faith and reduced their religion to a meaningless benevolence'. He believed that irrationality was a violent force that could not be suppressed, should not be ignored and was integral to much intelligence work. If excessive rationality and prudentialism had not denied and debased primitive and necessary passions, Zaehner believed,

> we might, perhaps, have been spared at least the worst excesses of twentieth-century barbarism: we might have been spared the sanguinary claptrap of blood and soil which for a moment became the religion of a great nation: we might even have been spared the moronic cult of lunacy preached by the Surrealists. If the twentieth century has taught us nothing else, it should have taught us that there is an element in man other than reason, and that if this element is neglected, it is liable to fester and to erupt into something monstrously evil.

Zaehner deplored 'the conversion of the American ideal of liberty into the most crassly materialist, soulless civilisation the world has ever seen', but equally despised Soviet Russia 'under the leadership of a Directoire of gloomy mediocrity'.[15]

Spycatcher recounts Wright talking for hours in Zaehner's All Souls rooms as the shadow of the college spires faded across the lawn outside (Zaehner's set overlooked a paved quadrangle where there was not a blade of grass). 'I'm sorry, Robin,' Wright began, 'a problem has come up. We're following up some old allegations. I'm afraid there's one that points at you.' He then recounted Volkov's reference to a Soviet spy in Persia. Zaehner was so hurt by the accusation that he dabbed tears from his eyes. 'I spent six years in the desert,' Wright remembered him replying. 'I stayed behind two years after Yalta, when everybody else went home. I got no honours, but I thought at least I had earned a degree of trust.' Zaehner felt sure that Volkov's spy, if he existed, was not English. 'There weren't many of us, and I'd vouch for everyone.' He suggested that the spy was an SIS agent rather than an officer, and suggested Rudolf ('Rudi') Hamburger, the first husband of Ursula Kuczynski @ SONIA. Wright left his interview with Zaehner feeling that 'Rees had been terribly, vindictively mistaken.'[16]

Rees had also fingered Stuart Hampshire, an Oxford philosopher who had joined Trevor-Roper's Radio Security Service in 1940. Hampshire's kinks especially suited intelligence work. 'I am capable of great dissimulation – that is one of my vanities,' he wrote in 1942. 'I am extremely vain about my capacity to perceive the moods and motives of other people.' He disclaimed deep loyalties: 'I find it very pleasant and easy to be pleasant and sympathetic to people, but there are only three or four people whose death would cause me the slightest pain; I like friends as a periodical source of pleasure, but their disappearance does not affect me.' Violence distressed him. 'I like gentleness, or the possibility of gentleness, above all other human qualities. I am preju- diced against successful and effective people.' All of these traits enhanced his official work. They were less valued by Wright, who would have been on high alert if he had known that Hampshire had once told Trevor-Roper, 'I like elaborate good manners and sophistication, and all forms of perversion.'[17]

During the war Hampshire specialized in analysing the activities of the central command of Heinrich Himmler's Schutzstaffel (SS) and gained expert knowledge of SS atrocities across Europe and in Russia. After the war, he interrogated several Nazi leaders in captivity. This experience transformed his attitude to politics and philosophy. 'I learnt how easy it had been to organise the vast enterprises of torture and murder, and to enrol willing workers in this field,' he recalled. 'Unmitigated evil and nastiness are as natural, it seemed, in educated human beings as generosity and sympathy: no more, and no less, natural, a fact that was obvious to Shakespeare, but not previously evident to me.'[18]

Hampshire's intelligence work gave him a lifelong interest in the 'processes of deception, intrigue, treachery, and mystification', he wrote later. 'The deception and intrigue sometimes go so far that any normal interest in literal truth is lost along the way, because the truth is buried beneath layer after layer of corrupt intention.' After the war, he worked, probably for MI5, in San Francisco during the opening session of the United Nations and in Paris for the implementation of the Marshall Plan. These experiences left him with 'difficulty in imagining that purity of intention and undivided purposes can be the normal case in politics. I believe that very many people feel divided between openness and concealment, between innocence and experience; and, outside politics, they often find themselves divided between love and hatred of their own homes and of their own habits.' At the suggestion of Dick White, Hampshire was asked in 1966 by the Cabinet Secretary, Burke Trend, to review the activities of GCHQ at Cheltenham, the costs of gathering SIGINT and the future extent of Anglo-American cooperation. Shortly afterwards, Wright turned to leading an investigation of him. Despite doubts about his friendship with Burgess, who may have made a tentative attempt to recruit him to the cause in 1937, Hampshire was exonerated in 1967. Wright was perhaps in mind when Hampshire later wrote: 'there is a black hole of duplicity and intrigue into which the plans of politicians and intelligence officers may altogether disappear, because they may forget what they are supposed to be doing, lost in the intricacies of political manoeuvre.'[19]

For fourteen years Hampshire was then left in peace until a Saturday in 1981 when a journalist from the Observer showed him the draft of an article, which was due to be published next day, insinuating that he was under plausible suspicion of having been a Soviet agent. Like so many such pieces, it dramatized and made false links with little regard for truth or probability. Hampshire appealed for help to the formidable lawyer Lord Goodman, then Master of University College, Oxford and former chairman of the Observer Trust and of the Newspaper Publishers Association. A telephone call was made to the acting editor of the paper: eight words were enough to convince the *Observer* not to run the story. 'Arnold Goodman here: Stuart Hampshire is with me,' he said before replacing the receiver. In a letter to *The Times*, which was drafted with Goodman's help, Hampshire protested against the twisting methods used in pursuit of espionage press stunts. There had been 'one or two definitely false and defamatory statements' in the spiked *Observer* attack on him.

> But most of the article was innuendo. For example, it was rightly stated that I had been interrogated in the early sixties about my relations with Professor Blunt and with others in wartime intelligence. But the writer had omitted to say that nearly everyone who had been associated with secret military intelligence in the war, and with Professor Blunt, had been interrogated at that time, and this was a very large class.
>
> The method of the proposed article was genteel British McCarthyism, playing on guilt by association and with dark allusions to sources in the secret service. I remonstrated with the journalist, a persuasive friend remonstrated with the acting editor, and after an interval we were told that the article would not appear. The editor of the newspaper later expressed his regret.
>
> This episode raises questions. Ought not this selling of newspapers with the aid of speculative spy stories to come to an end now? Ought we not to question the cant about public service when the methods of investigative journalism are applied to people who are obliged by the original conditions of their service to conceal much of what they know? Ought not former members of the security service to be discouraged from hawking stories around Fleet Street . . .?
>
> Do we want a demoralised intelligence service and demoralised security services?[20]

Anthony Blunt and Andrew Boyle

From 10 September until 22 October 1979 a television serialization of John le Carré's novel *Tinker, Tailor, Soldier, Spy* was broadcast on English television. Le Carré had used some traits of the MI5 officer John Bingham @ Lord Clanmorris for the character of George Smiley in his novels; but Alec Guinness, who played the part of Smiley on television, aped the mannerisms of Maurice Oldfield. On 6 November, fifteen years after Blunt's confession in Portman Square, Andrew Boyle published *The Climate of Treason: Five Who Spied for Russia*. In the book Boyle dropped hints about Blunt's identity without naming him. *Private Eye* however published a parody *Spectator* article headlined 'The Fourth Man' under the byline of 'Sir Anthony Blunt'. 'The simultaneous appearance of the Tinker Tailor T.V. series & Boyle's Climate of Treason has created a somewhat feverish public opinion which the Press is trying to serve,' Dick White wrote in January 1980. '"Moles" are of course Le Carré's invention & there is no doubt that his gruesome imagination has caught on.' He regretted that Boyle's book had not been indicted by reviewers for 'its many inaccuracies & misinterpretations', but had instead been endorsed by glib 'pundits' such as Malcolm Muggeridge.[21]

Margaret Thatcher had become Prime Minister in May 1979. She felt that as Blunt had betrayed his country, there was no reason to protect him unless his exposure would jeopardize national security or embarrass the Crown. On 15 November, in a written answer to a parliamentary question, she confirmed that he had been recruited to work for Russian intelligence before the war, had acted as a talent-spotter while a don at Cambridge and had passed official secrets to Moscow while employed in the Security Service in 1940–5. She called him 'contemptible and repugnant'. Blunt's knighthood was annulled. All night the BBC reported this news in sombre, stilted tones as if a head of state had died. The weekend, to judge from the tone of broadcasts, was spent in astounded mourning. In retrospect, Thatcher's 'outing' of Blunt seems the opening salvo of her campaign against Whitehall traditions and old-guard hierarchy. It was the end of the six-month honeymoon opening of her premiership and the start of serious business rather as the anti-monarchical upsurge after the death of Diana, Princess of Wales in 1997 was the defining moment that ended Tony Blair's honeymoon as Prime Minister.

The *Sunday Telegraph* on 18 November rushed into a story that Blunt's treachery had been responsible for the deaths of forty-nine wartime SOE agents behind enemy lines in the Netherlands. There was not a jot of truth in the report, which the *Telegraph* refused to retract, on the basis that traitors do not deserve apologies and can have any dirt chucked at them with impunity. Tales proliferated that Blunt had seduced and then blackmailed Cambridge undergraduates, that he was a paedophile who preyed on children, that he had connived in selling fake pictures by authenticating forgeries and that he had an ill-gotten fortune stashed offshore. The *Sunday Express* editor John Junor, who believed 'only poofs drink rosé' and that 'AIDS was a fair punishment for buggery', called Blunt 'a treacherous communist poof'. Muggeridge, in *Time* magazine, began with false premises – 'homosexuals tend to sympathize with revolutionary causes, and to find in espionage a congenial occupation' – and continued with spurious generalizations. 'The same gifts which make homosexuals often accomplished actors equip them for spying, which is a kind of acting, while their inevitable exclusion from the satisfaction of parenthood gives them a grudge against society, and therefore an instinctive sympathy with efforts to overthrow it.'[22]

On 20 November Blunt held a press conference in the offices of *The Times*. Only journalists from that newspaper, the *Guardian* and television newsrooms were admitted. Resentful of their exclusion, other newspapers burst into puritanical indignation that Blunt had been served white wine with smoked trout over lunch with the newspaper's deputy editor: they thought he should have been served crusts and gruel. The next day's front-page headlines included 'DAMN YOUR CONSCIENCE! The British deserve better than this load of phoney humbug, Blunt' (*Daily Express – the voice of Britain*, 21 November) and 'THE SPY WITH NO SHAME – A performance of supreme insolence' (*Daily Mail*, 21 November). The *Daily Mail* editorial raged with vindictive threats that:

> the Establishment . . . cannot any longer continue to deceive the nation. The time for the truth is now. And we must have it.
>
> If we do not, let them be warned: The truth *will* eventually be discovered, and then, no parade of consciences, however high-born, however mighty, will protect the Establishment from the rightful wrath of the British people.[23]

Two contrary voices were juxtaposed on the letters page of *The Times*. Sir Michael Howard, then Chichele Professor in the History of War at Oxford, decried 'the witch-hunt in Westminster and elsewhere'. As the author of an official but suppressed *Strategic Deception in the Second World War*, he gave a temperate explanation: 'When an enemy agent is discovered, the natural instinct of the security authorities is not to expose but to use him, and the greater his importance the stronger this instinct will be. Not only is he a mine of useful information, but if his employers are unaware that he has been "blown", they will keep in contact with him. He can then be used as a double agent, feeding them misinformation.' For MI5, Howard reminded readers, 'the value of keeping Professor Blunt as a card in their hands rather than discarding him by handing him over to justice must have been a major factor in the minds of those who made the decision'. He doubted if 'the country would really have been better off if Professor Blunt had been made to stand trial for treason in 1964'. The letter beneath Howard's came from a pompous dunce named Russell Burlingham, well known as the club bore of the Reform and as the bane of staff at the nearby London Library. 'Never has Mrs Thatcher shown her political resolution to better advantage than in her spontaneous decision to drag this shabby little history into the light of day. In doing so she has struck her shrewdest blow for British liberty and exposed spurious "liberal" values; and the moral impact will be quite as decisive in its effect, and as far-reaching, as any of her radical economic initiatives.'[24]

Blunt's intellectual gifts, homosexuality and bodily posture were pilloried. He was attacked as snobbish, cold, imperious and sexually predatory in a hate campaign that gave a propaganda victory to Moscow. Commentators never paused in their diatribes against the old school tie, Cambridge and homosexuality to recall the triumphs at Bletchley, where public schoolboys had abounded, where Cambridge graduates had led its inaugural phase and where Alan Turing was *genius loci*. Chapman Pincher in the Beaverbrook press's London evening news-paper called Blunt a 'revolting individual', and inveighed against the Foreign Office 'as a natural home for homosexuals, drunks and unstable weirdoes in general'. Between hard covers, too, Pincher abused Blunt as toffee-nosed, spiteful and – a deadly charge in an increasingly anti-elitist age – 'widely disliked for his intellectual arrogance, holding those whom he considered lesser mortals in contempt'. No admiration was permitted for Blunt's brilliant mind and scholarship, although it is reductive to think of him primarily as a spy. 'Blunt was only really happy when he was doing research,' wrote his Courtauld colleague Peter

Kidson. 'He was one of those true intellectuals for whom there is no experience to compare with the eureka moment, when an obsessive problem finally dissolves into a pattern of intelligible connections.'[25]

What of Boyle and his book? '*The Climate of Treason* is riveting but not very intelligent,' Frederic Raphael wrote at the time. It might be faulted, but it could not be ignored. It had, if not a bias, at least an entrenched basis to its ideas and procedures which is usually overlooked. Boyle was a devout Catholic: his brother was a Catholic priest; he corresponded with Cardinal Heenan and other Catholic clergy; he sent his son to the great Jesuit boarding school in Lancashire, Stonyhurst. The Catholic influence is marked in Boyle's references to sex. He referred to the 'abnormal sexual proclivities' of Burgess, who (he claimed without substantiation) 'introduced Maclean . . . to the sad pleasures of sodomy' at Cambridge: 'boasting about it as if he had thereby earned the Victoria Cross for valour beyond the call of duty'. Boyle's tone implied that the western world had been degrading itself since the Declaration of the Rights of Man in 1789 or since Martin Luther's protest at Wittenberg in 1517. Boyle approached the book, so he told George Carey-Foster when seeking an interview in 1978, with curiosity about the 'spiritual distemper that prevailed among resentful, guilt-laden young men and women at our Universities, and which the Comintern and other Soviet agencies capitalised on brilliantly'. He was enterprising in using the US Freedom of Information Act to obtain CIA and FBI documents, although he sometimes misunderstood or perhaps was swamped by them. He interviewed hundreds of witnesses, took impressionistic hand-written notes rather than recordings, and was overwhelmed not only by his proliferating material but by the din of conflicting voices. One can only be impressed at how hard he worked to meet his deadlines.[26]

Some of the reviews were informed. 'After the lapse of a generation, the mechanics of petty treachery become unimportant,' wrote Trevor-Roper in the *Spectator*. He judged that Boyle 'reveals nothing that was not known – perhaps more accurately known – to authority, and merely gives occasion for belated public persecution.' Histories of espionage that answered general questions about human tendencies, institutional development and social systems had more value than those that presented an accretion of irrelevant and distracting factual detail. In the *London Review of Books* Neal Ascherson found *The Climate of Treason* too unforgiving: 'Boyle is a bit of a prig. Nobody gets away with anything. Political hindsight dominates.' He noted that Boyle dismissed Maclean's book on *British Foreign Policy since Suez* as 'ponderous' whereas, wrote Ascherson, it is 'penetrating and very readable': he wondered whether Boyle had actually read it.[27]

Isaiah Berlin was surprised to be quoted in *The Climate of Treason* – sometimes inaccurately – because he had understood that his talk with Boyle at the Athenaeum had been on a non-attributable basis. In his complaint to Boyle, he noted factual errors, such as the statement that he and Burgess had flown on 'a VIP flight' to the USA in September 1940 when they had in truth travelled by a Cunard liner from Liverpool to Quebec in July of that year. Berlin rebutted Boyle's statement that, after meeting Maclean in wartime Washington, he had thought him 'abnormal and unhealthy' – a phrase of Boyle's that indicated his Catholic distaste for homosexuality. He also denied Boyle's story that Maclean had cast a recruiting fly over Berlin by asking him in Washington, 'why don't you join *us*?'[28]

Patrick Reilly thought that Boyle had little idea how either the Foreign Office or an embassy worked. He skewered some of Boyle's errors, such as the claim that Burgess had learnt about the VENONA-inspired investigation into the Washington leakages of 1944, and had warned Maclean when the latter was passing through London, from his old post in the US capital on his way to Cairo, in the autumn of 1948. But the first information about the 1944 leak did not reach London until January 1949. It is inconceivable that Burgess, who was then wasting time in the Office's Far Eastern Department, would have had access to VENONA material. Reilly denied crucial details of Boyle's account of the FO handling of Maclean's case.

Dick White had no respect for Boyle or *The Climate of Treason*. 'The first edition is crammed with inaccuracies & yet . . . he remains complacently satisfied that he is now accepted as the greatest authority on the subject of "moles"', White briefed Trevor-Roper in 1980. The worst mistakes were made, said White, when Boyle became entangled by his American material. Boyle's obstinacy in insisting that Wilfrid Mann, whom White knew to be a double agent turned by the Americans, was the Fifth Man also vexed White. 'I think it is important to debunk Boyle once & for all. His *Climate of Treason* has to some extent created a climate of opinion which is dangerously provocative of a witch-hunt. His only bull's eye was Blunt. Rees gave him that but it was already widely known in Fleet Street before *Climate* was published.' White was altogether dismissive of Boyle's efforts: 'I don't think the book has power at all, only luck that it was published in the wake of the showing on T.V. of Tinker Tailor Soldier Spy which created a feverish public interest in "moles"'. The real misfortune of the publicity whirlwind aroused by Thatcher's parliamentary statement was that it convinced critics of the Establishment that 'there have been a whole bucket full of pardons issued to cover up numberless moles in Government. This is not so.'[29]

Thoughtless and banal over-simplifications about the English class system permeated Boyle's text (neither Scotland nor Wales had any part). Burgess was described as belonging to 'the vulgarly ostentatious Pitt Club, a decadent right-wing group, as well as to the élitist and secretive Apostles', although the Pitt was boisterous rather than decadent and fogeyish rather than vulgar. The two Cambridge spies who confessed in 1964 received the equivalent of 'Royal Pardons', wrote Boyle, 'exonerated at the discretion of the two secret services concerned, partly for the sake of expediency and partly as a reward for the important light they were able to shed on the pattern of treachery inside the British Establishment'. Boyle's gloss on the episode in which Burgess revealed his and Blunt's secrets to Rees, who disclosed them to Rosamond Lehmann, runs: 'Thanks to the narrow, tightly enmeshed relationships which still characterized the structure of the British ruling class, whether at the centre of power or on the outer fringes, the gossip about Burgess did not spread beyond his intellectual friends.' But Lehmann's father was a rentier living in a pleasure villa on the banks of the Thames while Rees's father was a nonconformist clergyman: neither was remotely 'ruling class'. And outside totalitarian states, which class – rich, poor, middling, learned, outdoorsy – blabs like police informers? The experiences, for example, of France and the Netherlands under German occupation in the 1940s and during the unsettled period after their liberation suggest that informers were envious or vindictive neighbours, quarrelsome in-laws, disgruntled employees or other despicable types. It is hard to know what Boyle expected of Lehmann: it is hard to think what she could, with decency, have done.[30]

Wright had retired to a stud farm in Tasmania in 1976. He was embittered not only by the dismissal of his conspiracy theories, but also by the refusal of the Security Service to take account of his fifteen years at the Admiralty when computing the amount of his pension.

The lucrative fame of *The Climate of Treason* must have unsettled his jealous spirit. He took his grudges to Lord Rothschild, who bought him air tickets back to England so that they could discuss Wright's hopes of writing his memoirs. In 1980 he arrived at Rothschild's home with a ten-page typescript about Soviet penetration, to which he gave the hackneyed title 'The Cancer in our Midst'. Rothschild was hypersensitive about his reputation and perplexed by insinuations that as a friend of Blunt and Burgess he must have been a Soviet spy. He evidently hoped that he would be exonerated if Wright brought his experiences into the public domain. He invited Pincher to meet Wright; the two men collaborated; and Pincher wrote his hasty, shoddy book, *Their Trade is Treachery*.

Their Trade is Treachery, published in 1981, publicly revealed for the first time the investigation of Hollis, who had died in 1973, and suggested that Hollis had been guilty. Wright's secret help was indispensable to Pincher, who had a second informant – a mischievous wretch, with confidential access, who had once leaked to the *Sunday Times* the fact that Sir Geoffrey Harrison had been forced to retire as Ambassador in Moscow in 1968 after sexual entrapment by a Russian woman domestic. Pincher opened *Their Trade* with a series of falsehoods. He said that Lord Trend's inquiry of 1974–5 indicated that in addition to Blunt 'there had been at least one "Super-mole", and possibly two, with unrestricted opportunity for burrowing into secrets'. Readers could be excused for believing Pincher when he declared with such firmness, 'Lord Trend concluded that there was a strong *prima facie* case that MI5 had been deeply penetrated over many years by someone who was not Blunt. He named Hollis as the likeliest suspect.' It was Trend's view, so Pincher avowed, that 'Hollis had not cleared himself during his interrogation. His answers to searching questions had been unconvincing, and his memory had been at fault only when it suited him.' Moreover, the former Cabinet Secretary supposedly concluded, 'Hollis had consistently frustrated attempts by loyal MI5 officers to investigate the obvious penetration of their service.' In fact, Trend had said nothing resembling this. Pincher also indulged in the obligatory cant about class conspiracy: he called Trend 'the epitome of the Establishment', and a stalwart of 'the old boys' network', which was untrue if it meant that Trend was partial, socially discriminatory or nepotistic.[31]

In 1987 came Wright's ghosted and scrappily edited memoirs

Spycatcher, full of animus and confusion, to reanimate the attack-dogs on Hollis. 'When I read Wright's book, with its paranoid self-righteousness, its gloating record of persecution,' wrote Trevor-Roper, 'I was reminded of that other half-crazed witch-hunter in our history, Titus Oates, who also could not be totally refuted, for the Popish Plot was not a complete myth: a small nucleus of truth lay buried under the unscrupulously manufactured hysteria.' *Spycatcher* was published in Australia, to evade prosecution in London under the Official Secrets Act, and received an inordinate marketing boost from an ill-fated attempt by the British government in the Supreme Court of New South Wales to prevent its publication there. The luckless Cabinet Secretary, Sir Robert Armstrong, was sent to Sydney to testify on behalf of the Thatcher administration: he found himself in an impossible situation, and was drenched in the spittle of journalistic mockery. Many London newspapers treated Wright as a rebel-hero against authority, as a brave maverick, as a lone fighter against long odds. There was little criticism of his irresponsibility, fixations, vindictiveness, elisions, errors and conceit. One of Whitehall's great objections to *Spycatcher* was its references to GCHQ – 'the last really secret aspect of British government', as the historians Richard Aldrich and Rory Cormac say. At this time even Cabinet ministers did not know that it was twice the size of MI5 and SIS combined.[32]

Thatcher, whose autobiography seldom alludes to intelligence matters, presided over a vigilant and even aggressive regime – probably incited by Maurice Oldfield's hard-line successors at SIS – to protect official secrets. She vetoed publication of Michael Howard's officially commissioned history of wartime deception operations (finally published in 1990), while the Cabinet Office forbade publication of Howard's essay on the double agent GARBO, who had been discussed in previous books by Masterman and Montagu. During the first five years of Thatcher's administration, the Official Secrets Act was invoked once every eighteen weeks. The blanket of official silence on security matters created opportunities for the sensationalists and fabricators among writers of espionage history.

A renewed internal security investigation in 1988 concluded that the case against Hollis, which culminated in two interviews with him, was so meagre that it should not have been pursued. The prolongation of the divisive hunt for MI5 traitors was attributable to Wright's dishonesty and invention of evidence, his leading of witnesses (including Blunt) during questioning, 'His tendency to select a solution, then tailor the evidence to fit it', and 'His standard manoeuvre when worsted in argument of taking refuge in mystery ("If you knew what I know")'. To this indictment by Christopher Andrew must be added the weak analysis by investigators associated with Wright and the bias derived from Golitsyn's baneful delusions. The case against Hollis, White wrote in 1988, was 'highly contrived & purely circumstantial'. Wright's conspiracy theories were, he said, deceptions.[33]

'Only out for the money'

Even if one or two fingers had been amputated it would be easy to count on one hand the number of authors of espionage histories who practised scrupulous exactitude as they added to the heap of books responsible for what White called 'the spy torment'. This section will examine the motives, methods and plausibility of other leaders of the genre, which has excited newspaper stories and the public mind since 1979. The first of these was Donald McCormick, who was foreign manager of the *Sunday Times* in 1963–73 and a prolific author under his own name and using the alias of Richard Deacon. The others were John Costello and Anthony Cave Brown.

The books of McCormick @ Deacon included *The Identity of Jack the Ripper* (1959) and *Erotic Literature: A Connoisseur's Guide* (1992). Cannibalism, Unidentified Flying Objects, libertarian economics and apartheid were among his enthusiasms. Fantasists, tricksters, escapists and impostors intrigued him. He wrote a biography of the arms dealer and champion self-mythologizer Sir Basil Zaharoff, and an admiring study *Taken for a Ride: The History of Cons and Con-Men* (1976). He enjoyed hoaxing readers, invented anonymous sources, fabricated documents and described himself with a wink as 'a very clever man, who enjoys his quiet fun'. He had a canny sense of what would ring true and what would sell. One academic critic called him 'a charlatan, who took a dishonest, mischievous approach to gathering evidence', and whose books are 'riddled with inaccuracy, misrepresentation, poorly supported judgements that are far away from reality . . . and cognitive conceit'. Even an admirer conceded, 'I suppose his exactitude is not that of a scholar, but of a journalist.'[34]

McCormick @ Deacon profited by denigrating the ancient univer-sities to his credulous readers. In *The British Connection* (1979) he claimed that 'sodomy and communism' were both 'popular' in Oxford and Cambridge universities before 1939, 'especially among those of the upper strata of society'. At Oxford, he maintained, for he was always brazen in extrapolating minority examples into a mass movement, 'homosexuality was so much the "in" thing that many heteros posed as homos', while Cambridge, he claimed risibly, 'had a preponderance of homosexual dons'.[35]

One of his targets was the Cambridge economist Arthur Pigou. He depicted Pigou as gun-running for Russian revolutionaries, and recording his activities in an enciphered diary. According to Deacon's remunerative fantasies, Pigou ranked with Klugmann as a secret Cambridge recruiter, masterminded the stealing of the keys to Philip Noel-Baker's dispatch box and cultivated drunken, jumpy and unsporting Burgess by taking him rock-climbing in Wales. Noël Annan asked White about Pigou's supposed Soviet spy work. 'We looked into the matter of Deacon's allegations & had nothing to corroborate them,' White replied. There was a monosyllable that White always mistrusted unless it was accompanied by the tightest evidence, 'link'. Deacon had written of 'a link' between Pigou and the triple agent Theodore Rothstein: 'one can only ask what sort of "link"? The word may only be emotively used for the purposes of a purely circumstantial case.' Elsewhere in *The British Connection* similarly feeble 'links' were used to imply that Guy Liddell of MI5 and the atomic scientist Sir Rudolf Peierls had been Soviet spies.[36]

Trails of guilt by association were also laid by John Costello. Costello was pertinacious in tracking sources and indefatigable in producing bestsellers. His driving energy and intensity of temperament could seem attractive. But a histrionic element in the myth he created about himself, his dramatic sense of his activities and influence, and an underlying suspicious hostility were on the debit side. His bitterness against the Cambridge academic Christopher Andrew, whose painstaking research and careful conclusions belied the conspiracy theorists, showed the animus of someone whose world felt threatened by studious calm. Costello's big book about the wider context of the Blunt case, *Mask of Treachery* (1988), tapped rich veins of documentary material, but was flawed by its methods and assumptions. After a survey of the setbacks of Liddell's career, starting with the ARCOS raid in 1927, Costello concluded: 'Either Liddell suffered from a bad run of luck that was so disastrous as to be incomprehensible; or he was incompetent to the point of criminal negligence; or he was the grand-daddy Soviet mole in the British intelligence services.' After two pages of bullet points listing circumstantial facts as if they were tight evidential links, Costello deployed mixed metaphors ('the mechanism of intellectual treachery is woven from subtle deceits'), psycho-babble ('his connoisseurship grew in defiance of his stern military father and was nourished by a doting musical mother') and clichés about the English class system that together are a sure indicator of woolly thinking. 'The Liddells – like the Blunts – were a family with aristocratic connexions dropping down the social scale. The backbiting cynicism of the homosexual milieu which he enjoyed may have fed a deep-seated resentment against the Establishment . . . Liddell's artistic temperament, like Blunt's, shaped by similar adolescent resentments against the underlying philistinism of British society, may well have sown the seeds of later treachery.' These half-baked suppositions and callow prejudices were the flimsy foundations for the pillorying of Liddell in the 1980s.[37]

'There never has been & never could be any suspicion of Guy Liddell,' White insisted to Trevor-Roper in 1980. 'Only unscrupulous & malicious people . . . could possibly suggest it.' Accusers relied on 'completely futile' tales of 'friendship with Burgess & Blunt, Guy as the man who warned Burgess & Maclean to escape, suppression of an item of evidence warning of Pearl Harbour [sic]'. Liddell was even blamed by Costello and 'the awful Deacon' for the failure of the ARCOS raid. It was all 'so silly', especially as Liddell certainly 'detested Burgess'. White knew as a fact that when Blunt recommended Burgess to the Security Service, 'it was Guy who blocked his recruitment or any form of access to MI5'. In White's mind Deacon was twinned with Costello, who telephoned him in 1989 seeking information on a pre-war American case which White would not give him. 'He said that he was due to give a lecture to the CIA at Langley that day,' White told Noël Annan. 'I wonder what that will do for the so-called Special Relationship!' Costello was 'only out for the money', White thought. 'He may be industrious in reading everything but is totally indiscriminate in evaluating source material.'[38]

Among the common preoccupations of Costello and Deacon was the Cambridge discussion-group the Apostles, of which Blunt and

Burgess had been members. This innocuous society, with its private slang and rituals, its strict search for truth and its pitiless testing of false propositions was hated by Fleet Street hacks to whom its values were a standing reproach. The disputations of the Apostles were based, according to Christopher Brooke, who joined in the 1940s, on 'a belief that we *can* learn, and a determination that we *will* learn, from people of the most opposite opinions'. The latitude of their outlook was antithetical to the enraged over-simplifications beloved by reporters and editors alike. The linguistic precision, the empathy with opponents, the tolerance of irregularities were equally alien to Fleet Street: journalists represented the group as a nexus of treason and an example of all that was rotten about highly educated, over-sophisticated, offensively urbane men. The Apostles, wrote Malcolm Muggeridge (former deputy editor of the *Daily Telegraph*), 'combined culture, Communism and the love that nowadays all too readily dares to speak its name'. Men like Maynard Keynes, Ludwig Wittgenstein, Bertrand Russell and G. H. Hardy were 'dreadful people', the *News of the World* columnist Woodrow Wyatt insisted. Deacon, who was a devotee of the *News of the World*, wrote a whole insalubrious book about the Apostles. The 'homosexual faction within the Apostles' was 'mafia-like' in its enlistment of young dupes, he claimed. 'As history has shown over two thousand years or more, a homosexual mafia is by far the most dangerous' of recruiting bodies.[39]

Anthony Cave Brown was another of the authors who seized the chances made by the secret services' ultra-reticence about their operational history. 'He is a monster: gross, loud, aggressive, vulgar,' Trevor-Roper told Annan in 1994. 'He accumulates material but is very unreliable in his use of it, laying on his social prejudices and circumstantial colour quite irresponsibly, pretending to have met and known people whom, at most, he has only trapped into a telephone conversation. I am told that his only contact with Menzies was one telephone call in the course of which Menzies only uttered one world, *viz*: "No". But in his book he appears as a welcome guest at Menzies' country house – the evening shadows lengthening as his host uncorked another bottle of Krug.' Cave Brown was a dipsomaniac: Fred Winterbotham, the RAF officer charged with circulating ULTRA intelligence during the war, once returned home after Sunday-morning church to find that Cave Brown had in the meantime arrived to quiz him, climbed through a window, found a bottle of his whisky and drunk it. Cave Brown had

the knack of turning his verbose, turgid books into bestsellers. In one
he depicted the Apostles as 'bound together by that queer trinity of the
thirties, communism, Catholicism and sodomy. Hence the need for . . .
secrecy, for the Establishment had outlawed all three.' It is true that the
majority view of the Apostles was anti-Christian, and that a minority
were anti-capitalist, but false to claim that they treated Stalin's purges
as 'trivial compared to the sufferings of millions who were unemployed'.
The Apostles were not Stalinists any more than 'the Establishment' had
proscribed either communism or Catholicism. Journalists were,
however, enthralled by such caricatures: more sober writers than Cave
Brown have deprecated the Apostles as 'a self-appointed, secret group
of cultural elitists', harbouring 'unusual sexual relationships' and with
tentacles requiring 'nothing less than an investigation into Britain's
ruling class'.[40]

Alister Watson and Dennis Proctor were the first professed communists to be elected to the Apostles in 1927. This was at a time when
Marxism-Leninism had made negligible inroads into the university,
and was therefore not a factor in considering 'embryos', as candidates
for the Apostles were called. Blunt was neither a communist nor politically aware when elected in 1928: after his conversion to communism,
he seldom attended. 'Embryos' with doctrinaire minds were unwelcome
in a society that was speculative, sceptical and fluid in its ideas. John
Cornford was rejected as a candidate because, as Proctor told MI5
twenty years later, 'his overt membership of the Communist Party
meant that he had not got an open mind. Possession of an open mind
was a condition of membership.' Fellow-travellers without a party card
were eligible, for Burgess was elected in 1932; but according to Victor
Rothschild, who was elected on the same day as Burgess, endless discussions on communist themes were considered dull.[41]

What was it that made journalists feel threatened by the Apostles
and virulent in their attacks? Elevated thinking, privileged emotions
and the cultivation of sensibilities stuck in their gorge. 'I believe in
aristocracy,' the archetypal Apostle E. M. Forster had written in his
credo of 1939:

> Not an aristocracy of power, based upon rank and influence, but an
> aristocracy of the sensitive, the considerate and the plucky. Its
> members are to be found in all nations and classes, and all through

the ages, and there is a secret understanding between them when they meet. They represent the true human tradition, the one permanent victory of our queer race over cruelty and chaos. Thousands of them perish in obscurity, a few are great names. They are sensitive for others as well as for themselves, they are considerate without being fussy, their pluck is not swankiness but the power to endure, and they can take a joke.

This sort of thinking was abominated by the populist journalism of the 1980s. Men like Ray ('Dark Satanic') Mills, the self-styled 'Angry Voice' of the *Daily Star*, who declared his 'political philosophy' as 'hang 'em, flog 'em, castrate 'em, send 'em back' and who enjoyed the office nickname of Biffo (Big ignorant fucker from Oldham), hated intellectuals and their 'cretinous students'. In a decade of panic about AIDS, Mills decried 'wooftahs, pooftahs, nancy boys, queers' and wished 'a blight on them all'. The preference of the Apostles had been for 'less chastity and more delicacy', as Forster wrote. 'I do not feel my aristocracy are a real aristocracy if they thwart their bodies, since bodies are the instruments through which we register and enjoy the world.' English demotic journalists, by contrast, attacked other people's sexual pleasures unless they were conducted at the emotional level of a television sitcom.[42]

Maurice Oldfield and Chapman Pincher

One of the cruellest cases of money-grubbing victimization involved Maurice Oldfield. Born on a kitchen table in Derbyshire's Peak District in 1915, he was the eldest of eleven children of a tenant farmer. As a boy he lived in a two-up, two-down cottage, and laboured on his family's remote sheep-farm. He won a scholarship to Manchester University, where he graduated with a first-class degree and was elected to a fellowship in history. Not enough people thought it wrong that at Manchester there were sexually segregated students unions, one for men and the other for women, until the 1950s. In Manchester he had a love affair with a fellow student, Jimmy Crompton: he did not mention this, and possibly some other early experiences, when he underwent vetting as an intelligence officer. Altogether his career belied the stereotype of the Establishment as an impermeably class-bound congeries of inefficient snobs. After showing his talents while working for SIME in the 1940s, he was posted in 1950 to the SIS station in Singapore, with a remit covering south-east Asia and the east. He remained peripatetic when he became head of station in Singapore in 1956. He had particular success in using unofficial agents, or Friends, among airline crews. The International Olympic Committee was another source of Friends. In 1959 he was chosen as SIS representative in Washington, and was seventh Chief of the Service in 1973–8.

Hugh Trevor-Roper, who knew Oldfield, 'thought him likeable but . . . rather a bumbler. I could only reconcile his reputation with my impression by assuming that he deliberately simulated stupidity to conceal Machiavellian cunning: but I don't myself believe this rationalisation', Oldfield was the first chief of SIS to give formal briefings to the leader of the opposition, in this case Margaret Thatcher. Mutual admiration developed between the two of them. Pincher later claimed to have been Oldfield's conduit to Thatcher: in fact Oldfield already had a direct route through James Scott-Hopkins, a former SIS officer who was Tory MP for the Derbyshire constituency containing Oldfield's family farm.[43]

After retiring from SIS in 1978, Oldfield went to Oxford as a visiting Fellow at All Souls; but in 1979 Thatcher recalled him as coordinator of security intelligence in Northern Ireland. In March 1980 – four months after Thatcher's public naming of Blunt and in the thick of the toxic clouds of homophobia – a rumour was circulated that Oldfield had evaded his twenty-four-hour Special Branch protection team in Belfast and had visited the Highwayman public house at Comber where he propositioned another man in the urinals. Although this seems unlikely on several counts, the tales were repeated in London, and Sir Robert Armstrong, who was Thatcher's security adviser as well as Cabinet Secretary, summoned Oldfield for interview in Whitehall. 'I was utterly aghast to be having to question Maurice on such matters – he was the ultimate loyal civil servant', Armstrong recalled thirty years later. He thought it strange that although the allegations originated from Northern Ireland, no material from this phase of Oldfield's career was put before him. There were only reports of 'questionable friendships' during overseas postings. 'There were no suggestions of impropriety in the physical sense', to use the stilted euphemisms of the 1980s, but 'incontrovertible evidence that he preferred the company of men',

Armstrong said. 'Maurice made no attempt to deny it; he just sat, sad and broken, and apologized for having lied on his positive vetting forms when they homed in on sexuality.'[44]

Oldfield tendered his resignation, and had his vetting clearance withdrawn. He underwent two interrogations by MI5's Cecil Shipp, whom he assured that his sexual exchanges with young men had ended when he was in his mid-twenties. His flat was besieged by reporters hoping to intercept a rent boy whom they could bribe into lubricious extravagances. Oldfield soon fell mortally ill with stomach cancer. In March 1981 he was in his hospital room, surrounded by brothers and sisters, when two policemen ushered in Thatcher. The siblings stood to leave, but she said, 'No, stay, stay,' and talked with them agreeably for some time. Then she asked for some moments alone with the dying man. When the Oldfields trooped back after her departure, they found their brother, hitherto calm about his illness, distraught and weeping. It was the first time that any of them had seen him tearful. In answer to their question what was wrong, he replied: 'Mrs Thatcher asked if I was homosexual. I had to tell her.' It was the first time that he had mentioned his sexuality to any of his family. He died a few days later.[45]

The 1980s was a time of vile prejudice against both people with AIDS and male homosexuality. 'The homosexuals who brought this plague upon us should be locked up,' an editorial in Pincher's newspaper the *Daily Express* approvingly quoted a Solihull grandmother as saying in 1986. 'Burning is too good for them. Bury them in a pit, and pour on quick-lime.' Pincher certainly dragged sexual aspersions into his writings whenever he could. Herbert Norman, whom Cornford and Klugmann had converted to communism when he was at Trinity in the 1930s and who killed himself while Canadian Ambassador in Cairo in 1957, is stigmatized as 'a known homosexual' in Pincher's *Too Secret Too Long* (1984) – an ill-made, misleading, self-confident book. Pincher cited as a source Norman's biographer James Barros, who however treats this allegation as a slur which originated obscurely and for which there is no evidence except its repetition.[46]

'I have to look after my old age,' Chapman Pincher said in 1986. Though his personal myth was that he was a man of the world, he had narrow sexual prejudices. In his potboiler *Traitors*, published in 1987, for example, he called Blunt, Burgess, Driberg and Maclean 'gay deceivers', and Blunt's brother Wilfrid 'a self-confessed homosexual', as if homosexuality was still a crime to be confessed. He cited unnamed psychiatrists as authorities for his belief that 'what are referred to as "disturbed" homosexuals, like Burgess, feel themselves driven to take revenge on authority, of which the state is an obvious embodiment. Freudians further suggest that this is often the result of upbringing by a hostile or uncaring father and that traitors are hitting back at paternalistic authority'. Pincher condemned Vassall's 'sexual abnormality', and judged the appointment to Moscow of a man so 'obvious' in his 'perversions' as 'a severe indictment of our security services'. He explained: 'homosexuality is often so compulsive that those addicted to it are driven to take fearful risks to find partners. The risks are compounded by the strange need of many homosexuals to indulge themselves with . . . guttersnipes . . . called in the homosexual fraternity "rough trade".' Pincher had a new and lucrative target in Oldfield: 'a surreptitious homosexual' of 'staggering duplicity', who held 'the highest secret-service position in the land', but had been unable 'to control his compulsion' for 'rough trade'. The danger was that 'compulsive homosexuality is easily recognized by others of the fraternity', which therefore exacerbated 'the blackmail danger'. Pincher's obsession with Oldfield's 'unfortunate sexual habits' led him to tell impossible tales of foreign waiters and rent boys being taken to a Westminster flat which was under guard by Scotland Yard protection officers and covered throughout by listening devices.[47]

Pincher's so-called 'scoop' was to find a security officer who believed that a young oriental man, whom he had seen at Oldfield's flat in Westminster in 1978, had been a sex-worker. Encouraged by Pincher's publicity, newspapers reported as an agreed fact that Oldfield was, in the *Daily Telegraph*'s stilted circumlocution, 'a man with a known penchant for what is colloquially described as "rough trade"'. In response to this press storm, Margaret Thatcher stated in April 1987 that Oldfield's homosexuality had been a potential although not an actual security risk. Labour's former Foreign Secretary David Owen said with absurd over-statement that this admission was 'a devastating blow to the credibility of the security services', and aggressively referred to the former SIS chief as 'Maurice Oldfield' as if, like Blunt, he deserved to be stripped of his knighthood. The Labour backbencher whose parliamentary question had led to Blunt's naming eight years earlier chimed in to say that if the tales of Oldfield's 'disgusting behaviour' were true, it disgraced the whole country.[48]

Martin Pearce, Oldfield's biographer, has shown that the slinking youth was in fact a thirty-eight-year-old paediatrician named Michael Chan, whose family Oldfield had befriended in Singapore a quarter of a century earlier. Chan, who became a Commissioner for Racial Equality in the 1990s and a member of the Press Complaints Commission, received a life peerage in 2001. Such was the reality of the 'trade' with whom Pincher imagined Oldfield to be having sex. When Oldfield's friend Anthony Cavendish challenged Pincher about including the dead man in a book entitled *Traitors*, and using such tosh, Pincher replied with a wink: 'You may have a pension, Tony. I need to look after mine.' George Kennedy Young, Vice Chief of SIS in 1959–61, told the *Daily Telegraph* of this bestselling book, 'Chapman Pincher has done the KGB's work for them.' The historian Alistair Horne, ex-MI5/SIME, called Pincher 'a self-serving, disreputable man'. Margaret Thatcher was tetchy when her toady Woodrow Wyatt told her, on the basis of *Traitors*, that Oldfield was 'a homosexual who went in for the rough trade'. A few days later Wyatt discussed 'the Oldfield revelations' with Rupert Murdoch, who laughed with pride at the recent *Sun* headline, 'Tinker, Tailor, Poofter, Spy'.[49]

The personal history that took Oldfield from some early fun in bed with Jimmy Crompton to the misery of Margaret Thatcher's well-meant bedside visit had a security risk of zero. Spurious allegations, wild guesses and grubby innuendo continue to fester three decades after Pincher's *Traitors*. The facts are forgotten or ignored by journalists who still invoke Oldfield's name whenever an 'Establishment sex scandal' is thought to have occurred. The internet has empowered conspiracy theorists to spread mindless conjectures and nasty fantasies as if they are hard facts. Baseless 'links' even connect him to child abuse.[50]

Chapman Pincher lived to the age of a hundred, trying to the end to sully the truth about Soviet penetration agents or, as the *Daily Mail* preferred to say, 'still working away to find proof absolute about Hollis's betrayal, which many people now accept'. With people like Pincher, said an MI5 officer's wife Lady Clanmorris, 'the KGB does not need a disinformation department'. M. R. D. Foot, former intelligence officer and official historian of SOE, was quoted in one obituary: 'My view of the man would be sulphuric. The stuff he produced on the intelligence services was almost totally inaccurate.'[51]

Few writers brought 'a calming sense of reality into the mad world of journalistic spy writing', regretted Dick White in 1989. 'In the massive destruction that the journalists have wrought, several worthy people who are dead have lost their reputations. But the reputation of individuals is only one aspect of the matter.' Costello, among others, 'feeds the Americans with the sort of stuff they like to read & to believe, the condemnation of the entire British ruling class. One has to say that the damage he has done is worth comparing with the damage done by the spies themselves. As to the Services wh. have been so unmercifully battered I fear for the morale of their members & the effect on future security.' A year later, when Cairncross was publicly identified by Gordievsky as the Fifth Man, Trevor-Roper recapitulated the aims and achievements of the Cambridge ring of five. 'Their intention was to destroy Western civilisation, which they held to be doomed, and to replace it by Stalinist communism, which they supposed to be perfect, or at least perfectible.' Their faith in the historic inevitability of the dictatorship of the proletariat proved 'totally, diametrically and for themselves tragically wrong', continued Trevor-Roper. 'The system which they idealised, and to which they sold themselves, is bankrupt. The West, of which they despaired as irreformable, is reformed.' The enduring legacy of the ring of five in Britain 'was a poison of suspicion which, for a generation, has infected the already enclosed and stifling atmosphere of secret intelligence'.[52]

The deceptive publicity that began with *The Climate of Treason* gulled millions of readers in Britain and abroad, and demeaned the men and women of intelligence and moral purpose who had joined the secret services. The mole-hunters of the 1980s were foul-minded, mercenary and pernicious. Their besmirching of individuals and institutions changed the political culture and electoral moods of Britain far beyond any achievement of Moscow agents or agencies.

Envoi

The Union of Soviet Socialist Republics and the United Kingdom coexisted as rival powers for over seventy years. For four of those years they were allies in a global war which extended the power of the USSR into the satellite states of eastern Europe just as the UK began its unprecedented programme of decolonization; but for most of the period between 1917 and 1991 there was a deadly antagonism between them. The two conglomerated states were bound together by their hostile preoccupations with one another: their ideologies, armaments, diplomacy, propaganda and secret services vied for the same prizes. In espionage and counter-espionage they paced and marked one another: Moscow watched and learnt from London in the 1920s, by courtesy of the Ewer–Hayes espionage network, just as London learnt its counter-espionage from watching and turning Moscow's agents and sub-agents. During the short spell of Anglo-Soviet intelligence cooperation in Iran during 1944–5 this mutual education was explicit. Western commentators often dwell on Moscow's successes with such agents as Blake and Philby, but understate the maladroitness of the KGB and its anterior agencies, and seldom mention the irrecuperable setback to communist espionage caused by the mass expulsion from London of Soviet representatives in 1971.

A primary intention of this book is to test the entrenched assumptions about upper-class corruption and Establishment cover-ups that began with the disappearance of Burgess and Maclean in 1951, intensified after Philby's defection in 1963 and became unassailable after Blunt's public shaming in 1979. As avowed Marxists, the Cambridge spies justified their espionage activities in the language of class struggle. Their propagandist explanations were magnified and distorted by journalists who wanted to profit from angry headlines and indignant columns. The notions prevailed that Burgess and Maclean had got their jobs in the Foreign Office by exploiting the old-school-tie network; that they had been shielded from exposure as communist spies by the class loyalties of other diplomats; that in 1962–3 Philby had been allowed to avoid arrest by fleeing to the Soviet Union as part of a class-bound Establishment cover-up; that when clinching evidence forced Anthony Blunt's confession of espionage in 1964, his knighthood and post in the Royal Household had saved him from criminal trial.

This book has shown that none of the Cambridge five was upper class or descended from the traditional ruling orders. The immunity from prosecution given to Blunt and Cairncross showed no more favouritism than did the authorities' handling of the largely working-class Ewer–Hayes network of the 1920s or the lower-middle-class Meredith–Vernon network of the 1930s. The Soviet handlers of Percy Glading and Klaus Fuchs, among others, were moreover enabled to leave the country rather than detained to testify as potentially uncontrollable witnesses in criminal trials. Indeed spy trials – those of Glading, Nunn May, Fuchs, Marshall, Blake and Vassall among others – were carefully managed in their evidence, and are a poor guide to the facts behind the cases. Prosecutions and jury trials were avoided not in order to protect members of privileged classes, but because the clinching evidence – such as VENONA decrypts or material from defectors – could not be aired in open court. Juries in any case were chary of state prosecutions of the leakers of official secrets. 'The difficulty', said the Attorney General Sir Michael Havers in 1985, 'is getting a jury willing to convict on the facts in Official Secrets cases.' The standards of proof needed in anything but show-trials and kangaroo courts are more exacting than those needed by editors to justify inflammatory headlines.[1]

The advantages for the security services of cultivating and developing a spy as an informant should be obvious, even if some journalists denounce the authorities for doing so. Barack Obama's administration was reviled by right-wing Americans after Umar Abdulmutallab, the Nigerian who tried to explode an aircraft flying from Amsterdam to Detroit in 2009, was given a Miranda warning, indicating his right to keep silent in police custody. This upholding of legal rights and civil liberties proved to be an intelligence success. Abdulmutallab volunteered information after being informed of his right to avoid self-incrimination.

Other conventional interpretations are challenged in this book. I argue that the security lapses in the recruitment of wartime officials in London during 1939–41 were less grievous or numerous than those in Washington after 1941. I show that the culture of departmental trust, and the mild vetting system used in London until 1951, seemed preferable at the time to Gestapo methods, Stalinist purges, American loyalty tests or HUAC scapegoating. I suggest that the preoccupation with class loyalties and social exclusion, which has dominated histories of communist espionage in Britain, is a species of self-serving Marxism which relies on illusory or falsified readings of the English class system (social identities in Ireland, Scotland and Wales have no part in this narrative). Burgess lied about the protection of his career by fellow Old Etonians, and much of the other class analysis is factually unsound. My belief is that the dynamics of departments in government ministries and agency were gender-bound more than class-bound. The monopoly of power and influence by men, and the exclusion of all but a few women from anything other than secretarial services, was dominant in the nature of both their management and the complicity and co-operation among colleagues. This new insight will seem self-evident to some readers, while others will not relinquish their primary loyalty to class analysis.

What else must be said of the whips and scourges which have belaboured England's Establishment since the 1950s? They have been wielded by journalists, by fantasists and by others worming their way to political power. Governing institutions, notably the Security Service and the Foreign Office, have been subjected to ill-informed or malicious attacks. This book however demonstrates that MI5 was not the resting-place of inflexible blimps, superannuated Indian policemen, expensively educated silly asses or obtuse reactionaries. The Security Service's officers were generally subtle, patient, responsive and astute, although never super-human or infallible. They preferred to play long games rather than to score quick results. Their achievements, as recounted in this book, are as considerable as could reasonably be expected. It needs to be stressed, though, that there is an irreconcilable antagonism between the intelligence services and populists. The former are concerned with risk assessment, with calibrations of possibilities and likelihoods, and with managing future difficulties. The latter believe that the future cannot be predicted with rational precision, that imprudence is a form of moral courage, that thoughtless subjectivity is a valid mode in risk assessment, and that anyone who pretends to make expert forecasts is manipulating opinion for discreditable purposes.

The quiet intelligence of diplomacy, like the desk-work of counter-espionage officers, is often less respected than the emotive noise of parliamentarians. 'There is nothing dramatic about the success of a diplomatist,' said the nineteenth-century Foreign Secretary Lord Salisbury. 'His virtues are composed of a series of microscopic advantages: of a judicious suggestion here, an opportune civility there, a wise concession at one moment and a far-sighted persistence at another; of sleepless tact, immovable calmness, unshakeable patience.' These virtues are seldom understood or admired by the populace. The attacks on the Diplomatic Service beginning in the 1950s by George Brown, Richard Crossman and others were intentionally crowd-pleasing and destructive. Vituperation of political opponents was not new; but systematic denigration of an administrative cadre was historically unprecedented. This onslaught was intended to neutralize, subdue and weaken government departments for the benefit of socialist programmes. The aim was to force civil servants into submission to the will of politicians claiming to represent the will of the people: to curb officials in their guidance of policy-thinking, in their dispelling of false hopes and in their predictions of coming snares.[2]

Government by the knowledgeable – epistocracy – has been superseded in most of the English-speaking world by a version of democracy that elevates opinion above knowledge. When Michael Gove, a Cabinet minister campaigning for Brexit during the European referendum of 2016, made his unforgivable remark, 'People in this country have had enough of experts,' he was parroting attitudes that had first arisen in political discourse after the defections of 1951. He was stoking the attack on knowledge and informed judgement, fostering the populist delusion that one person's opinion is as good as any other, and pretending that it is improper to value trained minds and rational expertise higher than instincts, inklings, hunches and over-emotional fudge. The process whereby public leaders and experienced minds began to capitulate to people less informed than themselves started when Burgess and Maclean hurried aboard the night boat to Saint Malo.[3]

In Anthony Powell's words, 'The intellectual arrogance of clever people, intolerable though it often is, is nothing to the intellectual arrogance of ignorant people.' It is a democratic illusion that the voters of a democracy are more immune than those of totalitarian states from the distortion of reality. Democracy is a volatile system with which to direct and empower international policy. Citizens in any nation state can lose their sense of proportion or their aversion to conflict under the impetus of patriotism. Aggression is the outcome of national pride and of an overriding belief in the value of national sovereignty.[4]

There is a good reason for the expertise of MI5 to be called 'intelligence work'. It requires brainwork as well as desk-work: it requires checking, reassessing and constant thought. These proficiencies do not always fit with the national temper. Intelligence, whether individual or departmental, together with official competence, can be unwelcome to those who prefer to face risks with stubborn denial of their existence or with a roulette player's ruinous trust in luck. 'The British always think that they have something in hand,' Lord Vansittart wrote in retirement in the 1950s. 'At first it was vague superiority: "one Briton can beat three foreigners".' When that failed in 1914–18, Vansittart continued, 'they banked on geographical detachment and, when that failed too, they stopped thinking.'[5]

Acknowledgements

The later drafts of this book were slashed, binned, rethought, intensified and given exactitude during the intellectually sumptuous months when I was a visiting Fellow at All Souls College, Oxford in 2016. There is no toadying in my co-dedication of the book to the Warden and Fellows: in their college my thoughts 'began to burnish, sprout, and swell'; my work was invigorated by their vital ideas and unstinting stimuli; my debt to them is fathomless. It is invidious, perhaps, to mention individuals, but sitting in the Codrington Library, a few yards from the figure of Dmitri Levitin, crouched over his sources like a jaguar ready to spring on luscious prey, inspired me to read and read, and to read yet more, and to organize, clarify and revise. My college mentor, the Junior Dean George Woudhuysen, was unfailingly considerate: he managed the remarkable task of being both youthful and protectively avuncular; he mixed gravity with glee, and wielded the gentlest of prods. Without William Waldegrave it would have been impossible to write this book: the moral courage and good sense of his initiative as Chancellor of the Duchy of Lancaster in 1992 to declassify tranches of documents held by MI5, and to release them in the National Archives, were indispensable. I have followed reading recommendations, ideas, factual leads and corrections of nuance provided by John Drury, Gabriel Gorodetsky, Jane Humphries, Jonathan Katz, Dmitri Levitin, Avner Offer, Nicholas Rodger, Judith Scheele, Stephen Smith, Sir Keith Thomas and Sir John Vickers. The generosity of mind and disciplined creative ideas of Francesco Ademollo, Sarah Beaver, Margaret Bent, Edel Bhreathnach, Francis Brown, Clare Bucknell, Vince Crawford, Wolfgang Ernst, Sir Noel Malcolm, Jesse Norman, Philipp Northaft, Erik Panzer, Catriona Seth, Péter-Dániel Szántó, Frederick Wilmot-Smith and Andrew Wynn Owen were more enlivening and suggestive than they can know.

The intense scrutiny given to my manuscript by its copy-editor, Peter James, was stupendous, and saved me from mortifying blunders. The technical experience and intuitions of Christopher Phipps corrected many anomalies and slips found while he compiled the index. I am beholden to Iain Hunt for his help with illustrations and much else. Henry Hemming has been generous in advising on illustrations, and Valerie Lippay has kindly agreed to the use of the photograph of her mother Olga Gray. Gill Bennett and Cécile Fabre sacrificed their valuable time to read draft chapters of the book, and made supportive suggestions for improvements. I am grateful for further ideas, facts, corrections and references to the Reverend William C. Beaver, Lady Bullard, Jeremy Catto, Patric Dickinson (Clarenceux King of Arms), Minoo Dinshaw, Sir Brian Harrison, Ivo Hesmondhalgh, Sheila Markham, Tom Perrin, Timothy Pleydell-Bouverie, Basil Postan, Otto Saumarez Smith, James Southern, James Stourton, † Giles Waterfield and Michael Wheeler. Roy Foster, Lady Antonia Fraser, Flora Fraser, Munro Price, Stuart Proffitt, Andrew Roberts, John Saumarez Smith and Charles Sebag-Montefiore have prompted me to read books that have informed my own.

Notions that are developed in this book were first tested in papers given to the Algae group at the Athenaeum (led by Dan Cohn-Sherbok), the S. G. Gardiner Society at Christ Church, Oxford (at the invitation of Joshua Hillis), the Modern History Seminar at St John's College, Oxford (convened by Joshua Bennett, Sam Brewitt-Taylor, Matthew Grimley and Sîan Pooley), the Visiting Fellows' seminar at All Souls (organized by Marco Gentile and Cecilia Heyes), the Highgate Literary and Scientific Institute (where Hilary Laurie is the impresario), the Oriel Colloquium on Universities, Security and Intelligence Studies (mustered by Liam Gearon), and the British Studies seminar at the University of Texas at Austin (at which Wm. Roger Louis is the presiding genius). The Master and Fellows of Selwyn College, Cambridge, where I stayed during my Cambridge research, have my gratitude for their hospitality and companionship.

Miranda Carter, Ted Harrison and Andrew Lownie are longstanding friends: their books on Blunt, Philby and Burgess have been models for me. Lownie moreover has shown princely generosity in sending me references and scanned documents. Geoff Andrews and Martin Pearce are newer acquaintances, who at our meetings and in their biographies of James Klugmann and Maurice Oldfield have given me welcome pointers. When Nicola Lacey's biography of H. L. A. Hart was first published, I read it for pleasure: returning to it after almost twenty years, the enjoyment was undiminished; it remains a model of lucidity and balance which I have tried to emulate. My reliance at surface level and deep below on the works of Sir Christopher Andrew, Jonathan Haslam, Victor Madeira, Kevin Quinlan and Stephen Smith is comprehensive. The influence of the writings of David Burke and Nigel West pervade several chapters.

I thank the archivists and document-fetchers at the following institutions: All Souls College, Oxford (papers of John Sparrow); Balliol College, Oxford (papers of Sir Harold Nicolson); the Bodleian Library, Oxford (papers of Lady Asquith of Yarnbury, Sir Isaiah Berlin, Lord Brand, Lord Inverchapel, Sir Patrick Reilly, Anthony Sampson, Lord Sherfield, Viscount Simon, Lord Somervell of Harrow, the Earl of Stockton, Lord Wilson of Rievaulx, Earl Winterton and Sir Laming Worthington-Evans); the British Library (papers of Anthony Blunt); Cambridge University Library (the papers of Earl Baldwin of Bewdley, Andrew Boyle, the Marquess of Crewe, Joseph Needham, Sir Michael Postan, Viscount Templewood and Vickers Ltd); Christ Church, Oxford (papers of Lord Bradwell and Lord Dacre of Glanton); Churchill College, Cambridge (papers of Sir Alexander Cadogan and Sir Eric Phipps); Durham Cathedral Library (papers of Herbert Hensley Henson); House of Lords Record Office (papers of Lord Beaverbrook and Sir Patrick Hannon); Humanities Research Center, University of Texas at Austin (papers of Maurice Cranston, Kay Dick and Francis King); King's College, Cambridge (papers of Lord Annan, Lord Keynes and Joan Robinson); the National Archives, Kew (papers of the Foreign Office, the Foreign & Commonwealth Office, the Home Office, MI5, the Premier's Office and the Ministry of Supply); the Wren Library, Trinity College, Cambridge (papers of Lord Butler of Saffron Walden and Maurice Dobb); and Worcester College, Oxford (papers of Sir John Masterman, and college records). The amenities of the London Library, Cambridge University Library and the Codrington Library at All Souls were invaluable to my delving in secondary material.

For allowing me to quote from the Dacre papers at Christ Church, I thank Professor Blair Worden and the Literary Estate of Lord Dacre of Glanton. Extracts from the Cadogan and Phipps journals are reproduced by permission of the Master and Fellows of Churchill College,

Cambridge. Quotations from the unpublished diaries of Harold Macmillan are by consent of the Harold Macmillan Book Trust. Unpublished Annan and Keynes material appears by courtesy of the Provost and Scholars of King's College, Cambridge. I thank the Master and Fellows of Trinity College, Cambridge for their agreement to my use of archival material from the Wren Library. Jane Reilly has kindly agreed to my quotations from the unpublished papers of her father Sir Patrick Reilly, and Cathy Rosenberg has likewise enabled me to quote from a letter of her uncle Francis King.

This book was completed before the publication in 2017 of five books on which I would otherwise have drawn: Anne Applebaum, *Red Famine: Stalin's War on Ukraine* (Allen Lane); Mihir Bose, *Silver: The Spy Who Fooled the Nazis* (Fonthill); Helen Fry, *The London Cage: The Secret History of Britain's World War II Interrogation Centre* (Yale); Hamish MacGibbon, *Maverick Spy: Stalin's Super-Agent in World War II* (Tauris); and Odd Arne Westad, *The Cold War: A World History* (Allen Lane).

When I started to write *Enemies Within*, Rory Allan of Christ Church was the ideal reader in my head whom I had to keep amused. This dashing, glamorous and valiant young sprite seemed pleased in the last weeks of his life to know that he would be the primary dedicatee. Jenny Davenport and Christopher Phipps scoffed at my sillier provisional ideas, challenged my lazier assumptions, warned when the tone of my drafts was too testy and sustained me with their calm and merry sanity. For the umpteenth time I thank them.

NOTES

Chapter 1: The Moscow Apparatus

1. Sir John Balfour, *Not Too Correct an Aureole: The Recollections of a Diplomat* (Wilton: Michael Russell, 1983), p. 89; *Documents on British Policy Overseas* (hereafter *DBPO*), series 1, vol. 6 (London: HMSO, 1991), p. 324.
2. In this paragraph and throughout this chapter I have followed the ideas and even the phrases of an indispensable guide, Stephen A. Smith's *Russia in Revolution: An Empire in Crisis, 1890 to 1928* (Oxford: Oxford University Press, 2017).
3. Christopher Andrew and Oleg Gordievsky, *KGB: The Inside Story of its Foreign Operations from Lenin to Gorbachev* (London: Hodder & Stoughton, 1990), pp. 1–2.
4. Victor Sebestyen, *Lenin the Dictator: An Intimate Portrait* (London: Weidenfeld & Nicolson, 2017), p. 99.
5. The preceding paragraphs follow Daniel Beer, *The House of the Dead: Siberian Exile under the Tsars* (London: Allen Lane, 2016).
6. R. C. Zaehner, *Concordant Discord: The Interdependence of Faiths* (Oxford: Clarendon Press, 1970), p. 418.
7. Stephen A. Smith, 'Towards a Global History of Communism', in Smith, ed., *The Oxford Handbook of the History of Communism* (Oxford: Oxford University Press, 2014), p. 7; Gareth Stedman Jones, *Karl Marx: Greatness and Illusion* (London: Allen Lane, 2016), pp. 339, 342.
8. Smith, 'Towards a Global History of Communism', pp. 6–7.
9. Giles Ury, *Labour and the Gulag: Russia and the Seduction of the British Left* (London: Backbite, 2017), p. 163.
10. Smith, *Russia in Revolution*, pp. 183–7.
11. Sebestyen, *Lenin the Dictator*, pp. 348, 387–8.
12. Mark DeWolfe Howe, ed., *Holmes–Laski Letters: The Correspondence of Mr Justice Holmes and Harold Laski, 1916–1935*, vol. 2 (Cambridge, Mass.: Harvard University Press, 1953), pp. 829–30.

13. Lars T. Lih, 'Lenin and Bolshevism', in Smith, ed., *Oxford Handbook of History of Communism*, p. 68.

14. Cambridge University Library, Vickers microfilm R346, Emile Cohn to Sir Vincent Caillard, 15 September 1922.

15. Georges Agabekov, *OGPU: The Russian Secret Terror* (New York: Brentano, 1931), pp. ix, 266.

16. Christopher Andrew and Vasili Mitrokhin, *The Mitrokhin Archive: The KGB in Europe and the West* (London: Allen Lane, 1999), p. 38; Nadezhda Mandelstam, *Hope against Hope* (London: Collins, 1971), pp. 14, 79-80.

17. Lord D'Abernon, *An Ambassador of Peace*, vol. 1 (London: Hodder & Stoughton, 1929), pp. 312-13.

18. The National Archives (hereafter NA) FO 371/10495, N2488/2140/38, Sir Eyre Crowe, minute of 22 March 1924; Smith, *Russia in Revolution*, pp. 164, 188, 383-4.

19. George Slocombe, *The Tumult and the Shouting* (New York: Macmillan, 1936), p. 266; Sir Reader Bullard, *The Camels Must Go* (London: Faber & Faber, 1961), p. 159; Julian and Margaret Bullard, eds, *Inside Stalin's Russia: The Diaries of Reader Bullard 1930-1934* (Charlbury: Day Books, 2000), p. 15; Christopher Andrew, *The Defence of the Realm: The Authorized History of MI5* (London: Allen Lane, 2009), p. 174n.; Jonathan Haslam, *Near and Distant Neighbours: A New History of Soviet Intelligence* (Oxford: Oxford University Press, 2015), p. xv.

20. Colonel Josiah Wedgwood, 'Bulgarian Terrors', *Manchester Guardian*, 24 April 1925, p. 12.

21. Alexander Vatlin, 'The Evolution of the Comintern, 1919-1943', in Smith, ed., *Oxford Handbook of History of Communism*, pp. 188, 190; Andrew Boyle, *The Climate of Treason: Five Who Spied for Russia* (London: Hutchinson, 1979), p. 100.

22. Lord Vansittart, *The Mist Procession* (London: Hutchinson, 1958), p. 361.

23. *Documents on British Foreign Policy*, series 1A, vol. 1 (London: HMSO, 1966), p. 728.

24. Kevin McDermott, 'Stalin and Stalinism', in Smith, ed., *Oxford Handbook of History of Communism*, pp. 73-4, 77.

25. Smith, *Russia in Revolution*, p. 389.

26. *Documents on British Foreign Policy, 1919-1939*, series 2, vol. 7 (London: HMSO, 1958), pp. 97, 123, 138.

27. House of Commons debates, vol. 114, cols 2940 & 2942, 16 April 1919; W. N. Ewer, 'After the Break', *Labour Monthly*, 9 (July 1927), p. 414.

28. NA KV 2/2670, serial 54a, minute from Paris, 10 December 1929.

29. Cambridge, Wren Library, Trinity College, Dobb papers DD/4, Dobb, 'The Russian Revolution', paper to Pembroke College's Martlet Society, 1920.

30. Sir Owen O'Malley, *The Phantom Caravan* (London: John Murray, 1954), pp. 70, 72, 86, 214; Bullard, *Inside Stalin's Russia*, p. 19.

31. Haslam, *Near and Distant Neighbours*, p. 39.

32. Boris Volodarsky, *Stalin's Agent: The Life and Death of Alexander Orlov* (Oxford: Oxford University Press, 2014), pp. 163-5; Haslam, *Near and Distant Neighbours*, p. 57.

33. Elizabeth Poretsky, *Our Own People: A Memoir of 'Ignace Reiss' and his Friends* (Oxford: Oxford University Press, 1969), p. 74.

34. *Ibid.*, pp. 102–3.

35. *Ibid.*, pp. 69, 71.

36. Peter Holquist, '"Information is the Alpha and Omega of our Work": Bolshevik Surveillance in its Pan-European Context', *Journal of Modern History*, 69 (1997), p. 415; Poretsky, *Our Own People*, p. 109.

37. Boris Volodarsky, 'Unknown Agabekov', *Intelligence and National Security*, 28 (2013), p. 893; 'OGPU Deserter Mystery: Story of his Work against Britain', *Morning Post*, 3 July 1930; NA KV 2/2398.

38. Andrew and Gordievsky, *KGB*, pp. 179–80.

39. NA FO 371/10495, N6941/2140/38, despatches 787 & 812 of R. M. Hodgson, Moscow, 22 & 30 August 1924; Lord D'Abernon, *An Ambassador of Peace*, vol. 3 (London: Hodder & Stoughton, 1930), pp. 190–1.

40. Andrew and Mitrokhin, *Mitrokhin Archive*, p. 47.

41. George Slocombe, *A Mirror to Geneva: Its Growth, Grandeur and Decay* (New York: Henry Holt, 1938), p. 5.

42. NA FO 850/2, Y775/775/650, report of Valentine Vivian dated 20 February 1937, and undated minute of Sir Robert Vansittart.

43. Basil Liddell Hart, *Europe in Arms* (London: Faber & Faber, 1937), p. 13; Cambridge, Churchill College archives, ACAD 1/9, diary of Sir Alexander Cadogan, 26 January 1940; NA FO 371/21198, R1687/224/92, minutes of Sir Owen O'Malley, Sir Orme Sargent and Sir Alexander Cadogan, 11 March 1937.

44. Andrew and Gordievsky, *KGB*, pp. 180–2.

45. *DBPO*, series 1, vol. 2 (London: HMSO, 1985), pp. 650–1.

46. Balfour, *Not Too Correct*, pp. 89, 92; Simon Sebag Montefiore, *Stalin: The Court of the Red Tsar* (London: Weidenfeld & Nicolson, 2003), pp. 205–6.

47. Balfour, *Not Too Correct*, pp. 89, 92.

48. Sebag Montefiore, *Stalin: Red Tsar*, pp. 168–76.

49. *Ibid.*, pp. 176, 196, 287–8.

50. D. N. Pritt, *The Zinoviev Trial* (London: Gollancz, 1936), pp. 4, 20, 21, 29; Pritt, 'How the trial struck a British lawyer', *News Chronicle*, 3 September 1936, reproduced in Anon., *The Moscow Trial (1936)* (London: Anglo-Russian Parliamentary Committee, 1936), pp. 10–11.

51. Balfour, *Not Too Correct*, pp. 96–7; Sebag Montefiore, *Stalin: Red Tsar*, pp. 422–3.

52. *DBPO*, series 1, vol. 11 (London: Routledge, 2017), p. 16; Oxford, Bodleian Library, Mss Eng c 6888, f. 90, Hugh Trevor-Roper to Sir Patrick Reilly, undated [mid-December 1959]; Mandelstam, *Hope against Hope*, p. 34.

53. J. Arch Getty and Oleg Naumov, *The Road to Terror: Stalin and the Self-Destruction of the Bolsheviks, 1932–1939* (New Haven: Yale University Press, 1999), p. 557; David Holloway, *Stalin and the Bomb: The Soviet Union and Atomic Energy, 1939–1956* (New Haven: Yale University Press, 1994), p. 273.

Chapter 2: The Intelligence Division

1. William Camden, *The History of the Most Renowned and Victorious Princess Elizabeth . . .* (London: Harper & Amery, 1675 edition), book 3, p. 364.

2. Sir Victor Wellesley, *Diplomacy in Fetters* (London: Hutchinson, 1944), p. 16.

3. See John Carswell, *The South Sea Bubble* (Stroud: Alan Sutton, 1993 edition).

4. Andrew Lang, *Pickle the Spy, or the incognito of Prince Charles* (London: Longman, 1897), pp. 5–6, 194, 285; Jacqueline Riding, *Jacobites: A New History of the '45 Rebellion* (London: Bloomsbury, 2016), pp. 223, 230, 321. See also Lesley Lewis, *Connoisseurs and Secret Agents in Eighteenth-Century Italy* (London: Chatto & Windus, 1961).

5. Adam Zamoyski, *Phantom Terror: The Threat of Revolution and the Repression of Liberty, 1789–1848* (London: Collins, 2014), p. 150.

6. George Augustus Sala, *Gaslight and Daylight with some London scenes they shine upon* (London: Chapman & Hall, 1859), pp. 88-91; Gareth Stedman Jones, *Karl Marx: Greatness and Illusion* (London: Allen Lane, 2016), pp. 315, 317, 321.

7. Brian Stewart and Samantha Newbery, *Why Spy? The Art of Intelligence* (London: Hurst, 2015), pp. 67, 100; Viscount Mersey, *A Picture of Life, 1872–1940* (London: John Murray, 1941), p. 362.

8. William Beaver, *Under Every Leaf: How Britain Played the Greater Game from Afghanistan to Asia* (London: Biteback, 2012), p. 1.

9. *Ibid.*, p. 16.

10. *Ibid.*, p. 44.

11. Major General Lord Edward Gleichen, *A Guardsman's Memories: A Book of Recollections* (Edinburgh: Blackwood, 1932), p. 176.

12. Andrew Gailey, *The Lost Imperialist: Lord Dufferin, Memory and Mythmaking in an Age of Celebrity* (London: John Murray, 2015), p. 231.

13. Lord Vansittart, *The Mist Procession* (London: Hutchinson, 1958), p. 194; Beaver, *Under Every Leaf*, p. 63.

14. Gleichen, *Guardsman's Memories*, p. 78; Beaver, *Under Every Leaf*, p. 4; J. Arch Getty, *Origins of the Great Purges: The Soviet Communist Party Reconsidered, 1933–1938* (Cambridge: Cambridge University Press, 1985), p. 103.

15. See generally Richard Davenport-Hines, *Dudley Docker: The Life and Times of a Trade Warrior* (Cambridge: Cambridge University Press, 1984), and Davenport-Hines, 'The Ottoman Empire in Decline: The Business Imperialism of Sir Vincent Caillard, 1883-1898', in Robert Turrell and Jean-Jacques van Helten, eds, *The City and the Empire* (London: Institute of Commonwealth Studies, 1985).

16. Beaver, *Under Every Leaf*, p. 293; Gleichen, *Guardsman's Memories*, p. 188.

17. Sir Henry Hozier, *The Seven Weeks' War: Its Antecedents and its Incidents* (London: Macmillan, 1867), pp. 113–14.

18. Mersey, *Picture of Life*, pp. 185-6.

19. Gailey, *Lost Imperialist*, pp. 229-30; Stephen Gwynn, ed., *The Letters and Friendships of Sir Cecil Spring Rice*, vol. 1 (London: Constable, 1929), p. 301.

20. I follow in this paragraph and elsewhere an informative source: Matthew Seligmann, *Spies in Uniform: British Military and Naval Intelligence on the Eve of the First World War* (Oxford: Oxford University Press, 2006).

21. Sir Kenneth Strong, *Intelligence at the Top: The Recollections of an Intelligence Officer* (London: Cassell, 1968), p. 220; Donald Lindsay, *Forgotten General: A Life of Andrew Thorne* (Wilton: Michael Russell, 1987), pp. 103–13.

22. Lord Eustace Percy, *Some Memories* (London: Eyre & Spottiswoode, 1958), p. 11.

23. A. J. A. Morris, *The Scaremongers: The Advocacy of War and Rearmament, 1896–1914* (London: Routledge & Kegan Paul, 1984), pp. 107-8, 156–7; J. Lee Thompson, *Northcliffe: Press Baron in Politics, 1865–1922* (London: John Murray, 2000), p. 134; Beaver, *Under Every Leaf*, pp. 290–1.

24. Vansittart, *Mist Procession*, p. 109; Oxford, Bodleian Library, Inverchapel papers, box 19, Lord Eustace Percy to Archie Clark Kerr, 3 October 1913.

25. Percy Savage, *Savage of Scotland Yard* (London: Hutchinson, 1934), quoted in 'German Spy Organisation Smashed', in Dennis Wheatley, ed., *A Century of Spy Stories* (London: Hutchinson, 1938), pp. 93–5.

26. John Bew, *Citizen Clem: A Biography of Attlee* (London: Quercus, 2016), pp. 105–6.

Chapter 3: The Whitehall Frame of Mind

1. Cambridge University Library, Templewood papers 2/37, memorandum by Sir Basil Thomson, 1918.

2. Stuart Ball, ed., *Parliament and Politics in the Age of Baldwin and MacDonald: The Headlam Diaries, 1923–1935* (London: The Historians' Press, 1992), p. 121.

3. Leonard Woolf, *Downhill All the Way: An Autobiography of the Years 1919–1939* (London: Hogarth Press, 1967), pp. 18–20.

4. Durham Cathedral Library, diary of Herbert Hensley Henson, 7 May 1919.

5. Lord D'Abernon, *An Ambassador of Peace*, vol. 1 (London: Hodder & Stoughton, 1929), pp. 20, 22.

6. 'Lenin's courier sentenced', *The Times*, 3 November 1920, p. 5; 'Letters for Lenin', *Manchester Guardian*, 3 November 1920, p. 9; Giles Ury, *Labour and the Gulag: Russia and the Seduction of the British Left* (London: Backbite, 2017), pp. 53–5.

7. 'M.P. to Meet Sedition Charge', *Manchester Guardian*, 13 November 1920, p. 10.

8. 'Mr. Malone Held to be a Dangerous Person', *Manchester Guardian*, 20 November 1920, p. 12; NA KV 2/1905, minute 57 of 6 March 1934; NA KV 2/1907, minute 793, Courtenay Young to Roger Fulford, 5 April 1942.

9. Graham Greene, *Stamboul Train* (London: Heinemann, 1932), p. 132; NA FO 371/10478, N3844/104/38, Comintern to CPGB, 7 April 1924.

10. Gill Bennett, *Churchill's Man of Mystery: Desmond Morton and the World of Intelligence* (London: Routledge, 2006), p. 43; Hugh Trevor-Roper, *The Wartime Journals*, ed. Richard Davenport-Hines (London: I. B. Tauris, 2012), p. 149; Brian Stewart and Samantha Newbery, *Why Spy? The Art of Intelligence* (London: Hurst, 2015), p. 7.

11. Stuart Ball, ed., *Conservative Politics in National and Imperial Crisis: Letters from Britain to the Viceroy of India, 1926–31* (Farnham: Ashgate, 2014), p. 127; Gabriel Gorodetsky, ed., *The Maisky Diaries: Red Ambassador to the Court of St James's, 1932–1943* (New Haven: Yale University Press, 2015), p. 10.

12. NA KV 2/997, no serial, unsigned report 'James McGuirk Hughes', December 1925, and serial 39a, A. W. G. Tomlins, 'McGuirk Hughes', 16 February 1926.

13. Oxford, Bodleian Library, Mss Eng c 6565, journal of Sir Donald Somervell, 1937, 'The Macmahon [sic] case'.

14. Bennett, *Churchill's Man of Mystery*, pp. 76–7.

15. Lady Donaldson of Kingsbridge, *The British Council: The First Fifty Years* (London: Cape, 1984), p. 44.

16. *Documents on British Foreign Policy*, series 2, vol. 1 (London: HMSO, 1946), pp. 478–9.

17. Mark DeWolfe Howe, ed., *Holmes–Laski Letters: The Correspondence of Mr Justice Holmes and Harold Laski, 1916–1935*, vol. 2 (Cambridge, Mass.: Harvard University Press, 1953), p. 1200.

18. Kenneth Young, ed., *The Diaries of Sir Robert Bruce Lockhart, 1915–1938* (London: Macmillan, 1973), pp. 204, 355–6; Oxford, Bodleian Library, Mss Eng c 6918, unpublished memoirs of Sir Patrick Reilly, f. 206.

19. Bennett, *Churchill's Man of Mystery*, p. 58.

20. Cambridge, Churchill College archives, ACAD 1/8, diary of Sir Alexander Cadogan, 16 November 1939; Anthony Reed and David Fisher, *Colonel Z: The Life and Times of a Master of Spies* (London: Hodder & Stoughton, 1984).

21. Nigel West, ed., *The Guy Liddell Diaries: MI5's Director of Counter-Espionage in World War II*, vol. 1: *1939–1942* (London: Routledge, 2005), pp. 68, 77.

22. Lord D'Abernon, *An Ambassador of Peace*, vol. 3 (London: Hodder & Stoughton, 1930), p. 59; Christopher Andrew, *The Defence of the Realm: The Authorized History of MI5* (London: Allen Lane, 2009), p. 144.

23. D'Abernon, *Ambassador of Peace*, vol. 3, p. 31; Sir Owen O'Malley, *The Phantom Caravan* (London: John Murray, 1954), p. 45; Cambridge, Churchill College archives, Phipps papers 3/3, Sir Maurice Hankey to Sir Eric Phipps, 11 January 1938.

24. Lord Vansittart, *The Mist Procession* (London: Hutchinson, 1958), p. 44; Ball, *Conservative Politics*, p. 132.

25. James Ramsden, ed., *George Lyttelton's Commonplace Book* (Settrington: Stone Trough, 2002), p. 63.

26. Vansittart, *Mist Procession*, p. 369; Sir Victor Wellesley, *Diplomacy in Fetters* (London: Hutchinson, 1944), pp. 178–80, 183. These themes are explored in Julie Gottlieb, 'Guilty Women', *Foreign Policy, and Appeasement in Inter-War Britain* (Basingstoke: Palgrave Macmillan, 2015).

27. N. J. Crowson, ed., *Fleet Street, Press Barons and Politics: The Journals of Collin Brooks, 1932–1940* (London: Royal Historical Society, 1998), p. 37.

28. Vansittart, *Mist Procession*, p. 148; Sir Rupert Hart-Davis, ed., *The Lyttelton Hart-Davis Letters*, vol. 1 (London: John Murray, 1978), pp. 15, 80; Oxford, Bodleian Library, Mss Eng c 6565, diary of Sir Donald Somervell, 21 April 1934.

29. Edward Pearce, *The Golden Talking-Shop: The Oxford Union Debates Empire, World War, Revolution, & Women* (Oxford: Oxford University Press, 2016), p. 392.

30. Edwin T. Woodhall, 'Secret Service Days', in Dennis Wheatley, ed., *A Century of Spy Stories* (London: Hutchinson, 1938), p. 58.

31. Andrew, *Defence of the Realm*, pp. 41–2, 59.

32. Tom Bower, *The Perfect English Spy: Sir Dick White and the Secret Service, 1935–90* (London: Heinemann, 1995), pp. 26-7; Henry Hemming, *M: Maxwell Knight, MI5's Greatest Spymaster* (London: Preface, 2017), p. 76.

33. 'Captain H. M. Miller: Service in War and Peace', *The Times*, 15 June 1934, p. 21.

34. Oxford, Christ Church archives, Dacre 10/48, Sir Dick White to Hugh Trevor-Roper, 6 January 1980; Sir John Masterman, *On the Chariot Wheel: An Autobiography* (Oxford: Oxford University Press, 1975), p. 218; Somerset Maugham, *Strictly Personal* (London: Heinemann, 1942), p. 156.

35. Andrew, *Defence of the Realm*, p. 129.

36. Victor Madeira, *Britannia and the Bear: The Anglo-Russian Intelligence Wars, 1917–1929* (Woodbridge: Boydell Press, 2014), pp. 9, 131–2; Ball, *Conservative Politics*, p. 148; David Aaronovitch, *Party Animals: My Family and Other Communists* (London: Cape, 2016), p. 13.

37. Ball, *Conservative Politics*, p. 271; James Stourton, *Kenneth Clark: Life, Art and Civilisation* (London: Collins, 2016), p. 274; J. D. Bernal, 'The End of a Political Illusion', *Cambridge Left*, 1 (Summer 1933), p. 12; NA KV 2/4091, serial 202a, summary of CPGB bugging, 5 February 1951.

38. Vansittart, *Mist Procession*, p. 54; Sir David Kelly, *The Ruling Few, or the Human Background to Diplomacy* (London: Hollis & Carter, 1952), p. 210; 'Captain H. M. Miller: Service in War and Peace', *The Times*, 15 June 1934, p. 21; NA KV 4/224, serial 4a, Alan Roger, 'Most Secret. Russian Relations and Activities in Persia', nd [August 1944]; NA KV 2/2797, serial 373a, Report 'Mrs George [sic] Moody', 4 November 1953.

39. Masterman, *Chariot Wheel*, pp. 28, 218, 219–20; Villiers David, *Advice to my Godchildren* (London: Maggs, 2012), p. 11; Crowson, *Fleet Street*, pp. 64, 87.

40. Gaynor Johnson, ed., *Our Man in Berlin: The Diary of Sir Eric Phipps, 1933–1937* (Basingstoke: Palgrave Macmillan, 2008), pp. 56–8; John Herman, *The Paris Embassy of Sir Eric Phipps: Anglo-French Relations and the Foreign Office, 1937–1939* (Brighton: Sussex Academic Press, 1998), pp. 13, 52–3.

41. Sir Owen O'Malley, *The Phantom Caravan* (London: John Murray, 1954), pp. 241, 245.

42. Sir Michael Postan, *Fact and Relevance* (Cambridge: Cambridge University Press, 1971), p. 164; Donald Moggridge, ed., *Collected Writings of John Maynard Keynes*, vol. 10 (London: Macmillan, 1972), p. 447.

43. Andrew, *Defence of the Realm*, p. 42; Alan Danchev and Daniel Todman,

eds, *War Diaries, 1939–1945: Field Marshal Lord Alanbrooke* (London: Weidenfeld & Nicolson, 2001), p. 509.

44. Lord Beveridge, *Power and Influence* (London: Hodder & Stoughton, 1953), p. 3; Anthony Eden, House of Commons debates, 18 June 1951, vol. 489, col. 32.

45. F. H. Hinsley and C. A. G. Simkins, *British Intelligence in the Second World War*, vol. 4: *Security and Counter-Intelligence* (London: HMSO, 1990), pp. 57–8.

46. George Antrobus, *King's Messenger, 1918–1940: Memoirs of a Silver Greyhound* (London: Herbert Jenkins, 1941), p. 150; Lord Gladwyn, *Memoirs* (London: Weidenfeld & Nicolson, 1972), p. 57.

47. John Drury, *Music at Midnight: The Life and Poetry of George Herbert* (London: Allen Lane, 2013), p. 57; Sir Ivone Kirkpatrick, *The Inner Circle: Memoirs* (London: Macmillan, 1959), pp. 32, 39.

48. Drury, *Music at Midnight*, p. 6; O'Malley, *Phantom Caravan*, p. 35; Sir Bernard Burrows, *Diplomat in a Changing World* (London: Memoir Club, 2001), p. 22.

49. Sheila Grant Duff, *The Parting of the Ways* (London: Peter Owen, 1982), p. 127; Cambridge, Churchill College archives, ACAD 1/9, diary of Sir Alexander Cadogan, 25 January 1940; Wellesley, *Diplomacy in Fetters*, p. 130; Wilfrid Vernon, House of Commons debates, 4 March 1948, vol. 448, col. 616; West, *Guy Liddell Diaries*, vol. 1, p. 305.

50. Charles Ritchie, *The Siren Years: Undiplomatic Diaries, 1937–1945* (London: Macmillan, 1974), p. 77; Crowson, *Fleet Street*, p. 103; Philip Jordan, *There is No Return* (London: Cresset Press, 1938), p. 93.

51. 'Rebuilding the Fleet', *Observer*, 12 July 1936, p. 22.

52. *DBPO*, series 1, volume 6, pp. 206–9; Goronwy Rees, *A Chapter of Accidents* (London: Chatto & Windus, 1972), p. 94; Wilfred Macartney, *Walls Have Mouths: A Record of Ten Years' Penal Servitude* (London: Gollancz, 1936), p. 384.

53. Michael Young, *The Chipped White Cups of Dover: A Discussion of the Possibility of a New Progressive Party* (London: Unit 2, 1960), p. 6.

54. J. D. Gregory, *On the Edge of Diplomacy: Rambles and Reflections, 1902–1928* (London: Hutchinson, 1929), pp. 242–3.

Chapter 4: *The Vigilance Detectives*

1. House of Commons debates, vol. 166, 12 July 1923, cols 1697, 1705; vol. 448, 11 March 1948, cols 1554 & 1557.

2. Durham Cathedral Library, Henson papers vol. 23, diary of Herbert Hensley Henson, 30 August 1918.

3. 'Police Grievances', *Manchester Guardian*, 5 May 1919.

4. Stanley Salvidge, *Salvidge of Liverpool: Behind the Political Scene, 1890–1928* (London: Hodder & Stoughton, 1934), p. 177.

5. John Callaghan and Kevin Morgan, 'The Open Conspiracy of the Communist Party and the Case of W. N. Ewer, Communist and Anti-Communist', *Historical Journal*, 49 (2006), p. 558.

6. NA KV 2/1016, serial 59A, précis of Ewer file, K. L. L. Sissmore, 16 October 1925; Ewer, quoted in Callaghan and Morgan, 'Open Conspiracy', p. 554.

7. NA KV 2/1016, serial 3, Sir Victor Wellesley to Ministry of Labour, 7 February 1919; serial 4, Note 'W. Norman Ewer', Hugh M. Miller, 17 February 1919.

8. Giles Ury, *Labour and the Gulag: Russia and the Seduction of the British Left* (London: Backbite, 2017), pp. 124–5.

9. 'Mr Edgar Lansbury's "Extravagance": Bankruptcy Proceedings', *Manchester Guardian*, 20 December 1927, p. 12.

10. Anne Olivier Bell, ed., *The Diary of Virginia Woolf*, vol. 3 (London: Hogarth Press, 1980), p. 199; NA KV 2/1033, minute 2, Oswald Harker to Joseph Ball, 29 September 1922; 13 & 14, Notes by Harker of 28 September & 14 November 1923; serial 33a, Norman Ewer to George Slocombe, 1 December 1925; serial 50a, Oswald Frewen to Clare Sheridan, 31 January 1926; 77a, Clare Sheridan, 'I Shadowed Kameneff', *Evening Standard*, 25 August 1936; Clare Sheridan, *Russian Portraits* (London: Cape, 1921), pp. 14, 18, 21, 24, 26–8.

11. 'Diamonds in Day-Light: Lenin's "Jewel Box" a War Chest', *Observer*, 26 September 1920.

12. Sheridan, 'I Shadowed Kameneff'; Sheridan, *Russian Portraits*, pp. 38–9.

13. 'A Forged Russian Newspaper: Police Official's "Indiscretion"', *Manchester Guardian*, 4 March 1921, p. 10.

14. NA KV 2/989, serial 2a, Harker, 'Re Federated Press of America', 27 June 1928.

15. Francis Beckett, *Stalin's British Victims* (Stroud: Sutton, 2004), p. 26.

16. J. D. Gregory, *On the Edge of Diplomacy: Rambles and Reflections, 1902–1928* (London: Hutchinson, 1929), p. 269.

17. George Slocombe, *The Tumult and the Shouting* (New York: Macmillan, 1936), p. 26.

18. *Ibid.*, pp. 18, 20.

19. *Ibid.*, p. 48.

20. George Slocombe, 'Winning the War', *Daily Herald*, 20 July 1918, p. 13; Slocombe, 'A Letter to Lenin', *Daily Herald*, 24 August 1918, p. 4; NA KV 2/485, serial 5, H. D. Goldsmith to S. Menzies, 30 August 1918.

21. Sir Francis Meynell, *My Lives* (London: Bodley Head, 1971), p. 112; George Slocombe, *Men in Arms* (London: Heinemann, 1936), pp. 17, 37.

22. NA KV 2/485, serial 6, Home Office Warrant on 12, Woodend, Sutton, 30 November 1921; Ewer to Slocombe, intercepted letter 1 April 1922.

23. NA KV 2/2379, serial 17a, Guy Liddell, New Scotland Yard, to N. Watson, 13 November 1928.

24. A. J. P. Taylor, *English History, 1914–1945* (Oxford: Clarendon Press, 1965), pp. 218, 225; 'No Case against Communist Editor', *Manchester Guardian*, 14 August 1924, p. 14.

25. Thomas Jones, *Whitehall Diary*, ed. Keith Middlemas, vol. 1 (Oxford: Oxford University Press, 1969), p. 300; Ury, *Labour and Gulag*, pp. 228–9, 287–8, 423, 597 n.55; Gill Bennett, '*A Most Extraordinary and Mysterious Business': The Zinoviev Letter of 1924* (London: Foreign & Commonwealth Office, 1999), p. 59. I rely at all points in this section on Bennett's authoritative account.

26. Lord Vansittart, *The Mist Procession* (London: Hutchinson, 1958), p. 96.

27. NA KV 2/1016, batch 192 of 18 November 1925 and batch 195 of 26 November 1925.

28. Stuart Ball, ed., *Parliament and Politics in the Age of Baldwin and MacDonald: The Headlam Diaries, 1923–1935* (London: The Historians' Press, 1992), p. 98. Edward Langston is identified, with ingenious pertinacity, in Timothy Phillips, *The Secret Twenties: British Intelligence, the Russians and the Jazz Age* (London: Granta, 2017).

29. 'Prologue by Compton Mackenzie', in Wilfred Macartney, *Walls Have Mouths: A Record of Ten Years' Penal Servitude* (London: Gollancz, 1936), p. 18.

30. Gill Bennett, *Churchill's Man of Mystery: Desmond Morton and the World of Intelligence* (London: Routledge, 2006), p. 94.

31. Stuart Ball, ed., *Conservative Politics in National and Imperial Crisis: Letters from Britain to the Viceroy of India, 1926–31* (Farnham: Ashgate, 2014), pp. 141, 142, 144, 244.

32. Bennett, *Churchill's Man of Mystery*, p. 95.

33. Information from Patric Dickinson, Clarenceux King of Arms.

34. Nigel West and Oleg Tsarev, *The Crown Jewels: The British Secrets at the Heart of the KGB Archive* (London: HarperCollins, 1998), pp. 149–50.

35. NA KV 2/989, serial 63a, Oswald Harker to Sir Vernon Kell, 24 July 1928.

36. NA KV 2/990, serial 104a, Report of visit to Allen at Bournemouth, Harker, 12 April 1929.

37. NA KV 2/990, serial 105a, note by Harker, 29 April 1929; Report of meeting with Allen at Southampton on 18 May, Harker, 21 May 1929.

38. 'The Shock to Tory Liverpool – Leaders Dumbfounded', *Manchester Guardian*, 7 March 1923.

39. Ball, *Conservative Politics*, p. 321.

40. Ball, *Parliament and Politics in the Age of Baldwin and MacDonald*, p. 118.

41. Oxford, Bodleian Library, Mss Eng c 6565, diary of Sir Donald Somervell, 10 March 1934; 'Cabinet Secrets in Book', *Manchester Guardian*, 21 March 1934, p. 4.

42. NA KV 2/990, serial 109a, Report of Harker's meeting on 18 May with Allen at Southampton, 21 May 1929.

43. Ury, *Labour and Gulag*, p. 200; NA KV 2/1016, no serial (item following serial 8612), intercepted undated letter, Ewer to Palme Dutt [December 1929].

44. KV 2/485, serial 205a, Note 'George Slocombe', 29 April 1930; serial 253a, note of Harker's conversation with Sir Arthur Willert, 22 August 1930.

45. NA KV 2/1016, serial untraced, 'Revolutionary Matters', 21 September 1931; 'And his Pal', *Daily Worker*, 27 August 1936; Callaghan and Morgan, 'Open Conspiracy', pp. 562-3.

46. Beckett, *Stalin's British Victims*, pp. 62, 70–1; NA KV 2/1017, serial 1105z, Extract from B.4.c report by Maxwell Knight on interview with William Norman Ewer on 27.1.50.

47. NA KV 2/1017, serial 1105z, Extract from B.4.c report by Maxwell Knight on interview with William Norman Ewer on 27.1.50.

48. Brian Stewart and Samantha Newbery, *Why Spy? The Art of Intelligence* (London: Hurst, 2015), pp. 6-7.

Chapter 5: The Cipher Spies

1. Julian and Margaret Bullard, eds, *Inside Stalin's Russia: The Diaries of Reader Bullard, 1934–1939* (Charlbury: Day Books, 2000), p. 237; Lord Vansittart, *The Mist Procession* (London: Hutchinson, 1958), pp. 49, 60.

2. Wilfred Macartney, *Walls Have Mouths: A Record of Ten Years' Penal Servitude* (London: Gollancz, 1936), p. 208.

3. Oxford, Bodleian Library, Mss Eng c 6917, unpublished memoirs of Sir Patrick Reilly, f. 7; George Antrobus, *King's Messenger, 1918–1940: Memoirs of a Silver Greyhound* (London: Herbert Jenkins, 1941), pp. 98–101. In this chapter I rely throughout on Nick Barratt's excellent biography of his great-uncle Ernest Oldham, *The Forgotten Spy* (London: Blink, 2015).

4. J. D. Gregory, *On the Edge of Diplomacy: Rambles and Reflections, 1902–1928* (London: Hutchinson, 1929), p. 274; Vansittart, *Mist Procession*, p. 376.

5. Antrobus, *King's Messenger*, p. 16; Stuart Ball, ed., *Conservative Politics in*

National and Imperial Crisis: Letters from Britain to the Viceroy of India, 1926–31 (Farnham: Ashgate, 2014), p. 165; George Slocombe, *A Mirror to Geneva: Its Growth, Grandeur and Decay* (New York: Henry Holt, 1938), p. 171.

6. Antrobus, *King's Messenger*, pp. 186–7.
7. *Ibid.*, p. 63; 'Commander Cotesworth', *The Times*, 23 September 1937, p. 14.
8. Antrobus, *King's Messenger*, pp. 13, 154; T. E. Lawrence, *Seven Pillars of Wisdom: A Triumph* (London: Cape, 1935), p. 660.
9. Kenneth Young, ed., *The Diaries of Sir Robert Bruce Lockhart, 1915–1938* (London: Macmillan, 1973), p. 97; Emily Russell, ed., *A Constant Heart: The War Diaries of Maud Russell, 1938–1945* (Stanbridge: Dovecot Press, 2017), p. 137.
10. Sir Owen O'Malley, *The Phantom Caravan* (London: John Murray, 1954), p. 77; Antrobus, *King's Messenger*, p. 12.
11. Slocombe, *Mirror to Geneva*, pp. 48–9.
12. Antrobus, *King's Messenger*, p. 188.
13. Martin Pearce, *Spymaster: The Life of Britain's Most Decorated Cold War Spy and Head of MI6, Sir Maurice Oldfield* (London: Bantam, 2016), p. 61; NA KV 2/2670, serial 21a, Wilfred Dunderdale, 'Grigori Zinovievich BESODOVSKY', c. 23 October 1929; Elizabeth Poretsky, *Our Own People: A Memoir of 'Ignace Reiss' and his Friends* (Oxford: Oxford University Press, 1969), p. 74.
14. Slocombe, *Mirror to Geneva*, p. 43; Antrobus, *King's Messenger*, p. 86.
15. William E. Duff, *A Time for Spies: Theodore Stephanovitch Mally and the Era of the Great Illegals* (Nashville, Tenn.: Vanderbilt University Press, 1999), p. 82.
16. *Ibid.*, p. 55; Poretsky, *Our Own People*, pp. 102–3, 214.
17. NA KV 2/808, serial 48a, 'Jules Hotel, Jermyn St., W.1', report by T. A. Robertson, 28 August 1933.
18. Antrobus, *King's Messenger*, p. 188.
19. *Ibid.*, pp. 172–3, 189.
20. Nigel West and Oleg Tsarev, *The Crown Jewels: The British Secrets at the Heart of the KGB Archives* (London: HarperCollins, 1998), p. 75; Barratt, *Forgotten Spy*, p. 239.
21. NA KV 2/809, serial 128a, 20 September 1939, report on bank accounts of King and Oake.
22. NA KV 2/805, serial 55x, expurgated copy (prepared for USA) of Jane Archer interrogations of Walter Krivitsky, [? prepared April 1941]; West and Tsarev, *Crown Jewels*, pp. 76–7.
23. NA KV 2/810, no serial, 'Leakages from the Communications Department',

Valentine Vivian, 30 October 1939; NA KV 2/809, serial 132c, interrogation of Raymond Oake, 25 September 1939.

24. West and Tsarev, *Crown Jewels*, p. 81.

25. Viscount Simon, *Retrospect* (London: Hutchinson, 1952), pp. 202–3.

26. NA KV 2/809, serial 123a, 'Hans PIECK, Dutch; information from Mr C. PARLANTI', 15 September 1939.

27. West and Tsarev, *Crown Jewels*, pp. 92-3.

28. Barratt, *Forgotten Spy*, p. 250.

29. West and Tsarev, *Crown Jewels*, p. 90.

30. D. C. Watt, 'John Herbert King: A Soviet Source in the Foreign Office', *Intelligence and National Security*, 3 (1988), pp. 62–82.

31. E. M. Forster, *Two Cheers for Democracy* (London: Edward Arnold, 1951), p. 78.

32. Kevin Quinlan, *The Secret War between the Wars: MI5 in the 1920s and 1930s* (Woodbridge: Boydell Press, 2014), p. 143.

33. Robert Gale Woolbert, 'Recent Books on International Relations', *Foreign Affairs*, 18 (April 1940), p. 574; Malcolm Cowley, 'Krivitsky', *New Republic*, 22 January 1940, pp. 120–3; Hans Bak, ed., *The Long Voyage: Selected Letters of Malcolm Cowley, 1915-1987* (Cambridge, Mass.: Harvard University Press, 2014), pp. 258–9; Whittaker Chambers, *Witness* (London: André Deutsch, 1953), p. 233.

34. NA KV 2/802, serial 9a, Victor Mallet to Gladwyn Jebb, 3 September 1939, with enclosure 'Most Secret Memorandum by Mr Mallet'.

35. NA KV 2/809, serial 107a, G.H.S. [?] to Jane Sissmore, 25 March 1938, and serial 132b, interrogation of King, 25 September 1939; Cambridge, Churchill College archives, ACAD 1/8, diary of Sir Alexander Cadogan, 26 September 1939.

36. Cambridge, Churchill College archives, ACAD 1/8, diary of Sir Alexander Cadogan, 25 September 1939.

37. NA KV 2/810, no serial, 'Leakages from the Communications Department', Valentine Vivian, 30 October 1939; Cambridge, Churchill College archives, ACAD 1/8, diary of Sir Alexander Cadogan, 21 September 1939, & ACAD 1/9, 26 January 1940.

38. James Lees-Milne, *Prophesying Peace* (London: Chatto & Windus, 1977), p. 123.

39. Quinlan, *Secret War*, p. 146.

40. *Ibid.*, p. 139.

41. *Ibid.*, p. 141.

42. NA KV 2/805, serial 55x, expurgated copy (prepared for USA) of Jane Archer interrogations of Walter Krivitsky, [? prepared April 1941].

43. *Ibid.*

44. NA KV 2/804, serial 1a, Archer, 'Report re interview with Krivitsky', 23 January 1940, 10 February 1940, 3 March 1940.

45. NA KV 2/810, no serial, 'Leakages from the Communications Department', Valentine Vivian, 30 October 1939; Christopher Andrew, *The Defence of the Realm: The Authorized History of MI5* (London: Allen Lane, 2009), pp. 267–8.

46. Bak, *Long Voyage*, p. 318.

Chapter 6: *The Blueprint Spies*

1. Cambridge University Library, Vickers papers 546, Percy Westmacott to F. D. Rose, 18 March 1865.

2. Cecil L'Estrange Malone, *The Russian Republic* (London: Allen & Unwin, 1920), pp. 15–16; Cambridge University Library, Vickers microfilm R286, General Sir Noel Birch to Field Marshal Sir George Milne, April 1929 (incompletely dated).

3. NA FO 371/14055, 4254/4254/42, report of James Marshall-Cornwall, 23 August 1929, especially appendix F; Ewan Butler, *Mason-Mac: The Life of Lieutenant-General Sir Noel Mason-MacFarlane* (London: Macmillan, 1972), pp. 43–5.

4. Gill Bennett, *Churchill's Man of Mystery: Desmond Morton and the World of Intelligence* (London: Routledge, 2007), pp. 136, 148.

5. NA SUPP 3/16, Charles de Gaulle, 'Economic Mobilisation in Foreign Countries', *Revue Militaire Française*, no. 151 (January 1934), translated by Committee of Imperial Defence and circulated as PSO 249; Roger Faligot and Rémi Kauffer, *L'Hermine Rouge de Shanghai* (Rennes: Les Portes du Large, 2005).

6. NA KV 2/989, serial 77a, note on interview on 7 September with A. Allen at Bournemouth, by Oswald Harker, 11 September 1928.

7. 'Prologue by Compton Mackenzie', in Wilfred Macartney, *Walls Have Mouths: A Record of Ten Years' Penal Servitude* (London: Gollancz, 1936), pp. 10–11.

8. *Ibid.*, pp. 15–16, 20–1.

9. *Documents on British Foreign Policy, 1919–1939*, series 2, vol. 7 (London: HMSO, 1958), pp. 73, 74, 76, 139.

10. Hugh Dalton, House of Commons debates, 11 March 1926, vol. 192, col. 2736; Richard Overy, *The Morbid Age: Britain between the Wars* (London: Allen Lane, 2009), p. 192; Cambridge University Library, Vickers microfilm R333, Sir Mark Webster Jenkinson to Sir Basil Zaharoff, 16 July 1935.

11. Graham Greene, *A Gun for Sale* (London: Heinemann, 1936), p. 147; Christina Stead, *The House of All Nations* (London: Angus & Robertson,

1974 edition), p. 81; Lord Vansittart, *The Mist Procession* (London: Hutchinson, 1958), p. 231.

12. NA FO 371/18760, A 633/633/45, Report on Leading Personalities of the USA, January 1935; Thomas Hachey, 'American Profiles on Capitol Hill: A Confidential Study for the British Foreign Office in 1943', *Wisconsin Magazine of History*, 57 (Winter 1973–4), p. 147; William E. Dodd and Martha Dodd, eds, *Ambassador Dodd's Diary, 1933–1938* (London: Gollancz, 1941), pp. 75–6; NA KV 2/4036, serial 11xa, Peter Rhodes, 'Oxford and Rearmament', *Isis*, 11 March 1936; see also Wayne Cole, *Senator Gerald P. Nye and American Foreign Relations* (Minneapolis: University of Minnesota Press, 1962) and John E. Wiltz, *In Search of Peace: The Senate Munitions Enquiry, 1934–36* (Baton Rouge: Louisiana State University Press, 1963).

13. Sir Ivone Kirkpatrick, *The Inner Circle: Memoirs* (London: Macmillan, 1959), p. 50.

14. NA KV 2/992, serial 116b, Ba2 report by HOPS, 'Secret', 20 November 1934.

15. NA KV 2/2202, serial 378b, 'Stuart Havelock HOLLINGDALE – Interview of Edward Spence CALVERT', 27 April 1953.

16. NA KV 2/992, serial 126b, report by HOPS, 'FSU Aldershot', circa 4 December 1934.

17. NA KV 2/993, serial 155b, Ba2 report by HOPS, 10 January 1935.

18. NA KV 2/994, serial 447a, Ba2 report by HOPS, 30 August 1937; *The Strange Case of Major Vernon* (London: National Council for Civil Liberties, 1938), p. 16.

19. 'The Dismissal of a Communist', *The Times*, 24 October 1928.

20. NA KV 2/1180, serial 24a, H.F.B., 'Visit to Scotland', 3 December 1929; Giles Udy, *Labour and the Gulag: Russia and the Seduction of the British Left* (London: Backbite, 2017), pp. 129-32.

21. Victor Madeira, *Britannia and the Bear: The Anglo-Russian Intelligence Wars, 1917–1929* (Woodbridge: Boydell Press, 2014), p. 8.

22. The preceding paragraph is drawn from material in NA KV 2/2796 and 2797; 'Rebuilding the Fleet', *Observer*, 12 July 1936, p. 22.

23. Henry Hemming, *M: Maxwell Knight, MI5's Greatest Spymaster* (London: Preface, 2017), p. 73.

24. 'Inquest on Lord Loughborough', *The Times*, 7 August 1929, p. 7; Kenneth Young, ed., *The Diaries of Sir Robert Bruce Lockhart, 1915–1938* (London: Macmillan, 1973), pp. 103–4; Alan Clark, ed., *'A Good Innings': The Private Papers of Viscount Lee of Fareham* (London: John Murray, 1974), p. 11.

25. David Burke, *The Spy Who Came in from the Co-op: Melita Norwood and the Ending of Cold War Espionage* (Woodbridge: Boydell Press, 2008), pp. 76–7.

26. Elizabeth Poretsky, *Our Own People: A Memoir of 'Ignace Reiss' and his Friends* (Oxford: Oxford University Press, 1969), p. 128; Christopher Andrew and Oleg Gordievsky, *KGB: The Inside Story of its Foreign Operations from Lenin to Gorbachev* (London: Hodder & Stoughton, 1990), p. 173.

27. William E. Duff, *A Time for Spies: Theodore Stephanovitch Mally and the Era of the Great Illegals* (Nashville, Tenn.: Vanderbilt University Press, 1999), pp. 141, 216–17, discredits the inventions of John Costello, *Mask of Treachery: Spies, Lies, Buggery and Betrayal, the First Documented Dossier of Anthony Blunt's Cambridge Spy Ring* (New York: William Morrow, 1988), pp. 282–6.

28. Burke, *Spy from the Co-op*, p. 90.

29. Vansittart, *Mist Procession*, p. 177; Anthony Cave Brown, *'C': The Secret Life of Sir Stewart Menzies, Spymaster to Winston Churchill* (New York: Macmillan, 1987), p. 510.

30. 'Prologue by Compton Mackenzie', in Macartney, *Walls Have Mouths*, pp. 21–3.

31. David Caute, *The Fellow-Travellers: A Postscript to the Enlightenment* (London: Weidenfeld & Nicolson, 1973), pp. 119–20.

32. Dudley Collard, *Soviet Justice and the Trial of Radek and Others* (London: Gollancz, 1937), pp. 36, 99, 106, 109; NA KV 2/2159, serial 52a, 'Re the Glading Case', nd [March 1938].

33. Oxford, Bodleian Library, Mss Eng c 6565, journal of Lord Somervell of Harrow, 1937, 'The Macmahon [sic] case'.

34. Burke, *Spy from the Co-op*, pp. 101–2.

35. 'Charges under Official Secrets Act', *Manchester Guardian*, 15 March 1938.

36. 'Mr Justice Hawke', *The Times*, 31 October 1941, p. 9.

37. 'Official Secrets Act', *The Times*, 15 March 1938, p. 7.

38. Nigel West, ed., *The Guy Liddell Diaries: MI5's Director of Counter-Espionage in World War II*, vol. 1: *1939–1942* (London: Routledge, 2005), p. 35.

39. Oxford, Bodleian Library, Mss Eng c 6565, journal of Lord Somervell of Harrow, 21 April 1934; R. F. V. Heuston, *Lives of the Lord Chancellors, 1940–1970* (Oxford: Oxford University Press, 1987), p. 149; Richard Ollard, ed., *The Diaries of A. L. Rowse* (London: Allen Lane, 2003), pp. 218–20.

Chapter 7: The Little Clans

1. Sir David Kelly, *The Ruling Few, or the Human Background to Diplomacy* (London: Hollis & Carter, 1952), p. 9; Richard Bassett, *Last Imperialist: A Portrait of Julian Amery* (Settrington: Stone Trough, 2015), p. 43.

2. G. M. Young, *Last Essays* (London: Rupert Hart-Davis, 1950), p. 97; Edward Pearce, *The Golden Talking-Shop: The Oxford Union Debates Empire, World War, Revolution, & Women* (Oxford: Oxford University Press, 2016), p. 369.

3. David Footman, *Dead Yesterday* (London: White Lion, 1974), p. 135.

4. Cyril Connolly, *The Missing Diplomats* (London: Queen Anne Press, 1952), pp. 15–16.

5. John le Carré introduction to Bruce Page, David Leitch and Phillip Knightley, *Philby: The Spy Who Betrayed a Generation* (London: André Deutsch, 1968), pp. 9–10, 12, 14; Andrew Boyle, *The Climate of Treason: Five Who Spied for Russia* (London: Hutchinson, 1979), p. 42; Leo Abse, 'The Judas Syndrome', *Spectator*, 20 March 1982, pp. 11–12.

6. Miranda Carter, *Anthony Blunt: His Lives* (London: Macmillan, 2001), pp. 1, 16–17; Robert Cecil, *A Divided Life: A Biography of Donald Maclean* (London: Bodley Head, 1988), pp. 8–9.

7. Nigel West and Oleg Tsarev, *The Crown Jewels: The British Secrets at the Heart of the KGB Archives* (London: HarperCollins, 1998), pp. 210–11.

8. NA KV 2/1118, serial 56b, Valentine Vivian to Guy Liddell, 24 September 1940.

9. Sir Reader Bullard, *Two Kings in Arabia: Letters from Jeddah, 1923–5 and 1936–9*, ed. E. C. Hodgkin (Reading: Ithaca Press, 1993), pp. 48–9.

10. John Costello and Oleg Tsarev, *Deadly Illusions* (London: Century, 1993), p. 116.

11. Tim [I. I.] Milne, *Kim Philby: The Unknown Story of the KGB's Master Spy* (London: Backbite, 2014), p. 3.

12. Brian Urquhart, *A Life in Peace and War* (London: Weidenfeld & Nicolson, 1987), pp. 16, 19.

13. Milne, *Philby*, pp. 5, 8.

14. Urquhart, *Peace and War*, p. 20.

15. *Ibid.*, p. 24.

16. Richard Wollheim, 'Jesus Christie', *London Review of Books*, 3 October 1985; Urquhart, *Peace and War*, pp. 21, 23–4.

17. Milne, *Philby*, p. 4.

18. Durham Cathedral Library, Henson papers vol. 34, diary of Herbert Hensley Henson, 11 November 1922.

19. Lord Vansittart, *The Mist Procession* (London: Hutchinson, 1958), pp. 311, 315, 318.

20. Steve Nicholson, *The Censorship of British Drama, 1900–1968*, vol. 1 (Exeter: University of Exeter Press, 203), pp. 196–7.

21. Urquhart, *Peace and War*, p. 17; Footman, *Dead Yesterday*, pp. 136, 154–5; David Footman, *Pig and Pepper* (London: Derek Verschoyle, 1954 edition), p. 278.

22. Bullard, *Two Kings*, pp. 77, 239; NA KV 2/1118, serials 54a & 56a, Sir Harold Farquhar to Guy Liddell, 12 September 1940, and Guy Liddell to Valentine Vivian, 19 September 1940; NA KV 2/1119, serials 67a & 76b, Lord Lloyd to Oswald Harker, 14 November 1940, and Sir Alexander Cadogan to Lord Lloyd, 12 December 1940.

23. Patrick Seale and Maureen McConville, *Philby: The Long Road to Moscow* (London: Hamish Hamilton, 1973), pp. 1, 9.

24. Vansittart, *Mist Procession*, p. 232; Alan Maclean, *No, I Tell a Lie, It was the Tuesday: A Trudge through the Life of Alan Maclean* (London: Kyle Cathie, 1997), pp. 8, 11, 12–13.

25. Sir John Masterman, *On the Chariot Wheel: An Autobiography* (Oxford: Oxford University Press, 1975), p. 18; Oxford, Worcester College archives, MT/1920, Reverend George Chitty to Dean of Worcester, 22 December 1919.

26. T. Cuthbert Worsley, *Flannelled Fool* (London: Alan Ross, 1965), p. 47.

27. Geoff Andrews, *Shadow Man: At the Heart of the Cambridge Spy Circle* (London: I. B. Tauris, 2015), pp. 22–3.

28. NA KV 2/4150, serial 693a, Skardon, 'Interview with Mrs. DUNBAR in Paris on 2.12.53'.

29. James Delbourgo, *Collecting the World: The Life and Curiosity of Hans Sloane* (London: Allen Lane, 2017), p. xxviii; Kenneth Andrews, *Trade, Plunder and Settlement: Maritime Enterprise and the Genesis of the British Empire, 1480–1630* (Cambridge: Cambridge University Press, 1984), pp. 363–4.

30. Kelly, *Ruling Few*, p. 51; NA KV 2/4140, serial 18a, 'Selection Board 7 May 1935', questionnaire completed by Lt Col. J. H. Foster.

31. Donald Somervell, *The Future of Public School Education* (Oxford: Humphrey Milford, 1918), p. 19; Minoo Dinshaw, *Outlandish Knight: The Byzantine Life of Steven Runciman* (London: Allen Lane, 2016), p. 39; Cyril Connolly, *Enemies of Promise* (London: Routledge & Kegan Paul, 1949 edition), pp. 192, 214.

32. Masterman, *Chariot Wheel*, p. 32.

33. Jeremy Lewis, *Cyril Connolly* (London: Cape, 1997), p. 118; A. J. Ayer, *Part of my Life* (London: Collins, 1977), pp. 59–60.

34. NA KV 2/4110, serial 467a, Skardon, 'Interview with Murray Gladstone', 26 November 1953.

35. Carter, *Blunt*, p. 3.

36. BL, Add Mss 88902/1, memoir of Anthony Blunt.

37. Footman, *Dead Yesterday*, pp. 157–8, 159, 163.

38. *Ibid.*, p. 134; Worsley, *Flannelled Fool*, p. 47.

39. Footman, *Dead Yesterday*, pp. 142, 146; Worsley, *Flannelled Fool*, p. 45.

40. Carter, *Blunt*, p. 24.

41. BL, Add Mss 88902/1, memoir of Anthony Blunt; Louis MacNeice, *The Strings are False* (London: Faber & Faber, 1965), p. 95.

42. MacNeice, *Strings*, p. 97.

43. James Stourton, *Kenneth Clark: Life, Art and Civilisation* (London: Collins, 2016), pp. 20–2.

Chapter 8: The Cambridge Cell

1. Victor Madeira, *Britannia and the Bear: The Anglo-Russian Intelligence Wars, 1917–1929* (Woodbridge: Boydell Press, 2014), pp. 29, 43, 97.

2. Edward Pearce, *The Golden Talking-Shop: The Oxford Union Debates Empire, World War, Revolution, & Women* (Oxford: Oxford University Press, 2016), p. 268; Cambridge, Wren Library, Trinity College, Dobb papers DD/44, 'The Cultural Revolution in the USSR', Dobb's lecture at Bedford College, London, 1 October 1932; Cyril Connolly, *The Condemned Playground* (London: Routledge, 1945), p. 136; M. Y. Lang, 'The Growth of the Student Movement', in Carmel Haden Guest, ed., *David Guest: A Scientist Fights for Freedom (1911–1938)* (London: Lawrence & Wishart, 1939), p. 87; W. H. Auden, *Prose*, vol. 2, ed. Edward Mendelson (London: Faber & Faber, 2002), p. 242.

3. Paul Valéry, *Analects* (London: Routledge & Kegan Paul, 1970), p. 45; NA KV 2/4141, serial 128a, Skardon, 'Interview with Mrs CURZON on 31.5.51'; James Stourton, *Kenneth Clark: Life, Art and Civilisation* (London: Collins, 2016), p. 30.

4. David Fowler, '"Student Power" at Worcester: The Undergraduate Career of Arthur Reade, a Student Revolutionary of the 1920s', *Worcester College Record* (2010), pp. 91, 93.

5. *Ibid.*, pp. 95-6; Lewis Farnell, *An Oxonian Looks Back* (London: Martin Hopkinson, 1934), p. 297.

6. NA KV 2/1540, serial 17a, W. A. [illegible] to Harker, 3 August 1928; serial 26a, Arthur Reade to Norman Ewer, 11 January 1930; serial 27a, Reade to Ewer, 14 January 1930.

7. Edward Sackville-West, 'The Romantic Travellers', *Listener*, 22 February 1951, pp. 297–8; Frances Partridge, *Diaries, 1939–1972* (London: Weidenfeld & Nicolson, 2000), p. 200.

8. Editorial, 'Free Trips to Oxford for Selected Workers', *Plebs*, 19 (April 1927), pp. 123–4.

9. Cambridge, Wren Library, Trinity College, Dobb papers DD/4, Dobb, 'The Russian Revolution', paper to Pembroke College's Martlet Society, 1920.

10. Cambridge, Wren Library, Trinity College, Dobb papers DD/16, 'Report on Russian Visit: Forgotten Reply to Keynes', 1925.

11. Philip Toynbee, *Friends Apart* (London: MacGibbon & Kee, 1954), p. 62.

12. Hugh Lloyd-Jones, Valerie Pearl and Blair Worden, eds, *History and Imagination: Essays in Honour of H. R. Trevor-Roper* (London: Duckworth, 1981), p. 358; Michael Burn, *Turned towards the Sun: An Autobiography* (Norwich: Michael Russell, 2003), p. 61.

13. Sir Bertram Falle, House of Commons debates, vol. 161, col. 2698, 20 July 1923; John Steegman, *Cambridge: As It was and as It is Today* (London: Batsford, 1940), p. 41.

14. C. W. Guillebaud, 'Politics and the Undergraduate in Oxford and in Cambridge', *Cambridge Review*, 55 (26 January 1934), p. 186; Noel Annan, *The Dons: Mentors, Eccentrics and Geniuses* (London: HarperCollins, 1999), p. 244.

15. Oxford, Christ Church archives, Dacre papers 17/1/2, Hugh Trevor-Roper to Lady Alexandra Howard-Johnston, 13 February 1954; Austin, Texas, Humanities Research Center, Francis King papers 2/4, Maurice Cranston to Francis King, 8 May 1954.

16. 'The Case against Mr Tom Mann', *Manchester Guardian*, 4 July 1934, p. 14; 'Sedition!', *Manchester Guardian*, 5 July 1934, p. 8.

17. 'The Trenchard Plan', *Manchester Guardian*, 12 May 1933, p. 8; 'London Police Changes: Militarising the Force', *Manchester Guardian*, 24 May 1933, p. 5; David Guest, 'Democracy and the State', *Student's Vanguard* (June–July 1933), quoted in Haden Guest, *David Guest*, pp. 17–18.

18. James Ramsden, ed., *George Lyttelton's Commonplace Book* (Settrington: Stone Trough, 2002), p. 102.

19. Geoff Andrews, *Shadow Man: At the Heart of the Cambridge Spy Circle* (London: I. B. Tauris, 2015), p. 36.

20. Patrick Seale and Maureen McConville, *Philby: The Long Road to Moscow* (London: Hamish Hamilton, 1973), p. 37.

21. Lang, 'Growth of the Student Movement', in Haden Guest, *David Guest*, pp. 91–3, 104–5.

22. *Ibid.*, pp. 88–9.

23. F. C., 'Conversations with Communists', *Cambridge Review*, 56 (8 February 1935), p. 226; Cyril Connolly, *The Missing Diplomats* (London: Queen Anne Press, 1952), p. 17.

24. NA KV 2/4106, serial 317a, Note by Courtenay Young, 23 October 1951; NA KV 2/4138, serial 1560a, Guy Burgess to Sir Harold Nicolson, 1 February 1963.

25. Toynbee, *Friends Apart*, p. 61; R. W. Johnson, *Look Back in Laughter: Oxford's Post-War Golden Age* (Newbury: Threshold Press, 2015), pp. 168–9.

26. Simon Haxey [Arthur Wynn and Peggy Moxon], *Tory M.P.* (London: Gollancz, 1939), p. 31.

27. NA KV 2/4140, serial 6, Donald Maclean to William Ridsdale, 5 April 1950.

28. Mark DeWolfe Howe, ed., *Holmes–Laski Letters: The Correspondence of Mr Justice Holmes and Harold Laski, 1916-1935*, vol. 2 (Cambridge, Mass.: Harvard University Press, 1953), p. 1063; F. M. Hardie, 'Public Opinion: Pacifism and the Oxford Union', *Political Quarterly*, 4 (April 1933), p. 268; NA KV 2/4036, serial 11xa, Peter Rhodes, 'Oxford and Rearmament', *Isis*, 11 March 1936; Mark A. Bradley, *A Very Principled Boy: The Life of Duncan Lee, Red Spy and Cold Warrior* (New York: Basic Books, 2014), p. 23.

29. Mary McCarthy, *Novels and Stories, 1942-1963* (New York: Library of America, 2017), p. 111.

30. Jenifer Hart, *Ask Me No More: An Autobiography* (London: Peter Halban, 1998), p. 75; Nicola Lacey, *A Life of H. L. A. Hart: The Nightmare and the Noble Dream* (Oxford: Oxford University Press, 2004), pp. 63-7.

31. Steegman, *Cambridge*, p. 97.

32. Sir Brian Harrison, ed., *The History of the University of Oxford*, vol. 8 (Oxford: Clarendon Press, 1994), pp. 377-81; Janet Morgan, ed., *The Backbench Diaries of Richard Crossman* (London: Hamish Hamilton, 1981), pp. 228-9; Jonathan Haslam, *The Vices of Integrity: E. H. Carr, 1892-1982* (London: Verso, 1999), p. 175.

33. This paragraph follows Henry Hemming, *M: Maxwell Knight, MI5's Greatest Spymaster* (London: Preface, 2017), pp. 99-103, 128-9, 169.

34. I owe this paragraph to material generously supplied by Geoff Andrews.

35. 'Lord Lindsay of Birker', *Manchester Guardian*, 19 March 1952, p. 4.

36. G. D. H. Cole, *A History of Socialist Thought: Communism and Social Democracy, 1914-1931*, vol. 4 (London: Macmillan, 1958), pp. 7-8; 'Death of G. D. H. Cole', *Manchester Guardian*, 15 January 1959, p. 3; Naomi Mitchison and Royden Harrison, 'Appreciations', *Manchester Guardian*, 19 January 1959, p. 4.

37. Robert Pearce, ed., *Patrick Gordon Walker: Political Diaries, 1932-1971* (London: The Historians' Press, 1991), pp. 57-9.

38. NA KV 2/4140, serial 19a, Top Secret, 'CURZON', J. C. Robertson, 30 April 1951.

39. NA KV 2/4157, serial 1017z, minute of Roger Hollis, 26 June 1957; also serial 1017a, Courtenay Young, 'Secret Note for File', 24 July 1957.

40. Peter Broda, *Scientist Spies: A Memoir of my Three Parents and the Atom Bomb* (Kibworth Beauchamp: Matador, 2011), pp. 23-4.

41. NA KV 2/4150, serial 642a, 'Interview with J. R. CUMMING BRUCE', Skardon, 21 July 1953; S.B.R.C., 'The Union Society', *Cambridge Review*, 55 (2 February 1934), p. 216; Herbert Hensley Henson, *Retrospect of an*

Unimportant Life, vol. 3 (Oxford: Oxford University Press, 1950), pp. 254, 277, 280.

42. Tim [I. I.] Milne, *Kim Philby: The Unknown Story of the KGB's Master Spy* (London: Backbite, 2014), p. 36; NA KV 2/1012, serial 5w, Maurice Dobb to Alexander Tudor-Hart, 2 December 1930.

43. John Cornford, 'Left?', *Cambridge Left*, 1 (Summer 1933), pp. 25, 29; Julian and Margaret Bullard, eds, *Inside Stalin's Russia: The Diaries of Reader Bullard, 1930-1934* (Charlbury: Day Books, 2000), p. 240; Minoo Dinshaw, *Outlandish Knight: The Byzantine Life of Steven Runciman* (London: Allen Lane, 2016), pp. 212-13.

44. Favourable views of him are given in R. W. Bowen, ed., *E. H. Norman: His Life and Scholarship* (Toronto: Toronto University Press, 1984) and R. W. Bowen, *Innocence is Not Enough: The Life and Death of Herbert Norman* (Vancouver: Douglas & Macintyre, 1986).

45. The preceding paragraphs are drawn from Charles Rycroft, 'Memoirs of an Old Bolshevik' (1969), in *Psychoanalysis and Beyond* (London: Chatto & Windus, 1985), pp. 206, 208-11.

46. Andrew Boyle, *The Climate of Treason: Five Who Spied for Russia* (London: Hutchinson, 1979), p. 72.

47. D.M., 'Dare Doggerel. Nov 11', *Silver Crescent*, December 1933, p. 3.

48. Donald Maclean, untitled review of R. D. Charques, *Contemporary Literature and Social Revolution*, in *Cambridge Left*, 1 (Winter 1933-4), pp. ii-iii.

49. Pat Sloan, ed., *John Cornford: A Memoir* (Dunfermline: Borderline Press, 1938), pp. 104-5; Robert Cecil, *A Divided Life: A Biography of Donald Maclean* (London: Bodley Head, 1988), p. 31.

50. Robin Cecil, 'Legends Spies Tell', *Encounter*, 50 (April 1978), p. 9; NA KV 2/4150, serial 642a, 'Interview with J. R. CUMMING BRUCE', Skardon, 21 July 1953.

51. Michael Straight, *After Long Silence* (London: Collins, 1983), pp. 65, 71, 98; Peter Parker, *Housman Country: Into the Heart of England* (London: Little, Brown, 2016), p. 157.

52. Donald Moggridge, ed., *The Collected Writings of John Maynard Keynes*, vol. 21 (Cambridge: Cambridge University Press, 1982), pp. 494-5.

Chapter 9: The Vienna Comrades

1. George Slocombe, 'France in Revolt', *Labour Monthly*, 1 (September 1921), p. 282; J. D. Gregory, *Dollfuss and his Times* (London: Hutchinson, 1935), pp. 95-6.

2. Eric Gedye, *Fallen Bastions: The Central European Tragedy* (London: Gollancz, 1939), p. 112; Gregory, *Dollfuss*, pp. 165-6.

3. Gregory, *Dollfuss*, pp. 163–5.
4. George Slocombe, *The Tumult and the Shouting* (New York: Macmillan, 1936), p. 425.
5. George Antrobus, *King's Messenger, 1918–1940: Memoirs of a Silver Greyhound* (London: Herbert Jenkins, 1941), p. 221; Naomi Mitchison, *Vienna Diary* (London: Gollancz, 1934), p. 36.
6. Slocombe, *Tumult and Shouting*, p. 423; Gedye, *Fallen Bastions*, p. 89; William E. Dodd and Martha Dodd, eds, *Ambassador Dodd's Diary, 1933–1938* (London: Gollancz, 1941), p. 85.
7. NA KV 2/1014, serial 143b, Arthur Martin, interview with sources, 3 October 1951.
8. Gedye, *Fallen Bastions*, p. 111.
9. *Ibid.*, p. 114.
10. Sir Maurice Bowra and Dame Margaret Cole in William Rodgers, ed., *Hugh Gaitskell, 1906–1963* (London: Thames & Hudson, 1964), pp. 28, 46–7; Lord Elwyn-Jones, *In My Time* (London: Weidenfeld & Nicolson, 1983), p. 33; F. Elwyn Jones, 'An Austrian Relief Fund', *Cambridge Review*, 55 (9 March 1934), p. 308; Gedye, *Fallen Bastions*, p. 123.
11. NA KV 2/1603, serial 39a, letter from Alexander Tudor-Hart [Room Z1, Passage hotel, Moscow] to May Linnard, intercepted 11 May 1931; NA KV 2/1012, serial 5w, intercepted letter from Maurice Dobb to Alexander Tudor-Hart, 2 December 1930.
12. Genrikh Borovik (with Phillip Knightley), *The Philby Files: The Secret Life of the Master Spy – KGB Archives Revealed* (London: Little, Brown, 1994), pp. 27–9, 32.
13. Philip Jordan, *Say that She were Gone* (London: Heinemann, 1940), pp. 40–1.
14. Whittaker Chambers, *Witness* (London: André Deutsch, 1953), p. 233.
15. R. F. V. Heuston, *Lives of the Lord Chancellors, 1940–1970* (Oxford: Clarendon Press, 1987), p. 50; Gabriel Gorodetsky, ed., *The Maisky Diaries: Red Ambassador to the Court of St James's, 1932–1943* (New Haven: Yale University Press, 2015), pp. 110–11; 'Lords and Foreign Policy: The Primate on Events in Austria – a Step to Stability', *The Times*, 30 March 1938, p. 7.
16. Sir George Rendel, *The Sword and the Olive: Recollections of Diplomacy and the Foreign Service, 1913–1954* (London: John Murray, 1957), p. 261.

Chapter 10: The Ring of Five

1. NA KV 2/4167, serial 4a, Report by J.O., 27 January 1931.
2. NA KV 2/4167, serial 56a, Sir Arthur Willert to Harker, 12 November

1934; NA FO 1093/48, Sir Vincent Caillard to Henry Asquith, 1 February 1916, and Caillard to Basil Zaharoff, 4 February 1916.

3. Peter Smolka, *Forty Thousand against the Arctic: Russia's Polar Empire* (London: Hutchinson, 1937), pp. 13, 72, 77, 82.

4. John Costello and Oleg Tsarev, *Deadly Illusions* (London: Century, 1993), p. 175.

5. David Guest, 'Democracy and the State', *Student's Vanguard* (June–July 1933), reproduced in Carmel Haden Guest, ed., *David Guest: A Scientist Fights for Freedom* (London: Lawrence & Wishart, 1939), p. 217.

6. Costello and Tsarev, *Deadly Illusions*, pp. 179–80.

7. NA KV 2/4153, serial 857a, G. R. Mitchell, 'Note', 11 January 1956; Costello and Tsarev, *Deadly Illusions*, p. 192.

8. Sir Owen O'Malley, *The Phantom Caravan* (London: John Murray, 1954), p. 37; Donald Gillies, *Radical Diplomat: The Life of Archibald Clark Kerr, Lord Inverchapel, 1882–1951* (London: I. B. Tauris, 1999), p. 30; Valentine Lawford, *Bound for Diplomacy* (London: John Murray, 1963), p. 235.

9. Costello and Tsarev, *Deadly Illusions*, pp. 193–5.

10. Cyril Connolly, *The Missing Diplomats* (London: Queen Anne Press, 1952), pp. 17–18, 21; Lord Vansittart, 'The Great Foreign Office Mystery', *Sunday Dispatch*, 10 June 1951, p. 4; Percy Hoskins, 'Missing Diplomats', *Argosy*, January 1953, p. 55.

11. Humphrey Slater, *The Conspirator* (London: John Lehmann, 1948), pp. 59–60, 90, 125.

12. Genrikh Borovik (with Phillip Knightley), *The Philby Files: The Secret Life of the Master Spy – KGB Archives Revealed* (London: Little, Brown, 1994), pp. 48–9.

13. Sir Reader Bullard, *The Camel Must Go* (London: Faber & Faber, 1961), pp.166–7; Costello and Tsarev, *Deadly Illusions*, p. 224.

14. Costello and Tsarev, *Deadly Illusions*, pp. 226, 228, 239.

15. NA KV 2/804.

16. Costello and Tsarev, *Deadly Illusions*, p. 208.

17. Alexander Foote, *Handbook for Spies* (New York: Doubleday, 1949), pp. 18–19, 23, 27; Ruth Werner, *Sonya's Report* (London: Chatto & Windus, 1991), pp. 193–4.

18. J. D. Bernal, 'The End of a Political Illusion', *Cambridge Left*, 1 (Summer 1933), pp. 11-12, 14; Robert Cecil, *A Divided Life: A Biography of Donald Maclean* (London: Bodley Head, 1988), p. 33.

19. Wilfred Macartney, *Walls Have Mouths: A Record of Ten Years' Penal Servitude* (London: Gollancz, 1936), pp. 433–5; Edmund Wilson, *The Thirties: From Notebooks and Diaries* (New York: Farrar, Straus & Giroux,

1980), p. 525; David Footman, *Balkan Holiday* (London: Heinemann, 1935), p. 124.

20. Philip Jordan, *Say that She were Gone* (London: Heinemann, 1940), pp. 179–80.

21. Jon Snow, 'Francis Graham-Harrison', *Guardian*, 7 January 2002; NA KV 2/4139, serial 1579b, 'Interview with Francis L. T. Graham-Harrison', 29 May 1963; NA KV 2/4106, serial 320b, Skardon, 'Interview with Rosamond Lehmann on 20.10.51', 29 October 1951.

22. NA KV 2/4106, serial 313a, George Macaulay Trevelyan to Talks Department of BBC, 5 December 1935; James Lees-Milne, *Harold Nicolson: A Biography, 1930–1968* (London: Chatto & Windus, 1981), p. 135.

23. Footman, *Balkan Holiday*, pp. 167, 174, 195, 201; David Footman, *Pemberton* (London: Cresset Press, 1943), p. 10.

24. J.S., 'New Short Stories', *The Times*, 15 July 1938, p. 22; David Footman, 'Goronwy Rees', *Encounter*, 56 (January 1981), p. 32.

25. Costello and Tsarev, *Deadly Illusions*, pp. 236–7.

26. Tom Bower, *The Perfect English Spy: Sir Dick White and the Secret War, 1935–90* (London: Heinemann, 1995), pp. 23, 35.

27. Andrew Boyle, *The Climate of Treason: Five Who Spied for Russia* (London: Hutchinson, 1979), p. 218.

28. Peter Kidson, 'Anthony Frederick Blunt', *Biographical Memoirs of Fellows of the British Academy*, vol. 13 (Oxford: Oxford University Press, 2014), pp. 29–30.

29. Miranda Carter, *Anthony Blunt: His Lives* (London: Macmillan, 2001), pp. 186–7.

30. In this section I draw on conversation with Geoff Andrews, 1 February 2017, about his forthcoming biography of Cairncross, provisionally entitled *The Virtues of Disloyalty*, and an email from Andrews of 17 February 2017.

31. Nigel West and Oleg Tsarev, *The Crown Jewels: The British Secrets at the Heart of the KGB Archives* (London: HarperCollins, 1998), pp. 204–6.

32. *Ibid.*, pp. 207–9.

33. Igor Damaskin, *Kitty Harris: The Spy with Seventeen Names* (London: St Ermin's Press, 2001), p. 168.

34. Gaynor Johnson, ed., *Our Man in Berlin: The Diary of Sir Eric Phipps, 1933–1937* (Basingstoke: Palgrave Macmillan, 1998), pp. 38, 92, 94, 97, 195; *Hitler's Table Talk, 1941–1944: His Private Conversations*, trans. Norman Cameron and R. H. Stevens (London: Weidenfeld & Nicolson, 1953), p. 488.

35. John Herman, *The Paris Embassy of Sir Eric Phipps: Anglo-French Relations and the Foreign Office, 1937–1939* (Brighton: Sussex Academic Press, 1998), p. 111; Cambridge, Churchill College archives, Phipps papers I 3/2, Sir Eric Phipps to Duff Cooper, 8 December 1938.

36. Philip Jordan, *Russian Glory* (London: Cresset Press, 1942), pp. 1–2.

37. Philip Jordan, *Say that She were Gone*, p. 90; Costello and Tsarev, *Deadly Illusions*, p. 174.

38. Gill Bennett, *Churchill's Man of Mystery: Desmond Morton and the World of Intelligence* (London: Routledge, 2007), pp. 260–1.

39. 'Lieut.-Col. M. R. Chidson: Rescue of Dutch Diamonds', *The Times*, 4 October 1957, p. 13.

40. Boyle, *Climate of Treason*, p. 76; Justin Evans, 'How humble is "humble"?', *Liverpool Post*, 5 December 1979; Leslie Mitchell, *Maurice Bowra: A Life* (Oxford: Oxford University Press, 2009), p. 125; Jenny Rees, *Looking for Mr Nobody: The Secret Life of Goronwy Rees* (London: Weidenfeld & Nicolson, 1994), p. 54.

41. Elizabeth Bowen, *Death of the Heart* (London: Cape, 1938), pp. 75–6; Oxford, Bodleian Library, Berlin Ms 256, Stuart Hampshire to Isaiah Berlin, [nd; October 1936]; Rees, *Mr Nobody*, pp. 85–6.

42. Stuart Hampshire, *Innocence and Experience* (London: Allen Lane, 1989), pp. 5–6; Louis MacNeice, *The Strings are False* (London: Faber & Faber, 1965), p. 168.

43. Rees, *Mr Nobody*, p. 91.

44. A. L. Rowse, *All Souls and Appeasement: A Contribution to Contemporary History* (London: Macmillan, 1961), p. 32.

45. Sidney Aster, ed., *Appeasement and All Souls: A Portrait with Documents, 1937–1939* (Cambridge: Royal Historical Society, 2004), pp. 166–8, 225; Nigel West and Oleg Tsarev, *The Crown Jewels: The British Secrets at the Heart of the KGB Archives*, p. 143.

46. NA KV 2/4106, serial 328b, 'Top Secret', 14 November 1951; Gabriel Gorodetsky, ed., *The Maisky Diaries: Red Ambassador to the Court of St James's, 1932–1943* (New Haven: Yale University Press, 2015), p. 212; Jonathan Haslam, *Near and Distant Neighbours: A New History of Soviet Intelligence* (Oxford: Oxford University Press, 2015), p. 103.

47. Richard Overy, *The Morbid Age: Britain between the Wars* (London: Allen Lane, 2009), pp. 297–8.

48. Sir Maurice Peterson, *Both Sides of the Curtain* (London: Constable, 1950), p. 198.

Chapter 11: The People's War

1. Patrick Seale and Maureen McConville, *Philby: The Long Road to Moscow* (London: Hamish Hamilton, 1973), p. 127; Crane Brinton, *The United States and Britain* (Oxford: Oxford University Press, 1945), p. 70; Leslie Mitchell, *Maurice Bowra: A Life* (Oxford: Oxford University Press, 2009),

p. 243; Evelyn Waugh, *The Sword of Honour Trilogy* (London: Everyman, 1994), p. 272.

2. Sir John Masterman, *On the Chariot Wheel: An Autobiography* (Oxford: Oxford University Press, 1975), p. 218.

3. Oxford, Christ Church archives, Dacre 10/48, Dick White to Hugh Trevor-Roper, 10 February 1980.

4. J. C. Masterman, *The Case of the Four Friends: A Diversion in Pre-Detection* (London: Hodder & Stoughton, 1956), pp. 70–1; Andrew Boyle, *The Climate of Treason: Five Who Spied for Russia* (London: Hutchinson, 1979), p. 451.

5. Oxford, Christ Church archives, Dacre papers 10/50, Cyril Mills to Hugh Trevor-Roper 19 January 1985.

6. Nicola Lacey, *A Life of H. L. A. Hart: The Nightmare and the Noble Dream* (Oxford: Oxford University Press, 2004), pp. 38, 48, 85, 89.

7. *Ibid.*, pp. 90–1; Jenifer Hart, *Ask Me No More: An Autobiography* (London: Peter Halban, 1998), pp. 211–12.

8. Oxford, Bodleian Library, Berlin Ms 256, Stuart Hampshire to Isaiah Berlin, 9 March 1945; William Waldegrave, *A Different Kind of Weather: A Memoir* (London: Constable, 2015), p. 106.

9. NA KV 2/1540, serial 35a, Arthur Reade to Harold Stannard, 4 October 1939, and Stannard to Sir Vernon Kell, 11 October 1939; NA KV 2/1541, serial 54a, G. Lennox of War Office to S. C. Strong, MI5, 21 December 1940, minute 83 by D. G. White, 16 August 1948, minute 96 by H. Loftus Browne, 2 October 1951; Stuart Ball, ed., *Parliament and Politics in the Age of Churchill and Attlee: The Headlam Diaries, 1935–1951* (Cambridge: Cambridge University Press, 1999), p. 207.

10. NA KV 2/2159, serial 84a, Dudley Collard to Colonel William Hinchley Cooke, 3 July 1940; serial 92a, Lt Col. W. A. Alexander to Commander Kenneth Carpmael, 1 October 1941.

11. NA KV 2/4168, serial 117x, F. Beaumont Nesbitt to Sir Vernon Kell, 12 January 1940; *ibid.*, serial 121b, 'Note Re Harry Peter Smolka alias Smollett', 4 February 1940; *ibid.*, serial 133a, Dick White to I.P.I., 8 June 1940; NA KV 2/4169, Roger Hollis minute 155 of 13 August 1941.

12. Graham Ross, *The Foreign Office and the Kremlin: British Documents on Anglo-Soviet Relations, 1941–45* (Cambridge: Cambridge University Press, 1984), p. 198.

13. NA KV 2/4169, serial 173a, Richard Brooman-White to Roger Fulford, 12 September 1942.

14. The preceding paragraph derives from NA HW 15/25, Venona transcript of 26 August 1944; NA KV 2/4036, minute 40 of Peter Ramsbotham, 14 May 1942; digest of items in NA KV 2/4037.

15. Mark A. Bradley, *A Very Principled Boy: The Life of Duncan Lee, Red Spy and Cold Warrior* (New York: Basic Books, 2014), p. 168.

16. *Ibid.*, pp. 65–6; Allen Weinstein and Alexander Vassiliev, *The Haunted Wood: Soviet Espionage in America – the Stalin Era* (New York: Random House, 1999), p. 252; Don S. Kirschner, *Cold War Exile: The Unclosed Case of Maurice Halperin* (Columbia: University of Missouri Press, 1995), p. 69.

17. Kirschner, *Cold War Exile*, pp. 72–3.

18. Bradley, *Principled Boy*, p. 19.

19. This characterization follows Kathryn Olmstead, *Red Spy Queen: A Biography of Elizabeth Bentley* (Chapel Hill: University of North Carolina Press, 2002).

20. This paragraph relies upon Kirschner, *Cold War Exile*.

21. In the preceding section I follow John Earl Haynes and Harvey Klehr, *Venona: Decoding Soviet Espionage in America* (New Haven: Yale University Press, 1999), pp. 131, 134–6.

22. Ball, *Churchill and Attlee*, pp. 270–1.

23. Nigel West, ed., *The Guy Liddell Diaries: MI5's Director of Counter-Espionage in World War II*, vol. 1: *1939–1942* (London: Routledge, 2005), pp. 90–2.

24. Alex Danchev and Daniel Todman, eds, *War Diaries, 1939–1945: Field Marshal Lord Alanbrooke* (London: Weidenfeld & Nicolson, 2001), p. 400; Sir Hardy Amies, *Just So Far* (London: Collins, 1954), p. 109.

25. F. H. Hinsley and C. A. G. Simkins, *British Intelligence in the Second World War*, vol. 4: *Security and Counter-Intelligence* (London: HMSO, 1990), p. 53.

26. *Ibid.*, p. 57.

27. Hart, *Ask Me No More*, p. 96; Hinsley and Simkins, *British Intelligence*, vol. 4, p. 39; Nigel West, ed., *The Guy Liddell Diaries: MI5's Director of Counter-Espionage in World War II*, vol. 2: *1942–1945* (London: Routledge, 2005), pp. 63–4.

28. Hinsley and Simkins, *British Intelligence*, vol. 4, p. 288.

29. Tom Bower, *The Perfect English Spy: Sir Dick White and the Secret War, 1935–90* (London: Heinemann, 1995), p. 43.

30. West, *Liddell Diaries*, vol. 1, pp. 98, 256.

31. NA KV 2/1456, serial 83a, Kim Philby to Helenus Milmo, 30 November 1943, answering serial 80x, Milmo to Philby re Plan Squealer, 24 November 1943; Calder Walton, *Empire of Secrets: British Intelligence, the Cold War and the Twilight of Empire* (London: Harper Press, 2013), p. 65; Brian Stewart and Samantha Newbery, *Why Spy? The Art of Intelligence* (London: Hurst, 2015), p. 104.

32. Gabriel Gorodetsky, ed., *The Maisky Diaries: Red Ambassador to the Court*

of St James's, 1932–1943 (New Haven: Yale University Press, 2015), pp. 287–8.

33. Christopher Murphy, *Security and Special Operations: SOE and MI5 during the Second World War* (New York: Palgrave Macmillan, 2006), pp. 4–5; 'Mr Norman Mott', *The Times*, 18 February 1987.

34. West, *Liddell Diaries*, vol. 1, pp. 98–9; Malcolm Muggeridge, *Chronicles of Wasted Time: The Infernal Grove* (London: Collins, 1973), pp. 103–4.

35. Ben Pimlott, ed., *The Second World War Diary of Hugh Dalton, 1940–45* (London: Cape, 1986), p. 62.

36. Dennis Wheatley, *The Deception Planners* (London: Hutchinson, 1980), p. 30; NA KV 2/2839, minute 88, Major Rupert Speir, 21 June 1941; information from Professor Michael Wheeler, historian of the Athenaeum, 11 October 2016.

37. Gorodetsky, *Maisky Diaries*, pp. 231, 238, 239.

38. Hinsley and Simkins, *British Intelligence*, vol. 4, pp. 306–7.

39. Ross, *Foreign Office and Kremlin*, p. 73; Jonathan Haslam, *Near and Distant Neighbours: A New History of Soviet Intelligence* (Oxford: Oxford University Press, 2015), pp. 106–7, 115.

40. Hinsley and Simkins, *British Intelligence*, vol. 4, p. 83.

41. Philip Jordan, *Russian Glory* (London: Cresset Press, 1942), pp. 24, 107–8.

42. Earl of Avon, *The Eden Memoirs: The Reckoning* (London: Cassell, 1965), pp. 287, 302–3; Pimlott, *Dalton War Diaries*, p. 341.

43. Ross, *Foreign Office and Kremlin*, pp. 106–7, 116–17; Anthony Glees, *The Secrets of the Service: British Intelligence and Communist Subversion, 1939–1951* (London: Cape, 1987), pp. 44, 46; Jonathan Haslam, *The Vices of Integrity: E. H. Carr, 1892–1982* (London: Verso, 1999), pp. 94–6, 108–10.

44. Ross, *Foreign Office and Kremlin*, pp. 128–30.

45. John Harvey, ed., *The War Diaries of Oliver Harvey*, vol. 2 (London: Collins, 1978), p. 219; Donald Gillies, *Radical Diplomat: The Life of Archibald Clark Kerr, Lord Inverchapel, 1882–1951* (London: I. B. Tauris, 1999), p. 141.

46. Glees, *Secrets of Service*, pp. 204–5.

47. 'Mr Attlee and the "New Model Army": Russia Parallels Cromwell's Feat', *Manchester Guardian*, 22 February 1943, p. 3; Ball, *Churchill and Attlee*, p. 356.

48. Ross, *Foreign Office and Kremlin*, p. 216.

49. Gorodetsky, *Maisky Diaries*, p. 487; Waugh, *Sword of Honour Trilogy*, pp. 495–6, 508; 'Stalin the Great', *Listener*, 16 December 1943, p. 688. The Sword of Stalingrad is now on display in a Volgograd museum devoted to the battle.

50. Tim Garton Ash, 'Orwell's List', *New York Review of Books*, 25 September 2003; Danchev and Todman, *Alanbrooke Diaries*, p. 516.

51. Zbyněk Zeman and Antonin Klimek, *The Life of Edvard Beneš, 1884–1948: Czechoslovakia in Peace and War* (Oxford: Clarendon Press, 1997), pp. 68, 272; Harvey, *War Diaries of Oliver Harvey*, pp. 378–9.

52. Sir Maurice Peterson, *Both Sides of the Curtain* (London: Constable, 1950), p. 259; Sir Owen O'Malley, *The Phantom Caravan* (London: John Murray, 1954), p. 228; Sir John Colville, *The Fringes of Power: Downing Street Diaries, 1939–1955* (London: Hodder & Stoughton, 1985), p. 555.

53. Jordan, *Russian Glory*, p. 128.

54. Ross, *Foreign Office and Kremlin*, p. 198.

55. O'Malley, *Phantom Caravan*, pp. 230–1; *DBPO*, series 1, vol. 6 (London: HMSO, 1991), pp. 15–18.

56. *Ibid.*, p. 79.

57. Sir William Dugdale, *Settling the Bill* (London: Endeavour, 2011), pp. 137–8.

58. Sir Victor Wellesley, *Diplomacy in Fetters* (London: Hutchinson, 1944), p. 141.

Chapter 12: The Desk Officers

1. NA KV 2/1181, serials 288b and 288c, 'Bob Stewart', 9 December 1943.

2. Genrikh Borovik (with Phillip Knightley), *The Philby Files: The Secret Life of the Master Spy – KGB Archives Revealed* (London: Little, Brown, 1994), pp. 208–9.

3. Patrick Seale and Maureen McConville, *Philby: The Long Road to Moscow* (London: Hamish Hamilton, 1973), p. 135.

4. Hugh Trevor-Roper, *The Secret World: Behind the Curtain of British Intelligence in World War II and the Cold War*, ed. Edward Harrison (London: I. B. Tauris, 2014), p. 79.

5. Seale and McConville, *Philby*, p. 132.

6. Kim Philby, *My Silent War* (London: MacGibbon & Kee, 1968), pp. 37, 167.

7. Seale and McConville, *Philby*, p. 164.

8. J. C. Masterman, *The Case of the Four Friends: A Diversion in Pre-Detection* (London: Hodder & Stoughton, 1956), pp. 80-1.

9. Graham Greene, *Collected Essays* (London: Bodley Head, 1969), p. 418; Hugh Trevor-Roper, *The Wartime Journals*, ed. Richard Davenport-Hines (London: I. B. Tauris, 2012), p. 170; Anthony Cave Brown, *Treason in the Blood: H. St. John Philby, Kim Philby and the Spy Case of the Century* (London: Robert Hale, 1995), p. 291.

10. Oxford, Christ Church archives, Dacre papers 13/4, diary of Hugh Trevor-Roper, 25 November 1967.

11. NA KV 2/4169, serial 223a, 'Copies of notes on meetings attended by

SMOLLETT, found with BURGESS' correspondence at Courtauld Institute of Art in November, 1951': 1 February and 24 May 1942.

12. Oxford, Bodleian Library, Mss Eng c 6918, unpublished memoirs of Sir Patrick Reilly, ff. 204–5, 217.

13. NA KV 2/4140, serial 19a, Top Secret, 'CURZON', J. C. Robertson, 30 April 1951.

14. John Costello and Oleg Tsarev, *Deadly Illusions* (London: Century, 1993), p. 219; Charles Ritchie, *The Siren Years: Undiplomatic Diaries, 1937–1945* (London: Macmillan, 1974), p. 56.

15. Lord Eccles, *By Safe Hand: Letters of Sybil & David Eccles, 1939–42* (London: Bodley Head, 1983), pp. 254–5, 263.

16. Donald Gillies, *Radical Diplomat: The Life of Archibald Clark Kerr, Lord Inverchapel, 1882–1951* (London: I. B. Tauris, 1999), p. 217.

17. Frank Giles, *Sundry Times: An Autobiography* (London: John Murray, 1987), pp. 49, 52, 60.

18. Gillies, *Radical Diplomat*, p. 213.

19. Sir John Balfour, *Not Too Correct an Aureole: The Recollections of a Diplomat* (Wilton: Michael Russell, 1983), p. 113; NA KV 2/4150, serial 625a, George Carey-Foster to Dick White, 4 February 1953, enclosing George Middleton's statement of 18 December 1952.

20. Sir Isaiah Berlin, *Affirming: Letters, 1975–1997*, ed. Henry Hardy and Mark Pottle (London: Chatto & Windus, 2015), p. 120.

21. Trevor-Roper, *War Journals*, p. 161.

22. NA KV 2/4111, serial 497a, Skardon, 'JAMES POPE-HENNESSY', 21 January 1954; James Lees-Milne, *Ancestral Voices* (London: Chatto & Windus, 1975), pp. 256-7; Cambridge, King's College archives, NGA 5/1/290, Charles Fletcher-Cooke to Noël Annan, 25 November 1943; James Lees-Milne, *Prophesying Peace* (London: Chatto & Windus, 1977), p. 136.

23. KV 2/4109, serial 432a, Skardon, 'Interview with William RIDSDALE on 8.12.52', 11 December 1952.

24. Alan Maclean, *No, I Tell a Lie, It was the Tuesday: A Trudge through the Life of Alan Maclean* (London: Kyle Cathie, 1997), pp. 71–2.

25. Tom Bower, *The Perfect English Spy: Sir Dick White and the Secret War, 1935–90* (London: Heinemann, 1995), p. 113.

26. Nigel West and Oleg Tsarev, *The Crown Jewels: The British Secrets at the Heart of the KGB Archives* (London: HarperCollins, 1998), pp. 136–7.

27. Christopher Andrew, *The Defence of the Realm: The Authorized History of MI5* (London: Allen Lane, 2009), p. 270.

28. Jonathan Haslam, *Near and Distant Neighbours: A New History of Soviet Intelligence* (Oxford: Oxford University Press, 2015), p. 127.

29. West and Tsarev, *Crown Jewels*, p. 153.

30. Malcolm Muggeridge, *Chronicles of Wasted Time: The Infernal Grove* (London: Collins, 1973), pp. 106–7; Bower, *Perfect English Spy*, p. 47; John Costello, *Mask of Treachery: Spies, Lies, Buggery and Betrayal, the First Documented Dossier of Anthony Blunt's Cambridge Spy Ring* (New York: William Morrow, 1988), p. 390; Stephen Koch, *Double Lives: Stalin, Willi Münzenberg and the Seduction of the Intellectuals* (London: HarperCollins, 1995), p. 200.

31. British Library, Add Mss 88902/1, unpublished Blunt memoir, f. 50.

32. Goronwy Rees, *A Chapter of Accidents* (London: Chatto & Windus, 1972), p. 155; British Library, Add Mss 88902/1, ff. 51, 53.

33. N. J. Crowson, ed., *Fleet Street, Press Barons and Politics: The Journals of Collin Brooks, 1932–1940* (London: Royal Historical Society, 1998), p. 52.

34. In this section I follow Stephen Roskill, *Hankey: Man of Secrets*, vol. 3 (London: Collins, 1974), chapters 12–15.

Chapter 13: The Atomic Spies

1. David Footman, *Balkan Holiday* (London: Heinemann, 1935), p. 97; Jonathan Haslam, *Near and Distant Neighbours: A New History of Soviet Intelligence* (Oxford: Oxford University Press, 2015), p. 140; NA KV 4/224, serial 3a, Alan Roger, 'Top Secret Report on dealings with Russians', 23 July 1944.

2. Oxford, Christ Church archives, Dacre 10/50, Cyril Mills to Hugh Dacre, 19 January 1985.

3. Gill Bennett, 'The CORBY Case: The Defection of Igor Gouzenko, September 1945', in FCO Historians, *From World War to Cold War: The Records of the FO Permanent Under-Secretary's Department, 1939–51*, http://issuu.com/fcohistorians/docs/pusdessays/3.

4. *DBPO*, series 1, vol. 11 (London: Routledge, 2017), pp. 26–9, 66.

5. *DBPO*, series 1, vol. 6 (London: HMSO, 1991), p. 320.

6. Peter Broda, *Scientist Spies: A Memoir of my Three Parents and the Atom Bomb* (Kibworth Beauchamp: Matador, 2011), p. 100.

7. Eric Hobsbawm, *Interesting Times: A Twentieth-Century Life* (London: Allen Lane, 2002), p. 112; Broda, *Scientist Spies*, pp. 108–9.

8. Andrew Brown, *The Neutron and the Bomb: A Biography of Sir James Chadwick* (Oxford: Oxford University Press, 1997), p. 323.

9. Broda, *Scientist Spies*, p. 141.

10. Brown, *Neutron and Bomb*, p. 308.

11. *DBPO*, series 1, vol. 2 (London: HMSO, 1985), pp. 367, 525–6, 556–7.

12. Broda, *Scientist Spies*, p. 145; Cambridge, Churchill College archives, ACAD 1/15, diary of Sir Alexander Cadogan, 19 September 1945.

588   NOTES TO PAGES 337–50

13. Broda, *Scientist Spies*, pp. 175–6.
14. *Ibid.*, pp. 180–1.
15. Alan Moorehead, *The Traitors: The Double Life of Fuchs, Pontecorvo and Nunn May* (London: Hamish Hamilton, 1952), pp. 12, 26; Phillip Knightley, *Philby: The Life and Views of the KGB Masterspy* (London: André Deutsch, 1988), p. 187.
16. Moorehead, *Traitors*, pp. 44–5.
17. Robert Chadwell Williams, *Klaus Fuchs, Atom Spy* (Cambridge, Mass.: Harvard University Press, 1987), p. 29; Max Perutz, 'Spying made easy', *London Review of Books*, 25 June 1987, p. 6.
18. Tom Bower, *The Perfect English Spy: Sir Dick White and the Secret War, 1935–90* (London: Heinemann, 1995), pp. 93–4; Brown, *Neutron and Bomb*, p. 252.
19. Ruth Werner, *Sonya's Report* (London: Chatto & Windus, 1991), pp. 150, 244.
20. *DBPO*, series 1, vol. 6, pp. 64–5; Graham Ross, *The Foreign Office and the Kremlin: British Documents on Anglo-Soviet Relations, 1941–45* (Cambridge: Cambridge University Press, 1984), p. 227.
21. *DBPO*, series 1, vol. 2, pp. 530–1.
22. Allen Weinstein and Alexander Vassiliev, *The Haunted Wood: Soviet Espionage in America – the Stalin Era* (New York: Random House, 1999), p. 313.
23. Norman Moss, *Klaus Fuchs: The Man Who Stole the Atom Bomb* (London: Grafton, 1987), p. 200.
24. NA KV 2/2797, serial 373a, Report 'Mrs Moody', 15 September 1954.
25. Wilfrid Vernon, House of Commons debates, 8 October 1946, vol. 427, cols 121-2; NA KV 2/2202, serial 378b, 'Stuart Havelock HOLLINGDALE – Interview with Edward Spence CALVERT', 27 April 1953.
26. Oxford, Worcester College archives, WOR PRO 10/1/75, Richard Butler to Sir J. C. Masterman, 8 May 1953; Werner, *Sonya's Report*, p. 278.
27. This section follows John Earl Haynes and Harvey Klehr, *Venona: Decoding Soviet Espionage in America* (New Haven: Yale University Press, 1999).
28. NA KV 4/471, diary of Guy Liddell, 21 November 1949.
29. Alan Maclean, *No, I Tell a Lie, It was the Tuesday: A Trudge through the Life of Alan Maclean* (London: Kyle Cathie, 1997), p. 101.
30. Moss, *Fuchs*, pp. 69, 149.
31. Werner, *Sonya's Report*, p. 303; NA KV 2/2796, minute 306, Evelyn McBarnet, 24 November 1950.
32. Graham Greene, *Collected Essays* (London: Bodley Head, 1969), p. 414.
33. 'Ten Year Sentence on Estate Agent', *The Times*, 17 May 1952, p. 3; Josh Ireland, *The Traitors: A True Story of Blood, Betrayal and Deceit* (London:

John Murray, 2017), pp. 113–14; Markus Wolf, *Man without a Face: Autobiography of Communism's Greatest Spymaster* (London: Cape, 1997), pp. 227–31.

34. https://en.wikipedia.org/wiki/Theodore_Hall, accessed 2 February 2017; Haynes and Klehr, *Venona*, pp. 314–17.

35. David Holloway, *Stalin and the Bomb: The Soviet Union and Atomic Energy, 1939–1956* (New Haven: Yale University Press, 1994), p. 217; Simon Ings, *Stalin and the Scientists: A History of Triumph and Tragedy, 1905–1953* (London: Faber & Faber, 2016), p. 393.

Chapter 14: The Cold War

1. Crane Brinton, *The United States and Britain* (Oxford: Oxford University Press, 1945), p. 69; Angela Thirkell, *Love among the Ruins* (London: Hamish Hamilton, 1948), pp. 133–5, 190–1.

2. Oxford, Worcester College archives, Masterman papers, WOR PRO 10/1/128/1, Lord Normanbrook to Sir J. C. Masterman, 25 March 1965; Sir Dick White to Sir J. C. Masterman, 5 October 1967.

3. Christopher Andrew, *The Defence of the Realm: The Authorized History of MI5* (London: Allen Lane, 2009), p. 321; Tom Buchanan, *East Wind: China and the British Left, 1925–1976* (Oxford: Oxford University Press, 2013), p. 56.

4. Cambridge, Churchill College archives, ACAD 1/15, diary of Sir Alexander Cadogan, 9 & 14 November 1945; Tom Bower, *The Perfect English Spy: Sir Dick White and the Secret War, 1935–90* (London: Heinemann, 1995), p. 76.

5. *DBPO*, series 1, vol. 11 (London: Routledge, 2017), pp. 36–7.

6. Oxford, Bodleian Library, papers of Lord Sherfield, vol. 483, Sir Edmund Hall-Patch to Roger Makins, 11 March 1946.

7. Patrick Howarth, *Intelligence Chief Extraordinary: The Life of the Ninth Duke of Portland* (London: Bodley Head, 1986), pp. 16–17, 59, 223; *DBPO*, series 1, vol. 6 (London: HMSO, 1991), p. 19.

8. Kim Philby, *My Silent War* (London: MacGibbon & Kee, 1968), pp. 84–5; Oxford, Bodleian Library, Mss Eng c 6918, unpublished memoirs of Sir Patrick Reilly, f. 211.

9. George Blake, *No Other Choice: An Autobiography* (London: Cape, 1990), p. 100.

10. Oxford, Bodleian Library, Mss Eng c 6918, Reilly, f. 239.

11. *DBPO*, series 1, vol. 11, p. 19.

12. Brian Stewart and Samantha Newbery, *Why Spy? The Art of Intelligence* (London: Hurst, 2015), p. 7; Calder Walton, *Empire of Secrets: British*

Intelligence, the Cold War and the Twilight of Empire (London: Harper Press, 2013), p. 113. I am indebted to the latter source in the section that follows.

13. Wilfrid Vernon, House of Commons debates, 23 January 1948, vol. 446, cols 580-3; Buchanan, *East Wind*, pp. 106, 107, 109.

14. Walton, *Empire of Secrets*, p. 331.

15. *DBPO*, series 1, vol. 6, pp. 206–9.

16. *DBPO*, series 1, vol. 11, p. 101.

17. *Ibid.*, pp. 76, 157.

18. Walton, *Empire of Secrets*, p. 115.

19. 'Blood Runs in Palestine Violence', *Life*, 12 August 1946, p. 22; David Leitch, 'Explosion at the King David Hotel', in Michael Sissons and Philip French, eds, *Age of Austerity* (London: Hodder & Stoughton, 1963), p. 59.

20. Jonathan Haslam, *The Vices of Integrity: E. H. Carr, 1892–1982* (London: Verso, 1999), p. 152.

21. *DBPO*, series 1, vol. 11, pp. 161, 254–5.

22. Mark A. Bradley, *A Very Principled Boy: The Life of Duncan Lee, Red Spy and Cold Warrior* (New York: Basic Books, 2014), pp. 136–8.

23. *Ibid.*, p. 156.

24. Allen Weinstein and Alexander Vassiliev, *The Haunted Wood: Soviet Espionage in America – the Stalin Era* (New York: Random House, 1999), pp. 8, 18.

25. Thomas Hachey, 'American Profiles on Capitol Hill: A Confidential Study for the British Foreign Office in 1943', *Wisconsin Magazine of History*, 57 (Winter 1973–4), p. 153.

26. Anon., *Laurence Duggan, 1905–1948: In Memoriam* (Stamford, Conn.: Overbrook Press, 1949), pp. ix–x, 78, 91.

27. Eleanor Roosevelt, 'My Day', in *ibid.*, pp. 26–8.

28. NA KV 4/471, diary of Guy Liddell, 31 January & 11 April 1949.

29. Andrew, *Defence of the Realm*, p. 382; Norman Moss, *Klaus Fuchs: The Man Who Stole the Atom Bomb* (London: Grafton, 1987), pp. 202–3.

30. 'Civil Service Purge', *Manchester Guardian*, 4 May 1948, p. 3; 'Security Tests for Ministers', *Observer*, 12 March 1950, p. 5.

31. Andrew, *Defence of the Realm*, p. 384.

32. Phillip Knightley, *Philby: The Life and Views of the KGB Masterspy* (London: André Deutsch, 1988), pp. 135–6.

33. *Ibid.*, p. 138.

34. *DBPO*, series 1, vol. 11, pp. 51–2.

35. Martin Pearce, *Spymaster: The Life of Britain's Most Decorated Cold War Spy and Head of MI6, Sir Maurice Oldfield* (London: Bantam, 2016),

pp. 75–6; Alexander Foote, *Handbook for Spies* (New York: Doubleday, 1949), pp. 208, 228.

36. Evelyn Waugh, *Scott-King's Modern Europe* (London: Chapman & Hall, 1947), pp. 64–5; Pearce, *Spymaster*, pp. 108–9.

Chapter 15: The Alcoholic Panic

1. Patrick Seale and Maureen McConville, *Philby: The Long Road to Moscow* (London: Hamish Hamilton, 1973), pp. 202–3.

2. Lord Bethell, *The Great Betrayal: The Untold Story of Kim Philby's Biggest Coup* (London: Hodder & Stoughton, 1984), p. 97; Lorna Almonds Windmill, *A British Achilles: The Story of George, Second Earl Jellicoe* (London: Pen & Sword, 2005), p. 119.

3. Richard Bassett, *Last Imperialist: A Portrait of Julian Amery* (Settrington: Stone Trough, 2015), pp. 137–42.

4. Tom Mangold, *Cold Warrior: James Jesus Angleton, the CIA's Master Spy Hunter* (London: Simon & Schuster, 1991), p. 64.

5. William Waldegrave, *A Different Kind of Weather: A Memoir* (London: Constable, 2015), p. 99; Oxford, Bodleian Library, Mss Eng c 6920, ff. 252–3.

6. Cambridge, Churchill College archives, ACAD 1/15, diary of Sir Alexander Cadogan, 30 August & 1 September 1945; *DBPO*, series 1, vol. 6 (London: HMSO, 1991), p. 243; 'Mr McNeil angers his own party', *Manchester Guardian*, 12 August 1954, p. 1; 'London Correspondence', *Manchester Guardian*, 13 October 1955, p. 6.

7. *DBPO*, series 1, vol. 6, pp. 345, 346, 349.

8. NA KV 2/4110, serial 468a, G. R. Mitchell, 'Philip Dennis PROCTOR', 3 December 1953; James Lees-Milne, *Ancestral Voices* (London: Chatto & Windus, 1975), pp. 256–7.

9. Stewart Purvis and Jeff Hulbert, *Guy Burgess: The Spy Who Knew Everyone* (London: Backbite, 2016), pp. 208–9.

10. Nigel West and Oleg Tsarev, *The Crown Jewels: The British Secrets at the Heart of the KGB Archive* (London: HarperCollins, 1998), p. 176.

11. NA KV 2/4101, serial 21a, Vivian to Carey-Foster, Top Secret, 19 January 1950.

12. Sir Bernard Burrows, *Diplomat in a Changing World* (London: Memoir Club, 2001), p. 59.

13. Lord Greenhill of Harrow, *More by Accident* (privately printed, 1992), p. 73.

14. Windmill, *British Achilles*, p. 121.

15. W. H. Auden, *Prose*, vol. 1 (Princeton: Princeton University Press, 1996), p. 451.

16. NA KV 2/4143, serial 284a, George Carey-Foster to J. C. Robertson, 25 June 1951; Sir John Balfour, *Not Too Correct an Aureole: The Recollections of a Diplomat* (Wilton: Michael Russell, 1983), p. 114.

17. Jonathan Haslam, *Near and Distant Neighbours: A New History of Soviet Intelligence* (Oxford: Oxford University Press, 2015), p. 169; John Costello, *Mask of Treachery: Spies, Lies, Buggery and Betrayal, the First Documented Dossier of Anthony Blunt's Cambridge Spy Ring* (New York: William Morrow, 1988), pp. 554–5; Wilfrid Mann, *Was There a Fifth Man?* (London: Pergamon, 1982), p. 84; Michael Holzman, *James Jesus Angleton: The CIA and the Craft of Counter-Intelligence* (Amherst: University of Massachusetts Press, 2008), pp. 121–2.

18. NA KV 2/4140, serial 12, Robin J. W. Hooper, minute of 8 January 1950.

19. NA KV 2/4148, serial 567c, 'Interview with Humphrey SLATER – 11th July 1952', Richard Thistlethwaite, 12 July 1952; Humphrey Slater, *The Conspirator* (London: John Lehmann, 1948), p. 119.

20. Ferdinand Mount, *Cold Cream* (London: Bloomsbury, 2008), pp. 47–8.

21. NA KV 2/4140, serial 3a, Strictly Personal and Confidential, Edwin Chapman-Andrews to George Middleton, 10 May 1950.

22. Crane Brinton, *The United States and Britain* (Oxford: Oxford University Press, 1945), p. 71; Brian Urquhart, *A Life in Peace and War* (London: Weidenfeld & Nicolson, 1987), p. 117.

23. Mount, *Cold Cream*, p. 50; NA KV 2/4105, serial 245z, Telecheck on PAD 4841 (Philip Toynbee's number), Cyril Connolly to Dennis Weaver of *News Chronicle*, 18 July 1951; NA KV 2/4144, serial 316a 'CULME-SEYMOUR', A. S. Martin report, 12 July 1951.

24. Cyril Connolly, *The Missing Diplomats* (London: Queen Anne Press, 1952), p. 29.

25. Philip Toynbee, 'Alger Hiss and His Friends', *Observer*, 18 March 1951, p. 4; NA KV 2/4144, serial 316a, 'CULME-SEYMOUR', Martin report, 12 July 1951. Skardon surmised that the Judas epithet had been thrown at Slater, but Toynbee is more likely.

26. NA KV 2/4101, serial 91a, Guy Liddell, Top Secret, 2 June 1951.

27. Andrew Lownie, *Stalin's Englishman: The Lives of Guy Burgess* (London: Hodder & Stoughton, 2015), p. 232.

28. Andrew Boyle, *The Climate of Treason: Five Who Spied for Russia* (London: Hutchinson, 1979), p. 373; Alan Campbell, *Colleagues and Friends* (Wilton: Michael Russell, 1988), pp. 16–17.

29. J. C. Masterman, *The Case of the Four Friends: A Diversion in Pre-Detection* (London: Hodder & Stoughton, 1956), p. 203.

30. NA KV 2/4101, serial 36a, Guy Burgess to Guy Liddell, 5am, [16 February 1950]. Written on the back of an Apostles' dinner invitation.

31. Anthony Cavendish, *Inside Intelligence* (London: HarperCollins, 1990), p. 62.

32. W. A. P. Manser, 'Do you want me to kill him?', *Spectator*, 19 May 1995, p. 14.

33. Philip Jordan, *Russian Glory* (London: Cresset Press, 1942), p. 104; NA KV 2/4132, serial 1325z, journal of Stephen Spender, 7 February 1960.

Chapter 16: *The Missing Diplomats*

1. NA KV 2/4106, serial 274b, Top Secret, 'The BURGESS–MACLEAN Case', 22 August 1951.

2. Stephen Harper, 'A Phone Call Began It', *Daily Express*, 19 April 1962; Don Seaman, 'Burgess Knew Atom Spy', *Daily Express*, 13 June 1951; Andrew Lownie, *Stalin's Englishman: The Lives of Guy Burgess* (London: Hodder & Stoughton, 2015), p. 248.

3. NA KV 2/4102, serial 129a, Courtenay Young, 8 June 1951; Harper, 'A Phone Call Began It', *Daily Express*, 19 April 1962.

4. NA KV 4/473, diary of Guy Liddell, 24 July 1951; 'A Spectator's Notebook', *Spectator*, 31 July 1952, p. 5.

5. 'M.I.5 SILLITOE TAKES A (Burgess–Maclean) HOLIDAY', *Daily Express*, 22 August 1951.

6. Philip Jordan, *There is No Return* (London: Cresset Press, 1938), pp. 159–60.

7. 'Philip', *Manchester Guardian*, 7 June 1951, p. 6; Andrew Boyle, *The Climate of Treason: Five Who Spied for Russia* (London: Hutchinson, 1979), pp. 382–3.

8. NA KV 2/4144, serial 343y, R. T. Reed, Note on Mrs Maclean, 13 August 1951; NA FCO 158/26, minute of 3 September 1951 by Patrick Reilly, minute of 4 September by Herbert Morrison.

9. Oxford, Bodleian Library, Mss Eng c 6920, f. 245.

10. NA KV 2/4142, serial 186b, Lord Talbot de Malahide to Dick White, 5 June 1951; Alex Danchev and Daniel Todman, eds, *War Diaries, 1939–1945: Field Marshal Lord Alanbrooke* (London: Weidenfeld & Nicolson, 2001), p. 518.

11. Oxford, Bodleian Library, papers of Viscount Simon, vol. 99, Simon, 'The Mystery of Maclean and Burgess', 11 June 1951.

12. Alan Maclean, *No, I Tell a Lie, It was the Tuesday: A Trudge through the Life of Alan Maclean* (London: Kyle Cathie, 1997), pp. 96–8; James Lees-Milne, *Harold Nicolson: A Biography, 1930–1968* (London: Chatto & Windus, 1981), p. 247; Miles Jebb, ed., *The Diaries of Cynthia Gladwyn* (London: Constable, 1995), p. 131; Tom Buchanan, *East Wind: China and the British Left, 1925–1976* (Oxford: Oxford University Press, 2012), p. 131.

13. Constance Babington Smith, ed., *Letters to a Friend from Rose Macaulay, 1950-1952* (London: Collins, 1961), pp. 149-50; Charlotte Mosley, ed., *The Letters of Nancy Mitford* (London: Hodder & Stoughton, 1993), p. 278; Selina Hastings, *Rosamond Lehmann* (London: Chatto & Windus, 2002), pp. 292-3; NA KV 2/4106, serial 320b, W. J. Skardon, 'Interview with Rosamond Lehmann on 29.10.51', 31 October 1951.

14. 'Burgess One of "Nicest Men I Know": He Blamed U.S. for War Drift', *Daily Mail*, 18 June 1951; Tom Bower, *The Perfect English Spy: Sir Dick White and the Secret Service, 1935-90* (London: Heinemann, 1995), p. 118.

15. Sir Isaiah Berlin, *Affirming: Letters, 1975-1997*, ed. Henry Hardy and Mark Pottle (London: Chatto & Windus, 2015), p. 525.

16. Oxford, Bodleian Library, Berlin Ms 256, Stuart Hampshire to Isaiah Berlin, 17 February 1952; Miranda Carter, *Anthony Blunt: His Lives* (London: Macmillan, 2001), p. 347.

17. Bonnie Kime Scott, ed., *Selected Letters of Rebecca West* (New Haven and London: Yale University Press, 2000), pp. 282-3; Oxford, Bodleian Library, Macmillan D/8/121, diary of Harold Macmillan, 17 July 1951; NA KV 2/4108, serial 375a, Secret, George Carey-Foster, 6 March 1952; Hector McNeil, 'Were the diplomats eloping from reality?', *New Chronicle*, 28 January 1955.

18. NA KV 2/4102, serial 114a, Skardon, 'Interview with Mrs BASSETT 7.5.51'; Maclean, *No, I Tell a Lie*, pp. 102-4.

19. Bower, *Perfect English Spy*, pp. 114, 263.

20. NA KV 2/4102, serial 188b, Fred Warner, memorandum 'Mr Guy de F Burgess', forwarded by Sir David Kelly to Carey-Foster, 14 June 1951.

21. NA KV 2/2586, serial 61a, J. C. Robertson, 'Interview with Mr Sefton Delmer, 8.8.52', 9 August 1952.

22. Ernest Ashwick, 'Maclean Alive – The Proof: A Secret Number Hides His Cash Hoard', *Daily Express*, 6 June 1952; NA KV 2/4148, minute 565, C. A. G. Simkins, 10 July 1952.

23. Nora Beloff, *Transit of Britain: A Report on Britain's Changing Role in the Post-War World* (London: Collins, 1973), p. 107; NA KV 2/4150, serial 690a, [Evelyn McBarnet?], 'Melinda MACLEAN's letter to Mrs Dunbar', 30 November 1953; Peter Catterall, ed., *The Macmillan Diaries: The Cabinet Years, 1950-1957* (London: Macmillan, 2003), pp. 266-7; NA KV 2/4150, serial 647a, 'SECRET. Telecheck on Philby's Line', 17 September 1953.

24. Kim Philby, *My Silent War* (London: MacGibbon & Kee, 1968), pp. 137-8.

25. Patrick Seale and Maureen McConville, *Philby: The Long Road to Moscow* (London: Hamish Hamilton, 1973), pp. 217-18; NA KV 2/4105, serial 234c, PEACH telecheck, 10 July 1951.

26. Peter Carter-Ruck, 'Sir Helenus Milmo, Philby's Interrogator', *Guardian*, 3 September 1988.

27. Philby, *My Silent War*, p. 143.

28. Stan Cohen, *States of Denial: Knowing about Atrocities and Suffering* (Cambridge: Polity, 2001), p. 6.

29. NA KV 2/4170, serial 233c, Note to B2a, by Alan Roger, 15 March 1952.

30. NA KV 2/1604, serial 227a, A. F. Burbidge, report 'Edith Tudor-Hart', 1 December 1951.

31. NA KV 2/4091, serial B2a, Donald Winnicott to Edith Tudor-Hart, 2 January 1952.

32. NA KV 2/4091, serial 180b, 'Interview with Edith TUDOR-HART on 8.1.52', Skardon, 9 January 1952.

33. NA KV 2/996, serial 731b, 'Interview with Wilfred Foulston VERNON on 4.2.52', Skardon, 5 February 1952.

34. Stan Cohen, *Folk Devils and Moral Panics: The Creation of the Mods and Rockers* (London: MacGibbon & Kee, 1972), pp. 9, 191.

Chapter 17: The Establishment

1. W. N. Ewer, 'Sir Austen Von Hindenburg', *Labour Monthly*, 9 (March 1927), pp. 154, 159; Ivan Maisky, *Who Helped Hitler?* (London: Hutchinson, 1964), pp. 45–6.

2. Ben Pimlott, *Hugh Dalton* (London: Cape, 1985), p. 270; House of Commons debates, vol. 387, 18 March 1943, cols 1391, 1401–3; House of Commons debates, vol. 390, 22 June 1943, col. 1074; Sir George Rendel, *The Sword and the Olive: Recollections of Diplomacy and the Foreign Service, 1913–1954* (London: John Murray, 1957), pp. 200, 206.

3. Sir Eric Phipps, 'Foreign Office Reform', *The Times*, 3 February 1943, p. 5.

4. Markus Wolf, *Man without a Face: The Autobiography of Communism's Greatest Spymaster* (London: Jonathan Cape, 1991), p. 227.

5. Cambridge, Churchill College archives, ACAD 1/17, diary of Sir Alexander Cadogan, 19 January 1951, 19 February 1951, 29 July 1951, 8 October 1951; Peter Catterall, ed., *The Macmillan Diaries: The Cabinet Years, 1950–1957* (London: Macmillan, 2003), pp. 266–7.

6. Graham Ross, *The Foreign Office and the Kremlin: British Documents on Anglo-Soviet Relations, 1941–45* (Cambridge: Cambridge University Press, 1984), p. 174; Randolph Churchill, 'The Privacy of the Individual', *Spectator*, 23 May 1958, p. 649.

7. NA FCO 158/26, Top Secret, Lord Talbot de Malahide to Sir Patrick Dean, 23 September 1953.

8. Nancy Mitford, *Don't Tell Alfred* (London: Hamish Hamilton, 1960), p. 25.

9. Bonnie Kime Scott, ed., *Selected Letters of Rebecca West* (New Haven and London: Yale University Press, 2000), pp. 282–3.

10. Anthony Glees, *The Secrets of the Service: British Intelligence and Communist Subversion, 1939–1951* (London: Cape, 1987), pp. 117–19, 123–9.

11. Ian Colvin, 'Now Germany joins the race for atom power', *Sunday Express*, 7 March 1954; NA FO 371/109637, CW1194/7, minute of Michael Palliser, 12 March 1954.

12. Sefton Delmer, 'An ex-spy tells me about Burgess', *Daily Express*, 15 March 1954.

13. NA FO 371/109637, CW1194/15, minutes of M. A. Palliser and G. A. Barnes, 2 April 1954.

14. Graham Lord, 'John Junor: a bigot and blatant hypocrite', *Press Gazette*, 10 April 2013; NA PREM 11/762, Top Secret. Note by J. R. Colville, 30 September 1954.

15. Sefton Delmer, 'How Dead is Hitler?', *Daily Express*, 22 March 1955; NA FO 371/109637, CW1194/11, minute of Sir Frank Roberts, 27 March 1955, and of Sir Anthony Nutting, 29 March 1955.

16. NA KV 2/1636, serial 34a, 'Extract from War Office Papers for William MARSHALL', 13 May 1952, and serial 32a, Lambert Titchener to G. A. Carey-Foster, 9 May 1952.

17. NA KV 2/1638, serial 972aa, Marshall's statement to Special Branch, 13 June 1952; *ibid.*, serial 972, B2a report, 'The Case of William Martin Marshall', 19 June 1952.

18. NA FCO 158/209, Sir Alvary Gascoigne to Sir William Strang, Personal & Secret, 27 June 1952.

19. NA KV 2/1641, serial 220a, W. J. Skardon, report 'William Martin Marshall: Interview at Wormwood Scrubs on 19.2.53', 24 February 1953.

20. 'Sefton Delmer flies to the Petrov hearings and asks – Where was MI5?', *Daily Express*, 18 May 1954.

21. Tom Bower, *The Perfect English Spy: Sir Dick White and the Secret Service, 1935–90* (London: Heinemann, 1995), pp. 152–3.

22. 'Burgess and Maclean Soviet Spies for Years', *Manchester Guardian*, 19 September 1955, p. 1.

23. 'W. N. Ewer writes', *Daily Herald*, 19 September 1955, pp. 1–2.

24. 'Foreign Office Scandal', *Daily Mirror*, 20 September 1955, p. 1.

25. Henry Fairlie, 'Political Commentary', *Spectator*, 22 September 1955, pp. 5–6.

26. 'Burgess and Maclean Case Discussed on ITV', *Manchester Guardian*, 26 September 1955, p. 14.

27. George Brown, 'FO Flops: Spies Are Not the Only Trouble', *Sunday Pictorial*, 25 September 1955, p. 11.

28. E. P. Thompson, *Writing by Candlelight* (London: Merlin Press, 1980), p. 116; NA KV 2/4153, serial 820b, B. A. Hill, 'Top Secret', 26 September 1955. Brown was ennobled as Lord George-Brown in 1970.

29. Mark Amory, ed., *The Letters of Ann Fleming* (London: Collins Harvill, 1985), p. 161.

30. Lord Morrison of Lambeth, *Herbert Morrison: An Autobiography* (London: Odhams, 1960), pp. 274, 277, 313–14.

31. Glees, *Secrets of the Service*, pp. 6–7.

32. Nicola Lacey, *A Life of H. L. A. Hart: The Nightmare and the Noble Dream* (Oxford: Oxford University Press, 2004), p. 24; Edward Pearce, *The Golden Talking-Shop: The Oxford Union Debates Empire, World War, Revolution, & Women* (Oxford: Oxford University Press, 2016), p. 622; Charles Fletcher-Cooke, 'Table-Talk', *Observer*, 3 August 1952, p. 5; Janet Morgan, ed., *The Backbench Diaries of Richard Crossman* (London: Hamish Hamilton, 1981), p. 1003.

33. Richard Crossman, 'Why has the truth been hidden so long?', *Daily Mirror*, 20 September 1955, p. 4; Crossman, House of Commons debates, 7 November 1955, vol. 545, cols 1534-6.

34. Herbert Morrison, House of Commons debates, 7 November 1955, vol. 545, cols 1509–10.

35. NA KV 2/4153, serial 847b, R. T. Reed, 'The Disappearance of Burgess and Maclean', 16 December 1955.

36. NA KV 2/4153, serial 849b, Courtenay Young, 'Top Secret', 29 December 1955.

37. Michael Young, *The Chipped White Cups of Dover: A Discussion of the Possibility of a New Progressive Party* (London: Unit 2, 1960), pp. 5–6.

38. George Blake, *No Other Choice: An Autobiography* (London: Cape, 1990), pp. 139, 187.

39. *Ibid.*, pp. 197–9.

40. Bower, *Perfect English Spy*, pp. 267-8.

41. Oxford, Bodleian Library, Macmillan D/42/23 & D/42/32, diary of Harold Macmillan, 4 & 14 May 1961.

42. Peter Catterall, ed., *The Macmillan Diaries: Prime Minister and After, 1957–1963* (London: Macmillan, 2011), pp. 450–1; Oxford, Bodleian Library, Macmillan D/45/23, diary of 16 February 1962; Chapman Pincher, *Traitors: The Labyrinths of Treason* (London: Sidgwick & Jackson, 1987), pp. 9-10.

43. Oxford, Bodleian Library, Mss Eng c 6925, ff. 208, 258–9, 272, 276, 290; Donald Maclean, *British Foreign Policy since Suez, 1956–1968* (London: Hodder & Stoughton, 1970), p. 331.

44. Oxford, Christ Church archives, Bradwell papers B/10, Tom Driberg, 'Burgess: My Theory about the Warrants', 23 April 1962.

45. Tim [I. I.] Milne, *Kim Philby: The Unknown Story of the KGB's Master Spy* (London: Backbite, 2014), pp. 104-5.
46. David Footman, *Dead Yesterday* (London: White Lion, 1974), p. 163; Bruce Page, David Leitch and Phillip Knightley, *Philby: The Spy Who Betrayed a Generation* (London: André Deutsch, 1968), pp. 22-3.
47. The preceding paragraph summarizes Richard Davenport-Hines, *An English Affair: Sex, Class and Power in the Age of Profumo* (London: Collins, 2013).
48. Tony Benn, *Out of the Wilderness: Diaries, 1963-1967* (London: Hutchinson, 1987), p. 183; 'Who Runs This Country Anyhow?', *Sunday Mirror*, 23 June 1963, pp. 1-2; Richard Crossman, 'The Peril of the Whitehall Mandarins', *Sunday Mirror*, 23 June 1963, p. 8; Malcolm Muggeridge, 'The Slow, Sure Death of the Upper Classes, *Sunday Mirror*, 23 June 1963, p. 7; Cambridge University Library, Add 9429/IG/430, Andrew Boyle, notes of interview with Malcolm Muggeridge, 16 July 1977.
49. James Cameron, 'Why the World is Mocking Britain', *Sunday Mirror*, 23 June 1963, p. 9.
50. Nora Beloff, *Transit of Britain: A Report on Britain's Changing Role in the Post-War World* (London: Collins, 1973), pp. 199-200; James Ramsden, ed., *George Lyttelton's Commonplace Book* (York: Stone Trough, 2002), pp. 42-3.
51. Donald McLachlan, 'In Defence of our Secret Service', *Sunday Telegraph*, 8 October 1967.

Chapter 18: *The Brotherhood of Perverted Men*

1. Sir Rupert Grayson, 'Greatest risk', *Daily Telegraph*, 28 April 1987.
2. Richard Davenport-Hines, *Sex, Death and Punishment: Attitudes to Sex and Sexuality in Britain since the Renaissance* (London: Collins, 1990), p. 297; George Melly, *Rum, Bum, and Concertina* (London: Weidenfeld & Nicolson, 1977), p. 12.
3. Oxford, Bodleian Library, Inverchapel papers, box 17, Harold Nicolson to Archie Clark Kerr, 1 July 1911; box 18, Nicolson to Clark Kerr, 14 January 1912; John Julius Norwich, ed., *The Duff Cooper Diaries, 1915-1951* (London: Weidenfeld & Nicolson, 2005), p. 37.
4. Sir John Balfour, *Not Too Correct an Aureole: The Recollections of a Diplomat* (Wilton: Michael Russell, 1983), p. 10; Sir Maurice Peterson, *Both Sides of the Curtain* (London: Constable, 1950), pp. 64-5.
5. Charles Ritchie, *The Siren Years: Undiplomatic Diaries, 1937-1945* (London: Macmillan, 1974), p. 92.
6. Hardy Amies, *Just So Far* (London: Collins, 1954), p. 98; Hugh Trevor-Roper, *The Wartime Journals*, ed. Richard Davenport-Hines (London:

I. B. Tauris, 2012), p. 68; Anthony Cavendish, *Inside Intelligence* (London: Collins, 1990), p. 160.

7. Suleyman Seydi, 'Intelligence and Counter-Intelligence Activities in Iran during the Second World War', *Middle Eastern Studies*, 46 (September 2010), pp. 733–50; NA KV 4/224, serial 3b, Alan Roger, DSO in Tehran, 'Top Secret. Soviet S.I.S. Activities and the VAZIRI case', 6 August 1944; serial 4a, Alan Roger, 'Most Secret. Russian Relations and Activities in Persia', [August 1944]; serial 10a, Alan Roger, 'Cooperation with Russian Security', 28 December 1944; serial 14a, Alan Roger, 'Information about Russian intelligence gained from cooperation between DSO and Russian security authorities', 7 March 1945.

8. Sir Alistair Horne, *But What Do You Actually Do? A Literary Vagabondage* (London: Weidenfeld & Nicolson, 2011), p. 55.

9. N. J. Crowson, ed., *Fleet Street, Press Barons and Politics: The Journals of Collin Brooks, 1932–1940* (London: Royal Historical Society, 1998), p. 69; Peter Wildeblood, *Against the Law* (London: Weidenfeld & Nicolson, 1955), p. 36; Sefton Delmer, *Black Boomerang* (London: Secker & Warburg, 1962), p. 179.

10. Alastair Forbes, 'Whitehall in Queer Street', *Sunday Dispatch*, 10 June 1951, p. 4; George Wigg, House of Commons debates, 11 June 1951, vol. 488, col. 1672; Oxford, Bodleian Library, Macmillan D/8/120, diary of Harold Macmillan, 16 July 1951.

11. NA KV 2/4102, serial 145b, Maxwell Knight, 'Re the MACLEAN–BURGESS Case', 12 June 1951; NA KV 2/4102, serial 101d, Skardon, 'Top Secret', 'Interview with Jack HEWIT on 5.6.51', 6 June 1951; NA KV 2/4109, serial 409a, Skardon, 'Note', 27 September 1952.

12. Alan Campbell, *Colleagues and Friends* (Wilton: Michael Russell, 1988), p. 18; Andrew Boyle, *The Climate of Treason: Five Who Spied for Russia* (London: Hutchinson, 1979), p. 398.

13. NA FCO 158/206, 'Top Secret. Strictly Personal and Confidential. The Problem of Homosexuality in Relation to Employment in the Foreign Service', 8 October 1951.

14. NA FCO 158/206, Report of Cadogan committee, 1 November 1951.

15. NA KV 2/4104, serial 198b, Skardon, 'Guy BURGESS' [interview with Philip Toynbee], 22 June 1951; House of Lords debates, vol. 194, col. 738, 22 November 1955.

16. Robert Cecil, *A Divided Life: A Biography of Donald Maclean* (London: Bodley Head, 1988), p. 193.

17. NA KV 2/4109, serial 405a, A. F. Burbidge, 'Note', 27 August 1952.

18. Lord Montagu of Beaulieu, *Wheels within Wheels: An Unconventional Life* (London: Weidenfeld & Nicolson, 2000), p. 100.

19. Oxford, Christ Church archives, Dacre papers 17/1/2, Hugh Trevor-Roper to Lady Alexandra Howard-Johnson, 9 January 1954; Davenport-Hines, *Sex, Death and Punishment*, pp. 303–4; Peter Wildeblood, 'Telephone Tapping', *Spectator*, 5 July 1957, p. 16.

20. Brian Lewis, *Wolfenden's Witnesses: Homosexuality in Post-War Britain* (Basingstoke: Palgrave Macmillan, 2016), pp. 96–102.

21. House of Lords debates, 19 May 1954, vol. 187, cols 756–7.

22. David Footman, *Balkan Holiday* (London: Heinemann, 1935), p. 204; Wildeblood, *Against the Law*, p. 128; Oxford, Bodleian Library, Macmillan papers D/40/130, diary of Harold Macmillan, 11 December 1960; HLRO BBK H/177, Arthur Christiansen to Lord Beaverbrook, 10 November 1955.

23. 'The Squalid Truth', *Sunday Pictorial*, 25 September 1955, p. 1; Hugh Cudlipp, *At Your Peril: A Mid-Century View of the Exciting Changes of the Press in Britain and a Press View of the Exciting Changes of Mid-Century* (London: Weidenfeld & Nicolson, 1962), p. 317.

24. 'Who is Hiding the Man Who Tipped Off These Sex Perverts?', *Sunday Pictorial*, 25 September 1955, p. 1; Lord Rawlinson of Ewell, *A Price Too High: An Autobiography* (London: Weidenfeld & Nicolson, 1989), p. 37.

25. 'Guy Burgess Stripped Bare! Now I will show how he was the greatest traitor of them all! His closest friend speaks at last', *People*, 11 March 1956, p. 3.

26. 'He Kept Blackmail Letters in his Room. Guy Burgess Stripped Bare! Men in High Places made Friends with this Traitor', *People*, 18 March 1956, p. 3; Sir Isaiah Berlin, *Affirming: Letters, 1975–1997*, ed. Henry Hardy and Mark Pottle (London: Chatto & Windus, 2015), p. 524.

27. Lewis, *Wolfenden's Witnesses*, pp. 106-26, especially 106-7, 111.

28. *Ibid.*, pp. 144–7.

29. Ian Fleming, *Goldfinger* (London: Cape, 1959), chapter 19, pp. 313–14.

30. John Vassall, *Vassall: The Autobiography of a Spy* (London: Sidgwick & Jackson, 1975), p. 21; Rebecca West, *The Meaning of Treason* (London: Virago, 1982), pp. 361–2.

31. Vassall, *Vassall*, p. 39.

32. John Deane Potter, 'Twilight Traitors', *News of the World*, 28 October 1962, p. 15.

33. Humanities Research Center, University of Texas at Austin, Dick papers 28/1, Francis King to Kay Dick, 27 April 1975.

34. Michael Straight, *After Long Silence* (London: Collins, 1983), p. 63.

35. Cambridge, King's College archives, NGA 5/1/290, Charles Fletcher-Cooke to Noël Annan, 23 November 1943.

36. Charles Fletcher-Cooke, 'The Salzburg Festival', *Observer*, 11 August 1946, p. 3; Charles Fletcher-Cooke, 'Table-Talk', *Observer*, 3 August 1952, p. 5;

'Commons Discusses a "Peter Pan"', *Manchester Guardian*, 11 December 1953, p. 3.

37. Cambridge, Trinity College, Butler of Saffron Walden papers G/40, Charles Fletcher-Cooke to Molly Butler, 18 July 1963; Charles Fletcher-Cooke, 'End of Term', *Spectator*, 5 August 1960, p. 207; Oxford, Bodleian Library, Macmillan papers D/48/96, diary of Harold Macmillan, 5 March 1963.

38. Oxford, Bodleian Library, Macmillan papers D/48/85, diary of Harold Macmillan, 21 February 1963. Some of Fletcher-Cooke's letters to Noël Annan, deposited in the archives at King's College, Cambridge, are withheld from scrutiny at his request until the mid-twenty-first century. These may cover the circumstances of his ministerial resignation in 1963.

39. NA KV 2/4139, serial 1580a, Note by R. C. Symonds, 13 June 1963.

Chapter 19: The Exiles

1. *DBPO*, series 3, vol. 1 (London: Stationery Office, 1997), pp. 299–300.

2. Philip Williams, ed., *The Diary of Hugh Gaitskell, 1945–1956* (London: Cape, 1983), p. 507.

3. 'My Mission, by Guy Burgess' and 'Whom do they fool?', *Sunday Express*, 19 February 1956.

4. Tom Driberg, 'They May Be Heroes', *Reynolds News*, 25 February 1956; NA KV 2/4115, serial 689a, Burgess to Tom Driberg, 15 March 1956.

5. NA KV 2/4116, serial 790a, Eve Bassett to Guy Burgess, 9 August 1956.

6. NA KV 2/4118, serial 857c, Note by Robertson, 24 October 1956.

7. 'No Sort of Traitors?', *Manchester Guardian*, 30 November 1956, p. 6.

8. Edward Crankshaw, 'Unbelievable', *Observer*, 9 December 1956, p. 13; Alan Pryce-Jones, 'Meddling Diplomatist', *Times Literary Supplement*, 14 December 1956, p. 751.

9. NA KV 2/4128, serial 1156a, Eve Bassett to Guy Burgess, 26 December 1958.

10. Miranda Carter, *Anthony Blunt: His Lives* (London: Macmillan, 2001), p. 272.

11. Alan Maclean, *No, I Tell a Lie, It was the Tuesday: A Trudge through the Life of Alan Maclean* (London: Kyle Cathie, 1997), p. 99.

12. NA KV 2/4156, serial 981a, Donald Maclean to Philip Toynbee, 28 February 1957.

13. NA KV 2/4155, serial 933a, Donald Maclean to Lady Maclean, 17 August 1956; Don Kirschner, *Cold War Exile: The Unclosed Case of Maurice Halperin* (Columbia: University of Missouri Press, 1995), p. 212; Eleanor Philby, *Kim Philby: The Spy I Loved* (London: Hamish Hamilton, 1968), p. 116.

14. Nora Beloff, *Transit of Britain: A Report on Britain's Changing Role in the Post-War World* (London: Collins, 1973), p. 108.

15. NA KV 2/4128, serial 1176a, Edward Crankshaw, 'Burgess and Maclean', 21 January 1959, enclosed with Sir Patrick Reilly to Sir Patrick Dean, 23 January 1959.

16. NA KV 2/4128, serial 1157a, Sir Harold Nicolson to Guy Burgess, 4 January 1959; Alan Brien, 'Debased Coinage', *Spectator*, 5 February 1960, p. 177; Michael Young, *The Chipped White Cups of Dover: A Discussion of the Possibility of a New Progressive Party* (London: Unit 2, 1960), pp. 3–4.

17. Oxford, Bodleian Library, Macmillan D/42/43, diary of Harold Macmillan, 19 May 1961; Stephen A. Smith, 'Towards a Global History of Communism', in Smith, ed., *The Oxford Handbook of the History of Communism* (Oxford: Oxford University Press, 2014), p. 13; *DBPO*, series 3, vol. 1, p. 142.

18. Lara Feigel and John Sutherland, eds, *New Selected Journals, 1939–1995: Stephen Spender* (London: Faber & Faber, 2012), p. 268; 'My pals in MI5 by Burgess', *Daily Herald*, 24 April 1962.

19. Patrick Seale and Maureen McConville, *Philby: The Long Road to Moscow* (London: Hamish Hamilton, 1973), pp. 225–6.

20. Jeremy Lewis, *David Astor: A Life in Print* (London: Cape, 2016), p. 248.

21. Richard Davenport-Hines and Adam Sisman, eds, *One Hundred Letters from Hugh Trevor-Roper* (Oxford: Oxford University Press, 2014), p. 397.

22. NA FO 371/64085, C6781/C6781/3G, Sir Henry Mack, Vienna, to Sir Patrick Dean, 2 May 1947; Graham Greene, *Ways of Escape* (London: Bodley Head, 1980), p. 126.

23. NA KV 2/4170, serial 318a, Interrogation of Peter Smolka by Arthur Martin, 2 October 1961.

24. Peter Wright, *Spycatcher: The Candid Autobiography of a Senior Intelligence Officer* (New York: Viking, 1987), p. 173; Michael Holzman, *James Jesus Angleton, the CIA, and the Craft of Counterintelligence* (Amherst: University of Massachusetts Press, 2008), p. 346 (where, however, it is wrongly stated that Solomon was thirty years older than Philby).

25. Chapman Pincher, *Their Trade is Treachery* (London: Sidgwick & Jackson, 1981), p. 64; Davenport-Hines and Sisman, *One Hundred Letters*, p. 397; Martin Pearce, *Spymaster: The Life of Britain's Most Decorated Cold War Spy and Head of MI6, Sir Maurice Oldfield* (London: Bantam, 2016), p. 212.

26. Oxford, Christ Church archives, Dacre papers 13/5, diary of Hugh Trevor-Roper, 25 November 1967.

27. Oxford, Christ Church archives, Dacre papers 10/45, Dick White to Hugh Trevor-Roper, 14 January 1968.

28. Tom Mangold, *Cold Warrior: James Jesus Angleton, the CIA's Master Spy*

Hunter (London: Simon & Schuster, 1991), pp. 66–7; Holzman, *Angleton*, p. 206.

29. 'Danger: The Old Pals' Act', *Daily Mirror* editorial, 3 July 1963, p. 2.

30. W. N. Ewer, 'Poor Burgess – The Tragic Heretic who was always an Unhappy Misfit', *Daily Herald*, 2 September 1963.

31. Oxford, Christ Church archives, Dacre papers 10/45, Dick White to Hugh Trevor-Roper, 14 January 1968.

32. Ian Fleming, 'If I Were Prime Minister', *Spectator*, 9 October 1959, p. 466; Ian Fleming, *You Only Live Twice* (London: Cape, 1964), chapter 8, pp. 103–4.

33. Oxford, Bodleian Library, Mss Eng c 6925, ff. 246–7.

34. Oxford, Worcester College archives, WOR/PRO 10/1/128/1, Dick White to Masterman, 5 October 1967, and Masterman to White, 7 October 1967; Phillip Knightley, David Leitch, Bruce Page and Hugo Young, 'Government and the Press', *The Times*, 23 November 1967, p. 11.

35. Oxford, Christ Church archives, Dacre papers 10/45, White to Trevor-Roper, 14 January 1968.

36. Oxford, Christ Church archives, Dacre papers 10/45, Bruce Page to Hugh Trevor-Roper, 5 January 1968.

37. Holzman, *Angleton*, p. 204.

38. Oxford, Worcester College archives, WOR/PRO 10/1/128/1, Lord Normanbrook to Sir J. C. Masterman, 25 March 1965; and White to Masterman, 20 May 1968.

39. Richard Deacon, *The History of the British Secret Service* (London: Muller, 1969), p. 402.

40. Oxford, Worcester College archives, WOR/PRO/10/1/128/1, Masterman to White, 16 May 1968; Sir John Masterman, *The Double-Cross System in the War of 1939 to 1945* (New Haven: Yale University Press, 1972), p. 188.

41. *DBPO*, series 3, vol. 1, pp. 68, 287, 300.

42. *Ibid.*, pp. 92, 214, 292; Lord Greenhill of Harrow, *More by Accident* (York: Wilton, 1992), p. 121.

43. Christopher Andrew and Oleg Gordievsky, *KGB: The Inside Story of its Foreign Operations from Lenin to Gorbachev* (London: Hodder & Stoughton, 1990), p. 435.

44. *DBPO*, series 3, vol. 1, pp. 339–40.

45. *Ibid.*, pp. 309–10.

46. NA KV 2/4138, serial 1559a, Guy Burgess to Sir Roy Harrod, 29 January 1963.

47. House of Lords debates, 27 July 1971, vol. 323, col. 279, and 27 October 1971, vol. 324, col. 723.

48. Gill Bennett, *Six Moments of Crisis: Inside British Foreign Policy* (Oxford: Oxford University Press, 2013), p. 127.

49. *Ibid.*, p. 135.

50. Andrew and Gordievsky, *KGB*, p. 436.

51. Patrick Keatley, 'Spy Charges May Follow Lialine Case', *Guardian*, 2 October 1971, p. 1; Robert Kaiser, 'A Who's Who of Spies by Philby', *ibid.*, p. 3.

52. Arthur Lewis, House of Commons debates, 27 October 1971, vol. 823, cols 2034–6.

53. *DBPO*, series 3, vol. 1, p. 423; *DBPO*, series 3, vol. 3 (London: Stationery Office, 2001), p. 88; *DBPO*, series 3, vol. 8 (London: Routledge, 2012), pp. 381, 384.

Chapter 20: The Mole Hunts

1. Evelyn Waugh, *The Sword of Honour Trilogy* (London: Everyman, 1994), pp. 151, 307.

2. Graham Greene, *Collected Essays* (London: Bodley Head, 1969), p. 414.

3. Christopher Andrew, *The Defence of the Realm: The Authorized History of MI5* (London: Allen Lane, 2009), p. 437.

4. Markus Wolf, *Man without a Face: The Autobiography of Communism's Greatest Spy Master* (London: Cape, 1997), pp. 174–5.

5. Andrew, *Defence of the Realm*, pp. 503-5.

6. *Ibid.*, pp. 438–9.

7. Peter Wright, *Spycatcher: The Candid Autobiography of a Senior Intelligence Officer* (New York: Viking, 1987), p. 13.

8. Jenifer Hart, *Ask Me No More: An Autobiography* (London: Peter Halban, 1998), pp. 77-9; Sir Isaiah Berlin, *Affirming: Letters, 1975–1997*, ed. Henry Hardy and Mark Pottle (London: Chatto & Windus, 2015), p. 215; Cambridge, King's College archives, NGA 5/1/1029, Dick White to Noël Annan, 25 October 1990.

9. Wright, *Spycatcher*, p. 265.

10. *Ibid.*, pp. 265–6.

11. *Ibid.*, pp. 265–6, 267; Hart, *Ask Me No More*, p. 53.

12. Oxford, Christ Church archives, Dacre papers 10/48, Ewen Montagu to Hugh Trevor-Roper, 3 January 1980, and Dick White to Trevor-Roper, 6 January 1980.

13. Berlin, *Affirming*, p. 525.

14. R. C. Zaehner, *Concordant Discord: The Interdependence of Faiths* (Oxford: Clarendon Press, 1970), p. 6.

15. *Ibid.*, pp. 395–6, 416, 432-3.

16. Wright, *Spycatcher*, pp. 244–6.

17. Hugh Trevor-Roper, *The Wartime Journals*, ed. Richard Davenport-Hines (London: I. B. Tauris, 2012), pp. 67–8.

18. Sir Stuart Hampshire, *Innocence and Experience* (London: Allen Lane, 1989), p. 8.

19. *Ibid.*, pp. 10–11.

20. Sir Stuart Hampshire, 'Danger of taste for spy stories', *The Times*, 1 December 1981, p. 11.

21. Oxford, Christ Church archives, Dacre papers 10/48, White to Trevor-Roper, 6 January 1980.

22. Graham Lord, 'John Junor: a bigot and blatant hypocrite', *Press Gazette*, 10 April 2013; Miranda Carter, *Blunt: His Lives* (London: Macmillan, 2001), pp. 475, 481; Malcolm Muggeridge, 'The Eclipse of the Gentleman', *Time*, 3 December 1979.

23. 'DAMN YOUR CONSCIENCE!:, *Daily Express*, 21 November 1979, p. 1; 'Daily Mail Comment', *Daily Mail*, 21 November 1979, p. 6.

24. Sir Michael Howard, 'Professor Blunt and security', *The Times*, 21 November 1979, p. 15; Russell Burlingham, *ibid*.

25. Chapman Pincher, 'Newest twists in the Blunt tale', *Evening News*, 17 March 1980; Chapman Pincher, *Traitors: The Labyrinths of Treason* (London: Sidgwick & Jackson, 1987), p. 161; Peter Kidson, 'Anthony Frederick Blunt', *Biographical Memoirs of Fellows of the British Academy*, vol. 13 (Cambridge University Press, 2014), pp. 36–7.

26. Frederic Raphael, *There and Then: Personal Terms 6* (Manchester: Carcanet, 2013), p. 141; Andrew Boyle, *The Climate of Treason: Five Who Spied for Russia* (London: Hutchinson, 1979), pp. 107, 151, 184; Cambridge University Library, Add 9429/1G/35, Andrew Boyle to George Carey-Foster, 17 August 1978.

27. Hugh Trevor-Roper, 'The unholy trinity', *Spectator*, 17 November 1979, p. 22; Neal Ascherson, 'What sort of traitors?', *London Review of Books*, 7 February 1980, p. 6.

28. Boyle, *Climate of Treason*, pp. 197, 291–2; Berlin, *Affirming*, pp. 117–21.

29. Oxford, Christ Church archives, Dacre papers 10/48, Dick White to Hugh Trevor-Roper, 25 January 1980.

30. Boyle, *Climate of Treason*, pp. 11, 87, 156, 218.

31. Chapman Pincher, *Their Trade is Treachery* (London: Sidgwick & Jackson, 1981), pp. 1–2; Chapman Pincher, *Too Secret Too Long: The Great Betrayal of Britain's Crucial Secrets and the Cover-up* (London: Sidgwick & Jackson, 1984), p. 517.

32. Hugh Trevor-Roper, 'The Real Harm Done by the Fifth Man', *Daily Telegraph*, 21 October 1990; Richard Aldrich and Rory Cormac, *The Black Door: Spies, Secret Intelligence and British Prime Ministers* (London: Collins, 2016), pp. 366–7.

33. Andrew, *Defence of the Realm*, pp. 519-20; Cambridge, King's College archives, NGA 5/1/1029, Dick White to Noël Annan, 13 May 1988.

34. Robert Leeson, ed., *Hayek: A Collaborative Biography: Part III – Fraud, Fascism and Free Market Religion* (London: Palgrave Macmillan, 2015), pp. ix, 33, 215, 223.

35. Richard Deacon, *The British Connection: Russia's Manipulation of British Individuals and Institutions* (London: Hamish Hamilton, 1979), pp. 51–2.

36. Cambridge, King's College archives, NGA 5/1/1029, Dick White to Noël Annan, 13 May 1988.

37. John Costello, *Mask of Treachery: Spies, Lies, Buggery and Betrayal, the First Documented Dossier of Anthony Blunt's Cambridge Spy Ring* (New York: William Morrow, 1988), p. 605.

38. Oxford, Christ Church archives, Dacre 10/48, Dick White to Hugh Trevor-Roper, 6 January 1980; Cambridge, King's College archives, NGA 5/1/1029, Dick White to Noël Annan, 10 May 1989.

39. Christopher N. L. Brooke, *A History of the University of Cambridge*, vol. 4 (Cambridge: Cambridge University Press, 1993), p. 127; Malcolm Muggeridge, 'The Eclipse of the Gentleman', *Time*, 3 December 1979; Sarah Curtis, ed., *The Journals of Woodrow Wyatt*, vol. 1 (London: Macmillan, 1998), p. 229; Richard Deacon, *The Cambridge Apostles: A History of Cambridge University's Elite Intellectual Secret Society* (London: Robert Boyce, 1985), pp. 61, 68.

40. Richard Davenport-Hines and Adam Sisman, eds, *One Hundred Letters from Hugh Trevor-Roper* (Oxford: Oxford University Press, 2014), pp. 397–8; Anthony Cave Brown, *'C': The Secret Life of Sir Stewart Menzies, Spymaster to Winston Churchill* (New York: Macmillan, 1987), p. 173; Tom Bower, *The Perfect English Spy: Sir Dick White and the Secret Service, 1935–90* (London: Heinemann, 1995), p. 129; Michael Holzman, *James Jesus Angleton: The CIA and the Craft of Counterintelligence* (Amherst: University of Massachusetts Press, 2008), p. 100.

41. NA KV 2/4119, serial 468a, G. R. Mitchell, 'Philip Dennis PROCTOR', 3 December 1953.

42. E. M. Forster, *Two Cheers for Democracy* (London: Edward Arnold, 1951), pp. 82–3; Ray Mills, 'The Angry Voice', *Daily Star*, 2 September & 9 September 1986.

43. Oxford, Christ Church archives, Dacre papers 10/46, Hugh Trevor-Roper to Donald McCormick, 30 October 1981.

44. Martin Pearce, *Spymaster: The Life of Britain's Most Decorated Cold War Spy and Head of MI6, Sir Maurice Oldfield* (London: Bantam, 2016), p. 331.

45. *Ibid.*, p. 335.

46. Richard Davenport-Hines, *Sex, Death and Punishment: Attitudes to Sex and Sexuality in Britain since the Renaissance* (London: Collins, 1990), p. 1; Pincher, *Too Secret Too Long*, pp. 387, 417; James Barros, *No Sense of Evil: Espionage – The Case of Herbert Norman* (Toronto: Deneau, 1986), p. 9.

47. Anthony Cavendish, *Inside Intelligence* (London: Collins, 1990), p. 160; Pincher, *Traitors*, pp. 103, 104, 105, 107, 111–13.

48. 'After Oldfield', *Daily Telegraph*, 25 April 1987; Richard Evans, 'Ex-MI6 chief a homosexual says Thatcher', *The Times*, 24 April 1987, p. 1; Michael Evans, 'Inquiry call on ex-MI6 chief', *The Times*, 20 April 1987, p. 18.

49. Pearce, *Spymaster*, pp. 339, 343, 344; Curtis, *Journals of Woodrow Wyatt*, vol. 1, pp. 333, 335.

50. Pearce, *Spymaster*, p. 329.

51. Geoffrey Levy, 'The Spycatcher of Fleet Street whose Scoops Spooked PMs', *Daily Mail*, 7 August 2014; 'Chapman Pincher', *Daily Telegraph*, 6 August 2014.

52. Cambridge, King's College archives, NGA 5/1/1029, Dick White to Noël Annan, 13 April 1989; Hugh Trevor-Roper, 'The Real Harm Done by the Fifth Man', *Daily Telegraph*, 21 October 1990.

Envoi

1. Sarah Curtis, ed., *The Journals of Woodrow Wyatt*, vol. 1 (London: Macmillan, 1998), p. 10.

2. Alan Campbell, *Colleagues and Friends* (Wilton: Michael Russell, 1988), p. 134.

3. Tim Shipman, *All Out War: The Full Story of Brexit* (London: William Collins, 2016), p. 329; Arron Banks, *The Bad Boys of Brexit: Tales of Mischief, Mayhem & Guerrilla Warfare in the EU Referendum Campaign* (London: Biteback, 2016), p. 279; Craig Oliver, *Unleashing Demons: The Inside Story of Brexit* (London: Hodder & Stoughton, 2016), p. 280. Gove's admirers have since claimed, as if this might mute the outrage, that he intended to say, 'People in this country have had enough of experts from organizations with acronyms saying that they know what is best.'

4. Anthony Powell, *A Writer's Notebook* (London: Heinemann, 2000), p. 49.

5. Lord Vansittart, *The Mist Procession* (London: Hutchinson, 1958), p. 351.

Index

Annan, Noël (*later* Baron Annan) 416, 479, 535, 536, 537
Anschluss (Nazi annexation of Austria; 1938) 213, 238–9, 260
anti-American sentiment 349, 363, 489, 522
anti-British sentiment 359
anti-colonialism 188, 209, 359
anti-German sentiment 44, 288
anti-semitism 12–13, 30, 95, 102, 275, 277–8, 494
Anti-Socialist Union 66, 107
anti-war organizations 152, 159, 211, 224–5; *see also* pacifism
Antrobus, George 117–20, 123, 126, 130, 131, 145, 146
Antwerp 35
Apostles (Cambridge University society) 397, 531, 536–7, 538–9
appeasement 59, 170, 260, 265, 266, 267–8
Aragon, Louis 222
Archer, John 287
Archer, Kathleen 'Jane' (*née* Sissmore) 24, 64–5, 105–6, 113, 124, 142, 145, 340; debriefing of Walter Krivitsky 142–4, 162, 170, 248, 323
ARCOS (All Russian Co-operative Society) 86, 93, 98; police raid (1927) 49, 98, 103–5, 536; repercussions of raid 60, 62, 94, 104–5, 125, 150, 158, 166, 355
Ardagh, Sir John 39, 41
Argonne National Laboratory, Illinois 335
armaments manufacture 11, 126, 147–54, 157–8, 160, 164, 230; propaganda against 152–3, 220; *see also* Vickers; Woolwich, Royal Ordnance Factories
Armenia 125, 374
Armistice Day protest (1933) 224–5
Armstrong, Sir Robert (*later* Baron Armstrong of Ilminster) 533, 540–41
Armstrong & Co Ltd (engineering and ship-building company) 147
Army Education Department 302
Army and Navy Club 380
Army Security Agency (United States; ASA) 346
Arsenal football club 180
ASA (US Army Security Agency) 346
Ascherson, Neal 529–30
Ascona, Switzerland 400
Ashanti wars 41, 42
Ashton, Henry 227
Ashwick, Ernest 417
Asquith, H.H., 1st Earl of Oxford and Asquith 48, 215, 240
Asquith, Margot, Countess of Oxford and Asquith 214
Associated Press (press agency) 241
Association of Scientific Workers 354
Astor, David 417, 440, 495
Astor, Nancy, Viscountess 214, 263
Astor, Waldorf, 2nd Viscount 87, 277

Astor of Hever, John Jacob Astor, 1st Baron 440
atheism and atheists 8–9, 49, 71, 249, 380
Athenaeum (club) 65, 251, 292, 293, 298
Athens 136, 360, 382
Athlone, Alexander Cambridge, 1st Earl of 331
Athlone, Princess Alice, Countess of 331
atomic energy, development of 344–5, 347, 506
atomic and nuclear weapons: development 297, 327–8, 333–6, 340, 342, 349, 350–51, 432; testing and deployment 335, 342–3, 351–2, 370, 393; *see also* nuclear disarmament campaigns
atomic spies 73, 263, 300, 328, 330–52, 370, 505; *see also* Fuchs, Klaus; Mann, Wilfrid; May, Trevor Nunn; Norwood, Melita; Pontecorvo, Bruno; Rosenberg, Julius and Ethel
Attlee, Clement Attlee, 1st Earl: at Oxford 215; as demobbed soldier 47; addresses Red Army anniversary celebration 298; Prime Minister 331, 343, 355, 445; and Soviet espionage 331; and atomic weapons development 343; and appointment of Sillitoe as Director General of MI5 355; and withdrawal of British forces from Greece 360–61; and Zionist terrorism 362, 363; and Anglo-American Special Relationship 364; and vetting of Whitehall staff 369, 370; and Korean war 393; at Philip Jordan's memorial service 409; and Hector McNeil 414
Attlee, Violet, Countess 409
Auden, W.H. 197, 218, 388, 397, 406
Australia 361, 437–8, 533; Royal Commission on Espionage (1954–5) 437, 438
Austria: 18th and 19th centuries 35, 37; 'Red Vienna' (1918–34) 14, 22, 155, 229–31; civil war and rise of fascism 231–4, 238; *Anschluss* (1938) 213, 238–9, 260; Soviet zone of occupation 302; *see also* Austro-Hungarian empire; Salzburg; Vienna
Austrian Intelligence Bureau 69
Austro-Hungarian empire 49, 69; end of 48
Austro-Prussian war (1866) 41
aviation spies 154–7, 277, 344, 424–5
Ayer, Sir A.J. 'Freddie' 191, 474

Babington, Anthony 34
Baldwin, Calvin 285
Baldwin of Bewdley, Stanley Baldwin, 1st Earl 63, 103, 153, 182, 215, 243
Balfour, Arthur Balfour, 1st Earl of 215
Balfour, Sir John 'Jock' 3, 317–18, 359, 388, 460
Ball, Sir Joseph 99
Balliol College, Oxford 173, 215, 217, 325
Balogh, Thomas (*later* Baron Balogh) 325
Balzac, Honoré de 227